ENCYCLOPEDIA OF
SOCIETY AND CULTURE

IN THE
MEDIEVAL
WORLD

■ **VOLUME IV** ■

(sacred sites to writing)

PAM J. CRABTREE, Editor in Chief

Facts On File
An imprint of Infobase Publishing

Encyclopedia of Society and Culture in the Medieval World

Copyright © 2008 by Infobase Publishing

Facts On File, Inc.
An imprint of Infobase Publishing
132 West 31st Street
New York NY 10001

Library of Congress Cataloging-in-Publication Data

Encyclopedia of society and culture in the medieval world / Pam J. Crabtree, editor in chief.
p. cm.
Includes bibliographical references and index.
ISBN-13: 978-0-8160-6936-1 (set)
ISBN-10: 0-8160-6936-0 (set)
1. Civilization, Medieval—Encyclopedias. 2. Civilization—History—Encyclopedias. I. Crabtree, Pam J.
CB351.E53 2008
909.0703—dc22   2007036571

You can find Facts On File on the World Wide Web at http://www.factsonfile.com

Text design by James Scotto-Lavino
Cover design by Takeshi Takahashi
Maps by Dale Williams

Printed in the United States of America

VB Hermitage 10 9 8 7 6 5 4 3 2 1

This book is printed on acid-free paper and contains 30 percent postconsumer recycled content.

Contents

Advisers and Contributors

EDITOR IN CHIEF
Pam J. Crabtree
Associate Professor of Anthropology
New York University

ADVISORY BOARD
Mario Azevedo
Professor of Epidemiology and Biostatistics
Professor of History and Scholar-in-Residence
Jackson State University

R. Hunt Davis
Professor Emeritus of History and African Studies
University of Florida

Laura Lee Junker
Associate Professor of Anthropology, Director of
    Graduate Studies
University of Illinois at Chicago

Eloise Quiñones Keber
Professor of Art History
Baruch College and The Graduate Center of the City
    University of New York

S. M. Ghazanfar
Professor of Economics Emeritus
University of Idaho

CONTRIBUTORS
Charles W. Abbott, Ph.D., is currently revising his dissertation on Nigerian hometown associations and ethnic unions toward a book. His chapter "Nigerians in North America: New frontiers, old associations?" appears in the edited volume *The New African Diaspora in North America* (Lexington Books).

Olutayo Charles Adesina, Ph.D., teaches at the Department of History, University of Ibadan, Nigeria. He is the author of "The Underground Foreign Exchange Market in Ibadan during Devaluation," in *Money Struggles and City Life: Devaluation in Ibadan and Other Urban Centres in Southern Nigeria, 1986–96* (2002), and "Teaching History in Twentieth Century Nigeria: The Challenges of Change," in *History in Africa: A Journal of Method*, vol. 33 (2006).

Massoud Abdel Alim is a writer, editor, and trainer for Fortune 1000 companies. He has an M.S. and M.B.A. and has written for many business and medical publications. He has lived in the Arab world and is especially interested in Islamic history.

Mark W. Allen, Ph.D., is associate professor of anthropology in the Department of Geography and Anthropology at California State Polytechnic University, Pomona. His most recent publications include coediting *The Archaeology of Warfare: Prehistories of Raiding and Conquest* (University Press of Florida, 2006) and "Hillforts and the Cycling of Maori Chiefdoms: Do Good Fences Make Good Neighbors?" in R. Reycraft and J. Railey (eds.), *Global Perspectives on the Collapse of Complex Society* (University of New Mexico Press, 2007).

Miguel Arisa is finishing his doctoral studies in art history at the Graduate Center, City University of New York. He teaches at Technical Career Institutes and is a regular lecturer at the Cloisters and a docent at the Metropolitan Museum of Art, New York.

Rose Aslan is a graduate student in Arab and Islamic civilizations at the American University in Cairo, Egypt. Her research interests include Sufi hermeneutics, Qur'anic exegesis, and Islamic theology.

Peri Bearman is associate director of the Islamic Legal Studies Program at Harvard Law School. She founded the journal

Islamic Law and Society and is an editor of the *Encyclopaedia of Islam,* New Edition, and coeditor, with Rudolph Peters and Frank E. Vogel, of *The Islamic School of Law: Evolution, Devolution, and Progress* (Cambridge, Mass. 2005) and, with Wolfhart Heinrichs and Bernard G. Weiss, of *The Law Applied: Contextualizing the Islamic Shari'a* (I. B. Tauris, 2007). An article by her hand on Islamic law in contemporary application appears in Oxford's *Encyclopedia of the Modern World* (Oxford University Press, 2008).

Kirk H. Beetz, Ph.D., emeritus, has published over two dozen books and more than 900 articles. His books span topics from endangered mammal species to children's literature, including *Exploring C. S. Lewis' "The Chronicles of Narnia"* (2000). His recent writings have focused on the history and culture of ancient Japan.

Anne Berthelot (Docteur ès Lettres) is professor of French and medieval studies at the University of Connecticut. She specializes in Arthurian literature with a comparatist approach. She has published several books on this topic, including *King Arthur and the Round Table* and, more recently, *La Légende du roi Arthur.*

Amy Hackney Blackwell has degrees in history from Duke University and Vanderbilt University and a J.D. from the University of Virginia. Her books include *Mythology for Dummies* (2002), *LSAT for Dummies* (2004), *The Everything Irish History and Heritage Book* (2004), and *Essential Dictionary of Law* (2004). She has contributed to the *Encyclopedia of World Nations and Cultures* (2006), *Alternative Energy* (2006), and *Chemical Compounds* (2006).

Robert Bollt, Ph.D., (University Hawai'i at Mānoa, 2005), specializes in the archaeology of East Polynesia. His concentration is on the Austral Islands, where he found and excavated the earliest-known site to-date. He is the author of *Peva: the Archaeology of an Austral Island Settlement* (Bishop Museum Press, 2007). He has also excavated sites in Hawai'i and the Marquesas. Primary interests include Polynesia material culture (mainly lithics), and patterns of long-distance exchange among islands, which is achieved by using geochemical sourcing analyses to trace stone tools to their geological source of origin. He also enjoys experimental archaeology, especially adze making. Additional interests include Polynesian subsistence strategies, human-environment relations, sociopolitical transformation, and warfare.

Scott D. Briggs is a freelance writer, essayist, and critic who has been active in the professional, amateur and small-press literary fields for more than 20 years, specializing in horror, fantasy, and science fiction literature; film; and rock and roll, pop, alternative, and modern classical music. He has written essays for upcoming critical anthologies on the popular authors Thomas Harris and William Peter Blatty for McFarland & Co. and essays and reviews for various publications and music and arts journals, including Necronomicon Press, *NY Arts Magazine,* and *The Big Takeover* music magazine.

Flordeliz T. Bugarin, Ph.D., currently teaches cultural anthropology and archaeology at Howard University. She has written articles on children in the archaeological record, African studies, and historical archaeology.

Gregory R. Campbell is professor of anthropology at the University of Montana, Missoula. He is the author of numerous works about indigenous peoples of North America.

Alice V. Clark, Ph. D., is associate professor and coordinator of music history and literature at Loyola University New Orleans. Her scholarship, which focuses on aspects of the medieval motet, appears in *The Journal of Musicology, The Journal of Musicological Research*, and *Plainsong and Medieval Music,* as well as collections such as *Fauvel Studies,* and she has contributed an article on the medieval motet to the *On-line Reference Book for Medieval Studies* (the-orb.net).

Julia Marta Clapp is pursuing her doctorate in art history at the Graduate Center, City University of New York. Her research interests include modern and pre-Columbian Latin American art.

Leah A. J. Cohen is an independent writer and editorial consultant with a master's degree in geography from the University of Florida. She specializes in Africa area studies and food security. She was a senior author for the *Encyclopedia of African History and Culture*, volumes 4 and 5 (2005).

Justin Corfield, Ph.D., teaches history and international relations at Geelong Grammar School, Australia. He is the coauthor of *Historical Dictionary of Cambodia* (2003) and has written extensively on Asia, Australia, and European colonial history.

Arden Decker is a Ph.D. candidate in the history of art at the Graduate Center, City University of New York. Her research interests include Mesoamerican art as well as modern and contemporary art of Mexico.

Kathryn M. de Luna, M.A., teaches and is completing her doctorate in African history at Northwestern University. Her research uses alternative sources, particularly the reconstruction of dead languages, to elucidate early African economic, social, and political life.

Haig Der-Houssikian, Ph.D., is professor emeritus (2003), linguistics, at the University of Florida, Gainesville. His research and publication interests are in morphology, Creolization, and sub-Saharan Africa.

Kathryn Dickason is a graduate student in religious studies at New York University. Her previous projects have explored medieval religious women, heretical movements, and hagiographies. She is currently engaged in art historical research centered on the performative and liturgical functions of religious iconography in the Middle Ages.

Prof. Dr. Detlev Ellmers is now retired. From 1971 to 2002 he was director of the German Maritime Museum at Bremerhaven. He is author of studies in maritime archaeology and maritime history.

Karen E. Flint, Ph.D., teaches African history at the University of North Carolina, Charlotte. She is the author of several journal articles and an upcoming book on the history of health and healing in Southeastern Africa (Ohio University Press).

Alessia Frassani is a Ph.D. candidate at the Graduate Center of the City University of New York. Her research interests include the art and civilizations of ancient Oaxaca and issues surrounding the cultural interaction between the Old and New Worlds.

J. J. George is working on his Ph.D. at the Graduate Center, City University of New York. His research area is pre-Columbian art and architecture.

Mohammad Gharipour is visiting lecturer at Southern Polytechnic State University and a Ph.D. candidate at the College of Architecture at Georgia Institute of Technology. He has published extensively in magazines, journals, encyclopedias, and monographs. His area of expertise is architecture and garden design in Islamic countries.

S. M. Ghazanfar, Ph.D., is professor of economics (1968-2002, emeritus, 2002) at the University of Idaho, Moscow; he continues to teach occasionally (2005-06, 2006-07) as adjunct faculty. His recent books include an edited volume, *Medieval Islamic Economic Thought: Filling the "Great Gap" in European Economics* (Routledge-Curzon, 2003) and *Islamic Civilization—History, Contributions, and Influence: A Compendium of Literature* (Scarecrow Press, 2006). He also contributed to the 2001 PBS television documentary *Islam: Empire of Faith*.

Sebastian Guenther, Ph.D., is associate professor at the Department of Near and Middle Eastern Civilizations, University of Toronto, Canada. His research focuses on classical Arabic literature and the intellectual history of Islam. His most recent publications include the edited volume *Ideas, Images, and Methods of Portrayal: Insights into Classical Arabic Literature and Islam* (Brill 2005), contributions to the *Encyclopaedia of the Qur'an*, and "Medieval Muslim Thinkers on Educational Theory" (*Comparative Education Review* 50.3). He is currently writing a book on Islam's classical philosophies of education.

Kenneth R. Hall, Ph.D., is professor of history at Ball State University, teaching assorted courses in Asian and comparative world history. His publications include *Maritime Diasporas in the Indian Ocean, 960-1775* (Brill, 2006); *Structure and Society in Early South India* (Oxford, 2001/2005); *Maritime Trade and State Development in Early Southeast Asia* (Hawaii, 1985); *Trade and Statecraft in the Age of the Colas* (Abhinav, 1980/1997); *The Origin of Southeast Asian Statecraft* (Michigan, 1975), and the extended study of "An Economic History of Early Southeast Asia" in the *Cambridge History of Southeast Asia* (1992).

George Hambrecht is a doctoral candidate at the CUNY Graduate Center in New York City. He has published in *Archaeologica Islandica* and the *Stanford Journal of Archaeology* and has papers in press in an upcoming volume of *Historical Ecology*.

Jean Shepherd Hamm, Ph.D., is assistant professor in the Clemmer College of Education at East Tennessee State University. She holds bachelor's and master's degrees from Radford University and a doctorate from Virginia Tech. In addition to her work training future teachers, her interests include writing, history, literature, and women's studies.

Muhammed Hassanali is an independent scholar of Islamic studies in Cleveland, Ohio. He has contributed to *Encyclopedia of Antislavery and Abolition* (Greenwood 2006) and to *The Greenwood Encyclopedia of Love, Courtship, and Sexuality through History* (Greenwood forthcoming).

Angela Herren, Ph.D., teaches pre-Columbian art and architecture as an assistant professor in the Department of Art and Latin American Studies at the University of North Carolina at Charlotte. A specialist on painted manuscripts from central Mexico, she completed a 2005 dissertation entitled "Portraying the Mexica Past: A Comparative Study of Accounts of Origin in Codex Azcatitlan, Codex Boturni, and Codex Aubin."

Bret Hinsch received his Ph.D. in history and East Asian languages from Harvard University and is currently professor of history at Foguang University in Taiwan. He is author of *Women in Early Imperial China* (Rowman & Littlefield, 2002).

Rasheed Hosein, ABD, is currently the director of outreach for the Center for Middle Eastern Studies at the University of Chicago and an instructor of Arabic language and literature for the Graham School of General Studies at the University of Chicago. His dissertation topic is Thaqif and Quraysh in the late Jahiliyyah and early Islamic periods (AD 590-750).

Charles B. Hutchison, Ph.D., is an assistant professor at the University of North Carolina at Charlotte. He is the author of *Teaching in America: A Cross-Cultural Guide for International Teachers and Their Employers* and the forthcoming *Teaching Diverse and Urban Learners,* and the recipient of Recognition and Key to the City of Boston. His articles have appeared in several journals, including *Phi Delta Kappan, Intercultural Education, Cultural Studies of Science Education,* and *School Science and Mathematics.* He also has significant international educational experiences. He teaches and provides professional development workshops in science education, urban education, and international and cross-cultural education.

Suhail Islam, Ph. D., teaches world and comparative literature and Asian studies at Nazareth College of Rochester. He wrote "Bengal Famine," which appeared in *The Historical Companion to Postcolonial Literature* (Edinburgh University Press, 2005). A chapter entitled "The Wretched of the Nations," written with Syed Hasssan, appears in the book *Genocide, War Crimes, and the West: The Culture of Impunity* (Zed Books, 2004).

Dolly Jørgensen is currently a Ph.D. candidate in history at the University of Virginia. She has worked for over 12 years in environmental engineering consulting and has researched environmental issues in the medieval period, including forestry management and urban sanitation.

Keith Jordan, ABD, M.Phil., is a Ph.D. candidate in pre-Columbian art history at the Graduate Center of the City University of New York. He is currently finishing his doctoral dissertation, entitled "Stone Trees Transplanted? Central Mexican Stelae of the Epiclassic and Early Postclassic and the Question of Maya 'Influence.'"

Laura Lee Junker, Ph.D., is a professor in the Department of Anthropology at the University of Illinois at Chicago and an adjunct curator at the Field Museum of Natural History in Chicago. She specializes in the archaeology of historic period Southeast Asia, with archaeological projects in the Philippines, Laos, and Vietnam. She is the author of *Raiding, Trading and Feasting: The Political Economy of Philippine Chiefdoms* (University of Hawaii Press, 1999) and the coauthor of *Forager-Traders in South and Southeast Asia: Long Term Histories* (Cambridge University Press, 2002).

Bashir A. Kazimee, AIA, is professor of architecture at Washington State University. He is the author of *Place, Meaning and Form in the Architecture and Urban Structure of Eastern Islamic Cities* with Rahmani (Edwin Mellen Press, 2003). His collaborative project "Sustainable Development: A Comprehensive Urban Regenerative Proposal for Pullman, Washington" was awarded the global IAA/UN Gold Medal by the International Academy of Architecture in 1996.

Nam C. Kim is a doctoral candidate in the Anthropology Department at the University of Illinois at Chicago. Holding M.A. degrees in anthropology and political science, he is currently conducting archaeological fieldwork in Vietnam on the relationship between warfare and the rise of complex societies. He is coauthor of "Social Violence and War" (with Lawrence Keeley) in the *Encyclopedia of Archaeology* (Elsevier Publications, 2007).

Christian Lange, Ph.D., is lecturer in Islamic studies at the School of Divinity, University of Edinburgh. He is the author of *Justice, Punishment and the Medieval Muslim Imagination* (Cambridge University Press, 2008).

Russell M. Lawson, Ph.D., is associate professor of history and chair of the Division of General Studies at Bacone College in Oklahoma. He is the author of *Science in the Ancient World* (2004), *The Land between the Rivers: Thomas Nuttall's Ascent of the Arkansas, 1819* (2004), and *Passaconaway's Realm: John Evans and the Exploration of Mount Washington* (2002, 2004).

Marcos Martinón-Torres, Ph.D., is lecturer in archaeological science at the Institute of Archaeology, University College, London. He specializes on the scientific analysis of archaeological remains from medieval and early modern metallurgical activities. He has coedited *Archaeology, History and Science: Integrating Approaches to Ancient Materials* (Left Coast Press, 2007).

Katelin Mason is a graduate student of Islamic studies with research interests in medieval intellectual history and philosophy. She completed her M.A. in Hinduism and Islam at George Washington University (2006) and a B.A. in Middle East studies, also at GWU (2003). She currently works at Harvard University Fine Arts Library's Aga Khan Collection in acquisitions for Islamic and European language material.

Renee McGarry is a student in the Ph.D. program in art history at the City University of New York Graduate Center. Her research interests include Aztec sculpture of the natural world and religious manuscripts from the post-Conquest period.

Elizabeth Morán, Ph.D., teaches African, Mesoamerican, and Caribbean art history at Christopher Newport University. She has recently received an NEH award to participate in the Summer Institute Oaxaca: Crossroads of a Continent, Oaxaca City, Mexico.

Penny Morrill, Ph.D., teaches pre-Columbian and early colonial Mesoamerican art at Hood College, Frederick, Maryland. She has an essay, "The Queen of Heaven Reigns in New Spain: The Triumph of Eternity in the Casa del Deán Murals," in a Brill anthology, *Woman and Art in Early Modern Latin America* (2006). She has authored several books on modern Mexican silver: *Mexican Silver: 20th Century Handwrought*

Silver Jewelry and Metalwork (4th edition, 2007), *Silver Masters of Mexico: Héctor Aguilar and the Taller Borda* (1996), and *Maestros de Plata: William Spratling and the Mexican Silver Renaissance*, a catalog for a traveling exhibit (2002–2004).

Caryn E. Neumann, Ph.D., teaches history in Ohio Wesleyan University's Black World Studies Department. She is a former managing editor of the *Journal of Women's History*.

Daniel S. Nicolae is a fellow at Edinburgh University's Islamic and Middle Eastern Studies Department. He is the coauthor of *Lehrbuch des Klassischen Syrisch* (Harrassowitz, 2008).

Lisa Niziolek is a Ph.D. candidate in anthropology at the University of Illinois at Chicago. Her research interests include craft specialization, pottery production, pre-state societies in the Philippines, Neolithic Ireland, and the geochemical analysis of archaeological materials.

Tanure Ojaide, Ph.D., teaches at the University of North Carolina at Charlotte, where he is the Frank Graham Porter Professor of Africana Studies. He specializes in African and pan-African literatures, art, and folklore. In addition to winning many literary prizes for his poetry, he has many scholarly publications, including *Poetic Imagination in Black Africa* (1996), *Poetry, Performance and Art: Udje Dance Songs of the Urhobo People* (2002), and with Joseph Obi, *Texts and Contexts: Culture, Society, and Politics in Modern African Poetry* (2004).

Penelope Ojeda de Huala is a Ph.D. candidate in art history at the Graduate Center of the City University of New York, where she studies pre-Columbian to contemporary art of Latin America. Her research focus is Guatemala and Peru, particularly the enduring thoughts and practices of indigenous cultures as manifested in art.

Sophie Oosterwijk, Ph.D., is currently a lecturer in history of art at the University of Leicester and honorary editor of the journal *Church Monuments*. She has published widely on medieval childhood, which was the subject of her Ph.D. thesis and of her forthcoming monograph with Brepols Publishers.

Michael J. O'Neal, Ph.D., is a writer who lives in Moscow, Idaho. He is a frequent contributor to reference and educational books, including *Lives and Works: Young Adult Authors* (1999), *The Crusades* (2005), and *America in the 1920s* (2006).

Dianne White Oyler, Ph.D., teaches African history at Fayetteville State University. She is the author of *The History of the N'ko Alphabet and Its Role in Mande Transnational Identity: Words as Weapons* (2005) as well as articles in the refereed journals *Research in African Literature*, the *Mande Studies Journal*, and the *International Journal of African Historical Studies*.

Sharon Pruitt, Ph.D., currently teaches art history at East Carolina University's School of Art and Design. Her research interest includes both African and African American art and culture. She contributed essays to the following books: *African Studies: A Survey of Africa and the African Diaspora* (Carolina Academic Press, 1993), *Introduction to Kenya: An Interdisciplinary Approach* (Carolina Academic Press, 1993), *Issues in Contemporary African Art* (International Society for the Study of Africa at Binghamton University, 1998), *Contemporary Textures: Multidimensionality in Nigerian Art* (International Society for the Study of Africa at Binghamton University, 1999), *Black American Intellectualism and Culture* (JAI Press, Inc., 1999), *A Century of African American Art: The Paul R. Jones Collection* (Rutgers University Press, 2004), and *Engines of the Black Power Movement: Essays on the Influence of Civil Rights Actions, Arts, and Islam* (McFarland and Company, Inc., 2007).

Babak Rahimi, Ph.D, is assistant professor of Iranian and Islamic studies at the University of California, San Diego. He is the author of numerous articles on Iran, Iraq, and Turkey; he is also completing a book project, titled *Between Carnival and Mourning: Muharram Rituals and the Rise of the Early Modern Iranian Public Sphere, 1587-1666 C.E.*

Andrew Rippin, Ph,D,, F.R.S.C., is professor of Islamic history and dean of the faculty of humanities at the University of Victoria, Canada. He is author of *Muslims: Their Religious Beliefs and Practices* (third edition, Routledge, 2005) and *The Qur'an and Its Interpretative Tradition* (Ashgate, 2001).

Bradley Skeen, M.A., has taught at the University of Minnesota, Webster University, and Washington University. He is a specialist in magic, religion, and philosophy in late antiquity and has contributed to research in that field in *Die Zeitschrift für Papyrologie und Epigraphik*, among other journals.

John Soderberg, Ph.D., is the managing director of the Evolutionary Anthropology Laboratory at the University of Minnesota. His research focuses on the links between religion and urbanism in early medieval northern Europe.

Ilicia Sprey, Ph.D., teaches Asian and European history courses in the Department of History, Saint Joseph's College, Indiana. As a medievalist, she has written on intercultural, diplomatic, social, and economic relations in the premodern world and is the author of *The Ancient World: Civilizations of the Near East and Southwest Asia* (M. E. Sharpe, 2007).

Alan M. Stahl, Ph.D., is curator of numismatics at Princeton University. Among his numismatic publications are *The Merovingian Coinage of the Region of Metz* (Louvain-la-Neuve, 1982), *The Venetian Tornesello: A Medieval Colonial Coinage* (American Numismatic Society, 1985), and *Zecca: The Mint of Venice in the Middle Ages* (John Hopkins University Press, 2000). He has also written extensively on medieval Venetian history.

Tom Streissguth is a freelance author, editor, and journalist who has published more than 70 nonfiction and reference books. His most recent titles include *Clay v. United States, Genghis Khan's Mongol Empire, Library in a Book: Hate Crimes, Eyewitness History: The Roaring Twenties,* and the *Greenhaven Encyclopedia of the Middle Ages.*

Ananda Cohen Suarez is a Ph.D. student at the Graduate Center of the City University of New York, specializing in pre-Columbian and colonial Latin American art history. She is particularly interested in cross-cultural encounters, vernacular religious art, and manuscript production in the early colonial Americas.

Tina L Thurston, Ph.D., teaches archaeology at the University at Buffalo, State University of New York's Department of Anthropology. She works regularly in northern Europe, studying the development of Iron Age and early medieval states and the meanings of continuity and change in cultural landscapes. She is the author of *Landscapes of Power, Landscapes of Conflict: State Formation in the South Scandinavian Iron Age* (Kluwer, 2001) and recently edited *Seeking A Richer Harvest: The Archaeology of Subsistence Intensification, Innovation and Change* (Springer, 2007).

David W. Tschanz, Ph.D., has degrees in history and epidemiology and works for Saudi Aramco Medical Services in Dhahran, Saudi Arabia. He is the editor of the military history journal *Cry "Havoc!"* and was contributing editor of *COMMAND* magazine, specializing in medical military history. He is currently at work on his seventh book.

David Vallilee is an independent scholar.

Julie-Ann Vickers is completing a Ph.D. in medieval Italian history at the University of Cambridge, United Kingdom. Her thesis looks at monastic forgery in southern Italy during the central middle ages.

Lawrence Waldron, M.F.A., is an associate professor and doctoral candidate at the City University of New York, specializing in non-Western fields of art history and culture. He has presented and published various articles on the art and culture of the pre-Columbian Caribbean and Southeast Asia.

Alasdair Watson, B.A., is an Arabic linguist and translator. He is currently studying for his master's degree in translation studies at Edinburgh University, Scotland.

J. Tia Wheeler is a Ph.D. candidate at the University of St. Andrews. Her specialization within medieval Islamic history is interaction between the Middle East and Central Asia.

Shana Worthen, Ph.D., currently teaches history of technology at the University of Arkansas at Little Rock. Her essay "On Mills and Meaning" was published in *Wind and Water in the Middle Ages: Fluid Technologies from Antiquity to the Renaissance,* ed. Steven A. Walton (ACMRS, 2006).

Bailey K. Young is professor of history at Eastern Illinois University and co-director of the Walhain Castle Excavation Project in Belgium. His recent publications include articles on Merovingian archaeology in *Ancient Europe 8000 B.C.-A.D. 1000. Encyclopedia of the Barbarian World,* edited by Peter Bogucki and Pam Crabtree (Charles Scribners' Sons, 2004); "Rites funéraires et stratégie politique: le cas des tombes royales", in L. Baray, ed., *Archéologie des pratiques funéraires. Approches critiques* (Mt. Beuvray Archaeological Center, 2004); and "Le Tennessee Valley Authority: de l'archéologie de sauvetage à une politique de longue terme" in Jean-Paul Demoule (ed), *L'archéologie préventive dans le monde. Apports de l'archéologie préventive à la connaissance du passée* (La Découverte, 2007).

Almaz Zewde, Ph.D., currently teaches education and social change and several interdisciplinary courses at Howard University, Department of African Studies. She has authored book chapters and journal articles on African health and development issues. Her research synthesizing works on African development discourse is due within the next few years.

List of Illustrations

List of Maps and Primary Source Documents

Entries S to Z

► sacred sites

INTRODUCTION

In most traditional religions the place that is sacred is the place where ritual is performed. For many areas of the world, such as the Americas and much of Africa and Australasia, this remained true throughout the Middle Ages. The hearts of cities were grand backdrops for the display of ritual, most often animal sacrifice, whether in the Hindu temples of India and Southeast Asia; atop the giant pyramids in the cities of the Mississippians, Aztecs, and Incas; or in the palace complexes of China. The famous stone walls of Great Zimbabwe in southern Africa were not city walls in the usual sense, but they served to limit the space of the royal compound from the houses of the city's populace to create a sacred space for ritual. But ritual could also make much more private spaces sacred. East Asian homes contained shrines to the family ancestors and household gods, while in Africa blacksmithing forges were made sacred by the deposit of magical talismans under the foundations and by rituals of exorcism and consecration conducted by ecstatic priestesses.

Still, the great story of religion in the Middle Ages is the emergence of the three Abrahamic faiths as world religions. Even for these faiths, the synagogue, the church, and the mosque, where rituals are performed, remain the most familiar sacred places (though sacred talk—the sermon—holds a much more important place than sacred action compared with traditional religions). The nature of these new religions created a new sense of sacred place.

Although Judaism has older roots, the destruction of the temple in Jerusalem in 70 C.E. called for a fundamental transformation in its character that was not fully established until formation of the sacred texts the Mishnah (ca. 200 C.E.) and the Talmud (ca. 500 C.E.). Christianity, too, began at the turn of the era but came to its full prominence only with the conversion of the Roman Empire under Constantine (314). Islam arose entirely within the medieval period, in the seventh century. All three are religions of the book, whose primary means of devotion was reading a sacred scripture. The sacred sites important to each religion were those mentioned in the scriptures (in the case of Islam, in the Hadith—accounts of Muhammad's life and sayings—rather than strictly in the Koran). Thus pilgrimage, a visit by the faithful to the historical locations described in the text, became an important part of all three faiths.

The Hebrew Bible describes a whole series of religious rituals proper to Judaism, which are centered on sacrifice at the Jerusalem temple and are not radically different from those of other traditional religions. However, the destruction of the temple and the exile from Israel (a ban that the Romans did not strictly enforce) made the practice of this traditional cult impossible. The study of sacred scripture became a substitute for the original cult; indeed, much of the new Talmudic scripture produced at the beginning of the Middle Ages concerns intense and detailed debates about the correct procedures and customs to follow in every minute detail of the temple cult, precisely because it could no longer actually be realized. The substitution of text for cult was so complete that when in the 350s the Apostate Roman Emperor Julian undertook to rebuild the temple (never completed because of his death), Jewish religious leaders were far from enthusiastic over his offers to allow them to renew cultic practice there. Nevertheless, prayer performed at the ruins of the temple (but not inside them, for entry is forbidden to Jews by Talmudic law) is considered especially holy; one of the things they must pray for there is the restoration of temple by the coming messiah. For this reason, and in light of the entire history of Jerusalem, the city and the land of Israel as a whole was a destination of pilgrimage to Jews throughout the Middle Ages.

Christians, too, considered Jerusalem and Israel, as the scene of Jesus' life and ministry, to be their own sacred place, and pilgrimages to the Holy Land were being made in late antiquity. One impetus of the Crusades was the belief that those sacred lands ought to be under Christian political control. Since journeys to a place as far distant from western Europe as Jerusalem was impractical, however, medieval Christians began to make pilgrimage to sites considered holy because they supposedly contained relics of the persons described in the New Testament, such as the body of James the Apostle in the cathedral at Santiago de Compostela in northwestern Spain. Pilgrimages also could be made to churches containing the relics of later saints. In fact, an entire itinerary was developed, describing the spiritual merits of the pilgrim that derived from the importance of the relics visited, the distance traveled, and the personal inconvenience endured. (Walking up flights of steps on one's knees was considered beneficial, for example.)

Pilgrimage is an even more central feature of Islam. Every Muslim (unless prevented by some extraordinary circumstance) is required to make at least one pilgrimage to Mecca (the hajj) to view the places important in the early history of Islam there and at the neighboring city of Medina. Jerusalem, the site of Muhammad's ascension to heaven in Islamic tradition, is equally an object of Islamic pilgrimage as much as in Judaism and Christianity. Islamic authorities built two shrines on the Temple Mount, the Dome of the Rock, from where the prophet is said to have ascended, and the al-Aqsa Mosque.

AFRICA

BY TOM STREISSGUTH

The religious worldview known as animism has been present in Africa for thousands of years. By one definition, animism finds spiritual force in natural surroundings. Spirits inhabit lakes, rivers, forests, mountains, and deserts, providing essential water, food, and soil to those living nearby and protecting such places from desecration by outsiders. Unlike the monotheistic faiths that arose in the Middle East and which arrived in Africa in the centuries just before and during the early medieval period, the animism of Africa was not expounded in books; its doctrines changed with each society, often with each individual community. Through the medieval period animist beliefs on the African continent were an integral part of everyday life; they were learned within families and understood by all members of African communities, providing a basic framework for their perception of the world and for understanding the workings of fate and the natural world.

Animist belief was not under the guard of experts or scholars, nor was the faith renewed by regular visits or prayers in sanctified buildings. There were few sanctified locations at all; rather the entire natural world was understood as the abode of spirits—good or bad, benevolent or malevolent. Manifestations of otherworldly energies were seen in natural phenomena, such as a volcanic eruption, which often marked a location as important. Particular locales, as a result of human or natural events or merely through their appearance, were also sacred or taboo. African societies perceived certain forest groves, remote mountains, empty deserts, or bodies of water as having a strong connection with the unseen world, making them appropriate places for sacrifice or propitiation of the spirits. Other places threatened death or other misfortune for those who unwisely trespassed.

The Yoruba of Nigeria, whose kingdom flourished in the medieval period, marked off sacred groves outside their villages. One of the most enduring was the abode of the river goddess Osun, who inhabited a forest near the city of Osogbo. The goddess of the Osun River, she bestowed fertility, healing power, and protection on all those who came to worship her at the river's edge. Mount Kenya, or Kirinyaga, was known to the Kikuyu of eastern Africa as the home of Nagai, the god who created the world. According to tradition, Ngai bestowed on the Kikuyu the surrounding land and granted worldly goods and good fortune in exchange for sacrifices made to the mountain.

Beginning in the 15th century the Dogon of Mali inhabited several hundred villages lying along a series of sandstone ridges—the cliffs of Bandiagara—that are 125 miles in length and reach 2,000 feet in elevation. Sacred places in this area are associated with the cult of Binu; they were (and still are) used for ancestor worship, sacrifices, and communication with the spirits. In the Dogon story of creation the sky god Amma made the god Nomo, who was transformed into several pairs of twins. One of these offspring was sacrificed by Amma by having its body cut up and scattered; where the limbs and organs of the body came to rest a sacred place was made and a shrine was raised. The shrines contained the spirits of ancestors and the representation of a protective totemic animal. The Dogon mythology extended its conception of sacred place to the star Sirius and its invisible companion, known as Sirius B, a smaller companion star that was not known to European astronomers until well after the invention of the telescope.

Supernatural power also was associated with monuments and tombs left by earlier, vanished civilizations. In the upper Nile Valley the kingdom of Kush grew rich from the trade in iron, gold, and textiles; fought Roman legions to a standstill; and extended its authority throughout what is now northern Sudan and as far west as Lake Chad, at the southern limit of the Sahara. Modeling their society on the Egyptian realm, the Kushites worshiped the Egyptian gods and, like the Egyptians, preserved the bodies of their rulers within elaborate pyramids. The kingdom of Kush fell by the third century of the Common Era, after its defeat by a king of the Ethiopian realm of Axum. Near the Kushitic capital of Meroë, on the east bank of the river, more than 200 pyramids remained, testifying to the power and wealth of Kush over an empty desert plain. To the north the much larger pyramids and monuments of the Egyptian civilization were considered evil symbols of a false pagan religion by the Christians who inhabited the lower Nile Valley under Byzantine rule in the early medieval period. Many Egyptian monuments were destroyed, their tombs robbed of treasure, their inscriptions erased, and their stone used for the construction of new cities such as medieval Cairo.

The physical remains of ancient Egypt could never be erased, however, and the Nile Valley and the surrounding deserts contained thousands of temples and monuments marking out sites considered sacred to the gods. The temple of Amun in the Siwa oasis was the site of a famous oracle once consulted by Alexander the Great. The oasis resisted the Islamic conquest for several centuries, becoming a sanctuary for medieval Christian pilgrims and way station for anchorites who made their homes in the remote desert to be closer to the divine.

Mount Horeb, rising in the Sinai Peninsula, was considered sacred by Jews, Muslims, and Christians. According to tradition, Moses received the tablets of the law and the Ten Commandments on the mountain's slopes. A sixth-century monastery, Saint Catherine's, provided a resting place for pilgrims and remains in operation to this day—the oldest functioning Christian monastery in the world. Religious monuments were scattered throughout the nearby landscape. By Jewish tradition the law tablets of Moses were contained within the Ark of the Covenant, which vanished from its sanctuary in Jerusalem and, according to common belief in Ethiopia, was taken south by Menelik, the son of King Solomon and the Queen of Sheba. A medieval treasury was built near the Church of Saint Mary in Axum to house the Ark. It has remained a holy shrine, and viewing of it is still forbidden to all but the priest appointed for life to guard the Ark.

Near Axum is Lalibela, the site of monolithic Christian churches that were originally founded during the reign of Gebre Mesqel Lalibela in the late 12th century. After making a pilgrimage to Jerusalem, this ruler returned to Ethiopia and attempted to recreate what he had seen in Jerusalem, which fell to the Muslims in 1187 after nearly a century of rule by Christian crusaders from Europe. Eleven churches were hewn directly out of rock. The largest, the Bete Medhane Alem, contains the Lalibela cross and is the largest monolithic church in the world. Bele Golgotha holds the tomb of King Lalibela. The churches were built over a long period of time; some may have been constructed from the remains of earlier fortifications that were raised during the time of Axum Empire.

Rock paintings created by the San are common signifiers of sacred space in the deserts of southwestern Africa. In the Kalahari the site of Tsodilo contains more than 4,000 rock paintings created over many thousands of years. The paintings are made from mineral pigments, mostly red ochre, and depict wild game and hunters. More recent paintings that date from as early as the sixth century show domesticated animals and abstract shapes. The San consider this ancient outdoor gallery to be the abode of ancestors. A similar purpose is seen in Ambohimanga, a hill that marks a royal precinct and burial ground on the island nation of Madagascar and where a palace was built in the 15th century. The site encompasses fountains and pools whose waters were used for the purification of dead kings as well as shrines and altars and certain trees and groves considered to have spiritual significance.

In Uganda the royal tombs at Kasubi mark a sacred precinct within the national capital at Kampala. Historians believe the site may have been venerated by the Luo, a people who migrated into Uganda from the north in the 15th century. The site was later adopted as a royal burying ground, maintained by clans with specific tasks: the Nalinga as spiritual guardians, the Ngo who maintain the site, and the Lubungas, who control access by visitors. The site of Kasubi is characteristic of a feature common to many African religions, which hold that long-dead ancestors and important individuals are still present in the world, overseeing the fortunes of their clans and people as powerful spirits who also demand attention and care of their final resting places. Shrines of durable stone are often raised to mark the sites and warn off passersby. The task of maintaining these shrines and gravesites is too important to be left to untrained people or casual visitors; such places are placed under the care of certain lineages that enjoy the high status that comes with their obligations.

THE AMERICAS

BY ALESSIA FRASSANI

The sociopolitical developments that took place in the Americas between 600 and 1500 triggered the construction of large cities with centrally located sacred structures like temples and pyramids. At the same time Native Americans continued the ancient tradition of celebrating natural forces by visiting and worshipping natural sacred places, such as caves, mountaintops, and springs, set far from residential areas. Spanish documents dating around the mid-16th century, at the time of the Spanish conquest, provide historical information to complement the archaeological findings of Amerindian sacred sites. Caves, mountaintops, and temples alike were dedicated to specific gods and attended by specialized priests. In these places people sought to ensure their well-being by controlling natural forces, such as rain and earthquakes, on which their survival depended.

The word *pyramid* is a misnomer that describes the most important ritual structure that archaeologists have identified in the Americas. Unlike the Egyptians, Native Americans rarely used pyramids as tombs, and even American pyramids in which burials have been found never served the mere function of monuments or mausoleums. Rather they were prominent urban features, stages of ritual activities, and reminders of the gods' power.

The mound-building tradition of the Adena (ca. 1000–ca. 100 B.C.E.) and Hopewell (ca. 200 B.C.E.–ca. 400 C.E.) cultures was continued between 700 and the time of European contact by the Mississippian civilization. (De Soto reached the region in 1539) Cahokia, in southern Illinois, just 8 miles from the present-day city of Saint Louis, hosted at its height more than 20,000 people. Mounds were built in several stages and resemble Mesoamerican pyramids, with large steps and central staircases. Pyramids are found within large enclosures. One side of the pyramid serves as a ritual stage and faces a plaza for public gatherings. Effigy mounds are found in the northern Woodlands and Great Lakes areas. They date 200 to 400 years later than the Adena Serpent Mound in modern-day Ohio but belong to the same tradition. The animals depicted are mostly bears and birds, although occasionally other mammals and geometric figures appear. The mounds were burial places, and individual and communal graves have been mostly found in the heart or head of the animal depicted, suggesting perhaps that the animal was a totem clan for the family of the deceased.

The ancient city of Teotihuacán in central Mexico, site of the impressive Pyramid of the Moon, continued to be a sacred site even after its decline around 600. The Aztec gave the city its present name, which means "Place of Becoming Gods," acknowledging the deep and sacred relation that connected them to their ancestors. The largest pyramid in Mesoamerica, however, is found in Cholula, in the Mexican state of Puebla. Although it was first built around 200 B.C.E., the city of Cholula and its pyramid gained political, economic, and religious preeminence in Mesoamerica around 700 to 800 C.E. The pyramid was dedicated to the cult of Quetzalcoatl, the Feathered Serpent, a supreme god of creation and civilization in ancient Middle America. Rulers came to the city to receive their honorific titles during ceremonies that were carried out at the pyramid. The pyramid has the characteristic Mesoamerican stepped construction and appears to have been surrounded by numerous plazas and smaller platforms.

Two pyramid-temples, standing side by side, dominated the sacred precinct at the heart of the Aztec capital of Tenochtitlán. One shrine was called Tonacatepetl, "Hill of Sustenance," and was presided over by Tlaloc, the rain god. The other temple was a reproduction of Coatepec, the hill where the Aztec patron god, Huitzilopochtli, was born. In the 1980s archaeological excavations at the main temple revealed enormous caches of offerings, ranging from fine gold and jade pieces to humble ceramic pots. The offerings were brought from all over Mesoamerica by tribute payers' subjects and sanctified the economic and political hegemony of the Aztec Empire.

Chichén Itzá is the most prominent Mayan site of the Postclassic Period, flourishing from about 750 to 1200. It

*Stone serpent, Aztec culture, Mexico, ca. 1325–1521. Stone serpents were common architectural elements; a wall of serpents (*coatepantli*) was often used to delimit sacred spaces within a ceremonial area.*
(© The Trustees of the British Museum)

CAHOKIA MOUND 72

The Mississippian city of Cahokia is laid out on a grid well aligned to the cardinal points. The central structure is the enormous earthen ceremonial platform now called Monk's Mound. The main plaza of the city and other important earthen ceremonial mounds are laid on the south axis, while other structures of a more purely ceremonial nature, including the mysterious "woodhenge," are laid out on the west axis, extending toward the Mississippi River.

The southern axis terminates about a mile from Monk's Mound at a small artificial ridge known to archaeologists as mound 72. It lies just to the east of a straight line extending from the center of Monk's Mound and, unlike any other structure at the site, is aligned northwest to southeast. Excavation of the mound in the 1980s revealed that it is the marker of the most extravagant burials ever made in medieval North America north of Mexico. Radiocarbon dating of wood in the grave indicates that it was made in about 1000 C.E. The figure whose grave it appears to be is a middle-aged man who almost certainly was the ruler of Cahokia and who must have somehow been extraordinary even beyond that status to rate such treatment. He is laid out on a bed of seashells arranged in the pattern of a peregrine falcon, the image of the creator god in Mississippian belief. His grave goods consist of both ceremonial regalia and weapons.

The most extraordinary thing about the grave is that it also contains the skeletons of approximately 250 other individuals. Many had their heads and hands cut off, strongly suggesting that the process of burial included the offering of human sacrifice. That such sacrifices were common at Cahokia is indicated by the presence of pots in the shape of human heads, which archaeologists believe commemorated the identity of the victims after the flesh had rotted from their skulls. That practice might well indicate the sacrifice of prisoners of war, but a disproportionate number of the burials in Mound 72 were of pubescent girls, who must have been chosen for some other reason, perhaps to become the king's wives in the next world. Such an extravagant ceremony of sacrifice was probably a public spectacle. The site of the grave suggests that it must have remained an important sacred site after the actual burial ceremonies were completed.

dominated the northern Yucatán Peninsula, a lowland and arid area of Mexico. Several monumental structures make Chichén Itzá an exemplary late Mayan sacred site. The so-called El Castillo is a pyramid with nine terraces and staircases on all four sides. Like Cholula, the temple is dedicated to the Feathered Serpent, known in Yucatán as Kukulkan. Archaeologists and historians have long speculated about the political and religious connection between Chichén Itzá and central Mexico because of the widespread cult of the Feathered Serpent. The name of the site, which translates to "At the Mouth of the Well of the Itza People," indicates the importance of the natural wells, known as cenotes, among the Maya. Lacking rivers, Yucatán depended on wells for water. Chichén Itzá was built in proximity of two major wells, one of which, the Cenote of Sacrifice, was used only for religious purposes. It is reached through a sacred elevated way from El Castillo and continued to attract pilgrims even after the city was abandoned. From the depths of the Cenote of Sacrifice archaeologists have extracted gold, jade, pottery, and human bones. As in the sacred precinct of Tenochtitlán, tributes and offerings to the gods made in Chichén Itzá not only exalted the supernatural power of the deities but also fostered social cohesion among the various civilizations of southern Mesoamerica.

Sacred places in South America, and especially in the central Andes, are better described as *huacas*, which in the language of the Inca indicate sacred places or shrines, either human made or natural, where gods and ancestors are venerated. At the time of the Inca (15th and 16th centuries) the emperor was considered a *huaca*, and people worshipped mountain passes and stones where the ruler walked and rested during his journeys. Imperial burials or sacred places of origin were also *huacas*. These sites were found along imaginary straight lines that ideally connected every shrine to the most sacred place for the Inca, the city of Cuzco, considered the center of the empire and its political and spiritual capital. The most important *huaca* was considered the parent of the smaller *huacas*, referred to as siblings.

Besides the religious prestige they emanated, *huacas* were important economically. Priests and women devoted their entire lives to the maintenance of the cult at their *huacas*. Although historical information about these shrines is known for the Inca only at the time of the Spanish conquest, civilizations before that period probably worshipped *huacas* as well. The Inca actually appropriated *huacas* of the territories they conquered, superimposing the imperial cult to preexisting deities. The site of Pachacamac, the supreme god creator of the coastal region, is located just south of Lima, the modern capital of Peru. Although the Inca claimed that it was founded by the emperor Thupa Inca, archaeological excavations have proved that the *huaca* had been visited for at least 500 years, before the Inca added their contribution in the 15th century. The island of Titicaca in the Andean lake by the same name was also an accepted place of origin of the Inca. Incan rulers created an imperial cult around the sun, the supreme deity in the highland, and worshipped a rock on the island where, according to tradition, the sun was born. Archaeologists have found evidence that pilgrims gathered from all over the Andes to watch the sunrises and sunsets at Lake Titicaca and made offerings to the sun god.

ASIA AND THE PACIFIC

BY KENNETH HALL

China's early ritual tradition was shaped by its developing Confucian states. The imperial courts and their accompanying ritual and urban complexes celebrated the role of the Chinese emperor as the source of an orderly and productive society. Early imperial art not only stressed Confucian secularity but also respected preexisting popular concerns about ancestors and the realm of nature. Sensitivity to nature encouraged the Chinese and their Japanese and Korean neighbors to use wood as the primary building material for both public and religious buildings. China's architecture also celebrated the orderly use of space, consistent with what became known as feng shui—a practice based on the writings of the scholar Zhu Xi (ca. 1126–ca. 1200) regarding the placement and arrangement of space to achieve harmony with the natural surroundings.

Chinese courts and their urban surroundings consisted of properly placed public buildings; the residences of officials; Buddhist, Dao, and Confucian temples; and the marketplaces, public squares, and homes of the resident nonelite. Deliberately planned, these urban centers were laid out in a grid pattern on a north–south axis. North was positive, sacred, and traditionally associated with the realm of the supportive ancestors and celestial divine. South was negative, potentially dangerous, and associated with malevolent spirits and threatening outsiders. East and west marked the middle ground, where the sacred and secular intersected. Burial grounds, including royal tombs, were placed outside this orderly urban ritualistic, administrative, and residential realm, because they contained the unpredictable spirits of the dead.

The imperial palace compound was in the north; beyond the palace and outside the northern city walls was an imperial park that included a large artificial lake and served as a royal hunting preserve and private space for the emperor and his court. The palace compound inside the city wall included imperial academies (where the children of government officials received their education), a Hall of Ritual (the site of

An image thought to be of Shiva, from the Kashmir-Smast caves, Mardan, North-West Frontier, Pakistan, ca. seventh through ninth centuries; several Hindu caves with wooden architectural interiors and sacred images have been found in this region. (© The Trustees of the British Museum)

Confucian ceremonies), a Hall of Spirits (where the Chinese spirit pantheon was acknowledged), and a Hall of Learning (where the imperial examinations were administered). At the extreme north was the emperor's private residence, in a gardenlike setting containing carefully placed groupings of plants and rocks, winding streams, and pathways. Inspired by Dao and Buddhist religious doctrines, these natural elements satisfied the emperor's need for a sense of universal order beyond the secular orderliness of his surrounding imperial compound. Symbolically only the emperor, in his residential compound, was able to bridge the two realms.

Consistent with Confucian logic that emphasized secularity over the celestial, imperial tombs celebrated human existence. By the Tang Dynasty (618–907) royal tombs, which have been found near Xi'an in northern China and Nanjing in southern China, were set off by *pailou*, or large commemorative archways. A tomb's *pailou* served as an aboveground entranceway into an "urban" area complete with broad avenues ("spirit ways") that contained larger-than-life human and animal statuary, ritual halls, and elaborate gardens. The spirit ways led to the burial mound, which was located above the tomb entrance. A vertical shaft connected the mound to the underground burial chamber. In front of each Tang tomb was a memorial stone marker inscribed with the worldly accomplishments of the deceased. Tang tombs are also known for their three-colored glazed pottery figures of horses and human figures intended to accompany the deceased in their death.

The Chinese (like other Asians) did not think of themselves necessarily as members of a single church but compartmentalized their religions according to need. The worshipper went to a temple of the divinity he or she believed to have the most potential to secure the desired results. In China no ties bound a worshipper to a priest.

Chinese religion was centered ultimately on the family and combined elements of Daoism, Buddhism, and Confucianism daily practices. Acknowledgment of Buddhist or Confucian gods in family ritual was limited to lighting three sticks of incense in the morning and evening: one outside the back door for wandering ghosts, one for the Fireplace God in the kitchen, and one for the ancestors before their tablets in the main hall. The Fireplace God was especially important because he was likely to report inappropriate behavior to his superior gods.

While properly worshipped ancestors were the family's benevolent protectors, ghosts were ancestors who had no descendents to acknowledge them. The Chinese believed that three souls left the human body at death: one soul stayed in the grave and was like a stranger, another traveled to the otherworld to be judged as a member of the wider universe or condemned to the realm of demons, and the third soul stayed with the ancestral tablet and remained a family relative.

Ancestral tablets were stone, metal, or wooden tablets on ancestral altars, with accompanying urns meant for incense sticks and food offerings. In Chinese homes ancestral tablets stated the names of male ancestors and their wives. These family ancestors were honored in the home as well as in community or family clan temples and at grave sites. The Chinese believed that deceased ancestors who were not properly worshipped might become harmful ghosts rather than benevolent and loyal ancestors.

Buddhist statuary, temple art, and ritual tradition spread from India to Tibet and China in the early first millennium. Buddhism moved along the Silk Road from northwestern India across central Asia and the Indian Ocean maritime passageway used for the spice trade. The religion's path into China was marked by pilgrimage and monastic sites. The fifth-century Longmen Grotto complex in China's northwest Henan Province consists of more than 100,000 statues in a series of caves and temples. At the grotto Indian stupas (dome-shaped structures) transformed into pagodas—multitiered towers that became the focal point of Buddhist temples throughout East Asia.

The architects of India's medieval religious sites drew inspiration from forms of religious devotion introduced during the era. The Bhakti devotional tradition in Hinduism and the Mahayana Buddhist tradition in Buddhism encouraged devotees to embrace the divine through personal devotion and moral commitment, expressed by gifts, prayer, and ritual performance. The earliest Indian temples were third-century Buddhist and Hindu meditation sites cut into the faces of the mountains near Ajanta (ca. 200–ca. 600) and Ellora (ca. 600–ca. 1000), west of modern-day Mumbai and elsewhere in northwestern India, where the monastic compounds consisted of one or more chapels for worship. The oldest chapels contain abstract representations of the Buddha as stupas crafted out of solid stone. Later, the Buddha and the Hindu gods Vishnu and Siva were depicted in statuary accompanied by icons or representations of Mahayana Buddhist and Hindu divinity. Buddhist and Hindu texts were carved in stone images and painted on shrine walls. By 600 freestanding Buddhist shrines and Hindu temples across Asia adopted and adapted the art and architecture portrayed in these early mountain temples.

In northern India a fluted melon-shaped cushion called an *amalaka* crowned most Hindu temples; in southern India rounded stupas topped the spires. These decorations reflected an adaptation of earlier temple art that culminated in depictions of the *linga* (the male phallus), a symbol of the Hindu god Shiva, the lord of fertility. Hindu temples usually included the image of a divine being, with a spire above the image pointing to the god's celestial home and a hall in front of the image

Silver Buddha on a bronze lotus base, Borneo, Indonesia, eighth or ninth century; such sculptures were carried to the islands of Southeast Asia by pilgrims returning from the Buddhist holy land in eastern India. (© The Trustees of the British Museum)

for worshippers to pray. Preliminary iconography, stone and cast-metal (normally bronze) icons, and wall murals inspired by the oral and textual traditions of the temple's god prepared the worshipper to embrace the god in his inner sanctum.

A medieval Indian temple was a sacred space normally dedicated to the god Vishnu or Shiva or an alternate form or personality of either god, known as an avatar. After entering a temple, the worshipper prepared to embrace the god by meditating on the numerous statuary, stone carvings, and wall murals. These visual images were intended to help worshippers recall sacred stories that portray the various personalities associated with the divine and prepare them to proceed on their pilgrimages. Temple worship included prayer at several supplemental altars, culminating in entry to the innermost shrine of the temple, where the worshipper encountered the most sacred temple icon of the divine. Temple worship was partly a reciprocal exchange between the worshipper and the god. The worshipper normally presented a material offering, such as money or food, to the icon of the god. In theory, the god consumed the offering and was then spiritually present to receive the prayers of the worshipper.

At that moment the second aspect of temple worship began, in which the worshipper internalized the god to experience and temporarily become one with the divine presence. In preparation the worshipper cleared his or her mind of all external thoughts and centered attention exclusively on the god. To do this, the worshipper focused on the aspects of the god portrayed in the temple iconography and statuary: the depictions of the Lord's hands and legs, the items in the god's hands, and the posture and facial expression associated with the well-known oral and written traditions concerning the god. The worshipper might also invoke a chant or hymn, ring a bronze bell, light a candle or oil lamp, or burn incense to ensure a successful prayer.

Beginning in the sixth century artisans in the new monarchies of Southeast Asia redefined and modified Indian temple art to fit their cultural needs. Among the earliest ritual complexes, the late eighth-century monument called the Borobudur in central Java set the standard. The worshipper symbolically entered the Borobudur as a pilgrim, moving physically and spiritually from the materialism of the secular world to the abstractions of the divine. The pilgrim first encountered elaborate stone relief engravings of Indian Buddhist texts at the base of the Borobudur, moved through intermediate terraces of Mahayana Buddhist statuary, and finally reached a large stupa at the top of the monument. The ninth-century Prambanan complex of temples, on the other side of the sacred volcanic mountain from the Borobudur, contained the definitive Loro Jonggrang Hindu temples dedicated to Vishnu, Shiva, Brahman, and their subordinate deities (including the Buddha) and local spirits, mixing Indian religions and traditional Javanese ritual traditions.

Cambodia's 12th-century Angkor Wat, dedicated to the Hindu god Vishnu; the Mahayana Buddhist Angkor Thom Bayon; and the 11th- and 12th-century Bagan Theravada Buddhist complex in Burma (present-day Myanmar) are the most impressive among the later temple sites. Like other temple builders of that era, the architects of the Cambodian temples drew inspiration from the Indian architectural tradition but prominently incorporated local variations consistent with their unique cultural heritage.

The Shinto religion of Japan is a collection of local nature-worshipping cults that revere spirits called *kami*, which are celebrated in traditional Japanese myth and ritual. *Kami* include mythical gods and goddesses associated with objects of nature or features of the landscape, like trees, rocks, waters, or mountains. The most revered *kami* became the patron, or *ujigami*, of a familial clan or community.

Shinto in the early medieval era addressed people's earthly needs rather than providing a doctrinal path to salvation. It had no single founder but developed out of the communal rites and symbolic expressions of ancient Japanese society. In the sixth century it was paired with Buddhism, which provided the answers to the philosophical questions that Shinto did not. Only then did the word *Shinto*, which means "the way of the gods," emerge to distinguish local religious practices from those of Buddhism.

Among the *ujigami*, the sun goddess Amaterasu ranked highest as the guardian deity of Japan. Other Shinto divinities included the spirits of the deceased, the most important of whom were emperors, heroes, and other significant historical figures. *Kami* were initially worshipped and presented with offerings at sacred rocks and, from the sixth century, at shrines that had territorial associations with individual *kami* spirits. The earliest of these were Izumo (659) in west-central Japan, which honors the deities of the Izumo family clan, and Ise (690) in east-central Japan, which honors the guardian deity of the Yamato imperial clan.

A Shinto shrine is usually simple and naturalistic in style, surrounded by tall trees or set in a mountain location. The shrines have ponds, fountains, or streams, which are believed to cleanse the worshipper as well as the ritual site. Shinto shrines are framed by simple open gateways to the sacred grounds. The center of a shrine is a sacred space framed by a large rope that symbolically holds open the doors of Amaterasu's cave, preventing her from reentering and thus saving the world from eternal night. The shrine's altar may have a sacred object associated with the local *kami*, in which the *kami* spirit may temporarily reside at the call of the worshipper.

A Shinto service began with worshippers clapping their hands or making other noises to summon the *kami*. A period of prayer followed, and the service concluded with worshippers offering small gifts as symbolic sacrifices. At some time during the year a shrine would be the site of a community festival, with a carnival-like atmosphere that celebrated the relationship between the people and the *kami*—a relationship that served as the basis of the continuing success of the community. Shinto shrines were the sites of personal appeals for divine assistance; community and patriotic celebrations; and traditional ritual commemorations of certain life achievements, especially births and marriages. A Shinto priest served as an intermediary between the earth deity and ancestors on the one hand and the human community on the other. *Ujigami*, the supreme guardian spirits, could only be accessed by commoners through the intervention of aristocratic patrons or their associated Shinto priests.

The heaviest concentration of medieval ritual sites in Japan was in the imperial capital cities of Nara and Kyoto in central Japan and in the earliest shogunate capital at Kamakura south of modern Tokyo in the north. The Todaiji Buddhist temple in Nara, built in 743, is among the finest of the early ritual sites. At that time Buddhism was practiced by the emperor and his court and thus was the state religion. The temple building and its statue, like other Japanese civil and ritual structures of that era, were modeled on the art and architecture of contemporary China's Tang Dynasty. The Todaiji temple was built to symbolically unify all the Buddhist temples throughout Japan and their elite patrons under the centralized political and spiritual leadership of the emperor Shomu (724–49). According to Japanese legend, 2.6 million people participated in its construction.

Inside the Todaiji temple is the massive Daibutsu ("Great Buddha") statue. At a height of 49 feet and a weight of 500 tons, the Daibutsu is the world's largest cast-bronze Buddha. Its ears are 8.25 feet long, and its hands can hold 20 people. The structure is held up by thick wooden pillars. One pillar in the rear of the temple has a hole through it said to be the size of the Buddha's nostril. By tradition any person able to pass through that hole is a candidate for entrance to heaven. The Buddha is seated in a meditation posture on a lotus throne (symbolic of purity and the foundation for the "flowering" of knowledge), presiding over the various levels of the universe. With outstretched hands, the Buddha willingly offers truth and knowledge to his faithful devotees. The giant Buddha statue is housed in a wooden structure rising 157 feet, making it the world's largest building made of wood.

Social life in medieval Pacific Island communities centered on group performances and rituals held at local meeting grounds. Community assemblies convened inside a large wooden hall adjacent to the meeting grounds, where speeches, songs, and ritual processions took place. The proceedings frequently ended in gift exchanges between the meeting hosts and their guests, acknowledged by ceremonial physical contact (such as the touching of noses among the New Zealand Maori), and a concluding ceremonial sharing of food.

The spectacular ritual city at Nan Madol on the southeast shore of Temwen Island, off the coast of Pohnpei in modern Micronesia, and the mysterious stone heads of the Easter Island, which date from roughly 400, are representative of higher levels of ritual performance in the medieval Pacific Islands. However, neither site offers any explanation of the rituals beyond the archaeological remains.

Nan Madol was built by the line of kings of the Saudeleur Dynasty. At its peak between the eighth and 13th centuries the city consisted of a coral reef of 92 human-made islets intersected by a network of artificially constructed canals and waterways. Most of the islets were rectangular-shaped basalt rock platforms made of coral rubble. The islets were surrounded by seawalls of loglike basalt stone, each weighing up to 5 tons and measuring more than 15 feet long. The seawalls, standing up to 50 feet high and 20 feet wide, were built to protect the islets from the high waves of ocean storms. The ritual sector of the city consisted of 58 islets that were the site of elaborate funeral rituals, the residences of priests, and royal tombs surrounded by walls up to 25 feet tall. Administrators used another city sector, consisting of 34 islets, where the nobility also lived.

EUROPE

BY AMY HACKNEY BLACKWELL

Sacred sites were very important to medieval Europeans. People visited shrines and cathedrals to pray for help in all matters. They asked to have their illnesses cured, prayed to have children, asked for advice, and tried to ensure their eternal salvation. Although they could pray for these things anywhere, they hoped that prayers made at sacred sites would be more effective. They hoped that the saint or holy figure associated with the site would take a special interest in petitions made at that location and would look favorably on them.

Sites were considered sacred to Europeans if they had some religious significance. In this case, the religions in question were Judaism and Christianity, both Roman Catholic and Eastern Orthodox. Sites became sacred in several ways. If Jesus or one of the apostles was said to have been born, to have died, or to have taught in a particular place, that location might be considered sacred. Likewise, if a saint or holy person worked, performed miracles, or died in a place, that spot would hold special significance. A church that held a holy relic, such as the body or even a small piece of the skeleton of a saint, often would be considered particularly sacred. Sometimes people saw visions of the Virgin Mary or Jesus, and thereafter people would consider the locations of these visions to be sacred sites.

Sacred sites were everywhere. Many medieval towns housed the relics of their own local saints, who were not widely known but nevertheless had spiritual significance to the people who claimed them. Ireland, France, Spain, and Italy, in particular, had large numbers of saints and sacred sites associated with miracles, though sacred sites were plentiful in other areas as well.

Pilgrimages, or journeys to sacred sites, were an important activity to medieval Christians. Starting in the 10th century many religious leaders taught their believers that they could earn spiritual credits called indulgences if they completed one of the three main pilgrimages. These three were the journey to the Holy Land, specifically Jerusalem; the journey along the Via Francigena (for those coming from France or other parts of northwestern Europe) to Rome; and the journey on the Way of Saint James (El Camino de Santiago) to Santiago de Compostela in northwestern Spain. Pilgrimages to Rome and Jerusalem could be combined, because most travelers heading to the Holy Land had to pass through Rome on the way. Many sacred sites on pilgrimage routes sold badges that travelers could wear to show that they had been to those places. People who made it all the way to Jerusalem often attached a scallop shell to their hats to mark their accomplishment. Not all pilgrimages took months. Some could be accomplished in a matter of days. For example, the pilgrims in Chaucer's *Canterbury Tales* were on their way from Southwark to Canterbury in England, to visit the shrine of Thomas Becket (the archbishop of Canterbury who was assassinated in 1170 by knights of King Henry II), a journey that took at most several days for travelers who stopped to tell stories on the way.

Five cities were considered particularly important to Christians. These cities were the Pentarchy, the five cities that were centers of the early church. According to tradition, five patriarchs had settled in these cities to establish Christianity. Peter and Paul supposedly went to Rome; Peter also traveled to Antioch. James settled in Jerusalem. Andrew went to Constantinople. Mark settled in Alexandria, Egypt. All of these cities rose and fell in Christian prominence throughout the medieval period; Rome, Jerusalem, and Constantinople emerged as the most important.

The Holy Land, the part of the Near East where the events of the Bible occurred, attracted both Christians and Jews. Jerusalem had been the holy city of the Jews since about 1000 B.C.E. and had been a destination for religious pilgrimages

Pilgrim badge from Walsingham showing the Annunciation (Britain, 14th century) (© Museum of London)

since that time. Other towns and cities around Jerusalem also attracted visitors. This region was ruled by Muslims for much of the medieval period, with brief periods of Christian rule, but Christians and Jews managed to visit it to pay homage to its sacred sites throughout the period from 500 to 1500.

Jews had been banned from Jerusalem in the second century by the Roman emperor Hadrian, but the Islamic caliph Umar ibn al-Khattab opened the city back to them in the seventh century. Medieval Jews especially liked to visit the site of the old temple in Jerusalem. The Temple Mount was the site of the Holy Temple, the center of organized worship, and the holiest place in Judaism. The First Temple (as it was known) had been built by Solomon in the 10th century B.C.E. and destroyed by the Babylonians in the sixth century B.C.E. The Second Temple, built on the site of the first between 535 and 516 B.C.E., was destroyed by the Romans in 70 C.E. The outer walls continued to stand over the centuries. The famous Western Wall is the retaining wall that supports the western side of the Temple Mount. According to Jewish tradition, the emperor Titus left it standing to remind the Jews that Rome had conquered them, but the Jews regarded it as a sign of God's promise that they were his chosen people. The wall immediately became a popular site for prayer and attracted numerous Jewish pilgrims every year.

Christians were more interested in the Church of the Holy Sepulchre, built by the emperor Constantine in the fourth century over the spot in Jerusalem where Jesus was said to have been crucified. This church was deeply revered by Christians in Europe. It was destroyed by the Egyptians in the 11th century, one of the events that precipitated the First Crusade in 1099. The Christian conquerors rebuilt the Church of the Holy Sepulchre and converted the Muslim sites of the Dome of the Rock and al-Aqsa Mosque to Christian places.

Other sacred sites in Israel were important to Jews and Christians. People visited Nazareth because it was Jesus' adult hometown. Bethlehem was particularly important to Christians in its role as the birthplace of Jesus. Bethlehem's Church of the Nativity was built by Constantine in 330 over a cave called the Holy Crypt, where Jesus was believed to have been born. Close to the Holy Crypt was a grotto where Jerome, an early church father, translated the Bible into Latin in about 400. For Jews, Bethlehem was sacred as the birthplace of the biblical king David, father of Solomon. The tomb of the Jewish woman Rachel, the wife of Jacob in the Hebrew Bible, was also a sacred site to Jews and was traditionally believed to be on the outskirts of Bethlehem.

Constantinople was an important city to both Roman Catholic and Eastern Orthodox Christians. The church Hagia Sophia, or Holy Wisdom, was one of the largest and most beautiful churches in the world at the time, and many visitors reported being struck by awe upon seeing it. The bishop of Constantinople, known as the ecumenical patriarch, had his seat at Constantinople. After the Great Schism of 1054, which split apart the eastern and western churches, Constantinople became the most important city in the Eastern Orthodox Church, and the bishop of Constantinople took responsibility for administering Orthodox churches in non-Orthodox regions.

Within western Europe, Rome was the most important holy city. Christian tradition held that the saints Peter and Paul had founded churches there and died within the city. The pope's seat was in Rome, and the city was full of churches and shrines. The church of Santa Maria Sopra Minerva, built on the site of an ancient Roman temple to the goddess Minerva, housed the headless body of Saint Catherine of Siena (her head was in Siena) who had died there in 1380. Santa Maria Maggiore was a major church built in the fifth century and dedicated to the Virgin Mary. It contained an icon of Mary supposedly painted by the evangelist Luke, a silver urn containing the fragments of the Christ child's cradle, and the grave of Saint Jerome, translator of the Latin Vulgate bible.

A road called the Via Francigena became the main route for pilgrims heading to Rome in the 900s. Although its route varied depending on where pilgrims started, by tradition one end was in Canterbury, England, and the other was in Brindisi (Italy), the main port of disembarkation for the Holy Land. Numerous shrines lay along the way. Santiago de Compostela was a cathedral in Galicia, Spain, said to mark the burial site of the apostle James. According to tradition, James's body was brought to Spain and buried after he died in Jerusalem. The site supposedly became known to Christians after a shepherd saw a bright light glowing over the burial site. James became the patron saint of the local people, who believed that he had helped them in their battle against the Moors.

Another road, called the Way of Saint James, was the main route to Santiago de Compostela. The trail had several departure points in France, among the, Paris and Arles. The trails met up in the Pyrenees and led on to Galicia. Thousands of people from all over Europe visited the shrine during the medieval period. Another major medieval pilgrimage was the journey to Nidaros, Norway, the site of the Christ Church (also known as Nidaros Cathedral), built in the 12th century. This cathedral was built over the tomb of Saint Olaf, who had brought Christianity to Norway and the other Scandinavian territories in the 10th century. People flocked there every year on July 29, hoping to gain spiritual favors by visiting the reliquary that housed Olaf's bones.

There were literally thousands of other sacred sites in medieval Europe, some quite significant and well known. Glastonbury, England, was said to be the place where Joseph of Arimathea built the first church in England during the first century. He was thought to have brought with him from Jerusalem the Holy Grail, the chalice Jesus used at the Last Supper, and placed it in the church. Legend said that when he got off the boat on arrival he struck the ground with his staff, which caused a hawthorn tree to grow. This tree, called the Holy Thorn, attracted many medieval pilgrims.

Saint Patrick's Purgatory was a pilgrimage to Station Island in County Donegal, Ireland. During the fifth century Saint Patrick was said to have felt some doubts about the success of his mission. God showed him a pit in the ground called Purgatory, a place where Christians would be purified before entering heaven. People came from all over Europe to visit this site, and monks would often spend a month at a time there, fasting and meditating.

Assisi in Italy attracted its share of visitors. Saint Francis of Assisi was canonized in 1228, and shortly thereafter Pope Gregory IX had a basilica built in Assisi in his honor. Saint Clare, the other saint associated with Assisi, was herself a medieval pilgrim who had visited the major sacred sites. She was canonized in 1255. Pilgrims came to Assisi to visit Santa

Chiara, the church built in her honor, where her remains had been buried under the altar.

Mount Athos in Greece was on a peninsula that was supposedly visited by the Virgin Mary, sailing with the evangelist John on her way to visit Lazarus, the man Jesus raised from the dead. Mary was so taken with the beauty of the mountain that she asked Jesus to give it to her for a garden. Monks moved there in the third or fourth century and banned all women except the blessed Virgin. It became a major holy site for both Orthodox and Roman Catholic Christians.

THE ISLAMIC WORLD
by Rose Aslan

The three most sacred places of Islam are Mecca, Medina, and Jerusalem. Mecca was the birthplace of the prophet Muhammad and home to the Kaaba, a rectangular, hollow, cube-shaped structure made of stones that Muslims believe was first built by Adam and was restored by Abraham with help from his son Ishmael. After the deaths of Abraham and Ishmael, the people started to forget their monotheistic heritage and fell back into idol worship. By the time Muhammad was born, Mecca was the center of polytheism in the Arabian Peninsula because the Kaaba was a major site of pilgrimage for polytheists.

When Muhammad gained control of Mecca in 630, he purified the Kaaba by smashing the 365 idols placed inside and around it and sanctified it in the name of God. Since then Mecca has been the most sacred place to Muslims around the world. Muslims pray in the direction of the Kaaba, and it is the destination of the hajj, or pilgrimage, which is one of the five pillars of Islamic practice. The Kaaba is so sacred to Islam that only Muslims were allowed to enter the borders of the cities of Mecca and Medina, and pilgrims to those cities were required to enter a special state of purity, wherein men donned only two pieces of unstitched white cloth while they carried out the rituals. (Women were allowed to wear ordinary clothes, which among Muslims must cover their entire bodies except for their faces, hands, and feet.) Each station of the hajj holds symbolic meaning; pilgrims would go through a spiritual cleansing, following the footsteps of Abraham, Ishmael, and Ishmael's mother, Hagar.

For Muslims the entire universe, including the earth, is sacred because it is part of the creation of God. In the early years of their religion Muslims prayed privately in their homes, especially because they faced harsh persecution from the polytheists who were against the new monotheistic religion. In 622 Muhammad decided to create a self-contained sacred space that would separate the mundane world from the spiritual. Thus he built the first mosque in Quba, a village on the outskirts of Medina. Soon after, the Prophet built a bigger mosque in Medina, which became the focal point for the Muslim community. The mosque in Medina was very simple, consisting of four unbaked brick mud walls, pillars made of dry palm tree trunks, and a shaded area covered by palm branches. Having undergone several updates throughout the centuries, the mosque remains an important center of worship for Muslims from around the world.

Jerusalem holds special significance to Muslims for several reasons. First, the Koran narrates stories of ancient prophets from Jerusalem, such as Solomon and David, who are also mentioned in the Jewish holy book, the Torah. Jerusalem has such a special significance that Muslims used to pray in the direction of that city, before the Kaaba in Mecca became the focal point. In addition, Muslims believe that in 620 the archangel Gabriel transported Muhammad from Mecca to Jerusalem. In Jerusalem he was said to have stood on the Dome of the Rock, which is where the Al-Aqsa Mosque now stands, and was then taken to the heavens. Afterward the Prophet descended again to Jerusalem, where he met the ancient prophets mentioned in the Koran and led them in prayer. In the Middle Ages, Muslims also believed that the Dome of the Rock was the site of the legendary Temple of Solomon.

Unlike prayer halls in Christian churches, mosques have many functions beyond being a place for prayer. In the time of the Prophet the mosque also functioned as a town hall, a

Model of the Church of the Holy Sepulchre in Bethlehem, late 17th century; the church is one of the holiest sites in Christendom and the focus of pilgrimage, especially during the medieval era of the Crusades. (© The Trustees of the British Museum)

shelter for the homeless, and a general meeting and socializing area. The wives of the Prophet had rooms built for them adjacent to the mosque that opened onto the main courtyard. Thus, the mosque was a vibrant center for the thriving Muslim community and had great importance in early Muslim society.

After the spread of Islam, mosques were built everywhere Muslims settled, often built according to the regional style. The common term for "mosque" in Arabic is *masjid*, the root of which means "to prostrate" or "to kneel"; thus a *masjid* is a place for prostrating oneself to God. Another type of mosque, often very large, is the *jamaa*, or "a place of gathering." Traditionally the *jamaa* is where the community would pray on Fridays, the Sabbath for Muslims, while *masjids* are more commonly used for the five daily prayers. Basic features inside mosques include a prayer hall covered with a carpet and a prayer niche, or mihrab, that indicates the direction of Mecca. In front of the mosque is usually a *minbar*, which comprises a set of steps leading to a platform from which the imam, or leader of the congregation, gives a sermon every Friday. Mosques can be decorated with ornate calligraphy and motifs of inanimate objects, but art depicting humans or animals was strictly forbidden. Decorations are intended to affect worshippers' emotions and often incorporate verses from the Koran to remind people of God.

Typically, mosques have ablution fountains built either outside or within the courtyard. Worshippers perform the ritual Islamic ablutions, symbolically ridding themselves of the dirt of the mundane world in preparation for entering the sacred and spiritual space of the mosque.

During the Umayyad (661–750) and Abbasid (750–1258) dynasties, most mosques were built following hypostyle architecture, with a flat roof supported by many columns. Within its rectangular or square plan, the mosque included an enclosed prayer hall and an open-air courtyard in the center. This layout was designed to create an atmosphere of spirituality, with the rows of pillars and arcades conveying the feeling of the infinite as a symbol of God. The spatial design emphasized the sanctity of the place of worship. Hypostyle mosques spread from Medina to North Africa, Sicily, South Asia, Persia, and Spain. A classical example of a hypostyle mosque is that of the Mosque of Cordoba in Spain (built between 784 and 786), which has more than 850 columns. Another mosque layout built during the medieval era used *iwans*, vaulted spaces that opened onto a courtyard. Usually a courtyard would have one to four *iwans*, one of which was used for prayer. The use of *iwans* was influenced by pre-Islamic Sassanid (226–651) architectural styles of Persia and they were developed during the Seljuk Empire (1077–1308) in Persia.

Pilgrim bottle, Syria, ca. 1330–50; glass vessels were popular containers for mementoes, since the contents (bones of saints or the earth or water from sacred sites) remained both safe and visible. (© The Trustees of the British Museum)

With the rise of the Ottoman Empire (1453–1923) mosque architecture was transformed by the introduction of the central dome. A large dome, often with smaller domes built around it, was built over the main prayer hall. The Suleymaniye Mosque in Istanbul, built between 1550 and 1557, is an example of central-dome architecture. According to some scholars, the symbol of the single large dome that covers the main prayer space affirmed the unity and uniqueness of God.

Traditionally, Muslims are buried in unmarked graves as an acknowledgment of the insignificance of the body after death. Yet a person who had reached a high level of spirituality could be honored after death by having a structure with a dome built on top of the grave. This tradition was common throughout the Islamic world. Sufi saints, religious leaders, and members of Muhammad's family were buried in this manner. Some of Islam's most sacred sites include the tombs of the Prophet and his wives and daughters in Medina and the tombs of his grandchildren in Egypt, Syria, and Iraq. Almost every Islamic town has at least one shrine commemorating a saint. Mass pilgrimages usually take place only to the grave sites of well-known members of the Prophet's family or of Sufi saints; other burial sites are mainly visited only by local residents.

A tomb might be a simple four-walled structure with a dome, but it could be ornate with more than one dome, large rooms, a prayer niche, and sometimes an adjacent mosque. A mausoleum, or *maqam*, is covered with a gravestone and sometimes was surrounded by grating. In the medieval period mausoleums of holy people were often visited by local residents and pilgrims who traveled far to receive blessings from the deceased. Folk tradition held that saints' bodies never decompose and that the saints could give blessings to the living who visited their tombs. Thus visitors to a shrine would show the dead saint great respect and ask for blessings and help in their lives. Another type of mausoleum, called a

mashhad, was built as a memorial of someone's vision of a saint but was not a grave. *Mashhads* were also places of pilgrimage, although they were not as popular as *maqams*.

See also ARCHITECTURE; ART; BUILDING TECHNIQUES AND MATERIALS; CALENDARS AND CLOCKS; CITIES; CRAFTS; DEATH AND BURIAL PRACTICES; ECONOMY; EMPIRES AND DYNASTIES; FAMILY; FESTIVALS; GOVERNMENT ORGANIZATION; NATURAL DISASTERS; RELIGION AND COSMOLOGY; ROADS AND BRIDGES; SETTLEMENT PATTERNS; SOCIAL ORGANIZATION; TOWNS AND VILLAGES; TRADE AND EXCHANGE; WAR AND CONQUEST.

Asia and the Pacific

～ *Excerpt from the Hindu Agni Purana (ca. eighth through 11th centuries)* ～

Agni said: I will now describe the fruits of making temples for the residence of Vasudeva and other deities. He who attempts to erect temples for gods is freed from the sins of a thousand births. Those who think of building a temple in their minds are freed from the sins of a hundred births. Those who approve of a man's building a temple for Krishna go to the region of Acyuta [Vishnu] freed from sins. Having desired to build a temple for Hari, a man immediately takes a million of his generations, past and future, to the region of Vishnu. The departed manes of the person who builds a temple for Krishna live in the region of Vishnu, well adorned and freed from the sufferings of hell. The construction of a temple for a deity dissipates even the sin of Brahmanicide. By building a temple one reaps the fruit which he does not even gain by celebrating a sacrifice. By building a temple one acquires the fruits of bathing at all the sacred shrines. The construction of a temple, which gives heaven, by a religious or an irreligious man, yields the fruit reaped by persons slain in a battle undertaken on behalf of the celestials. By making one temple one goes to heaven; by making three one goes to the region of Brahma; by making five one goes to the region of Shambhu; by making eight one goes to the region of Hari. By making sixteen one attains all objects of enjoyment and emancipation. A poor man, by building the smallest temple, reaps the same benefit which a rich man does by building the biggest temple for Vishnu. Having acquired wealth and built a temple with a small portion of it, a person

acquires piety and gains favours from Hari. By making a temple with a lakh of rupees, or a thousand, or a hundred, or fifty, a man goes where the Garuda-emblemed deity resides. He who in his childhood even sportively makes a temple of Vasudeva with sand, goes to his region. He who builds temples of Vishnu at sacred places, shrines, and hermitages, reaps three-fold fruits. Those who decorate the temple of Vishnu with scents, flowers, and sacred mud, go to the city of the Lord. Having erected a temple for Hari, a man, either fallen, about to fall, or half-fallen, reaps twofold fruits. He who brings about the fall of a man is the protector of one fallen. By making a temple for Vishnu one attains to his region. As long as the collection of bricks of Hari's temple exists, the founder of his family lives gloriously in the region of Vishnu. He becomes pious and adorable both in this world and in the next.

He who builds a temple for Krishna, the son of Vasudeva, is born as a man of good deeds and his family is purified. He who builds temples for Vishnu, Rudra, the sun-god, and other deities, acquires fame. . . .

By building temples for other gods, a man reaps the same fruit which he does by building one for Vishnu. By building temples for Shiva, Brahma, the sun, Candi, and Lakshmi-, one acquires religious merit. Greater merit is acquired by installing images. In the sacrifice attendant upon the setting up of an idol there is no end of fruits. One made of wood gives greater merit than one made of clay; one made of bricks yields more than a wooden one. One made of stone yields more than one made of bricks. Images made of gold and other metals yield the greatest religious merit. Sins accumulated in seven births are dissipated even at the very commencement. One building a temple goes to heaven; he never goes to hell. Having saved one hundred of his family, he takes them to the region of Vishnu. Yama said to his emissaries: 'Do not bring to hell persons who have built temples and adored idols. Bring those to my view who have not built temples. Range thus rightly and follow my commands. . . .

By building a golden temple one is freed from all sins. He who has built a temple for Vishnu reaps the great fruit which one gains by celebrating sacrifices every day.

By building a temple for the Lord he takes his family, a hundred generations past and a hundred to come, to the region of Acyuta. Vishnu is identical with the seven worlds. He who builds a temple for him saves the endless worlds and himself attains immortality. As long as the bricks will last, the maker [of the temple] will live for so many thousands of years in heaven. The maker of the idol attains the region of Vishnu and he who consecrates the installation of the same is immersed in Hari. The person who builds a temple and an image, as well as he who consecrates them, come before him.

From: Manmatha Nath Dutta, *A Prose English Translation of Agni Purana* (Calcutta: H. C. Das Elysium Press, 1903).

Europe

∽ Annalist of Nieder-Altaich: "The Great German Pilgrimage of 1064–65" ∽

An almost incredible multitude set out for Jerusalem this year to worship at the sepulcher of the Lord. So many people took part in the pilgrimage and so much has been said about it that, lest its omission seem serious, we should briefly summarize here what transpired.

The leading personages who took part in the pilgrimage were Archbishop Siegfried of Metz, Bishop William of Utrecht, Bishop Otto of Ratisbon, and Bishop Gunther of Bamberg. Bishop Gunther, though younger than the others, was not inferior to the rest in wisdom and strength of spirit. Although now, after his death, we can scarcely record it without sorrowful groans Gunther was at that time the glory and pillar of the whole realm. Those who were acquainted with his secrets used to say that in many virtues he was perfection itself, down to the most minute details.

These leaders were followed by a multitude of counts and princes, rich and poor, whose numbers seemed to exceed twelve thousand. As soon as they had crossed the river known as the Morava, they fell at once into constant danger from thieves and brigands. Prudently avoiding these dangers, they cautiously made their way to the city of Constantinople. . . .

They left Constantinople a few days later and, after passing through various difficulties and tribulations, came to Latakia. . . .

While they were staying for a few days in Latakia, they began to meet each day many people returning from Jerusalem. The returning parties told of the deaths of an uncounted number of their companions. They also shouted about and displayed their own recent and still bloody wounds. They bore witness publicly that no one could pass along that route because the whole land was occupied by a most ferocious tribe of Arabs who thirsted for human blood.

The question before the pilgrims was what to do and where to turn. First of all, they quickly agreed in council to deny their own wishes and to put all hope in the Lord. They knew that, living or dying, they belonged to the Lord and so, with all their wits about them, they set out through the pagan territory toward the holy city. . . .

Harassed by various trials and tribulations, the pilgrims at last made their way through the whole country to the city called Caesarea. There they celebrated Holy Thursday, which fell that year on March 24. They even congratulated themselves on having escaped all danger,

(continued)

(continues)

since it was reckoned that the journey from there to Jerusalem would take no more than two days.

On the following day, Good Friday [March 25, 1065] about the second hour of the day, [about 6:30–8 a.m.] just as they were leaving Kafar Sallam, they suddenly fell into the hands of the Arabs who leaped on them like famished wolves on long awaited prey. They slaughtered the first pilgrims pitiably, tearing them to pieces. At first our people tried to fight back, but they were quickly forced, as poor men, to take refuge in the village. After they had fled, who can explain in words how many men were killed there, how many types of death there were, or how much calamity and grief there was? Bishop William of Utrecht, badly wounded and stripped of his clothes, was left lying on the ground with many others to die a miserable death. The three remaining bishops, together with a considerable crowd of various kinds of people, occupied a certain walled building with two stone towers. Here they prepared to defend themselves, so long as God allowed it. . . .

For three whole days both sides fought with full force. Our men, though handicapped by hunger, thirst, and lack of sleep, were fighting for their salvation and their lives. The enemy gnashed their teeth like ravening wolves, since it seemed that they were not to be allowed to swallow the prey which they bad grasped in their jaws.

At last, on Easter Sunday, about the ninth hour of the day, [mid-afternoon] a truce was called and eight pagan leaders were allowed to climb up into the tower, where the bishops were, to find out how much money the bishops would pay for their lives and for permission to leave.

As soon as they had climbed up, the one who seemed to be their chief approached Bishop Gunther, whom he took to be the leader of the pilgrims. The sheik removed the linen cloth with which his head was covered, and wrapped it around the neck of the seated bishop. "Now that I have taken you," he said, "all of these men are in my power and I shall hang you and as many of the others as I wish from a tree." . . . As soon as the interpreter made known what the sheik had done and said, Gunther, who was not at all terrified by the numerical strength of the surrounding enemy, immediately leaped up and knocked the pagan to the ground with a single blow of his fist. . . . Thus the assault of the attacking pagans was quelled for that day.

On the following day, about the ninth hour, the governor of the King of Babylon [al-Mustansir, the Fatamid Caliph of Cairo] who ruled the city of Ramla, came at last with a large host to liberate our men. . . . The governor took charge of those who had been captured and tied up by the pilgrims and opened the gate so that our men could leave. They made their way, after leaving, to Ramla, where, at the invitation of the governor and townspeople, they rested for two weeks. They were finally allowed to leave and on April 12 they entered the holy city.

From: Annalist of Nieder-Altaich, "The
Great German Pilgrimage of 1064–65,"
trans. James Brundage, Internet
Medieval Sourcebook.

The Islamic World

～ *Nasir-i Khusrau: Excerpt from* Diary of a Journey through Syria and Palestine (1046–52) ～

By the wayside I noticed, in quantities, plants of rue, which grows here of its own accord on these hills, and in the desert places. In the village of Kariat-al-'Anab there is a fine spring of sweet water gushing out from under a stone, and they have placed all around troughs, with small buildings contiguous [for the shelter of travelers]. From this village we proceeded onward, the road leading upward, and I had imagined that we should come to a mountain; and then, going down on the further side, that we should arrive at the Holy City. But after we had continued our upward road some way, a great plain opened out in front of us, part of which was stony, and part of it good soil; and here, as it were, on the summit of the mountain, lay before our view Bait al Mukaddas [the Holy City]. From Tripoli, which is by the seashore, to the Holy City is fifty-six leagues; and from Balkh to the Holy City, eight hundred and seventy-six leagues. It was the 5th of Ramadan, of the year 438 [5th March, 1047 C.E.] that I thus came to the Holy City; and the full space of a solar year had elapsed since I set out from home, having all that time never ceased to travel onward, for in no place had I yet sojourned to enjoy repose. Now, the men of Syria, and of the neighbouring parts, call the Holy City by the name of Kuds [the Holy]; and the people of these provinces, if they are unable to make the pilgrimage [to Mecca], will go up at the appointed season to Jerusalem, and there perform their rites, and upon the feast day slay the sacrifice, as is customary to do [at Mecca on the same day]. There are years when as many as twenty thousand people will be present at Jerusalem during the first days of the [pilgrimage] month of Dhu-l Hijjah; for they bring their children also with them in order to celebrate their circumcision.

From all the countries of the Greeks, too, and from other lands, the Christians and the Jews come up to Jerusalem in great numbers in order to make their visitation of the Church [of the Resurrection] and the Synagogue that is there; and this great Church at Jerusalem we shall describe further on in its proper place.

The country and villages round the Holy City are situated upon the hillsides; the land is well cultivated, and they grow corn, olives, and figs; there are also many kinds of trees here. In all the country round there is no spring water for irrigation, and yet the produce is very abundant, and the prices are moderate. Many of the chief men harvest as much as 50,000 Manns weight [or about 16,800 gallons] of olive-oil. It is kept in tanks and in pits, and they export thereof to other countries. It is said that drought never visits the soil of Syria. I heard from a certain person, on whose word I can rely, that the Prophet—peace be upon him, and the benediction of Allah!—was seen in a dream by a saintly man, who addressed him, saying, "O Prophet of God, give me assurance for ever of my daily bread;" and the Prophet—peace be upon him!—replied: "Verily it shall be warranted unto thee, even by the bread and oil of Syria."

I now purpose to make a description of the Holy City. Jerusalem is a city set on a hill, and there is no water therein, except what falls in rain. The villages round have springs of water, but the Holy City has no springs. The city is enclosed by strong walls of stone, mortared, and there are iron gates. Round about the city there are no trees, for it is all built on the rock. Jerusalem is a very great city, and, at the time of my visit, there were in it twenty thousand men. It has high, well-built, and clean bazaars. All the streets are paved with slabs of stone; and wheresoever there was a hill or a height, they have cut it down and made it level, so that as soon as the rain falls the whole place is washed clean. There are in the city numerous artificers, and each craft has a separate bazaar. The mosque lies at the [south] east quarter of the city, whereby the eastern city wall forms also the wall of the mosque. When you have passed out of the mosque, there lies before you a great level plain, called the Sahirah, which, it is said, will be the place of the Resurrection, where all mankind shall be gathered together. For this reason men from all parts of the world come hither to make their sojourn in the Holy City till death overtakes them, in order that when the day fixed by God—be He praised and exalted!—shall arrive, they may thus be ready and present at the appointed place.

From: Nasir-i Khusrau, *Diary of a Journey through Syria and Palestine*, trans. Guy Le Strange (London: Palestine Pilgrims' Text Society, 1893).

FURTHER READING

Elad Amikam, *Medieval Jerusalem and Islamic Worship: Holy Places, Ceremonies, Pilgrimage* (Leiden, Netherlands: Brill, 1995).

Brian S. Bauer, *The Sacred Landscape of the Inca: The Cusco Ceque System* (Austin: University of Texas Press, 1998).

David L. Carmichael, *Sacred Sites, Sacred Places* (London: Routledge, 1994).

Henry Louis Gates and Anthony Appiah, *Africana: The Encyclopedia of the African and African-American Experience* (New York: Basic Civitas Books, 1999).

Joseph M. Kitagawa, ed., *The Religious Traditions of Asia* (New York: MacMillan, 1989).

John S. Mbiti, *Introduction to African Religion* (Oxford, U.K.: Harcourt Heinemann, 1991).

Kenneth W. Morgan, *Reaching for the Moon: On Asian Religious Paths* (Chambersburg, Pa.: Anima, 1991).

Jon Ortner, Ian W. Mabbett, James Goodman, et al., *Angkor: Celestial Temples of the Khmer* (New York: Abbeville Press, 2002).

Lawrence E. Sullivan, ed., *Native Religions and Cultures of Central and South America* (New York: Continuum, 2002).

Richard Townsend, ed., *The Ancient Americas: Art from Sacred Landscapes* (Chicago: Art Institute of Chicago, 1992).

John Ure, *Pilgrimage: The Great Adventure of the Middle Ages* (New York: Carroll and Graf, 2006).

Diana Webb, *Medieval European Pilgrimage, c. 700– c. 1500* (Houndmills, U.K., Palgrave, 2002).

► scandals and corruption

INTRODUCTION

The study of scandals and corruption in any historical period entails a special difficulty. The society under investigation will have its own conceptions of what is scandalous and corrupt, which might be very different from those of the modern investigator and reader. For instance, the prevalence of anti-Semitism in medieval Europe seems shocking from the modern viewpoint, but in the Middle Ages anti-Semitic views were so thoroughly enmeshed in popular culture that it was the fact that Jews were allowed to live in Christendom that seemed scandalous to nearly everyone in the community. Whenever a ruler expelled Jews from his territories, it was trumpeted as a virtuous act and offered as compensation to the public for unpopular measures, such as raising taxes.

In the traditional cultures of the Middle Ages, social mores were set by religion. Jews seemed to violate the social consensus of both Christendom and Islam (and in Islam, Christians did as well) by refusing to convert to the one faith accepted by the community. The failure to conform was perceived as blasphemy. More ordinary forms of corruption (political and economic) were characterized as idolatry (the worship of man-made ideas or objects as opposed to the "one true god") because religious authority established what was right and just. Also, in China and Japan, Buddhism was perceived as a foreign religion and in different eras could either be supported as possessing a superior culture and spirituality or persecuted as a corrupting alien influence. At the same time, the possibility of reform relied on restoring the ideals sanctioned by religion, whether based on revealed scripture, the will of the ancestors, or simple tradition.

Medieval rulers inevitably claimed divine sanction, if not divine status, and with it the ability to intervene with divinity on the behalf of the community; this very claim, in fact, more than mere governance, was seen as the most vital role of the ruler in premodern times. The occurrence of natural disasters, such as plague or famine, scandalously undermined the authority of medieval rulers because it seemed to demonstrate the withdrawal of divine sanction. This led to a curious situation in many places in the medieval world, from the Byzantine city of Ephesus to Great Zimbabwe, but nowhere more clearly than in the civilization of the Maya. Successful agriculture increased the population, but the growth in population demanded more agricultural resources. The response was not conservation but more prayer and sacrifice, which often consumed more agricultural resources. Eventually, the environment became degraded and agricultural production, population, and local civilization all collapsed together.

Recent research has helped to reveal how the elite classes of Mayan society responded to this cycle. Far from being unaware of it, they recognized the threat to their own power that the degradation of the land could cause. Animals such as white-tailed deer and jaguars were vital to the religious ceremonies that displayed the elite's power as well as to defining their own identity. Not only was the meat of the sacrificed animals distributed to the people as a form of beneficence, but their hides and body parts also were used in religious rituals and even dramas, displays that served to enforce the elite's power over society. When the population of these animals declined in the wild, the Mayans' response was not to stop hunting them, but rather to kill more in the belief that increasing sacrifices would restore the balance between the human and divine world as well as bolster the elites' position in their urban centers. The failure of this policy led to a more severe agricultural crisis and the eventual collapse of Mayan culture.

A universal scandal was the corruption of officials. Before the reforms of the modern age it would have been unusual to have a transaction with a government official that did not involve a bribe. Islamic tax collectors limited themselves to bribes extorted from *dhimmi* (non-Muslims), but those were institutionalized. Although simony, the selling of church offices, was specifically prohibited by canon law, it was openly understood in western Europe that appointment to any church office with an income attached would be accompanied by a payment to the nobleman or bishop in whose gift it was by a bribe equal to 10 years of the office's revenues. Even the vaunted Chinese civil service, selected by competitive examination in Confucian philosophy and meant to put government power in the hands of disinterested bureaucrats with no wealth or power of their own, was regularly corrupted by bribery. Throughout the whole Middle Ages, fewer than half of civil service positions went to examinees; the remainder were filled by the sons of wealthy aristocratic families who bribed either examination officials or higher officials to circumvent the examination process entirely.

AFRICA

BY TOM STREISSGUTH

The decline of the Roman state in the fifth century invited the invasion of the Germanic Vandals into Roman territory in North Africa. The Vandals defeated the Roman defenders and overthrew their administration. For about a century what is now Tunisia and eastern Algeria was ruled by a Vandal dynasty. In the meantime, the Roman government had survived in Constantinople, the former eastern capital of the Roman state. In the sixth century the Eastern Roman Empire, or Byzantine Empire, began a reconquest of the Roman domains in North Africa and the eastern Mediterranean. The Vandal armies were defeated by the superior technology and firepower of the Byzantines, who deployed a powerful navy and companies of archers who easily overwhelmed defenders fighting with sword and shield.

To undermine Vandal authority in North Africa, the Byzantines had allied themselves with the Berbers, nomadic herders and hunters who had been living in the Sahara region for millennia. The Byzantine generals promised Berber chiefs autonomy in exchange for their assistance, but the Byzantines reneged on their promises soon after their conquest, a betrayal that ultimately brought their domain to a violent end. Instead of granting autonomy to the Berbers, the Byzantine governors attempted to restore the Roman administration and make tribute-paying vassals of the Berber tribes. They seized land and turned it over to the eastern Christian church, to army officers, or directly to the Byzantine emperor. These practices alienated a large part of the native African population, and the Byzantine rule in North Africa was marred by constant revolts of people who saw their Byzantine overlords as greedy and corrupt.

The Byzantines also attempted to bring North Africa under the control of the eastern Christian church and stamp out the Arian heresy that had been adopted by the Vandals. (The Arian heresy was a position held by some Christian believers in contradiction to the widely held belief in the divine nature of the Holy Trinity. Essentially, the Arians did not grant absolute divinity to the person of Jesus Christ.) The constant flux in Christian doctrine weakened Byzantine authority among the common people, who saw the Christian religion as little more than a tool of conquest and control employed by their new rulers. The church and the secular administration lost authority, and by the 640s North Africa had become an easy target for conquest by the armies of Islam.

To the south the empire of Axum in what is now central Ethiopia had grown wealthy from trade via the Red Sea port of Adulis. The merchants of Axum dealt in ivory, gold, salt, and valuable spices with the Middle East, India, and Persia. The rulers of the city showed a taste for grandiose displays of their wealth and power. The members of the royal family and wealthy aristocrats built ever-larger palaces on the hills surrounding the city and imported luxurious clothing and lavish furnishings for their homes. Giant stelae raised as monuments to the dead demanded a growing share of the city's workers and resources, while iron foundries used to fashion tools and weapons required the cutting of trees for use as firewood.

The rulers found themselves unable to deal with a worsening environmental crisis, as drought and deforestation in the surrounding region made food and water supplies scarce. Trade was undermined by the conquest of Arabia by the Muslims in the seventh century, and the Axumites began to lose control of their possessions on both sides of the Red Sea. By the early 10th century the Axumite dynasty was overthrown.

At this time the Mali Empire of the western Sahara was developing into the largest state in Africa. The king of Mali ruled a central district around the capital city, and the provinces were ruled by governors appointed by the king. The governors appointed district chiefs, who oversaw several villages, each of which had its own chief. Neighboring states that fell to Malian conquest were allowed to rule themselves but also were forced to make an annual tribute. By custom the governors were members of the royal family, or court favorites of the king, and the competition for the best appointments brought constant intrigue and plotting and an occasional outbreak of civil war and rebellion.

The treasuries were filled by tribute from vassal states, by duties on goods coming to or leaving the empire, and by revenues from land held directly by the king. The constant rivalry for appointments and the king's favors contributed to the downfall of the Mali Empire. By the 14th century the general population held the royal family in low esteem. A steep decline set in after the end of the reign of Mansa Suleiman in 1360. The royal court was troubled by assassinations, civil war, violent rivalries over the succession, and the frequent overthrow of the kings by their ambitious rivals. The loss of central authority encouraged the vassal states to break away. There were four different rulers of Mali between 1387 and 1390; in the meantime the weakening empire was attacked by Tuareg from the north, the rising Songhai realm in the east, and the Mossi from the south. In the 1430s the Tuareg captured the city of Timbuktu. Akil Akamalwal, the Tuareg ruler, was known for his sense of justice and piety, but his successors ruled as corrupt tyrants.

An important theme in this history was the conflict of Islam with traditional African religions. In the 1460s, when the emperor Soni Ali Ber arrived to rule Timbuktu, he found himself in conflict with a long-established group of Islamic ulemas, or religious scholars. Decrying these scholars as corrupt and incompetent, he forced them out of office and replaced them with his favorites, who melded African traditional beliefs with Islam. Despite these attempts at reform, the decline of Mali under the onslaught of invaders from Songhai and internal corruption proved impossible to stop. By the end of the 15th century the kings of Mali were appealing in vain to the Portuguese for help. By the middle of the 16th century the empire had disappeared.

The Songhai Empire that succeeded Mali, from the capital of Gao, reduced vassal states to provinces, also directly ruled by selected governors. The king appointed his favorites to become governors, and many of these officials did not hesitate to profit from their sinecures by directing tribute payments to their personal treasuries. Judges were rewarded for their services with land, slaves, and an annual salary paid in gold, a system that made such appointments a plum reward for those able to exercise personal influence, bribery, and guile.

The arrival of European explorers along the western coasts of Africa had a long-lasting impact on the social and political makeup of the native African states. The Portuguese, who first reached western Africa in the 15th century, originally came in search of a gold route that would bypass the trans-Saharan caravans controlled by Tuareg or Arab middlemen. Soon, however, Portuguese and other Europeans were developing an industrial slave market in order to provide labor for colonies in the Americas. To obtain slaves, they raided coastal regions and dealt with native kings who captured and traded prisoners from rival tribes.

Slavery was present in Africa before the arrival of Europeans. Africans were enslaved for crimes or for debt or were made slaves after being captured in warfare. The Saharan caravans that transported gold to North Africa and the Mediterranean regions also brought human cargo north from sub-Saharan Africa. But by custom most slaves could eventually buy or earn their freedom, and slavery was never practiced as a large-scale commercial industry.

Originally, slaves were simply captured by force, but as armed resistance developed along the coasts, the Europeans resorted to bribery and guile to obtain their human cargoes. The Europeans had guns, tools, glass work, ceramics, and other useful goods to use as barter in exchange for slaves. They found willing partners in the kings of Congo and other realms, who simply extended their practice of taking war captives into a commercial enterprise. Slaves were taken by bandits, large and organized parties of professional kidnappers, and through a perverted judicial system that turned accused wrongdoers, such as those accused of witchcraft, over to slave depots as punishment. The trade in slaves became such an integral part of the social and economic life of western Africa that many historians see slaving as the root cause of the corruption, violence, and poverty that still haunt this region of the world.

THE AMERICAS
by Tom Streissguth

By the time of the Middle Ages large empires were gathering strength in the Americas. Although these realms were separated by physical distance as well as by language and culture, they shared one characteristic: rulers who glorified and legitimized their power by showing how favored they were when the gods gave protection in war, sent good weather and timely rain, and allowed their subjects to prosper. When bad fortune threatened, the kings called down supernatural assistance. If assistance did not arrive, it revealed that the kings as merely human, which in some instances led to political turmoil, revolution, and ultimately their downfall.

The Mayan realm covered what is now southern Mexico, Guatemala, and Belize and was one of the wealthiest and most populous empires in the medieval world. Mayan cities numbered in the hundreds, with a few that sheltered tens of thousands of farmers and artisans. The Mayan rulers were considered to be deities, but, as it turned out, they possessed very worldly ambitions and flaws. They employed their resources in raising great armies for raids against their neighbors; they also built immense stone palaces, ceremonial pyramids, and ball courts to symbolize their power and wealth.

Over the span of a few generations in the ninth century Mayan society collapsed. From the records of civil wars that occurred beginning early in the medieval period, it is evident that ambition and the thirst for glory among the Mayan rulers was giving rise to violent conflict. Greedy for treasure, the Mayan leaders oriented the economy to deliver luxury goods to themselves and their retainers. They strove to outdo one another in the extravagance of their buildings and raised great armies to fight for dominance. While the clash among the Mayan princes and their city-states fragmented the society, a drought robbed ordinary people of their food supply.

With the population looking to them for help and guidance, the Mayan rulers were unable to provide the hoped-for deliverance. Irrigation works and canals fell into disrepair, wells dried up, and sparse groundwater disappeared. The Mayan priesthood failed in its vital task: to bring down assistance from Chac, the god of the rains. Without the mandate of the gods, the Mayan kings lost prestige in the eyes of their followers, who saw them as merely human and their taste for wealth and luxury as corrupt. Stressed by the drought and having exhausted the land's ability to sustain their society, the Maya tore their empire apart in civil conflict and revolution.

In the northern Yucatán Peninsula, a remnant of the Mayan realm survived. According to some historical traditions the Toltec king Topiltzin Quetzalcoatl arrived at Chichén

Itzá, in northeastern Yucatán, to establish a new empire in the late 10th century. The fall of the Mayan rulers to the south provided an object lesson for the leaders at Chichén Itzá. The absolute monarchy and wealthy aristocracy, which the economy had served at the expense of the rest of the population, was transformed into a society in which a strong merchant class traded in salt, chocolate, cotton, and other locally produced goods.

In the meantime, the maize cultivation upon which the Maya relied had already been exported to North America. Maize grew abundantly in the Mississippi River valley but required large cleared fields and farming collectives, which in turn gave rise to the first large cities north of the Rio Grande. Around the middle of the seventh century, a large community belonging to the Mississippian culture arose along the banks of the river near what is now East Saint Louis, Illinois.

The city, known to historians as Cahokia, supported itself by planting maize in the fertile bottomlands along the river. The Cahokians dug an artificial channel for the river's eastern tributaries to improve the water supply and make the transportation of wood easier. The city surrounded a huge earthen mound built around 1000. Monk's Mound, as it is known today, covers 15 acres and rises to a height of 100 feet, making it the largest earthen pyramid in North America. A temple on top of the mound was the home of the kings, who were expected to control the rains, the spring floods, and all other forces of nature for the benefit of their subjects.

The city eventually gathered as many as 15,000 people, making it the largest city in North America. By denuding forests along the Mississippi for firewood, however, the Cahokian culture stripped the land of essential protection against the river's devastating floods, while the artificial channels dug to improve irrigation flooded all too easily. In the 13th century the river floods overwhelmed the fields of maize, robbing the Cahokia of their staple food supply.

In the eyes of the people, the famine that resulted was a sign of incompetence on the part of their kings. Historians speculate that political unrest grew as the food supply dwindled. Monk's Mound itself carries abundant evidence of the unfolding events. At some point, a long palisade was built around the temple mound to protect it from hostile invaders and separate the aristocratic elite from the common people. A platform was built on one side of the mound so that the priestly ceremonies could be heard and seen by the people, making the efforts and practices of the priests more visible to them. The ceremonies failed to keep the city safe. An earthquake struck, destroying thousands of homes and buildings on the mound and in the surrounding area and starting fires throughout the city. The mound was rebuilt, but so poorly that it soon collapsed. A civil war then broke

out, and by the middle of the 14th century Cahokia was destroyed, its hundreds of mounds remaining as testimony to the city's former glory.

Far to the south, in what is now northern Peru, another maize culture known as Chimú was flourishing at this time. Chan Chan, the Chimú capital, covered 4 square miles and was the site of elaborate stone palace complexes, entirely barred to commoners and outsiders and reserved for the kings and their retainers. The palaces were used to store grain as well as the mummified remains of dead kings, who were left unburied to enjoy their palatial homes and attend important ceremonies. Each new king had to build his own palace and find a means to maintain it, a system that required the royalty of Chimú to constantly seize or find new sources of wealth.

The wealth of the city made its leaders arrogant and overconfident. In the middle of the 15th century, during the reign of the 11th king of Chimú, Minchacaman, an army of Inca soldiers under Capac Yupanqui, the brother of the Inca ruler Pachacuti (r. 1438–71), arrived at Cajamarca, an allied city to the east. Cajamarca quickly fell to the Incan army, and Chimú submitted to become a tributary state. Capac Yupanqui's success, however, made him suspect in the eyes of his brother. When he returned to the Incan capital of Cuzco, Pachacuti soon put him to death.

The Inca dominion ruled by Pachacuti had risen to dominate the Andean highlands and 1,000 miles of coastlands in what is now Peru and Ecuador. The Inca demanded tribute from subject princes, who preferred submission to resistance. But without accepted rules for the succession, the Inca monarchy was riven by constant factional disputes.

In the late 15th century, a violent melee among rivals to the throne led to the rise of Huayna Capac, still a teenager at the time. Two uncles were appointed as regents but found themselves unable to share power. After one uncle murdered the other, Huayna Capac (r. 1493–1525) took the reins, putting two of his brothers to death to avoid any further disputes. The constant strife among the Inca royal families over the succession would weaken the empire's defenses against the Spanish conquistadores who arrived with Francisco Pizarro in the early 16th century.

Much the same kind of infighting was undermining the Aztec Empire of central Mexico. A central figure in this story was Malintzin (ca. 1501–50), the daughter of an Aztec cacique, or chief. After the death of her father, she was given away by her mother, a greedy woman who wanted to control the inheritance and eliminate any claims her daughter had to royal power. To further these ends, Malintzin was sold off to the cacique of another city and traded several more times until she was presented to the Spanish conquistadores under the leadership of Hernán Cortés in 1519.

Christened Doña Marina by the Spaniards, she provided valuable service to Cortés as a translator who could speak both Mayan and Nahuatlan, the language of the Aztecs. Doña Marina may have seen the invaders as beneficent outsiders who could resolve the endless bickering and destructive corruption that had plagued the Aztec monarchy. What is known is that she helped opponents of the Aztec ruler Montezuma II (r. 1502–20) ally against him and with the Spaniards. Her role in the conquest of the Aztecs, however, has earned her widespread condemnation in the minds of Mexicans as a traitor who caused the fall of Mexico to European weapons and disease.

ASIA AND THE PACIFIC

BY KIRK H. BEETZ

From a perspective of hundreds of years later, medieval Asia and the Pacific seem to have been awash in scandals and corruption. The subject can be narrowed by the dependence of historians on written accounts of the scandals and corruption. Archaeology can help a little by identifying places that must have been brothels or gambling dens, but while such places would be scandalous in many societies, they may have been accepted as ordinary parts of life within their own cultures. Therefore, even with sound physical evidence of practices that some cultures would have regarded as immoral, without written documents confirming that in their own cultures such practices were considered scandalous, modern historians are still limited in their interpretations of medieval Asian and Pacific cultures.

Instructive in just how complex matters of scandal could be in a culture is the life of a 10th-century Tamil woman, Kodhai. Her adoptive father, Vishnucitta, was a devotee of Vishnu and was responsible for daily bringing garlands to Vishnu's temple to adorn the god. Kodhai made the garlands for Vishnucitta to take to Lord Vishnu, and as a youngster, she began trying on the garlands in secret before giving them to her father. This act was sacrilege because no person was to sully the garlands intended for Vishnu by wearing them first. Kodhai's father caught her and insisted that Kodhai stop trying on the garlands. She argued that she thought she should try on the garlands to make sure they were suitable for Vishnu. This discussion might have been the end of the matter, but instead, the very orthodox Vishnucitta revealed the scandalous behavior of his daughter to others and in doing so inspired events that reveal much about the nature of Indian society in the early medieval era.

It was discovered through visions that Vishnu was unhappy about receiving garlands that Kodhai had not worn because he liked her having tried them on before he received them. Instead of severely punishing Kodhai for her sacrilege, her community was flexible enough in its thinking not only to forgive her but to accept her as a spiritually gifted person. Instead of facing disgrace and exile, Kodhai became an Alvar, or a saint; known as Andal, she became one of the foremost religious writers of her time. In fact, people guilty of severe sacrilege were expected to be reborn as dung worms that would live for 80,000 years, but Andal was wed to Vishnu. Thus, even when scandalous behavior really is scandalous, people may choose to respond to that behavior in unorthodox ways.

Even when there are written accounts of scandal and corruption and people responded with expected revulsion and dismay, all may not have been as histories make it seem. For instance, Kassapa I, "the Usurper" (r. 477–95), king of Sri Lanka, murdered his father and usurped his brother, who fled the land. Thereafter, Kassapa built a stronghold called Sigiriya—even today one of the world's most spectacular feats of architectural engineering—built atop a 600-foot-high bluff with sheer sides. According to the chroniclers in Kassapa's era, Sigiriya was either a fortress in which Kassapa hid himself from his many enemies or a pleasure palace where he indulged his many depraved desires. In either case, he was a corrupt ruler who scandalized his subjects. In 495 his brother returned with an army, and Kassapa left the safety of his stronghold to lead his own army on the plains below; he became separated from his troops and fell on his sword rather than be captured. He would seem to have been a thoroughgoing reprobate.

Nevertheless, the accounts were written by monks who had received more favorable treatment from his brother. Sigiriya still has a small number of figures remaining from the hundreds that once adorned its murals, and they include beautiful, sensuous women; however, such figures are common to many Hindu places of worship, and archaeologists have identified several temples on Sigiriya. These temples and the meager fortifications suggest to some archaeologists that Sigiriya was a place of religious contemplation and that Kassapa was defending it from defilement when he perished.

Chronicles and tales from medieval India often tell of greedy Brahmans (priests), self-indulgent princes, scheming prostitutes, and cruel monarchs. Although considered very corrupt by Indians, it was nonetheless common for a king to be murdered by his son, for a brother to murder another over who should become king, and for a queen to poison the sons of concubines who might rival the queen's own favorite son for the throne. Indeed, it seems to have been a noteworthy achievement for a monarch to die of natural causes. Perhaps the most scandalous act occurred during the reign of Sasanka (r. ca. 600–ca. 625), founder of the Bengal kingdom of Gaur. Among the many misdeeds attributed to him, he murdered King Rajyavardhana of Thanesar (r. ca. 606) while meeting under a safe-conduct agreement, probably to discuss a peace treaty. This event triggered a long war in which Rajyavardhana's brother, Harshavardhana (r. 606–47), was driven back into the core of his kingdom. Sasanka became renowned in Bengal for supposedly creating the Bengali calendar, but one scandalous act overshadowed his good deeds as well as his other evil deeds: He reputedly chopped down the Boddhi tree in the shade of which Gautama Siddhartha (ca. 563–ca. 483 B.C.E.) had achieved enlightenment and become the Buddha. In Sasanka's own day this act would have seemed monstrous.

Other sources of scandal in medieval India seem mundane by comparison. Anyone acting out of his or her caste could become the subject of scandalized gossip, although in the early medieval era society was more forgiving of minor offenses against caste behavior than it was in the late medieval era. In cities people were scandalized by men who spent more on their favorite prostitutes than on their own families, prostitutes who became rich and took on the trappings and behavior of the aristocracy, and especially people who gambled away all their wealth on games of chance. In such matters, life was harsh. The man who spent all his wealth on a prostitute would be treated like the fool he was by the prostitute, who, having milked the man dry, moved on to other clients. The government tried to regulate gambling houses, even collecting taxes from the gambling houses, but those who gambled away everything seldom received any aid: They could go to prison if they did not pay their gambling debts, and they could become slaves of those to whom they owed money. It was often left to courts of law to deal with crimes of corruption. A common problem in courts of law was witnesses who lied in exchange for bribes, and judges were supposed to take this situation into account when making a decision.

In the many kingdoms of Southeast Asia murder and betrayal were common among the royal families and the social elite, in part because few kingdoms had clear rules for the succession of monarchs. Brothers, generals, and nobles often fought over who was to be the next ruler of a nation. Characteristic of significant scandals were the expenditures of the emperor Jayavarman VII (r. 1181–1215 or 1219) of the Khmer Empire. It was typical of monarchs of the region to aggrandize themselves with not only large temples but also statues of themselves. It was believed that statues of divine beings with the features of living people would make those people immortal. Among the Khmer the monarchs and members of the royal family wanted people in the future to worship them as if they were gods. Jayavarman VII took this desire to an extreme. He built a new capital city, Angkor Thom, as well as

many useful structures, including 101 hospitals. Further, he continued the Khmer tradition of waging war on neighbors. The 20,000 shrines he ordered built, as well the monuments of his new city, drained not only the treasury but also the people of the empire. His greed and pursuit of self-glorification badly weakened the empire.

Medieval Chinese chroniclers seem to have had a passion for recording the scandals and misdeeds of rulers and government officials. A common problem from the Tang Dynasty to the Ming Dynasty was unfairness in the government examinations that were used to identify talented bureaucrats. The examinations were based on Confucian principles, and candidates for government posts had to take a series of three, each successively qualifying those who passed for higher honors and respect. However, under the Tang only about 20 percent of government jobs went to people who took the examinations. Under the Song 40 percent of jobs went to examinees. Many who passed the examinations did not receive the government posts they were supposed to receive. Often government officials arranged for their children to be given posts without qualifying for them. In addition, aristocrats were given the opportunity to place relatives in government posts. In the 15th century people often purchased their way through the first level of examinations without taking them. Those who ran the examinations often were open to bribery. There is an account of a young man entering his examinations with coins strung on a lace on one of his shoes. The examiner asked him why he had the coins, and he replied that he had heard that those who wished to pass the examinations needed to have cash with them. The examiner understood and kept silent.

Perhaps no regimes were more corrupt than those of the empress Wu Hou (r. 690–705), the emperor Zhongzong (r. 684 and 705–10), and the empress Wei (r. 710–12), who reigned through a puppet emperor. Under these rulers the government became a criminal organization, with its members looting the treasury, kidnapping children of commoners into slavery, and selling government offices. Each of Zhongzong's daughters was given her own staff, and each sold appointments to her staff for 300,000 copper coins apiece. The daughters sold more than 1,400 government positions. In 710 Empress Wei poisoned her husband, Zhongzong, and tried to rule through a puppet emperor. In a coup Emperor Xuanzong (r. 712–56), called Minghuang (meaning the "brilliant emperor"), seized the throne. He put an end to much of the corruption of his predecessors and brought Tang China to its height of power, prosperity, and arts, but corruption eventually ruined his life. Scheming for power among government officials, not only in the capital but in the provinces, resulted in a revolt by his most trusted governor, An Lushan. Betrayed and trapped by his own guards, Xuanzong was made to murder the concubine he loved most and then was forced into exile, dying in 761.

EUROPE

by Bradley A. Skeen

In the intensely Christian culture of medieval Europe the transgression of Christian morality was scandalous. Adultery, for instance, was a scandalous act for all that the ideal of courtly love held by the aristocracy was inherently adulterous. Witchcraft, too, was scandalous, though before the 15th century it was considered a sort of delusion held by the simpleminded. Political corruption and the perceived hypocrisy of spiritual institutions that did too little to help the poor were scandalous precisely because they transgressed Christian morality, which claimed to overturn social hierarchy and which had originated in a movement of social protest against oppression. From the viewpoint of most medieval people two events or circumstances stand out as extraordinarily scandalous because they undermined the essential unity of western Christendom: the Babylonian captivity and the toleration of Jews within Christian culture.

Boniface VIII (r. 1294–1303) made the most far-reaching claims for papal authority of any pope. Faced with the prospect of the clergy of France being taxed by the crown, Boniface issued papal bulls, or proclamations, defending the immunity of the church from secular taxation and asserting the authority of the pope over secular rulers. Philip IV (r. 1285–1314) of France in return ordered the French clergy to cease obeying Boniface's decrees. Boniface then excommunicated the king. Philip sent a military force to Rome to arrest the pope, who was tortured in an attempt to force him to abdicate. Although he refused, Boniface died from his injuries within a few weeks.

France unduly influenced the election of Boniface's successors. After the short-lived Benedict XI (r. 1303–04), the Frenchman Clement V (r. 1305–14) was elected pope. He was a close ally of King Philip's and, as an inquisitor, had conducted the famous trial against the Knights Templars that had resulted in the confiscation of the order's property by the crown. Clement broke with all tradition and established his court outside Rome at the papal enclave in Avignon (then on the French border) and set a precedent for popes to reside at Avignon instead of Rome for the next century.

This change of papal residence is called the Babylonian captivity, after the exile of the elite classes of the kingdom of Judah in the city of Babylon described in the Hebrew scripture. Avignon was likened to Babylon, famous in the medieval mind for its decadence and idolatry, because of the

Pewter pilgrim badge of the head of Thomas Becket, who quarrelled with the king over the relations of the church and the state and was murdered by four knights in Canterbury Cathedral, Britain, 14th century (© Museum of London)

increasing perception of luxury and arrogance in the Avignon popes.

During the Babylonian captivity the popes were seen throughout Europe as being increasingly under the control of the French crown. However, in 1378 Gregory XI (r. 1370–78) returned the papal court to Rome. After his death in the same year, the college of cardinals elected the Neapolitan Urban VI (r. 1378–89) as his successor. The cardinals were appalled, however, by the development of a dangerous paranoia in Urban after his election, and they left Rome and elected the Swiss Clement VII (r. 1378–94) as pope. Clement moved to Avignon and was unable to take any effective action to remove Urban. As a result, the papacy, meant to be the single unifying authority of Christendom, was split by a schism between two popes, each excommunicated as an antipope by the other. Worse, each had his own college of cardinals to elect successors, perpetuating the crisis. A church council met at Pisa in 1408 to try to resolve the crisis by deposing both existing popes and electing a new one. But since there was still no effective means of ousting the other two claimants, this resulted in three popes holding office simultaneously.

This schism was intolerable and from 1414 to 1419 another council met at Konstanz (Constance) in present-day Switzerland under the authority of the emperor Sigismund (r. 1433–37) to settle the matter. The first important act of the council was to declare the doctrine of conciliarism, meaning that a council of the church has supreme authority in ecclesiastical matters and can depose and elect popes at will. Nevertheless, care was taken to find a candidate who would win the political backing not only of the emperor but also of other important secular rulers so that the deposition of the antipopes and the election of a new pope could be enforced. In 1417 a native Roman, Martin V (r. 1417–31), was elected. He reigned until 1431.

The Babylonian captivity and the schism that followed it seriously damaged the papacy and the Catholic Church. Not only did it undermine the authority of the papal office through the alternative doctrine of conciliarism, it also lessened the prestige of the Catholic hierarchy by suggesting that legitimate rivals to the established order were possible. This set the stage for the challenge to Rome's authority mounted by the Reformation that helped to bring about the end of the Middle Ages.

The modern world finds the existence of anti-Semitism within any society scandalous. But western Europe was a highly anti-Semitic culture, to such a degree that popular opinion found the existence of the Jews within a Christian civilization scandalous, resulting in various forms of persecution against them.

Many levels of justification were offered for the irrational system of belief underlying anti-Semitism. Jews were outsiders in Christian Europe and, like any minority community, seemed suspicious to many members of the majority community. Lurid depictions of supposed Jewish blasphemy and of the Jews' role in the Gospel accounts of the execution of Christ were the subjects of popular literature and religious drama. Church law forbade Christians to loan money at interest, and because most other professions were closed to them, many Jews took advantage of this lack of competition to become bankers. Christians who were forced to borrow from Jewish moneylenders found a cause for grievance.

A more pertinent justification for anti-Semitism was found in widely circulated rumors. The basic rumor, called the blood libel, went back to antiquity. It held that Jews celebrated the Passover seder (or feast, held on the Friday before the Christian celebration of Easter) by kidnapping, killing, and eating a Christian child. This story was regularly revived during the Christian Holy Week, and its incensed hearers

would not infrequently lynch local Jews. (There were many thousands such incidents all over Europe throughout the Middle Ages.) It was in the hope of escaping violence like this that many Jews at first welcomed the formation of ghettos (segregated sections of a city in which Jews were forced to live), though they ultimately provided no safety. While the Fourth Lateran Council (1215) forced Jews to wear distinctive badges or hats in a stigmatization reminiscent of lepers or prostitutes, anti-Semitic actions were for the most part officially discouraged by the church, though to little effect.

Medieval kings sometimes decided that it was incompatible with a Christian nation to have Jews as their subjects and expelled them from their domains. In 1290 Edward I (r. 1272–1307) expelled the Jews from England. His motive seems to have been partially economic. At the time of the expulsion he also declared that all money owed to Jews was instead to be paid to the crown. It was an extremely popular measure. Edward touted it as a concession to the English nobles and won from them a voluntary increase in their tax rate as a gesture of thanks. In 1492, after the capture of the city of Granada completed the Reconquista of Spain from the Moors, Ferdinand II (1452–1516) and Isabella (1451–1504) of Spain forced all remaining Jews and Muslims in Spain to choose between either converting to Christianity or leaving the country.

The kingdom of France presents a more complicated case. From 1315 to 1318 southern France experienced a severe famine, and this caused an increased need to borrow money from Jewish moneylenders with a corresponding rise in hostility toward them. In 1321 thousands of young peasants (called *pastoureaux*) abandoned the fields and began wandering from town to town, calling for repentance and denouncing the corruption of both church and state. They also circulated a new rumor concerning lepers. In medieval society people infected with leprosy were quarantined in special hospitals where they were legally required to live. They were forbidden to work but were provided for by charitable institutions controlled by the church. They were allowed to go out during the day to beg for alms but had to wear special identifying marks on their clothing. The new rumor claimed that the lepers had been bribed by foreign rulers (the king of Babylon—an utterly fantastic title—and the king of Granada) to poison the wells from which common drinking water was taken and thus murder everyone in Christian Europe. It was claimed further that the Jews had acted as intermediaries between the Christian lepers and the Islamic rulers.

Action on this rumor was very swift. Many lepers and Jews were lynched, but others were arrested and tried. Interrogated under torture, every detail of the conspiracy was confirmed by most defendants, who were then executed. Defendants who persistently denied the charges were either also executed on denunciations by others or else sentenced to be closely confined for the rest of their lives in prisons run by the Inquisition in the hope that they would eventually repent of their sins. These trials went on throughout France, and one result was that the same local governments that initiated the trials were able to take over administration of the endowments of the now empty leper hospitals. King Philip V (r. 1316–22) met with a group of Jewish leaders and accepted an enormous fine of 100,000 livres in lieu of expelling the entire Jewish community. His successor, Charles IV (r. 1322–28), nevertheless issued an expulsion order in 1323. Perhaps beginning in 1325, and certainly by 1338, the surviving lepers (if not the Jews) had been exonerated of all charges against them (upon reflection it was easy to see that they could not possibly have been true) and in some cases their confiscated property was returned.

A similar but even greater wave of anti-Semitism accompanied the Black Death that from 1347 to 1350 killed one-third of the entire population of Europe. With no medical or other means available to halt the plague, the identification of a conspiracy provided at least the illusion that something could be done. Accordingly, the story circulated (not only in France but also throughout western Europe) that the disease was caused by the Jews (no lepers this time) poisoning the wells at the behest of Islamic rulers. In this instance, the authorities generally resisted the accusation and pointed out that Jews were dying just like everyone else. But this did not prevent thousands of Jews from being lynched in mob violence. The Jews of the Rhineland fled to Poland and Russia in the face of this extraordinary anti-Semitic violence. Pope Clement VI issued two bulls in 1348 denouncing the conspiracy theory and proclaiming the Jews' innocence, but this had little effect.

The irrational anti-Semitic violence of these two episodes seems scandalous now, but the episodes are a measure of how the discontents of European culture could be projected onto the Jewish community. The Jews were passionately committed to preserving the traditional identity of their own community, but their very existence as something other became a provocative scandal to a medieval Christian Europe that was increasingly intolerant and uncertain of its own identity.

THE ISLAMIC WORLD

BY BRADLEY SKEEN

Muhammad set down in the Koran the kinds of corruption to which he felt civil government and society as a whole were prey. Perhaps he based his ideas on his observations of the various governments he encountered in his travels around the eastern Mediterranean. One of the corrupt practices he warned against was idolatry. Naturally, this means first the worship of gods other than the one god (Allah) and was meant to stigmatize the traditional religions of Arabia. But Muhammad also advanced a more subtle and important understanding of the term. Idolatry, according to the Koran, is a kind of arrogance that makes men prefer institutions and ways of life dependent on human reason or tradition rather than divine revelation. He stressed that this attitude could corrupt even those who professed Islam without their being aware of it because they had been led astray by the devil. Muhammad used the term to describe anyone who opposed his own teaching and secular rule, and it was later used within Islam to characterize any political opposition, whether by those in or by those out of power.

Closely related to idolatry is the sin of pride. Muhammad taught that pride is what keeps people from accepting the truth when it is shown to them, merely because it is contrary to their preconceived ideas. Perhaps he had in mind the considerable resistance to his own teaching that he encountered; however, it can have a more general meaning too, as when people refuse to accept legitimate criticism of a government they support. Muhammad taught that the same pride is what keeps people from seeing that they are mistreating those who are beneath them in a social or political hierarchy. Pride and idolatry, conceived of in this way, are both sins that Muslims were not to tolerate within themselves and which could corrupt even a devout Islamic state.

The Islamic philosophical tradition views the state as holding a balance between corruption and correction; according to this view, the state has a natural tendency to veer toward the human, which must be checked in order to restore its conformity to the tradition of divine revelation. The precarious nature of this balance can be seen in the case of the *dhimmi*—the Jews, Christians, Zoroastrians, and Sabians (Mandaeans). According to Muhammad's own practice as well as the writings of the Koran, together with Islamic legal tradition (sharia), these peoples were to be treated as second-class citizens. They had to pay a special tax, for example, and could not participate in the government. Their testimony could not be used in court to disprove that of a Muslim. They could be enslaved; the justification for this was that, as non-Muslims, they were guilty of idolatry as Muhammad had conceived of it in the Koran. On the other hand, it was also an official government practice throughout much of the Islamic world during the Middle Ages that when an individual *dhimmi* paid taxes, he was to be slapped on the face by government soldiers. Although it was not officially sanctioned, it was almost a universal practice that government tax collectors would also receive bribes from the *dhimmi* at the time that they collected the tax. These policies seem to be motivated by what Muhammad denounced as pride.

The difficulties that Islamic tradition had to negotiate can be seen in the well-known story from the oral tradition associated with Muhammad's life and teaching known as the Hadith. The story goes that toward the end of his life in 632 Muhammad, on a Thursday in June (he died the following Monday), fell ill and asked for pen and paper so that he could prepare a statement that would safeguard the righteousness of the Islamic world forever. One of his companions, Omar, who as the second caliph would conquer most of the Near East, responded that no such testament was necessary, since Muhammad was ill and should not trouble himself and since he had already produced the Koran.

The meaning of the story turns on the concepts of idolatry and pride. Sunni tradition interprets the story as a test by Muhammad to see whether his companions had succumbed to idolatry and believed that another authority besides the Koran was needed as the final word of divine revelation. Shia tradition, on the other hand, teaches that Muhammad's companions had succumbed to pride and refused to see the necessity of allowing Muhammad to write a will, knowing that if he did not, they would come to power after his death. Naturally, Shiites argue that Muhammad intended to name his cousin and son-in-law Ali as his successor. Sunnis argue in turn that the Shia tradition succumbs to both pride and idolatry in imagining that Muhammad could have been thwarted in this way and in believing that any document other than the Koran might have been necessary. Shiites see Omar's proud treatment of

Muhammad as a precursor or model for what they viewed as the corrupt governance of the Islamic world in later ages.

The first four caliphs were chosen from among Muhammad's companions and relatives and are generally referred to as the "righteous caliphs" (*rashidun*), especially in Sunni Islam. All four were not without certain controversies, however. The first caliph, Abu Bakr (r. 632–34), was elected by a consensus of the Islamic elders present in Medina at the time of Muhammad's death, but many Islamic tribesmen from outside Muhammad's inner circle did not initially endorse the election and had to be subdued through civil war. The caliph declared that his enemies were apostates, that is, that they had abandoned Islam and returned to the ways of idolatry, refusing to accept the divinely sanctioned succession. Since he was successful in overcoming his enemies, this claim is not disputed in Islamic tradition.

Omar (r. 634–44) served as the next caliph. Despite his phenomenal military success, Omar continued to live in remarkable simplicity and refused to establish a dynasty by naming a successor, following Muhammad's example. Nevertheless, he was assassinated by a slave whom he had ruled against in a legal case. The slave thought Omar had acted proudly in denying him what he considered justice.

The third caliph was Uthman ibn Affan (r. 644–56). He had a standard edition of the Koran made and circulated it throughout the Islamic world, destroying copies of alternative editions. Some of Muhammad's original companions ob-

Gold tanka of Sultan Qutb al-Din Mubarak Shah I, Delhi Sultanate, India, 1318; Mubarak Shah I ascended the throne of Delhi at the age of 18, having blinded the previous sultan, his brother Umar, a child of about six years old. His reign was short-lived and also ended violently when he was murdered by his favorite, Khusra Khan. (© The Trustees of the British Museum)

jected to this practice, so he had them publically flogged. He also filled the administrative posts of the Islamic Empire with his own relatives. He was assassinated by Omar's son, who could not tolerate these seemingly proud actions.

The fourth caliph was Ali, Muhammad's son-in-law and cousin (r. 656–61). He, too, was assassinated. The controversy that followed over his succession split Islam into the Shia and Sunni factions, which each view the other as idolatrously falling away from true Islam. Ali's son, Hassan, was proclaimed the new caliph, but this was unacceptable to Muawiyah, the governor of Egypt, who declared himself caliph and precipitated a civil war in which Hassan was defeated, largely through Muawiyah's subversion of Hassan's commanders through bribes and promises of offices. Their preference for their own advantage over the good of the Islamic world is a clear example of what Muhammad meant by "idolatry."

The Umayyad caliph Yazid I (r. 680–83) was characterized as falling into idolatry through becoming an alcoholic (ignoring the Koranic prohibition on wine) and obsessed with prostitutes to the neglect of his religious duties. The later caliph al-Walid II (r. 743-44) is presented in the same light. These historical characterizations go along with the loss of the popular mandate that was meant to support the caliphate and with outbreaks of rebellion and civil war. These scandalous descriptions are meant to explain the rulers' political failure, particularly the end of the Abbasid Dynasty in revolt. Because they lacked the consensus of religious elders throughout the Islamic community but succeeded through birthright and through civil war, they are presented as proud and idolatrous.

Despite its achievements in founding Baghdad (Iraq) and creating one of the great high points of medieval culture, the Abbasid Dynasty (750–1258) was viewed as tyrannical, and its rulers were blamed by Arab historians for allowing the Islamic world to fall into permanent division and for allowing the rule of Arabs over the Islamic world to be transferred to Turks. Just as they had founded Baghdad, their secular rule ended when they failed to protect the city from Mongol invaders, who sacked it in 1258. Accordingly, the historical tradition emphasizes the scandalous personal excesses of the Abbasid caliphs. Family members killed each other in the quest for political power. Al-Amin (r. 809–13) is presented in sources as a homosexual. Al-Mamum (r. 813–30) was unable to control the female members of his family (a great failing in traditional Arabic culture) and failed in a suit for divorce against his wife. Details of personal scandals like these are incorporated into historical texts about rulers as a form of judgment by historians against the rulers they are writing about. In general, Arab scholars presented the history of the caliphate as one of decline. As the Islamic world's rulers moved further away from Muhammad in family relationship and further from the divine example set by him, they inevitably moved toward idolatry and pride.

See also ALCHEMY AND MAGIC; AGRICULTURE; CITIES; CRIME AND PUNISHMENT; ECONOMY; EMPIRES AND DYNASTIES; EXPLORATION; FAMILY; FOREIGNERS AND BARBARIANS; GOVERNMENT ORGANIZATION; LAWS AND LEGAL CODES; MILITARY; NATURAL DISASTERS; PANDEMICS AND EPIDEMICS; RELIGION AND COSMOLOGY; RESISTANCE AND DISSENT; SLAVES AND SLAVERY; SOCIAL COLLAPSE AND ABANDONMENT; SOCIAL ORGANIZATION; TRADE AND EXCHANGE; TRANSPORTATION; WEAPONRY AND ARMOR; WAR AND CONQUEST.

Asia and the Pacific ~ *Excerpt from the Taika Reform Edicts (645)* ~

Commissioners were sent to all the provinces to take a record of the total numbers of the people. The Emperor on this occasion made an edict, as follows:

"In the times of all the Emperors, from antiquity downwards, subjects have been set apart for the purpose of making notable their reigns and handing down their names to posterity. Now the Omi and Muraji, the Tomo no Miyakko and the Kuni no Miyakko, have each one set apart their own vassals, whom they compel to labor at their arbitrary pleasure. Moreover, they cut off the hills and seas, the woods and plains, the ponds and rice-fields belonging to the provinces and districts, and appropriate them to themselves. Their contests are never-ceasing. Some engross to themselves many tens of thousands of shiro of rice-land, while others possess in all patches of ground too small to stick a needle into. When the time comes for the payment of taxes, the Omi, the Muraji, and the Tomo no Miyakko, first collect them for themselves and then hand over a share. In the case of repairs to palaces or the construction of misasagi, they each bring their own vassals, and do the work according to circumstances. The Book of Changes says, "Diminish that which is above: increase that which is below: if measures are framed according to the regulations, the resources of the State suffer no injury, and the people receive no hurt.

At the present time, the people are still few. And yet the powerful cut off portions of land and water, and converting them into private ground, sell it to the people, demanding the price yearly. From this time forward the sale of land is not allowed. Let no man without due authority make himself a landlord, engrossing to himself that which belongs to the helpless."

The people rejoiced.

From: W. G. Aston, trans. *Nihongi: Chronicles of Japan from the Earliest Times to A.D. 697* (London: Kegan, Paul, Trench, Trübner, 1896).

Europe

∽ *Lateran IV: Canon 68—On Jews (305)* ∽

In some provinces a difference in dress distinguishes the Jews or Saracens from the Christians, but in certain others such a confusion has grown up that they cannot be distinguished by any difference. Thus it happens at times that through error Christians have relations with the women of Jews or Saracens, and Jews and Saracens with Christian women. Therefore, that they may not, under pretext of error of this sort, excuse themselves in the future for the excesses of such prohibited intercourse, we decree that such Jews and Saracens of both sexes in every Christian province and at all times shall be marked off in the eyes of the public from other peoples through the character of their dress. Particularly, since it may be read in the writings of Moses [Numbers 15:37–41], that this very law has been enjoined upon them.

Moreover, during the last three days before Easter and especially on Good Friday, they shall not go forth in public at all, for the reason that some of them on these very days, as we hear, do not blush to go forth better dressed and are not afraid to mock the Christians who maintain the memory of the most holy Passion by wearing signs of mourning.

This, however, we forbid most severely, that any one should presume at all to break forth in insult to the Redeemer. And since we ought not to ignore any insult to Him who blotted out our disgraceful deeds, we command that such impudent fellows be checked by the secular princes by imposing them proper punishment so that they shall not at all presume to blaspheme Him who was crucified for us.

From: H. J. Schroeder, *Disciplinary Decrees of the General Councils: Text, Translation and Commentary* (St. Louis: B. Herder, 1937).

The Islamic World

∽ *Abul Hasan Ali Al-Masudi (Masoudi), Excerpt from* The Book of Golden Meadows *(ca. 940)* ∽

AL MAHDI AND HIS VIZIER YAKUB IBN DAUD

When Al Mahdi's father, Al Mansur, died, he left in the treasury nine hundred million and sixty thousand dirhems, and Abu Obaid allah, the first Vizier of Al Mahdi, advised the Caliph to be moderate in his expenses and to spare the public money. When Abu Obaid allah was deposed, his successor, Yakub ibn Daud, flattered the inclinations of the Caliph, and encouraged him to spend money, enjoy all sorts of pleasures, drink wine, and listen to music. By this means he succeeded in obtaining the entire administration of the State. One of the poets of the time composed an ode containing

(continued)

(continues)

the following lines: "Family of Abbas! your Caliphate is ruined! If you seek for the Vicar of God, you will find him with a wineflask on one side and a lute on the other."

Abu Haritha, the guardian of the treasure chambers, seeing that they had become empty, waited on Al Mahdi with the keys, and said: "Since you have spent all your treasures, what is the use of my keeping these keys? Give orders that they be taken from me." Al Mahdi replied: "Keep them still, for money will be coming in to you." He then dispatched messengers to all quarters in order to press the payment of the revenues, and in a very short time these sums arrived. They were so abundant that Abu Haritha had enough to do in receiving them and verifying the amount. During three days he did not appear before Al Mahdi, who at length said: "What is he about, that silly Bedouin Arab?" Being informed of the cause which kept him away, he sent for him and said: "What prevented your coming to see us?" "The arrival of cash," replied the other. "How foolish it was in you," said Al Mahdi, "to suppose that money would not come in to us!" "Commander of the Faithful," replied Abu Haritha, "if some unforeseen event happened which could not be surmounted without the aid of money, we should not have time to wait till you sent to have the cash brought in."

It is related that Al Mahdi made the pilgrimage one year, and passed by a milestone on which he saw something written. He stopped to see what it was, and read the following line: "O Mahdi! you would be truly excellent if you had not taken for a favorite Yakub, the son of Daud." He then said to a person who was with him: "Write underneath that: 'It shall still be so, in spite of the fellow who wrote that-bad luck attend him!'" . . . Rumors unfavorable to this minister had greatly multiplied. His enemies had discovered a point by which he might be attacked, and they reminded the Caliph of his having seconded Ibn Abd allah the alide in the revolt against Al Mansur.

One of Yakub's servants informed Al Mahdi that he had heard his master say: "The Caliph has built a pleasure-house, and spent on it fifty millions of dirhems out of the public money." The fact was that Al Mahdi had just founded the town of Isabad. Another time Al Mahdi was about to execute some project when Yakub said to him: "Commander of the Faithful, that is mere profusion." To this Al Mahdi answered: "Evil betide you! does not profusion befit persons of a noble race?"

At last Yakub got so tired of the post which he filled that he requested of Al Mahdi permission to give it up, but that favor he could not obtain. Al Mahdi then wished to try if he was still inclined toward the party of the alides, and sent for him, after taking his seat in a salon of which all the furniture was red. He himself had on red clothes, and behind him stood a young female slave dressed in red; before him was a garden filled with roses of all sorts. "Tell me, Yakub," said he, "what do you think of this salon of ours?" The other replied: "It is the very perfection of beauty. May God permit the Commander of the Faithful to enjoy it long!" "Well," said Al Mahdi, "all that it contains is yours, with this girl to crown your happiness, and, moreover, a sum of one hundred thousand dirhems." Yakub invoked God's blessing on the Caliph, who then said to him: "I have something to ask of you." On this, Yakub stood up from his seat, and exclaimed: "Commander of the Faithful, such words can only proceed from anger. May God protect me from your wrath." Al Mahdi replied: "I wish you to promise to do what I ask." Yakub answered: "I hear, and shall obey." "Swear by allah," said the Caliph. He swore. "Swear again by allah." He swore. "Swear again by allah." He swore for the third time, and the Caliph then said to him: "Lay your hand on my head and swear again." Yakub did so.

Al Mahdi, having thus obtained from him the firmest promise that could be made, said: "There is an alide, and I wish you to deliver me from the uneasiness which he causes me, and thus set my mind at rest. Here he is; I give him up to you." He then delivered the alide over to him, and bestowed on him the girl, with all the furniture that was in the salon and the money. When the alide was alone with him, he said: "Yakub, beware lest you have my blood to answer for before God. I am descended from Fatima, the daughter of Mohammed, on whom God's blessings and favors always repose." To this Yakub replied: "Tell me, sir, if there be good in you." The alide answered: "If you do good to me, I shall be grateful and pray for your happiness." . . . "Depart with my good wishes," said Yakub.

The girl heard all this conversation, and told a servant of hers to go and relate it to Al Mahdi, and to say in her name: "Such is the conduct of one whom in giving me to him you preferred to yourself; such is the return he makes you for your kindness." Al Mahdi immediately had the road watched, so that the alide was taken prisoner. He then sent for Yakub, and said to him: "What has become of that man?" Yakub replied: "I have delivered you from the uneasiness he gave you." "Is he dead?" "He is." "Swear by allah." "I swear by allah." . . . Al Mahdi then said to an attendant: "Boy, bring out to us those who are in that room." The boy opened the door, and there the alide was seen with the very money which Yakub had given him. Yakub was so much astounded that he was unable to utter a word. "Your life," said Al Mahdi, "is justly forfeited, and it is in my power to shed your blood, but I will not. Shut him up in the matbak." He had him confined in that dungeon, and gave orders that no one should ever speak to him or to any other about him. Yakub remained there during the rest of Al Mahdi's reign (over two years), and during the reign of Musa-al-Hadi, the son of Al Mahdi, and during five years and seven months of the reign of Haroun Al Rashid.

From: Charles F. Horne, ed., *The Sacred Books and Early Literature of the East*, Vol. 6, *Medieval Arabia* (New York: Parke, Austin, and Lipscomb, 1917).

FURTHER READING

Charles D. Benn, "Usurpation, Overthrow, and Corruption (684–712)," in his *China's Golden Age: Everyday Life in the Tang Dynasty* (New York: Oxford University Press, 2004).

Renate Blumenfeld-Kosinski, *Poets, Saints, and Visionaries of the Great Schism, 1378–1417* (University Park: Pennsylvania State University Press, 2006).

Joel Carmichael, *The Satanizing of the Jews: Origin and Development of Mystical Anti-Semitism* (New York: Fromm International, 1992).

Youssef M. Choueiri, *A Companion to the History of the Middle East* (Oxford, U.K.: Blackwell, 2005).

David C. Conrad, *Empires of Medieval West Africa: Ghana, Mali, and Songhay* (New York: Facts On File, 2005).

Marzieh Gail, *The Three Popes: An Account of the Great Schism When Rival Popes in Rome, Avignon, and Pisa Vied for the Rule of Christendom* (New York: Simon and Schuster, 1969).

Carlo Ginzburg, *Ecstasies: Deciphering the Witches' Sabbath*, trans. Raymond Rosenthal (New York: Penguin, 1991).

John Hemming, *The Conquest of the Incas* (New York: Harvest, 2003).

John Y. B. Hood, *Aquinas and the Jews* (Philadelphia: University of Pennsylvania Press, 1995).

R. Stephen Humphreys, *The History of the al-Tabari XV: The Crisis of the Early Caliphate* (Buffalo: State University of New York, Press, 1990).

John Keay, "Harsha-Vardhana," in his *India: A History* (New York: Atlantic Monthly Press, 2000).

Nehemia Levtzion and Jay Spaulding, eds. *Medieval West Africa: Views from Arab Scholars and Merchants* (Princeton, N.J.: Markus Wiener Publishers, 2002).

Richard S. Levy, ed., *Antisemitism: A Historical Encyclopedia of Prejudice and Persecution* (Santa Barbara, Calif.: ABC-CLIO, 2005).

Paul Lovejoy, *Transformations in Slavery: A History of Slavery in Africa* (New York: Cambridge University Press, 2000).

Charles C. Mann, *1491: New Revelations of the Americas before Columbus* (New York: Alfred A. Knopf, 2005).

Robert Michael and Philip Rosen, *Dictionary of Antisemitism from the Earliest Times to the Present* (Lanham, Md.: Scarecrow, 2007).

Roland Oliver and Anthony Atmore. *Medieval Africa, 1250–1800* (Cambridge, U.K.: Cambridge University Press, 2001).

Timothy Pauketat, *Cahokia: Domination and Ideology in the Mississippian World* (Lincoln: University of Nebraska Press, 2000).

Phillip H. Stump, *The Reforms of the Council of Constance (1414–1418)* (Leiden, Netherlands: E. J. Brill, 1994).

Denis Twitchet, "The Empress Wu," in *The Cambridge Encyclopedia of China*, ed. Brian Hook and Denis Twitchett (New York: Cambridge University Press, 1991).

▶ **science**

INTRODUCTION

Science is an invention of modern Western civilization. Its basic idea is that the natural world can be explained using a specialized form of logic called the scientific method. This entails observing facts in nature (for example, the motions of the planets through the night sky) and then formulating a hypothesis, or explanation, of how and why they move as they do. Then the scientist makes a prediction about how the system under observation or the object of study will behave in an experiment or test of the predictions. Finally, a theory is made that explains all of the facts, experimental results, and observations. This theory, in turn, will generate new predictions that have to be tested through experiment and lead to the theory's being changed or replaced with a new one, depending on how accurate its predictions are. In the case of planetary motion, the general theory of the planets' motion around the sun (rather than the ancient belief that planets moved around the earth) was proved by the accurate prediction not only of the return of Halley's comet in 1759 but also of its precise path through the sky.

Not coincidentally, the same return of Halley's comet was a confirmation of predictions based on Isaac Newton's theory of gravity. (In the nature of theories, this was accepted until Einstein's more precise understanding of gravity in the early 20th century forced it to be abandoned by scientists.) Newton's theory described gravity as a force of attraction that operated over a distance without any physical connection between the bodies involved (for example, the earth and the moon). This contravened the whole mechanistic principle of science as it had been developed in the century before Newton. But Newton was able to make this imaginative leap only because of his extensive, though ultimately futile, investigation of medieval alchemy, where action at a distance was taken for granted. This is an example of a more general foundation of the scientific method in the abstract thought of alchemists, theologians, and philosophers of the Middle Ages in Western Europe as well as in Islam.

A more general contribution of medieval thought to science is in understanding the idea of the natural world itself. Traditional peoples all over the world (including Greeks and Romans and early Christians, the precursors of medieval European and Islamic thinkers) believed that the world was a continuum between the material and the divine with many intervening stages, such as the human (which was believed to reconcile both extremes) and spiritual beings (among them, angels or jinn). This idea is sometimes known as the Great Chain of Being. It would not make any sense to separate merely the physical as being natural, since the spiritual and divine were just as much a part of nature as a whole. But Christian (and, to a lesser degree, Islamic) theologians were presented with a problem by alchemy, magic, and witchcraft.

Alchemists, in particular, sometimes claimed that in manipulating physical elements they had discovered and were able to use the same divine powers over nature that God used in creating the world. Magicians, witches, and the devil seemed to be able to work wonders in terms of cursing and healing, damaging crops, and causing various misfortunes. Their powers ranged from flying through the air to transforming people into animals (all powers that witches and the devil were believed to have in the Middle Ages).

Theologians, especially at the end of the Middle Ages as witch persecutions became more common, had to formulate a distinction between the power of God and the powers of men and the devil. Alchemists, on the one hand, and the devil and his minions, on the other, either operated through deception and illusion or else caused wonders that might not be able to be immediately explained but were nevertheless performed through natural means by the manipulation of the physical laws of nature that God had ordained. God, however, achieved miracles that contravened the natural order (such as raising the dead and the other miracles attributed to Jesus in the New Testament or the miracle of transubstantiation performed during the Eucharist) and which the devil or human agency could not duplicate. God's actions were said for the first time to come from outside the natural world, that is, to be supernatural. This separation of the natural and supernatural was a vital precondition for the later creation of science.

Because God is not separated from the physical universe, the study of physical phenomena was a specifically religious concern for medieval thinkers. Christian and Muslim philosophers in the Middle Ages both viewed astronomy, for instance, as a form of worshipping God, since it was an investigation into the perfection of his work. The foundation for this kind of investigation necessarily began with the revealed scriptures of the Bible or the Koran. In fact, within Islam astronomy was sometimes encouraged by religious authorities for this reason, but it was also sometimes condemned (meaning that astronomical books were burned) as though it implied that the revelation of the Koran was incomplete and needed to be supplemented by new learning. For the priests of the Mayan civilization of the Americas the stars themselves were a form of divine revelation and the predictability of their movements the guarantee of religious truth.

Concerning the Middle Ages itself, it is often more useful to speak of technology rather than science. Craftsmen worked slowly through trial and error based on experience to improve their control of nature and the technological systems they knew. The development of the compass in Asia, for instance, took centuries from the first discovery of the magnetic properties of the loadstone. The independent invention of the blast furnace in Europe and China is another patient development of this type. Rarely, the invention of whole new technological devices, such as printing with movable type, would come in a flash of inspiration, as seems to have happened independently in medieval Korea and Germany. Chinese alchemists, working as they always did on a chemical formula that would bring immortality and freedom from the physical restraints of the body, discovered gunpowder entirely by accident. Even the elite scholars supported by royal courts in China and India, in the Mayan cities, or in the House of Wisdom in Baghdad worked always within tradition, trying to improve it incrementally, rather than working against received wisdom, trying to disprove it—the skepticism that is the hallmark of the Scientific Revolution.

AFRICA

BY BRADLEY A. SKEEN

Science in its strict sense did not exist before the 17th century, when it was created in Europe by early scientists like Galileo and Descartes. The scientific method with its testing of hypotheses by experiment and the formulation of explanatory, falsifiable theories was developed from many traditions: from mathematical and geometrical proofs that went back to antiquity, from the graphical representation of equations as developed by Scholastic philosophers in the Middle Ages, and from traditions of verification through experiment in fields such as optics, ballistics, and, perhaps surprisingly, the pseudoscience of alchemy, among others. So the history of these precursors of science, which did exist in the Middle Ages, is an important part of the history of science as a scholarly discipline.

The worldview of medieval Africa (and with few exceptions that of the Middle Ages all over the world) can generally be thought of as religious rather than scientific. Africans believed in gods and spirits and their operation in the world through a rational (in the sense of being self-consistent but nevertheless not scientific) system that can be called magic in English for want of a better term. African thought about the gods and magic was in general symbolic and expressive of human relationships (for example, imagining the gods to govern over humankind and the world in the same way that parents govern over their children and their household) and expressive of the human tendency to project their own condition onto the world (for instance, imagining that might animals think and act like people and that phenomena like storms might do so as well or might at least be controlled by a person, such as a witch), rather than being motivated by practical considerations about how to control and influence nature through specific technological means.

The anthropologist Robin Horton has refined scholarly understanding of the traditional African worldview. Africans looked to the realm of the spiritual and the divine both as a means of understanding the everyday world around them and as means of controlling it, through rituals, prayers, and spells. In such a worldview, language is taken as precisely equivalent to reality, and to invoke the existence of or change in a thing is all that can be done to accomplish it. In this view, invoking the sky, through words, to rain is the most important practical step to ensure the rains necessary for agriculture. Ordering a fever to go away is an effective means of treating malaria. (Actually, as Horton points out, this form of treatment may well be preferable to using untested—and in the medieval context untestable—herbal medicines that could well prove poisonous.) This does not mean that other actions might not be taken that seem more practical from the viewpoint of Western science, but they would always be understood by the Africans performing them as being effective through their linguistic or quasi-linguistic (ritual) component. Words have meaning derived from tradition (from authority or consensus within the community). In African tradition, language is used to act, not to explain, and the truth of words or ideas is always within a social context and can never be absolute. As long as these conditions prevailed, African culture could not move away from its traditional religious worldview; there was no way to criticize tradition or imagine an alternative, and Africans did not do so except through contact with the West in periods later than the Middle Ages.

Egypt played a prominent role in the development of the scientific tradition in late antiquity, and its importance continued in the early Middle Ages, especially as a mediator of Hellenistic science to the Islamic world. In Sub-Saharan Africa, however, science was largely limited to technological systems, often borrowed from Mediterranean cultures, without a scientific discipline to support them. We often think of technological change today being driven by science, but this is a fairly recent phenomenon. In medieval Africa, as in much of the world throughout human history, technology was maintained by a tradition that was capable of only accepting small changes, arrived at through accident or trial and error methods.

EGYPT

In the third century B.C.E. the Greek kings of Egypt established a museum in their capital of Alexandria. This institution attracted the leading scholars of antiquity. Egypt became a center of scientific learning and technological advances throughout the Hellenistic and Roman periods. The geometrical *Elements* of Euclid and the *Almagest* (a treatise on astronomy and geography) of Claudius Ptolemy were written in Alexandria, to name only two of the Greek works that had wide influence on Christian, Islamic, and Indian learned culture in the Middle Ages. Great strides in technology were made in Alexandria, such as a working model of a steam engine, even if they were not always given wide practical application. By the beginning of the medieval period (the fifth and sixth centuries) the level of learning in Egypt was sharply declining because the museum had been destroyed by mob violence instigated by the Christian bishops of Alexandria. It was the subject of sectarian conflict because it was a "pagan" temple as well as a center of learning.

One scientific subject, however, alchemy, developed rapidly in Egypt at the beginning of the Middle Ages. Although it was developed by scholars working in the Greek communities in Egypt, there is no evidence that alchemy owed anything to pre-Greek ancient Egyptian culture. Nevertheless, because of the extreme antiquity of Egyptian civilization, some Greek alchemists claimed that their work was based on the translation of ancient Egyptian hieroglyphic texts. Because of continuing fascination with Egypt, this claim was perpetuated throughout the ages, and even some modern scholars look for precursors of alchemy in ancient Egypt. However, alchemy seems to have derived entirely from Greek ideas and to have originally functioned with a Greek cultural context.

The first alchemist was Bolus of Mendes (a city near Alexandria in Egypt). He composed a book called *Physical Properties and Mysteries* (*Physica et mystica*) in the second century B.C.E, which was divided into four chapters on gold, silver, gems, and purple dye. In order to emphasize the link of his work to earlier Greek science, Bolus published the book under the name of an earlier Greek philosopher, Democritus, who was the first thinker to speculate that material substances might be made out of small particles he called atoms. This ancient form of publication is called pseudepigraphy. Bolus's book is lost, but it appears from references in later writers that he dealt with the physical properties of each of the four substances and described the process of purifying and refining them as well as various chemical reactions they participated in. Gold, silver, and gems were valuable commodities in antiquity as well as today.

Purple dye was manufactured from the sea-snail murex, was extremely costly, and could be used only by aristocrats. Roman law regulated the width of the purple stripe that senators were allowed to wear on their clothes. By the fifth century C.E. Christian bishops also added purple-dyed ornament to their clothing. Only the emperor was allowed to wear an entirely purple garment; for anyone else to wear or even possess such a costume was a capital crime because it was considered tantamount to treason. Thus the science of purple dye production was as important as that of gold refining. Bolus characterizes the chemical reactions he describes in highly metaphorical terms, as though the metals and acids in the chemical process were fighting each other or marrying each other, and uses many further extravagances. This kind of language was eventually elaborated into a sort of secret code by which alchemists described chemical reactions, which is not necessarily fully understood today. Bolus also describes how each of the substances could be made, or at least simulated, artificially.

In its early stages of development, alchemy probably did not make extravagant claims of physical transmutation of elements and had little concern for the spiritual or mystical state of the alchemist. However, perfectly ordinary chemical reactions were represented by alchemists as resulting in transmutation. Alchemists were very interested in color and tended to assume that anything golden in color was gold. The kind of procedure that might have encouraged belief in the possibility of transmutation is the combination of copper and arsenic into copper arsenide which is, indeed, silver in color.

Surprisingly, many early alchemical procedures used existing scientific principles to produce tricks, not unlike those of a modern stage magician. These seem to have functioned by way of demonstrations that could be made at formal dinner parties (an important Greek social location) in order for the alchemist to make an impression on potential patrons and interest them in financially supporting his research. (Most alchemists were male, though an important exception was Maria the Jewess, inventor of the double boiler.) For example, a brief handbook attributed pseudepigraphically to Democritus that was written in fifth-century Egypt gives instructions on how to treat bronze plates, goblets, and utensils so that they appear, at least, to be made out of gold. Other such books describe the use of the purple dye of the murex to make water appear to turn into wine before the diners' eyes.

However, by the fifth and sixth century the nature of alchemy had undergone a fundamental transformation itself. Alchemy remained concerned with the investigation of the physical properties of matter, but it had become, like Greek philosophy as a whole, almost religious in character. A new level of theological meaning and purpose had been added above the investigation of chemical reactions. Alchemical texts of a wholly different nature began to appear. These generally claimed to have been transcribed from hieroglyphic texts and were pseudepigraphically attributed to the Egyptian god Thoth, known in Greek as Hermes Trismegistus (Thrice-Great Hermes). In other words, they were not now primarily technical but theological texts.

One brief text written most likely in the sixth century in Alexandria is known as the Emerald Tablet because it claims to have been copied from an inscription in Egyptian hieroglyphs made on an emerald tablet in remotest antiquity. It contains the famous alchemical formula "as below, so above," meaning that there is a direct correspondence between the physical world on earth and the divine world in the heavens. Manipulating an element on one level, therefore, has an effect on the other. The tablet teaches that the alchemist is seeking a physical quality (later called the "philosopher's stone") that is the physical correspondence to God. This quality or substance contains within itself all four elements that the Greeks believed composed matter: fire, air, water, and earth. The control of this principle would allow the alchemist to transmute metals, but that becomes a secondary goal subordinate to the salvation of the alchemist's soul. The work of this divine principle is described in the same language used in philosophical texts to describe the ascent of the soul to heaven and its mystical union with God. At the same time that the physical transmutation of the elements is effected the alchemist's soul is clarified and divinized. The alchemist essentially becomes like God and assumes the creative role of God.

The *Turba philosophorum* (The Philosophical Circle), from the same era as the Emerald Tablet, was also translated into Arabic and later into Latin. It purports to be the summary of a sort of alchemical conference held by the philosopher Pythagoras (sixth century B.C.E.) and his students, including Democritus and Socrates and many other famous Greek philosophers. However, these are figures that never had any contact with one another and never held any of the doctrines ascribed to them here, since they all lived centuries before the development of alchemy. It is another case of the names of ancient authorities being used in an attempt to integrate alchemy into traditional Greek philosophy.

The *Turba* begins with a discussion of the four elements conceived of by Greek science and attempts to prove their traditionally accepted characteristics through logical demonstration. It quickly moves to a complicated discussion of the sun. The *Turba* takes the sun as the physical object that corresponds to God. But just as God is one and solitary (and monotheism was hardly foreign to Greek thought of this period), the sun, as the visible God, must also be the sole source of light in the universe. It is then asserted that the light of the moon, planets, and stars is all reflected sunlight. That moonlight is reflected sunlight was well understood in antiquity and in the Middle Ages, but it was generally supposed that the planets and stars shone by their own light, since they have no apparent phases like those of the moon. So the *Turba* advances what we know to be a true scientific discovery—that the planets shine by reflected sunlight—but beginning from theological principles that cannot bear scientific scrutiny. Thus, the concept amounts to an inspired guess.

The further inference that the stars reflect sunlight is made simply by analogy with the moon and planets and is, in fact, quite reasonable for the Middle Ages (for all that it is wrong) because there was at that time no way to prove that the stars were bodies similar to the sun but considerably farther away. This argument is also used in an attempt to logically demonstrate the existence of God. But the supposed proof's circular reasoning merely begs the question. The argument is made that the sun as a unique physical object implies the existence of a unique divine object, whereas the uniqueness of the sun had earlier been established by equating it with a physical manifestation of God. A second proof of God's existence is offered by stating that the sense of sight is able to discern the difference between colors; in the same way, reason is able to discern the different grades of reality between the physical and the divine. Hence divinity, as an object of human perception, must be real. But the analogy is quite false, since reason is not a sense like sight.

The *Turba* asserts that God created the four elements and then used alchemical processes to create the physical and spiritual world (including immaterial entities such as angels and human souls) around us. From this premise, it would follow that the laws of alchemy exist in nature and can be discovered by reason and further that the alchemist, by discovering and using them, makes himself godlike. The second half of the *Turba* turns to describing a sequence of chemical reactions in the peculiar metaphorical language of alchemy. For all of its logical fallacies, the *Turba* nevertheless makes an attempt to understand the natural world through reason. It should be observed that it does not exclude God from the natural world as part of a separate supernatural realm. It is insistent that physical laws are uniform throughout a single unitary world and that every part of it can be known and explained through reason. These are basic scientific concepts.

Alchemy in early medieval Egypt was probably limited to practice by the remaining minority of adherents of traditional Greek religion ("pagan," in Christian terms), but their writings were nevertheless taken up by later intellectuals in the Islamic world and Christian Europe. Both the Emerald Tablet and the *Turba philosophorum* were translated into Arabic in the ninth century and into Latin in the 12th. They became paramount texts in the development of alchemy both in the Islamic world and in the European Middle Ages and Renaissance. They insured that later alchemical work would be suffused with religious mysticism but at the same time propagated a tradition of physical investigation of nature that eventually led to modern scientific chemistry.

ETHIOPIA

Ethiopians understood the universe through a system of astronomy borrowed from ancient Egypt in pre-Hellenistic times. The most important function of astronomy was to regulate the calendar. The Ethiopian kings converted to Christianity in the early fourth century and added the Christian tradition of the Easter *computus*, a calculation that allowed churchmen to fix the date of Easter each year and then of the rest of the liturgical calendar. Astrology never gained importance in Ethiopia.

Monks of the Ethiopian Church, however, developed an interest in the First Book of Enoch (I Enoch). The text is also called the Ethiopian book of Enoch because it first became known to Western scholars in the 18th century from its Ethiopic translation. The book itself was composed in Judea in the third century B.C.E. in Aramaic. Fragments of the Aramaic text have been discovered among the Dead Sea Scrolls, while fragments of a Greek translation have been recovered from archaeological digs in Egypt. The book was well known in antiquity, however, even though it was dismissed from the canon of scripture by both the rabbinical authorities in Judaism and by the early Christian Church. It is, however, treated as a canonical book of scripture in the Ethiopian Orthodox Church. I Enoch supplied the predominant astronomical learning of medieval Ethiopia.

The section of I Enoch known as the "Book of the Itinerary of the Luminaries of Heaven" describes a vision of the biblical patriarch Enoch (Genesis 1:18, 5:24) in which the angel Uriel gives him a tour of the heavens and describes to him the motions of the stars and planets. The author of I Enoch shows little or no knowledge of Babylonian or Hellenistic scientific astronomy. The text presents an astronomical system based on that of the Hebrew Bible: The earth is a flat disk (with Jerusalem in the center) surrounded by a ring of gigantic mountains beyond which are limitless oceans; the sky is a solid dome covering the earth. The sun enters the sky by passing through one of six gates in the eastern part of the dome and then passes out through a corresponding gate in the west. These gates are simply 10 degree arc sections on the portion of the horizon on which dawn and sunset occur.

The sun, moon, and planets travel in chariots drawn by the winds. The lengths of day and night vary according to the height of the gate used at particular times of the year. During the night the sun journeys around the outside of the dome to return to the eastern gates. The moon follows the same paths and uses the same gates as the sun. The stars form an army ("the host of heaven") commanded by the angel Uriel and encamped around the heavenly gates. The visible planets, including the moon, are their captains. The moon is known to shine with reflected sunlight and is said to be the same size as the sun (because of the nearly identical apparent size of the two bodies) and one-seventh as bright as the sun.

I Enoch includes various computations to reconcile the 354-day period of 12 lunar months with the 365-day solar year, but these computations are imprecise compared with ancient Greek or Medieval Islamic computations. Nevertheless, Enoch is told that many human beings mistakenly use astronomical calendrical reckonings different from those he has been shown and hence hold religious festivals on the wrong days. In fact, many technical passages are highly corrupt in the manuscript tradition, suggesting that mathematical astronomical concepts were not well understood by the Ethiopian monastic scribes responsible for copying the text.

Medieval Ethiopia possessed sophisticated metalworking and shipping industries whose technologies had been borrowed from Egypt. But Ethiopia had its own stoneworking tradition. Going back to prehistoric times, when the erection of stone monoliths was commonplace in the Ethiopian highlands, Ethiopian masons routinely worked with exceptionally large blocks of stone. At the beginning of the medieval period the stonemasons of the Ethiopian kingdom of Axum had such confidence in their tradition that they undertook to create the largest single blocks of stone quarried in the Middle Ages or at any other time or in any area of the world. The kings of Axum commissioned for themselves grave stelae. Half a dozen of these were more than 65 feet high, while the largest was up to 108 feet high. That is the largest single piece of stone ever quarried. An idea of the skill and technological sophistication involved in cutting, dressing, and transporting these stelae can be derived from that fact that one of these enormous stones was transported to Rome in the 20th century while Italy was the colonial power in Ethiopia. When it was returned to Ethiopia, it had to be cut in half to overcome the difficulties of transporting so large and heavy an object, even using modern technology.

The Ethiopian emperor Gebre Mesqel Lalibela (r. 1189–1229) drew on the tradition of Ethiopian stone cutting in creating a group of 13 churches in Tigray when, inspired by a dream, he made the city his capital and renamed it after himself. The town is built on massive granite outcroppings, and Gebre had the churches built by cutting down into the stone, carving them like sculptures rather than traditional buildings. Rooms were relieved inside, however, so they are fully functional as buildings, even as they are still engaged in the bedrock. The largest, the Bete Medhane Alam (House of the Savior of the World), was relieved to a depth of 134 feet, making it the largest monolithic structure in the world.

Although agriculture is often romanticized as a natural pursuit, it is a science used to control nature as much as anything else and was one of the essential technologies whose development led to the birth of civilization. Ethiopians used a number of domestic crops and animals imported from Egypt and the Near East. However, Ethiopian farmers in the Middle Ages produced an important new crop by the usual method of domesticating plants through the selective breeding of wild ancestors. In this case, the plant was the coffee bean, which was domesticated in the province of Kaffa. Domestication, a process that would have taken many generations, was probably not complete before the ninth century. In earlier times other plants such as teff had also been domesticated in Ethiopia.

SUB-SAHARAN AFRICA

Sub-Saharan Africa suffered from a relative poverty in the scientific understanding of the world and in technologies used to control the human environment. In terms of astronomy and geography, medieval African peoples (outside of those cultures dominated by Islam) do not seem to have received anything from the Mediterranean world. It is clear, in fact, that we cannot speak about science in this region but only about cosmological and astral myths. For instance, the sky was believed to be a solid dome over the earth, so that if one walked to the edge of the world it would become impossible to stand up straight as the dome bent down to meet the earth. (While this is similar to older Greek or Hebrew views, it seems in this case to be a parallel rather than borrowing, since many peoples throughout the world held the same belief, based on the circular character of the horizon.)

Just as Semitic culture explained the relationship between the earth and heaven by the metaphor of a ladder and Greeks by the flight of birds, Africans tended to represent this idea through the hanging silken string of the spider. The spider was the messenger of the gods, and other gods would travel between the two realms on the spider's thread. The idea that the stars are organized into constellations seems to have been known, but the limits and characters of the constellations varied from one group to the next and owed nothing to Hellenistic astronomy. Use of a solar (365-day) calendar was unknown; time was commonly reckoned in lunar months and by seasons.

The suggestion is sometimes made by archaeoastronomers that certain astronomically significant alignments exist in the buildings of the southern African city of Great Zimbabwe. What they mean by this is that if one were to have looked out of a certain window at a specific time of day on a precise day of the year toward a certain visible point on the horizon, one would have seen an astronomically important event, such as the year's first rising of a particular star. It is very difficulty, however, to draw definite conclusions from such speculations without the aid of written records to confirm that such procedures were undertaken and would have had some meaning to the culture in question. Moreover, in cultures that have left written records of their interest in astronomy, such alignments do not play a very significant role. Thus, conclusions based on this kind of evidence must remain highly speculative.

The most sophisticated technologies in sub-Saharan Africa were those related to metallurgy. The archaeologist Peter Schmidt has advanced the suggestion that ironworking technology was invented independently in Africa. But the chief argument he uses to support this view is that ironworking was integrated into traditional Africa systems of belief, for example, by the use of ritual to guarantee the success of the smelting process. Any culture integrates what it borrows, however. Ironworking was similarly integrated into medieval European culture (where it was not invented), and rituals and prayers associated with the patron saint Barbara were used by European smiths. It is more likely that iron technology was invented once, in the ancient Near East in the second millennium B.C.E. and from there was diffused to Africa just as it was to Europe and East Asia. Early (premedieval) centers of African ironworking existed at Meroë in the Nile valley and at Nok in Nigeria. Considerable inventiveness was shown in the adaptation of this technology to local conditions. Some cultures, however, such as the Bushmen of the Kalahari, continued to use stone tools and knew nothing of metalworking.

Copper working appears to have been reinvented independently during the Middle Ages in central Africa, where copper ore is abundant. There is no older period of bronze-based technology in Africa as in the Near East, and indigenous copper and bronze production appears quite late. The specific formulas for making bronze may well have been imported from Islamic or Ethiopian sources, however.

The techniques of agriculture were widespread in medieval Africa (though some peoples still lived as hunter-gatherers), having borrowed from the near East in antiquity. Crops like millet and sorghum were domesticated by the precursors of Egyptian civilization (ca. 5000 B.C.E) and spread by the ancestors of the Bantu peoples in early times. They took these crops, along with domestic livestock, as they migrated across the continent. Other crops, such as yams and bananas, were imported from East Asia probably also in antiquity and were widespread by the Middle Ages. But sub-Saharan African agriculture never became as intensive and productive as those in many other areas of the world because of problems in climate and geography that could not be solved.

THE AMERICAS

BY MICHAEL J. O'NEAL

The word *science* creates images of modern-day researchers working in laboratories, conducting experiments under controlled conditions and then publishing their findings so that other scientists can verify them. Science in the medieval Americas—and throughout much of the medieval world—did not conform to these modern methods. Rather, science was based on close observation of the workings of the natural world and on trial and error over many generations.

Further, much of modern-day science is conducted as a quest for knowledge for its own sake. Scientists want to understand the principles that underlie the workings of the universe. Science during the medieval period, in contrast, was more practical. People were more interested in finding ways to exert some control over their environment to help ensure their survival. Thus, medieval science could be characterized more as "technology" than science. It was the application of observations about the physical world to a whole range of activities: agriculture, measurement, construction, engineering, mining and metalwork, forestry management, food preservation, and a host of other concerns. Many of these activities required an understanding of mathematics, especially geometry.

A final distinction between modern-day science and science as it was practiced in the medieval Americas has to do with the distinction between the physical and spiritual worlds. In the modern era scientists maintain a sharp distinction between the physical and spiritual. They regard spiritual beliefs—a belief in God, along with such matters as ethics and morality—as matters entirely separate from pure science. In the medieval Americas, in contrast, the physical and spiritual worlds were intimately linked. Every aspect of people's lives had religious significance. They saw the universe as composed of spiritual and divine forces that affected them every moment of their lives. The role of scientific thought was to understand those forces and put them to use for the benefit of people.

Ancient Americans were scientists. They were keen observers and experimenters. For example, they made early observations in the fields of astronomy, biology, chemistry, geology, and physics. As astronomers, they learned about the movements of heavenly objects and used those observations to create calendars and to predict changes in the seasons. They observed the "hole" in the Big Dipper long before European astronomers did. In fact, so keen was the interest of the medieval Americans in astronomy that priests and astronomers were often one and the same. Science throughout much of the medieval world was associated with magic, with understanding the power and will of the gods, so the earliest scientists were shamans, priests, and others who claimed knowledge of the divine and could read it in the heavens.

Ancient Americans typically did not have any way to understand the underlying scientific principles that gave rise to phenomena in the natural world. They did, however, observe the effects of those principles and applied them to their daily lives. A good example comes from the field of physics. During lightning storms they learned to throw pieces of cedarwood onto a bonfire to ward off the lightning. Even though they could not have fully understood the physics that explained why this was successful, successful it was. When cedar burns, it emits a negative electrical charge that repelled the negative electrical charge in the atmosphere that produces lightning. Such an observation would have been made over many generations, adding to medieval Americans' storehouse of knowledge about the workings of their physical world.

LAND MANAGEMENT

The primary resource that ancient Americans had at their disposal was the land they occupied. But the nature of this land, and the resources it provided, varied widely: the fro-

zen regions of far North America, the plains that dominated central North America, the woodlands of eastern North America, the desert regions of the American Southwest and modern-day Mexico, the highland regions of the South American Andes, the rain forests of South America, and the coastal regions occupied by tribes throughout the Americas, including the islands of the Caribbean.

Each of these environments required different methods of adaptation, particularly in the area of food production. In the frozen north, where crops could not be grown, Native Americans applied the principles of buoyancy to construct boats that enabled them to hunt at sea—and they had to understand the properties of the materials out of which those boats were built to ensure their seaworthiness and durability.

In many other regions, food was relatively abundant. A good example was the Eastern Woodlands of North America. In the dense forests of this region, stretching from modern-day eastern Canada down through the eastern third of the United States, game animals were hunted, and the forests provided nuts, berries, acorns, and fruits for human consumption. Nevertheless, the Eastern Woodlands tribes supplemented with agriculture and grew such crops as gourds, pumpkins, squash, beans, and corn. Accordingly, Eastern Woodlands tribes had to make scientific observations about crops, planting cycles (based on astronomical observations), the fertility of soil, and the management of land for agricultural purposes.

The Plains Indians faced a different set of challenges. These tribes relied primarily on large game, such as deer, antelope, elk, and especially buffalo. To manage the land for food purposes, they set large fires at the margins of the Great Plains to create what were in effect "buffalo farms," or large, open game preserves. In many places, fires were also used to open up living spaces. In particular, fire eliminated the low brush that provided habitat for snakes, rodents, and other undesirable species. In other words, they used fire to alter their environment, in much the same way later scientists would.

The Plains Indians also used fire to clear agricultural land. Many Native American communities relied on "slash and burn" farming techniques. They cut down trees in forested areas to clear fields of 20 to perhaps 200 acres. After they cut the trees, they burned off the rubble and stumps and planted such crops as maize (corn), squash, and beans. They learned that such ground was exceptionally fertile, for the ash provided valuable nutrients for the soil, particularly potash, which boosts the development of fruits and vegetables. Similar practices were followed in the Peruvian Andes, where scientists estimate that as much as 1.5 million acres were cleared by slash-and-burn methods. Incidentally, many of those Peruvian fields were in the form of terraced gardens, requiring the people to function as scientists in terracing the fields and constructing walls that were durable. They also had to function as hydrologists to ensure an adequate supply of water.

In the South American rain forests the quality of the soil tended to be poor, largely because the persistent rains leached away nutrients. Accordingly, rain-forest dwellers, acting as scientists, found ways to manage the land. One technique was to avoid annual crops and plant perennial crops that would provide food for many years. To accomplish this, rain-forest dwellers may have built immense earthen mounds. On these mounds they planted fruit and nut trees. Another technique was to compost the soil. Scientists believe that during the pre-Columbian centuries some parts of the Amazon rain forests were, in effect, huge compost heaps, where people scraped off soil for use in agriculture and landscaped gardens, leaving a layer of it behind. This layer continued to "brew" with nutrients and microorganisms, turning debris and the soil under it into new rich topsoil. Again, by observing the workings of nature and the way soil is produced and fed and then altering their environment in beneficial ways, people were acting as scientists.

ENGINEERING AND CONSTRUCTION

In North America perhaps one of the best examples of the application of scientific principles to engineering and construction comes from the mound-building Mississippian cultures, which flourished from about 700 or 800 until about 1400 to 1500. These cultures, as the name suggests, extended throughout the Mississippi River valley, with concentrations in modern-day Illinois. These cultures are noted for their construction of enormous mounds, or elevated earthworks, that formed the centers of their community. One of the best-known examples is the Cahokia culture, which flourished in modern-day Illinois where the Mississippi, Missouri, and Illinois rivers meet. The Cahokians required an enormous labor force and millions of man-hours to construct the 120 large mounds in the area, including Monks Mound, which covers an area of 14 acres. In addition to the mounds themselves, homes, granaries, ceremonial centers, burial grounds, stockades, and similar structures were constructed on the sites and often had to be rebuilt or refurbished as time went on. All of these activities were directed by the social and religious elites, who applied scientific principles to their construction.

The Cahokia mounds show an understanding of geometry and astronomy. The mounds are not laid out in a simple helter-skelter fashion. The Cahokians positioned the mounds in a way that reflected their understanding of the structure of the universe. In particular, archaeologists have noted that the mounds create patterns of perfect equilateral triangles (triangles whose three sides are of equal length). Further, the

mounds are oriented to face the cardinal points of the compass. In this respect, the mounds may have served a function similar to that of the Stonehenge monuments in England. By positioning the mounds to reflect the culture's understanding of astronomy, the elites who directed their construction turned the sites into hubs that bound the community together, not just materially but spiritually as well.

This type of understanding of the principles of geometry and their relationship to astronomy were exhibited through the medieval Americas, particularly in pre-Columbian Mesoamerica. Some historians of science use the term *design science* to refer to the activities of the Maya, the Aztec, and other cultures that inhabited Mesoamerica. Design science refers to methods of thought that integrate knowledge about land, terrain, geometry, building materials, architecture, design, and art to create structures that were both functional and aesthetically pleasing. Mathematicians have studied, for example, the kivas, or dug-out ceremonial centers, many of them found in the southwestern United States but also in Mexico. These kivas and their environs served as hubs, where elites resided and where craft production took place. They were connected by roads that integrated the outlying communities. The structure of the kivas demonstrate a solid understanding of geometrical forms, including circles, squares, and spirals, as well as more complex matters, such as the relationship of a circle's radius to its diameter.

MATHEMATICS

In addition to geometry, many Mesoamerican cultures showed an understanding of more abstract mathematics. The ancient Maya occupied the Yucatán Peninsula in modern-day Mexico, Belize, Guatemala, and Honduras. They began to inhabit the region in roughly 2000 B.C.E., reached the peak of their influence in the early centuries of the Common Era, and began to decline in about 900.

In studying Mayan history and culture, historians refer to the Classic Period, extending from about 250 to 900, the period of the Maya's greatest achievements. However, the so-called Postclassic Period of Maya history lasted for hundreds of years more, until the arrival of the Spanish in the early 16th century The earlier decline and collapse of the lowland Maya took place largely in the south; the more northern Yucatán Peninsula cities, such as Chichén Itzá, Edzná, Uxmal, and Cobá, continued to develop and exhibit some of the characteristics of the Classic Period throughout the Postclassic Period.

In the 16th century Spanish explorers arrived on the Yucatán Peninsula. Eventually they overran the regions inhabited by the Maya, Aztec, and other Postclassic cultures. Unfortunately, the early Spanish explorers and missionaries saw Mayan religious beliefs as the work of the devil and had the evidence of them destroyed, including not only religious artifacts but also written texts on a wide variety of subjects. Only a handful of these manuscripts survived and are housed in museums in Paris, France; Dresden, Germany; and Madrid, Spain. They date to the Postclassic Period but probably were based on texts originally written in the Classic Period.

Historians of science are especially intrigued by the Mayan system of mathematics, which they applied to such other fields as astronomy and architecture. A similar system was also used by the Olmec of the first millennium B.C.E. Much of this complex system has been preserved in painted manuscripts and carved hieroglyphic calendrical texts. Mayan mathematics used a vigesimal system, that is, one based on the number 20 (from the Latin word for "20th"). Such a system probably evolved because people often counted with their fingers and toes; when they reached the number 20, they had, in effect, to start over with a new set of 20, in much the same way that modern systems of mathematics are based on the number 10, a decimal system derived from Hindu mathematics, and its multiples.

Thus, in Mayam texts the numeral 1 was represented by a thick dot, 2 by two dots, and so on. The numeral 5 was represented by a straight horizontal line, 6 by one dot above a line, 7 by two dots above a line, and so on. The numeral 10 was then represented by two horizontal lines, 11 by a dot above two lines, and so on up to 15, represented by three lines, and so on up to 20, represented by a single dot above a shell representing zero. The Maya were among a handful of world civilizations to develop the concept of zero. At higher numbers, position in vertical columns of numbers also determined value in multiples of 20, just as in our system, the numeral 5 has a different value depending on whether it is in the "tens column" or "hundreds column" of a decimal count.

The Maya used two calendars. One was a 260-day ritual calendar that consisted of 13 periods, each with 20 days. Days and periods were associated with various gods. The other calendar was a solar (civil) calendar consisting of 360 days, with 18 periods each consisting of 20 days (with a five-day period at the end regarded as unlucky). The two calendars "caught up" with each other after 18,980 days, or 52 solar years or 73 ritual years, a period known as a Calendar Round. The Maya also kept track of eclipses and planetary cycles, observing that the planet Venus returned to its original celestial position after two 52-year cycles. In fact, they held a great celebration after 104 years—that is, after two 52-year solar cycles or one 104-year cycle of Venus.

It is necessary to recognize that the Maya also counted history from a fixed point in the past, calculated by days and multiples of days, in a system known as a Long Count. For their purposes they calculated that the world had been created on August 12, 3113 B.C.E., and they dated many of their historical monuments in terms of the number of days that had passed since Creation. In the Classic Period Guatemalan city of Tikal, for example, a historical marker dates a structure as having been built 1,253,912 days after the date when the world was created., arriving at a date equivalent in our system to 320 C.E. Put differently, counting did not determine the structure of the calendar; instead, the structure of the calendar determined counting, enabling the Maya to incorporate into their mathematical system their conception of the gods, Creation, the movement of heavenly bodies, and the like.

The Aztec of Mexico, too, had a relatively sophisticated system of mathematics, with application to astronomy and calendrics, that shared some features with Maya computation but was less complex. Like the Maya, the Aztec used a vigesimal system   and observed a ritual calendar of 260 days and a solar calendar of 360 plus 5 years. They, too, celebrated the ending of a calendar round of 52 years and a great cycle of 102 years that coincided with the ending of a Venus cycle Longer periods, however, were calculated by 52-year cycles rather than by a fixed date in the past.

The Aztec system was applied in two primary ways. One was in conducting commerce in the marketplaces of cities and towns. The large market of Tlatelolco, the sister city of the Mexica (Aztec) capital of Tenochtitlan, was visited by as many as 50,000 people a day, although local markets attracted much less traffic. Thus, Aztec arithmetic was applied daily to the computation of weights and measures for goods as well as for their prices. The other application was in land ownership. Mathematics enabled the Aztec to keep accurate records of the size, boundaries, and value of land. This, in turn, enabled the authorities to calculate the amount of tax the landowner owed to the state. Records show that the Aztec system of land measurement, based on the principles of geometry, were remarkably accurate and consistent. They were based on a unit of measurement called the quahuitl.

The Inca of Andean South America did not have a writing system, but they were nevertheless able to store mathematical information in the form of knots in strings. These devices were called quipu. The quipu was important to the administration of the Inca Empire because it allowed the authorities to keep track of all manner of information. The quipu was made up of strings. These strings were then knotted to form numbers, using a base 10 number system. The system was also "positional," meaning that the value of a numeral depended on its position in a larger number—in much the same way that modern arithmetical systems are positional. Thus, for example, the number 476 would be represented on the quipu with six knots at the end of the string. After a space, seven knots were used to represent seven 10s. Again a space would follow, and then four knots represented four 100s. The system continued for larger numbers, with, for example, an additional group of knots representing 1,000s, 10,000s, and occasionally even 100,000s.

The knots in each group were all touching. The spacing of groups of knots had to be highly regular and consistent, primarily because zero was represented by the absence of knots; without consistent spacing, the absence of knots could have been interpreted as the normal spacing between groups of knots rather than as a zero. Additionally, the Inca system had one peculiarity, having to do with the style of the knots. In the unit position (that is, the 1s), one style of knot was used to represent the numeral 1, with a different style for units greater than 1.

The Inca had to have a way of distinguishing strings from one another so that they could keep track of what the strings were counting. They did this in two ways. One was color, so that, for example, a green string might have been used to keep track of the number of cattle, while a white string might have been used to count sheep. The courts used this method. Colors represented the nature of the crime with which an accused was charged; the number of knots was used to record the length of a prison sentence. Sometimes, the colors had symbolic value. Thus, red was used to count items associated with war, while white was used to record the number of items associated with peacetime uses. Another method was to use subsidiary strings tied to the middle of the main string. Again, the courts used this method to record the nature of the punishment a convicted criminal had to undergo.

In each town the Inca king appointed a person called the *quipucamayoc*, or "keeper of the knots." In larger cities the number of these people might have been as high as 30. These people were, in effect, government statisticians. They used the quipu to record census data and data about agricultural production, livestock, and weapons. A system of relay runners conveyed the information recorded to the capital city of Cuzco.

The Inca system of arithmetic had one other peculiarity worth mentioning. In the modern world numbers are thought of as abstract. That is, the number "5" has a meaning entirely apart from the objects counted with this number. Whether we count five sheep or five trees, the "5" has a consistent, abstract meaning. The Inca, however, regarded numbers in a different way. Different words were used to indicate number, depending on the nature of the items being counted. Consider, for example, the numeral 2. Different words were used to refer to a pair of matched items, two unrelated items, an object that could be divided into two parts, or two items that are bound together (such as an ox and a cart).

In addition to the quipu, the Inca also had a mathematical tool called a *yupana*. The *yupana* served much the same purpose as the strings, but it also may have functioned as a kind of abacus, or calculating tool. In 1596 a Spanish priest named José de Acosta published a book titled *Historia natural moral de las Indias*. This book was based on his experience of living with the Inca from 1571 to 1586. He described the *yupana* as a "calculator" that functioned with the use of maize kernels. He told how, instead of using pen and paper to make "a very difficult computation," they instead manipulated the maize kernels, moving them about and solving problems "without making the smallest mistake." He went on to say that when it came to matters of practical arithmetic, the Inca could solve problems faster than the Spanish could on paper. Unfortunately, Acosta never learned the principles underlying the use of this tool, so he was never able to provide a more detailed description of how it worked. His narrative, though, provides the modern world with a tantalizing glimpse of Incan mathematics.

MEDICINE

An important part of the scientific achievements of any civilization is its ability to find treatments for illness and disease. Again, much of what might have been known about medical lore in Mesoamerica has been lost because the invading Spaniards destroyed the manuscripts. Some of this knowledge was later reconstructed, and modern paleopathologists—those who study disease and illness by examining preserved tissues from ancient times—have been able to add to that knowledge. Generally, medical practitioners in the medieval Americas were shamans. Like the astronomer-shamans discussed earlier, shamans who practiced medicine were believed to have had access to supernatural power and wisdom.

Medicine throughout the Americas was studied from two orientations. One was the spiritual. Among the Aztec, for example, it was believed that illness and even some forms of injury were the result of having offended the gods. The goal of the shaman was to help the patient determine which god and then to make restitution.

The other orientation was more practical. Ancient Americans knew, of course, that injury could result from wars, accidents, and similar events. Thus, in addition to consulting the gods, they developed practical remedies and treatments. In common with ancient civilizations the world over, they made wide use of herbs and other medicinal plants. One manuscript catalogues 132 medicinal plants the Aztec used. Modern people who think of themselves as addicted to chocolate might take heart in knowing that healers in Mesoamerica recognized the therapeutic benefits of chocolate (derived from the Nahuatl word *chocolatl*) and cocoa (derived from the Mayan word *cacao*). They used it not only to deliver other medicines but also as a medicine in its own right. They used it to help people gain weight, to stimulate the nervous system, and to improve digestion and elimination. They also used it to treat anemia, poor appetite, gout, kidney stones, fevers, and, in paste form, burns. Interestingly, modern medical researchers have confirmed what the ancient Americans knew. Chocolate has been shown to be an effective cough medicine. More important, consumed in moderation, it is a good source of polyphenols, or chemicals that protect the heart.

Additionally, ancient Americans used medicinal plants to treat fever, infection, skin rashes, urinary and digestive complaints, chest pain, bleeding, anemia, and a host of other ailments. Many of these herbal remedies have a solid scientific basis. For example, the ingredient in aspirin that reduces fever is found in willow bark, and willow bark teas were commonly used to treat fever; sometimes, chewing on the bark accomplished the same goal. Mesoamericans also learned to bind wounds, makes casts for broken bones, and perform certain types of surgery. For this purposes, they used extremely sharp scalpels made of obsidian.

ASIA AND THE PACIFIC
by Amy Hackney Blackwell

Science was quite well developed in medieval Asia. Scientists in China and India studied chemistry, biology, physics, mathematics, astronomy, and pharmacology. They had well-reasoned medical theories that were based largely on observation and experimentation. Chinese rulers throughout the medieval period encouraged scientific innovation and sponsored court scientists, such as Shen Kua (1030–93), Su Song (1020–1101), and Wei Pu of the Song Dynasty (960–1279). India produced its own important scholars, including Aryabhata (476–ca. 550) and Bhaskara II (1114–ca. 1185). Even in areas with less-sophisticated cultures, science was important. For example, Pacific islanders were excellent astronomers and grew expert at assessing the way ocean currents and wind patterns affected their sailing.

CHEMISTRY AND METALLURGY

Chinese scientists performed a number of experiments on the chemical properties of substances. Chinese chemistry experiments resulted in several useful inventions. It is said that matches were first invented in the seventh century by Chinese court ladies who lacked tinder to start fires for cooking. They took small sticks and coated the ends in sulfur, which, when struck, would ignite.

During the seventh century the Chinese developed a process of making brandy that grew out of a scientific discovery made by central Asian peoples. During the third century these people had observed that when wine froze, parts of it remained liquid. Chinese chemists and winemakers repeated this experiment and determined that the remaining liquid was pure alcohol. They discovered that freezing was a reliable test for the alcohol content of wine and also that the pure alcohol could be skimmed off and sold as distilled wine or brandy.

Indian alchemists experimented with chemistry in their efforts to create various potions and tonics. The 10th-century alchemist Nagarjuna (b. 931) wrote several books in which he describes how to purify metals and how to prepare compounds of mercury; he also provides recipes for Ayurvedic (holistic) medicines. Indian chemists knew how to distill substances, how to make good dyes, and how to make glass.

Medieval Indians knew a great deal about metallurgy and were expert ironworkers. Metalworkers could extract such metals as silver and gold from ores and purify them. Indian iron was famous in the ancient Greek and Roman worlds because it did not rust, and medieval metalworkers retained the secret of quality tempered steel. An iron pillar erected in Delhi during the fifth century still stands today, free of rust.

The Chinese learned how to smelt steel in the third century, but they improved the technique during the medieval period. Ironworks used hydraulic bellows powered by waterwheels to run their furnaces. In the 11th century scientists discovered that bituminous coke, a type of coal, made a good source of fuel for the furnaces. Like their European and Islamic counterparts, Chinese alchemists performed various chemical experiments in their efforts to produce love potions and an elixir of immortality. These experiments eventually led to the invention of one of the most important chemical compounds in history: gunpowder.

Although Chinese alchemists were experimenting with mixtures of saltpeter in the fourth century, most historians agree that gunpowder was invented in China in the ninth century. This invention may have been an unintended result of alchemists' experiments aimed at finding a potion that could make people immortal. Chinese alchemists had been using saltpeter since the first century, and by the late fifth century they had discovered how to identify pure saltpeter by its purple flame. Alchemists also knew sulfur well. The first-known reference to mixing the two together appears in a text from the mid-ninth century. The writer reports that heating sulfur and saltpeter with honey and realgar, an arsenic sulfide commonly used in Chinese medicine, resulted in smoke and flames that could burn down an entire house.

Gunpowder opened the door to a whole new level of military technology. By the 11th century Chinese soldiers had come up with multiple uses for gunpowder and could make different formulas for different purposes. The military handbook *Wujing zongyao* (Collection of the Most Important Military Techniques), written in 1044, describes different recipes for gunpowder that vary the saltpeter and nitrate content to achieve different effects. Once they understood the chemistry behind the explosions, people began experimenting with the physical properties of different containers. Soldiers learned how to make bombs that would emit poison smoke or incendiary bombs that would explode when flung from a catapult. Soldiers filled cast-iron cylinders with gunpowder to make grenades and land mines.

The first rockets appeared during the 10th century. Archers made what they called fire arrows, wooden arrows wrapped in a casing that contained gunpowder. The archers would light a fuse at the end of the arrow and then fire it. Ideally, the gunpowder would explode on impact. Before long soldiers had begun putting gunpowder into metal casings and firing them from metal tubes. In the 13th century Chinese soldiers used these weapons against the Mongols, creating explosions that reportedly flung shrapnel 2,000 feet.

It did not take Chinese scientists and soldiers long to create machines that could take greater advantage of gunpowder. The *Huolongjing* (Fire Drake Manual), written in the late 14th century, contains numerous descriptions of firearms and gunpowder recipes. It describes weapons, such as several mines joined to single fuses, grenades, and multistage rockets. It also describes early firearms. The fire lance was a short-range spear that shot poison darts, shrapnel, and flames. Early cannons could fire metal balls filled with gunpowder that exploded on impact. The first handguns were basically muzzles with fuses that could be lit to fire off the ammunition. The book also describes handguns with locks similar to matchlock guns; these guns could be fired by pulling a trigger.

The Chinese tried to keep their recipe for gunpowder secret, but they had little luck, and the formula for gunpowder rapidly spread throughout medieval Asia, Europe, and the Islamic world. The Mongols were using gunpowder by the 13th century. Gunpowder had entered India by the 14th century. The Koreans developed their own recipe during the late 14th century, using potassium nitrate in the mix. Korean soldiers created their own version of the fire arrow, the *singijeon*, during the 14th century. The *singijeon* came in three sizes. These sizes were calibrated to hit targets at different distances; the archers adjusted fuse lengths so that the missile would explode when it hit its target, not before. During the 15th century the Koreans invented the *hwacha*, a cart with several slots for launching *singijeon*, which functioned as a multiple-rocket launcher.

Gunpowder was not used only for military purposes. One of the most popular uses of the substance was in fireworks. The first fireworks seem to have appeared in China in the 12th century. Fireworks soon became customary at festivals and celebrations, and the art of making them turned into a respected profession. Pyrotechnicians experimented with different chemical compounds to create different colors and used different shells to create different shapes of sparks in the air. Fireworks technology also spread throughout Asia, and fireworks displays became very popular in Japan and India.

Another practical result of scientific experimentation was the invention of paper and the subsequent invention of printing with movable type. Both of these inventions required a good understanding of chemistry, to make the pulp for paper and to create useful inks, and of the physical properties of the equipment involved. Many Asian cultures devised methods of making a sort of paper long before the Chinese wet-pulp method arrived. People in ancient China, India, and Sumatra, for example, made a sort of paper out of bark or bamboo beaten together to form a thin, flat surface. These types of paper were not as strong as pulp paper or Egyptian papyrus.

Paper made from wood pulp was actually invented before the medieval period, probably around 105. The process of making paper was complicated and required a good understanding of the physical properties of fibers and technical skill to build and use the equipment. First the papermaker would shave and crush wood and bark to a fine pulp and dissolve it in water. He would then pour the mixture onto a wooden frame and shake it to level it out. He would lift the frame and shake it to let the water drain out and then turn the new sheet of paper out onto a cloth to dry.

Paper technology continued to evolve and spread during the medieval period. The Chinese began making toilet paper in the sixth century, and by the 14th century they had perfected the technique of making soft, absorbent paper that could even hold perfume. Papermaking spread from China to Korea and Japan around 600, with people there adapting the recipe to use local ingredients, such as mulberry wood in Japan. Papermaking technology arrived in India in the seventh century. In China this technology was applied to the creation of exchange certificates and paper money in the 10th century.

Basic block printing was invented in ancient times, but the more complicated and flexible technique of printing with movable type did not appear until the 11th century in China. Around 1040 the inventor Bi Sheng devised a method of making character types out of fired clay that was described by the contemporary scientist Shen Kua. These types could fit into an iron plate glued to an iron frame with a type of glue that set hard when heated. The types could be reused, but they were fragile and broke easily, and they did not hold ink well. These defects were somewhat remedied by the invention of wooden type by Wang Zhen (fl. 1290–1333) in the late 13th century. Wooden types, however, wore down easily and had to be carved by hand. Wang Zhen attempted to use the wooden types to make tin casts, but this process did not work well because the tin did not take ink well.

The Korean Chae Yun-ui is often credited with being the first person to create useful metal movable type in the early 13th century. He used bronze-casting methods that were well developed by that time. He first carved characters into wood and then pressed these letters into sand to form negative impressions. He then poured molten bronze over the sand, creating the bronze type. Bronze movable type had made its way to China by 1490.

PHYSICS

Historians do not agree on exactly when and where the compass was invented, but the evidence suggests that the first use of the magnetism to determine direction occurred in the 11th century in China. Scientists had begun experimenting with magnetism much earlier. During the seventh or eighth century Chinese scientists had made iron needles take a magnetic charge by rubbing them with magnetite or by heating them and then holding them in a north-south orientation as they cooled. From there scientists devised ways to make actual compasses by fixing magnetic needles to a device in which they could move freely. The main ways of doing this were floating the needle in water, hanging it from a silk thread, or placing it atop a thin shaft. The first compasses were wet compasses. A book written around 1040 describes a bowl of water in which floated an iron needle that always pointed south; the device was helpful to armies trying to determine direction at night.

The 11th-century scientist Shen Kua is credited with being the first person to discover true north by using a magnetic compass to identify the direction of the North Pole and using this information to determine the actual location of the North Star. This information made it easier for sailors to use magnetic compasses in navigation. Shen Kua describes in his writing how magicians and fortune-tellers in the late 11th century used dry compasses made with needles hung from silk threads to help them in their divinations. In the 11th and 12th centuries engineers used compass technology to improve the existing south-pointing chariot, a type of chariot, invented in the third century, on which a figure always pointed south; engineers added to it an odometer, another old invention that found new life in the medieval period.

By the 12th century people were using compasses to help them navigate at night or when clouds obscured the position of the sun and stars. Dry compasses with wooden frames shaped like tortoise shells appeared in the 12th or the 13th century. Box compasses, small compasses in wooden boxes with hinged lids, appeared in the 13th century and were small and portable. The faces of compasses were marked with north, south, and other celestial landmarks. Despite the appearance of more convenient dry compasses, Chinese sailors continued to favor wet compasses throughout the medieval period. Compass technology spread west from China through the Mongol world and into India. It is said that Europeans first learned of the compass from Mongols in Persia in the 13th century.

Physics had other applications, some of them frivolous. For example, starting in the fourth century the Chinese understood aerodynamics well enough to build horizontal propellers, like a helicopter's rotors. Toy makers and children made use of this technology throughout the medieval period, creating flying tops called bamboo dragonflies. These devices had blades of bamboo set at the correct angles to make the devices fly. The user would pull a cord to send the rotor spinning up a bamboo pole and fly into the air. The design of medieval Chinese rotors was one of the inspirations to modern pioneers of aeronautics.

Chinese people developed many methods for powering equipment, such as mills. Engineers had already developed gears and waterwheels in the first century. During the medieval period they put this technology to use in mills and blast furnaces. In the 14th century Chinese engineers borrowed windmill technology from the Islamic world. They developed their own version of the design with horizontal instead of vertical blades, using rigging techniques from Chinese boats, or junks, to affix the sails.

Su Song was especially famous for the hydraulic clock tower he designed and built in Kaifeng in 1088. This clock used an escapement mechanism to control its pendulum, using gears to keep the pendulum's motion regular. The hydraulic-powered mechanism used a chain drive to transmit power among the clock's gears. Su Song describes the design of his clock and of clock making in general in a book he wrote on the subject in 1092. Shen Kua also experimented with clock design, creating an improved version of the clepsydra water clock.

Engineers in medieval China spent a good deal of effort designing revolving or rotating bookcases. These bookcases used gears and brakes to allow bookshelves to move in and out of the repository smoothly and with little effort. Civil engineers invented various locks and gates for canals. The most significant of these was the pound lock, invented in 984. This type of lock used gates to regulate the movement of barges on the canals, mainly to prevent bandits from robbing the merchants as they sailed.

MEDICINE

Chinese medical scientists studied human physiology and anatomy and had a good understanding of the position of organs within the human body. They believed that the body needed to be in balance and that all treatments must take into account the whole patient, not just the illness. Though many modern Western scientists disparage traditional Chinese medical practice, Chinese doctors did use a great deal of observation of their patients and of the natural world to reach conclusions, methods that are the foundation of modern scientific theory. For example, early medieval researchers noticed that the urine of some patients tasted sweet, which they determined either by tasting it or by putting some urine in a saucer to see if it attracted ants. This observation enabled them to diagnose the disease diabetes.

Chinese medical theory relied on the assumption that the human body contained 12 pathways, each of which passed through various organs and points on the skin. Each pathway corresponded with an internal organ. Half of the pathways were yin, and half were yang, corresponding to the positive and negative energy sources in Daoist philosophy. Energy called chi moved through each of those pathways in a preordained schedule that took 24 hours to cover the entire body. Chi and blood both nourished the body as they flowed through their respective pathways. Chinese doctors believed that illness and pain resulted from the imbalance or blockage of chi and blood.

Before treating a patient, a Chinese doctor performed a thorough scientific examination to diagnose the causes of illness. He would examine a patient's tongue, listen to the patient's breathing and bodily noises, smell the patient's body odors, feel the patient's pulse, palpate the patient's internal organs, and question the patient thoroughly about his or her symptoms. This information would tell the doctor which energy pathways were blocked and accordingly tell him which acupressure points to stimulate with needles or burning herbs.

Moxibustion and acupuncture were two of the main techniques Chinese doctors used to treat patients. Moxibustion is the practice of using burning mugwort, an herb, on acupressure points in order to stimulate blood flow and relieve various symptoms. Acupuncture uses many small needles to stimulate those same points. Both of these techniques required that the practitioner study anatomy at great length to learn the locations of the many acupressure points in the body. Stimulating acupressure points on a patient's body could restore the proper flow.

Some of the most important developments of acupressure theory and Chinese medicine occurred during the medieval period. During the seventh century Sun Simiao (581–682), sometimes called China's king of medicine, wrote two major medical texts, the *Beiji qian jin yao fang* (Essential Formulas for Emergencies Worth a Thousand Pieces of Gold) and the *Qian jin yi fang*, a supplement to the previous text. Sun Simiao wrote about the physician's duty to treat all patients equally regardless of class, wealth, education, or beauty. The Song Dynasty physician Wang Wei Yi wrote a treatise on acupuncture and moxibustion. By the 14th century many physicians claimed expertise on the use of acupressure to correct energy imbalances.

Chinese doctors also used herbal concoctions and dietary modifications to treat patients. Instead of using a standard preparation for every patient suffering from a given disease, doctors used their understanding of chemistry and the properties of herbs and bodies to customize herbal treatments for each patient. Doctors classified foods according to their wetness or dryness and their heating or cooling properties, and prescribed foods that would correct their patients' imbalances. Chinese physicians also knew about the medicinal properties of many plants and minerals, both through their own experimentation and from manuals written by scholars in the field. For example, the 11th-century scientist Su Song wrote the *Ben cao tu jing* (Atlas of Materia Medica, 1070), a book on pharmacology and related topics, such as botany and metallurgy. One of the drugs he recommends in this book is the stimulant ephedrine.

The idea of external pathogens causing disease appeared during the Ming Dynasty (1368–1644). The Ming Dynasty scientist Wu You Ke was the first Chinese physician to posit the "warm disease" theory, which held that warm pathogens caused illness after entering the body through the mouth and nose. He describes this theory in the *Wen yi lun* (Treatise on Acute Epidemic Warmth).

In India doctors practiced Ayurvedic medicine, which was quite advanced by the beginning of the medieval period. The 11th-century scholar Chakrapani Dutta was one of the most famous students of Ayurveda; his work *Chakradutta* is still considered a valuable treatise on the topic. Ayurvedic doctors had to train for seven years and pass a test before they could practice on their own. Even after finishing their studies, doctors were expected to continue learning by making observations, by meeting with colleagues, and by talking to local people about their own natural remedies. Ayurvedic medical treatment was based on thorough observation of patients. An Ayurvedic doctor would conduct a detailed examination of his patient, examining the tongue, skin, veins, hair, and pulse. He would then prescribe herbs and other treatments, such as massage, designed to balance the patient's *doshas*.

Like traditional Chinese doctors, Ayurvedic practitioners used herbs, diet, and a holistic approach to treating patients. Ayurveda taught that the human body contained three types of humors, called *doshas*. *Vata* controlled the nervous system, *pitta* controlled digestion and energy, and *kapha* controlled mucus and lubrication. An overabundance of any one of these would create symptoms. Practitioners believed that one of the best ways to keep the *doshas* in balance was through diet. Ayurveda taught that every food had different properties that could increase or decrease particular *doshas*.

ASTRONOMY AND MATHEMATICS

The first treatises on astronomy written in India date to the fifth century, at the beginning of the classical period of Indian astronomy. The astronomer Aryabhata believed that the earth rotated on its axis and determined that the moon was illuminated by the sun. He describes his theories in a book called *Aryabhatiya*. Bhaskara II wrote about gravity and created models of planetary orbits, which he discusses in the *Siddhanta-shiromani*. Both of these works found their way to the Islamic world, where they influenced other astronomers.

The classical period of mathematics in India lasted from 400 to 1200. Aryabhata and Bhaskara II contributed to this field as well as to astronomy. Indian mathematicians studied a number of concepts. They learned about trigonometry from contact with Hellenistic Greeks and expanded the subject themselves. They also worked with the concept of zero, decimal numbers, negative numbers, and algebra.

The Kerala school of astronomy and mathematics was founded in the 14th century to study astronomy and mathematics. It was founded by Madhava of Sangamagrama (1350–1425), a mathematician who specialized in sine and cosine calculations. The school's scholars created a number of formulas to describe infinite series for trigonometric functions and some series expansions of calculus. They worked with geometry, algebra, decimal floating point numbers, and nonlinear equations. They also formulated models to define the position of the moon at any given moment and to estimate the orbits of the planets. Notable scholars of this school included Narayanan Pandit (1340–1400), who worked with algebra and higher order equations, and Parameshvaran (1370–1460), an expert on astronomy and one of the creators of the mean value theorem, a fundamental principle in calculus.

The Chinese scientist Shen Kua studied geology and climatic activity during the 11th century. Based on changes he observed in the landscape, he suggested that climate must change over time. Shen Kua also studied the sun, moon, and planets. He observed lunar and solar eclipses and concluded based on their progress that the sun and moon must be round,

not flat. With the astronomer Wei Pu, Shen Kua developed a model of planetary motion which hypothesized correctly that planets undergo some retrograde motion. The pair of scientists spent five years recording the moon's position five times every night and produced a new model describing the movement of the sun and moon. Another contemporary astronomer, Su Song, wrote an atlas of the heavens with detailed maps of the night sky.

Astronomy made it possible for people to colonize the islands of the Pacific Ocean. For many peoples of the Asia and the Pacific region, navigation on the ocean was a critical skill. Compasses and sextants did not exist in much of the region. Chinese and Indian sailors started using compasses in the 11th and 12th centuries, but magnetic compasses never reached the Pacific islands. Before the advent of mechanical navigation devices, sailors everywhere relied on the sun and the stars to tell them where they were. Pacific islanders continued to use these techniques throughout the medieval period. Celestial navigation was entirely adequate for allowing islanders to sail outrigger canoes vast distances across the ocean.

Islanders created star maps through intense observation of the night sky over many years. They also plotted the relative positions of islands and markers around them, such as coral reefs or shoals. They could use this combination of geographical markers to create a kind of artificial compass. Navigators used a "star structure" to divide the horizon into sections. Each star in the night sky would rise and set at a different point, some rotating entirely in a northern arc and some in an arc to the south. A navigator would choose 16 stars to observe, selecting them on the basis of their positions in the sky, in an effort to create a 32-point celestial archway with the North Star at its top. This structure was called a sidereal compass, a structure that allowed an ocean navigator to determine his position relative to stars, islands, and other oceanic markers. He would also take into account weather patterns, such as winds and ocean currents.

In Micronesia, for example, a navigator could stand on an island and revolve in a circle, reciting the islands and stars that lay in any given direction. Good navigators could do this for the entire network of islands. They also knew the stars and landmarks that marked sea-lanes, pathways that lay on the same celestial coordinates. Sailors could use shells and sticks to lay out maps that described the stars and the landmarks on any given route. The Maori were said to take on every voyage one or two men who were expert astronomers, with good vision and a vast knowledge of the positions of the stars. Polynesian sailors knew a tremendous amount about the stars; they had names for a large number of them and knew how they behaved throughout the year.

EUROPE

BY BRADLEY A. SKEEN

Science is a systematic means of investigating nature. Today the scientist asks a question about the natural world, makes a falsifiable prediction in answer to that question (a hypothesis), tests that hypothesis through experiment, and then formulates a theory that explains the results of the experiment. The theory is used to generate more questions (ways of testing the theory's predictions), which then lead to more experiments. Science is constantly changing in its understanding of nature, approaching but never reaching a complete and final description of the world. Science, therefore, has no use for authority or tradition; no theory is so prestigious or accepted that it cannot be challenged and replaced.

Modern science developed in a specific time and place in Europe during the 17th century. There was, strictly speaking, no science in the Middle Ages or in any earlier period. However, many factors that led to the development of science did exist in the Middle Ages, such as Aristotelian formal logic, the idea of mathematical proof, and various forms of natural philosophy. The Latin word *scientia*, from which the word *science* is derived, refers to any systematic body of knowledge or of theology, such as the science of painting or even a pseudoscience, such as astrology; many sciences of this kind were practiced in the Middle Ages. Medieval thought never abandoned the Aristotelian syllogism by which knowledge is derived from deductions based on supposedly self-evident (that is, unexamined) first principles, precisely the opposite of the inductive scientific methodology developed in the 17th century; these later methods set out to disprove theoretical propositions.

In medieval Europe the systematic investigation of nature was undertaken for a religious purpose, to glorify God. Unlike the science of today, it did not serve a practical purpose in terms of producing new technology. The Scholastic philosophers, who used logic to study nature, were not in contact with the workmen who made improvements in milling technology, water pumps, and the design of boats and other devices that advanced considerably during the Middle Ages. This situation was markedly different from the Islamic world or China, where abstract theory and practical design were carried out by the same men. An exception is in the science of optics. In the 13th century Scholastic research into the interaction of light with lenses led directly to the invention of eyeglasses and the magnifying glass; of course, these instruments were used for reading and so were of special interest to the scholars.

BYZANTINE SCIENCE

There was little original philosophical thought in the Byzantine Empire during the Middle Ages. Despite having access to virtually the whole of Greek scientific literature or perhaps because of that fact, Byzantine intellectuals limited themselves to expounding and commenting on ancient writers of natural philosophy, like Aristotle (384–322 B.C.E.). Perhaps the most original of these was the Christian philosopher John Philoponus (d. ca. 570), who wrote to criticize Aristotle and to prove that he was wrong wherever he disagreed with the authority of the Bible (for example, in Aristotle's belief that the world has existed and will exist forever, compared to the historical context of its creation and destruction according to Christian theology).

Philoponus also made more general attacks on Aristotle's physics, suggesting that Aristotle was wrong by insisting that heavier bodies fall faster than lighter ones (the very issue that most directly led to the development of science in the 17th century). Philoponus suggested that this assertion could easily be disproved by experiment, but it is not clear whether he actually conducted such an experiment. It is certain that his speculation was not widely accepted and did not spark a change in the character of natural historical investigation. While in his writings Philoponus simply appeals to one authority over another, he does suggest to his Islamic and Western readers (his works were quickly suppressed in the Byzantine world because he held heretical theological opinions) that Aristotle was far from infallible and that even so revered an authority could be questioned.

EARLY MEDIEVAL SCIENCE

The political and social collapse of the Western Roman Empire had a devastating effect on scientific knowledge. The chief intellectual language of the Roman Empire had been Greek, and in the West all knowledge of the Greek language and almost all of the information in Greek books were lost. Authors like Boethius (ca. 480–524) translated some Greek philosophical works into Latin. The chief scientific author available in the Latin Middle Ages was Pliny the Elder (23–79), whose encyclopedic *Naturalis historia* (Natural History) gives a systematic account of the physical world hopelessly mixed up with magic, superstition, and pseudoscience. Early medieval authors concerned with nature, like Isidore of Seville (ca. 560–636) or the Venerable Bede (672 or 673–735), could do little but repeat and summarize Pliny. Bede, however, did begin the medieval genre of the *computus*, manuals describing how to calculate the correct date of Easter each year.

The situation for learning improved somewhat under the first Holy Roman Emperor, Charlemagne (r. 800–14), who established a central school at his palace in Aachen and encouraged each bishop in western Europe to found schools. Alcuin (ca. 732–804), the director of the palace school, oversaw the collection of surviving manuscripts of ancient Latin texts along with their reproduction and distribution to schools and monasteries. One scholar produced by this resurgence of education was John Scotus Erigena (ca. 810–ca. 877). In his *De divisione naturae* (Division of Nature), he describes the creation of the world based on Byzantine theology and the work of Dionysius the Areopagite (ca. 500)—as a pouring out of God and a descent toward a point beyond which creation was no longer possible: physical matter. This work formed the background for all later medieval thought about the physical world.

The first Western scholar to study Arabic science in Spain was Gerbert d'Aurillac (ca. 945–1003), who became Pope Sylvester II in 999. He learned and disseminated in Europe the modern Arabic numerals and the abacus. He also learned enough about engineering to design the first hydraulic pipe organ in western Europe since Roman times. In part because of his ability to carry out mathematical operations in his head, which seemed like a miracle to anyone trained in the cumbersome Roman numerical system, he was widely believed in his lifetime to be a magician; later many medieval magical books falsely circulated under his name. Gerbert's recourse to Arabic culture, which had much better preserved the scientific and scholarly heritage of the Roman Empire, was a foreshadowing of developments in the next few centuries.

PETER ABÉLARD

Peter Abélard (1079–ca. 1142) was the most important philosopher in the period between the founding of the universities in the 10th century and the reception of Arabic science. He was also a prominent poet and composer. He is well known in popular culture today because of his scandalous affair with a student he was tutoring, Héloïse (ca. 1098–1164), with whom he exchanged letters, over 100 of which have been preserved.

Abélard was not directly interested in natural philosophy, but he produced a logical framework that both authorized and limited scientific investigation within the Catholic tradition and that is important in understanding the intellectual foundation of scientific methodology down to the present day. In his book *Sic et non* (Yes and No), Abélard assembles a list of 158 theological questions, such as whether priests should be celibate, and a catalog of relevant biblical texts and patristic texts (works that deal with the writings of the church fathers) on each, some of which seem clearly to give the answer yes and others just as clearly the answer no. The point of the exercise is not to try to reach a conclusion on any individual issue, and Abélard does not attempt to do so. However, in the introduction he summarizes the methods by which such contradictory texts must be treated. Each text must be analyzed: How is language used in each quotation? What is the context?

The Chaucer astrolabe, the earliest-known European astrolabe, Britain, 1326 (© The Trustees of the British Museum)

Is the author speaking in his own voice, or is he perhaps stating a position that he refutes in the next sentence? Abélard shows that the literal meaning of authoritative texts cannot be used to resolve the issue at hand; only a process of rational investigation based on logic can do so. This philosophy provides the Scholastic justification of the investigation of nature through observation and experiment rather than through the acceptance of the revealed texts of the Bible.

In the *Theologia Christiana* (Christian Theology), on the other hand, Abélard sets a clear boundary for the use of human reason within the Catholic intellectual framework that prevailed in the Middle Ages. He attacks the use of dialectic (logic) over and against revelation with arguments that can be applied not only to the investigation of nature in the Middle Ages but even to modern science. He opposes the proposition that everything can be explained by human reason, that we ought to accept only what can be demonstrated by reason and reject appeals to authority unless the authority's position can be validated through reason. He insists that reason is limited and that complete knowledge must depend on revelation, yet he concedes that only authorities who agree with reason as far as reason goes can be trusted when they move beyond it. In his view, reason can reveal the truth about the physical world, but logic must to yield to authority in such matters as theology, whose premises cannot be investigated by the human senses and reasoning faculty.

THE RECEPTION OF ARABIC SCIENCE

In the 12th century scientific works written in Arabic (including ancient books that had earlier been translated from Greek into Arabic) began to be translated into Latin by Christian scholars working in Spain. Copies of these translations were quickly disseminated all over western Europe and became the standard for scientific learning at the universities. The new philosophical learning posed difficulties for the priests who began to work with it, insofar as its authors were either ancient "pagans" or Islamic "infidels." Using human reason, this new learning also sought to discover knowledge that could stand apart from the divine revelation that established the church's privileged position in medieval culture. These problems were soon resolved by Thomas Aquinas (1225–74) in his *Summa theologica* (Summary of Theology) and other works. In these works, incorporating Aristotelian science, he presents a new philosophical system that was acceptable to the worldview of medieval Christianity. Thomistic science undertakes to examine the world as the work of God.

Aristotle wrote technical treatises on almost every branch of science, from biology to the physics of motion. These now came into Europe together with extensive commentaries by Arabic philosophers. Other ancient works were received also, such as the astronomical writings of Ptolemy (second century) and the medical works of Galen (129–ca. 99). The most important element of the Aristotelian science adopted by the Scholastic thinkers, however, was logic. In his *Prior Analytics*, Aristotle develops a formal system of deductive reasoning that is capable of producing new knowledge and that was adopted as the main method of investigation by medieval philosophers. An Aristotelian syllogism combines two facts (which must be self-evidently true to ensure the validity of the process) to produce a new deduction that is not yet known. A syllogism involves a major premise, a minor premise, and a conclusion: *Major premise*: Socrates is a man. *Minor premise*: All men are mortal. *Synthesis*: Socrates is mortal.

This intellectual procedure is valid if its premises are in fact true, but it tends to produce results that confirm the premises even if they are mistaken. Logic was well suited to medieval thought, which proceeded from premises of divine revelation that by definition could not be examined.

The reception of Greek and Arabic learning brought with it also a host of pseudosciences that enjoyed the same prestige as texts and systems treating the legitimate investigation of nature. These were mostly forms of divination, which is a system that attempts to foresee future events, particularly whether the outcome of a decision made in the present will be favorable or unfavorable. People turned to divination whenever they had to make decisions whose outcomes could not be rationally predicted—for instance, whether a business venture or a marriage would be successful. These systems of occult science included astrology, which seeks to use the precision of astronomical observation and calculation to support a form of astral divination. During the Middle Ages astrology in particular became an almost universal aid in medical prognosis. Another class of divination was physiognomy, a system that claims to be able to reveal a human being's character and future based on an analysis of physical appearance. Numerology attempts to understand and even manipulate nature by reducing language to mathematics and carrying out various operations and transformations on the revealed numbers. One of the most important manuals of these kinds of pseudoscience translated from the Arabic into Latin in the 12th century was the *Picatrix*. It also provides information on how to raise and interrogate the spirits of the dead and how to make pacts with demonic beings.

New forms of alchemy also came into Europe from the Arab world through the work of translators in Spain. Even though alchemy's purpose to transform base metals into gold was impossible to achieve, its emphasis on physical experimentation in a laboratory made alchemy an important precursor to modern science. Such early scientists as Isaac Newton (1642–1727) and Robert Boyle (1627–91) in the 17th century began by working in alchemy and moved beyond it when they found many of its claims fraudulent. However, the real purpose of alchemy was not physical investigation at all but the spiritual transformation of the alchemist in a process akin to mysticism.

ROGER BACON

The Franciscan friar Roger Bacon (ca. 1220–92), who taught at Oxford and Paris and acquired the Scholastic nickname of Doctor Mirabilis ("miraculously learned"), is sometimes called the first scientist, but that title is something of an exaggeration. He was practical minded and wanted to see and understand things for himself, but he did not develop this disposition into scientific methodology as Galileo (1564–1642) later did. Bacon rejected the widely held Scholastic idea that knowledge about the physical world can be achieved through reason without observation and investigation. He opposed contemporary theological methods for the same reason and insisted that analysis of the Bible should start with reading the texts in the original language. (He may have learned Greek himself.) Bacon's interest in mathematics was also practical rather than theoretical: in its use in physics (his geometrical description of vision), astronomy and astrology, and cartography.

Bacon's interests made him turn toward practical sciences, like optics and alchemy. He advanced the understanding of optics received from Arabic science, which was just becoming known in Europe during his lifetime. He was the first to understand that the rainbow, which he reproduced by passing sunlight through a beaker of water, was the division of the light into its constituent parts, or spectrum. He also proved for the first time that rainbows could not appear more than 42 degrees above the horizon. Bacon's work with lenses led him to invent the magnifying glass and lay the foundations for the discovery of such later instruments as eyeglasses, the telescope, and the microscope. Much of his work in optics was based on practical experiments with lenses, pinholes, and other devices; he later expressed the results of these experiments in a geometrical form. This practice led him to call for the development of a new method of experimental science for testing the validity of theory, analogous to logic for testing the validity of arguments, but he could not advance a general form of such a method outside of his special field of optics.

Bacon's alchemical investigations led him to examine gunpowder (then newly introduced to Europe from China); he was the first to publish the formula for its manufacture. He was aware of the invention of the steam engine in antiquity and believed that it could probably be adapted to propel vehicles—thoughts that show a remarkable power to imagine beyond the limits of mechanical engineering as it existed in Bacon's lifetime. Bacon laid out the plan to publish a universal encyclopedia that would have undoubtedly been a stimulus to scientific development, as was the work of the encyclopedists in the 17th and 18th centuries, but he never produced more than a few fragments.

Bacon is often portrayed as a martyr to science who was silenced by the church, but in fact his main scientific work, the *Opus maius* (Major Work), was written by the special commission of Pope Clement IV (d. 1268) in 1266 to 1267. It is by no means certain that Bacon was ever actually put under house arrest (and hence forbidden to publish), but if he was, this arrest would likely have been for his sympathies with the radical Spiritual Franciscans or for his insistence on the deterministic influence of astrology rather than for his investigation of nature. Many alchemical and even magical books written during the Middle Ages were published under Bacon's name in an attempt to gain authority for themselves.

WILLIAM OF OCKHAM

William of Ockham (ca. 1285–ca. 1349) taught philosophy at the London Greyfriars Franciscan monastery. (He studied at Oxford but did not take a master's or a doctor's degree.) He is chiefly remembered now in connection with Ockham's razor. This is a logical principle suggesting that unnecessary steps in reasoning should not be introduced into argument and that simpler arguments are more likely to be true than are more complex ones. As important as this concept is to scientific reasoning, Ockham did not invent what was an inevitable part of the practice of philosophy going back to ancient times. The attribution to Ockham was made in the 19th century, probably because of the particularly ruthless and effective way he used it to dismantle and to simplify Aristotle's arguments.

NICOLE ORESME

Scholastic philosophers were often drawn to problems in physics because they considered them inseparable from problems in theology. For instance, the problem of how force causes a body to move and how the body remains in motion after it has no further contact with that force seemed to these philosophers intimately connected to the problem of how divine grace is carried in the Eucharistic host. Similarly, investigation of the problem of whether and how the quality of love (*charitas*) varies at different times in an individual (that is, how love is increased by the Holy Spirit) led to quite remarkable advances in the understanding of motion (both require the understanding of the degree of change over time) and even to the mathematicization of science.

Nicole Oresme (ca. 1325–82) studied at the University in Paris and briefly served as a professor there before becoming the bishop of Lisieux in Normandy. He was also a courtier to the kings of France and to the popes in Avignon. He was one of the first scholars to write extensively in a vernacular language (French, in his case) rather than in Latin, an important step away from medieval and toward modern practices. Oresme became interested in the work of a group of scholars at Merton College, Oxford, had carried out from around 1325 to 50. They had realized that the velocity of an object could be represented as a ratio between the force that impelled it and the factors that caused resistance to its motion (such as friction). Although no one in the Middle Ages used the notation of modern algebraic equations, this discovery was the first time that a physical property had been defined in mathematical terms and could be represented in modern signs as $V=F/R$. The very idea of finding the velocity of an object in motion, rather than the force that propelled it, which was all that had interested Aristotle, arose from the Scholastic interest in changing qualities in general, such as love, health, age, virtue, or warmth.

Several scholars quickly realized that this new discovery could be represented geometrically. The earliest such system (1351) was developed by Giovanni di Casali (d. ca. 1375). However, a more complete system, and the one that influenced the later development of science, was made by Oresme. He began with a simple example: Suppose one has a rod anchored by a pin at one end and begins to rotate it. Different sections of the rod will move different distances in the same time and so have different velocities. If one rotates the rod and marks its old and new positions by lines, the resulting figure will be a triangle whose height is proportional to the velocity. Thus, the end near the pin will have moved hardly at all, and the height of the triangle at that point will be low. The more distant end will have moved much farther and therefore faster, so the height of the triangle will be greater. The hypotenuse of the triangle will slope upward, indicating the increase in velocity uniformly from one end of the rod to the other.

Oresme realized that a more powerful form of representation could be had if the baseline were not the position of some physical object like a rod but an abstract representation of the passage of time. This theory in itself is not startling since Aristotle had often represented time through the use of a straight line passing through various temporal points. However, Oresme's innovation was to plot velocity as a function of time perpendicular to the baseline. In this way an object traveling at a constant speed would also have a velocity the same height above the time line and produce the geometric form of a rectangle. An object that was constantly accelerating at a uniform rate, however, would have ever higher velocities and so make a right triangle, just as in the original example.

Oresme's geometric representation contained the same key features as the system of graphic representation developed by René Descartes (1596–1650) in the 17th century; Descartes' system became an indispensable tool of the scientific revolution, the plotting of velocity against time. It was precisely identical to the graphical system that Galileo used to prove the validity of his own theories, by showing through experiment that the slope of the line representing acceleration was the same for heavier and lighter objects. Oresme's work, then, helped to lay the foundation for the scientific revolution. Oresme is often said to have anticipated Galileo's proof that acceleration due to gravity is uniform regardless of the mass of the falling objects (thus disproving a key Aristotelian proposition). It did not occur to Oresme, however, to apply the results of his abstract geometrical diagrams to real-world objects, and it would hardly have been possible for him to do so for technical reasons, such as the lack of any practical timekeeping device that could have taken the necessary measurements. While Oresme was able to represent continuous acceleration through his geometrical illustration, he did not apply his theories to the study of falling bodies.

Oresme did challenge Aristotle in the area of astronomy, though. He disproved Aristotle's arguments against the possibility that the earth was moving and showed, using Ockham's razor, that the heliocentric theory (the belief that the sun is at the center of the solar system) was simpler and therefore more likely to be true than Aristotle's geocentric theory (the belief that the sun, moon, planets, and stars revolve around the earth). Even here, however, Oresme wished only to show that Aristotle's logic was faulty; he did not move from this logical demonstration to the suggestion that the heliocentric model of the solar system was a physical fact. Copernicus (1473–1543) in the 16th century did not actually suggest that his defense of the heliocentric theory was anything more than a simpler and more accurate way of calculating celestial motion. The difference in the reception of the two thinkers (the former went unnoticed, and the latter helped to start the scientific revolution) was that the scholarly community in general had in the meantime become interested in the scientific investigation of nature through observation and experiment.

NICHOLAS OF CUSA

Nicholas of Cusa (1401–64), generally known as Cusanus, was a German bishop and cardinal who worked to restore the prestige of the Papacy after the end of the Babylonian captivity in Avignon and the period of rival popes. He also acted as a papal ambassador to the patriarch of Constantinople, working to reunite Catholic and Orthodox Christianity. His chief scientific work was *De docta ingnorantia* (On Learned Ignorance, 1440).

Cusanus argued that the earth and the heavenly bodies of the sun, moon, planets, and fixed stars were made of material substances. Since they consisted of matter, they would be subject to the Fall, that is, the punishment of Adam and Eve when they were expelled from the Garden of Eden. Indeed, Scholastic teaching held that the Fall applied to the whole physical world. Cusanus thought that Aristotle's generally accepted opinion that the earth was at the precise center of the universe and that the heavenly bodies moved in perfect circles must be wrong. Those qualities represented perfect forms, but if the earth and stars were fallen in the Christian sense, they could not be perfect. While this argument is interesting within the context of the history of Scholastic philosophy, it does not contain any persuasive scientific proof of the claims made.

Much of Cusanus's detailed argument consisted of numerological (pseudoscientific number mysticism) calculations. Nevertheless, when such early scientists as Copernicus, Galileo, Brahe (1546–1601), and Kepler (1571–1630) began to offer mathematical and observational proofs of the heliocentric model of the solar system, the physical imperfections of heavenly bodies, such as sunspots and lunar craters, and the elliptical nature of the orbits of the planets, these scientists all pointed to Cusanus's theories as their starting point, in part to help make their ideas acceptable to ecclesiastical authorities. In the more practical sphere of optics, Cusanus was the first to use concave lenses to correct myopic eyesight. His work on infinitesimal motion contributed to the later development of calculus.

THE ISLAMIC WORLD
BY KATELIN MASON

A historical account of science in the Islamic world could be arranged according to individual scientist or by discipline, yet both methods are unable to express fully the spirit of scientific inquiry during the rise of the Islamic Empire. Scientists did not live in vacuums—they were in isolation neither from one another nor from other fields of study. Often engaged in numerous disciplines, these scholars were diverse in their interests and talents. Abu ar-Rayhan al-Biruni (973–1048), a renowned astronomer, was also a gifted astrologer, geographer, historian, mathematician, and scientist of the physical and natural sciences. Ibn Sina (980–1037), the physician known in the West as Avicenna and who composed *Al-qanun fi al-tibb* (The Canon of Medicine), was an Aristotelian philosopher, mathematician, astronomer, and metaphysician. Mercantile cities became centers of scientific exchange and development, while vast libraries, centers of learning, and translation and travel enabled exchange of the vibrant thought emerging with the rise of Islam. This exchange of ideas suggests division by discipline rather than by scientist, facilitating a discourse that considers these scholars in relation to one another. It should be kept in mind, though, that most of the scientists mentioned were masters of several sciences. Only the most historically significant personages of each discipline are mentioned, while countless others provided the framework, data, and theory informing their thought and discoveries. A particular scientist may have been the most prominent in a field in which he is mentioned here, such as physics, yet also have been significant, but not historically critical, to the field of mathematics.

The phrase *Islamic science* has been scrutinized extensively because of the ambiguity of its terms. Today *science* refers to the physical and natural sciences, and the word *Islamic* implies something intrinsically Muslim. In fact, Islamic science is Islamic only insofar as it is science occurring within the sphere of influence of Islam (Morocco to China), regardless of religion or ethnicity. The phrase *Arab science* is often used to designate the same subject. Here, *Arab* replaces *Islamic* because of the dominant use of the Arabic language in the majority of scientific writings. While the term no longer implies science exclusively by Muslims, it is similarly flawed in its exclusionary properties. *Arab science* implies that the scientific tradition of the Islamic world was developed alone by Arabs—conceptually more contentious and inaccurate than the implication that all science within these regions was practiced by people of the Islamic faith. This is because these regions, including the Arab world itself, are made up of highly diverse ethnic populaces. Finally, Islamic science would be inconceivable without the contributions of the Persian and Indian civilizations.

The linguistic nature of the Koran is nuanced and sophisticated, such that it is viewed as having inevitably sparked an intellectual revolution in the Islamic world. It enabled the growth of science by providing a rich vocabulary with which to detail the theory and practice of science. Furthermore, the Koran sparked the founding of the Islamic religious sciences, such as theology and jurisprudence, which, in turn, gave rise to the other branches of Islamic science. The sayings of the Prophet (Hadith) also propelled Islamic science by establishing several foundational branches of knowledge, including *ilm al-rijal* (science of biographies of narrators of Hadith), and the related *ilm al-ansab* (science of genealogy) and *ilm al-tarikh* (science of history). These religious sciences helped create the epistemological framework of Islamic science.

Science was a major part of society in the Islamic world, thriving in its most vibrant cities, such as Baghdad, Cairo, Córdoba, and Gundishapur. The Koran and Hadith ask Muslims to seek knowledge and truth, which they did with fervor. These religious messages encouraged and allowed Islamic rulers to support scientific endeavors. One of the greatest sources of pride of an urban center was its claim to scientific knowledge, as this implied adherence to Islam and intellectual and societal prowess vis-à-vis other cities. The prominent position of science in society is evidenced by the establishment of schools of translation, medicine, and science.

The synthesizing of Indian, Persian, and Greek knowledge into the corpus of Islamic thought allowed it to flourish. This knowledge entered the arena of Islamic thought through translation efforts, the most notable being that of ninth-century Abbasid Baghdad under the caliph Abu al-Abbas al-Mamun (r. 813–33). This initiative was continued by later caliphs and, to a lesser extent, throughout the Islamic world. In Baghdad the Abbasid caliph Harun ar-Rashid (r. 786–809) established the House of Wisdom (Bayt al-hikmah), while in 1005 the Fatimid caliph Abu Ali al-Hakim (r. 996–?1021) founded Dar al-ilm (House of Knowledge), housing approximately 1 million volumes. There were a number of great translators, but the most prolific was the Nestorian Christian Hunayn ibn Ishaq al-Ibadi (808–73), who translated an enormous volume of Greek medical, philosophical, and scientific works into Syriac and Arabic in the school of Baghdad. Through their knowledge of Arabic and extensive translations, scientists of all ethnic and cultural backgrounds could communicate with one another, in person or through text, across thousands of miles or hundreds of years.

Any division of the intellectual sciences of the Islamic world is somewhat limited insofar as these sciences must be understood as parts of a whole—reinforcing, assessing, critiquing, and informing one another. The divisions listed are primarily for clarity of understanding. The philosopher Abu Nasr al-Farabi (ca. 87–ca. 950) and the historian Ibn Khaldun (1332–1406), among others, divided the sciences into several branches. Still, this should not be understood as anything more than classification for the purpose of positioning the sciences in relation to one another and tracking their maturity. In anatomy one may classify the parts of the body, but the complete separation of its parts would render each incomprehensible and meaningless. Similarly, science in the Islamic world, while divided rhetorically into disciplines, remains an integral whole whose parts continue to nurture one another.

ASTRONOMY

While pre-Islamic Arabs had some familiarity with astronomy for creating calendars, it was not until the incorporation of Greek, Indian, and Persian astronomy that this developed formally into a science. The pursuit of astronomy in the Islamic world was dictated by interest in both the predictive study of astrology as well as in the application of astronomical data. Astrological prediction was sought particularly by rulers seeking strategic guidance, although many viewed this as heretical, implying lack of faith in God. While astronomy was used for finding the direction of the *qibla* (which Muslims face to pray) and travel, it was also motivated by that enchantment with the heavens felt by virtually all before the modern era. Despite their close relationship, astronomy and astrology were maintained, at least in rhetoric, as separate disciplines.

Indian and Persian astronomical texts were first translated into Arabic in the eighth century. Most notably, Ibrahim al-Fazari (d. 777); his son, Muhammad al-Fazari (d. ca. 796–806); and Yaqub ibn Tariq (d. 796) compiled the *Zij al-sindhind*, the crown of Indian achievement in astronomy, from the *Surya siddhanta* and the works of the Indian astronomer Brahmagupta (598–668). It would remain the most important work of astronomy until the ninth century. The Persian *Zij al-shah* (555), a collection of astronomical tables compiled over two centuries and representing the height of Persian astronomy, was translated into Arabic by Abu al-Hasan al-Tamimi. Both of the latter were critical texts that helped inform Islamic astronomical thought. Ultimately, Greek texts, in particular Ptolemy's *Almagest*, were most utilized by Islamic astronomers. Translated, commentated upon, and revised

continuously, the *Almagest* also served as a primer and starting point for original astronomical thought.

Muhammad al-Fazari was also the inventor of the astrolabe, a scientific instrument used for calculating the data found through astronomical observation. Al-Fazari and Yaqub ibn Tariq applied the Indian sine function to astronomy, making calculations far easier, yet these men are most significant for their introduction of the major Indian and Persian astronomy texts into Islamic thought. It was not until the ninth century that the Hellenistic tradition would be added to the now-thriving field of astronomy in the Islamic world.

The full translations of the *Almagest* that began to appear in the ninth century provided a wealth of astronomical techniques, theory, and data of utmost importance for the formulation of Islamic astronomy. The first of these translations was

The Wonders of Creation and the Oddities of Existence, *page from a manuscript, Egypt or Syria, ca. 1375–1425; this book, compiled in 1270 by Zakariya Qazwini, covers the fields of geography, astronomy, astrology, and natural history, in a mixture of science and superstition.* (© The Trustees of the British Museum)

completed by al-Hajjaj ibn Matar (ca. 800), followed by that of a non-Muslim member of the Sabian sect of Harran, Thabit ibn Qurra (ca. 836–901), in the latter part of the century. Ibn Qurra's was a substantial improvement from the first rendition of the *Almagest*, utilizing the blossoming vocabulary of Arabic. In addition to his translation efforts, Thabit ibn Qurra is noted for expositing the theory of trepidation (oscillation of the equinoxes) first proposed by Theon of Alexandria (fourth century C.E.), which he explained by adding a ninth planet to the Ptolemaic model. In addition to these great achievements, Thabit ibn Qurra used Euclid's *Elements* to demonstrate Ptolemy's model of the motion of a planetary body on an eccentric course. He is also considered the first to discuss the velocity of a moving object at a particular point.

Abu Abd Allah al-Battani (ca. 858–929), an associate of Thabit ibn Qurra, continued the latter's pursuits in general while abandoning trepidation theory. Al-Battani's keen observational skills enabled him to discover the behavior of the solar apsides. He created a new method of establishing the sighting of the new moon and a detailed study of eclipses. Al-Battani's works remained important throughout medieval Islamic astronomy and were utilized in Europe as late as the 18th century.

Muhammad Ibn Musa al-Khwarizmi's (ca. 780–ca. 850) *Zij al-sindhind* (not to be confused with the Sanskrit text translated under the same title in the earlier 700s) is the first original text of Islamic astronomy, with solar, lunar, and planetary tables and commentary. Here al-Khwarizmi makes use both of Indian and Greek elements. Insofar as al-Khwarizmi does not merge these elements fluidly, this work represents the early stage of the synthesizing of pre-Islamic sciences into the corpus of Islamic science.

The verification of Greek, Indian, and pre-Islamic Persian astronomy coupled with the avid pursuit of new data led to the formation of a collective astronomy project with centers in Baghdad and Damascus through the patronage of the caliph al-Mamun. This resulted in the *Zij al-mumtahan*, which contained critical corrections of Ptolemaic data, most notably the demonstration that the apogee of the sun moves with the fixed stars. With increased production of commentaries on and revisions of pre-Islamic astronomical texts came an awareness of problematic data therein. As Hellenistic astronomy propounded theories constructed upon data, the demonstrated variance of this data with new observations led to the pursuit of new theories. Habash al-Hasib's (d. ca. 870) *al-Zij al-damashqi* represents one such work, in which, while revising Ptolemy, he made trigonometry an essential component of astronomical science.

Progress in 10th- and 11th-century trigonometry combined with the founding of several large observatories led to increases both in corrections of Ptolemaic astronomy as well as to an expansion of original astronomical thought. During this period Abd al-Rahman al-Sufi of Rayy produced the *Kitab suwar al-kuwakib al-thabita* (Book of the Fixed Stars), which refined the cataloging of stars in the *Almagest*. Also during this time, Abu al-Hassan Ali bin Yunus (d. 1009) of Cairo helped to fully synthesize pre-Islamic astronomical thought into the body of Islamic astronomy. *Al-zij al-hakim al-kabirun* contains a history of astronomy until his times, along with revisions and new observational data. The 10th century was also important for instrument building and writing on instruments of observation by figures such as Abu Mahmud Hamid al-Khujandi (d. 1000), who wrote on astronomical instruments and built a sextant at Rayy.

Abu ar-Rayhan al-Biruni of Khwarizmi was a master scientist for whom astronomy was just one of several subjects in which he excelled. He mentions Abu al-Wafa al-Buzjani (d. 998) and Abu Nasr Mansur Ibn Iraq (960–1036) as his teachers. Following the tradition of these researchers, al-Biruni was a mathematical astronomer, making expert use of applied trigonometry. Al-Biruni used his linguistic skills to access the Persian, Greek, Syriac, Indian, and Arabic astronomical traditions, producing more than 150 works on almost all branches of science and philosophy. His *al-Qanun al-masudi* (Masudi Canon) is most notable for its simultaneous depth and comprehensiveness concurrent with its synthesis of pre-Islamic astronomy. Al-Biruni was a scholar of many fields of science but was primarily an astronomer and astrologer. His role as astronomer was intimately connected with his love of mathematics, which he made use of in his formulation of treatises on such critical subjects as shadows, astrolabes, and geographic coordinates. In addition to al-Biruni's immense scientific achievements was his establishment of astronomy and the mathematical sciences as distinct from metaphysics and philosophy, particularly Aristotelian presuppositions. The points that al-Biruni raised, such as a lack of "natural" reasons why the heavenly bodies must move on a particular course is demonstrative of his epistemologically revolutionary attitude. Al-Biruni's *Al-asila wa al-ajwaba* provides the content of his exchanges with Ibn Sina, the foremost Aristotelian philosopher of the Islamic world. In this text al-Biruni clearly asserts himself as a mathematician and not a philosopher. This conscientious decision colored al-Biruni's thought and shaped the future of the Islamic scientific tradition.

New elements of Indian astronomy and astronomical discoveries in the 10th and 11th centuries led to the solidification of Islamic astronomy as a discipline unto itself. Astrology was increasingly condemned, moving the patronage of astronomy from royal courts to mosques and observatories. Greater interest in astronomical precision for religious purposes, such as prayer times and the direction of prayer, also encouraged this shift of patronage.

The 11th century was shaped by more questioning of Aristotelian and Ptolemaic presuppositions. These critics and astronomers included Abu Ubayd al-Juzjani (d. 1070) who in his *Tarkib al-aflak* questions the equant problem of the Ptolemaic model. An anonymous work from Andalusia titled *Al-istidrak ala batlamyus* lists further objections to Ptolemaic astronomy. Pointed critiques also came from Abu Ali al-Hasan ibn al-Haytham (965–1039), often known by his Latinized name of Alhazen, in his *Al-shukuk ala batlamyus* (Doubts concerning Ptolemy), which listed his concerns with the Hellenistic philosophical and astronomical traditions, in particular, the questions he held in regard to the Ptolemaic models and their alleged inconsistencies. The inconsistencies laid out by Ibn al-Haytham were taken up readily by such towering scientific figures as Muayyad al-Din al-Urdi (d. 1266), Nasir ad-Din at-Tusi (1201–74), Qutb al-Din al-Shirazi (d. 1311), Sadr al-Sharia al-Bukhari (d. 1374), Ibn al-Shatir (d. 1375), to name only a few of those who rigorously investigated and refined the Ptolemaic astronomical tradition and in turn fortified Islamic astronomy.

The 12th century witnessed the growth of planetary theory by Western astronomers, including Ibn Bajjah (ca. 1095–1138); Muhammad ibn Abd al-Malik ibn Tufayl (d. ca. 1185); Abu al-Walid ibn Rushd (1126–98), known in the West as Averroës; and Abu Ishaq al-Bitruji (d. 1204). These theorists sought to resuscitate Aristotelian astronomy after rejecting aspects of Ptolemaic thought, in particular, eccentrics and epicycles. Al-Bitruji created an alternative model, which still adhered to Aristotelian motion theory.

The 13th and 14th centuries witnessed the favoring of philosophy over astronomy in the Western lands of Islam, while in the Eastern lands it continued to flourish with such scholars as Nasir ad-Din at-Tusi, Qutb al-Din al-Shirazi, and Ibn al-Shatir. At-Tusi's "Tusi Couple" was an alternative to Ptolemy's problematic equant theory. Al-Shirazi, the student of at-Tusi, discussed the possibility of a heliocentric model extensively, while Ibn al-Shatir brought astronomy further from the equant problem of Ptolemaic astronomy by adding another epicycle. Ibn al-Shatir was also able to show through trigonometric demonstration that the earth is not located precisely at the center of the universe.

MATHEMATICS

The incorporation of the Indian numerical system into Islamic science brought about solutions to many difficult mathematical questions and made arithmetic a substantially easier enterprise than it had been. Yet preexisting modes of arithmetic such as the Babylonian sexagesimal system that was based on the number 60 remained in use, particularly for astronomy where the Indian and Babylonian modes were both used.

The development of algebra was aided by the translation of Diophantus's *Arithmetica*. This translation was produced at approximately the same time that al-Khwarizmi was writing the first significant work of Islamic mathematics during the early ninth century, *Kitab al-jabr wa al-muqabalah* (Book of Compulsion and Comparison). Here al-Khwarizmi's quest for a comprehensive system for solving linear and quadratic equations is achieved, earning him the title that he shares with Diophantus, "Father of Algebra." The word *algebra*, in fact, derives from the title of this text, "*al-jabr*" ("compulsion"), used in his solution of quadratic equations by this mathematical principle.

The interrelationship of arithmetic, algebra, and geometry helped each of these grow further in the fertile intellectual climate established by Islam. Abu Bakr al-Karaji was focused on extrapolating arithmetical laws and applying these to algebra. Thabit ibn Qurra used geometry as a lens for his conception algebra, while others, such as Abu Abd Allah Muhammad ibn Isa al-Mahani (d. 880) used algebra for volumetric quantification in geometry. The use of conic sections to solve cubic equations was another significant development whereby geometric solutions were applied to algebraic problems, thus enabling the finding of roots more efficaciously than through the traditional route of algebraic solutions. It was with Omar Khayyam (1048?–1131), however, that the use of conic sections would be used to solve third-order equations.

Algebraic geometry was furthered by Sharaf al-Din al-Tusi (d. 1213), through the process of expressing the intersection of two lines algebraically. Additionally, al-Tusi developed the concept of a maximum and introduced the notion of derivatives. This relationship of arithmetic, algebra, and geometry helped Islamic mathematics extend the knowledge transmitted by Greek civilization. When trigonometry from India was added to this body of knowledge, its development quickened. New branches of mathematics emerged, including those devoted to asymptotic behavior, infinitesimal objects, and intermediate analysis.

OPTICS

Greek knowledge of optics was conveyed to the Islamic world during the early translation movements of the eighth century. These translations included research on vision, rays, reflection, mirrors, the atmosphere, and burning mirrors, to name only a few. Along with this transmission of optics texts were the production of original works by Islamic scientists, including Ibn Masawaih (d. 857), Hunayn ibn Ishaq al-Ibadi, Qusta ibn Luqa al-Balabakki (fl. 860–900), and Thabit ibn Qurra. Yaqub ibn Ishaq al-Kindi (d. ca. 870) also wrote texts on an array of subjects pertaining to optics from an Aristotelian and Euclidean perspective. During the 10th century Abu Sad al-Ala ibn Sahl contributed substantially to the field of dioptrics, refracting and focusing light using burning lenses and mirrors. He also wrote on the science of refraction and developed the constant ratio. Ibn al-Haytham's work is inconceivable without the developments advanced by this important predecessor.

Ibn al-Haytham, in his *Kitab fi al-manazir* (Book of Optics), dated 1270, created the foremost text and achievement of Islamic optical research. Ibn al-Haytham essentially deconstructed Hellenistic optics and rewrote many of its principles. Euclid and Ptolemy had propounded the view of extramission, where a ray extends from the eye to the perceived object, while Aristotle had supported the notion of intromission that involves a form passing from the object to the eye. Rejecting both of these views, Ibn al-Haytham introduced an original theory of vision, holding that light reflected by the object is received by the eye. Ibn al-Haytham is also responsible for the so-called Alhazen's problem, after his Western name, which involves locating the point of reflection on a concave or convex spherical mirror in relation to the positioning of the visible object and eye. Making use of physiological, mathematical and medical advances, Ibn al-Haytham was able to transform optics fundamentally. His use of controlled experimentation was adopted by Kamal al-Din al-Farisi (d. 1319), who further revised optics and wrote commentaries on Ibn al-Haytham's works. Al-Farisi is responsible for having demonstrated the refractory causes underlying the shapes of the first and second arcs of rainbows.

PHYSICS

While the Aristotelian scientific tradition was essential to the formulation of all Islamic science, it was particularly true of the physical sciences. Even where Aristotle's theories were rejected, as was the case with the physics of motion, this rejection and reformulation was innately tied to its starting point in Aristotle. The field of physics developed in tandem with other fields, especially astronomy and optics. Several major achievements of Islamic physics stand out as particularly noteworthy, including the theory of inclination and the laying of the foundation for the discovery of the concepts of impetus and momentum in later centuries. Some of the outstanding physicists include Ibn Bajjah (Avempace) (d. 1138) who made great strides in his efforts to quantify projectile motion. Ibn al-Haytham, in addition to his successes in optics, was also responsible for discovering the principle of inertia.

Al-Biruni, in addition to his other accomplishments, was also an exceptional theoretical and experimental physicist, evidenced in his exchange with Ibn Sina that included debate on the Aristotelian theories of motion. Al-Biruni critiqued these theories on the basis of analytical reasoning and experimentation. His commitment to physics resulted in his final objection to the heliocentric system, an objection based not on philosophy but physics. Al-Biruni and al-Khazini (fl. 1115–30) used the works of Archimedes to develop the science of measuring specific weights as well as of balance. Al-Khazini's research on centers of gravity, mechanics, and hydrostatics (the study of liquids at rest and the pressures exerted by or on them) culminated in his text *Kitab mizan al-hikma* (The Book of the Balance of Wisdom).

A fascinating branch of Islamic physics was *ilm al-hiya*, or the science of useful devices. This forerunner of technology was essentially playful in nature, yet it led to some significant technological developments and discoveries of physical principles. While such figures as the Banu Musa brothers (ninth century) and al-Biruni had an interest in mechanics and in simple machines, it was al-Khazini who took this interest in a new direction. With his studies of mechanics, hydrostatics, and the center of gravity in relation to the subject of balance, al-Khazini helped to establish the quirky yet intellectually rigorous science of ingenious devices. This branch of physics reached fruition with al-Khazini's successor, Abu al-Izz al-Jazari (fl. ca. 1200) in his *Al-jami bain al-ilm wal-amal al-nafi fi sinatat al-hiyal* (The Book of Knowledge of Ingenious Mechanical Devices). Al-Khazini's most substantial contribution, however, lies in his research on the measurement of specific weights and his research on balance. This research was continued by such scholars as Qaysar al-Hanafi (b. 1178 or 1179), who applied his expertise to the making of celestial globes and waterwheels based on the principles of physics.

CHEMISTRY

The word *chemistry* derives from the Arabic word *al-kimiya*, which means "alchemy," the predecessor of chemistry as it is understood in the 21st century. The study of alchemy in the Islamic world was shaped by its roots in Alexandria and China. Almost from the inception of Islam, alchemy was a science whose significance was found in its three component functions. The original goal of alchemy was to turn base metal into gold. This material function became entwined with a second symbolic function that was, to mystics, fundamentally more real. This symbolic function of alchemy was that of spiritual alchemy, intimately connected with and in many aspects inseparable from the science of the conversion of metals. The spiritual function refers to the transformation of the soul of the practitioner from base metal into gold; in other words, the attempt to convert one's base instincts and nature into the purest substance through spiritual purification and unification with God. The third type of alchemy refers to what is today known as chemistry.

Muhammad ibn Zakariya ar-Razi (ca. 865–d. ca. 923–25), known in the West as Rhazes, developed chemistry from its alchemical father, Jabir ibn Hayyan (ca. 721–ca. 815). One of ar-Razi's most significant contributions to this field is his categorical distinction of the classes of animal, vegetable, and mineral. Another important discovery of Islamic chemistry was the mercury-sulfur theory, which prepared the path for the development of acid-base theory.

MEDICINE

Islamic medicine is the combination of the primarily theoretical tradition of Galen and the primarily observational tradition of Hippocrates with the theoretical light and applied practice of Indian and Persian medicine. Medicine was connected to both philosophy and to alchemy—to philosophy in its link between the wise man and the physician, both known in Arabic as *hakim*, and to the alchemical tradition through the relation between body and soul, both of which fell within the sphere of alchemy.

The historical background of Islamic medicine originates in the schools of Gundishapur and of Alexandria. The Gundishapur tradition was influenced deeply by the Hippocratic, Zoroastrian Persian, and Indian medical traditions. The physicians and rulers of Gundishapur actively sought to incorporate foreign medical knowledge, sending scholars to India to bring back texts and physicians who could train those of Gundishapur. The Alexandrian tradition was primarily the merging of Greek and Egyptian medicine. This school was most important for transmitting the works of Hippocrates, Galen, Rufus of Ephesus, Paul of Aegina, and Dioscorides to Muslim physicians for study and assimilation into the corpus of Islamic medical knowledge.

The first physician of Islam, al-Harith ibn Kaladah (sixth to seventh centuries), who was educated in Gundishapur, lived at the time of the Prophet. Initially, Arabs considered this science suspect, with its roots in so many other traditions. According to prophetic instruction to "seek knowledge, even in China," however, it soon became acceptable to learn from all known medical traditions. Their foreign nature was ameliorated by their total absorption into the Islamic tradition. What could not be reconciled with the Islamic faith was ignored or practiced by certain physicians while not being incorporated into the popular corpus of Islamic medicine.

The essential sources informing Islamic medicine are the Koran and Hadith. The Koran contains both the principles of Islamic medicine and certain specific instructions, while the medical knowledge of the Hadith, (*al-Tibb al-nabawi*, or "prophetic medicine") contains principles as well as extensive detail on health and hygienic practices. These are the bases of Islamic medicine, which were conjoined with Greek, Indian, and Persian elements.

In the nascent years of the Islamic Empire, physicians were often of Christian or Zoroastrian origin. When the caliph al-Mamun was suffering from dyspepsia, he called upon the most renowned Christian doctor of Gundishapur, Jirgis Bukhtyishu (fl. eighth century). The caliph was impressed with Jirjis's facility as a physician and sought to bring the Persian physicians of Gundishapur to Baghdad to establish a school of medicine. The Christian Masawaih family also moved to Baghdad, where Ibn al-Masawaih flourished as a leading physician.

The translation of Greek texts that began with the Umayyad Dynasty was launched into full force with the coming of the Abbasids. Ibn Muqaffa (d. 760) translated several Pahlavi medical texts of critical importance to Islamic medicine. Hunayn ibn-Ishaq al-Ibadi is the most significant translator of this period. He immigrated to Gundishapur to study with Ibn Masawaih (before the latter's move to Baghdad), but Ibn Masawaih discouraged al-Abadi's pursuit of medical knowledge. Al-Abadi was not deterred from his studies, however, and developed into one of the most significant founders of the Islamic scientific tradition.

The *Firdaws al-hikmah* (Paradise of Wisdom) of Ali ibn Rabban al-Tabbari (fl. ninth century) was a true synthesis of Hippocratic, Galenic, Indian, and Persian medicine. This text prepared the way for al-Tabbari's student Muhammad ibn Zakariya ar-Razi (Rhazes) who, while conducting limited theoretical critiques, is most significant for the clinical and applied knowledge that he used to construct his book on smallpox and measles, *Kitab fi al-jadari wa al-hasba* (Smallpox and Measles) Other key works of ar-Razi include treatises on diabetes and hay fever as well as the *Kitab al-tibb al-mansuri* (Manuri Book of Medicine), which provided a valuable overview of medical theory. Ar-Razi's *Al-hawi fi al-tibb* (Comprehensive Book of Medicine) is a voluminous work filling some 21 volumes. In this work ar-Razi produced a compendium of clinical observation in which he makes some critiques of Galen based on his own clinical experience. Rather than relying on theoretical medicine and inference, as in the Galenic tradition, ar-Razi's primary mode of acquiring knowledge was through a series of controlled experiments. Ali ibn Abbas al-Majusi (d. 994) sought in his *Kitab al-malaki* (The Royal Book, also known as the Complete Book of the Medical Art) to provide the theoretical and structural gaps present in ar-Razi's *Al-hawi*. The *Kitab al-tasrif li-man ajaz an at-taalif* (Book for Medical Practitioners), by Abu al-Qasim (d. 1013), is a 30-volume set that collects all known medical knowledge at his time. While focusing on clinical medicine, this text is most valuable for its section on surgical practices.

ABU ALI AL-HUSAYN IBN ABD ALLAH IBN SINA (980–1037)

Known as Avicenna in Europe, Ibn Sina was one of the greatest scientists in history. He wrote about astronomy, chemistry, mathematics, medicine, philosophy, physics, and theology. Of his more than 450 publications about 240 survive, mostly about medicine and philosophy. He is often called part of the Hellenistic Islamic scientific tradition because his work often included the ideas and discoveries of ancient Greek philosophers, especially Aristotle.

His most influential book was *Al-qanun fi al-tibb*, or the Canon of Medicine (published ca. 1020). This was an encyclopedia of medical knowledge that was commonly used as a textbook in the Islamic world and Europe in the 1700s. Among the book's many important contributions to the study of medicine was Ibn Sina's pointing out that to make someone healthy, a physician needs to know what a healthy body is. He introduced the idea of experimenting with physiology as part of learning how a healthy body functions. Ibn Sina contributed to public health by identifying infectious diseases and trying to determine how they were transmitted. He noted that diseases could be spread by water and soil as well as by air.

Ibn Sina was born in the town of Balkh in what was then Khorasan, now in Afghanistan. His father was a scholar who saw to it that his son had a good education. Ibn Sina had memorized the Koran by age seven, and he was said to have surpassed his teachers by age 14. In his teens he found the writings of Aristotle to be particularly absorbing. By age 18, he had become a well-known physician. During much of his adult life he migrated from place to place, hoping to settle down, and he even held important government posts, but wars and political intrigues usually caused him to move. In the course of his moves he was attended by many students, some of whom helped him with his research and writing. He dictated much of the Canon of Medicine to students, sometimes while on horseback. The last 12 years of his life he spent as the physician and scientific adviser in the court of the emir Ala al-Dawla of Isfahan. He died on June 18, 1037, while accompanying al-Dawla on a military campaign.

The foremost text of Islamic medicine, however, is Ibn Sina's *Qanun fi al-tibb*. This grand work of synthesis includes text that is rich in theoretical knowledge on anatomy, physiology, pathology, and therapy. The *Qanun* remained the primary work of medical knowledge in the Islamic world and the West until the 17th century. Like all texts, and especially those that are the greatest, the *Qunan* received criticism, particularly by pharmacologists, including Ibn al-Jazzar (d. 980) and Ibn Zuhr (ca. 1090–1162), known in the West as Avenzoar or Abumeron, who viewed this text as inefficacious because of its theoretical rather than applied nature. Other important texts include the anatomical work on the pulmonary circulation of blood of Ibn an-Nafis (d. 1288) and one on experimental anatomy by Abd al-Latif al-Baghdadi (d. 1231). The full incorporation of medicine into society during the 12th and 13th centuries led to the development of advanced medical facilities, clinical research, and endowments for medical study.

BOTANY AND ZOOLOGY

The 12th-century scientist of Spain, al-Ghafiqi (d. 1165) produced highly detailed botanical accounts, considered by the historian of science George Sarton to be the most precise in Islamic history. Also significant is Abu Zakariyya Yahya's (12th century) *Kitab al-falahah* (Book of Agriculture), which contains detailed descriptions of almost 600 plants and advice for the cultivation of trees and vines, listing their diseases, cures, and preferred soil composition.

Zoology in the Islamic world reached its peak with such scholars as al-Jawaliqi (12th century), al-Jahiz with his *Kitab al-haywan* (Book of Animals) and al-Damiri (d. 1405) who wrote *al-Hayat haywarz* (Life of Animals), the most prominent work of Islamic zoological thought. These authors focused primarily on classification, description, and behavior. Other zoologists pursued scientific zoology along with the allegorical and religious connotations of certain animals, exemplified by the text *Ajaih al-makhluqat* (The Wonders of Creation) of Abu Yahya al-Qazwini (14th century).

See also AGRICULTURE; ALCHEMY AND MAGIC; ARCHITECTURE; ASTRONOMY; BUILDING TECHNIQUES AND MATERIALS; CALENDARS AND CLOCKS; CLIMATE AND GEOGRAPHY; ECONOMY; EDUCATION; FESTIVALS; FOOD AND DIET; FORESTS AND FORESTRY; HEALTH AND DISEASE; INVENTIONS; LANGUAGE; METALLURGY; MILLS AND MILLING; MINING, QUARRYING, AND SALT MAKING; NUMBERS AND COUNTING; OCCUPATIONS; RELIGION AND COSMOLOGY; ROADS AND BRIDGES; SEAFARING AND NAVIGATION; SHIPS AND SHIPBUILDING; STORAGE AND PRESERVATION; TRADE AND EXCHANGE; WEAPONRY AND ARMOR; WEIGHTS AND MEASURES; WRITING.

Africa

∽ Excerpt from the Emerald Tablet of Hermes (undated) ∽

This is true and remote from all cover of falsehood. Whatever is below is similar to that which is above. Through this the marvels of the work of one thing are procured and perfected.

Also, as all things are made from one, by the consideration of one, so all things were made from this one, by conjunction.

The father of it is the sun, the mother the moon.

The wind bore it in the womb. Its nurse is the earth, the mother of all perfection.

Its power is perfected.

If it is turned into earth,

separate the earth from the fire, the subtle and thin from the crude and course, prudently, with modesty and wisdom.

This ascends from the earth into the sky and again descends from the sky to the earth, and receives the power and efficacy of things above and of things below. By this means you will acquire the glory of the whole world, and so you will drive away all shadows and blindness.

For this by its fortitude snatches the palm from all other fortitude and power. For it is able to penetrate and subdue everything subtle and everything crude and hard. By this means the world was founded and hence the marvelous conjunctions of it and admirable effects, since this is the way by which these marvels may be brought about.

And because of this they have called me Hermes Tristmegistus since I have the three parts of the wisdom and Philosophy of the whole universe.

My speech is finished which I have spoken concerning the solar work.

From: Tenny L. Davis, "The Emerald Tablet of Hermes Tristmegistus: Three Latin Versions Which Were Current among Later Alchemists," *Journal of Chemical Education* 3, no. 8 (1926): 863–875.

Europe

∽ Roger Bacon: "On Experimental Science" (1268) ∽

Having laid down the main points of the wisdom of the Latins as regards language, mathematics and optics, I wish now to review the principles of wisdom from the point of view of experimental science, because without experiment it is impossible to know anything thoroughly.

There are two ways of acquiring knowledge, one through reason, the other by experiment. Argument reaches a conclusion and compels us to admit it, but it neither makes us certain nor so annihilates doubt that the mind rests calm in the intuition of truth, unless it finds this certitude by way of experience. Thus many have arguments toward attainable facts, but because they have not experienced them, they overlook them and neither avoid a harmful nor follow a beneficial course. Even if a man that has never seen fire, proves by good reasoning that fire burns, and devours and destroys things, nevertheless the mind of one hearing his arguments would never be convinced, nor would he avoid fire until he puts his hand or some combustible thing into it in order to prove by experiment what the argument taught. But after the fact of combustion is experienced, the mind is satisfied and lies calm in the certainty of truth. Hence argument is not enough, but experience is.

This is evident even in mathematics, where demonstration is the surest. The mind of a man that receives that clearest of demonstrations concerning the equilateral triangle without experiment will never stick to the conclusion nor act upon it till confirmed by experiment by means of the intersection of two circles from either section of which two lines are drawn to the ends of a given line. Then one receives the conclusion without doubt. . . .

(continued)

(continues)

Whoever wishes without proof to revel in the truths of things need only know how to neglect experience. This is evident from examples. Authors write many things and the people cling to them through arguments which they make without experiment, that are utterly false. It is commonly believed among all classes that one can break adamant only with the blood of a goat, and philosophers and theologians strengthen this myth. But it is not yet proved by adamant being broken by blood of this kind, as much as it is argued to this conclusion. And yet, even without the blood it can be broken with ease. I have seen this with my eyes; and this must needs be because gems cannot be cut out save by the breaking of the stone. . . . Again it is popularly said that cold water in a vase freezes more quickly than hot; and the argument for this is that contrary is excited by the contrary, like enemies running together. . . .

Experience is of two kinds. One is through the external senses: such are the experiments that are made upon the heaven through instruments in regard to facts there, and the facts on earth that we prove in various ways to be certain in our own sight. And facts that are not true in places where we are, we know through other wise

men that have experienced them. Thus Aristotle with the authority of Alexander sent 2,000 men throughout various parts of the earth in order to learn at first hand everything on the surface of the world, as Pliny says in his *Natural History*. And this experience is human and philosophical just as far as a man is able to make use of the beneficent grace given to him, but such experience is not enough for man, because it does not give full certainty as regards corporeal things because of their complexity and touches the spiritual not at all. Hence man's intellect must be aided in another way, and thus the patriarchs and prophets who first gave science to the world secured inner light and did not rest entirely on the senses. So also many of the faithful since Christ. For grace makes many things clear to the faithful, and there is divine inspiration not alone concerning spiritual but even about corporeal things. In accordance with which Ptolemy says in the *Centilogium* that there is a double way of coming to the knowledge of things, one through the experiments of science, the other through divine inspiration, which latter is far the better as he says.

From: Oliver J. Thatcher, ed., *The Library of Original Sources*, Vol. 5: *The Early Medieval World* (Milwaukee, Wis.: University Research Extension Co., 1901).

The Islamic World

∼ Adelard of Bath: Excerpt from Natural Questions (ca. 1137) ∼

ADELARD: You will remember, Nephew, how seven years ago when you were almost a child in the learning of the French, and I sent you along with the rest of my hearers to study with a man of high reputation, it was agreed between us that I should devote myself to the best of my ability to the study of Arabic, while you on your part were to acquire the inconsistencies of French ideas.

NEPHEW: I remember, and all the more because, when departing, you bound me under a solemn promise to be a diligent student of philosophy.

The result was that I applied myself with great diligence to this study. Whether what I have said is correct, the present occasion will give you an opportunity of

discovering; since when you have often set them forth, I, as hearer only, have marked the opinions of the Saracens, and many of them seem to me quite absurd; I shall, therefore, for a time cease to exercise this patience, and when you utter these views, shall attack them where it seems good to me to do so.

To me it seems that you go too far in your praise of the Arabs, and show prejudice in your disparagement of the learning of our philosophers. Our reward will be that you will have gained some fruit of your toil; if you give good answers, and I make a good showing as your opponent, you will see that my promise has been well kept.

ADELARD: You perhaps take a little more on you than you ought; but as this arrangement will be profitable not only to you but to many others, I will pardon your forwardness, making however this one stipulation, that when I adduce something unfamiliar, people are to think not that I am putting forward an idea of my own, but am giving the views of the Arabs. If anything I say displeases the less educated, I do not want them to be displeased with me also: I know too well what is the fate which attends upon the teachers of the truth with the common herd, and consequently shall plead the case of the Arabs, not my own. . . .

How the Globe Is Supported in the Middle of the Air

NEPHEW: . . . I will put the first question that comes into my head: How is it that this earth of ours which supports all weights (I am speaking not of simples, but of compounds), how is it that it remains in the same place, or by what is it supported? If all heavy bodies, such as stone, wood, etc., require support, and cannot through their weight be supported by the air, then much more does the earth, which is heavier than everything else put together, require to be supported, nor can it be held in position by so unstable a body as the air. Hence it is contrary to reason that it should maintain its position.

ADELARD: Certainly it is inexpedient that it should fall, and that we also shall not fall along with it. I will show that its remaining in its position is in accordance with reason. From the character of its primary qualities, we know that the earth has weight; that which has weight is more secure in the lowest position; and everything is naturally fond of that which preserves its life, and tends towards that for which it has a liking. It follows therefore that everything which is earthy tends towards the lowest possible position. But in the case of anything round, it is clear that the middle and the lowest are the same, and therefore all earthy things tend towards the middle position. Now the middle position is a simple and indivisible middle point, and it is therefore clear that all earthy things tend towards a local and simple point. But this local point is not several but one, and must necessarily be occupied by one thing, not by several; but to it, as has been said, all things tend: consequently each one thing presses on something else, since all and sundry are hastening to the same point. Now the point to which all weighty bodies are hastening is that to which they are falling, for the fall of weighty bodies is merely a hastening to a middle point. By the point to which they are falling I mean the fixed middle point. The place to which they are falling-the middle point -remains fixed; and therefore, while falling into a stable position, they yet remain fixed, unless some force be impressed on them as a result of which they are diverted from their natural course. The very opposite then is the case to what you thought; and you will now see clearly that it is what you thought to be a reason for falling which gives stability and coherence to heavy bodies. They are, therefore, in some way sup ported by the point to which they are hastening; and if it should move in any direction, all the things which are affected towards it would also of necessity move, though of course in that selfsame spot we have not the first but the second cause of stability: for, in accordance with the reason previously given, the first cause of this equilibrium is the property of the subject, the second the stability of the point which it makes for.

From: Adelard of Bath, *Dodi Ve-Nechdi*, ed. and trans. H. Gollancz (London: Oxford University Press, 1920).

FURTHER READING

Marcia Ascher and Robert Ascher, *Mathematics of the Incas: Code of the Quipu* (Mineola, N.Y.: Dover, 1997).

Osman Bakr, *Classification of Knowledge in Islam* (Kuala Lumpur, Malaysia: Institute for Policy Research, 1992).

Hans Dieter Betz, ed. *The Greek Magical Papyri in Translation, Including the Demotic Spells* (Chicago: University of Chicago Press, 1992).

Sally Anderson Chappell, *Cahokia: Mirror of the Universe* (Chicago: University of Chicago Press, 2002).

Terry S. Childs, "'After All, a Hoe Bought a Wife': The Social Dimensions of Ironworking among the Toro of East Africa." In *The Social Dynamics of Technology: Practice, Politics, and World Views*, ed. Marcia-Anne Dobres and Christopher R. Hoffman (Washington, D.C.: Smithsonian Institution Press, 1999).

Eduard J. Dijksterhuis, *The Mechanization of the World Picture: Pythagoras to Newton*, trans. C. Dikshoorn (Oxford, U.K.: Clarendon Press, 1961).

Chris Hardaker, "Native American Geometry." Available online. URL: http://www.earthmeasure.com/Anthro/Past/pastindex.html. Downloaded on February 25, 2008.

Eric John Holmyard, *Alchemy* (Baltimore, Md.: Penguin, 1968).

Toby E. Huff, *The Rise of Early Modern Science: Islam, China, and the West*, 2nd ed. (Cambridge, U.K.: Cambridge University Press, 2003).

E. Isaac, trans., "I (Ethiopic Apocalypse of) Enoch." In *The Old Testament Pseudepigrapha*, ed. James H. Charlesworth (Garden City, N.Y.: Doubleday, 1983–1985).

Muzaffar Iqbal, *Islam and Science* (Aldershot, U.K.: Ashgate, 2002).

Abdul Hai Khalid, *Maya Math, Maya Indians, and Indian Maya: Reflections on Numbers, History and Religion*. Available online. URL: http://math.mohawkcollege.ca/ocma/conf05/Post_Conf05/Abdul_MAYA_MATH.doc. Downloaded on December 7, 2007.

David C. Lindberg, *The Beginnings of Western Science: The European Scientific Tradition in Philosophical, Religious, and Institutional Context, Prehistory to A.D. 1450*, 2nd ed. (Chicago: University of Chicago Press, 2007).

Seyyed Hossein Nasr, *Science and Civilization in Islam* (Cambridge, Mass.: Harvard University Press, 1968).

Joseph Needham, *Science and Civilisation in China* (Cambridge, U.K.: Cambridge University Press, 1954).

Otto Neugebauer, "Notes on Ethiopic Astronomy." In his *Astronomy and History: Selected Essays* (New York: Springer-Verlag, 1983).

Patricia J. O'Brien and Hanne D. Christiansen, "An Ancient Maya Measurement System," *American Antiquity* 51, no. 1 (1986): 136–151.

George Saliba, *A History of Arabic Astronomy: Planetary Theories during the Golden Age of Islam* (New York: New York University Press, 1994).

Peter R. Schmidt, *Iron Technology in East Africa: Symbolism, Science, and Archaeology* (Bloomington: Indiana University Press, 1997).

René Taton, ed., *History of Science: Ancient and Medieval Science from the Beginning to 1450*, trans. A. J. Pomerans (New York: Basic Books, 1964).

Lynn Thorndike, *A History of Magic and Experimental Science* (New York: MacMillan, 1923).

► seafaring and navigation

INTRODUCTION

It seems as though every culture that lived beside the sea ventured out into the sea. Even when they had only small boats, people made daring voyages to other lands. Sometimes the voyages were accidental. Fishermen were occasionally blown by storms to unfamiliar shores. If they made it home, their stories could interest other sailors, who might try to visit the newly discovered land.

Such voyages were not necessarily made with big ships capable of withstanding great storms. In the Americas people sailed the seas in dugout canoes and kayaks. The Inuit of the north were masters at sailing far from shore to hunt whales and other prey, using only kayaks and paddles. Other coastal Americans found boating along shores to be faster than walking across land. In some places, they may have been safer traveling in dugouts than they would have been crossing land. For instance, Mayan traders often voyaged by canoe along the coasts of Mesoamerica to carry trade goods to coastal cities; otherwise they might have had to make their way through dense forest or across open lands of kingdoms that were at war.

The Polynesians are often cited as history's most amazing seafarers. They used canoes to explore almost all of the Pacific Ocean, voyaging across thousands of miles of ocean. Their boats were often double-hulled with a platform that could carry about a dozen people plus livestock, such as pigs. Theirs was a hit-or-miss strategy of exploration, with no guarantees that they would find land on which to settle. There is no telling how many Polynesians perished in attempts to discover uninhabited lands. Once they knew where they were going, they used constellations at night and the motion of waves to determine where they were in the ocean. The Polynesian navigator knew the direction and size of waves for various parts of the ocean and through them could determine what direction his boat should go.

Danger was always part of seafaring. Even the gigantic ships of China in the 1400s could be capsized by a large wave or by a severe storm. Medieval societies tried to improve safety by building beacons along the shore to serve as guides for navigators, who often remained close to the shoreline instead of venturing out into trackless sea. In Europe and the Near East sailors sometimes wrote guidebooks for sailing where they had sailed. These books were often dry affairs, recounting little of the exotic places the sailors had visited and instead describing how to determine where one was by the sort of land nearby, the prevailing winds, and the currents.

The compass was developed in China, probably during the Han Dynasty. It consisted of spoon-shaped magnetized iron hung from a string to tell miners which direction they were going when mining for metal ore or digging tunnels. In the mid-1000s a Chinese writer described a magnetized needle used for navigation. It was an iron needle on wood that floated in water, allowing the needle to orient itself to magnetic north. The compass was not a perfect solution for navigating, because it pointed to magnetic north rather than true north; a navigator still had to know the stars of the night sky and other indications of where the ship was. Even so, the Islamic world took to navigating with magnetized iron embedded in wood and set afloat, and Europeans were using such a compass by the 1240s.

There were human hazards as well as natural ones. Pirates often sailed in the major trade routes of the sea, sometimes becoming powerful enough to conquer coast land and establish kingdoms. A particularly nettlesome lot preyed on ships in the sea lane that passed north of Borneo and Sumatra and south of Malaysia. The pirates were bold enough to try attacking one of the great Chinese fleets of the 1400s and were nearly destroyed. Keeping shipping lanes open was a priority for any seafaring culture, and governments often built navies just to keep pirates away. Even after it destroyed its remarkable navy of oceangoing vessels, China maintained a navy to protect its coasts from pirates. Thus it was that medieval peoples had several reasons for seafaring that mattered enough to them to bear the risks of going out to sea, whether it was northwestern South Americans using balsa wood boats to venture into the rich fishing grounds of the open sea to their west or traders sailing the Indian Ocean to find riches from trade or exploration.

AFRICA

by Charles W. Abbott

Seafaring in medieval Africa was most visible on the Swahili coast of East Africa, where Swahili sailors made their homes in a variety of small cities stretching along 2,000 miles of coastline from Mogadishu in present-day Somalia south to Sofala in present-day Mozambique. These regional and long-distance traders used sailing ships driven by the monsoon winds. The East African ships might sail as far as Persia (Iran) or India.

Seafaring existed in western Africa as well, where sail power was less utilized and where the preferred vessel was the large dugout canoe. In contrast to the East African voyages, western African sea routes never circled fully north around the "bulge" of Africa (current-day Mauritania and Morocco) to reach Europe. Strong ocean currents prevented such travel, and there was no effective maritime link between western Africa and Europe until Portuguese mariners improved Atlantic sailing expertise after 1400. Until that time, western African coastal trade routes turned from the ocean waters to travel up rivers and inland to meet caravans tied to the camel-based trans-Saharan trade.

Moving farther south, seafaring on the coastline between the Congo River and Mozambique was limited to fishing and local and regional trade. Seafaring was less developed than in western or eastern Africa, and evidence suggests little or no linkage to trade networks with Europe or Asia. South of the Congo River's mouth at the Atlantic Ocean, the environment for maritime trade was not favorable. Parts of southern Africa (such as current-day Namibia) consisted of deserts. Elsewhere the coast fronted narrow beaches isolated from the continental interior by high escarpments. Travel upriver by canoe was interrupted near the coast by high waterfalls where interior rivers plunged over cliffs on their way to the sea.

The Swahili coast trade is the best-documented instance of African seafaring in medieval times. It linked Africans with literate and largely Muslim communities in Arabia, the Red Sea, the Gulf of Aden, and the coast of India. The trade is thus documented by abundant written records (largely in Arabic) as well as by archaeological and linguistic evidence.

Seafaring on the Swahili Coast relied on the seasonally alternating monsoon winds. These winds blew from the southwest toward India from April to October; they then reversed and blew from the northeast from November to March. Relying on the monsoons, Africans could sail northward in the spring and return to their home port within the year. Navigation and travel was facilitated by the relatively calm seas and by a variety of coastal islands (such as Zanzibar, Pemba, and Lamu) that provided sites for berthing ships. Sailors navigated their ships into sheltered inlets for trade, and the coast possessed many calm beaches on which ships could be safely landed at high tide and then unloaded when the tide ran out. Offshore coral reefs posed a hazard but were easily avoided, and they sheltered beaches and ports from the open sea.

Navigation was largely accomplished by remaining close to the coast when possible, by orienting with the sun and stars, and through careful observation of currents and plants that were characteristic of different portions of the Indian Ocean. African skill and the favorable environment combined to make journeys common between the African coast and the Comoros Islands (200 miles east of present-day Mozambique) and Madagascar (300 miles offshore). Africans knew these islands well, sailed to them regularly, and traded with their inhabitants.

Seafaring has a long tradition in western Africa, but the historical record is more obscure. The dugout canoe, constructed by hollowing out a single log and sharpening the prow, was the craft of choice. Such canoes varied widely in size: the largest ones were big enough to hold 40 sailors and considerable cargo or 100 men and minimal cargo if fitted for war. Such large canoes, sometimes equipped with sails or outriggers, were used for fishing five or more miles off the coast. Canoe trade upriver from the coast was important along such rivers as the Niger, Senegal, and Gambia. Canoe routes typically hugged the shoreline. In other areas—especially from present-day Ghana east to Cameroon—the heaviest traveled routes often threaded a path behind coastal sandbars. Heavily laden canoes full of cargo could follow lagoons and a maze of creeks, sometimes traveling parallel to the coastline but away from the open sea for dozens of miles at a time.

In the eastern half of the African continent, coastal regions were linked to the rest of the world by the Indian Ocean. In the western half of the African continent, coastal regions were isolated by the Atlantic Ocean. The Atlantic was a barrier to the wider world, with formidable winds and currents that made Europe inaccessible by sea. Coastal Africans of the west were good mariners, but prudence and technology dictated that they stay closer to the coast than the Swahili did, though fishing 5 or more miles offshore was common.

In contrast to Swahili contact with the Comoros Islands and Madagascar, many islands off the coast of western Africa were uninhabited until European discovery. The Cape Verde Archipelago, 300 miles west of the Cape Verde Peninsula, was uninhabited until Portuguese discovery in the 1450s. Other islands such as São Tomé (180 miles west of Gabon, discovered in 1470) and Príncipe (150 miles west of Gabon) have similar histories of isolation until Portuguese discovery and settlement after 1450. The island of Bioko (also known as Fernando Póo) is much closer to the African mainland and was settled by Africans centuries earlier. About 60 miles southwest of the Cameroon coast the island's 9,000-foot peak is visible from the African mainland. Bantu-speaking Africans sailed to it and settled it from the mainland long before Portuguese contact in 1472.

One key factor in western Africa's maritime isolation from Europe was the Canary Current, a strong, swift, cold-water current flowing south past present-day Morocco and Mauritania. The current is strongest north of the Cape Verde Peninsula, which deflects part of the current west toward the Cape Verde Islands and the Americas. Europeans who sailed coastwise south with the current were unable, even in their large sailing ships, to return the same way against the prevailing winds and waters. Only by first sailing hundreds of miles west into the open sea could they avoid the Canary Current and return to Europe under sail. For Africans, canoe travel north of the Cape Verde Peninsula was physically grueling and economically pointless. The Canary Current opposed their progress, and the wind blew toward the open sea. African mariners exploring in that direction would have paddled furiously against the current in order to advance slowly past an empty desert of fog-shrouded beaches and dangerous reefs. The isolation imposed by the Canary Current is a key reason medieval western Africa was linked to Europe not by oceanic routes around the bulge of Africa but through the Sahara Desert via camel-based caravans.

The way in which western African seafarers in Senegambia and the Upper Guinea coast (present-day Guinea-Bissau, Guinea, Sierra Leone, Liberia, and Ivory Coast) linked their canoe-based networks to the trans-Saharan trade has been detailed. The sailors knew the coast well, fishing miles off the coast during the day and coming back to shore at night. The coast was characterized by daunting currents, dangerous reefs, sharp volcanic rocks, and shifting sandbars. The strong Guinea Current pushed consistently southeast, but during the rainy season it weakened and the winds reversed, making coastwise travel to the northwest easier. African merchants in this region would travel southeast to secure cargos of kola nuts and then journey back northwest, turning inland up rivers such as the Gambia or Senegal to network with the Sahara-based trade.

On the Upper Guinea coast the canoe men were from a variety of small ethnic groups such as the Biafada and Kru, and they traveled upriver to trade with Mande-speaking caravan merchants. Farther west along the coast, in modern-day Ghana, the canoe men were Fante. Still farther west, in modern-day Nigeria, the creeks of the Niger Delta were inhabited by Ijaw. Ijaw in the Niger Delta specialized in fishing and salt boiling in coastal mangrove swamps unsuitable for agriculture. They then exchanged salt fish for agricultural products that traders brought down the Niger River in large canoes from hundreds of miles in the interior.

South of the Congo River there is less evidence for seafaring in the service of long-distance trade. Along a vast extent of central and southern Africa, extending from the Congo River on the Atlantic Coast around the Cape of Good Hope (in present-day South Africa) to present-day Mozambique, where the Swahili trade begins, evidence of seafaring generally is more modest. Here, seafaring seems to have served primarily fishing and local and regional trade. Coastal peoples made salt and fished, exchanging these products for farm produce from the interior.

In much of southern Africa high escarpments impede movement to the interior. River navigation is interrupted by waterfalls within 30 miles of the ocean on the Congo and on most rivers south of it. Congo River canoe traffic resumed upriver above the falls to serve the inland trade, but cargo had to be portaged around the falls. With few exceptions, coastal plains in southern Africa are narrow and hemmed in by mountain escarpments, which quickly climb several thousand feet. Eventually, the coastal scene becomes inhospitable desert. In parts of southern Africa much of the population lived inland, and much of the economic activity was centered there.

Events after 1400 foreshadowed changes to come. The Chinese fleet under Admiral Zheng He made seven journeys to the outside world in the 1400s—the fourth voyage of 1413 to 1415 reached the Swahili coast. But the Chinese presence was short-lived. Portuguese exploration in the 1400s had a more durable impact, because Portuguese trading ships identified profitable markets and began to appear regularly on the African coast. As the Portuguese presence grew, the contact resulted in new trade relationships, with some Portuguese traders marrying into local communities. The children of these marriages, fluent in local languages and with kinship ties to coastal African communities, were well suited to sail and trade on the African coast.

Historians have never confirmed the Arab historian al-Umari's report of a large Malian sea voyage in the early

1300s. In al-Umari's histories the Malian ruler Mansa (king) Musa asserted that his own predecessor on the throne had dispatched a convoy of 200 ships to explore the sea off the coast of western Africa. After a single ship came back, the king assembled an even larger convoy and joined it on a second exploration, from which no one returned. Al-Umari's history recounts this event, but no evidence has been found to corroborate it.

THE AMERICAS

BY LAWRENCE WALDRON

In ancient times Amerindians had proved themselves the ablest of small-craft mariners. They traveled enormous distances in simple canoes without so much as outriggers or sails. American geography may have aided in their coverage of such vast areas in that the Pacific Coast of the Americas presented an almost unbroken line from Alaska to Argentina. Only occasionally would choppy seas and powerful currents have impeded the exploration and settlement of the Americas by sea. Paleo-Indians, the first settlers from Asia, traveled the entire length of America in the early centuries after their arrival. Knowledge of coastal features, routes, and seasonal variations gained on these ancient journeys would have been retained in oral, ritual, and practical traditions. Some of these may have been passed down well into the Common Era.

Modern archaeologists have discovered widespread contacts between different Common Era cultures up and down the western regions of the Americas. Ethnicities along the coast of the Pacific Northwest, western Mexico, and Pacific South America have all left archaeological evidence that they traveled far beyond their territories in search of whaling, fishing, and trading opportunities and were aware of one another. With land almost always in their sight and with the sun, moon, and stars as their guide, Native American seamen in swift and maneuverable vessels were able to ply the Pacific and the Atlantic coastlines. Coastal boating was often circuitous, with travelers going back and forth along known littoral, or seashore, passages in response to seasonal needs.

While their small watercraft were never used for carrying them beyond the American landmasses out into the high seas, Common Era Amerindians established a widespread network of maritime trade that reached from arctic Alaska to tropical Guatemala to alpine Bolivia and many regions between. Thanks to river travel and maritime seafaring, the people of the Americas were afforded at least intermittent access to resources from one of the widest varieties of natural environments on earth. Kingdoms and empires that had never met face to face were thus able to export and import animal and marine products, semiprecious stones and precious metals, herbal and mineral medicines alongside various cultural, religious, and social influences.

Although the Indians on the coast of British Columbia, the Jalisco in western Mexico, and the Maya in Yucatán all developed distinct seafaring strategies, most water travel in the Americas was confined to inland freshwater. Rivers, lakes, marshes, and swamps were the most common freshwater and mixed-water environments. A range of watercraft was developed in response to the varied conditions of these waters, from vessels made of skin to dugout canoes, log rafts, and wooden boats.

Navigation on rivers was often merely a matter of maintaining mental maps of river courses, whereas wider-ranging open-water travel employed stellar, solar, lunar, and barometric navigation. Knowledge of the various constellations and their positions in the sky from season to season was a customary part of many native religious and seafaring traditions. Likewise, the movements of the sun and phases of the moon were expertly tracked by both landlocked and aquatic travelers. Awareness—sometimes used in the hunt—of seasonal changes in wind direction and of the varieties, speeds, and densities of cloud cover were also part of the seaman's toolkit. The keen observation and memorization of all these factors enabled seafarers to maintain their orientation amid powerful tides and currents, disorienting battles with large ocean mammals and rough seas, and even bad weather.

Since both the Maya and, later, the Aztec used paper for making books and other documents, it is possible that their mariners drew maps and star charts. However, no such examples seem to have survived the book burnings of the Spanish conquest. Colonial era Christian friars would have appreciated immediately the link between Indian astronomy and native religion and thus destroyed these symbols of the ideological systems they were competing with. In destroying them, they also erased any inscribed evidence of the specifics of Amerindian navigation. Nevertheless, cave art, stelae, ceramics, textiles, folktales, and monumental architecture all retain a partial record of Amerindian stellar constellations and their cultural significance to groups such as the Inuit, Chumash, Anasazi, Maya, Tupinamba, and Inca, among dozens of other ethnicities.

Navigation on the North American Great Lakes, the swamps and estuaries of Mexico, Andean lakes and ponds, and other bodies of inland water was accomplished by simple sighting of landmarks. However, when navigating on long trips out to sea in search of whales and fish, Northwest Coast and Andean mariners used their intimate familiarity with the species of marine and avian life that marked certain distances from land as well as key latitudes, water depths, and water temperatures, all of which helped them approximate their bearings.

With the growth of such massive civilizations as the Mississippian, Maya, Toltec, and Aztec, there was an increased need for conquest, tribute, and long-distance trade. While much of this trade was done on foot, a large part was also done by boat, whether up and down the great rivers or along the coasts of the Gulf of Mexico and around the Caribbean. Large dugout canoes, able to carry dozens of people and tons of goods, were the favored vessels. Depending on their size, dugout canoes were equally well suited to the many turns and tangles of eastern Mexico's estuaries as to the open-water ferrying of passengers and goods between Yucatán and its offshore islands. Smaller canoes were favored for passage on the great Central American rivers, especially in areas where water depth varied with the seasons or because of rocks and rapids.

While Maya contact with the Mississippian cultures from Louisiana to Florida remains largely unproved, Maya canoeists have left evidence of their seafaring in most other regions around the Caribbean. Maya trading canoes occasionally ventured far into the Caribbean, and there is evidence of contact between Yucatán Maya traders and the Taíno kingdoms of the Greater Antilles. In order to cross the Yucatán Channel into the Caribbean islands, Maya canoe traders braved powerful currents, which threatened to sweep them north and trap them in circular tides between North America and northern Cuba. Their expertise at open-water canoeing is borne out by the various jade objects, honeycombs, and other uniquely Central American objects found on islands from Cuba to Antigua, all appearing to have arrived there from Guatemala and Yucatán. Likewise, Taíno objects have been found in Mesoamerica, including a carved spatula found at Altun-Ha in a Maya grave in Belize. This means that canoe travel between Yucatán Maya and the Caribbean Taíno was bilateral.

The Caribbean objects found in Mesoamerica testify to a much wider maritime connection between three separate regions of the Americas, namely Central and South America and the Antilles. As Maya traders disembarked from their dugout canoes on the coasts of western Cuba sometime in the first millennium, they united most of the Americas through maritime trade for a brief moment in history. In this encounter formidable canoeists from Mesoamerica would have encountered their counterparts from the Caribbean kingdoms. These Caribbean Indians were, in fact, the descendants of accustomed seafarers who had arrived in these islands three millennia before from South America and who had maintained indirect trade contact with the South American mainland.

The Taíno and Maya were not the only boaters plying the Caribbean. In the latter days of the great Taíno kingdoms, Carib canoeists arrived in the Caribbean from the Guianas, paddling the largest canoes in the region around the Caribbean. According to Columbus and other early Spanish explorers, some Carib canoes held up to 100 people. It was no comfort to the Taíno caciques (chiefs) that many of these canoeists were, in fact, fearsome warriors intent on making inroads into their territory. The Carib expansion out of the Orinoco-Amazon littoral was the last major marine migration of Indians before the conquest of the Americas and in the Greater Antilles; their arrival predated that of the Spaniards by only two centuries.

Although many parts of the Andes and coastal portions of eastern South America are known to be among the driest areas on earth, the people in these regions of present-day Ecuador, Peru, and Bolivia became adept seafarers in order to search for food. While their landscape could be arid and precipitous, the cool waters off the coasts of these countries provided the best fishing resources in the Americas. Towns and cities located far inland maintained either direct political control over fishermen on the coast or otherwise sought to establish long-term trade partnerships that gave them access to rich coastal food sources, such as anchovies, shellfish, turtle meat, and eggs.

The Manteño and Huancavilca seafarers of Ecuador used balsa-wood boats to sail far out to sea in search of spondylus shells for use in their religious rituals. The Ecuadorian mariners were also known to have sailed as far north as western Mexico on trade expeditions for their imperial lords in Moche and Inca Peru. Moche boaters or seafaring ethnicities in Moche employ often facilitated long-distance pilgrimages up and down the Pacific Coast with their cleverly bundled reed boats. Such vessels were also used on shorter runs to the islands off the coasts where bird and bat droppings (guano) were gathered to be used as fertilizer back on the farms in the mountains and foothills. Before European contact, the Inca inherited many customs and overseas pilgrimage routes from the seventh-century Moche and earlier civilizations. Throughout their empire, royal entourages arrived at the traditional holy sites (huacas) with offerings of shells, ceramics, and other materials they had brought down the coast from Cuzco in reed boats.

ASIA AND THE PACIFIC
BY ROBERT BOLLT

In the Middle Ages, China was a world leader in seafaring and navigation. During the Han Dynasty (202 B.C.E.–220 C.E.) the Chinese developed their own type of sailing vessel, known as the junk, and began making long-distance ocean voyages in the first centuries of the Common Era. The stern-mounted rudder seems to have been invented around the first century; the device was more effective for steering than using oarsmen for that purpose. These sturdy sailing ships employed stern-mounted rudders long before the Western world adopted them. Before the development of the compass in the 11th century, Chinese seafaring relied, as it had for thousands of years, upon the monsoon winds, which blow north in the summer months and south in the winter months. Dead reckoning was a principal means of navigation. It is the process of estimating one's present position by keeping a record of the ship's movement, that is, the course and speed from its last position. The ship's initial position usually was obtained by a fix on an object on land. Dead reckoning also was used to predict future positions by projecting course and speed from its present position. It provides only an approximate position, as it does not take into account the effects of currents, errors, and other external factors. The scientist Shen Kuo (1031–95) first described a magnetic needle compass and its importance for navigation by the discovery of true north. Slightly later we have descriptions of a new type of junk that contained separate watertight bulkhead compartments, which safeguarded the ship against sinking if one compartment happened to be breached.

The medieval Chinese Tang (618–907) and Song (960–1279) dynasties saw considerable seafaring activity. Prior to that time Chinese seafarers had been venturing into Southeast Asia and even the Indian Ocean for centuries. (In insular Southeast Asia seafaring had, of course, been a way of life for many thousands of years.) Chinese merchants would travel first to Southeast Asia and then into the Indian Ocean, even venturing as far as the Middle East and the Red Sea. China traded with Malaysia, India, Sri Lanka, the Arabian Peninsula, Egypt, and Ethiopia. Chinese descriptions of trade routes into East Africa date from the eight century. In turn, Chinese ports hosted mariners from all over, as far west as Morocco; Muslim travelers visited china in the late first millennium.

It was the Ming Dynasty (1388–1644), however, that saw the most dramatic advances in Chinese exploration. From 1405 to 1433 the government sent out a series of the largest exploratory expeditions the world had ever seen. The Chinese admiral Zheng He commanded these fleets, which consisted of hundreds of ships and thousands of sailors. Zheng He sailed to the Indian Ocean seven times, with the goal of establishing a Chinese presence abroad and securing imperial control over trade. The massive nine-masted treasure ships that comprised much of his fleets were the largest vessels ever developed on earth up until that time.

The first three voyages visited Southeast Asia, India, and Sri Lanka (then called Ceylon), the fourth went as far as the Persian Gulf and the Arabian Peninsula, and the remainder ventured into East Africa. Zheng He brought back to China such exotic animals as giraffes to adorn the Ming gardens as well as emissaries from foreign lands. With the seventh voyage of the treasure fleet, Ming exploration abruptly ceased. Zheng He himself died during the expedition and was buried at sea. While these missions could have resulted in unprecedented Chinese expansion abroad, the Ming Dynasty did not find much of value outside China and was content to maintain trade with its nearest neighbors (Southeast Asia and Japan) instead, as the country had for centuries. The ships were left to rot and fall to pieces in harbor. In fact, many of Zheng He's charts were deliberately destroyed; eventually, the technology of the ships was forgotten as well.

In the Middle Ages trade between Japan and China was well documented. In the mid-first millennium the Japanese had little experience in long-distance voyaging and navigation, but they gradually improved their skills and technology to trade items such as silk, porcelain, sandalwood, and tea. Chinese ports with trading links to Japan were Ningbo and Hangzhou; Japan also traded with Korea during the Three Kingdoms Period (ca. 300–670) and with the Ryukyu Islands. (Influence from both China and Japan have shaped the unique Ryukyu culture.) Japan continued active trade with its neighbors until the advent of the Tokugawa Shogunate in 1600, when the country effectively shut itself off from the outside world—though limited exchange did occur, especially with the Ryukyu Islands.

Piracy was another form of Japanese seafaring that was prevalent from the 13th century until the Japanese invasions of Korea in the late 1500s. During this turbulent period of civil strife Japanese pirates raided Chinese, Koreans, and even Japanese coastlines and ships. These pirates, known as Wōkòu (Japanese bandits), flourished for more than 100 years. Pirate activity concentrated on the Korean peninsula. Japanese piracy became enough of a problem for the Chinese Ming Dynasty to construct coastal fortifications, develop divisions of antipirate troops, and impose sanctions on trade with Japan. They were also a major incentive for Korea to maintain a navy.

Another important player in the medieval world of seafaring was India. Indian ports and merchants were a vital link in the spice trade between the Middle East and Southeast Asia in the late first millennium. Important spices included musk, ambergris, camphor, and sandalwood. Indian cultural influence on the islands of Java and Borneo fueled the demand there for incense. The Moluccas of northern Indonesia and the southern Philippines were known as the Spice

Islands. In the Middle Ages they were the sole source of such valuable goods as mace, clove, and nutmeg, commodities that had been circulating into India and the Arabian Peninsula for centuries, dating to ancient times. Arabic influence there became stronger after the 1300s, as China's Ming Dynasty interest in long-distance trade waned. In addition to Islam, Arabic influence also brought with it the sultanate form of government, which replaced local chiefdoms. Spice Islands products first passed through India and Sri Lanka before making their way to the Arabian peninsula and the Persian Gulf and then sometimes into East Africa.

By around 1000 the last great human expansion on Earth was taking place—the colonization of the eastern Pacific by the Polynesians. Originating in western Polynesia (Samoa, Tonga, and Fiji), which had been colonized by around 1000 B.C.E., the Polynesians, for reasons that are unknown, expanded into the eastern Pacific and colonized the islands there only around 2,000 years later. They then proceeded to settle virtually every island in the eastern Pacific. At the margins they settled remote Hawaii, New Zealand, and Easter Island. The South American sweet potato throughout eastern Polynesia in prehistory is one line of proof that Polynesians reached the continent and brought this tuber back with them, and it is possible that they reached North America as well.

The Polynesians were remarkable because they navigated throughout the vast eastern Pacific Ocean using only natural means (the sun, stars, waves, currents, birds, and winds), in what were probably large double-hulled sailing canoes equipped with cultigens and domesticated animals (pigs, dogs, and chickens) for settlement. It is due to their incredible skill in traversing long distances of empty ocean that the Polynesian are often considered to have been the greatest seafarers and navigators ever.

No one island or archipelago in eastern Polynesia can be proved to have been the earliest settled. Dates from the earliest sites are nearly identical. The period of around 1000 to 1450 is generally known as the Archaic Period, during which similar artifacts, such as fishhooks, ornaments, and adzes, were made and used throughout East Polynesia. This homogeneity is attributed to exchange via long-distance voyaging, when settlers would try to obtain as many necessities as possible from their original homes and elsewhere. Oral traditions speak of long-distance voyages between islands and archipelagos, and archaeological evidence continues to confirm this. Long-distance voyaging was essential not only for survival but also to maintain a sense of identity with one's ancestral place of origin. However, after about 1450 archaeologists note a distinct drop in exotic goods and believe that interaction gradually declined as populations became more self-sufficient.

While we do not have written documentation for these events, archaeologists can trace stone tool material to its parent source, which is sometimes hundreds and sometimes thousands of miles from where it was later found. By the time of European contact many islands of Polynesia had completely lost touch with even their nearest neighbors. Elsewhere in the Pacific, the Torres Strait Islands off the coast of Australia link the continent with New Guinea. The islands around the northernmost tip of Australia, Cape York, have been home to aboriginal seafarers since time immemorial. The many islands of Melanesia and Micronesia have similarly been practicing long-distance seafaring and traditional navigation for thousands of years, for which there is archaeological evidence of trade before, during, and after what we refer to as the Middle Ages.

EUROPE

BY DETLEV ELLMERS

Seafaring is the use of boats and ships on the ocean for fishing, for transport of goods or passengers, for hostile actions, or for combinations of several purposes. Ports and harbors along the coasts act as interfaces, which on the one hand are connected by sea routes and on the other hand provide access into their hinterlands by rivers and roads. Navigation is the method of getting from place to place across water that seems to be featureless.

On the coast of western Europe seaports were urban, but along the North Sea and Baltic coasts harbors were rural. Angles and Saxons from the southern shores of the North Sea raided and settled in England from the third to fifth centuries using mere rowing boats. The Vikings, using sailing vessels, raided nearly all European shores beginning in the eighth century. Seagoing ships were the most cost-effective means of transportation, and maritime trade became increasingly the motive for medieval seafaring. By the eighth century seasonal beach markets in rural areas had grown into maritime trading centers. By the 12th and 13th centuries many of these maritime centers had become the urban seaports of the Hanseatic League (an alliance of trading guilds), and in these northern regions seafaring was an urban profession.

The men who sailed the ships or cared for them settled their families at the seaports. Skippers had their ships built to order and hired their crews. A typical crew for a Bremen (Germany) ship in the late 14th century consisted of 10 men: a helmsman, a cook, and eight sailors, working in two watches. Such a ship was provisioned with rusk, a kind of hard and crisp bread, as the main food, along with salted meat, smoked bacon, salted herring, stockfish, dried legumes, groat, and beer for the crew, with better beer reserved for any officers and guests. French and Mediterranean crews drank wine instead of beer. Fresh water and fresh vegetables could be taken on at intermediate harbors that were reachable within a few days. Originally the skipper and merchant were the same person; by about 1300, however, merchants began to stay at home, ordering merchandise by letter from many different places at the same time, and skippers were turned into mere carriers.

Fishing and trading ships gradually extended their voyages. In the 13th century Hanseatic ships sailed the North Sea and Baltic, and Italian ships stayed in the Mediterranean. A century later Hanseatic ships voyaged out to Iceland and down to Vizcaya in Spain, while Venice and Genoa sent great galleys north to Flanders. Also in the 14th century urban Dutch fishermen began using bigger ships to engage in deep-sea fishing for herring. By the 15th century the Portuguese, seeking trade with India, sailed along the western coast of Africa and reached their aim in 1498, while the Spaniards crossed the Atlantic in 1492 and established trade with America.

In general, medieval ships sailed within sight of the coastline. Sailors recognized where they were by means of natural landmarks on the shore, such as promontories, hills of specific shape, trees, or the mouths of rivers. Man-made landmarks—grave mounds in early medieval Scandinavia and England and church towers in Christian Europe—served the same purpose. Sailors also added special marks. In Scandinavia they built stone piles, and in the late Viking Age wooden beacons marked inlets to harbors. On the Continent the first wooden beacons appeared in 1225. Later, stone towers were erected. In the Mediterranean lighthouses seem to have been used without interruption since Roman times. Farther north, coastal beacons and towers got lanterns—in England in the 13th century and in the Baltic in the 14th century. At this same time, floating seamarks were added as navigational aids. To maintain these seamarks port authorities collected taxes from incoming ships.

On the ship itself the lead remained the most indispensable nautical instrument. It was used for measuring the depth of the water and for bringing samples up from the seabed as additional clues to orientation. Along the Atlantic coast and in the English Channel and the North Sea, sailors carefully watched the tidal streams and waited until these streams could carry them into or out of harbors, most of which were situated upstream of rivers. Medieval ships, which could not cruise very well against the wind, had to wait until it blew in the necessary direction. When a storm threatened, the skipper had to find a safe berth as quickly as possible in the shelter of a promontory, island, or river inlet. It was necessary for him to know all the berths along his course that could give shelter against a gale approaching from any possible direction. Knowledge was passed down orally to younger sailors.

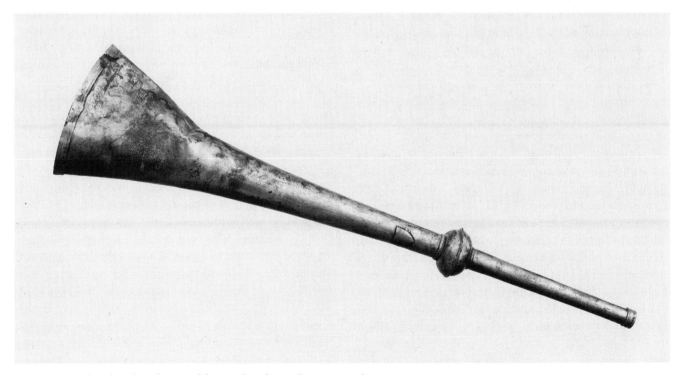

Brass trumpet, thought to have been used for signaling ship to ship at sea, 14th century (© Museum of London)

Early medieval ships could reach coasts beyond the horizon only by watching the North Star on starlit nights. This limited their distance to what they could sail in one night. Those who wanted to sail from Jutland or Norway to the British Isles could not cross the North Sea directly but had to follow the Frisian coast. It was the Irish hermits who managed to move from one island to another far out into the Atlantic and in so doing started deep-sea navigation. In the late eighth century Norwegian Vikings for the first time directly crossed the North Sea to raid coastal settlements in northern England. In contact with Irishmen they developed deep-sea navigation, settled Iceland (in 870) and Greenland (in 985), and about 1000 reached America.

To cover the long distances between the islands, they needed a favorable wind that would direct them to their aim. This meant that the weather vane on top of the mast became a necessary nautical instrument. Before starting, they had to estimate that the wind would blow constantly in the same direction for 12 to 24 hours in small seas and up to seven days in wide seas. About 1240 the first mention is recorded of using a magnetic stone to navigate to Iceland. An iron needle was inserted in a straw, magnetized by the stone, and left to float in a water-filled bowl, where it would always point to the north. With this rough compass sailors knew where north was even in the daytime or on cloudy nights when the North Star was not visible.

Italian sailors in the 13th century combined three elements into a more advanced system of navigation. First, they converted the magnetic needle into a real compass, with a compass card divided into 32 directions that was fixed to the needle to turn with it. By watching this compass the helmsman could steer a straight course in any of the 32 directions. While steering with 32 directions is less precise than using the modern compass of 360 degrees, in European waters this lack of precision did not matter, since after a few days land became visible and the course could be corrected. Second, the Italians used written sailing instructions with compass courses and distances from one harbor to the other. Third, the multitude of compass courses enabled them to transfer these sailing instructions to the first nautical charts, the so-called portolan (from the Latin *portus*, meaning "port") charts of the Mediterranean, which show a spiderweb of compass courses instead of latitudes and longitudes. This three-part system turned out to be a most important step forward in navigation. In the 15th century the Portuguese and Spanish used the system as the basis for the deep-sea navigation of their discovery expeditions. At the same time, in the North Sea and Baltic Sea only two elements of the system were adopted: the compass and written sailing instructions. The first nautical chart was not created there before 1543.

THE ISLAMIC WORLD

BY MUHAMMED HASSAN ALI

Ships had sailed the Mediterranean Sea since ancient times. The Romans had controlled virtually all the lands surrounding it, turning it into a highway of commercial activity. But by the Middle Ages this control had divided, with Muslims influencing the lands east of the Mediterranean while Europe held sway over the lands west of the Mediterranean. This dynamic turned the Mediterranean highway into a frontier. The early Muslims lacked seafaring knowledge and relied on the Copts, Syrians, and Greeks recruited from the coastlands of the conquered provinces to sail their ships.

In early medieval time the Fatimids built a new capital Cairo to rival Baghdad. Cairo was not only a strategic center but also an inland port providing the Nile traffic a gateway into the Mediterranean. It also became a major transshipment point between the Mediterranean and the Southern Seas, eventually overshadowing the port at Alexandria. At the beginning of the first millennium, the Fatimid navy controlled both the Red Sea (as far south as Yemen) and the eastern Mediterranean seaways. At its height Fatimid naval power was respected from Sicily to Sind.

Muslim conquest consolidated the lands around the Red Sea and Arabian Sea, thus bringing stability to that region. The Tang Dynasty (618–907) brought stability to China, and as a result commercial activity in the Indian Ocean benefited. Muslim and Chinese ships plied the sea so regularly that a number of handbooks were written that provided detailed accounts of ports, sea routes, navigational references, and information about the cultures of the various inhabitants that might be encountered. Ships brought goods from as far away as India and China to the Muslim capital of Baghdad along the Tigris.

Initially the ships sailed close to land, always keeping the shoreline in sight. While this is a relatively safe practice, it results in a longer voyage than a straight ocean passage. The Muslims were familiar with using the stars to navigate across the featureless desert and brought similar techniques to seafaring. Their contributions opened the way to sailing across the ocean and greatly reduced the time it took to get from one point to another. Scheduling the voyage to coincide with favorable monsoon winds reduced the time even further.

Relying on the monsoon winds of the Indian Ocean, Muslim merchants sailed regularly from Arabia to China and back. From October to May the favorable northeast trade wind and strong southwesterly current sent many Arabian dhows south with date harvests. When the strong southwest trade wind blew from June to September, the dhows sailed home again to Arabia on the northern current. The ships carried peanuts and sesame from Sudan; textiles and vegetables from Egypt; sheep from Somalia; and coffee, wheat, sorghum, and raisins from Yemen. Hundreds of dhows docked every day to unload or transship goods at ports like Al Hudaydah (northern Yemen), Hadramawt (southern Yemen), Mogadishu (Somalia), and Suez.

The Arabian Gulf, which was relatively easy to navigate, provided another route linking Arabia to India. Small boats could sail along the coastline, always keeping the shore in sight. The voyage could be made without knowledge of the stars and was not dependent on the monsoon winds. The discovery of the sea route between the Arabian Gulf and China was an event equal in importance to the discovery by the Portuguese of the sea route to India. It was one thing to cross the Indian Ocean with the monsoon to Gujarat or the Malabar coast or even to sail south of Sri Lanka and turn north to the Bay of Bengal or east to Malaya—but it was quite another to make the far longer voyage to Canton through a lesser-known sea with its own pattern of winds, to say nothing of the perpetual danger of piracy and the typhoons of the South China Sea. Still, in early Islamic times, direct sailing to Canton via the Arabian Gulf seems to have been common practice. The *bahr al-hind* (Sea of India) or the *bahr al-sin* (Sea of China), as the Indian Ocean was often called, was thought to have been made up of several different seas, each with its own unique characteristics.

The first full description of the use of the magnetic compass for navigation in the Muslim world was by Baylak al-Qibjaqi in his *Kitab kanz al-tujjar fi marifat al-ahjar* (Treasure Book of Merchants in Travels), written in Egypt in 1282. He describes the floating compass, which was a magnet embedded in wood in an assembly typically shaped like a fish. The "fish" was put in a bowl of water, whereupon it would align with the meridian. These designs were often sealed with tar or wax to make them waterproof as they floated on water. There was also the dry compass, which consisted of two magnetic needles attached to opposite sides of a disk. The disk rested on a funnel in a way that allowed it to pivot about its axis. The disk and funnel were placed in a box, which was then sealed by a plate of glass that prevented the disk from dropping.

Fixing a position at sea and setting a course out of sight of land was done by determining the ship's latitude. Another method of measuring the polestar's height above the horizon was by using the *kamal*. The *kamal* was a small rectangle of wood attached to a cord that was calibrated by knots along its length. Each knot represented the latitude of a particular port. The navigator held the cord in his teeth at a certain knot and held the *kamal* at eye level at the cord's full length, aligning the lower edge of the rectangular plaque with the horizon. When the upper edge intersected the polestar, the ship was on the latitude of the desired port. Distance east and west was

SINBAD'S WORLD

There are seven adventures of Sinbad the sailor in *One Thousand and One Nights*, often called *The Arabian Nights*. Much of the content of the tales about Sinbad derives from other literary sources, primarily from Greek literature, but other aspects of the tales reflect the seafaring of the medieval Islamic world. The locations in the tales suggest the city-states of East Africa and the seas of southern Asia. Sinbad's home was Basra, a city on the river Shatt-al-Arab, about 75 miles north of the Persian Gulf. An island in the river is still called Jazirat as-Sindibad, meaning Sinbad's Island, where he supposedly lived when he was not at sea. The plot of the fourth voyage of Sinbad seems to be taken from a couple of Greek sources, but its descriptions of a narcotic that could have been made from hemp suggest that its locale was India. In the fifth voyage the Old Man of the Sea rides Sinbad with his legs twisted around Sinbad's neck, a practice derived from masters' riding of slaves in Africa. Sinbad also encounters apes, suggesting the locale is Africa. In the sixth voyage Sinbad visits Serendib, or Sri Lanka.

Basra was a city of wonders in medieval times. Most of its residents were Shia Muslims, but there were sizable minorities of Sunni Muslims, Orthodox Christians, and Madean Gnostics. On any day one could venture into the city's markets and see people from Christian Europe, al-Andalus, North Africa, sub-Saharan Africa, Bulgaria, India, Sri Lanka, Malaysia, Indonesia, and China, each garbed in his or her national dress. Local agriculture brought livestock, dates, rice, wheat, millet, and barley to the city. Sinbad was a wealthy man, because of the riches he brought home with him from his voyages, and he would have lived in a tall city house of stone and brick, with high ceilings of brick on the first floor and of wood on the others. The outside would be plain except for a door of fine wood opening on an alley. His living quarters on the second and third floors would have been filled with rugs, pillows, and other textiles, where he and his wife from the seventh voyage would have had privacy. The fourth floor would have entertained guests, and its windows would have opened on narrow streets teeming with activity.

measured by time, not in hours but in *zam*, three-hour increments—the length of a watch on board—measured by the burning of a standardized stick of incense.

Astrolabes (also called "the mathematical jewel") could take altitude measurements of the sun, tell time during the day or night, or find the time of a celestial event (like sunrise, sunset, or the culminant or zenith of a star). These astronomical and analogue computers of their time are two-dimensional models of the heavens. A highly sophisticated form of the astrolabe was developed in the 11th century in Toledo, Spain. The universal astrolabe was a breakthrough because it could be used in any location (previous ones had been designed for a specific latitude and longitude locations).

The earliest evidence for the existence of a navigational calendar is an almanac compiled in 1271 by al-Malik al-Ashraf. It is an example of how knowledge from disparate lands was amalgamated into a coherent whole. The almanac contains Syriac months as well as Persian months. The equinoxes, solstices, and prominent stars are designated according to the Bedouin system. Measurements of shadow lengths throughout the year are included. The days are marked to allow correlation with the Roman Julian calendar. It also has useful information on times to sow and reap, on insect pests,

healthy and unhealthy seasons, and so on. It included the dates of departure and arrival of ships from India, Qalhat, Hormoz, al-Shihr, Mogadishu, and Egypt. The entries in the almanac reveal a highly synchronized system of regular shipping and interregional trade that was also tied in with the oceangoing merchant convoys.

Ahmad ibn Majid (b. ca. 1432) was a master navigator and knew virtually all the sea routes from the Red Sea to East Africa and from East Africa to China. His navigational knowledge was compiled in his book *Kitab al-fawaid fi usul ilm al-bahr wa l-qawaid* (Book of Useful Information on the Principles and Rules of Navigation), written in 1490. Among the topics addressed is the history and basic principles of navigation, the difference between coastal and open-sea sailing, star positions, accounts of the monsoon and other seasonal winds and typhoons.

See also ASTRONOMY; CALENDARS AND CLOCKS; CLIMATE AND GEOGRAPHY; ECONOMY; EXPLORATION; HUNTING, FISHING, AND GATHERING; MIGRATION AND POPULATION MOVEMENTS; MILITARY; MINING, QUARRYING, AND SALT MAKING; SHIPS AND SHIPBUILDING; STORAGE AND PRESERVATION; TRADE AND EXCHANGE; WAR AND CONQUEST.

Europe

∼ *Excerpt from* The Travels of John de Marignolli (1339–53) ∼

There is ZAYTUN also, a wondrous fine seaport and a city of incredible size, where our Minor Friars have, three very fine churches, passing rich and elegant; and they have a bath also and *a fondaco* which serves as a depot for all the merchants. They have also some fine bells of the best quality, two of which were made to my order, and set up with all due form in the very middle of the Saracen community. One of these we ordered to be called Johannina, and the other Antonina.

We quitted Zaytun on St. Stephen's day, and on the Wednesday of Holy Week we arrived at Columbum. Wishing then to visit the Shrine of St. Thomas the Apostle, and to sail thence to the Holy Land, we embarked on board certain junks, from Lower India which is called Minubar. We encountered so many storms, commencing from St. George's Eve, and were so dashed about by them, that sixty times and more we were all but swamped in the depths of the sea, and it

was only by divine miracle that we escaped. And such wondrous things we beheld! The sea as if in flames, and fire-spitting dragons flying by, and as they passed they slew persons on board the other junks, whilst ours remained untouched, by God's grace, and by virtue of the body of Christ which I carried with me, and through the merits of the glorious Virgin and St. Clare. And having brought all the Christians to penitential mourning, even whilst the gale still blew we made sail, committing ourselves to the Divine guidance, and caring only for the safety of souls. Thus led by the Divine mercy, on the morrow of the Invention of the Holy Cross we found ourselves brought safely into port in a harbour of Seyllan, called PERVILIS, over against Paradise.

From: Sir Henry Yule, *Cathay and the Way Thither: Being a Collection of Medieval Notices of China* (London: Hakluyt Society, 1913–1916).

~ The Seven Voyages of Sinbad the Sailor: Excerpt from the Sixth Voyage (ca. 800–ca. 1400) ~

Compelled by Fate and Fortune, I resolved to undertake another voyage, and, buying me fine and costly merchandise meet for foreign trade, made it up into bales, with which I journeyed from Baghdad to Bassorah.

Here I found a great ship ready for sea and full of merchants and notables, who had with them goods of price, so I embarked my bales therein. And we left Bassorah in safety and good spirits under the safeguard of the King, the Preserver, and continued our voyage from place to place and from city to city, buying and selling and profiting and diverting ourselves with the sight of countries where strange folk dwell. And Fortune and the voyage smiled upon us till one day, as we went along, behold, the captain suddenly cried with a great cry and cast his turban on the deck. Then he buffeted his face like a woman and plucked out his beard and fell down in the waist of the ship well-nigh fainting for stress of grief and rage, and crying, "Oh, and alas for the ruin of my house and the orphanship of my poor children!" So all the merchants and sailors came round about him and asked him, "O master, what is the matter?" For the light had become night before, their sight. And he answered, saying: "Know, O folk, that we have wandered from our course and left the sea whose ways we wot, and come into a sea whose ways I know not, and unless Allah vouchsafe us a means of escape, we are all dead men. Wherefore pray ye to the Most High that He deliver us from this strait. Haply amongst you is one righteous whose prayers the Lord will accept." Then he arose and clomb the mast to see an there were any escape from that strait. And he would have loosed the sails, but the wind redoubled upon the ship and whirled her round thrice and drave her backward, whereupon her rudder brake and she fell off toward a high mountain.

With this the captain came down from the mast, saying: "There is no Majesty and there is no Might save in Allah, the Glorious, the Great, nor can man prevent that which is foreordained of Fate! By Allah, we are fallen on a place of sure destruction, and there is no way of escape for us, nor can any of us be saved!" Then we all fill a-weeping over ourselves and bidding one another farewell for that our days were come to an end, and we had lost an hopes of life. Presently the ship struck the mountain and broke up, and all and everything on board of her were plunged into the sea. Some of the merchants were drowned and others made shift to reach the shore and save themselves upon the mountain, I amongst the number. And when we got ashore, we found a great island, or rather peninsula, whose base was strewn with wreckage and crafts and goods and gear cast up by the sea from broken ships whose passengers had been drowned, and the quantity confounded count and calculation. So I climbed the cliffs into the inward of the isle and walked on inland till I came to a stream of sweet water that welled up at the nearest foot of the mountains and disappeared in the earth under the range of hills on the opposite side. But all the other passengers went over the mountains to the inner tracts, and, dispersing hither and thither, were confounded at what they saw and became like madmen at the sight of the wealth and treasures wherewith the shores were strewn. . . .

Then I fell to reproaching myself for my little wit in leaving my native land and betaking me again to travel after all I had suffered during my first five voyages, and when I had not made a single one without suffering more horrible perils and more terrible hardships than in its forerunners, and having no hope of escape from my present stress. . . . Then, sighing for myself, I set to work collecting a number of pieces of Chinese and Comorin aloes wood and I bound them together with ropes from the wreckage. Then I chose out from the broken-up ships straight planks of even size and fixed them firmly upon the aloes wood, making me a boat raft a little narrower than the channel of the stream, and I tied it tightly and firmly as though it were nailed. Then I loaded it with the goods, precious ores and jewels, and the union pearls which were like gravel, and the best of the ambergris crude and pure, together with what I had collected on the island and what was left me of victual and wild herbs. Lastly I lashed a piece of wood on either side, to serve me as oars, and launched it.

From: Richard F. Burton, trans.,
The Book of the Thousand Nights and a Night
(Kamashastra Society of Benares, 1885).

FURTHER READING

Ahmad al-Hassan and Donald Hill, *Islamic Technology: An Illustrated History* (New York: Cambridge University Press, 1992).

Salim al-Hassani, *1001 Inventions: Muslim Heritage in Our World* (Manchester, U.K.: Foundation for Science Technology and Civilization, 2006).

George E. Brooks, *Landlords and Strangers: Ecology, Society, and Trade in Western Africa, 1000–1630* (Boulder, Colo.: Westview Press, 1993).

John F. Haslett and Cameron M. Smith, "In the Wake of the Ancient Mariners," *Archaeology Magazine* (March/April 2002). Available online. URL: http://www.archaeology.org/0203/abstracts/mariners.html. Downloaded on September 27, 2007.

George Hourani, *Arab Seafaring: In the Indian Ocean in Ancient and Early Medieval Times* (Princeton, N.J.: Princeton University Press, 1995).

Archibald R. Lewis and Timothy J. Runyan, *European Naval and Maritime History, 300–1500* (Bloomington: Indiana University Press, 1985).

John Middleton, *The World of the Swahili: An African Mercantile Civilization* (New Haven, Conn., and London: Yale University Press, 1992).

Saudi Aramco World, *The Indian Ocean and Global Trade* (July–August 2005). Available online. URL: http://www.saudiaramcoworld.com/issue/200504/default.htm. Downloaded on October 9, 2007.

Robert Smith, "The Canoe in West African History," *Journal of African History* 11 (4) (1970): 515–533.

Eva G. R. Taylor, *The Haven-Finding Art: A History of Navigation from Odysseus to Captain Cook*, 2nd ed. (London: Hollis and Carter, 1971).

Richard W. Unger, *The Ship in the Medieval Economy 600–1600* (London: Croom Helm, 1980).

► settlement patterns

INTRODUCTION

Settlement patterns are the expression on the landscape of societies' ideas and values. They speak of what people valued in their economies, which sometimes is driven more by custom than by environment. For instance, lands in North Africa that for hundreds of years in the ancient world produced large crops of grains, vegetables, and fruits were changed from farmland to pastureland by Arab nomads, who valued their mobile pattern of life focused on the economics of herding, selling, and trading of domesticated animals, such as sheep, goats, and camels.

Settlement patterns further speak of social organization and shared social values. In some cultures the dominant settlement pattern was one of small settlements scattered across the land. Sometimes these settlements were composed of family groups, who lived in small clusters of houses near farmlands that they worked or pasturelands that they tended. Occasionally, the scattering was even less dense, with single homes on land tended by a single family. In early medieval England the single homestead, standing apart from other homesteads, was the preferred pattern of people who had resisted the Roman emphasis on city life. At times, settlements consisted of several families who jointly controlled the land around the settlement, with individual people being apportioned control but not ownership of part of the land according to their need and often according to their social standing. Such was the custom in most of medieval central Africa and many of the rural areas of the Near East.

In addition to economic and social reasons, religion and politics played significant roles in drawing people to live in towns and cities. The economic concerns may be the plainest, because they were often stark. In times of famine, natural disasters, or epidemic disease, people often abandoned their rural dwellings to go to a city in the hope of finding work that would earn them food to eat and a place to live. In one of the ironies of settlement patterns, economics could cause the opposite to happen. For example, in much of early medieval Europe many towns and cities of the Roman Empire were almost abandoned because of an economic collapse that resulted in urban dwellers having no means of earning what they needed in order to survive. They fled to the countryside to try to farm to support themselves. Even the city of Rome, which had millions of inhabitants in the Roman Empire, fell to a population of thousands.

Towns and cities had significant social advantages over villages and other small settlements. One was that large settlements tended to attract more consumer goods than did small, scattered settlements. If a person were a specialist in a craft, living where traders and others congregated on market day could increase demands for his or her products. Further, a large settlement usually offered better defense than did rural areas, where it could take days or even weeks to pull enough people together to form an effective military force. There were cultures in the medieval world that survived primarily by stealing the results of the labor of others, and a walled city was a common recourse for defense against such cultures. In a densely populated settlement professional, full-time soldiers could congregate and be supported by some of the surplus of goods produced by town or city dwellers and nearby farmlands, usually extracted in the form of taxes. Sometimes a central government took care of the maintenance of the troops, as was usually the case in the Islamic world, but sometimes communities took it upon themselves to pay for a small group of warriors, as was sometimes the case in medieval Japan and in parts of Arabia in Muhammad's time.

People also often congregated at centers of power. Centers of power could derive their authority from religion, politics, or both. In Europe and China monasteries and convents could attract large numbers of monks and nuns and appeal to even larger numbers of pilgrims, attracted to the spiritual teachings of the monasteries and convents or by sacred relics housed in the religious complexes. The settlements built around religious centers could become prosperous. Some settlements became political centers of power. On occasion they were established, as Cairo was, to be an administrative center; in other instances a burgeoning population center became the logical place for people to meet to discuss matters such as mutual defense and law and order. Not only national capitals but provincial ones as well could attract people to work for the people in power, to serve in government posts, and to provide services for the government officials and other residents. Medieval Mesoamerica has examples of how some settlements combined both religious and political power, often in the form of kings who had supernatural abilities. The mix was dangerous, and one reason the Maya left their cities may have been that they believed that their monarchs had lost their supernatural powers.

AFRICA

BY JUSTIN CORFIELD

In the medieval period people speaking Afro-Asiatic and Nilo-Saharan languages inhabited the areas of northern Africa; Saharan Africa west of Chad; the Songhai Empire in what is today central Mali; and present-day Ethiopia, Eritrea, Somalia, Sudan, and northern Uganda. People speaking Niger-Kordofanian languages most of whom were Bantu, lived in western Africa, central Africa, and much of southern Africa, excluding modern-day Namibia, Botswana, and South Africa. The Khoisan people lived in the Kalahari Desert, South Africa, and isolated pockets in present-day Burundi and central Angola.

In northern Africa before the arrival of Islam, many Roman, Greek, and Phoenician influences were adopted in the towns and cities along the Mediterranean coast of Africa. These were all permanent settlements that either became more prosperous or declined as a result of politics or trade. The influence of the Romans is evident in the layout of most large cities in this region, with major civic buildings located in the center along with the market and often the military command post. Many of the Roman temples were replaced by or converted into Christian churches during the medieval period. Although in ancient times the cities typically had walls, by the fifth century Rome's control of the Mediterranean had been unchallenged for so many centuries that many of the walls had either crumbled from neglect or, because of urban expansion, no longer represented a line of defense. The Vandals' emergence as a power in what is today Morocco and

Algeria and their capture of Carthage in 439 prompted the refortification of many cities and the abandonment of more outlying areas as people sought refuge in walled cities. The Romans finally launched an effort to retake the region, and their defeat of the Vandals at the battle of Ad Decimum in 533 led to the decline of numerous cities and towns. Timgad and Bagai were abandoned, and Leptis Magna succumbed to the encroaching desert. The decline of these cities is evident by only one major civic building, the baths at Tunes (modern-day Tunis), being dated to the period of Vandal rule from the 430s to the 530s.

From the 530s the Romans tried to rebuild their former settlements, with their work focusing on the churches and civic buildings. A large church was constructed at Leptis Magna, and baths were built at Carthage in honor of the Empress Theodora (d. 548), marking a new confidence in urban life. That confidence lasted only slightly more than a century. As Islam spread throughout North Africa in the seventh century, the cities were remodeled.

Inland settlements were isolated and invariably located near oases along trade routes, with camel tracks linking many of them. More remote yet were settlements in the Sahara Desert near salt-mining areas, like Taghaza and Taodeni, around the borders of present-day Algeria, Mauritania, and Mali. Other remote settlements became prosperous in new ways. Zawila in the Fezzan of southern Libya, a place of refuge for the Islamic Ibadites, soon emerged as a center of the slave trade. These settlements tended to be made from stone or mud brick, with all the villagers living within a strong outer wall, making the place capable of withstanding an attack by parties of bandits, brigands, or people from neighboring settlements. The oasis or well was in the center of the settlement, along with a small market. The use of date palms to provide shade in these settlements is evidenced by a painting found at a site near the banks of Wadi Oua Molin. The Arab writer Abu Abdullah al-Bakri (fl. 1068), who traveled through the region, describes some of these settlements, especially Awdaghurst, as having orchards, fig trees, vines, and fields of henna and gourds. He also mentions land devoted to sorghum and cotton around the settlement at Silla in the western African state of Tekrur.

The medieval kingdoms of Ghana (located in modern-day Mauritania), Mali, Kanem-Bornu, and Songhai had similar settlement patterns, with townships located at oases along trade routes or rivers. The kingdom of Ghana had grown rich from the alluvial gold found at Galam and Bure (present-day Guinea). Salt and gold were sold to Berber traders, who in return brought goods from the Mediterranean. This led to villages being built along the trade routes and also where supplies could be grown for sale to the traders.

Al-Bakri describes the capital of ancient Ghana as being surrounded by vegetable gardens, although he does not mention what was grown in them. However, many people in the region remained nomadic.

In Nubia in northeast Africa, almost all settlements were along the Nile River. Among the few more-isolated townships was Abu Negila, in northern Kordofan in hills that became known as the Abu Negila Hills. The major change in the settlements during the medieval period was the building of impressive churches and cathedrals in many of the towns. The most impressive was perhaps the cathedral at Faras, built on top of what is believed to have been a palace and dominating the township. Many churches date from 707, and the Faras cathedral dates from about 930. Other towns such as Aydhab, Suakin, and Badi, were built along the Red Sea. In the early medieval period Aydhab was an important location for Christian pilgrims heading to Jerusalem, but the town soon became just as important for Muslim making their pilgrimage, or hajj, to Mecca. The hajj led to the proliferation of settlements along the coast of the Red Sea.

In central Ethiopia settlements were located where the Funj Empire flourished during the 1400s. In Darfur in modern-day Sudan the main settlement of al-Fashir was located at the foot of the mountains in the west. Many people in the Darfur region remained nomadic, rearing camels and sheep on lands from the Nile to northern Darfur. Goods arrived in Darfur by caravan from Asyut in Upper Egypt and Kharga in southern Egypt, leading to some isolated settlements in northern Kordofan in central Sudan. Indeed Kharga, on the caravan route to Al Kufrah in southwest Libya and western Sudan that appears to have been largely abandoned during the early medieval period, managed to survive only because of the trade with Darfur.

In western Africa most settlements were located along rivers, with Koumbi Saleh, Kano, Old Oyo, and Kong being significant exceptions. By the late 13th century the Mali Empire, which grew rich on the trade of gold and salt, dominated the northern inland area of western Africa, centered on its great capital at Timbuktu. In the areas of modern-day Senegal and Gambia, settlements were known to have been built primarily along the coast, and a significant coastal trade with Morocco began. The lack of settlements from the region of Sierra Leone to the Komoé River was largely because of the density of the Guinea forest. Settlements like Axim and Mouri were built to take advantage of the gold around the Ankobra River, and other cities of modern-day Ghana—Begho, Bouna, and Bono-Manso—were established north of the forest region. The city of Benin in present-day Nigeria also appears to be of medieval foundation. In eastern Nigeria and Cameroon the Warri and Ijaw peoples established many settlements around

the Niger Delta, while farther up the Niger River settlements like Idah were established by the Igala people.

Because much of central Africa is forested, little is known about the pattern of settlements in the region. However, the Bobangi people, and farther inland the Ngbandi, Binza, and Mangbetu peoples, did establish villages along the Ubangi River. Additionally, the Kongo people occupied the plains and hills just south of the mouth of the river. In modern-day Zambia the Kalomo people built their settlements in clearings and constructed mounds to protect them not only from marauders but also from flooding from the nearby marshland. Over time old buildings were dismantled and the rubble added to the height of the mounds. However, despite the work involved in building their settlements, the Kalomo apparently did not live in one place continuously but stayed only until the fertility of the land was exhausted and then moved to another region, often returning to former mound villages a century or so later. By contrast, the Lozi people living along the east bank of the Zambezi River in modern-day western Zambia took advantage of the new topsoil provided by river floods to establish permanent settlements. On the coast of present-day Kenya, the settlement of Manda had elaborate sea and land walls.

The increase in coastal trade in southwestern Africa led to the establishment of some permanent townships, such as Benguela and Luanda in Angola. The increase in Arab traders also led to more settlements along the Africa's southeastern coast, such as Inhambane, Sofala, Quelimane, and Angoche in modern-day Mozambique. Because the structures in most of these settlements were made entirely from wood that has perished, information on the layouts of these settlements is mostly speculative. The exceptions are the stone buildings of the inland kingdom of Great Zimbabwe, which flourished between 1100 and 1500, and more than 150 other settlements across modern-day Zimbabwe and Mozambique. Raised platforms built of granite in the centers of many of these settlements may have been places of worship. Given its size, Great Zimbabwe may have been a royal palace, and its towers may have held large supplies of grain and other crops. Farther south, Khoisan people continued to live a nomadic existence, moving with changes in climate and locations of animals to hunt.

THE AMERICAS

BY J. J. GEORGE

Settlement patterns have been defined as the ways humans have disposed of themselves over the landscape on which they live. In other words, settlements are archaeologically discernible sites characterized by structures in relation to one another and forming patterns on the landscape with varying degrees of scale and complexity. The range of settlements in the Americas during the medieval period included camps, farmsteads, ceremonial clusters, villages, and cities.

North American settlement varied by region and time and never achieved the type of state-level urbanism seen in Mesoamerica and South America. Settlements of the Mississippian culture, most of which were developed along the floodplains of the Mississippi River and its tributaries, are consistent with chiefdom-level societies, with evidence of two or three levels of social hierarchy and monumental architecture. The largest center was usually a capital with subordinate centers. Cahokia (ca. 900–ca. 1100), for instance, near modern East Saint Louis, Illinois, was the largest Mississippian settlement, covering 5 square miles and containing more than 100 mounds. Located nearby were smaller subordinate sites, perhaps with a single mound and covering only a few acres. The Moundville, Big Ben, and Powers Phase settlements, which had emerged by the 11th century and were small polity centers with affiliated villages, hamlets, or farmsteads in outlying areas.

Southwest settlement development began roughly 6,000 years ago with the Anasazi, Mogolion, and Hohokam cultures beginning in the first millennium of the Common Era and extending, in related forms, to current times. Farmstead and hamlet communities consisting of four or five circular or rectangular pit houses with a total population of between 25 and 30 people developed by the sixth century. Between 750 and 1150 the Hohokam developed settlements with ball courts, platform mounds, and populations of up to 100 people. At about this time settlement groups in Chaco Canyon, New Mexico, centralized into apartment-like walled adobe compounds and broadly coalesced into some form of organized interaction sphere whose nature is debated. The period from 1250 to 1450 witnessed dramatic change. Irrigation canals reached their maximum extent and connected numerous communities. The Hohokam continued dispersed settlement patterns at some sites, but at other sites rectangular compounds enclosed several households and open-plaza work areas. In the Mogolion and Anasazi areas regional abandonment and population aggregation brought about by drought forced communities to join together. Contemporary pueblos such as the one at Taos, New Mexico, ultimately were derived from these trends.

In the Northeast, ceremonial centers appeared, followed by large villages covering one to several acres of elevated ground. The villages contained semipermanent houses and storage pits, and archaeologists have found evidence of maize agriculture. A typical house was a circular lodge 12 to 15 feet in diameter, presumably of the wigwam type, with a central hearth and enclosed by a palisade. In the Great Plains region hunter-gatherer complexes existed until the arrival of the Europeans, suggesting the temporary and recurrent occupations of a migratory culture. Loosely arranged village sites throughout the central Midwest show traces of bean and maize agriculture and earth-covered or rectangular lodges clustered together.

Central Mexico was distinguished early in the medieval period by peoples practicing agriculture, which resulted in the most intensive development of urbanism in Mesoamerica. Villages, towns, and cities were common. By the Postclassic Period (ca. 900–1530) innumerable small polities from towns to kingdoms to city-states dotted the landscape. Cities and feuding city-states came to define settlement in central Mexico. The collapse of Teotihuacán (ca. 100–ca. 750) led to the rise of Tula (ca. 850–ca. 1150), Cholula (ca. 400–ca. 800), and Xochicalco (ca. 700–ca. 1000). Tenochtitlán, which became Mexico City, was the center of power in the 15th and 16th centuries until the Spanish arrived in 1521. These cities and city-states not only dominated but also coordinated regional agricultural, trade, and tribute economies and localized political, economic, social, and ritual functions. The results were dynamic civic spaces to which local and regional tributaries were often subordinate. Affluent production zones ruled by dynasties of Mixtec and Zapotec origin in the Oaxaca region, to the south of the Aztec, demonstrated close social interaction. City-states also developed in the region, possibly in response to Aztec incursion.

Mayan settlements are grouped into highland and lowland developments. Highland settlements developed in mountainous regions running from Mexico through Guatemala to Honduras. Lowland regions, typically below 2,600 feet and covered in tropical forest, include the Petén region of northern Guatemala, the Yucatán Peninsula, and a transitional zone between the highland and lowland. Classic Period (ca. 200–ca. 900) lowland sites are the most studied. Mayan centers represented larger and more complex versions of residential clusters, which consisted of two or more residential groups separated by open space. A group averaged two to six units, with each unit comprising a family household. These centers varied greatly in size. The smallest may have covered less than half a square mile, whereas others, such as Tikal, extended over an area of some 50 square miles. Regardless of their function, Mayan centers and their residential clusters defined the community and became administrative centers of religious, economic, political, and social significance. The distance between the larger sites averaged 12 to 18 miles, whereas a whole range of smaller centers have been found at smaller intervals. Differences in size suggest different levels of political affiliation or control.

Overall, the location and prosperity of Mayan sites, as for human settlements generally, were determined by access to essential resources such as water and food. The centers in the Petén region, such as Tikal, El Mirador, and Uaxactun, are at or near the divide between drainage basins, indicating they controlled the portages for canoes across the Petén. Centers also developed along rivers; for example, among the centers near the Usumacinta River included Seibal, Yaxchilan, Piedras Negras, and Palenque. Seacoast trade determined the location of Cerros, Lamanai, and Tulum. Often a center would be located at the source of a resource with widespread demand; for example, Dzibilchaltun in northern Yucatán had access to coastal salt; Colha in Belize, good-quality flint; and Kaminaljuyu in the southern lowlands, obsidian. Centers established during the Postclassic Period (ca. 900–1530) in the Yucatán, including Uxmal, Chichén Itzá, and Mayapán, show the influence of the Toltec culture of central Mexico.

Although the most advanced civilizations in South America developed in the Andean region, scholars reanalyzing older work suggest a long indigenous sequence of settlement in the Amazon and Orinoco river basins, with populations clustering along floodplains in northeastern Brazil and Venezuela. Between the fifth and 15th centuries indigenous societies of considerable scale and cultural complexity developed. Most Amazon Basin sites were not urban and seem comparable to chiefs' domains, stratified chiefdoms, or small states. Many occupation sites are several miles long and densely packed with deep refuse piles. Among the best-known societies are the Marajoara culture (ca. 400–ca. 1100) of Marajó Island, the vast floodplain at the mouth of the Amazon in Brazil, and the Tapajós chiefdom on the lower Amazon, which occupied a large area of savanna, forest, and floodplain from 10th to the 16th centuries.

Scholars have subdivided Andean settlement into broad historical trends called the Horizon and Intermediate periods (ca. 500–1530). The Horizon Period features widespread similarities in the art and culture of various areas that may be associated with the power of a cult, state, or empire. Regional diversity, by contrast, is more characteristic of the intermediate periods. Together these periods help define settlement patterns and the manner in which various settlements interacted or related to one another.

The Wari and Tiwanaku cultures defined the Middle Horizon Period from the sixth to 11th centuries. Wari expansionism relied on militarism. Its original sphere was the area of Ayacucho, Peru, a sierran basin occupied previously by the Huarpa, who lived in villages and hamlets scattered over the mountain slopes. Initial Wari development was closely tied to Tiwanaku, but toward the end of the sixth century it broke completely free from Tiwanaku settlement patterns, establishing strategic valley sites such as Cerro Baúl and Cerro Mejía. Wari imperial strategy subsequently focused on ag-

ricultural areas. Ultimately the Wari composed an urban culture whose characteristic settlements were hierarchically arranged around a capital city connected by a series of roads and a strong army. After the Wari fell, towns of differing sizes and types appeared in the Cuzco Valley on slopes and in the Lucre Valley on hilltops, organized along local urban types.

Initial Tiwanakan settlement occurred south of Wari territory adjacent to Lake Titicaca, the richest agricultural area of the highlands. Expansion during the sixth through 11th centuries took various forms. Colonization brought people with stable occupations to low-lying agricultural zones, like the coastal towns of Arica and Tacna. In other areas expansion depended on a stable network of trade and exchange linking local settlement clusters. One theory suggests that unlike the Wari, the Tiwanaka settled in unifying complementary zones. Given the extreme ranges of the Andean topography, this theory implies that vertically integrated zones with various levels of productivity helped forge a coherent state entity.

The Chimú was a post-Wari society arising in northern Peru, in territory earlier occupied by the Moche, and spreading south and north between the 12th and 15th centuries. The great urban experiments of Chan Chan and Pikillakta define the Chimú culture, but most of the population lived outside those urban settlements in villages and hamlets. The Inca conquered the Chimú in the 15th century.

Historians generally agree that the Inca state began modestly, as a confederation of social groups under the rule of warrior leaders. The ascension of the ruler Pachacuti in 1438 signaled their greatest period of expansion. A victory over the Chanca catapulted the Inca on their imperial course, incorporating multitudes of polities, chiefdoms, and communities by force, diplomacy, and reciprocity. In less than 100 years the Inca consolidated all the territory from Santiago, Chile, to Quito, Ecuador—more than 3,400 miles—into the empire. The Spanish arrived in 1532 and soon thereafter defeated the Inca, thus ending purely indigenous development.

ASIA AND THE PACIFIC

BY LAURA LEE JUNKER

A *settlement system* is usually defined as the way in which a human population arranges itself over its regional landscape for the purpose of social, political, economic, and religious activities. Settlement patterns often are influenced by geographic and environmental features (for example, the distribution of critical resources and transport routes such as rivers), demographic factors (like population densities), political exigencies (for instance, whether political authority is concentrated or dispersed and the need to create borderlands with hostile neighbors), social factors (that is, ideas about segregation versus interaction of social classes, kin units, or ethnic groups), or cosmological ideals (such as determining the location and layout of settlements according to the directives of deities or worldviews). In such complex societies as empires, states, and chiefdoms, settlement systems are always hierarchical and often tied to the process of urbanization, with larger "central places" (that is, regional cities or "capitals") having specialized roles as administrative, commercial, or religious centers or all three.

Geographers and anthropologists have developed an ideal model of the spatial relationships between settlements in state-level societies, known as central place theory. They note that economies of scale in commodities production, efficiencies in transporting and distributing goods, and the need for political control of distant and potentially rebellious groups favor a lattice-like settlement pattern in which secondary centers are evenly spaced and equidistant from the capital. While this is an abstract model, settlement-pattern studies have shown that many medieval Asian states conformed at least loosely to this settlement arrangement.

Medieval India had a strongly urbanized landscape in which political, economic, military, and ideological power was concentrated in large cities like Bijapur, Delhi, Gaur, Madurai, and Vijayanagar, with populations in the hundreds of thousands spread over areas up to 15 square miles. These capital cities at the core of Hindu, Buddhist, and Islamic kingdoms and empires were the center of state administrative hierarchies; they supported industrial-level production of goods such as silk and cotton cloth, iron and steel, and stone beads; they had large international markets and served as the primary nodes for foreign trade; they had the state's finest military defenses and large artilleries for warfare; and they emphasized the spiritually based power of kings through elaborate temple complexes.

The necessity for homogeneous residential neighborhoods based on social caste and religion meant that medieval cities (as well as towns and villages) were rigidly ordered into differentiated housing zones. Secondary urban centers (smaller-scale and subordinate cities) tended be conform to central place theory with respect to location, particularly if they were prominent trade centers. However, archaeologists and historians studying this urbanized landscape emphasize that these secondary and tertiary cities in the settlement hierarchy did not usually start out as miniaturized versions of the capital, with its walled royal residences and sacred temple complexes at the center. Instead, secondary cities tended to form as centers with functionally specialized roles, including military camps, market centers, and religious pilgrimage sites, which became more functionally diverse as they took on new political, economic, and religious roles. Settlement in the

rural countryside consisted of dispersed, small-scale villages close to cultivated fields with houses built of perishable materials. These villages at the lower end of the regional settlement hierarchy were characterized by less residential segregation by caste than urban centers, household craft workshops oriented toward production of mundane domestic goods, and smaller-scale religious architecture and religious functionaries serving the immediate community.

In China it was in the medieval period, particularly during the Tang Dynasty (618–907), that an enduring model emerged for highly ordered and pragmatically designed cities and their accompanying regional hierarchy of outlying administrative centers. This model, epitomized by the seventh-century Tang imperial capital at Xi'an (known then as Ch'angan), persisted in later Chinese dynasties and served as a template for emerging urbanism and highly integrated states in Korea and Japan. Housing more than 1 million inhabitants within a 52-square-mile area, Xi'an was the largest city in the world in the seventh century. A 23-mile wall surrounded the neatly gridded city, which had numerous functionally distinguished "inner cities" all with gated walls, including an imperial palace complex in the center, government buildings directly to the south, nine enormous markets to the east and west (three specializing in international commerce), military armories to the south, and Buddhist and Daoist monasteries and temple complexes scattered throughout the city. The city was divided by streets laid in a grid into 108 discrete residential and commercial wards, also individually walled and gated, that functioned as administrative units for the urban peasantry serving the city in various economic roles. The ideal of walled enclosures around specialized areas of the city was copied on a smaller scale in the provincial capitals and other second-tier cities of the empire.

As in medieval India, these secondary political and commercial centers tended to conform spatially to the hexagonal lattices of central place theory, with roughly even spacing across the landscape to facilitate collection of taxes, transport of commodities, and the strict state surveillance necessary to quell rebellious populations. The vast majority of Tang people, however, were rural peasants occupying dispersed towns and villages of about 100 to 1,000 inhabitants who worked their own nearby fields or, more often, were tenants or virtual "serfs" to nearby aristocratic landlords living in extensive walled manor houses or land-owning monasteries.

While the general pattern of hierarchically ranked walled cities with this highly regimented layout persisted in China until the 17th century, significant changes in agricultural and industrial technologies in the later medieval period (beginning with in the Song Dynasty during the 10th–13th centuries and accelerating in the succeeding Yuan and Ming) led to massive overall population growth, the expansion of secondary cities in size and complexity, and a marked increase in the proportion of Chinese living in cities relative to rural areas. These settlement changes had profound social effects on the Chinese peasantry, who increasingly gained access to education, civil service and religious positions, and new opportunities for lucrative economic pursuits owing to their greater proximity to urban institutions.

Korean and Japanese societies of the early medieval period were influenced by Chinese forms of Buddhism, political administrative concepts such as merit-based civil service, written record keeping, and military organization, and Tang-style gridded and walled cities at the apex of highly ordered regional settlement hierarchies. Nara and Heian, the capitals and cores of two sequential centralized states in Japan between the eighth and 11th centuries, as well as the capitals of medieval Korean states like Silla were also laid out in the Chinese-style grid pattern, with walled and spatially segregated areas of the cities for imperial court ritual, state administration, commerce, Buddhist religious structures, and commoner residences. Secondary provincial capitals radiating out from Nara and Heian and reached by a well-constructed system of roads were smaller-scale versions of the dynastic capital. Regional planning ensured that these provincial centers were well situated to facilitate trade, taxation, labor and military conscription, and other aspects of state administration that flowed from the imperial center outward to the scattered hamlets of rice-farming peasants. Thus, regional settlement systems tended to conform relatively closely to an ideal lattice-like "central place" hierarchical pattern.

Perhaps the best historic description of village structure is that for the Korean state of Unified Silla in the seventh and eighth centuries. Villages or hamlets known as *ch'on*, consisting of about 10 houses with kin-related families who cooperated in agricultural labor and other economic activities, were the smallest administrative group in the settlement hierarchy. Several of these nearby villages were clustered for administration under a single local headman who kept the local census, collected taxes, and drafted family members for corvée labor (including farming or stock raising on government-owned lands, construction work, or other state projects).

By the 12th century, however, peasant uprisings, court intrigue, external military threats, and other factors had begun to unravel the strongly centralized state structures of both Korea and Japan. This process of political fragmentation and the consequent establishment of a radically different settlement system were particularly pronounced in Japan, where political, military, and economic authority was largely transferred from the weak imperial court into the hands of independent warlords (shoguns). For the first time large-scale

cities like Kamakura and Kyoto rivaled the imperial capital in size and complexity, with some topping 200,000 inhabitants and no longer subordinate within a hierarchical settlement system. These new cities were focused less on political administration than on commercial activities by freewheeling merchants and seagoing "pirates" under the protection of shoguns, who overlooked the commercial cities they largely ruled from massive, heavily fortified, multistoried palaces similar to the castles of feudal period lords in Europe during the medieval period. Surrounding small towns and villages comprised the residences and commercial establishments of the peasantry, who depended on the protection and patronage of the warlords and their attached warriors (samurai) for their economic livelihood and personal safety. While they were not as extreme as the late medieval Japanese polities, the once highly-centralized Korean states did become somewhat politically fragmented into similarly localized seats of power centered on "castle towns" in this period.

In Southeast Asia the great significance of maritime commerce and river-based transport routes into the island interiors meant that regional settlement patterns tended to be dendritic (meaning that they were linear and branching) rather than lattice-like in nature, with single large primate "centers" or cities located at the mouths of large rivers and in areas of good anchorage. Strategically located coastal trade ports, like Palembang (the capital of the Buddhist Srivijaya kingdom on Sumatra during the seventh to 11th centuries), Melaka (the capital of Melaka, Malay Peninsula, during the 15th–16th centuries), and Cotabato (the capital of the Magindanao Sultanate on the island of Mindanao in the Philippines during the 15th through 19th centuries) dominated the regional landscape in terms of size and complexity. These large trade entrepôts, housing up to 100,000 people, had palaces and administrative buildings, bustling international markets and craft-production areas, and the walled mansions of the aristocracy and wealthy foreign traders.

However, religious architecture was the most visible component of these urban centers, such as the spectacular Buddhist stupas and temples of Ayutthaya (Thailand) and Pegu (present-day Myanmar), the immense Hindu temple complex of Angkor Wat (modern-day Cambodia), and the brick mosques of Melaka and Aceh (Malay Peninsula).

"Secondary centers," used for bulking trade goods along interior rivers, were significantly smaller but had specialized craft activity, markets, and the presence of commercial administrators and aristocracy connected to the polity capital. Owing to the generally land-extensive nature of tropical agricultural systems and the household production of most domestic goods, the bulk of the farming population was scattered in small-scale villages organized around kin groups who relied on the middlemen economic brokers and political patrons at the secondary centers.

In the Pacific island chiefdoms, settlements tended to consist of small villages of closely related kinsmen scattered over the landscape in close proximity to coastal fishing resources and agricultural fields where taro, yams, banana, coconut, and breadfruit were intercropped. Unlike many complex polities, there were no large "towns" or "cities" with concentrated populations, but there were specialized settlements where chiefs resided (often with several wives, retainers, and artisans producing elite goods) or where community religious activities took place. At the center of the Tonga chiefdom between 1200 and 1500 was the large ceremonial and political center at Mu'a on the island of Tongatapu, consisting of an earthen fortification enclosing an area of almost 22,000 square miles, within which were large open spaces for ritual activities, coral-faced and stone-faced earthen tombs of chiefs, and numerous stepped earthen platforms (as high as about 16 feet) that probably supported perishable structures which were the aristocratic residences of chiefs, their kinsmen, priests and retainers.

In Tahiti these enclosed chiefs' ceremonial centers, known across the Pacific as *ahu* or *marae*, had stepped platforms more than 260 by 65 feet at their base and reaching a height of some 50 feet. Captain Cook described them as places of animal and human sacrifice by the high chiefs to propitiate the deities. On the northern island of New Zealand, Maori chiefs, their close associates, their wealth, and their precious stores of sweet potatoes and yams were housed in hilltop or ring-ditch fortified settlements known as *pa* (of which almost 6,000 have been recorded historically and archaeologically), while the vast majority of commoners lived undefended in scattered villages next to agricultural fields.

In focusing on settlement patterns in the large-scale empires, kingdoms, and chiefdoms of Asia and the Pacific, it is important to recognize that in many of the regions discussed, there was a mosaic of cultural groups that included smaller-scale tribal peoples, both swidden agriculturalists and hunter-gatherers, who lived in different types of ecological zones (mountainous areas or interior tropical or temperate forests) and had quite different settlement systems lacking the central place structures and specialized settlements of the complex polities that were their neighbors. Because many of these societies on the periphery of states were illiterate, we primarily rely on archaeological evidence and historic accounts of adjacent groups to construct a picture of their settlement systems in the medieval period.

In the Philippines (as elsewhere in Southeast Asia), upland tribal swidden agriculturalists like the Hanunoo and Magahat lived in small, one-roomed bamboo houses in semi-permanent villages of similar size (often less than 15 houses) scattered over the landscape near agricultural fields, with each village largely politically autonomous and providing for its own economic needs. Mobile rather than sedentary hunter-gatherer groups in the Philippines (such as the Agta) as well as the Ainu of northern Japan (an area marginal to the medieval shogunates farther south) and the whole continent of Australian aborigines had impermanent settlements that were moved periodically to different ecological zones to take advantage of the seasonal availability of resources. While the storable resources (for example, salmon and nuts) of the temperate zone Ainu allowed them to congregate in larger groups (as many as 100–150 people) and remain sedentary for most of the year, the tropical Southeast Asian hunter-gatherers and the Australian aborigines typically lived in small extended family groups (25–50) and sometimes moved their small settlements more than 12 times per year.

EUROPE

BY CHARLES W. ABBOTT

A full discussion of settlement patterns covers several phenomena. One is rural settlement structure: the arrangement of farmhouses relative to fields. Farmers can live clustered in villages and go out to their fields to work, or they can live isolated on individual farms, traveling into town to shop and meet friends. The rural settlement structure influences the texture of rural life. Combined with factors such as topography and vegetation, it contributes to a farming landscape's characteristic appearance—the way the landscape looks.

Another phenomenon is the size and spatial distribution of settlements: the structure of the urban system. (This is sometimes called "the urban system." The term *urban structure* refers to a separate topic: how a city is organized internally.) Economic geographers have analyzed and described such urban systems since the 1930s. The structure of the urban system is closely associated with still another phenomenon: patterns of urban dominance and the zones in which particular cities have their influence. A country can be dominated by one gigantic town (as France now is by Paris or Mexico by Mexico City). Alternatively, a country can be characterized by a larger number of medium-sized cities, more like contemporary Germany.

To fully characterize Europe's settlement patterns, we would need two types of data: periodic censuses of population over the entire continent, and periodic cadastral surveys (which show property boundaries and related information). With few exceptions we have neither of those data sets. In some cases we have fragmentary cadastral surveys, often reporting the value of holdings for tax purposes but without much care to describe their exact location. A great data set bequeathed from the Middle Ages is the *Domesday Book*, which exhaustively surveyed the land assets, population, and mills of England in 1086.

Despite shortcomings in data, we can sketch out basic stylized facts. Let us begin with a historic contrast. At the dawn of the Middle Ages, around 500 C.E., most of Europe was thinly populated, and the total population was perhaps 25 million. Mediterranean city populations had shrunk from their earlier peaks. Over most of Europe farmers lived in small clusters of homesteads or in farm hamlets. Settlements were often separated from one another by forest, marsh, and all the unused land known as waste. Trade and travel were perilous, and many local communities were largely self-sufficient.

Europe by 1300 looked very different. It was richer and more urbanized. Its population had probably tripled, and its urban population had doubled from 10 percent to 20 percent. In many areas of northwest Europe scattered farm hamlets had been replaced by nucleated village settlements surrounded by open fields, with the land cultivated by heavy plows into long, narrow strips (rather than rectangular farm fields).

A time traveler to 1300 from Imperial Rome might not have been surprised to see the cities of northern Italy but would have been stunned by the almost equally dense network of cities in Flanders (the region around today's northern Belgium and southern Netherlands). The rough parity of wealth between northern Europe and Mediterranean lands would have been a surprise as well. Northern lands had long been a Roman frontier, but by 1300 most of western Europe was fully occupied. The salient frontier was to the east, where German colonists had been settling. Areas in western Europe that in 500 had been undeveloped border regions or waste now hosted monasteries. Europe's forests had shrunk massively from 500, the land put to pasture or to the plow.

In 1300 medieval Europe was near its peak of development; the population made full use of arable land for crops and of forests for firewood. Climatic shifts after the 1310s brought colder, wetter weather, with recurrent famines after 1315. The three years from 1348 to 1351 saw the Black Death, or plague, kill roughly a third of Europe's population, resulting in pervasive changes in wage rates as well as more subtle changes in culture and politics. There was no social collapse after the plague, but many marginal farm settlements shrank or were abandoned—in Britain, Italy, France, and more peripheral areas. Marginal farmland might be converted to pasture, with survivors migrating to better lands or to towns, where high mortality rates opened up opportunities for those who were still alive.

During our entire time of interest medieval Europe was largely a land of peasant farmers, and the overall urbanization rate never topped 20 percent. The average family was intimately engaged in agriculture and produced a small surplus to support those who lived in cities and did not farm. The average family produced most of its goods and services itself or bought them from nearby specialists, such as the village blacksmith. Still, within these constraints patterns of human settlement varied widely from one European region or locale to the next. Herders spent much of the year in rustic camps with their flocks. Miners, fishermen, and woodsmen had their own settlements oriented to their resources. Different forms of agriculture and production generated their own characteristic landscapes, landscapes that often varied within 10 to 20 miles because of soils and topography. In addition, the lands of southern Europe close to the Mediterranean (especially Italy) were more heavily urbanized than the lands farther north. Urbanization was more deeply rooted there, as were traditions of urban governance; trade was facilitated by the Mediterranean Sea.

In parts of northwest Europe in the centuries between 800 and 1200 farmers gathered themselves (or were gathered by their lords) from scattered homesteads into nucleated villages surrounded by open fields. This landscape was associated with heavy clay soils and gentle topography, where mounted knights could operate easily and where feudal institutions became deeply rooted. Parts of southern England and the Midlands exhibited this pattern, as did portions of northern France and the Rhineland. Four key features went together: the nucleated village, the open fields surrounding it, feudal lords as rulers or managers, and soils requiring the heavy plow.

Much has been written about the "open field" system: individual strips lay side by side but were owned and cultivated by different households, without any fencing to separate them. Strips were cultivated individually, but in synch with a communal calendar. With the spread of the "three-field system," one field had spring-sown crops, one had fall-sown crops, and one was fallowed for the year and used for pasture. An economically viable household owned strips in all three fields. Farmers were forced to follow the general calendar. After harvest, cattle and sheep were turned out on the entire field.

Some scholars have discerned in the open-field system the goal of reduced individual inequality or have perceived it as a form of communal production. Most current interpretations stress greater individualism: strips were owned and managed privately, and households did not always own equal amounts of land. Those who stress the role of private enterprise (rather than communal labor) note that a market for

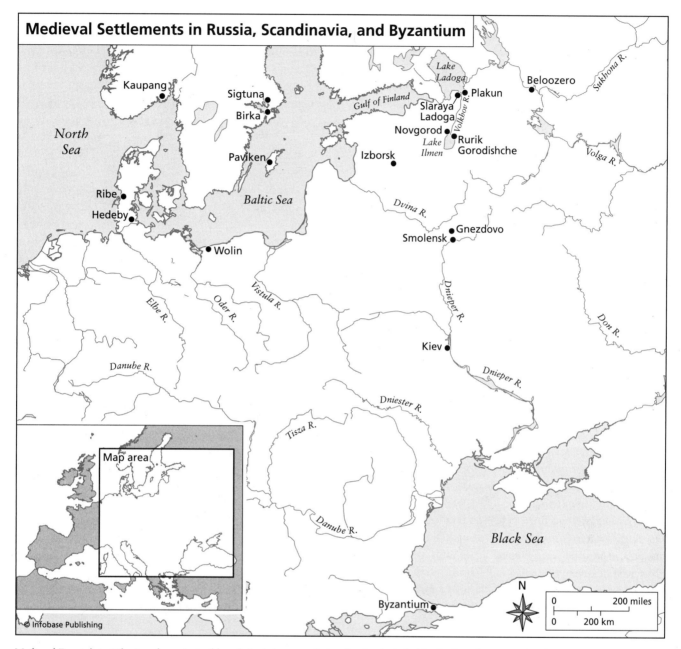

Medieval Settlements in Russia, Scandinavia, and Byzantium

Medieval Europe's peripheries, characterized by relatively low population density, included Spain, Scandinavia, most Alpine regions, Scotland, the Baltic, and eastern Europe more generally. People in these areas were engaged in economic activities that used land extensively, such as herding, stock raising, and growing grain for export. Some peripheral areas, such as the Baltic, eventually became large grain- and timber-exporting regions. This map shows the medieval settlements around the Baltic Sea and along key river routes in Russia.

plowing services and oxen hire was crucial in assembling the plow, team, and driver. The best interpretation of the open-field system is that it did not reflect communal production but was an elegant mix of public (grazing) and private (cultivation) property rights.

The open-field system, paradigmatic of the High Middle Ages, is characteristic of only parts of Europe. Not every place in Europe had them, nor did every place have the nucleated village—forested and hilly areas often did not, nor did regions with light and sandy soils. While Italy was full of cities, in some parts of Italy villages were absent, and farmhouses were in the fields. Many forest villages in Germany were "street villages," with houses spread out along a single street. If such a village enclosed a common grazing area, it took on a spindle shape and was known as an *Angerdorf*. As the German colonization of the east proceeded, settlers often established *Rundling*, or ring-fence, villages—houses facing outward in a ring, their backs defining a common grazing area for penning and keeping the livestock.

The difference between a village and town is not simply size but also function. A village might have been small, but in addition it was largely undifferentiated, a settlement of farmers. The mark of a town was not simply its larger size but its specialized tasks. Networks of towns existed in part to market agricultural products to urban inhabitants and to provide urban-based goods and services to farmers and rural dwellers. An architect might focus on a town's layout, and a demographer will ask how many people live there. An economic geographer will inquire how many different goods and services are sold in the town, how far people travel to do business there, and where the grain is shipped when it leaves the town market.

Farming villages blanketed the landscape with a certain regularity. A hierarchy of larger settlements emerged as well, especially as market exchange grew in importance. Nearby settlements provided a few basic services, while larger urban centers supplied a greater variety of services (including higher levels of government and ritual functions from specialized sites such as cathedrals).

Roads, canals, and seaborne shipping were the sinews of the urban system, and through them the 20 percent of Europeans who lived in cities and towns received their food. Europe thus possessed a network of towns that facilitated the marketing of food to feed lords, bishops, and other elites as well as urban-based craft workers. Urban crafts flowed in the other direction, from cities and towns to farm villages. The same basic arrangement held even if cities were parasitic on the peasantry, with urban elites commandeering food and returning little in exchange. It was only in the depths of the Viking Period (ca. 850–ca. 1050) that elites commonly imposed taxes in part by visiting various rural outposts in rotation with their retainers, eating their tax revenue from storehouses and then moving on to dine at another town.

Geographers characterize regions in terms of "core and periphery." Regional cores are characterized by high population densities, high incomes, concentrations of capital, the intensive use of land, and the presence of urban elites with considerable power and wealth. Peripheral areas are characterized by the opposite: lower populations, lower incomes (and also lower costs), and the extensive use of land relative to capital (grazing for meat and wool rather than market gardening or dairying, for example). Medieval Europe's core was centered on a line between its two most developed regions: northern Italy and Flanders. After 1114 seasonal trade fairs boomed midway between Italy and Flanders in Champagne, gradually fading after 1275 when seaborne trade linked Italian cities directly to the ports of the Atlantic.

The peripheries included Spain, Scandinavia, most Alpine regions, Scotland, the Baltic, and eastern Europe more generally. In the peripheral regions the population was much lower and engaged in economic activities that used land extensively, such as herding, stock raising, and growing grain for export. Some peripheral areas also came to specialize in activities such as labor migration—well before 1500, for example, Swiss men began leaving their mountain valleys to serve Italian counts as mercenaries. Much of Spain was devoted to the raising of sheep, with the wool manufactured into cloth in Flanders or Italy. Still other areas, such as the Baltic, eventually became large grain- and timber-exporting regions.

In Europe's core-periphery system, the network of towns and large cities grew sparser, and the towns grew smaller as one left Flanders or Lombardy and moved toward the periphery. Some researchers subscribe to the theory that dense farms, butter, and dairy production were near the core, while grains and lumber were produced in far regions accessible by sea. Cows, like Swiss mercenaries, could move out of the mountains on their own feet. A final factor worth noting is that cities had a higher mortality rate than rural areas and were not demographically self-sustaining until roughly the year 1800. Flows of food and raw wool were also matched by flows of young people moving toward towns and cities—only continual migration to towns enabled urban areas to maintain a constant population, let alone to grow in size.

THE ISLAMIC WORLD

BY BRADLEY A. SKEEN

In its origin Islam had a twin heritage of settlement patterns. Muhammad, the founder of Islam, was urban. He came from the Arabian city of Mecca and began to spread the new religion in the neighboring city of Medina. He also lived in exile for a time in the Ethiopian city of Axum. At the same time, the bulk of the population of the Arabian Peninsula, the first generation of converts, were nomadic tribesmen who lived by transhumance with herds kept on the Arabian plateau. Muhammad's ancestral occupation as a merchant took him to the Byzantine cities of the Mediterranean coast but also familiarized him with the camel caravans that crossed the Arabian deserts and that depended on the nomadic cultures of the region. The later history of Islam in the Middle Ages took place among both nomads and urbanites and was propagated, in part, through the interactions of the two ways of life. Muhammad also laid the ideological foundation for a third type of settlement pattern, the slave plantation. While these came about in the Islamic world as a result of the astounding military conquests of the seventh and eighth centuries,

Muhammad not only permitted slavery (as evidenced in the Koran) but also engaged in slave trading himself.

The homeland of Islam was in the Arabian Peninsula. Arabia, at more than 1.2 million square miles, is more than five times the size of California. Most of it is desert with huge expanses of dune seas, but the Nejd central plateau provided pasturage for horses, camels, sheep, and goats. At the beginning of the Middle Ages most Arabs lived in tribal groups devoted to nomadic animal husbandry in this area. Since the end of the last ice age more than 9,000 years earlier, the tropical regions of North Africa and Arabia had been undergoing increasing desertification. At the same time, the relatively rich agricultural system of Arabia produced an ever-growing population. Because of these two trends, waves of out-migration from Arabia have helped to shape the Near East since the earliest historical times. Migrants regularly moved, sometimes as conquerors, into the settled areas to the north, Mesopotamia and the Levant. The Semitic language group originated in Arabia but eventually became dominant throughout the Near East because of the out-migration. The Islamic conquests may be seen as the last out-migration of this kind.

Some Arab nomads worked in the caravan trade that crossed the northern part of the Arabian desert, trading goods between Mesopotamia and the Mediterranean coast and along the Red Sea coast, where frankincense, myrrh, and spices grew. There was also a trade in dates grown at desert oases. There were a string of small cities around the coast of the Arabian Peninsula that thrived on the overland trade of the peninsula and on the Indian Ocean trade between East and West. Mecca and Medina were among these cities.

The Arabia unified under Muhammad's rule (632 C.E) was essentially a pastoral society. Within 10 years the Islamic Caliphate found itself in possession of the entire Near East, from Thebes in Egypt to the mouth of the Tigris-Euphrates on the Persian Gulf, one of the most densely populated areas on earth. The region contained several large cities with populations of half a million or more (Alexandria, Antioch, and Babylon, among them). The bulk of the population, however, lived in small villages devoted to settled agriculture. The population represented a variety of language groups and ethnicities and was also religiously diverse, including Orthodox, Monophysite, and Nestorian Christians, "pagans," Jews, Manicheans, Zoroastrians, and small minority groups such as the Mandaeans. Under those circumstances there was some uncertainty about how to proceed.

The way of life of the conquered peoples seemed completely alien to the Arabian nomads. Their experience did not prepare them to understand the use of cities and farmland.

Moreover, the Arabs' new subjects did not practice the same religion that the Arabs themselves had fervently and recently adopted. Just as when the nomadic Mongols conquered urban and agricultural areas in northern China, serious thought was given to simply slaughtering or enslaving the population and clearing the land for pasturage. Cooler heads prevailed, however, and it was decided to let the peasants keep their land but as tenants, paying taxes to the Islamic state. In fact, very heavy taxes were imposed on the conquered people as non-Moslems, and they were often exacted in an unnecessarily brutal manner, through tax collectors and other officials insisting on bribes above the legally required payments and with the payment of taxes accompanied by public beatings— to remind the subjects that they were conquered people. The kind of oppressive treatment that the *dhimmi* or "peoples of the book" (Christians and Jews) suffered naturally led to frequent revolts in the first century or so of the Islamic conquest, especially in Egypt.

The conquered populations nevertheless presented still other problems. They were still not Muslims, and it was not immediately apparent whether compelling or even allowing them to convert was desirable. The compromise worked out to solve this problem was to found special garrison towns in the conquered territories that would allow Arab soldiers to live in isolation among the conquered populations. These garrisons included Kufa and Basra in Iraq and Fustat in Egypt, which was eventually incorporated into the later foundation of Cairo. These towns initially allowed the Arab population to maintain their traditional tribe and clan structures without their social cohesion being dissolved into the larger group of the conquered populations of the cities. Fustat was purposely built out of the remains of looted antiquities, such as the limestone facing of the pyramids, in order to emphasize the triumph of the new Islamic civilization. For the same reason, Basra was built on the site of an ancient Sassanian city that had been razed.

The revolts were ruthlessly put down. By the 10th and 11th centuries much of the problem presented by the subject peoples had been resolved as a majority (but by no means all) had converted to Islam. (Conversions seem to have been especially common after the massacres necessary to put down revolts.) Even so, the converts, called *mawali* in Arabic, faced discrimination for generations because they were still left outside the Arab social system and were only more gradually integrated into it.

By the ninth and 10th centuries Arab civilization had become reconciled to urban living, and the original garrison town had turned into important multiethnic cities with vibrant cultural and economic institutions. The later foundations of Baghdad (762) and Cairo (969) became two of the greatest cities in the medieval world, in terms of both their size (both with over 500,000 inhabitants) and their cultural achievements.

Outside of the initial Arab conquests in the Near East, the spread of Islamic civilization had an important influence on local settlement patterns. Although the Maghreb (northern Africa west of Egypt) had been conquered in the seventh century, the Fatimid rulers of Egypt unleashed a fresh wave of Arabic pastoralist tribes from Arabia into the area in the 12th century, owing to sectarian differences with the local rulers. These Banu Hilal tribes devastated the area and actually took much land out of agricultural production and turned it to pastoral use. On the other hand, the Arab colony in Spain, al-Andalus (711–1492), took on a sophisticated urban character in the great cultural centers of Seville, Córdoba and Granada. South of the Sahara, Djenné and Timbuktu became large mercantile cities and important centers for the spread of Islam to Africa through the madrassas at Sankore and other mosques.

The situation along the other axis of Islamic expansion, toward inner Asia, was quite different in its effects on settlement patterns. In this region most of the population was made up of Iranian or Turkic tribesmen who lived as nomads. They readily converted to Islam, perhaps because it seemed well suited to their way of life. The Seljuk and Ottoman Turks, originally brought into the Near East as mercenaries, went on to conquer and rule much of the Islamic world. Most Mongols outside of China eventually converted to Islam also, although their raids under Genghis Khan and his successors through inner Asia as far as Egypt in the 13th century led to a terrible economic and demographic collapse from which the northeastern Islamic world never recovered, with most of the Islamic cities in the area destroyed or greatly reduced in population. The Islamic cultural and political capital of Baghdad was sacked by the Mongols (1258) and never recovered its former prominence.

A third settlement pattern that the Arabs encouraged was plantation slavery. This practice had been invented by the Carthaginians in antiquity in order to exploit the vast agricultural resources of the Maghreb in North Africa. A relatively small population of masters and overseers (whose homes were most likely in nearby cities) lived on large estates in the countryside that were worked by hundreds or thousands of slaves, who lived on the estate in barracks little different from stables. Once they conquered North Africa in the second century B.C.E., the Romans took over the practice, referring to it as the *latifundia* system. It was later adopted by the Arabs when their military officers acquired large estates seized from the conquered peoples of the Near East. The concentration and mistreatment of slaves on these kinds of plantations led to a major slave revolt of East African captives (mainly from the Zandj region opposite Zanzibar) on a sugar plantation near Basra in 869 that lasted until 883 and had to be suppressed by military action. Muhammad's teaching that manumission of slaves was a pious action in itself and his instruction that only prisoners of war who refused to convert to Islam could be enslaved were for the most part ignored in the face of the immense profits available from trading and working slaves in a plantation system.

See also AGRICULTURE; ARCHITECTURE; BORDERS AND FRONTIERS; BUILDING TECHNIQUES AND MATERIALS; CITIES, CLIMATE AND GEOGRAPHY; CRAFTS; ECONOMY; EMPLOYMENT AND LABOR; FAMILY; FORESTS AND FORESTRY; GOVERNMENT ORGANIZATION; HOUSEHOLD GOODS; HUNTING, FISHING, AND GATHERING; LANGUAGE; MIGRATION AND POPULATION MOVEMENTS; MILITARY; MINING, QUARRYING, AND SALT MAKING; NATURAL DISASTERS; NOMADIC AND PASTORAL SOCIETIES; OCCUPATIONS; RELIGION AND COSMOLOGY; RESISTANCE AND DISSENT; ROADS AND BRIDGES; SACRED SITES; SCANDALS AND CORRUPTION; SEAFARING AND NAVIGATION; SLAVES AND SLAVERY; SOCIAL COLLAPSE AND ABANDONMENT; SOCIAL ORGANIZATION; STORAGE AND PRESERVATION; TOWNS AND VILLAGES; TRADE AND EXCHANGE; TRANSPORTATION; WAR AND CONQUEST.

FURTHER READING

Paul Bairoch, *Cities and Economic Development: From the Dawn of History to the Present*, trans. Christopher Braider (Chicago: University of Chicago Press, 1988).

Neville H. Chittick, *Manda: Excavations at an Island Port on the Kenya Coast* (Nairobi, Kenya: British Institute in Eastern Africa, 1984).

William E. Deal, *Handbook to Life in Medieval and Early Modern Japan* (New York: Oxford University Press, 2006).

Tom Dillehay, *The Settlement of the Americas: A New Prehistory* (New York: Basic Books, 2000).

Erwin A. Gutkind, ed., *International History of City Development*, 8 vols. (New York: Free Press of Glencoe, 1964–1972).

John Haywood, *Penguin Historical Atlas of Ancient Civilizations* (New York: Viking Penguin, 2005).

Paul M. Hohenberg and Lynn Hollen Lees, *The Making of Urban Europe, 1000–1994* (Cambridge, Mass.: Harvard University Press, 1995).

Richard Jones and Mark Page, *Medieval Villages in an English Landscape: Beginnings and Ends* (Macclesfield, U.K.: Windgatherer Press, 2006).

Heng Chye Kiang, *Cities of Aristocrats and Bureaucrats: The Development of Medieval Chinese Cityscapes* (Honolulu: University of Hawaii Press, 1999).

Harry A. Miskimin, "People, Food, and Space: Urban Size and the Late Medieval Economy," *History Teacher*, 27, no. 4 (1994): 391–403.

David Nicholas, *Urban Europe, 1100–1700* (New York: Palgrave Macmillan, 2003).

Charles S. Orwin and Christabel S. Lowry Orwin, *The Open Fields* (Oxford, U.K.: Clarendon Press, 1967).

Sydney Pollard, *Marginal Europe: The Contribution of Marginal Lands since the Middle Ages* (New York: Oxford University Press, 1997).

Norman J. G. Pounds, *An Historical Geography of Europe* (New York: Cambridge University Press, 1990).

Peter Robertshaw, *Early Pastoralists of South-Western Kenya* (Nairobi, Kenya: British Institute in Eastern Africa, 1990).

Marilyn Silberfein, ed., *Rural Settlement Structure and African Development* (Boulder, Colo.: Westview Press, 1998).

Evon Z. Vogt and Richard M. Leventhal, eds., *Prehistoric Settlement Patterns: Essays in Honor of Gordon R. Willey* (Albuquerque: University of New Mexico Press, 1983).

Gordon Randolph Willey, ed., *Prehistoric Settlement Patterns in the New World* (Westport, Conn.: Greenwood Press, 1981).

► ships and shipbuilding

INTRODUCTION

Ships and boats expanded the horizons of medieval people. With them, people could step beyond the boundaries of oceans, lakes, rivers, marshes, and swamps into places otherwise inaccessible to them. In central Africa boats enabled people in dense forests to create societies that extended for hundreds of miles near rivers and to build trade economies in which boats carried traders and their goods to trading towns along rivers. In the Americas boats allowed Mayan culture to spread along the coasts of mainland Mesoamerica and as far as islands in the Caribbean. In China boats gave people mastery of inland waterways that helped them transport goods and people for thousands of miles, and in India boats were essential to moving products on rivers to ports where the products could be loaded on seagoing vessels.

For the Islamic world boats and ships carried not only goods and passengers but also knowledge and technology, as well as offering Muslims real-life adventures to exotic lands. Without transportation on rivers and seas many of the faithful would not have been able to make required pilgrimages to the holy city of Mecca. In medieval Europe boats and ships became part of a vast network of trade, and European developments in shipbuilding reveal to the modern historian an arms race in which control of the sea could make empires. Perhaps the most amazing feats of seamanship were accomplished by Polynesians in their settlement of the Pacific on sturdy, well-balanced boats built to withstand the terrors of the ocean.

Environment had a profound effect on the technology of shipbuilding in the medieval world. Various environments required different solutions to the problems posed by navigating waters. In forests in the Americas and Africa travel by boat was often the fastest, safest method. Big ships would have been unsuitable to maneuvering in winding rivers among dense forests; that both Americans and Africans should create the canoe as a solution to traveling in places where small boats would have significant advantages over large ones is not surprising: Cultures in the Americas and Africa devised canoes that were narrow and light, for quick movement of small numbers of people and small loads of goods. Environment was not alone in influencing the building of boats and ships. Cultures put their own special demands on boats and ships. For instance, in western and central Africa cultures built war canoes—big canoes used to convey warriors swiftly along waterways, allowing armies to attack quickly and to maneuver around enemies that were shielded by swamps and rivers.

Of the developments in seafaring technology during the medieval era the most significant may have been the planking technique used for European caravels, the invention of bulkheads, the adaptation of the compass for navigation in open seas, the development of multiple masts with several sails, and the use of square sails in addition to triangular ones. All represented leaps forward in shipbuilding. The technique of creating a frame onto which planks were nailed edge to edge made for light, strong ships and gave European caravels an edge in technology in the late 1400s that allowed their ships to dominate the oceans of Asia as well as Europe. It also permitted a small European power such as Portugal to take control of major sea routes and Europeans to sail with confidence to the Americas. In a race to catch up to European shipbuilding, the use of planks and nails on frames was adapted to their ships by Asian sea powers.

Another significant development in shipbuilding technology probably began in China with the creation of bulkheads, which, during a storm or after an accident, gave Chinese ships an advantage over others by containing flooding to a single chamber in the case of a breach in the hull or deck. This development would become essential in shipbuilding, permitting ships to better endure the hazards of the oceans; when coupled with the compass, it would allow ships to be built bigger and to range farther away from shore, creating new sea-lanes for commerce. These shipbuilding technologies resulted in significant social changes; those cultures that did not adapt the advanced technologies tended to become marginalized. For instance, the city-states of East Africa declined in part because the ships of their Arab trading partners, who controlled the trading lanes along eastern Africa's coast, lost that control to sturdier caravels, whose frames gave them space to carry not only more cargo but also cannons for attack as well as defense.

AFRICA

BY MICHAEL J. O'NEAL

The chief problem historians and archaeologists have with studying ships and shipbuilding practices in medieval sub-Saharan Africa is that any such watercraft the people may have built were made of nondurable materials. These materials probably included reeds, poles, bark, and logs. Because they are nondurable, they decay over time, so the archaeological record is thin.

Accordingly, historians and archaeologists have to rely on other sources. One is language. If the language spoken by a people contained words that referred to boats or rafts, then clearly those people used such watercraft. However, in some language groups there were no such words. One good example is the Bantu-speaking peoples of southeast Africa. To the extent that historians can know for certain, it appears that these people did not use watercraft of any type, for the language did not contain words for boat, raft, or other watercraft. For fishing purposes, they used traps and weirs (fences placed in a river or stream for catching fish) and did not venture out into the waters of a river on a craft.

A second method is artwork. Some examples exist of artwork that depicts watercraft and people using them. Some of this artwork is in the form of rock art that dates back to ancient times; however, it is likely that cultures continued to build similar watercraft into the medieval period. It is believed, for example, that the Tongan-speaking people used canoes for purposes of trade along river routes. Although they did not always speak the same language as those with whom they traded, evidence suggests that they rowed the canoes to the banks of the river near the trading community and then indicated their presence through whistles and similar noises. After the nearby people brought goods for trade, the rowers moved along to the next community. A 16th-century painting depicts this process, though it is unknown which tribe the rowers of the boat were from.

A third method, related to the second, is to rely on the testimony of European explorers, such as the Portuguese, as well as the testimony of Islamic explorers. In the 16th and 17th centuries numerous Portuguese explorers roamed the continent. In their travel accounts, they often mention boats and rafts. In most cases, these primitive craft were used by fishermen. Explorers also made drawings of people using watercraft, and in some instances, they took back to Europe models they had made of the craft.

In southern and East Africa most of these craft were very simple. They consisted primarily of rafts and canoes. Rafts were made by lashing together lengths of wood or poles. Canoes were made from bark or from dugout logs. In the case of bark canoes, sheets of bark from such trees as the cottonwood—the bark of which comes off in sheets rather than in fragments—were lashed to a frame made of sticks. A sheet of bark was first heated to make it more flexible. In the case of dugout canoes, the size of the canoe was limited only by the size of available and suitable trees. In most cases throughout Africa boats were not propelled by rowing—that is, by oars fixed to the boat and pulled by a rower sitting backward. Rather, they were propelled by paddling, with the paddler facing forward, or by punting—that is, propelled by a long pole pushed into the riverbed or lake bed. While many such canoes were quite small, capable of carrying perhaps only two persons, some were up to 80 feet in length and could carry as many as 100 people. Most such craft were used on inland waterways, but along the Guinea coast and the Gold Coast fishermen ventured up to several miles at sea.

In addition to dugout canoes, boats made of lashed-together reeds were used on Lake Chad. On the East African coast dhows were in common use. The dhow was borrowed from North Africa and was usually a small boat with a triangular sail and a low mast. Some of the ships built in this region were in fact large, possibly as large as ancient Greek galleys and Scandinavian longboats. They were not as seaworthy, though, because they did not have an interior frame to give them support and to withstand the buffeting of heavy seas.

In this respect, historians distinguish among many different kinds of medieval boats. One of the distinctions they make is between boats with some kind of skeleton, or framework, and those that were merely a shell. In general, medieval African boats were of the shell variety. Even boats made of reeds were shell-like, and they floated because they were coated with some type of waterproof material.

In west-central Africa boats were more complex, primarily because many of the cultures that flourished in the region—Mali, Songhai, Ghana, Benin—were riverine cultures, depending on the Niger River and its tributaries for food, transportation, and trade. Evidence has been found that the people in this region made boats out of planks of wood and that the edges of the planks were rabbeted to form a tighter fit, then caulked to keep out the water. The boards were hewn with an adze, a chopping and carving tool made with a thin blade attached at right angles to a handle. Some of these boats may have been up to 60 feet long and had a carrying capacity of 6 tons. While western Africa made extensive use of plank boats, some evidence suggests that plank boats were also used in East Africa.

The Songhai culture made extensive use of boats and canoes, as did its predecessor, the kingdom of Mali. Much of the region was densely forested, making wood widely available for the construction of boats. Further, the population would have been highly motivated to used boats and canoes because of the nature of the terrain. Such was particularly true during the rainy season, when rivers ran high and the area was dotted with lakes, pools, lagoons, and marshes. Water transport was often the most efficient way to travel and to import supplies from outlying regions to the kingdom's cities. Even in the modern world boats are a primary means of transportation in the nation of Mali.

One of the tribes that the Songhai subdued was the Sorko. One of the primary duties of the Sorko was to build and operate boats on the Niger and throughout the kingdom. Some of these boats were dugout canoes. Others were plank boats called *kanta*. These boats were used to transport such commodities as rice but were also used as transportation for the kingdom's elite families. Considerable evidence, including testimony by later European and Islamic travelers, notes that a common occurrence was for goods to be carried by human porters along footpaths to the edges of rivers. There the goods would be loaded into boats for transportation to city markets.

THE AMERICAS
BY LAWRENCE WALDRON

Most of the watercraft used by Amerindians in the Common Era had been developed much earlier. The canoes, kayaks, umiaks, rafts, and reed boats of the Common Era all had their origins in very similar vessels used by archaic Indians. Nevertheless, Amerindian watercraft and their uses continued to evolve in response to the changing conditions of the people. As some ethnic groups migrated inland, they either eliminated watercraft as unnecessary or adapted large, sturdy seacraft to rivers, rapids, and swamps. The design, building materials, function, and size of watercraft all came under review from time to time as Indians changed their lifestyle, territory, or trading patterns. By far the most powerful factor affecting boat design was the craft's usefulness in obtaining food. Tied to these practical considerations, some boats became increasingly streamlined, lightweight, or maneuverable. Others became larger and sturdier in order to transport large crews and payloads, sometimes over much longer distances.

By the beginning of the Common Era there were several different varieties of stretched-skin boats in use throughout the varied environments of present-day Canada and the United States. As some groups adopted the technology of the skin boat, they also quickly changed its material construction to better suit their environment and the materials available to them.

The Indians of the North American woodlands may have adopted the idea of making boats by stretching membranes over wooden armatures from their westerly neighbors, the

Plains Indians. Crow and Arikara hunters and traders had been using such boats from ancient times, made by stretching a bison hide over a bentwood frame. However, Woodland Indians such as the Cayuga, Ojibwa, Micmac, and many Iroquois groups had no regular access to large mammals so they found an ingenious substitute. Theirs was a skin boat made not of animal hide but of tree bark. While tree bark might seem to be either too delicate or too brittle for use as a boatbuilding material, certain species of trees provide a hardy bark that can be soaked or beaten into a strong and flexible membrane.

Women usually did the fine but tedious work of preparing the bark and tying it to the gunwales with roots or animal sinew. Young men then bent and fastened the wooden frame into the desired shapes. In some cases crossbeams, thwarts, and other parts of the frame were forced into the hull only after it had been sewn together by the women. In this way the hull was stretched to an extreme tautness. Tree resin, animal fat, or both was then added to the stitching to waterproof the vessel.

Eastern Woodland Indians favored elm, birch, and linden bark. Some western groups, such as the northern Shoshone and Bannock ethnicities, also developed these bark vessels after switching from the wooden dugout canoes they had used before the Common Era. What distinguished many Woodland bark boats was that they did not follow the umiak and kayak design favored by earlier groups for stretched-hide craft. Rather, Woodlands boatbuilders used bark to construct a type of craft otherwise made only in wood, the canoe. This small, fast-moving bark canoe weighed no more than a small child and could be hoisted out of the water and carried from one river to another. Thus Woodland Indians moved across their territories with seemingly no more difficulty on water than on land.

Throughout much of the Americas and many of the Caribbean islands, the dugout canoe was the watercraft of choice. This often flat-bottomed vessel was easily adaptable to South American rivers, Mexican swamps, island-to-mainland ferrying, and even the open seas of the Caribbean and Gulf of Mexico. It had no rudder and was steered by boaters who used paddles that allowed them to face in the direction they were traveling. While canoes in North America often featured a pointed prow, those farther south, from the Rio Grande to the Amazon, tended to vary greatly in shape.

Classic Maya ceramic pots depict both historic and mythical figures riding in canoes with raised prows and sterns that curl upward and outward, serving not only as a decorative flourish but also to prevent splashing water from entering the hull. Maya imagery also illustrates a rather snub-nosed variety of canoe, which seemed to retain more of the purely cylindrical proportions of the tree from which it had been hewn. Central American canoes south of the Maya and South American canoes could be likewise cylindrical, lozenge shaped, or nearly rectangular. Some featured a narrow, flattened shelf along the gunwales, prow, or stern. Canoes found along the South American coasts and Caribbean islands featured a pot-bellied design in which the center of the hull was far wider than the extreme ends of the vessel.

In making a dugout canoe, a tree of a suitable variety and size was selected and felled. An oily or resinous species, such as Spanish cedar, was preferred because it could withstand water seepage and rotting. Trees could vary in height from those that would yield the typical 10- or 20-passenger to the 80- to 100-passenger canoes used by Carib and Maya seafarers. Once felled, the tree's bark was removed, after which the canoe could be fashioned by some reductive process. In one such process used by the Aztec and many others throughout the circum-Caribbean and South America, contained fires were set along the upside of the stripped log in order to render the wood there brittle and workable. Adzes were then used to chip away the fragile charcoal, leaving the characteristic dugout hull.

This cavity could be deepened by further charring but could also be stretched outward by another process involving saturation with hot water. Water was poured into the newly carved hull, after which hot rocks were dropped into the water. The hot, steaming liquid would render the wooden fibers of the carved log elastic, causing the hull to expand outward. The result was a canoe whose hull was rounded halfway along its length and wider than the tree from which it was originally carved.

Perhaps the most unusual American watercrafts were those developed by Andean Indians in ancient times but which have been used throughout the Common Era up to the present. Inca and other indigenous boatmen paddled or poled small reed boats across the sprawling Lake Titicaca. In these fibrous vessels Peruvian and Bolivian pilots transported family members, foodstuffs, and even their llamas. Fishermen also cast their nets into the lake from these buoyant vessels and either loaded on or hauled their catch home behind them.

The boats were fashioned from four or more bundles of totora reeds, a kind of thick grass that grew along the shores of slow-moving bodies of fresh water. The reeds were lashed together into a canoe-like shape, with an upward-curling prow and stern. Typically, a reed boat could last up to a year before it rotted or became waterlogged. The biodegradable vessel could then be used for any number of purposes, from fire kindling to construction filler. Since reed boats were quite narrow, lakeshore Andeans could not use them for all their

transportation needs. To supplement their fleets of reed boats, the Inca also built flat balsa log rafts for transporting much larger amounts of goods and animals across the vast expanses of Lake Titicaca. It is worth noting that while the unusual reed boat seems to have developed only in the Andes, it had a North American analogue in the marshlands of California. There, the Yokut Indians used *tule* grass to make rafts, which were similarly buoyant and biodegradable.

By the time of the European encounter, Native Americans had not developed large ships with masts, sails, compartmentalized bulkheads, or the like. Though maritime trade connections existed all along the western shores of the Americas and across the Caribbean Sea, Amerindians seem to have felt neither need for nor interest in explorations beyond the coastal and Caribbean archipelagos. Disconnected from other landmasses where maritime technologies had been circulating for millennia, Indians developed instead a unique variety of small vessels tailor-made to American trading, fishing, and hunting needs.

In turn, early European settlers observed that native watercrafts were much better suited to inland river travel than their large ships. They often adopted the technology of Indian vessels wholesale so that many designs remained virtually unchanged throughout the colonial period. Even the nomenclature of these Indian vessels was retained so that kayaks and umiaks are still called by those names and likewise the Arawak word *canoa* has been adopted to refer to a variety of vessels throughout the Americas, now generically called canoes.

ASIA AND THE PACIFIC

BY KENNETH HALL

Ships and local watercraft were crucial in the development of Asian and Pacific societies. Small dugouts and hulled wooden ships that have been recovered among regional coastal archaeological sites are smaller versions of the watercraft that dominated the trade route between Africa and China during the era before 1000 C.E. These were the prototypes for the Southeast Asian *jong*, China Sea junks, and western Indian Ocean dhows that European navigators encountered when they arrived in the 16th century.

During the medieval age Asians built, owned, and navigated ships that were often of considerable size and were the preferred source of transport for the international trade in the India-to-China maritime passageway. In the Middle East–to–India portion of this route, variations of the Middle Eastern and Indian dhows were preferred; from roughly 800 to 1000 the dhow was prominent among vessels sailing between India and China. From 1000 the Malay *jong* was the prototype for the large Chinese junks of up to 1,000 tons carrying capacity, which with redesigned *jong* were then preeminent in providing transport to the increased volume of trade merchandise along the India-to-China route.

During the medieval era Malayo-Polynesian seafarers continued to navigate the Pacific in ingeniously designed and built double-outrigger canoes. These boats consisted of two hulls connected by lashed crossbeams and covered with a central platform. Although referred to as a canoe, the vessel was wind-driven, using sails made of natural fiber matting. The two hulls gave the craft incredible stability and resiliency in the open ocean as well as the capacity to transport people and supplies over long distances. A medium-size boat 50 to 60 feet long could accommodate two dozen people and their belongings, including plants and animals to be introduced on the new islands they settled. Many 21st-century Polynesian sailors continue to use boats with the same basic design.

One sailing ship relief carved on central Java's ninth-century Buddhist stupa at Borobudur shows a sophisticated medium-size ship that used multiple masts, at least two types of sails (a canted square sail and a lugsail), a spritsail, quarter rudders, outriggers, and paddles that stuck out of portholes. A second Borobudur relief depicts similar ships but without outriggers. This second relief is consistent with contemporary cave paintings from Ajanta in western India, which show large, multi-masted ocean vessels without outriggers. The Chinese imperial records and the accounts of Chinese Buddhist pilgrims speak of the *kunlun bo*, "Southeast Asian ships," sailed by multiethnic Southeast Asia–based seamen that visited China's ports and provided most of the transport for China's Buddhist pilgrims en route to Southeast Asia and India from roughly 300 to 1000. The largest ones were said to be more than 164 feet in length and stood out of the water 13 to 15.4 feet and were thought to carry up to 600 to 700 persons with 10,000 bushels of cargo (250–1,000 tons). Like the ships depicted in the Borobudur reliefs, these ships had up to four sails made from natural fibers that were set in an off-center, oblique row so that they could better maximize the wind currents and sail at maximum speed during the Asian monsoon seasons.

Based on the evidence supplied by recoveries of early shipwrecks, it is now confirmed that before 1000 Southeast Asian *jong* and Chinese junks were constructed of several layers of thin, horizontal planks, normally up to 200 feet in length and lashed together using cords made from the fibers of a coconut; the several layers provided reinforcement against an outer plank breaking. Because of the shortage of iron in the shipbuilding areas of Southeast Asia, nails and clamps were not used. Chinese accounts report that this was also because of local belief that the heating used in the production of iron would give rise to shipboard fires. The resil-

Mountain and river landscape: sailing before the wind; ink on silk panel, Ming Dynasty, China, 1368–1644 (Freer Gallery of Art, Smithsonian Institution, Gift of Charles Lang Freer, F1916-136)

ient saltwater-soaked fiber lashing was preferred because it would not rust or pop out in a storm.

Recoveries of shipwrecks at South China Sea and Melaka Strait archaeological sites confirm these literary accounts.

Southeast Asian ships and boats had planks and frames fastened together with coconut palm ropes; the ship hulls were built by attaching planks on each side of a raised rib that was attached to a center keel. "Sewn plank" ships had stitches of fiber rope passing through holes drilled near the planks' edges within the seams. "Lashed lug" ships had the insides of their planks cut out so that the planks could be lashed to the ship frame. In either case, the frame of Southeast Asian ships was not watertight. These sewn and lashed ships were adequate for the luxury trade of the era before 1000, but new opportunities that came with the increased volume of the maritime trade route in the Song era, made this technology inadequate.

By the 13th and 14th centuries new dowel-fitted teak ships—which the initial 16th-century Portuguese visitors called *junco,* the transcription of the Malay *jong* and Chinese junk—provided greater rigidity for the ocean crossings of larger boats with a carrying capacity of up to 1,000 tons. These ships towered over the smaller Portuguese *nau* that had a carrying capacity of 400 tons. Common to the earlier *jong,* the new ships were neither nailed nor lashed but were built using up to three layers of planks held together by wooden dowels that were inserted from the inside into holes drilled at the seams. Southeast Asian *jong* had three to four sails (a bowsprit sail, a spritsail, a canted square sail, and a lugsail) made of woven rattan (bark fiber) and three rudders, one on each side and one in the middle, in contrast to the Portuguese, Chinese, Middle Eastern, and Indian ships of that era that used a single, stem-post rudder.

In contrast, Chinese junks built after 1000 did not have a keel at their center and were flat-bottomed. They had a single, large stern-mounted rudder (in contrast to the two Southeast Asian *jong* quarter rudders), which could be adjusted up or down according to the depth of the water. The rear rudder was critical to the junk's stability and was so large that up to three men had to control it during storms. Leeboards and centerboards attached to the hull also helped to stabilize the *junk.* By the 15th century the heavy rear rudders had holes drilled in them to allow for greater maneuverability.

The most notable feature the junk of that era was its watertight hold, separated by bulkheads, which reduced the likelihood of sinking should a single hole be made in the hull. Each division of the hold could be reached through separate hatches and ladders. This also allowed the spatial separation of different types of cargoes and differentiated human living space from transported commodities. By the 15th century Chinese ships had square-pallet bilge pumps that were used to pump water seepage from their holds. Like the *jong,* a junk's navigational flexibility resulted from its multiple rectangular sails (battens—from three to 12 on the largest junks), which could be readily angled, whether moved inward toward the ship's center to allow the junk to sail into the wind (by letting the wind cross the sail and pull it forward, similar to the uplift that occurs when wind crosses an airplane wing), or outward allowing the sails to catch the fullness of the wind currents from the rear.

Chinese ships hung flags from their masts both as identification and for good luck. Red and other brightly colored flags with Chinese writing on them were intended to please the dragon that Chinese sailors believed lived in the clouds, so the dragon would not cause endangering typhoons and other storms. All Chinese ships depended on the compass for navigation, supplemented by the sailors' knowledge of the stars and constellations and the detailed navigational charts that were critical to the movements of Chinese shipping—among these were the massive Ming "treasure fleets" commanded by the eunuch admiral Zheng He from 1405 to 1433. By the 15th century large freight-carrying China- and India-based junks and Java-based *jong* dominated the bulk carrying trade, supplemented by smaller vessels modeled on the *jong* or junk, which were based in the ports of Myanmar (Burma), Thailand, the Straits of Melaka, Vietnam, Korea, and Japan. These smaller regional craft frequently used slave laborers as sailors and were known for their acts of piracy as well as their alternative role as cargo carriers.

The largest ships were designed to maximize profits in the peaceful bulk-carrying trade, but lacked the speed to flee, outmaneuver, and combat the firepower of the earliest Portuguese and Spanish ships (only the early 15th-century Ming fleet had mounted cannons). After the arrival of the Europeans, Southeast Asian shipbuilders in Burma, Thailand, and Java built galleys of less than 200 tons capacity for military combat and constructed smaller and cannon-armed *jong* and junks that were able to neutralize the initial European advantage.

In the western Indian Ocean and in coastal India, several regional variants of the dhow were preeminent. The "Arab" dhows were commonly built in the Middle East and South Asia with a high stern and side rails sweeping low toward the bow before rising to a characteristic jutting prow. The largest medieval-era dhows reached up to 115 feet in length and could carry 400 tons. They had a rear rudder and a yoke-type steering gear system with chains leading from the ends of the yoke to the steering wheel. Dhows had two lateen (triangular) sails, in a fore-and-aft rig, unlike the square rig characteristic of early European sailing ships or the rectangular sails common to *jong* and junks. These lateen sails allowed the dhow to sail into the wind; as the wind crossed the sails that were filled with air the ship was pulled ahead.

Like the *jong,* the dhow was constructed from a center keel. It was not watertight with holds like the junk, but instead like the *jong* had coconut husks packed into its seams, which swelled when wet to prevent water seepage. Dhow construction started with the hull planking and later added the reinforcing framework. This planking had to be supported during construction, which required temporary supporting ribs or templates on the outside. As in the eastern Indian Ocean, the dhow sideboard planking was lashed or sewn together using coconut fiber cord acquired from India, which had been soaked in saltwater to give it strength. Teak from southern India was the preferred wood for dhow construction, and early dhows had teak masts that leaned forward a bit to catch the wind better and which also allowed their use in the loading and unloading of cargo. A feature unique to the dhow was its "thunderbox," the barrel-shaped structure overhanging the stern that served as the ship's sea toilet.

EUROPE

by Detlev Ellmers

In the Middle Ages no craftsmen had to work more carefully than did the shipwrights. The lives of everyone on board depended on the quality of the shipwrights' products. Well-tried techniques—for example, how to join planks—were passed from one generation to the next, resulting in highly specific shipbuilding traditions. Each technique produced watercraft for different purposes, whether from small boats for local fishing and ferrying to big vessels for long distance trade. The trading ships were the biggest movable objects made by men. The details of ship construction are best known from excavated craft, and these archaeological remains make it possible to identify different shipbuilding traditions and to understand their development over the centuries, as well as identifying local variations within one tradition. Many ship finds (sites where ships are found) in Scandinavian and British waters and along the southern shores of the Baltic and North seas give good direct information. Research in the Mediterranean and along the Atlantic shores of the Continent, where there have been only a few medieval ship finds, depends more on written and pictorial sources.

In Mediterranean seaports medieval shipwrights continued to make ships like the Romans had. For centuries they continued to use mortises and tenons to join the edges of the planking, until, in the late Middle Ages, they arrived at the simpler carvel construction. Like the Romans, they arranged two steering oars, one at each side of the stern, and adopted the sternpost rudder of Hanseatic cogs after 1300. In the late 10th century shipwrights began a momentous change in the rigging of large vessels. Instead of one large triangular sail (called a lateen sail), they added two sails, and later three minor ones, on two or three masts. This allowed smaller crews

to maneuver ships more easily, as the sails could be operated one after the other, with each being more manageable than a single large one.

The main type of warships—used in armed conflicts and for escorting trading vessels—were long, narrow galleys, designed for speed, created for large crews of oarsmen (about 100 in the ninth century, up to 230 beginning in the 12th century) who operated in two or more rows along each side. Auxiliary sails made the voyage out to the enemy easier but required a small extra crew of sailors. A third crew of warriors was on board to fight with hand weapons and catapults. The fleets of galleys and other supporting types of warships were built, equipped, and maintained in state arsenals, which became centers of many different crafts with a high degree of division of labor. The medieval arsenals at Barcelona or Venice are still to be seen.

After 1300 Venice and Genoa converted the galley into a special trading vessel, the "great galley." It was larger and broader than the fighting galley, and it carried little or no armament except where there was a risk of pirates. It made better headway under sail than when powered by oars, which were reduced in number to create greater cargo space, and it was more reliable than mere sailing ships. It carried passengers (often pilgrims to the Holy Land) and valuable cargoes and, as early as the 14th century, sailed as far north as Flanders.

All other types of Mediterranean trading vessels were summed up in the term *round ships*. Their name derived from the Roman *oneraria*, and they were tubby, spacious, and slow, propelled exclusively by sails. While the Venetian trading fleet remained that of the state, all other round ships were built in private shipyards, belonged to private shipowners, and transported cargoes and passengers for private merchants. In 1268 a record describes Venetian round ships as being about 85 feet long, 20 feet wide (with a length and beam proportion of 4.2), and about 21 feet high, with two masts for lateen sails, two complete decks, one forecastle for the crew, and a spacious quarterdeck for officers and high-ranking passengers.

Early medieval Scandinavia had no towns, so ships were built at rural estates. Many examples of these Scandinavian boats have been excavated. Typically, they are long and narrow open rowing boats (with a length and beam proportion between 5 and 7) propelled only by a single row of up to 20 oarsmen seated along each side and steered by a rudder on the starboard, or right, side of the hull (as it moved forward). From the keel, forming the backbone of the construction, stem and stern posts rose in elegant curves. The thin planks overlapped each other, with iron rivets joining the overlap. This overlapping construction is called clinker-built. Because of their shallow drafts, these light and sail-less boats landed by simply beaching at a convenient sandy shore. People used these boats to contact their neighbors, visit religious festivities and political meetings, and raid coastal settlements. Because those who rowed were also warriors, even small fleets could suddenly overcome settlers. It was in these boats that the Angles and Saxons raided England in the third and fourth centuries, settled there in the fifth century, and introduced their shipbuilding tradition into England. In the seventh century, without losing any of its raiding qualities, this type was outfitted to carry one square sail. Step by step the seaworthiness of these vessels increased (with a length and beam proportion of 4.5 to 6) until, in the late eighth century, the Vikings began to raid settlements along almost all the European shores and most European rivers.

For purposes of trade the Scandinavian and Anglo-Saxon shipbuilding tradition produced broad and high but open sailing boats. It was on these that the Vikings dared to cross the Atlantic for Iceland (beginning around 870) and Greenland (985). The archaeological evidence for these trading boats does not go back beyond the 10th century. Older, well-preserved boats, designed to transport people or to engage in battle, have been found sunk in boat graves or at sacrifice sites preserved in peat. But there was no religious reason to deposit trading vessels on the bottom in ritualized fashion. Thus no old trading vessels are found, although they might well date further back than the 10th century, especially since, in the first century C.E., Pliny knew of Germanic mariners making use of sails. Stimulated by increasing maritime trade, the first seaports were established in Scandinavia before 800. Shipbuilding gradually moved off the rural estates and became an urban profession, and the sizes of trading vessels expanded. The best-documented one (Skuldelev 1), built between 1030 and 1040 in western Norway, was about 52 feet long, 16 feet wide, and 7 feet high and could transport 20 to 25 tons of cargo; nevertheless, it was not the biggest of its time.

Outside the Mediterranean and Scandinavian regions, other shipbuilding traditions were developed. That of the cog started in the Frisian mud flats with small trading vessels on which Frisian trade entered the western Baltic before 800. Cogs had flat bottoms, straight stem and stern posts, and steep clinker-built sides. Their thick, wide planks were joined by iron nails. Before 1200 growing Hanseatic trade made the cogs in the Baltic and North seas the predominating trading vessels, using the new stern rudder instead of the Frisian side rudder. The best-documented cog, built at Bremen in 1380, was about 77 feet long, 25 feet wide, and 14 feet high and transported 80 to 84 tons of cargo, but its deck was not waterproof. It had a sheltered quarter for officers and high-ranking passengers in the aftercastle, while the crew, as usual, had to sleep on the open deck. In the event of hostile actions warriors were taken on board the trading cogs. In this tradition the small boat for fishing, inland traffic, and other purposes is known as a *kahn.*

Farther west, along both sides of the English Channel, the *hulc* was the predominant trading vessel from the eighth to the 11th centuries. The word means "dugout," and indeed this shipbuilding tradition began with an oval-shaped dugout. Remains of a dugout dating from around 1000 have been found near Utrecht. It had three additional strakes, or bands of hull planking, added to it, establishing the base of a roughly 56-foot-long, 12-foot-wide, and 4-foot-high seagoing boat. The *hulc* eventually grew to such size that, beginning around 1400, it displaced the cog—even in Hanseatic seaports. This *hulc,* for the first time outside the Mediterranean, had narrow accommodations for the crew in the forecastle and, after 1450, had three masts added to it.

The shipbuilding technique of carvel construction, consisting of heavy planks, edge to edge, nailed with wooden dowels only to frames, was thought to have originated in the Mediterranean. But an excavation from Port Berteau indicates its origin on the French Atlantic shore. This roughly 48-feet-long and 16-feet-wide trading vessel was built there, using carvel construction, in 600. It points to a decisive role for the Bretons in spreading carvel construction. By the 15th century all Europe was using the technique for large ships, because it allowed them to be made stronger and bigger than any other means. The carvel construction was supplemented with waterproof decks and the advantages of the other shipbuilding traditions (sternpost rudders, three masts, and accommodations for all people on board). Evidence from 1493 shows that this construction even allowed a gun deck to be built underneath the main deck through which heavy guns could shoot from gun ports that could be closed from inside for secure sailing. Thus, at the end of the Middle Ages, the Europeans had a ship superior to that of any other nation and they made worldwide use of it.

THE ISLAMIC WORLD

BY AMY HACKNEY BLACKWELL

People in the Islamic world made great use of sea transportation, sailing in the Red Sea, the Mediterranean, and across the Indian Ocean. Islamic ships were different from ships of the West, containing several design features that made them better able to handle the unpredictable conditions and changing winds of the region. Within the Mediterranean, many Islamic sailors used the boats typical of that region. These had square sails and flat bottoms and were constructed of planks nailed together. Their military ships included galleys, which could be rowed by teams of men. For the most part, however,

Islamic sailors used traditional Arab boats, usually called *dhows* in English. The people of the Muslim world did not call them by that name, and historians are not sure where the word comes from. Arabs called their vessels "sailing ships," or *marakib*, or they used specific technical terms for different types of dhows.

There were some 200 different styles of dhows known in the Muslim world. These included the *zanuq*; the *boum*; the *sanbuq*; the canoe-like *zaruq*; the Kuwaiti *batil*; the *mtepe* of Kenya; the felucca, which was common on the Nile and the Red Sea; and the *baghlah*, a dhow that sailed in the open ocean. Dhows typically did not have decks and were steered with tillers. Passengers who were not seafarers reportedly found them very uncomfortable to ride in, and often found overseas voyages terrifying.

Dhows had long, thin hulls. Most dhows were built of wooden planks lashed together with coir (coconut-husk fiber) ropes. Historians sometimes describe this method of joining planks as stitching, and Arab ships are described as being stitched together. The vessel was then waterproofed with grease. From a practical perspective, the dhow's design was ideal for sailing conditions in the Red Sea and Arabian Gulf. Waters in this area could be shallow and full of coral reefs and sandbars on which vessels might run aground. In the seventh century an Iraqi viceroy attempted to introduce to the Arabian Gulf ships of the nailed-together style being used in the Mediterranean. With their flat bottoms and square sails, they proved much more prone to running aground and suffering damage when they did so than the traditional dhows. Arab shipbuilders did not start nailing their ships together until the end of the 15th century, when Portuguese explorers arrived with cannons. Nailed ships tended to survive cannon attacks better than lashed dhows.

Unlike European ships, dhows were not distinguished from one another by the number of their masts. What made one type of dhow different from another was the shape of its hull. Small differences in the shape of bow and stern helped sailors identify types of ships. Some dhows also had elaborately carved sterns or bows, often in the shape of menacing faces and heads. Historians believe that these decorations and figureheads were meant to frighten either enemies or evil spirits.

The origin of the dhow's design is unknown. The 15th-century Omani sailor Ahmad ibn Majid-an-Najdi wrote a treatise on navigation in which he suggested that Arabs had learned how to build ships from Noah, who learned the art from the archangel Gabriel. He claimed that the stars of the constellation Ursa Major formed the shape of Noah's ark. Arab shipbuilders claimed to be able to see the outline of a *batil*, a style of dhow common in Kuwait, in the constellation. Historians surmise that this story must have been a very old

legend, and further that it proves that the shape of the Arab dhow had been invented long before the time this tale was written down.

A dhow might have from one to three masts. Each mast could hold one sail. Most ships in the Islamic world used settee or lateen sails. Ancient Arab boats used semitriangular sails called settee sails. These gradually evolved into the sharply triangular lateen sail, in contrast to the square sails common in the West. They were attached both fore and aft. They could be very tall. The top of a lateen sail came to a sharp point.

Historians disagree about the origins of the lateen sail. Lateen sails do not appear in European illustrations until Byzantine manuscripts of the ninth century, leading some historians to surmise that the design appeared in the Middle East during the Arab expansion of the seventh and eighth centuries and thereafter found its way into the Mediterranean. Lateen sails did not arrive in northern Europe until

Abduction by boat, from a manuscript of the Khamsa *(Quintet) by Amir Khusraw Dihlavi, opaque watercolor, ink, and gold on paper; Afghanistan; ca. 1496* (Freer Gallery of Art, Smithsonian Institution, Purchase, F1937-27)

the 14th century. Likewise in Asia most early medieval depictions of sails in India and China were of square sails. Although many scholars argue that the design originated in the Mediterranean and spread west to the Indian Ocean or vice versa, others believe that the lateen sail was invented on the Red Sea. Historians who support this viewpoint argue that square sails work very well in the large oceans of the Far East and Europe, but they are not effective in the seas around the Middle East.

Winds in the Red Sea and the Gulf of Aqaba constantly change directions, forcing sailors to fight their way into the wind quite frequently. Sailing close to the wind is very difficult with square sails because it is hard to change their alignment. The lateen sail's direction can be changed quickly, making it more flexible for sailing in and out of harbors and easier to sail into the wind. Multiple lateen sails provide good sailing speed while still allowing much more flexibility than is available with square-rigged vessels.

Sailing a boat into the wind can require sailors to make regular changes of direction, zigzagging across the wind in order to sail upwind. When sailing a dhow with a lateen sail into the wind, medieval Arab sailors generally avoided tacking, which involves changing the bow's direction across the wind. Instead, they preferred to wear around, or change course into the wind by turning the bow away from the wind and letting the stern turn. Dhows had small rudders that were not very effective at turning the boat into strong winds. It was easier to let a boat take the path of least resistance and sail in a nearly complete circle with the wind in order to change direction.

Arab dhows were large enough and maneuverable enough to travel from the Red Sea to India. Dhows were also maneuverable enough to make good pirate vessels. Pirates lurked near the shores of the Red Sea. Merchant ships would travel down the middle of the Red Sea to avoid attack. An Arab ship could carry 20 to 50 tons of cargo. Merchant ships generally delivered this cargo to the northern point of the Red Sea, from which it could make a quick journey to land markets. A merchant sea captain would employ a crew consisting of 10 to 30 men, depending on the size of his vessel.

The first known illustration of an Arab ship is that of the Hariri ship from 1237. This illustration appeared in a book of grammar written by Abu Muhammad al-Qasim ibn Ali al-Hariri. The illustration shows stitched planking, an anchor, and a central rudder mounted in the stern. There are other, earlier Arab depictions of ships, such as paintings of three-masted ships on ceramic bowls from the Balearic Islands from the 11th century, but these illustrations do not provide much detail.

Some Western historians have suggested that Arab peoples did not like to sail. This assessment is partially based on an eighth-century letter sent by Umar ibn al-Khattab, the second caliph of Islam (r. 634–44), refusing to allow the governor of Syria to invade Cyprus. The letter said that the sea was so large as to make ships seem tiny and was not to be trusted because it could easily kill people on it. Later, in the 12th century, other commentators noted that the Egyptian navy was incompetent and disobedient and ineffective at naval warfare. Nevertheless, other historians point out that Arab sailors from the Arabian Peninsula had large sailing fleets that traveled around the peninsula, down the east coast of Africa, and across the Indian Ocean and Bay of Bengal to trade and spread Islam. They note that the Arab poet Tarafah wrote verse about ships sailing on the sea back in the sixth century and that Arab scholars write about *khaliya safin*, or "great ships" that sailed in the sea. Some Arab writers refer to ships as *batsha*, with or without an adjective meaning "big." This term appears to have referred to both Christian and Muslim ships.

See also ARCHITECTURE; ART; ASTRONOMY; BUILDING TECHNIQUES AND MATERIALS; EXPLORATION; HUNTING, FISHING, AND GATHERING; MILITARY; SEAFARING AND NAVIGATION; TRADE AND EXCHANGE; TRANSPORTATION; WAR AND CONQUEST.

FURTHER READING

Tappan Adney and Howard I. Chapelle, *Bark Canoes and Skin Boats of North America* (Washington, D.C.: Smithsonian Institution Press, 1993).

Ralph A. Austen and Daniel Headrick, "The Role of Technology in the African Past," *African Studies Review* 26, nos. 3/4 (1983): 163–184.

George F. Bass, ed., *A History of Seafaring Based on Underwater Archaeology* (London: Thames and Hudson, 1972).

Roxanna Brown, *Turiang: A Fourteenth-Century Shipwreck in Southeast Asian Waters* (Pasadena, Calif.: Pacific Asia Museum, 2000).

Ole Crumlin-Pedersen and Olaf Olsen, eds., *The Skuldelev Ships I: Topography, Archaeology, History, Conservation and Display* (Roskilde, Denmark: Viking Ship Museum, 2002).

James P. Delgado, *Native American Shipwrecks* (London: Franklin Watts, 2000).

Ivan A. Donnelly, *China Junks and Other Native Crafts* (Singapore: Graham Brash Ltd., 1989).

Robert Gardiner and Richard W. Unger, eds., *Cogs, Caravels and Galleons: The Sailing Ship, 1000–1650* (London: Conway Maritime Press 1994).

George F. Hourani and John Carswell, *Arab Seafaring in the Indian Oean in Ancient and Early Medieval Times* (Princeton, N.J.: Princeton University Press, 1995).

Louise Levathes, *When China Ruled the Seas* (New York: Oxford University Press, 1994).

Sean McGrail, "Toward a Classification of Water Transport," *World Archeology* 16, no. 3 (1985): 289–303.

Eric Rieth, *The Medieval Wreck from Port Berteau II (Chaente-Maritime)*. In *Down the River to the Sea: Eighth International Symposium on Boat and Ship Archaeology*, ed. Jerzy Litwin (Gdańsk, Poland: Polish Maritime Museum, 2000).

Richard W. Unger, *The Ship in the Medieval Economy, 600–1600* (London: Croom Helm, 1980).

▶ slaves and slavery

INTRODUCTION

Slavery—the practice of owning another human being for the purpose of exploiting his or her labor—has existed since prehistoric times and almost universally around the world in antiquity and the Middle Ages and until modern times. There are still millions of slaves in the world today. Most likely, slavery became intensively practiced as part of the agricultural revolution in the Neolithic era around 10,000 years ago. Hunter-gatherers would have little use for slaves. Australian Aborigines, for instance, did not keep slaves, but some hunter-gatherers in North America did keep slaves.

Slave owners had to adapt themselves to the psychology of the system based on injustice and exploitation from which they profited. They had to adopt a calloused and detached attitude to human life and an indifference to human suffering that would make them seem very much out of place, for instance, in the modern Western world. Rape of female slaves was common (whether or not it was legal in a particular culture). While some institutions, such as Islamic sharia law, required that women impregnated by their masters be freed, in many other cultures, such as western Europe, the fathers of such children were expected to treat their offspring as slaves. In some cultures the murder or even physical mistreatment of slaves was theoretically illegal, but it was very unlikely that a mistreated slave would ever be able to successfully sue for freedom in such cases. In both Europe and the Islamic world slaves supposedly enjoyed this legal protection, but it was nevertheless legal for slaves in both cultures to be put to work on plantations, where the combination of a starvation diet and oppressive workloads made the average survival time about seven years.

In both the Islamic world and Europe systematic thought about slavery was predicated on the work of the ancient Greek philosopher Aristotle. In his *Politics* he had written that slaves are slaves by nature and that slaves benefit from slavery, since their inferior condition cries out for direction by their betters. Still, in the legal regime of his day Aristotle himself could have been enslaved merely through the misfortune of voyaging away from Athens and being captured by pirates. He could then have been legally sold to another Greek from any city other than Athens. As Aristotle was well aware, this is precisely what had happened to his fellow philosopher Diogenes. Aristotle's ideas kept slave owners from having to examine the true character of the relationship between themselves and the people they exploited.

Medieval religious institutions that stressed ideas of personal freedom and redemption, such as Christianity, Islam, and Buddhism, did not speak out against slavery but rather fully endorsed it. Saint Paul had permitted Christians to hold other Christians as slaves; however, after Christianity became the universal religion of Europe, the church generally did not allow Christians to be enslaved. Sharia law permitted Muslims to own slaves (and Muhammad himself had been a slave owner). Although Muslims could not be enslaved by other Muslims, slaves who converted were not to be freed on this account. The theory was that slavery was a suitable punishment for their earlier failure to convert. This was held to be true even in the case of slaves from sub-Saharan Africa and other isolated areas who had never heard of Islam until they came to be sold to Islamic masters.

Buddhist monasteries in China were supported by land grants. Their lands were usually worked agriculturally by slaves owned by the monastery so that the monks would not have to violate Buddhist teaching by having to kill insects while tending the fields. In 845 the Tang government of China confiscated more than 150,000 such slaves, partly on the ground that they were being mistreated by the monks beyond what was legally permissible even for slaves.

In general, there were two main ways in the Middle Ages by which people could become slaves. One was to be captured as a prisoner of war. This did not apply only or even especially to enemy soldiers, who would likely be hard to manage as slaves; women and children (the most desirable slaves) who happened to live in captured cities, towns, or villages could also be taken as slaves. The other common way people became slaves was through debt bondage (a practice still common in the third world today). In this scenario large landowners or other wealthy patrons loan money to small landowners or tenant farmers each year to buy seed and other necessities. The money is then repaid out of the profits from selling the harvest. But during bad years or through the mounting of interest on the debt over time, the farmer is eventually unable to meet the agreed payment schedule and must enter slavery or sell a child into slavery to discharge the debt. It was to discourage this practice that loaning money at interest was forbidden by Christianity and Islam. Even if Christians could not technically be forced into debt slavery by other Christians, they could still be forced into indentured servitude, a sort of temporary slavery lasting several years.

AFRICA

BY AMY HACKNEY BLACKWELL

Slavery was present throughout medieval Africa in various forms. Most African slaves were not chattel in the sense that American slaves were. Medieval African slavery was more an occupational classification; agricultural workers and domestic workers were often classified as slaves. In many cases, the people who functioned as slaves were really more equivalent to indentured servants, who were temporarily forced to work for another but who could expect to see freedom again. For most of the medieval period slaves were not a major commodity sold in large numbers on the open market, though Mali was known for its hugely profitable slave trade.

Slaves were common. Historians estimate that between one-third and one-half of the population in most sub-Saharan societies was enslaved. The medieval kingdoms of Ghana, Songhai, and Mali were all about one-third slaves. Slaves in medieval Africa were often prisoners of war who were brought to the homes of their captors and made to work. Sometimes vassal states would deliver specified numbers of male and female slaves to their overlords as a political tribute or as part of a treaty agreement. In other cases, convicted criminals and debtors could be forced to work as slaves for their victims' families. Sometimes slaves changed hands through dowries when people married. The children of slaves often became slaves themselves.

Many African slaves received wages for their work and often could earn their freedom. Depending on the society, free people could marry slaves. Ashanti slaves, for example, could themselves own slaves. They could also own property, marry, testify in court, and even be the heirs to their masters. Ashanti slaves often intermarried with their owners' families and their descendants intermingled to the point that their origins became obscure. Some slaves worked their way very high up in society. The freed slave Sakura, for example, seized the throne of the Mali Empire in about 1285.

In the Mali Empire slaves provided much of the agricultural and domestic labor. The slave trade flourished. Spanish observers around 1500 reported that the merchants of Mali were extremely rich and that they did a brisk business in buying and selling slaves on market days. Slaves of all ages were sold, including children. The king of Mali had numerous slaves in his palace, some of them doing domestic work and others serving as concubines.

Among the Songhai people and in the Bornu Empire, many agricultural workers functioned as vassals, akin to European peasants or serfs. Nobles owned or controlled large areas of land. The people who farmed the land had to pay tributes of crops and other goods to the landowners. Nobles might also control their movements and actions. They did not, however, ordinarily buy and sell large numbers of peasants. The Hausa people in the area of northern Nigeria organized their society into several social strata, ranging from lords at the top to free peasants to serfs bound to the land. The Bornu likewise ordered society into a feudal hierarchy. Nobles were at the top. Below them were freemen, who included freed slaves. Next came slaves, who were typically men and women captured in wars. At the bottom were descendants of slaves, who worked as laborers and as foot soldiers in the army.

The people of the Congo region were long accustomed to slavery. When groups went to war with one another, they would take prisoners home with them to serve as slaves. They also enslaved people convicted of crimes and people who could not pay off their debts. In many cases slaves could gradually earn back their freedom. In eastern Africa many households used slaves as domestic servants. Ethiopian slaves, for example, lived with families and were largely considered part of their owners' families. Slave owners had to feed, clothe, and care for the slaves who lived with them. Ethiopian slaves were allowed to move about freely, to conduct their own business, and to observe their own religions. Within the homes of their employers they performed domestic duties, such as cleaning, cooking, making clothing, and raising crops and livestock. Some male slave owners had sex with their female slaves.

A number of sub-Saharan Africans ended up as slaves in the Arab world. Starting in the 10th century Arab traders regularly crossed the desert with camel caravans. They would acquire Africans in Mali, Ghana, and other points south of the desert and transport them to North Africa. Slaves regularly moved from Ghana to Morocco and Tunisia, from Chad to Libya, and from the southern reaches of the Nile upriver. These traders transported about 6,000 slaves every year. Traders acquired more women than men because their Arab customers mainly wanted domestic servants and concubines. Some African men also were slaves, working as soldiers in North African armies or as eunuchs who guarded the women in harems. Many black African slaves married into North African society. Eunuchs were especially valuable in Muslim markets. Because Islamic law prohibited the mutilation of slaves, traders often castrated male slaves in Africa, at the point of purchase or at some point before entering Muslim territory.

The slave trade on the Indian Ocean coast began in the seventh century and lasted throughout the medieval period. Arab traders sailed to the African coast and acquired slaves from local traders who were generally black Arabs. These traders captured or bought African people and shipped them north to Yemen, Arabia, or even India. Like the Arab traders in the Sahara, they preferred female slaves to males. Many of these slaves passed through the island of Zanzibar, which became a major market in the Indian Ocean slave trade.

The Atlantic slave trade appeared much later than the Indian Ocean and Saharan trade routes. Portuguese slave traders began capturing people to be slaves in western Africa in the 15th century. Portuguese colonists in São Tomé and the New World wanted laborers to grow sugarcane, so they turned to Africa. Gomes Eannes de Zurara, a Portuguese chronicler, reported that starting in 1444 the Portuguese captured Africans by waging war on them in the name of Portugal and the saints. The Portuguese sailed to the Gulf of Arguin on the coast of Mauritania in ships called caravels, well armed and prepared to fight. They would land at night and attack fishing villages by surprise. According to Zurara, Portuguese soldiers attacked Africans with weapons, killing some of them and capturing the others. The embattled African people ran for their lives, some mothers dropping their children on the way as they ran for cover. Some hid in or under their huts. Others concealed themselves by jumping into the water and wrapping themselves in seaweed; a few drowned using this strategy. The Portuguese men managed to find many Africans who had hidden themselves and proceeded to capture them and take them to Europe as slaves.

Africans quickly learned to fight back against European slavers and became formidable opponents to the Portuguese. Prince Henry the Navigator instructed his soldiers that they should no longer simply attack and seize Africans but instead should buy them. The Portuguese captain João Fernandes spent a year on the coast of the Bay of Arguin in 1445, getting to know the local people and eventually paying them to capture and turn over other Africans to be slaves for Europeans. Portuguese traders solidified their claim to African slaves through the rest of the 15th century. The papal bull Dum Diversas, issued by Pope Nicholas V in 1452, granted Alfonso V of Portugal the right to make all pagans into slaves. Unlike traditional African slavery, these slaves were considered to be the property of their owners, and all their offspring would be considered slaves as well.

The Portuguese continued to invest in infrastructure within Africa that would help them capture Africans and ship them to markets. Elmina Castle, built by Portuguese traders and African laborers in Ghana in 1482, soon became an important stop on the slave-trading routes. The construction of this castle involved the coercion of the local African people, Fante of the Akan group, who were reluctant to allow a permanent Portuguese settlement on their land and put up armed resistance. Elmina's existence quickly transformed the culture of the region. The Portuguese formed alliances with some local African groups and punished groups that traded with non-Portuguese Europeans, which increased local tensions between Africans and paved the way for the larger slave trade that developed in the next centuries.

THE AMERICAS
BY MICHAEL J. O'NEAL

Normally, the words *slave* and *slavery* evoke images of plantations in the American South or the Caribbean, where large numbers of Africans—or Native Americans in the case of the Caribbean—were owned as chattel and forced to perform labor for their owners, usually under grueling and inhumane conditions. Under this type of slavery, called chattel slavery, people were regarded as property, or chattel, with almost no legal rights. They could be bought and sold, their children were automatically slaves, and slave owners had power of life and death over them.

Among native North American groups in the centuries before the arrival of Europeans, slavery as an organized institution did not exist, at least not to the extent to which it existed in other parts of the world or to which it would later exist in the New World. In particular, while the practice of holding slaves was fairly common, there was no organized slave trade, so slaves were not bought and sold at slave markets or imported by seagoing slave traders, and generally a slave's children were not automatically slaves. Most Native American bands usually had enough manpower to perform necessary work in their simple economies, although in many bands captive slaves were forced to perform menial duties, including cooking, building fires, digging roots, preparing hides, rowing canoes, and the like. Occasionally slaves were forced by their owners to assassinate members of other groups.

In some cases, forced labor may have been employed within the community to undertake major construction projects, such as the mounds characteristic of the Mississippian culture. One example is the Cahokia culture, which flourished in modern-day Illinois where the Mississippi, Missouri, and Illinois rivers meet. The Cahokians constructed at least 120 large mounds in the area, including one that covers an area of 14 acres. Historians estimate that it would have taken millions of man-hours to construct some of these mounds. Additionally, homes, granaries, ceremonial centers, burial grounds, stockades, and similar structures were constructed on the sites. These structures often had to be rebuilt or refurbished as time went on. Similarly, among the Pueblo peoples of the southwestern United States and northern Mexico, notably the Anasazi, people worked on large communal construction projects, including cliff-side dwellings and kivas, or dugout ceremonial centers.

The people who performed this labor, though, were not thought of as the "property" of the social and religious elites who directed the projects. They performed labor for "free" and perhaps under some duress, but they saw their labor as contributing to the welfare of the community, and when their tasks were complete, they returned to their families. In general, forced servitude was not a widespread practice among Native Americans. Where it was practiced, it was not based on race, nor was it necessarily a hereditary condition.

There were some exceptions, however. During times of war captives were seized and sometimes forced to perform labor. The nations of the American Northwest routinely formed raiding parties to seize slaves from other settlements, and some historians estimate that the number of slaves in the Northwest relative to the number of free people was quite high, perhaps as high as 30 percent. The practice of seizing captives in war was also common among the Natchez of the American Southeast. When the Natchez seized captives, they typically tortured and killed the men, but women and children were often forced into slavery.

Similarly, the Iroquois of the northeastern United States often conducted what were called mourning wars. These were raids launched against groups with which the Iroquois had previously done battle. Their purpose was to seize captives and take them back to the Iroquois as a way of compensating families for their losses during war. The prisoners were typically subjected to beatings and humiliation, including running the gauntlet (that is, running through a double line of armed men who attempted to strike the prisoners), where they were beaten and insulted, then given to the mourning families. Over time these captives were integrated into the nation. In most cases, they came to be regarded as kin, though they continued to be forced to perform hard labor. At the same time the seizing of captives depleted the manpower of the enemy nation, reducing its threat to the Iroquois.

A similar practice was also common among the Pawnee of the American Plains. The Pawnee placed a high value on family honor and status within the community. One measure of status was wealth; the most biting insult that could be hurled at another was to call him *ruti-kapakis-kawitat*, or the "one who is poor-ragged." Thus, the Pawnee frequently seized captives in battle and held them as slaves as a mark

AZTEC SLAVERY

The Aztec culture arose in the valley of Mexico in the 13th century. In time it became the most powerful empire in Mesoamerica. Aztec society identified the *tlacotin* as a distinct social class. These were slaves who were not captives in war. In many respects, slavery under the Aztec was similar to slavery as it was practiced in other Mesoamerican cultures. It was not based on race. It was not hereditary, so the children of a slave were not themselves slaves. Slaves could even own their own goods, and in fact, some slaves themselves owned slaves. They could purchase their liberty, they could be freed if they could demonstrate that their masters had treated them with cruelty, and a female slave was freed if she married her master or had a child by him. Slaves were, however, heritable property, meaning that when the master died, his slaves passed to his heirs, although sometimes a slave who had performed well was freed on the death of his master.

The customs and laws surrounding slavery among the Aztec had some marked peculiarities. A slave owner was legally bound to look after his slave. If, then, a slave who accompanied his master to the marketplace escaped and ran outside the walls of the city and then stepped in human excrement, he was able to appear before a judge and win his freedom, based on the notion that his master had neglected him. The successful slave was then washed, given new clothing, and granted his freedom. Further, it was actually against the law for a person to help prevent the escape of a slave. A person who did so could himself be declared a slave.

Another peculiarity was that a slave owner could not legally sell a slave without the slave's consent. The only exception was in the case of a slave whom the authorities declared incorrigible because of laziness or bad conduct. Such slaves were forced to wear wooden collars that identified them as incorrigible and that made it harder for them to run away. A slave who had changed hands four times often commanded a high price, for that slave could be purchased for blood sacrifice. But a collared slave who somehow managed to flee into a temple or a royal palace was given his freedom.

As in other Mesoamerican cultures, the Aztec could be enslaved as punishment for a crime. At the request of the wife of a murder victim, a murderer could, instead of being put to death, be given to the wife as a slave. Incorrigible sons could legally be sold into slavery, as could people in debt. Poor people could sell themselves into slavery and were given a year to enjoy their money and freedom before having to submit to their purchasers.

of status and wealth. Additionally, some Native American groups practiced peonage. Typically, the term *peon* refers to a person who is forced to perform labor as a way of working off debt, but it can also refer to the use of convict labor. The latter is the form that peonage took among Native Americans. Again, the "convicts" were typically prisoners who were seized during war. Often these prisoners were eventually released, but not before they had been forced to perform labor for their captives.

Yet another form of early North American slavery had to do with what could be called family extension. Particularly along the borderlands between what are now the United States and Mexico, Native Americans often formed raiding parties. One of the purposes of these raiding parties was to capture brides and others, who were then incorporated into the group. These people were taken against their will, making them slaves of sorts, but they were not forced to perform backbreaking labor and, in fact, became accepted members of their new group and had kin relationships with their captors. Sometimes the purpose of these seizures was simply to find brides for men. Sometimes the purpose was to prove a sense of honor and manhood by triumphing over a neighboring group. Sometimes the purpose was to extend the economic reach of the group. These captives, by being in effect members of two nations, often served as mediators and go-betweens in trade and other forms of economic and social exchange. They provided a necessary linkage between peoples who otherwise may have had no relationship with one another other than that of rivals for limited economic resources.

In Mesoamerica slavery was a much more formalized institution, ruled by laws and conventions that dictated who could become a slave, under what conditions people could become slaves, how slaves were to be treated, and how slaves could be released from servitude. For example, many people sold themselves, and even their families, into slavery as restitution for debt. Sometimes poor people, faced with starvation, sold themselves and their families as a way of surviving. Poor people often sold a son to a noble and then provided slave labor, often over the course of several generations, as a way of "keeping the son alive." Gamblers and prostitutes sometimes sold themselves into slavery as a way of raising funds, but they had a year to repay the money they received before they had to become slaves. Slave labor was almost certainly employed in the construction of the massive monumental architecture of Mesoamerican cities.

Crime was often punishable by slavery. Thieves were sold into slavery, but their families could redeem them; if the family restored the stolen property, the thief was released from slavery. The families of people executed for capital crimes were sold into slavery, and if a man was found guilty of treason, his family for five generations was sold into slavery. Typically, a man found guilty of murder was not executed but enslaved, given to the murder victim's family as a form of compensation. Additionally, many slaves, typically men, were held and then sacrificed to the gods. Throughout Mesoamerica it was a major crime to subject a free person to slavery. It was also a crime for a man to kill another man's slave; usually the guilty party was punished by becoming a slave to the owner whose slave was killed. Similarly, if a free man impregnated another man's slave and that slave died during childbirth, the free man became the other man's slave as compensation.

In South America the Incan culture, the dominant culture that emerged in the late 12th century and reached the peak of its influence in the century before the arrival of the Spanish, employed slave labor in the construction of its massive cities, temples, and monuments, and particularly its extensive network of roads. The Inca spread their influence primarily through persuasion. The empire was so powerful that when emissaries from the Inca approached a neighboring territory bearing gifts and "explained" to the people and their rulers the "advantages" of membership in the Incan state, these neighboring territories generally acquiesced.

While the Inca did not have an organized slave system, the state was all-powerful, with an emperor who ruled by divine right and a royal family and nobility. The state, in the persons of the emperor and the nobility, owned everything: land, produce, the products of manufacture, such as textiles and metalwork, and the like. The Incan state showed no mercy to anyone who opposed it, so the people lived in a kind of slavery. They were frequently drafted to perform public works projects.

The Incan state did not collect taxes in the form of money. Taxes could be paid in kind, with goods, but the usual practice was to perform labor for a certain period of time. This system is called corvée, or labor "paid" to the state in the place of taxes. Corvée was the system used to provide labor for public works projects. It was a form of slave labor, although the period during which it was performed could be as little as two weeks.

ASIA AND THE PACIFIC

BY LAURA LEE JUNKER

Historians and anthropologists have emphasized the wide range of relations referred to as "slavery" by early European observers of medieval Asia, the necessity of viewing slavery within specific cultural contexts, and the importance of avoiding any universal concepts of slavery. Late-medieval European writing on Asian and Pacific societies often refers to slavery in describing the ties between elite patrons in these societies (kings, chiefs, and other high-ranking individuals) and their clients (lower-ranking individuals, particularly commoners), a relationship that might be better described as "dependency." As opposed to these ties of dependency, the term *slavery* may be defined as a social and economic relationship in which someone is owned by another person in a legal sense and can be legally purchased, rented, mortgaged, bequeathed, or otherwise alienated like private property. In contrast, commoners in a dependency or serfdom relationship with an elite patron were generally obligated to pay tribute and to perform military, agricultural, craft, or other services to their benefactor, but their services and resources could not be transferred to another patron without consent.

The ways in which individuals could enter into the state of slavery as well as their ability to leave slave status varied according to cultural and historical circumstances in Asian and Pacific societies. A general contrast, however, can be noted between closed and open systems of slavery in Asia and the Pacific. The more rigid lineage-based systems of social class and political hierarchy in medieval India, China, Korea, and Japan created closed structures of slavery. In these systems slaves were segregated from nonslaves both ideologically and physically in their participation in political, social, and economic life, with little chance for any change in status. In contrast, slavery in Southeast Asian societies, with their more fluid social ranking systems and volatile political dynamics, followed an open pattern in which captured or purchased slaves and their progeny were eventually assimilated into the dominant society (often within one generation). Chiefdoms in the Pacific Islands, depending on their scale, tended to support both types of slave systems.

The concept of slavery was tied to traditions of caste, or *varna*, in medieval India. Historians have established that elements of the caste system existed since the Aryan advances into northern India in the first millennium B.C.E., well before the rise of the fourth-century Gupta Empire and continuing with the later medieval Islamic Mughals of the north and Hindu empires like Vijayanagara to the south. Medieval society was rigidly divided, in descending order of rank and privilege, into Brahmin (a priestly, aristocratic class), Kshatriya (a warrior class), Vaishya (a merchant class), and Shudra (a peasant and artisan class), with pariahs, or "untouchables," forming a group at the bottom; pariahs were not even considered a legitimate part of the caste system. Even though slavery (in the sense of "owned" individuals who could be bought and sold as commodities) had explicitly been outlawed by the medieval period, many scholars believe that the untouchables originated as a slave class consisting of prisoners of war, criminals, dissidents, tribal minorities, and others viewed as being outside of Indian society. Pariahs had few resources,

they were assigned tasks (such as handling the dead or butchering animals) that were considered polluting to other castes, they were segregated residentially, they were the object of taboos on social interactions with other groups, and they were socially defined as foreigners and outsiders; their children inherited their pariah status in perpetuity. In some ways, the pariah caste fit the model of a closed system of slavery.

China, through the early medieval Tang Empire (618–907), the Five Dynasties (907–60), and the later periods of Song (960–1279), Yuan (1279–1368), and Ming (1368–1644), maintained a highly stratified and hierarchical society, in which inequities in the allocation of land and resources, rights to sumptuary goods and a lavish lifestyle, access to education and political office, taxation, and judicial punishment were institutionalized in state regulations. In Tang society hereditary aristocrats were at the top of the rigid social and political order, followed by professional bureaucrats, Buddhist clergy, peasants, artisans, and merchants, all of whom could own slaves and appropriate their labor. Slaves were of two types, official and private, the former generally associated with the imperial court and government functionaries and acquired through foreign conquest, foreign tribute, and local imprisonment for crimes.

Successful military campaigns by the Tang in Korea, inner Mongolia, central Asia, and northern India in the early years of the Tang Dynasty resulted in the transport of massive numbers of foreign slaves into the empire. (Approximately 200,000 slaves were brought from northern Korea in 688.) Rulers of Tang-controlled foreign tributary states and tribal chieftaincies were obligated to send tribute, which often included slaves who possessed unique artistic, technical, or intellectual skills or who were physically exceptional. The king of Tokhāra (located north of present-day Afghanistan and Pakistan) sent a talented painter of Buddhist icons, while the kingdoms of Japan, Korea, and Burma periodically dispatched dance and music troupes and (in the case of Japan) shockingly hairy Ainu archers; the king of what is now Cambodia delivered albinos. Individuals internal to Tang society also became slaves when all of the relatives of a condemned criminal (particularly for crimes against the state, such as rebellion and sedition) were enslaved as part of judicial punishments. Many of the 40,000 "palace ladies" in Emperor Xuanzong's (r. 712–56) harem at the capital of Ch'angan were slaves of this type, including many highly educated women who served as scribes and teachers and oversaw silkworm raising and silk production for the palace.

Merchants and clergy, and sometimes entrepreneurial peasants, procured and exchanged slaves, who were seized on trading expeditions or were debt-bonded to their masters. It was officially illegal for individuals outside the government to buy, seize, or sell indigenous Chinese. (The Tang law code stipulated execution by strangulation for kidnapping other Chinese for enslavement.) However, these laws did not apply to aboriginal tribal peoples in the distant prefectures of the empire and most foreigners, and merchants evaded the prohibitions on local slave raiding by claiming that Chinese debtors were willingly selling themselves or family members as slaves to ease their family financial obligations. Highly skilled horse-riding Turks and Persian craftsmen as well as exceptionally beautiful women from Korea, Mongolia, and Vietnam were highly desirable commodities in the slave-trade market.

In the ninth century Buddhist monasteries were gaining what the Tang aristocracy viewed as dangerous levels of wealth and power, accumulating vast lands, industrial operations (such as silk factories), wealth in gold, and large numbers of slaves procured through debt-bondage arrangements or purchased from merchant slave traders. In 845 the Tang government confiscated 150,000 slaves from Buddhist temple complexes, slaves who ironically were acquired to allow the Buddhist monks to adhere to prohibitions against killing insects during agricultural work but who were often treated very poorly.

Whatever their source, slaves had very little social mobility once they passed into slave status since even debt-bonded slaves were rarely able to purchase themselves out of servitude; marriage (but not concubinage) with nonslaves was strictly forbidden, and children of slaves generally continued in their slave status for several generations. With few exceptions, social segregation of slaves from freemen in both domestic and public spheres, significant economic disenfranchisement, and cultural prohibitions against social mobility conformed to a closed system of slavery.

Medieval polities in Korea and Japan closely followed the Chinese imperial model of assigning foreign war captives as slave labor for newly created or expanded noblemen estates to reward aristocratic supporters. As with slaves in imperial China, intermarriage between social ranks and especially with foreign captives was largely forbidden, there were few possibilities for social mobility, and there was no real measure of economic independence. For example, when the United Silla Kingdom emerged in southern Korea in the seventh century through conquest of the rival polities of Paekche and Koguryo and the expulsion of the invading Tang of China, portions of the conquered land were distributed to Silla nobles as landed estates, along with tax revenue privileges and foreign war captives designated as personal slaves.

By the 10th-century ascendancy of the Koryo Kingdom in northern Korea, slavery had expanded and had been institutionalized for war captives and debt-bonded indigenous people, both groups passing on their slave status to subsequent generations. Government slaves performed manual labor as well as various administrative activities associated with the functioning of the state, while private slaves served aristocratic households and temples in various capacities. Similarly to the situation of Chinese polities of the period, the severity of tribute exactions and corvée (unpaid) labor demands on both slaves and peasants periodically led to popular peasant and slave uprisings, the most severe occurring throughout the 12th century, weakening the social order and opening Korea to Mongol invasion.

Although slave laborers (largely captives) are mentioned as early as the third century in Chinese descriptions of the coalescing Yamato Japanese state, in Japan the rigid social order and specific roles of slaves in this hierarchy are particularly well described for the Kamakura Shogunate (1185–1333) and later periods. The imperial court, the aristocracy, and the samurai warrior-elites were strongly segregated by lifestyle, wealth, and absolute authority from the mass of peasants and slaves (known as *eta*) at the bottom of the social scale. Peasants had heavy tax quotas, labor levies, and military conscription (draft) from the aristocracy controlling the landed estates but were free to use or invest remaining crops and goods they produced.

In contrast, members of the hereditary slave class, who constituted about 5 percent of the population, were largely descendants of war prisoners, criminals, or seized tribal populations not integrated into the feudal state. They had no rights to ownership of land or other economic resources, and they could be bought and sold like other personal property. They served on aristocratic estates and in Buddhist monasteries as landless laborers and in what were considered degrading occupations, such as curing leather and burying the dead. Slaves and their descendents were locked into their status by rigid social segregation and no legal economic routes to freedom, though some slaves and, particularly, indigent peasants turned to forms of banditry, fueling the need for samurai protectors for the nobility.

In Southeast Asian kingdoms and chiefdoms of the period—characterized by relatively low population levels, an abundance of rich agricultural land that could be intensively farmed given large labor inputs, and an emphasis on maritime raiding and trading for wealth—control of people rather than land or capital was a key aspect of political power. In societies where labor was a valuable asset, it is not surprising that institutionalized forms of slavery would become an integral part of the social and political fabric. Many medieval Southeast Asian cities, such as Angkor, Ayuthaya, Melaka, Aceh, Macassar, and Manila, had economies that were fueled by slave labor, and slaves were the most valuable form of movable property.

In addition to providing in some societies up to 50 percent of the agricultural labor, slaves in the maritime trade–oriented Southeast Asian kingdoms performed an astounding array of occupations. These included fishing, manning sailing vessels, building elite residences and public works, mining, producing crafts (pottery, weaving, and metallurgy), entertaining, serving as concubines or domestic servants, trading, interpreting, writing for illiterate masters, fighting as warriors, raiding to acquire additional slaves, and even functioning as high-ranking government ministers. Slaves were also movable property or forms of "wealth" that, like gold coins, fine textiles, and porcelain, could be used as exchangeable commodities to cement political alliances, to offer as trade products, and to function as part of a bride-price (payment by a prospective groom to a bride's family as part of the marriage contract).

Large-scale slave labor for commercialized production of commodities like textiles, bulk transport of trade goods, and other maritime trade–related activities at the most massive coastal trading ports in medieval Southeast Asia approached what historians call a slave mode of production. This involved centrally managing and housing slaves, making possible a level of production not otherwise available in a household-oriented economy. However, historians agree that the vast majority of Southeast Asian slaves were integrated at the household, kin-based level of production, becoming household members with a certain level of economic independence rather the nearly complete economic disenfranchisement (deprivation) characteristic of European colonial plantation systems.

In most Southeast Asian societies there were numerous paths by which an individual could enter into a state of slavery or bondage: inheritance, economic reversal, debt bondage, judicial punishment, and capture in warfare and raiding. While intergenerational inheritance of slave status was not inevitable and relatively rapid assimilation of slaves into the kin networks of their owners was common, the progeny of slaves often retained social identities as slaves for a generation or longer. Individuals and even larger kinship groups sometimes voluntarily entered into slavery as the result of economic hardship and the potential advantages of having a wealthy and generous owner. In other cases, a legally binding state of debt bondage to a specific owner was created as result of the failure of an individual to pay economic obligations (such as a bride-price contracted in a marriage negotiation or debts incurred in trading transactions). Many elites attempted to retain the perpetual services of their debt-bonded slaves by paying the bride-price for their offspring or securing other forms of debt with mounting interest. Judicial punishments were also a frequent origin of slave status when the criminal could not pay the imposed fines that generally settled serious infractions, such as murder, robbery, or a culturally defined lack of deference to aristocracy.

Finally, given the competition for productive labor in comparatively underpopulated medieval Southeast Asia, maritime slave raiding was widespread and large scale, and many slaves were foreign captives. The Sulu Sultanate of the southern Philippines transported about 200,000 to 300,000 foreign slaves from throughout the islands of Southeast Asia into the polity over three or four generations at the time of European contact. Historical accounts indicate that slaves of all types often eventually left the slave ranks by accumulating enough independent wealth to buy themselves out of bondage (particularly for debt-bonded and criminal slaves but also as ransom for captive foreign slaves) or by marrying nonslaves (which redefined their status or that of their children). Probably the most important factors in promoting an open slave system were the lack of strong cultural prohibitions against slaves (whether foreign or indigenous) marrying into commoner and even aristocratic families and the fluidity with which individuals crossed social class lines. Ironically, the loss of slaves through this process of social assimilation and redefinition encouraged the perpetuation and even expansion of slave raiding and other institutional sources of slave acquisition.

Among the island chiefdoms of the Pacific, like the Hawaiians, the Tahitians, the Tongans, the Marquesans, and the Maoris, slavery was generally a temporary condition of war captives, who served as household menials (farmers, fishers, craftsmen, and personal retainers) in return for protection by the lineage males in the patrilineal household into which they were integrated. Unlike in China and Southeast Asian polities, warfare was restricted to isolated island chains with more culturally and linguistically homogenous peoples; thus, captive slaves were likely to speak the same language as and share similar social norms with their captors, and the slaves often quickly assimilated into the household lineage as pseudokinsmen. However, for men in general, but particularly for the nobility and warrior-elite, captivity meant loss not only of social rank but also of spiritual essence, or mana. Social status and political authority were inherited at birth but could be denigrated by cowardice in battle, low-status marriages, capture in warfare, and other indignities, so enslavement by a rival chief was to be avoided at all costs, even if the warrior was later repatriated to his lineage through political negotiations.

In the larger-scale chiefdoms of Hawaii and Tahiti, captive slaves also faced the danger of ritual sacrifice to the deities as these societies evolved in the period immediately before European contact into theocratic polities ruled by divine leaders. Another trend in the later Hawaiian history is that an expanded scale of warfare aimed at large-scale territorial conquest meant that massive captive taking and transport were no longer feasible. Instead, conquering chiefs more often sent land administrators to newly annexed lands, which became alienated from their traditional lineage-based ownership, and in a sense all of the subjugated and landless people became "slaves" in the short-term.

EUROPE

BY TOM STREISSGUTH

Slavery was an integral part of ancient Roman society and trade. Roman slaves labored on agricultural estates, were employed to build aqueducts and roads, worked as household servants, and served in quarries and workshops. They were bought and sold throughout the empire and had no legal rights or personal property. The son or daughter of a slave was legally a slave and remained so unless granted freedom by the owner. Roman slave traders carried out a flourishing business along the coasts of the Mediterranean Sea and the Atlantic Ocean, where the open sea allowed for easy escape. Patrick, the patron saint of Ireland, was captured in such a raid and kept as a slave for 16 years on the European continent before finally escaping to his homeland, bringing the new faith of Christianity to the pagan Irish.

The fall of the Western Roman Empire in the fifth century did not end the use of slaves. The trade in slaves persisted throughout Europe, even as pagan societies were converted to Christianity and were thus, according to Christian doctrine, granted their freedom. Prisoners of war were still sold as slaves; an important slaving trade route linked the Slavic regions of the east to the Mediterranean region, and the cities of Marseille, Prague, and Constantinople had busy slave markets in which Slavs and other eastern pagans were sold to Muslim buyers from the Middle East and North Africa. Another slave trade route linked the Slavic lands to a large market in the Crimea, where slaves were sold to Arab buyers from the Middle East and later to merchants from the Ottoman realms in Asia Minor and southeastern Europe. An important trade in slaves also occurred on the Iberian Peninsula, where Jews free of religious constraints on slavery sold their captives through the Muslim caliphate established in Spain in the eighth century.

The waves of migration in northern and central Europe after the fall of the empire left in their wake chaos and disruption, making much of the population captives and slaves. The Magyars of the distant Eurasian steppes swept through central Europe and the Danube valley in the 10th century, capturing peasants and townspeople of Germany and Italy. Slaves were also taken by the Vikings in their many raids in the British Isles and on the European continent. The Vikings

of Sweden, also known as the Varangians, captured many slaves on their raids down the rivers of the Russian steppes, a practice that established a busy slave market in the northern Russian town of Novgorod and which made the word *Slav* synonymous with "slave."

In medieval Europe criminals and debtors could be enslaved as a legal punishment. Among the Germanic peoples certain crimes were punished by fines; if the accused was unable to pay the fine, he or she would have to surrender to the wronged party as a slave. It was a custom of the Franks and other Germanic peoples to take war captives as hostages for ransom, if the families of the captives were wealthy enough. Those who could not be ransomed became slaves, to be put to work on the estates of their captors. Some slaves were sold to pagan tribes for the purpose of human sacrifice—a practice eventually banned by Pope Gregory III (d. 741) and punished as an act of murder.

The church took the view that believers could not be held or sold as slaves, and the Christianization of peoples such as

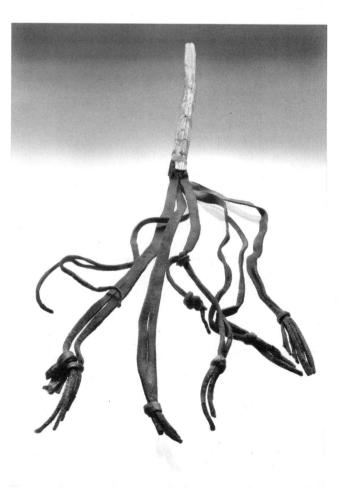

Leather whip from ca. the 11th century; under Anglo-Saxon law only a slave could be punished by flogging. (© Museum of London)

the Saxons ended much of the slave trade in northern Europe. In areas where Christians and nonbelievers lived in proximity, it was still legal to hold non-Christians, usually Muslims, as agricultural slaves or, more commonly, house servants. Conversion to the Christian faith often ended one's status as a slave and required the owner to grant the slave freedom.

Many of the church councils that set out official Christian doctrine dealt with the legal status of slaves owned by the church. By the Council of Agde, in the early sixth century, a bishop who freed a slave was obligated to pay the sum of 20 solidi for the care of the freed slave. The Third Council of Toledo (589) forbade Jews from holding Christians as slaves and decreed that the children of freed slaves could not lose their status. The Council of Worms (876) set a penance of two years for anyone found guilty of killing a slave and a penance of seven years for any woman who intentionally killed a female slave in a fit of jealousy. The 12th-century councils of London and Armagh prohibited the selling of Christians in pagan territories

Pope Gregory I (ca. 540–604) freed all slaves in his service, granted them property, and prevented anyone from collecting from them the price set for their freedom. Another church father, Saint Éloi (also known as Eligius, ca. 588?–660), the bishop of Noyon, was known to board ships bringing slaves to France and immediately redeem and free as many slaves as he could afford. Slavery persisted in the uncertain and famine-haunted times of early medieval Europe, however, and many people sold themselves into slavery simply for protection or to provide themselves with shelter and sustenance. Gradually, slavery evolved into serfdom, in which laborers worked the land and other productive property for the benefit of a feudal lord, who considered the serfs belonging to his estate to be a form of property. Serfdom gradually spread as feudal lords allowed slaves to inhabit private dwellings and in some cases offered them a formal declaration of manumission—freedom. It was customary for manumitted slaves to be granted enough property to keep themselves free of debt and a return to bondage.

Serfs lived in their own homes and could address grievances to the lord. They had the right to a portion of their land and produce for their own use and were considered full members of the church. This contrasted with the condition of slaves in Roman times, who were considered nonhumans without any legal rights whatsoever and who could not own property, be baptized into the church, or demand protection of the law. Even as slavery died out in western Europe, the institution persisted in the east and in the Mediterranean region. Bonded servants were common in the cities of Italy, and service for the repayment of debt remained a legal institution throughout Europe.

Captives taken by the Mongols in their raids into Poland and Hungary in the 13th century were sold at markets in Russia and central Asia, a trade facilitated by merchants from Genoa and Venice through their trading depots in the Crimea.

Although central Europe was ultimately spared conquest by the Mongols, Russian territory remained under the control of the Mongol khans of Astrakhan and Kazan, and slaving raids on Russian towns and villages remained an important occupation in these territories.

Gradually civil laws prohibited slavery altogether. The trade in slaves was forbidden in England in the early 12th century, although the English settlers colonizing Ireland often made slaves of Irish war captives. The keeping of thralls (slaves) in Scandinavia was abolished in the 14th century. Slavery was not abolished in Poland until the 15th century and in Lithuania a century later. In Russia slavery persisted until the 17th century, when slaves became serfs. In southeastern Europe, Christians taken as slaves by the army of the Ottoman Turks made up the Janissaries, a powerful faction of the Turkish army. Janissaries were often taken as boys and trained from a young age as soldiers and officers. After the medieval period they rose to prominence as an important political faction within the Ottoman Empire.

THE ISLAMIC WORLD
BY MASSOUD ABDEL ALIM

The institution of slavery was common to all major traditions in the ancient world—the Greeks, the Romans, the Byzantines, the ancient Hebrews, and the pre-Islamic Arabs all had slave populations. The emergence of Islam in the seventh century did not question the validity of the institution but rather accepted it and regulated its practice. The Koran contains several passages on the treatment of slaves, tacitly assuming the reality of the institution. Muhammad himself owned slaves, as did several of his military companions who could afford them. Muhammad built upon existing norms of slave ownership, and his successors took their cues from him. Islamic thought presumed that people were born free and that only the strictest rules governed the enslavement of a free person. A body of laws pertaining to slave ownership, slave status, slave trade, and the manumission (freeing) of slaves evolved in the Muslim world. Slavery was thus deemed to be permitted by Allah and became a legal status that was recognized and regulated by the sharia (Islamic law).

Slavery in Islam differed from slavery in Europe in several ways. In Islam both the Koran and the sharia permitted Muslim men sexual access to slave concubines, whereas European men attempting to have sexual relations with slaves were confronted with legal, social, and religious sanctions. Furthermore, in the

Islamic world the offspring of such unions might be recognized and legitimized by Muslim fathers; the father might also choose to recognize and free the slave mother herself. Such was not the case in the West, where such offspring remained anonymous and usually blended with the rest of the slave population.

A major consequence of this difference is that the Muslim world soon developed a far larger proportion of children of mixed racial and ethnic characteristics than did the Western world. Furthermore, race never became quite as definitive a characteristic of a person as it did in the West. Nevertheless, the Muslim world was not free of racial prejudice. Writing about black African slaves, the foremost 15th-century Islamic historian, Ibn Khaldun (1332–1406), wrote that "Negroes are in general characterized by levity, excitability, and great emotionalism."

A person could become a slave in one of four ways: by being born to a slave woman, by being taken captive in jihad (a holy war), as part of an annual tribute paid by the head of state of a conquered land, or by outright purchase. Because the Koran presumes the natural freedom of human beings, only unbelief can categorically qualify someone for enslavement. Moreover, Islamic jurists determined that unbelief justified continued slave status even after a slave had converted to Islam.

Conquered regions, most notably Mesopotamia, Egypt, Iran, North Africa, central Asia, and Spain, provided sources of slaves. Central Africa and East Africa also became sources of slaves, especially toward the end of the medieval era, when the supply of slaves from Europe diminished significantly. Most of these people, often cultural equals with the Arabs, eventually converted and were absorbed into mainstream Muslim culture. Skilled slaves were imported from outside the Islamic frontier—notably from Byzantium, India, China, and Southeast Asia—to serve as technicians or specialists. Unskilled slave labor was imported from Europe, the Eurasian steppes, and sub-Saharan Africa.

Slave markets thrived during the medieval era, and a brisk trade provided the Muslim world with a steady supply of domestic and menial labor via three main routes. European white slaves arrived overland through France and Spain, from eastern Europe through the Crimean Sea, and across the Mediterranean Sea. Venetian slave merchants figured particularly well in the trade and delivered cargo to Spanish and North African markets. African black slaves were similarly transported through several routes: from the West across the Sahara to Morocco and Tunisia and from Chad (west-central Africa) to Libya, and from the East up the Nile to Egypt and across the Red Sea and Indian Ocean to Arabia and the Persian Gulf. Turkish slaves were transported from the Eurasian steppes to Samarqand (and other Muslim cities) and eventually to Iran and Mesopotamia. Caucasian slaves crossed the

Dinar of Sultan al-Malik al-Zahir Baybars, a sultan of the Bahri line of the slave dynasty known as the Mamluks, Alexandria, Egypt, 1268 (© The Trustees of the British Museum)

narrow landmass between the Black Sea and the Caspian Sea for sale in Mosul, Iraq, and Aleppo, Syria.

Slaves were employed in all parts of the economy: They were domestic servants, agricultural workers, tradesmen and business agents, military recruits, and even leaders; they also occupied posts in the civil administration. In the social hierarchy of slavery, military slave commanders were at the top, while slaves working in agriculture for peasant owners were at the bottom.

The slave military was a uniquely Islamic institution. Military slaves were known in antiquity—in the form of armed bodyguards or local police—but they had no combat role in Greek and Roman armies. In addition, whereas European monarchs populated their officers corps from among their sons and those of the nobility, Islamic rulers chose instead to create a military with commanders whose allegiance would be to none other than the sultan or the caliph and who could never compete for power. Additionally, a slave military would not form a hereditary nobility, would have no conflicting loyalties, and would not build up power bases with the local populations—all characteristics especially well suited to autocratic rulers.

In the eastern portion of the empire slave recruits were largely white and drawn mostly from Turkey, the Eurasian steppes, and central Asia. In the West, Muslim Spain drew its military slaves from the Slavs and from the people of North Africa. Later, Ottomans took their recruits from the Balkans and the Caucasus. Most of these recruits had been part of vanquished populations. They were selected and purchased, usually early in adolescence or even before, converted and indoctrinated to Islamic thought and social norms, and ultimately made to serve the political objectives of the sultan. These former slave boys eventually became the soldiers, officers, and commanders in the Muslim armies. Some acquired considerable political power and even founded slave dynasties (for example, the Fatimids in Egypt).

Below the slave military were high-ranking slave civil servants, who populated the administration of the caliphs and sultans. They too came from the ranks of conquered populations. Despite conversion to Islam, they retained slave status since according to the sharia, this was required due to previous unbelief. Still, they could—and often did—rise to positions of influence, even that of vizier (the equivalent of a chief operating officer).

Eunuchs came next and acted as guards of harems, custodians of mosques, tombs, and shrines, and servants of the ruling dynasty. They were recruited from Slavic and Ethiopian populations especially but also from among Greek (Rum), west African, Indian, and even western European peoples.

Slaves working for merchants and craftsmen in cities and towns occupied the middle ranks of the hierarchy. Some even became responsible for their masters' businesses and could act as the owners' agents. Musicians, singers, dancers, and other performers of both genders were likely to be slaves in the medieval era. In slave society they were especially well regarded and well treated.

Among the lower rungs of the hierarchy were female slaves, who acted as domestic servants and concubines, since the sharia permitted sexual access to a slave girl or woman by her Muslim slave owner. Although prostitution was outlawed by the sharia, some female slaves were also hired out as prostitutes, a practice common in the pre-Islamic era.

At the bottom of the social hierarchy were the field workers in agriculture or those recruited for special public works projects, such as draining ditches for road construction or draining marshes in southern Iraq. These slaves, who were predominantly black, had the harshest lives and often the shortest life spans, which were often cut short by accidents, disease, and exhaustion. Thousands of African male slaves worked cotton, sugar, and rice plantations, some of which were owned by the state. One group, the Zanj from East Africa, who were brought to drain salt deposits in southern Iraq, became famous for a revolt against their masters.

The price and cost of slaves can be understood from medieval Egyptian sources. A dinar was a gold piece, and a dirham was a silver piece; the silver equivalent was 13.3 dirhams for one dinar. Black girls brought in 266 dirhams, adult black females 500 dirhams, black eunuchs 1,000–1,500 dirhams, and trained singers and performers 10,000–20,000 dirhams. White men from Turkey and central Asia who were targeted for the military brought in a minimum of 300 dirhams and often much more; a white girl could fetch at least 1,000 dinars, or over 13,000 dirhams. Relatively speaking, eunuchs were more valuable and more expensive than uncastrated males, younger people were more valuable than older people, and women were more valuable than men.

The sharia denied slaves any legal rights; they could not enter into contractual agreements, hold property, or inherit property. They could not hold office, perform or participate in religious functions, have any authority over others, or present testimony in court. Furthermore, the sharia did not fix any specific penalty for the maltreatment of slaves, although tradition dating back to Muhammad frowned upon such practice. Slaves also required the consent of their masters to marry. The rights of slaves included adequate food and shelter provided by the master and duties that were not excessive for a slave's ability or strength. Ideally, a master should look upon a slave with a kindly attitude and be moderate in his punishment when the slave transgressed. Fines incurred by a slave were the responsibility of the master.

The sharia provided several ways of emancipating a slave. First, the slave owner could make a formal declaration, which was duly recorded and given to the former slave. Second, the slave owner could enter into a written agreement in which the slave would pay a sum for his freedom. Third, the slave owner might liberate his slaves of his own free will, usually at a future date, such as upon his death, and might also require his heirs to free a slave upon his death. If a slave was maltreated, a judge might declare a slave free in yet another form of emancipation. In cases in which a slave woman gave birth to a son by her master, she acquired additional legal rights. Once freed, slaves were not wholly without discrimination, but manumission provided the legal means out of slavery.

Those *dhimmis* (non-Muslims who followed a religion that is tolerated under Islam) who could afford slaves were permitted to own them, but they could not own Muslim slaves, since Muslims could not be enslaved. Furthermore, *dhimmis* were obliged either to sell or to free a slave who had converted to Islam while working for them. Dhimmis could not have Muslim concubines, although Muslims certainly could and did have Christian and Jewish slave concubines. Typically, although Jews captured in eastern Europe were ransomed by other Jews, the same could not be said for Christians. Conversion of *dhimmi* slaves to one of the *dhimmi* religions—even if only partially—required the slave owner to free them. Conversion from Islam was a capital offense and was punishable by death. Conversion to Islam by a slave owned by a Muslim did not necessarily mean that the slave would be set free, since according to the sharia, the condition of slavery was due to the state of previous unbelief and could therefore continue.

By the end of the medieval era in the 15th century the slave system had become so entrenched that inevitably several Ottoman sultans were the sons of slave concubines. Moreover, the emergence of European Christian nation-states effectively dried up the traffic in white slavery for both genders. Henceforth, Africa became the main source of slaves, and the slave population, increasingly black, was permitted to rise further in Islamic society than had previously been possible.

See also ARCHITECTURE; CRIME AND PUNISHMENT; ECONOMY; EMPLOYMENT AND LABOR; FAMILY; FOREIGNERS AND BAR- BARIANS; GOVERNMENT ORGANIZATION; LAWS AND LEGAL CODES; MIGRATION AND POPULATION MOVEMENTS; OCCUPA- TIONS; RELIGION AND COSMOLOGY; RESISTANCE AND DISSENT; SEAFARING AND NAVIGATION; SOCIAL ORGANIZATION; TRADE AND EXCHANGE; WAR AND CONQUEST.

Europe

∼ Gregory of Tours: "Harsh Treatment of Serfs and Slaves" (ca. 575) ∼

(The widow of Godwin) married Rauching, a man of great vanity, swollen with pride, shameless in his arrogance, who acted towards those subject to him as though he were without any spark of human kindness, raging against them beyond the bounds of malice and stupidity and doing unspeakable injuries to them. For if, as was customary, a slave held a burning candle before him at dinner, he caused his shins to be bared, and placed the candle between them until the flame died; and he caused the same thing to be done with a second candle until the shins of the torchbearer were burned. But if the slave tried to cry out, or to move from one place to another, a naked sword threatened him; and he found great enjoyment in the man's tears. They say that at that time two of his slaves, a man and a girl, fell in love—a thing which often happens—and that when their affection for each other had lasted for a period of two years, they fled together to a church. When Rauching found this out he went to the priest of that place and asked him to return the two slaves immediately, saying that he had forgiven them. Then the priest said to him, "You know what veneration is due to the churches of God. You cannot take them unless you take an oath to allow them to remain together permanently, and you must also promise that they will be free from corporal punishment." But he, being in doubt and remaining silent for some time at length turned to the priest and put his hands upon the altar, saying, "They will never be separated by me, but rather I shall cause them to remain in wedlock; for though I was annoyed that they did such things without my advice, I am perfectly happy to observe that the man did not take the maid of another in wedlock, nor did she take the slave of another." The simple priest believed him and returned the two slaves who had been ostensibly pardoned. He took them, gave thanks, and returned to his house, and straightway ordered a tree to be cut down. Then he ordered the trunk to be opened with wedges and hollowed out, and a hole to be made in the ground to the depth of three or four feet, and the trunk to be placed therein. Then placing the girl as if she were dead, he ordered the slave to be thrown on top of her. And when the cover had been placed upon the trunk he filled the grave and buried them both alive, saying, "I have not broken my oath and I have not separated them."

From: Roy C. Cave and Herbert H. Coulson, *A Source Book for Medieval Economic History* (Milwaukee: Bruce Publishing Co., 1936).

The Islamic World

∼ Al-Tanukhi: Excerpt from **Ruminations and Reminiscences** (ca. 980) ∼

Another [man], I am told, was in a hurry to get rid of his money, and when only five thousand dinars were left, said he wanted to have done with it speedily in order that he might see what he would do afterwards. . . . I heard nothing of him for three years, and then one day at the Taq Gate seeing a slave clearing the way for a rider, raised my head and beheld my friend on a fine horse with a light silver-mounted saddle, fine clothes,

(continued)

(continues)

splendid underwear and fragrant with scent—now he was of a family of clerks and formerly in the days of his wealth, he used to ride the noblest chargers, with the grandest harness, and his clothes and accoutrements were of the magnificent style which the fortune inherited by him from his parents permitted. When he saw me, he called out: Fellow! I, knowing that his circumstances must have improved, kissed his thigh, and said: My lord, Abu so-and-so! He said Yes! What is this? I asked. He said: God has been merciful, praise be to Him! Home, home. I followed him 'till he had got to his door, and it was the old house repaired, all made into one court with a garden, covered over and stuccoed though not whitewashed, one single spacious sitting-room being left, whereas all the rest had been made part of the court. It made a good house, though not so lordly as of old. He brought me into a recess where he had in old times sought privacy, and which he had restored to its pristine magnificence, and which contained handsome furniture, though not of the former kind.

His establishment now consisted of four slaves, each of whom discharged two functions, and one old functionary whom I remembered as his servant of old, who was now re-established as porter, and a paid servant who acted as sa'is. He took his seat, and the slaves came and served him with clean plate of no great value, fruits modest both in quantity and quality, and food that was clean and sufficient, though not more. This we proceeded to eat, and then some excellent date-wine was set before me, and some date jelly, also of good quality, before him. A curtain was then drawn, and we heard some pleasant singing, while the fumes of fresh aloes, and of nadd rose together. I was curious to know how all this had come about, and when he was refreshed he said: Fellow, do you remember old times? I said I did. I am now, he continued, comfortably off, and the knowledge and experience of the world which I have gained are preferable in my opinion to my former wealth. Do you notice my furniture? It is not as grand as of old, but it is of the sort which counts as luxurious with the middle classes. The same is the case with my plate,

clothes, carriage, food, dessert, wine—and he went on with his enumeration, adding after each item "if it is not super-fine like the old, still it is fair and adequate and sufficient." Finally he came to his establishment, compared its present with its former size, and added: This does instead. Now I am freed from that terrible stress. . . .

I replied: That is all past, and praise be to God, who has replaced your loss, and delivered you from the trouble in which you were! But whence comes your present fortune and the singing-girl who is now entertaining us? He replied: She is one whom I purchased for a thousand dinars, thereby saving the singing-women's fees. My affairs are now in excellent order. I said: How do they come to be so? He replied that a servant of his father and a cousin of his in Egypt had died on one day, leaving thirty thousand dinars, which were sent to him . . . . So, he said, I thanked God, and made a resolution not to waste, but to economize, and live on my fortune 'till I die, being careful in my expenditure. So I had this house rebuilt, and purchased all its present contents, furniture, plate, clothing, mounts, slaves male and female, for 5000 dinars; five thousand more have been buried in the ground as a provision against emergencies. I have laid out ten thousand on agricultural land, producing annually enough to maintain the establishment which you have seen, with enough over each year to render it unnecessary for me to borrow before the time when the produce comes in. This is how my affairs proceed and I have been searching for you a whole year, hearing nothing about you, being anxious that you should see the restoration of my fortunes and their continued prosperity and maintenance, and after that, you infamous scoundrel, to have nothing more to do with you. Slaves, seize him by the foot! And they did drag me by the foot right out of the house, not permitting me to finish my liquor with him that day. After that when I met him riding in the streets he would smile if he saw me, and he would have nothing to do either with me or any of his former associates.

From: D. S. Margoliouth, ed., *The Table Talk of a Mesopotamian Judge* (London: Royal Asiatic Society, 1922).

FURTHER READING

Marc Bloch, *Slavery and Serfdom in the Middle Ages: Selected Essays* (Berkeley: University of California Press, 1975).

Pierre Dockés, *Medieval Slavery and Liberation* (Chicago: University of Chicago Press, 1982).

Herbert J. Foster, "Partners or Captives in Commerce? The Role of Africans in the Slave Trade," *Journal of Black Studies* 6, no. 4 (June 1976): 421–434.

Bernard Lewis, *Race and Slavery in the Middle East: An Historical Enquiry* (New York: Oxford University Press, 1990).

William Christie MacLeod, "Economic Aspects of Indigenous American Slavery," *American Anthropologist*, new series 30, no. 4 (1928): 632–650.

Anthony Reid, ed., *Slavery, Bondage, and Dependency in Southeast Asia* (New York: St. Martin's Press, 1983).

William A. Starna and Ralph Watkins, "Northern Iroquoian Slavery," *Ethnohistory* 38, no. 1 (1991): 34–57.

Hugh Thomas, *The Slave Trade* (New York, Simon and Schuster, 1997).

► social collapse and abandonment

INTRODUCTION

The history of the Old World in the Middle Ages was largely dictated by events in the relatively obscure region of inner Asia. The vast stretches of steppe from the Carpathians in Europe to the Gobi Desert north of China, from the Siberian forests in the north to the Hindu Kush mountains in the south, itself produced no great civilizations or cultural achievements, but its nomadic population shaped the medieval world. The out-migration of nomadic tribes from this area led ultimately to the destruction of the Western Roman Empire in 476 and continued to bring pressure to bear on Western culture until the defeat of the Magyars at the end of the first millennium C.E. It also led to the great pandemic of the Black Death, which killed as much as half of Europe's population between 1347 and 1350. When the steppe tribes were finally unified by Genghis Khan in the 12th century, they quickly conquered China and beyond that the largest empire ever seen, extending from Korea to Hungary and Egypt. Turkish tribesmen from inner Asia conquered the Islamic world more than once, but the Mongols had the most devastating effect on the development of Islamic civilization.

The destruction of Baghdad by the Mongols in 1258 did more damage than simply slaughtering the huge population of the city, more than tearing down the delicate and complex irrigation system on which Mesopotamian agriculture had always depended, more than destroying the library and research staff of the House of Wisdom. Islamic clerics saw this terrible calamity as the judgment of god against Islam as it had

evolved since Muhammad. In reaction, philosophical learning and the investigation of the natural world was denounced as blasphemous: the search for new knowledge implied that the revelation of the Koran was incomplete. Thousands of books of science and philosophy were burned all over the Islamic world. Greek intellectualism fell out of favor as a means of approaching and interpreting the Koran. The lifetime of the Prophet was seen as a privileged time; improvement on the era that had received the Koran seemed impossible, and to insist otherwise seemed blasphemous. Consequently, technological inventions and social reforms that had been created since that time were overturned. In particular, many astronomical observatories were destroyed as unique symbols of blasphemous curiosity and new learning. Although not all Muslims accepted this reaction, the fundamental change of view caused the Islamic world, which up to that time seemed in many ways more advanced and sophisticated than western Europe, to turn back in on itself and eventually loose the ability to react military, economically, or culturally to the west; it was largely colonized by European powers in the modern period.

Elsewhere in the world, many cultures destroyed themselves by their own success. A rising population puts pressure on the local landscape that can be sustained only by the most careful land management. The failure to shepherd resources results in a collapse of agriculture and hence of civilization. This story played itself out again and again during the Middle Ages, from Easter Island in the South Pacific to Angkor Wat in Cambodia to Great Zimbabwe in Africa to the Mayan civilization of Central America and to the Mississippian city today known as Cahokia in the center of North America. At Cahokia and on Easter Island a population brought under the tremendous pressure of famine responded with violence directed perhaps against the ruling elites but perhaps with little definite target, yet it seems that more often old centers of habitation were simply abandoned as the mismanaged lands that supported them failed.

At the very end of the Middle Ages the Americas underwent a pandemic crisis far worse even than the Black Death. Having lived in isolation from the Old World and the diseases endemic to its peoples, the population of the New World had absolutely no immunity to smallpox and other illnesses brought by the Spanish after 1492. By 1550 Old World diseases had spread throughout most of the New World, killing as much as 90 percent of the population. This, more than the concerted attacks of the relatively small number of conquistadors invading the Aztec and Inca empires, brought the downfall of the most sophisticated states in the Western Hemisphere.

AFRICA

BY BRADLEY SKEEN

Outside Egypt and the Phoenician and Greek colonies on the northern coast, the development of cities was late and rare in Africa. During the Middle Ages urbanization outside the Islamic sphere was usually brought about by unusual economic circumstances and tended to collapse either because those circumstances changed or because cultures did not adapt to the novel urban conditions. Such mundane facts are far removed from the conception of the "lost cities" in Africa of the popular imagination and even from the sometimes fantastic suppositions made by early investigators.

The beginning of the Middle Ages in the horn of Africa comes with the collapse of the kingdom of Kush (between 300 and 600), centered during this later period around the city of Meroë. Kush had become an important state in the eighth century B.C.E., when it had even briefly conquered Egypt. The heartland of Kush, however, was in the Nile Valley above the third cataract, corresponding to the northern part of modern-day Sudan.

At one time historians believed that some dramatic single event, such as the destruction of Meroë by an invading army, must have destroyed the kingdom of Kush and its civilization overnight. Such a romantic idea was fostered by the modern conditions of the ruins of the royal cemetery at Meroë, a group of more than 200 shattered pyramids half-buried by encroaching sand dunes. In fact, no archaeological evidence of such destruction (for example, a layer of burning) has been found there, so it seems rather that the city was gradually abandoned.

The royal house and aristocracy of Meroë had used the wealth they had gained from mediating trade between Egypt and East Africa to create an elite culture that modeled Egyptian civilization, but in an artificial and romanticizing way. This model included their miniature copy (at least compared with the gigantic Egyptian pyramids at Giza) of the pyramid form for their tombs—a practice that had long since been abandoned in Egypt itself—the worship of Egyptian gods, and the creation of a pseudohieroglyphic script (still undeciphered).

The collapse of Kush refers to the state's loss of its political cohesion—that is, local elites no longer could or would be controlled by the center—and the decline of the elite Egyptianizing culture. This collapse occurred because the trade between East Africa and Egypt shifted from overland routes passing through Kush to routes on the Red Sea and the Indian Ocean controlled by Axum. Without this income, the superstructure of the Meroitic monarchy, with its Egyptian pretensions and imperialist ambitions, could not be supported and fell away, leaving local economies, cultures, and political units that reverted to traditions very similar to those that had preceded the rise of Meroë. There was no longer any use for the imperial capital and its pyramids, so these were abandoned over time. What happened was a process of cultural change rather than destruction.

The kingdom of Axum dominated Ethiopia from the first century to the 10th century. It became especially important after the collapse of Meroë. Shortly after 300 the kings of Axum converted to Christianity, no more than a few years after the Roman Empire had done so. The wealth of the kingdom was based on control of the East African and Indian Ocean trade of the Roman (later Byzantine) Empire passing through the Red Sea.

Axum is best known for its royal cemetery, where 119 stone stelae were erected. The objects are slender slabs of stone up to 36 yards high, carved to resemble the facades of buildings. The tallest of these are probably the largest single pieces of stone ever quarried. At one time the cemetery seems also to have been decorated with gigantic carved thrones and colossal statues, but these were looted or destroyed before the beginning of archaeological investigation of the area. In general, the well-developed urban character of Axum and its subject cities, its sophisticated technology and engineering, and its extensive trade network made it the most sophisticated state in sub-Saharan Africa in the second half of the first millennium. The Western discovery of this ancient civilization led in the popular imagination to fantastic characterizations of its history—for example, making Axum the home of the Queen of Sheba, in this case fueled by local legends that survive from the kingdom's height. For instance, a church in Axum to this day claims to hold the Ark of the Covenant (the container of the tablets of the Mosaic Law) salvaged from the sack of Solomon's temple in Jerusalem.

The monarchy of Axum gained its power from the control of wealth that accrued from the trade passing through the Red Sea between Roman Egypt, East Africa, Arabia, and India. It used its resources to support grand displays of prestige in the gigantic monuments in the royal cemetery and to aggrandize its power in militaristic expansion (for example, the conquests of southwestern Arabia in the sixth century). It also built up an elite social structure based on the importation of foreign ideals, in this case those of the Eastern Roman or Byzantine Empire—for instance, in the use of Greek as an official language, the striking of a Byzantine standard coinage, and the adoption of Christianity. The mercantile wealth of Axum came to an end when Islamic control of the foreign ports linked through the Red Sea isolated Christian Axum. The elite culture collapsed when the source of wealth in foreign trade ended. In this case, however, the abandonment of urban centers and the end of elite culture left important changes in society as a whole, especially in the establishment of the Ethiopian Christian Church as an institution.

Weakened by its economic decline, the city of Axum was destroyed in the 10th century by the army of the Ethiopian queen Gudit (fl. 960), a figure as much legendary as historical. Thereafter, Ethiopian culture turned inward, retreated from the sea and contact with the Islamic and Orthodox Christian worlds, and devolved into a rural, feudal state.

No archaeological site in Africa has been as misunderstood as Great Zimbabwe (located in the modern-day state that is its namesake). Its European discoverers fantasized that these extensive ruins of large masonry walls in the interior of Africa must be the lost city of the Queen of Sheba of biblical fame. In fact, every effort was made, for political reasons, to argue that the city had been built by anyone other than native Africans. More rational explanations of Great Zimbabwe's rise and fall would have to await the application of scientific archaeology to the ruins in the mid-20th century.

Zimbabwe means "walled enclosure" in the Shona language, and the name Great Zimbabwe is applied to the center of a civilization that flourished between about 1250 and 1450 in modern Zimbabwe. Great Zimbabwe is today the ruined remains of a city that underwent rapid expansion in building and population growth after 1400 so that it reached a population of as many as 18,000 immediately prior to its sudden abandonment in 1450. It is surrounded by lesser *zimbabwes* comprising settlements of a few hundred or few thousand peoples. The dressed drystone walls of all these settlements enclosed small groups of huts and were surrounded by much larger numbers of huts that served as the dwelling places for the population at large. The walls must have separated a small but dominant political or religious elite. It is clear that the style of stonework is unrelated to that found anywhere else in the world; it evolved from older and simpler structures that had been built in that area several centuries before the creation of an urban center. These walls were built entirely for the purposes of display, since they would not have been suitable for any military purpose such as city walls are in other areas of the world. Great Zimbabwe probably began as a religious center, with stone walls used to mark off sacred space. Archaeologists generally accept that the Shona people who occupied the area of Great Zimbabwe at the time of European penetration into the area are the descendents of the Zimbabwe builders and that they share a language and culture that, according to their own historical traditions, was present in the area from 1000 or before.

The necessary precondition for the beginning of an urban center like Great Zimbabwe was wealth that could be concentrated in the hands of a ruling elite. Great Zimbabwe and its satellite communities were located on a plateau too high to be bothered by the tsetse fly infestation that makes living conditions so difficult throughout much of Africa because of this insect's spread of sleeping sickness. When the cattle-herding ancestors of the Shona people moved into this area, that fact alone must have greatly increased their wealth and prospects. However, a ruling elite controlled some greater source of wealth that allowed them to dominate their culture by conspicuous displays, such as the building of their walled enclosures. This source of wealth was probably a trade in gold. There is ample archaeological evidence for gold mining in the region contemporary with the development of urbanization. The extent of the trade has been revealed by the discovery inside Great Zimbabwe of manufactured goods from as far away as Persia, India, and China.

The rapid growth of Great Zimbabwe and its satellite communities posed the same problems that cities face everywhere in the world. However, the elite class of the Zimbabwe civilization seems to have failed to meet the demands of these problems with the fundamental changes in technology and agriculture that enable the growth of urban civilizations. No evidence of a sanitation system in Great Zimbabwe exists. In a city of 18,000 people the lack of a sanitation system would mean that human and animal waste would have piled up near places of habitation, with a consequent high incidence of disease and mortality. The area would soon have been stripped of firewood so that this vital commodity would have had to have been carted from ever increasing distances, hence become increasingly scarce and expensive. As labor was diverted away from the cattle-based agriculture that was the foundation of the society, dietary substitutions of cereal crops for the poor masses in Great Zimbabwe would have impacted their health and well-being. Even this form of agriculture would have become increasingly difficult as the fertility of farmland degraded. Building up over two or three centuries, such environmental deterioration would have made life in Great Zimbabwe unlivable for its inhabitants. Whatever problems existed would have been made worse by the rapid burst of population growth after 1400. It is no wonder, then, that the people living in Great Zimbabwe eventually broke their allegiance to the elite culture that had fostered urbanization and simply abandoned the city to return to the pastoral way of life of their ancestors.

THE AMERICAS

BY KEITH JORDAN

Several periods of social collapse punctuate the history of the Mississippian culture (ca. 750–ca. 1500) of the Eastern Woodlands in North America. Archaeological evidence shows that the power of the first great Mississippian center, the city of Cahokia in Illinois, began to decline in the mid-12th century. Local villages surrounding the site were abandoned, and a defensive palisade was built around the temples and the chief's houses at the center of the city. Perhaps to compensate for a decline in the chief's real power, chiefly costumes and symbols became more complex and elaborate. By a century later the city's population had declined by about 60 percent. At the same time there was a sharp decline in the manufacture of decorated objects that may have been used by chiefs to secure the loyalty of their followers. The growth of noble families may have led to increased competition at the top levels of the society.

Natural factors also played a role in Cahokia's demise. Two periods of drought, each about 25 years long, beset the area in the early 13th century, and there is geological evidence that local creeks started to fill up with silt, possibly causing flooding. There is also some evidence for a rise in the local water table. The Cahokians may have contributed to their own demise by deforesting the area for fuel and construction. In the late 13th century an earthquake may have damaged the main temple mound at the site, and a related chiefly center in East Saint Louis, Illinois, was burned, perhaps by invaders. The Cahokian population declined further until the city had almost completely been abandoned by 1400. However, the inhabitants of Cahokia did not merely "disappear" or "decline." They may well have migrated onto the Great Plains and left their farming lifestyle to take up buffalo hunting, as did the ancestors of the Osage, the Omaha, and the Quapaw Native Americans.

Individual Mississippian centers rose and fell over the next two centuries, but the culture as a whole seems to have collapsed decisively in the 16th century following the Spanish expedition of Hernando de Soto into the Southeast from Mexico. Although de Soto's journey through the Southeast was relatively brief and did not result in a Spanish conquest of the native peoples like what happened to the Aztec and the Inca, its legacy was just as deadly. De Soto's men and animals introduced into the area diseases for which the indigenous peoples had no immunity, leading to massive epidemics. These diseases created dramatic population decline and social chaos, and the knowledge of Mississippian religious and governmental lore died with the chiefs and priests, surviving into modern times only in fragmentary form.

Although popular and New Age writings are full of references to the mysterious "disappearance" of the Anasazi, or ancestral Pueblo, peoples of the North American Southwest, in fact several periods of site abandonment took place during the development of this culture. The huge and influential site of Chaco Canyon, New Mexico, was abandoned and lost its apparent political power in the early 12th century. The decline was probably the result of many factors rather than a single cause. Excess population growth may have led to overcrowding, thus exhausting the farming lands around the site, and skeletal remains bear some evidence of increasing malnutrition. According to scientific study of tree growth rings from the area, a major drought struck Chaco around 1090. While the rains resumed in the early 12th century, summer rains tended to arrive later and end earlier than they had previously done. Although construction continued at Chaco to around 1120, this did not stop the movement of people out of the canyon, and exotic goods, like copper bells from Mexico, ceased to be traded into the site. If the site was a powerful religious center controlled by ritual specialists, as some archaeologists think, the influence of religious leaders might have declined sharply when their rituals did not succeed in bringing needed rain in the face of the drought. Their followers, losing confidence, may then have abandoned them, and not even the eventual return of the rains was able to stop the process.

Man-made environmental problems may have compounded the natural ones. The Chacoans cut down whole forests for construction timber during the 10th and 11th centuries, altering the environment and leading to soil erosion. It is possible that the rulers of Chaco resettled at the site of Aztec, New Mexico, where Chaco building and burial traits last until around 1250, before finally taking over the trading center of Casas Grandes in northern Mexico in the 13th century. In any event, subsequent societies in the Southwest seem much more egalitarian, perhaps in reaction to the failure of the Chaco elite.

After the collapse of Chaco, Anasazi settlements flourished at Mesa Verde, Colorado, and in the San Juan River basin, but then these areas, too, were abandoned between around 1270 and 1300. Indeed, the whole northern Southwest or Four Corners region was drastically depopulated at this time, with the inhabitants moving south to become the historic Pueblo peoples encountered by Spanish explorers in the 16th century. The number of people in the Mesa Verde area, for example, dropped from around 15,000 to 7,000 by about 1280 and plummeted further in the next two decades. In some cases, the abandonment seems to have been quite orderly—people sealed up their houses and took their valuables with them. A drought struck the Four Corners between 1276 and 99, according to tree-ring data, and spread in the same direction as the migrations, from north to south, but again the drought seems to be just one of many contributing factors to the abandonment rather the primary cause of it.

Already in the early 13th century, the so-called Little Ice Age led to longer, colder winters in the Southwest, drier conditions, decreased spring sunlight, and shorter farming seasons. Natural phenomena alone do not account for the collapse of the Four Corners Anasazi. Some areas, like the San Juan River valley, were little affected by the drought but were abandoned nonetheless. Population growth at Anasazi settlements, in the absence of a strong unifying belief system as seems to have been present at Chaco, might have led to social conflict and chaos. The early Pueblos adopted or developed the kachina cult (ancestor worship) after the migration as an ideology promoting community cohesion and cooperation. There is evidence for widespread warfare in the Four Corners before the abandonment—skeletons showing signs of violent death, placement of settlements on easily defended cliffs, defensive towers, painted images of warriors, and whole sites burned and destroyed. This evidence suggests chronic conflict between communities over scarce natural resources, a pattern that continued among Pueblo groups up to the European invasions of the 16th and 17th centuries.

The decline of the Classic (ca. 250–ca. 850) Mayan city-states of the lowlands of Guatemala, Belize, southern Mexico, and western Honduras is one of the most-discussed, often hyped, and controversial social collapses in human history. As is the case with the Anasazi, pseudoscientific claims in current popular literature suggest that the Maya simply vanished from the earth. The Maya did not disappear; rather, at the end of the Classic Period they abandoned many settlements as well as the Classic institution of rule by individual divine kings. They did not decline as a whole culture—in fact, several Mayan cities went on to flourish and fall in succession in the Yucatán after the Classic Period, and Mayan states were warring and trading with each other as well as creating art at the time of the Spanish Conquest in the 16th century. Moreover, the "collapse" of the Maya did not take place all in one blow. Rather, it was a gradual process of abandonment of cities and institutions spread across more than a century. New construction had ceased at most Classic Mayan cities by the mid-ninth century, but some sites in Belize saw continuous habitation and construction up until the arrival of the Spanish. Royal inscriptions using the Long Count dating system, another hallmark of Classic Maya culture, ceased to be produced gradually, with the last-known recorded Long Count date in the lowlands corresponding to 910.

The causes of this change were many. There is evidence of increased and mutually destructive competitive warfare among the separate city-states as they tried to dominate each other, similar to the conditions that contributed to the decline of the classical Greek states. The goal of warfare for most of the Classic Period was to capture and sacrifice a rival king, so military operations were limited. At the time of the collapse this military conflict seems to have degenerated into outright wars of conquest. Fortifications became more common in the ninth century, and several cities show evidence of destruction. Populations in some cities grew quite large in the late Classic Period and may have exceeded the carrying capacity of Mayan agriculture. Deforestation and soil erosion may have led to the waning influence of Mayan kings, who as shamans were supposed to be magically responsible via their rituals for the fertility of the land.

At some cities like Copán, there is evidence that the power of nonroyal noble families grew to rival and ultimately eclipse the king's own power, and in general, Mayan royal families themselves grew, leading to conflicts among rival claimants to kingship. The rulers may have attempted to compensate for their problems at home by organizing more monumental construction in their own honor, leading to further environmental degradation. Invasion from central Mexico was once a popular theory for the collapse, but the evidence for large movements of foreigners into Mayan lands has been debunked, and many new artistic features once seen as evidence of Mexican "influence" are now recognized as local and Mayan in origin. Natural disasters have been suspected as additional culprits, and in fact, there is scientific evidence of severe droughts in the Yucatán in the ninth and 10th centuries. However, this drought did not affect the whole Mayan region, and the Yucatán was not abandoned but flourished during the "collapse." In addition, the abandonment of some sites was well under way before these droughts. As in North America, though natural disasters may have contributed to social collapse, they certainly were not the primary cause.

The great metropolis of Teotihuacán in the basin of Mexico met a catastrophic end around 650, and possibly as much as a century earlier. Though the city itself was not completely abandoned, most of its population of 125,000 to 200,000 left after the temples and elite residences at the center of the site were burned and destroyed. Foreign invasion is one possible explanation for the destruction, but internal social factors leading to a revolt or civil war seem more likely. As with the Maya, Teotihuacán's vast agricultural and building projects may have led to deforestation and natural disaster, which the leadership tried to remedy with religion through building more monuments, leading to social collapse in a vicious circle.

The Toltec capital of Tula in the central Mexican state of Hidalgo fell from power and was sacked and burned around 1150, according to archaeological data. The culprits were probably seminomadic Chichimec, migrants from the arid north of Mexico driven south by worsening climate conditions. Their ranks may have included some of the ancestors of the Aztec.

The city of Cerro Blanco, center of a powerful Moche state in northern Peru, fell upon hard times in the late sixth century, struck by a succession of natural disasters, including drought, floods, and possibly even an earthquake. Though the city recovered and was rebuilt, it lost much of its prestige, and the center of political power shifted to the site of Pampa Grande, while the ideology of Moche rulership weakened. By 800 Pampa Grande itself was abandoned after the palaces of the elite were burned and plundered, most likely by their disgruntled subjects.

Although some popular crank literature continues to assert that the Tiwanaku state of Bolivia and its influence collapsed in 12,000 B.C.E. owing to a cosmic catastrophe, the more sober archaeological truth is that its power declined between 1000 and 1100 C.E. The natural events that spurred its downfall were less than cosmic but were nonetheless significant. Core samples from lakes and glaciers in the Andes reveal that severe climate changes beset the region between 1000 and 1300, leading to a marked reduction in annual rainfall. The drought lasted for decades (at least) and caused the failure of the agricultural base of Tiwanaku civilization. The political sphere, or "empire," of the city collapsed, and its inhabitants may have ritually destroyed the site before they abandoned it.

ASIA AND THE PACIFIC
by Laura Lee Junker

In discussing cases of collapse of civilizations or societies in Asian and Pacific medieval history, it is important to understand that "collapse" generally involves the breakdown of social and political institutions that define particular societies but rarely involves the wholesale annihilation or disappearance of the people who made up that society. (Easter Island, as discussed here, may be seen as an exception.) The causes of social collapse in human history are diverse, as we will see in the examples outlined here. They may include conquest by a foreign group, environmental disasters or degradation affecting economic viability (for instance, drought, destruction by typhoons, disease and depopulation, ecological changes), social conflict within a society (such as competition for power or uprisings of disenfranchised groups), or more often a convergence of several factors. As the social fabric and structures of state organization begin to unravel as a result of these stresses, most of the population (particularly the nonelites, who are not part of the government) are generally absorbed into conquering nations or radically change their social and economic strategy to survive (that is, they make themselves over as a new form of society).

Medieval India between the fifth and 16th centuries had a fragmented political landscape consisting of numerous highly militaristic kingdoms and empires in which political structure and authority was defined and legitimated by religious ideals, including Buddhism in the early phases, followed by Hinduism and Islam. Large urban centers like Multan, Gaur, Tughlaqabad, and Vijayanagar were used as the anchors for territorial expansion and foreign trade that eventually reached central Asia, China, Africa, and the Near East. The political fortunes of these kingdoms and empires appear to have hinged on military might, the ability to claim ideological right through strategic use of religious fervor, and a powerful economy. The last included the capacity for industrial-level production of export commodities (such as silk, semiprecious stone beads, and indigo), efficient transport of goods by sea and land (allowing the polity to monopolize the lucrative foreign trade market), and massive agricultural production. When one or more of these military, economic and religious elements failed, dominant polities collapsed and ceded power to rising kingdoms.

Vijayanagar, the capital of the Hindu empire that ruled southern India in the 14th through 16th centuries, was overrun in 1565 by a conquering Islamic Mogul army from the north. The elites fled southward, leaving abandoned and in ruins religious and administrative architecture, critical irrigation systems, and commercial centers. Social, ideological, and economic collapse followed military conquest, since the remaining Hindu population (largely peasants) lost their religious center, state-defined systems of caste, large-scale state-run water-control systems that had made agriculture productive in the arid environment, and established links in international commerce.

Similarly, the sultanate of Bengal, in the 13th through 16th centuries, centered at the city of Gaur on the India-Bangladesh border, went from a regional powerhouse in foreign trade toward rapid collapse in the mid-16th century owing to an unfortunate confluence of factors: military invasion by the Afghan leader Sher Shah, the loss of commercial preeminence to competing trade powers, and a plague that decimated the demographic base of the state. In both cases external polities quickly filled the economic and political void in the regions.

While China tended to support extensive unified empires through this period, it also went through cycles of political fragmentation, collapse of state structures, and significant shifts in the social order. The Tang Dynasty (581–907) in China, with its demise at the end of the ninth century, is one of the best-studied cases of social collapse in medieval period Chinese societies. The Tang rulers, through military force and unprecedented economic expansion, forged an empire that unified what is now northern and southern China, expanded into northern Vietnam and northern Korea, and controlled western steppe trade routes by invading vast areas of central Asia. Most important, the empire exported its con-

Eleven-headed Kannon, Japan, 13th century; the bodhisattva Kannon is the manifestation of the wisdom and infinite compassion of the universal Buddha, who was especially popular among the Japanese of the 11th and 12th centuries, a time of social upheaval. (Freer Gallery of Art, Smithsonian Institution, Gift of Charles Lang Freer, F1904-350)

cepts of aristocratic privilege, court culture, highly centralized political rule, and a strong state control of commerce to Korea, Japan, and other distant lands, with the spectacular capital of Xi'an (then called Ch'angan, the largest city in the world) serving as a model for orderly and cultured society.

However, the social system in which noble pedigrees bought access to political authority and in which social and economic mobility was highly constrained soon cracked under the strain of social rebellion. Disenfranchised military leaders marched on the capital, and the emperor was forced to restore order by allowing the rebels to establish private fiefdoms within the rapidly decentralizing state. This was soon followed by a loosening of central management over commerce and markets, allowing the rise of a new independently wealthy merchant class. Faced with internal unrest from military governors, embittered and scheming aristocrats, a rising merchant class, bandit gangs of disenfranchised lower classes, and even scheming court eunuchs, the weakened Tang Dynasty fell military prey to antagonistic states along its borders (including the Tibetans and Turkish Uighurs). The final collapse of the Tang 907 ushered in a period of political fragmentation in the north and a decline of aristocratic ideals. Society was reshaped into one with unprecedented social mobility and economic opportunity. This new social pattern was reinforced in the new Southern Song state (907–1276) by Confucian scholars, who emphasized that the ideal society was one in which power and social action were centered at the local community level.

Both Korea and Japan saw repeated patterning of strongly centralized states, followed by social and political crisis and fragmentation into a political landscape of regional powers. In Korea the powerful kingdom of Silla (668–891) was patterned after the Tang as a highly centralized state ruled by hereditary aristocracy whose wealth contrasted sharply with the slavelike conditions of the commoners. However, the state soon disintegrated under peasant uprisings, the rise of independently powerful "castle lords" out of the besieged local aristocracy, the rise of new sects of Zen Buddhism that emphasized individualized spiritual enlightenment and agency, and economic instability driven by difficulties in tax collection and decentralization of sources of wealth and production. As in China, a cycle of political fragmentation was followed by unification by a powerful state (Koryo, 918–1392) which attempted to redress some of these internal social and economic issues through new concepts of merit in civil service, attempts at land distribution and tax reforms, and limits on aristocratic power. However, internal class conflict continued to plague the Koryo kingdom, weakening it to the point where the Mongol Yuan Empire in China was able to conquer Koryo and establish it as a client Yuan state.

In Southeast Asia the numerous tropical maritime trading kingdoms of the medieval period were notoriously socially unstable and politically fragile, owing at least partly to economies heavily reliant on foreign commerce, ethnic heterogeneity, and leaders with authority that derived from continual alliance building rather than fixed hereditary rights. Political cycling, in which regional power centers rose and fell with surprising rapidity, rather than enduring hegemony by a single polity, was the norm in the region. The Khmer state (ninth through 15th centuries), centered in present-day Cambodia, was unusually resilient but collapsed eventually as the result of military pressure and environmental factors. The Khmer state was politically consolidated out of a number of independent regional chiefdoms by King Jayavarman II (r. ca. 790–850), whose successors built the spectacular Hindu and than Buddhist-oriented centers of Angkor Thom and Angkor Wat, consisting of extensive complexes of temples, monuments, reservoirs, canals, and elite residential structures.

While the Khmer state gained great wealth through maritime commerce, their economic staple was large-scale wet-rice production supported through extensive irrigation and reservoir systems. Remarkable carved relief scenes on the temples and other public architecture emphasize the military power of the Khmer state as it expanded against its neighbors (Champa to the east, the Vietnamese in the north, the Thais to the west, and the Malays to the south) with sophisticated ships and a well-armed land-based military led by elephant-riding generals. However, the decline of Khmer political dominance in the region and the collapse of Khmer social fabric by the late 14th and early 15th centuries is attributed by scholars to a combination of economic, ecological, and military factors: a precipitous fall in agricultural surplus due to environmental changes and failure of irrigation technologies, military expansion of the rising Siamese people to the east and the invading Mongols to the north, and rapidly increasing malaria due to standing water in irrigated rice fields.

In the Pacific islands we have perhaps some of the strongest historical and archaeological evidence for the various environmental, technological, and social factors that lead to the so-called collapse and even near-disappearance of societies. Easter Island (or Rapa Nui), an isolated island in the southeastern Pacific settled by migrating Polynesians (probably Marquesans) sometime around 400 to 500, had serious ecological constraints, including its relatively small size (only about 100 square miles), no permanent rivers for water and crop irrigation (only three freshwater volcanic lakes in the rugged interior), few indigenous mammals and cultivatable plants, no highly productive shallow coral reefs for marine harvesting, and considerable distance from other islands (around 1,240 miles from the nearest inhabitable island) that

precluded trade as a safety net. In addition, many of the traditional equatorial crops of Polynesian colonizers would not grow well in the somewhat cooler climate of Easter Island, so chicken was their only domesticated animal, and sweet potato, yams, banana and gourds were their staple crops.

In the first thousand years after initial settlement the Easter Islanders flourished in the form of several socially stratified chiefdoms that supported themselves fairly adequately through farming and fishing and built an increasingly dense landscape of villages and chief's residences, represented archaeologically by the fortified village of Orongo, comprising 48 oval stone houses with earthen roofs. Ceremonial activity centered on *ahu*, large rectangular ceremonial platforms built of volcanic rock (a large one called Tongariki, measuring around 148 feet in length and 10 feet high). These often supported rows of huge stone statuary (the largest more than 30 feet high and weighing more than 50 tons), legless busts with outsized heads sporting topknot hairstyles and elongated earlobes that might represent sacred ancestors.

Archaeological evidence and contact period European accounts suggest that Easter Island society began a dramatic decline some time around 1500 to 1600. By the time of initial European discovery in 1722, the Dutch explorers found a population of 1,000 from an estimated high of 10,000 prior to 1600, a barren landscape largely devoid of trees, many of the ceremonial *ahu* in ruins, and little evidence for the social stratification and political complexity attested by archaeological research for earlier periods. Archaeological investigations and the study of oral traditions suggest that a combination of population increase beyond the carrying capacity of the environment, ecological degradation by the human population, and social conflict over dwindling resources all contributed to societal collapse.

Archaeological settlement studies show that the population continued to grow throughout the Easter Island occupation but reached critical levels in the century or so before European contact. Geological studies of the history of soil erosion and paleobotanical studies of changes in pollen preserved in ancient soils indicate that trees were slowly and then more rapidly depleted as populations used wood for fuel, for canoe and house building, and for wooden rollers to move the several-ton statues from interior quarries to coastal *ahu* and cleared fields for expanding agricultural fields. Erosion and heavy farming degraded the soils and reduced agricultural productivity, while fewer wood canoes curtailed fishing and negated the possibility of maritime "escape" routes off the island.

Social conflict and warfare between groups on the island are evidenced in the appearance of possible defensive lava tube "refuges" in the island interior, the building of the 2-

mile-long Poike Ditch to defend a peninsula on the island, the proliferation of obsidian spearheads, the destruction of *ahu*, and the emergence of intensified ritual that included a bird cult and possible cannibalistic rites. While archaeological evidence indicates that there were probably several territorially discrete chiefdoms on the island at the height of development, oral traditions collected after contact tell a story of apocalyptic war in the 17th century between enigmatic groups known as the "Long Ears" and "Short Ears" that resulted in annihilation of most of the population. Archaeological work on at least a dozen islands elsewhere in the Pacific (popularly known as the "Mystery Islands") has documented prehistoric occupation but no inhabitants at European contact, suggesting that eventual failure of societies on small, remote islands due to economic nonviability and social conflict is not an unusual outcome.

EUROPE

BY BRADLEY A. SKEEN

During the Middle Ages western Europe suffered three periods of social collapse that resulted in the transformation of society and the loss of whole villages, cities, and ways of life: the barbarian invasions that destroyed the Western Roman Empire in the fifth and sixth centuries; the renewed waves of barbarian invasions in the ninth and 10th centuries that led to the institution of feudalism; and the pandemic of bubonic plague that killed approximately one-half of the population in the middle 14th century. In addition, eastern Europe suffered two catastrophic invasions in the later Middle Ages that resulted in the Mongol occupation of Russia and the destruction of the Byzantine Empire.

In the fourth and fifth centuries a massive out-migration of nomadic tribes from central Asia had a domino effect all the way to the Roman Empire, with one group of people displacing another in a chain that stretched from beyond the Urals to the borders of the empire. In the sixth century another wave of Asiatic invaders, among them, the Avars, forced more Germans into former Roman territories, notably the Franks into France and the Lombards into Italy. The Lombard invasion of Italy in the 560s and 570s was especially devastating. Nearly every town in the Po valley was sacked. Refugees from the region fled to the sandbars north of the mouth of the Po, where they eventually founded the city of Venice.

In 541 and 542 a pandemic of bubonic plague, probably beginning in Ethiopia, swept over Europe, especially the Byzantine Empire. As many as 25,000,000 people died, including as much as 40 percent of the population of the Byzantine Empire. It came at the very moment that the emperor Justinian (r. 527–65) was making the last realistic attempt to reconquer the Western Roman Empire, forever dooming that project. As is typical of the plague, major outbreaks recurred in the Byzantine Empire about every generation for the next two centuries.

The cumulative effects of these disasters created an entirely different and much-impoverished world between 350 and 650. From a demographic perspective the population of Europe declined by more than half, perhaps much more. The usual estimate for Italy, the hardest-hit area, is that the population in 600 was only one-seventh of what it had been two centuries earlier. Very few population centers had been abandoned, but huge stretches of countryside that had contained rich villas and prosperous farms were completely depopulated. Large Roman cities, which once had populations of 100,000 or more, now had no more people than a village.

The case of Rome and its environs was one of the most extreme, but it was far from unique. The population of Rome and its port of Ostia in 400 must have been close to 1 million. By 600 Ostia had almost completely vanished, with most of the city buried under rubble and accumulated earth. In Rome itself the small remaining population lived in the ruins of public buildings. For example, the hollow spaces of the triumphal arches of the emperors were broken open and converted into dwellings. The Roman Forum, which had once been the political and economic center of the Western world, became a sheep pasture, with most of its temples and government buildings pulled down. The entire documentary history of the Roman Empire had been stored in government offices in Rome in 400; by 600 they had been destroyed. Roman factory complexes such as the pottery works at La Graufesenque in France, which produced more than 100,000 ceramic items of all kinds per month, or the water-powered flour mills such as those at Barbegal in France or on the Janiculum Hill in Rome, which produced 4 to 5 tons of flour per day, were abandoned and forgotten. In short, an entire civilization was destroyed during the course of those few centuries.

By 800, the year of the coronation of Charlemagne as the first Holy Roman Emperor (r. 800–14), western Europe had slowly recovered in terms of population and political institutions, even if it still lacked great urban centers, and its intellectual life was already centered on recovering the Roman past rather than making its own progress. But at this time, new incursions, usually in the form of violent raids, from outside peoples again broke up the cohesion of western Europe, in this case those of the Vikings from Scandinavia, of Asiatic Magyars moving from the eastern steppes into the region of modern-day Hungary and devastating Germany, and of Islamic forces from across the Mediterranean. This led to a breakdown of central authority and the waste of resources required for military reaction to the raids. In many local areas these raids were quite devastating (but it must also be said that Viking settlement led to the founding of many towns and the so-called Norman principalities in France and Sicily). More particularly, the institution of feudalism—in which political power was decentralized into the hands of noblemen holding castles serving as places of refuge in the countryside—was in place by the time order was generally restored about the year 1000. The raids left western Europe far more politically fragmented than it had been before.

By 1300 Europe had reached a population approaching 100 million, probably larger than the Roman Empire's at its height. But a pandemic of bubonic plague known as the Black Death killed between one-third and one-half of the total population between 1347 and 1350. Rural areas like Poland had lower death rates, while Italy, the most heavily urbanized part of Europe, is now thought to have had a death toll of at least two-thirds of its population. This again led to the abandonment of vast regions of countryside and its reversion from farmland to forest. The Jewish ghettos of Mainz, Strasbourg, and other Rhineland cities were completely depopulated, not through plague but through anti-Semitic violence—inspired by the general panic brought about by the crisis—that killed thousands of Jews and induced any survivors to flee as refugees. The Black Death also brought about the end of the feudal system of enserfed agricultural labor. Those peasants who survived found that the value of their labor, and with it their social mobility, had dramatically increased. They could now bargain for higher wages or readily find high-paying work in the towns and cities.

Eastern Slavic civilization was organized between the upper Dnieper and Don rivers into a federation of essentially independent principalities known as Kiev Rus, named for the most powerful of the small states. After an initial reconnaissance that resulted in an overwhelming victory at the Kalka river in 1223, Mongols led by Batu Khan (d. 1255), Genghis Khan's grandson, and Sabutai (ca. 1172–1245), Genghis's ablest subordinate, invaded Kiev Rus, completely overwhelmed all military resistance, and destroyed every major city (except Pskov and Novgorod in the northwest). Much of the surviving population fled to the uninhabited forests of the northeast. The foundation established by hundreds of Orthodox Christian monasteries in the area was instrumental in the survival of the Russian people and culture. The principality of Moscow was eventually built up in the area and became the ancestor of the modern Russian state. The Mongols continued their nomadic tradition and lived apart from their agriculturalist subjects, but they imposed heavy taxes that had to be paid throughout the medieval period. As a result, this period of Russian history is traditionally referred to as the Mongol Yoke, as though Russia were a beast of burden laboring under a yoke.

Arab invaders defeated forces of the Byzantine Empire at Yarmuk in Syria in 636, opening the way for the conquest of all Byzantine possessions in Asia south of the Tarsus Mountains (just northwest of the modern-day border between Turkey and Syria) and in Africa. Islamic forces frequently raided into Asia Minor, however, and as early as 674 they lay siege to Constantinople, the Byzantine capital, on the European coast just across the Bosporus from Asia Minor. That attempt, and several more in succeeding centuries, always failed. Byzantine fortunes rose and fell, but in 1204 Constantinople was captured for the first time, not by Muslims, however, but by Christian European crusaders who had been admitted to the city to help its defense. Byzantine rule of the city was eventually restored, but the fragmented empire never recovered. By 1354 Ottoman Turks invaded Europe, conquering much of the Balkans in the battle of Kosovo (1389), leaving Constantinople little more than a city-state. In 1453, Sultan Mehmed II, called the Conqueror (r. 1444–46 and 1451–81) finally captured the city, attacking it with an army of 80,000 men against about 7,000 defenders, bringing to an end more than 2,000 years of Roman and Byzantine history. A few Byzantine intellectuals, who either had fled to Italy earlier in the 15th century or actually escaped the siege itself on a Venetian fleet that broke out of the naval blockade, helped—particularly with their personal libraries—to spur the Renaissance and are primarily responsible for the modern world's fragmentary knowledge of ancient Greek literature. Undoubtedly, thousands more texts of Greek authors existed in Constantinople and were destroyed when the Turks sacked the city.

THE ISLAMIC WORLD

by Tom Streissguth

The Islamic conquests of the seventh and eighth centuries established the new faith from Afghanistan to the Middle East and North Africa. After the death of its founder, Muhammad (ca. 570–632), Islam spread from its home in Mecca and Medina in the Arabian Peninsula. Under the first caliphs, who combined political and religious authority, Islamic armies defeated the Sassanid Empire of Persia and the Byzantine armies in the Middle East and Egypt. The Muslims established the realm of al-Andalus in the Iberian Peninsula and advanced as far as Tours, in central France, where they were turned back in 732 at the battle of Tours by an army of Christian Franks and Burgundians.

A Muslim domain was also established on the island of Sicily in the early 10th century. The governors contended with constant raiding from armies of the Byzantine Empire, while civil war among different ruling factions further weakened the island's defenses. In the middle of the 10th century several emirs (governors) allied with the Normans, who were

Christians from northern Europe, and invited them to invade Sicily. The war between Muslim and Christian armies lasted a generation before the fall of Palermo in 1072. Muslim control ended, and in the following years Muslim civilians converted to Christianity or fled the island.

In Mesopotamia the Islamic civilization was attaining great heights in philosophy, science, mathematics, astronomy, and medicine. But the Muslim domain was too large to be effectively governed from a single capital, and its frontiers were vulnerable to raids and invasion. At the end of the 10th century nomadic tribes of central Asian Turks swept across the Amu Darya (Oxus) River and southward into Persia. The Turks invaded Khorasan and what is now eastern Iran, conquering the city of Nishapur. In 1040 the Turks won a key battle at Dandanakan. The Seljuk Empire that had been founded by a Turkish dynasty spread across Mesopotamia and the Middle East, holding cities for ransom and reducing them to ruins whenever they resisted. Behind the Turks followed new hordes of central Asian nomads who raided towns, ports, caravans, oases, and settled farms throughout the Middle East as far north as Azerbaijan and Asia Minor.

By the 1070s the Turks had reached Egypt. Governed by the Fatimid Dynasty, which ruled most of North Africa, Egypt had been devastated by a long drought and famine, and Fatimid control was challenged by the revolt of the Zirids, a family of local rulers who sought independence. A powerful confederation of Arab tribes known as the Banu Hilal was spreading into North Africa at the invitation of the Fatimids. Following the Banu Hilal invasion the Turks also arrived in the Nile Valley, uprooting the Fatimid administration and creating chaos wherever they went.

A new threat came to the Levant in the late 11th century, when the first wave of Christian crusaders landed on the Mediterranean shores of Palestine. Fired by their religious zeal and the promise of rich rewards of gold and land, the crusaders were led by a skilled military aristocracy charged by the pope with the task of recapturing the holy city of Jerusalem. The heavily armored knights and well-trained foot soldiers of Europe won a string of victories against the mobile Arab cavalry, besieging and taking the city of Antioch in Syria and finally reaching the walls of Jerusalem in June 1099. The Muslim governor of the city expelled all the Christians within the walls and fortified the walls with thousands of archers.

The Christians answered with mobile siege towers. These tall platforms were brought up to the city walls and used by the Christian infantry to storm across the ramparts on the morning of July 15. The fall of the city was followed by a massacre of its inhabitants. The Christians did not discriminate between civilian and soldier or spare Jews, Muslims, or fellow Christians; every inhabitant found was executed, and the bodies of the victims were piled high outside the city walls

and burned. The crusader realms that were established after this event usurped Muslim rulers from the Sinai Peninsula north to Antioch and the upper Euphrates valley (which became the Christian County of Edessa), although Christians always made up a minority in the region.

In Mesopotamia the Abbasid Caliphate that ruled from the city of Baghdad had survived the onslaught of the Turks in the 11th century. Dating from 751 the caliphs controlled tributary states from the Caspian Sea to the Persian Gulf. By the 13th century, however, the caliphate was in decline. The caliph himself had little authority, and true control of the realm had passed to military leaders among the Turks and Mamluks (a caste of soldiers that had risen from slavery to seize control of Egypt).

In the early 13th century, meanwhile, nomadic Mongol tribes inhabited the steppes north of China, in distant northeastern Asia. Their leader Genghis Khan (ca. 1162–1227) forged a powerful army of skilled cavalry fighters, drilled in complex maneuvers designed to confuse and outwit their enemies. Beginning in the 1220s the Mongols swept through central Asia, capturing the important city of Mary (formerly Merv), in what is now Turkmenistan and putting every single inhabitant, except for a few hundred useful artisans, to the sword. The cities of Bukhara, Urganch, and Samarqand fell in quick order, their inhabitants killed or scattered.

In Persia the Mongols often defeated their enemies with sheer terror. By utterly destroying cities that did not agree to surrender, they spread a fearsome reputation through the region, a reputation that persuaded many garrisons simply to give up without a fight. In cities that did resist, the Mongols slaughtered the men, enslaved women and children, and brought artisans home to serve them in their homeland in the Asian steppes.

Under Hülegü Khan (ca. 1217–65), the grandson of Genghis Khan, the Mongols reached Baghdad in 1258 and immediately demanded the surrender of the caliph. Confident of victory, the caliph failed to reinforce the city or gather reinforcements, and Hülegü soon had Baghdad surrounded. The city formally surrendered on February 10, and three days later the Mongols marched into the city, beginning a slaughter and reducing Baghdad to a smoking ruin. The Mongols destroyed every major public building in the city, including the magnificent Abbasid palaces, libraries, and mosques. The caliph himself was executed in a traditional Mongol way, by being rolled into a carpet and trampled to death by horses. The survivors fled Baghdad, many of them purposely spared by the Mongols to serve as messengers of the destruction awaiting anyone who refused to submit.

The Mongol invasion of Mesopotamia brought a centuries-long decline in the region. Irrigation canals and dams were destroyed, setting back agriculture and returning much of the land to desert. The abandonment of Baghdad and other important cities dealt a major blow to Islamic advancements in the sciences, while the caliphate itself moved to Egypt, where it came under the domination of the Mamluk warrior caste. In the late 13th century, after a Mongol army was defeated at the battle of Ain Jalut, in Syria, the Mongols retreated from Mesopotamia and the Mamluks extended their control into the region.

At this time the Christian Reconquista of the Iberian Peninsula was gathering force. After 1000 the caliphate of Córdoba began to break up. In 1085 Christian forces under the leadership of the king of Castile captured the key city of Toledo. In the early 12th century Aragon joined the campaign. The battle of Las Navas de Tolosa in 1212 was a crucial turning point in the campaign. This Christian victory further divided the Muslim governors of Iberia; within 50 years the cities of Córdoba and Cádiz had fallen, leaving a last Muslim outpost in the kingdom of Granada.

The unification of Castile and Aragon under Ferdinand and Isabella gave the final impetus to the Reconquista. After a series of defeats in the surrounding countryside, Granada finally fell to the Christians in 1492. The city was abandoned by its last ruler, Muhammad XI (Boabdil) (r. 1482–92), who left behind the magnificent Moorish palace of Alhambra. The Muslims who remained in Spain were stripped of their land and property and forced to convert to Christianity. The majority fled Iberia altogether, moving across the Mediterranean to North Africa, which remained in Muslim hands.

See also AGRICULTURE; ARCHITECTURE; BORDERS AND FRONTIERS; CALENDARS AND CLOCKS; CITIES; CLIMATE AND GEOGRAPHY; ECONOMY; EMPIRES AND DYNASTIES; FOREIGNERS AND BARBARIANS; FORESTS AND FORESTRY; GOVERNMENT ORGANIZATION; HEALTH AND DISEASE; MIGRATION AND POPULATION MOVEMENTS; MILITARY; NATURAL DISASTERS; PANDEMICS AND EPIDEMICS; RELIGION AND COSMOLOGY; RESISTANCE AND DISSENT; ROADS AND BRIDGES; SACRED SITES; SCANDALS AND CORRUPTION; SEAFARING AND NAVIGATION; SETTLEMENT PATTERNS; SOCIAL ORGANIZATION; TRADE AND EXCHANGE; TRANSPORTATION; WAR AND CONQUEST.

Europe

∼ An Anonymous Jewish Account of the Expulsion of Jews from Spain (1495) ∼

And in the year 5252 [1492], in the days of King Ferdinand, the Lord visited the remnant of his people a second time, and exiled them. After the King had captured the city of Granada from the Moors, and it had surrendered to him on the 7th of January of the year just mentioned, he ordered the expulsion of all the Jews in all parts of his kingdom—in the kingdoms of Castile, Catalonia, Aragon, Galicia, Majorca, Minorca, the Basque provinces, the islands of Sardinia and Sicily, and the kingdom of Valencia. Even before that the Queen had expelled them from the kingdom of Andalusia [1483].

The King gave them three months' time in which to leave. It was announced in public in every city on the first of May, which happened to be the 19th day of the Omer, and the term ended on the day before the 9th of Ab.

About their number there is no agreement, but, after many inquiries, I found that the most generally accepted estimate is 50,000 families, or, as others say, 53,000. They had houses, fields, vineyards, and cattle, and most of them were artisans. . . .

In the course of the three months' respite granted them they endeavoured to effect an arrangement permitting them to stay on in the country, and they felt confident of success. . . .

The agreement permitting them to remain in the country on the payment of a large sum of money was almost completed when it was frustrated by the interference of a prior who was called the Prior of Santa Cruz. Then the Queen gave an answer to the representatives of the Jews, similar to the saying of King Solomon: "The king's heart is in the hand of the Lord, as the rivers of water. God turneth it withersoever He will." She said furthermore: "Do you believe that this comes upon you from us? The Lord hath put this thing into the heart of the king."

Then they saw that there was evil determined against them by the King, and they gave up the hope of remaining. But the time had become short, and they had to hasten their exodus from Spain. They sold their houses, their landed estates, and their cattle for very small prices, to save themselves. The King did not allow them to carry silver and gold out of his country, so that they were compelled to exchange their silver and gold for merchandise of cloths and skins and other things.

One hundred and twenty thousand of them went to Portugal, according to a compact which a prominent man, Don Vidal bar Benveniste del Cavalleria, had made with the King of Portugal, and they paid one ducat for every soul, and the fourth part of all the merchandise they had carried thither; and he allowed them to stay in his country six months. This King acted much worse toward them than the King of Spain, and after the six months had elapsed he made slaves of all those that remained in his country, and banished seven hundred children to a remote island to settle it, and all of them died. . . .

Many of the exiled Spaniards went to Mohammedan countries, to Fez, Tlemçen, and the Berber provinces, under the King of Tunis. On account of their large numbers the Moors did not allow them into their cities, and many of them died in the fields from hunger, thirst, and lack of everything. The lions and bears, which are numerous in this country, killed some of them while they lay starving outside of the cities. A Jew in the kingdom of Tlemçen, named Abraham, the viceroy who ruled the kingdom, made part of them come to this kingdom, and he spent a large amount of money to help them. The Jews of Northern Africa were very charitable toward them. A part of those who went to Northern Africa, as they found no rest and no place that would receive them, returned to Spain, and became converts . . . .

When the edict of expulsion became known in the other countries, vessels came from Genoa to the Spanish harbors to carry away the Jews. The crews of these vessels, too, acted maliciously and meanly toward the Jews, robbed them, and delivered some of them to the famous pirate of that time who was called the Corsair of Genoa. To those who escaped and arrived at Genoa the people of the city showed themselves merciless, and oppressed and robbed them, and the cruelty of their wicked hearts went so far that they took the infants from the mothers' breasts.

Many ships with Jews, especially from Sicily, went to the city of Naples on the coast. The King of this country was friendly to the Jews, received them all, and was merciful towards them, and he helped them with money. The Jews that were at Naples supplied them with food as much as they could, and sent around to the other parts of Italy to collect money to sustain them. The Marranos in this city lent them money on pledges without interest; even the. Dominican Brotherhood acted mercifully toward them. On account of their very large number, all this was not enough. Some of them died by famine, others sold their children to Christians to sustain their life. Finally, a plague broke out among them, spread to Naples, and very many of them died, so that the living wearied of burying the dead.

Part of the exiled Spaniards went over sea to Turkey. Some of them were thrown into the sea and drowned, but those who arrived, there the King of Turkey received kindly, as they were artisans. He lent them money and settled many of them on an island, and gave them fields and estates. . . .

He who said unto His world, Enough, may He also say Enough unto our sufferings, and may He look down upon our impotence. May He turn again, and have compassion upon us, and hasten out salvation. Thus may it be Thy will!

From: Jacob Marcus, *The Jew in the Medieval World: A Sourcebook, 315–1791,* (New York: Jewish Publication Society, 1938).

The Islamic World

~ *Fulk of Chartres: "The Capture of Jerusalem" (1099)* ~

CHAPTER 27: THE SIEGE OF THE CITY OF JERUSALEM

On the seventh of June the Franks besieged Jerusalem. The city is located in a mountainous region, which is lacking in rivers, woods, and springs, except the Fountain of Siloam, where there is plenty of water, but it empties forth only at certain intervals. This fountain empties into the valley, at the foot of Mount

(continued)

(continues)

Zion, and flows into the course of the brook of Kedron, which, during the winter, flows through the valley of Jehosaphat. There are many cisterns, which furnish abundant water within the city. When filled by the winter rains and well cared for, they offer both men and beasts an unfailing supply at all times. Moreover, the city is laid out most beautifully, and cannot be criticized for too great length or as being disproportionately narrow. On the west is the tower of David, which is flanked on both sides by the broad wall of the city. The lower half of the wall is solid masonry, of square stones and mortar, sealed with molten lead. So strong is this wall that if fifteen or twenty men should be well supplied with provisions, they would never be taken by any army. . . .

When the Franks saw how difficult it would be to take the city, the leaders ordered scaling ladders to be made, hoping that by a brave assault it might be possible to surmount the walls by means 'of ladders and thus take the city, God helping. So the ladders were made, and on the day following the seventh, in the early morning, the leaders ordered the attack, and, with the trumpets sounding, a splendid assault was made on the city from all sides. The attack lasted till the sixth hour, but it was discovered that the city could not be entered by the use of ladders, which were few in number, and sadly we ceased the attack.

Then a council was held, and it was ordered that siege machines should be constructed by the artisans, so that by moving them close to the wall we might accomplish our purpose, with the aid of God. This was done. . . .

When the tower had been put together and had been covered with hides, it was moved nearer to the wall. Then knights, few in number, but brave, at the sound of the trumpet, took their places in the tower and began to shoot stones and arrows. The Saracens defended themselves vigorously, and, with slings, very skilfully hurled back burning firebrands, which had been dipped in oil and fresh fat. Many on both sides, fighting in this manner, often found themselves in the presence of death. . . .

On the following day the work again began at the sound of the trumpet, and to such purpose that the rams, by continual pounding, made a hole through one part of the wall. The Saracens suspended two beams before the opening, supporting them by ropes, so that by piling stones behind them they would make an obstacle to the rams. However, what they did for their own protection became, through the providence of God, the cause of their own destruction. For, when the tower was moved nearer to the wall, the ropes that supported the beams were cut; from these same beams the Franks constructed a bridge, which they cleverly extended from the tower to the wall. About this time one of the towers in the stone wall began to burn, for the men who worked our machines had been hurling firebrands upon it until the wooden beams within it caught fire. The flames and smoke soon became so bad that none of the defenders of this part of the wall were able to remain near this place. At the noon hour on Friday, with trumpets sounding, amid great commotion and shouting "God help us," the Franks entered the city. When the pagans saw one standard planted on the wall, they were completely demoralized, and all their former boldness vanished, and they turned to flee through the narrow streets of the city. Those who were already in rapid flight began to flee more rapidly.

Count Raymond and his men, who were attacking the wall on the other side, did not yet know of all this, until they saw the Saracens leap from the wall in front of them. Forthwith, they joyfully rushed into the city to pursue and kill the nefarious enemies, as their comrades were already doing. Some Saracens, Arabs, and Ethiopians took refuge in the tower of David, others fled to the temples of the Lord and of Solomon. A great fight took place in the court and porch of the temples, where they were unable to escape from our gladiators. Many fled to the roof of the temple of Solomon, and were shot with arrows, so that they fell to the ground dead. In this temple almost ten thousand were killed. Indeed, if you had been there you would have seen our feet colored to our ankles with the blood of the slain. But what more shall I relate? None of them were left alive; neither women nor children were spared.

From: Fulk of Chartres, "Gesta Francorum Jerusalem expugnantium," in Frederick Duncan and August C. Krey, eds., *Parallel Source Problems in Medieval History* (New York: Harper and Brothers, 1912).

FURTHER READING

Paul Bahn and John Flenley, *Easter Island, Earth Island* (New York: Thames and Hudson, 1992).

Peter Bellwood, *The Polynesians: Prehistory of an Island People* (London: Thames and Hudson, 1987).

Graham Connah, *African Civilizations: An Archaeological Perspective*, 2nd ed. (Cambridge, U.K.: Cambridge University Press, 2001).

Michael R. Drompp, *Tang China and the Collapse of the Uighur Empire: A Documentary History* (Boston: Brill Academic Publishers, 2004).

Susan Toby Evans, *Ancient Mexico and Central America: Archaeology and Culture History* (London: Thames and Hudson, 2004).

Leo de Hartog, *Russia and the Mongol Yoke: The History of the Russian Principalities and the Golden Horde, 1221–1502* (London: British Academic Press, 1992).

David Herlihy, *The Black Death and the Transformation of the West* (Cambridge, Mass.: Harvard University Press, 1997).

Charles Warren Hostler, *The Turks of Central Asia* (Westport, Conn.: Praeger, 2003).

Johan Huizinga, *The Waning of the Middle Ages* (New York: St. Martin's Press, 1985).

Jordanes, "The Origins and Deeds of the Goths," trans. Charles C. Mierow. Available online. URL: http://www.ucalgary.ca/~vandersp/Courses/texts/jordgeti.html. Downloaded on November 9, 2007.

John Kantner, *Ancient Puebloan Southwest* (Cambridge, U.K.: Cambridge University Press, 2004).

Lester K. Little, ed., *Plague and the End of Antiquity: The Pandemic of 541–750* (Cambridge, U.K.: Cambridge University Press, 2006).

Thomas F. Madden, *The New Concise History of the Crusades* (Lanham, Md.: Rowman and Littlefield, 2005).

David Morgan, *The Mongols* (Oxford, U.K.: Blackwell, 2007).

Stuart Munro-Hay, *Aksum: A Civilisation of Late Antiquity* (Edinburgh, U.K.: Edinburgh University Press, 1991).

Joseph F. O'Callaghan, *Reconquest and Crusade in Medieval Spain* (Philadelphia: University of Pennsylvania Press, 2004).

Robert Sewell, *A Forgotten Empire: Vijayanagar* (Boston: Adamant Media Corporation, 2006).

David Webster, *The Fall of the Ancient Maya: Solving the Mystery of the Maya Collapse* (London: Thames and Hudson, 2002).

Derek A. Welsby, *The Kingdom of Kush: The Napatan and Meroitic Empires* (Princeton, N.J.: Markus Wiener, 1998).

Philip Ziegler, *The Black Death* (New York: John Day, 1969).

► social organization

INTRODUCTION

When studying social organization, it is good to keep in mind that the terms used by historians, anthropologists, and archaeologists are ones created by people to describe cultures and customs that were not necessarily their own. For instance, people of hunter-gatherer cultures might have no understanding of what *hunter-gatherer* meant, and even if they came to understand the term, they might not perceive it as applying to themselves. Further, terms for describing social organization are subject to revision, not only by scholars but also by others who may adapt the terms for their own purposes. For example, at one time the term *feudal* was supposed to apply only to a social organization found in Europe during the medieval era. Many people found the concept to be useful when applied to other societies, thus creating descriptions of feudal societies in medieval Japan, ancient China, medieval India, and medieval Ethiopia. In recent times, the use of *feudal* has become even more muddied, because some historians have attacked the notion that Europe was ever truly "feudal," suggesting that the very concept of feudalism had more to do with historians misunderstanding what happened in medieval Europe than with what medieval Europeans themselves thought they were doing. This dispute over *feudal* has become ever-more complex, with some historians arguing that disparate parts of Europe were feudal at various times, while others were not. The essence of this conflict is that the terminology used for social organization is for convenience: Terms help people think about broad trends in human behavior that can explain how cultures functioned and why cultures survived or disappeared.

One way to evaluate a medieval culture's social organization is by how well it served the needs of the people living within the culture. At its most fundamental, this evaluation means discovering whether the social organization enabled people to survive long enough to bear children, raise those children, and pass on their social organization to those children. Sometimes, people barely survived long enough for their children to reach their late teens. Some cultures found ways of organizing their resources so that people lived much longer, although in most of the medieval world someone who lived into his or her seventies was considered to be remarkable. The Aztec culture provides an example of how this works in terms of historical analysis.

The Aztec represented a very successful culture; they were the greatest political and military power in their region for 200 to 300 years before the coming of the Spanish. Their social organization provided for the fundamental needs of an ever-growing population, and its support of a military caste proved very successful, because the military caste was able to suppress rival societies and provide thousands of captives for blood sacrifices that, they believed, kept the sun rising each morning. Still, the very aspects that made Aztec society successful contributed to its failure. A far too simple view of Aztec social collapse focuses on the idea that a small Spanish force had superior military technology. Even using superior armor and swords and riding horses, the small number of Spanish adventurers could have been overwhelmed by the

Aztec, who were very good at killing people. A key to the success of the Spanish was the hatred the neighbors of the Aztec had for them; the Aztec priestly class was despised, and their government was loathed. Thus, aspects of Aztec society that seemed to make it successful inspired outsiders to destroy it.

Therefore, care should be taken in evaluating a society's organization. A good question to ask is "How well did the society's organization adjust to changing circumstances?" In the Near East the Sassanian Empire did not adjust at all well to the surge of Islam; although Muslim leaders used some government bureaucrats from the Sassanian government in their own bureaucracies, over a period of about 100 years, they reorganized most former Sassanian lands into their own model of social organization, based on traditional Arab practices. On the other hand, the socially rigid Byzantine Empire, which created much resentment among its own people with its often oppressive social organization, managed to survive, even though it lost a great deal of important territory. Why did the Byzantine Empire remain a persistent threat to the Islamic world for centuries after the Sassanian Empire had disappeared? The answer to that could speak to why Islam was the biggest success in the Near East and why some societies manage to adjust, as the Byzantine society did, or succumb to new pressures, as the Sassanian society did.

Military power alone does not answer why one society is more resilient than another, although brute force was an ever-present factor in the societies of the medieval world. A stark example of this is what happened in central Asia in the 1200s. Cities of wealth existed on the many routes collectively called the Silk Road, a term invented by a historian. The slow drying up of the land was an important environmental factor in their decline, but cultures can survive changes in their environment by moving to new lands, as many Africans south of the Sahara did when the desert expanded southward, or by adjusting to the changing circumstances, as the Maya did. The Maya moved out of their cities and, despite suffering a severe drop in population, kept their culture alive by changing important aspects of their social organization, such as eliminating the roles of priest-kings and shifting from a focus on urban life to a focus on small, scattered communities. In the case of the cities of central Asia the settled peoples of the region were nearly annihilated by the Mongols.

Even though military power and natural disasters may manage to exterminate some societies, one of the lessons to be drawn from medieval social organization is that people are very resilient, and they can overcome great hardships. Examples of this can be found in medieval India. Muslims armies were able to conquer much of India in part because those armies brought with them new rules of warfare that were unfamiliar to Indians. But as India succumbed slowly to the military and political dominance of Islam, many Indians continued to live in their traditional ways. Over centuries, India's Muslims became ever more Indian in behavior and outlook; Indian social organization not only survived but indeed transformed the political practices of their new overlords. Examples abound from medieval times, such as the transformation of the Mongol invaders of China from nomads to settled people absorbed into China's social structure and the Norman overlords of England who gradually shifted from speaking French to speaking English and thinking of traditional British heroes, such as King Arthur, as their own heroes. What made some social organizations so valuable to their people that they retained much of their structure even after utter defeat by another culture? Answering that is part of the fun of learning about medieval social organization.

AFRICA
by Leah A. J. Cohen

Many of the organizational elements of societies in medieval Africa were the same as those from ancient history. For example, matrilineal (when descent is traced through the mother) and patrilineal (when descent is traced through the father) lineage systems still dictated social groupings, relationships, and hierarchies. Chiefdoms were common, and in many societies the elders' councils represented the lineages or clans within the society and made decisions with the support of those they represented, especially in the areas with lower population densities and for human groups living outside major civilization centers. Those human groups that had remained small and continued to make a living as hunter-gatherers were perhaps more egalitarian, making decisions by consensus. As a result of domesticating plants and animals in ancient times (and gaining the capacity to have surplus food), centrally governed city-states and empires had emerged. During the medieval period the spread of improved agricultural techniques and increased trade between groups within Africa and with those from outside of Africa brought different ideas and demands for new products and resources. All of these conditions resulted in the rise and fall of numerous city-states and many new empires during this period. While lineages may have still played a role in the social organization of people within these civilization centers, new principles based on structured government hierarchies, occupational caste systems, and religious hierarchies became more prominent.

LINEAGE- AND CLAN-BASED SOCIETIES

For the smaller human groups lineage (a type of kinship relation that groups people according to blood relations to a common ancestor) was the main organizational structure. These groups were usually engaged in hunting and gathering, farming, or herding, and there was little of the occupational specialization that led to differences in status and wealth as in the major civilization centers in Africa. In medieval Africa descent could be matrilineal, such as the Ashanti who lived in present-day Ghana around 1200 and the East African Bantu who were still hunter-gatherer, farmer, and herder groups at the start of the medieval period, or patrilineal, such as the Yoruba of present-day Nigeria, who may have been descendents of the ancient Nok civilization. Some groups were more or less egalitarian with decisions made by consensus or by a council of elders that represented each of the families or lineages in the society. A higher order division in this social structure was that of clans, which were also based on descent and grouped several lineages together. These cultures became known as segmentary societies after E. E. Evans-Pritchard developed the concept in his 1940 study of human groups in Sudan. The term *segmentary society* is commonly used to describe societies that are subdivided into kinship groups that are relatively equal in status and are part of larger more distant kinship groups.

Hierarchies did exist where lineages were differentiated, usually based on closeness of relation to the founder of the community or an important ancestor. Chiefdoms existed with the chief's lineage holding more social and political power than other community members, but that power was often exercised within a context of approval from the elders, who in turn had the approval of the families or lineages they represented. Within medieval Yoruba culture the council of elders was often more powerful than the leader.

AGE-SET AND AGE-GRADE SOCIETIES

An important organizing principle in some areas of eastern and southern Africa during the medieval period was that of age-sets and age-grades. Community members (usually only males) were born into an age-set with the boundaries for that group ranging from 4 to 14 years for each set. Members of each age-set developed close ties with each other that transcended lineage ties. As the age-set members grew older they passed through different age-grades, which assigned the age-set with specific roles and responsibilities. For example, among the Masai of East Africa men in the Moran age-grade were assigned the role of village warriors. This type of social structure was often found among Kushite peoples and the Nilotic people with whom they came in contact. The Oromo people (a Kushitic-speaking people) who lived in medieval eastern Africa were one of many African cultures that were organized based on an age-grade system. People were born into an age-set; for the Oromo the divisions were made ev-

ery eight years, but it varied from four- to 10-year divisions. Although societies that are organized into age-sets may have lineage and kinship links as well, the age-set crosses lineage and kinship boundaries and counteracts power and status that is inherited through lineages. Typically movement into an age-set was symbolized through traditional ceremonies.

HIERARCHICAL CITY-STATES AND EMPIRES

As the human population grew, trade expanded as the result of demand for Africa's slaves, gold, salt, ivory, and other natural resources. Because farmers and herders were able to produce enough food to feed people engaged in other livelihood activities, city-states with more complex social structures emerged all across the continent. In some areas the transition away from small-scale villages with little central governance began with lineage groups uniting under clans headed by chiefs that could trace their lineage back to an important or founding ancestor. Either alliances formed between clans, or powerful clans began to conquer new peoples and territories. Kingdoms, such as those of medieval Nubia, became known for their military expertise.

One example of this is the Yoruba, who had been organized into patrilineal descent groups prior to the 11th century and then started to form centrally organized city-states with leading chiefs. A council of elders advised the reigning monarch. In the more southern city-states in the forested areas this council had a substantial amount of political power and the elected monarch (*oba*) was more of a figurehead. Some city-states also had a council of military advisers in addition to the civilian council. There were a handful of reigning queens, but mostly these states were ruled by kings. Royal lineages existed but right to the throne could be denied for misconduct. In some of the city-states democratic elections were held for the *oba*. At the end of the medieval period systems were developing for occupational associations (such as for artists), religious groups, and other types of social groups. After the development of city-states, Yorubaland was organized around occupational guilds that crossed the lineage and clan groupings. These guilds answered to the *oba* of the region, who also had a council that provided advice and named his successor.

Another example of the transition from less to more hierarchical social organization comes from the Hausa people of present-day Nigeria. Around the 10th and 11th centuries Hausa people established several smaller villages and eventually city-states. Initially the villages were decentralized. As populations grew, so did the social and governmental structure. Each of the city-states was ruled by a *sarkis* and was enclosed in a wall, which also protected a sizable amount of farmland. It is thought that these city-states may have formed because access to land became more difficult

Male stone figure, Sierra Leone, Guinea, as early as the 15th century; the figure wears a headdress and bracelet reminiscent of the regalia of certain Temne chiefs and rides either an elephant or a lion, symbolic of a king's power. (National Museum of African Art, Smithsonian Institution, Photograph by Franko Khoury, Museum purchase, 85-1-3)

due to the migration of Berber pastoralists into northern Hausaland. These city-states had a ruling aristocracy that was centrally located around the palace, and skilled occupational classes (including weavers, tanners, and metalsmiths), merchants, and musicians all resided within the city's walls. Outside the walls lived the farmers who produced food for the city dwellers and the slave communities. The first centralized kingdom to develop from these city-states was Daura in the late 12th century. At the time that Islam swept the region with the migration of Fulani people from the north, the Hausa states of Gobir (north), Zamfara (east), Kebbi (west), and Yauri (south) were ruling the region.

More complex social systems developed as grand empires emerged during the medieval period. The Sudanic empires of present-day West Africa, which were Ghana (eighth through 11th centuries), Mali (13th through 15th centuries), and Songhai (which started as a smaller state in the ninth century and developed into an empire by the 15th century), are some of the most frequently cited kingdoms of medieval

Africa. Other highly stratified and centrally organized civilization centers included Nubia (3800 B.C.E. through the 12th century) in northeastern Africa, Kanem-Bornu (at least as early as the ninth through the 19th centuries) in central Africa, Axum (third–eighth centuries) in eastern Africa, and Mapungubwe (11th through the end of the 13th centuries), and Great Zimbabwe (11th–15th centuries) in southern Africa. To manage densely populated areas, centralized systems of governance were needed to create and enforce laws and regulations, to provide access to resources such as water, and to carry out conquests. For many of these civilizations class differences in status were fueled by an increase in specialized occupations and material wealth. Archaeologists often identify social stratification through differences in tombs and tomb markers, the remains of specialized occupations, and such signs as the size of houses, the existence of luxury goods, and the material with which houses were constructed. Additionally, in pastoral communities the size of the herd was also an indication of status. Within empire civilizations, in general, the existence of monumental architectural features such as palaces, churches, or mosques also indicated class differentiation.

In the medieval empires it was common to see social stratification with the ruling class under a highly revered king (or sometimes queen) with a network of religious scholars, advisers, judges, and government administrators at the top; a merchant class, specialized skilled craftspeople, and laborers in the middle; and slaves farmers, herders, and unskilled laborers at the bottom. At the top of the social hierarchy there was extreme luxury and ceremony with rich cloth, jewelry, foods, and servants. At the other end of the social hierarchy people were often enslaved from areas of new conquest.

Slavery in medieval Africa came in many forms. There were indigenous systems of slavery that were less brutal than the Arab or transatlantic slave trade systems. Often slaves were used to work the mines and salt-production industries. It was common for slaves to be put to work within the households of merchants or elites doing domestic chores. In some central African communities female slaves and their offspring were incorporated into the kinship of the household and were relatively well taken care of. In southern Africa there were slaves who inherited their status as slaves because one of their ancestors had committed a crime or had been captured during war. These societies also made such provisions for people who were destitute. These types of slaves lived in their own houses and could leave the community. Despite the fact that these conditions were better than those under chattel slavery, these slaves did not have their freedom. However, there are a few cases in which former slaves reached positions of high status (as military leaders, for example), which indicates a less rigid social structure, where an individual could move between social classes. Even though there are examples of this social mobility, it is suspected that this was not commonplace, and it depended on the society. For example, the Igbo of present-day Nigeria made a distinction between free men and those born without freedom. Even though those who were not considered free would be incorporated into the lineage of the household within which they worked, they did not have the social mobility to earn titles as other Igbo males did.

Women often held positions of high status in many of the cultures of medieval Africa. Before the widespread adoption of Christianity at the start of the medieval period in Nubia, women played a very unique role as warrior queens who fought in battle and reinforced the Isis cult religion. Other empires were led by females during this period. It is thought that in the 11th century Kanem's queen ruled over a multi-tiered governance system. Some Berber groups gave women the responsibility of passing on their oral histories.

The lineage-based social systems that were common in rural Africa also played a part in the social organization of the major civilization centers. For instance, the throne of the Ghana Empire was passed down from the ancestral founder of the empire matrilineally with the sons of the king's sister claiming right to the throne; other monarchies in the Sahel region were also matrilineal. The Ghana kings traced their descent group back to an ancestor who was thought to have originally settled the land. Most empire leaders acquired their positions through lineage and military might during this period. However, one exception is that of the Oromo culture, which elected its leader democratically.

The grand empires of medieval Africa had elaborate systems of leadership. By the start of the medieval period Ghana had a strong organizational system. The king ruled with the advice of a council that was made up of individuals from all the different social strata in the empire. For example, the king of Ghana was the leader of his subjects' traditional religion and was thought to have divine powers. This Mande kingdom had a multitiered system of governance that included units called *kafu*, which were the villages or towns that ranged from 10,000 to 50,000 people each. The leader (called the *mansa*, or king) of each *kafu* was considered to have divine powers and was revered by the people. These leaders were part of a confederation of *kafus* whose ultimate leader was the king of kings. The Ghana Empire had many structures that glorified the present and past kings, including a traditional priesthood that protected the tombs of previous kings. The kings were always dressed in fine robes and adorned with jewelry. The luxury enjoyed by the king and his closest associates was the result of the great wealth that the kingdom accumulated by controlling access to gold and its taxation in the trans-Saharan trade network. In southern Africa's Great Zimbabwe there was a palace where the chief lived and reigned. He was revered and considered to have divine powers. Portuguese writers from the 16th century recorded that he was approached from a crawl and everything he did was repeated by all in his court.

The medieval Buganda kingdoms located northwest of Lake Victoria (present-day Uganda) were organized based on lineages and clans with men of status serving as lineage leaders or elders who answered to the leaders of the clans. The king oversaw many tiers of officials that met regularly to discuss administrative and governing issues. Despite the lineage system, within Buganda society some individuals achieved mobility. Young men were often sent to the capital to serve as message bearers and to do other jobs for the court and elite. If they did well, they would be advanced to serve as a low-status chief. In this position they could earn the right to move up the social ladder. In general, outside the capital homes were organized around the chief's home, which was larger and better stocked. The chiefs collected taxes from their community members and then passed those taxes on to higher chiefs.

While many of the centrally organized civilizations of medieval Africa did not separate religion and the state (and, in fact, many cultures considered the king or queen to have divine powers), there were examples of empires that exercised religious tolerance. Within Christian Nubia, the king was also a priest, yet there is archaeological evidence that Muslims lived alongside Christians. When Muslims arrived in ancient Ghana, they initially existed in a separate Islamic community from the royal palace. The king allowed the practice of Islam and the construction of mosques, but he and many of his subjects continued to practice their traditional African religion. Most of the Muslim people lived in a separate city near the capital; however, Muslims did serve as advisers to the king and court. Within the Mali Empire, even after the adoption of Islam, it was not mandatory for all of the people to also adopt Islam.

For the most part the city-states and empires of this period were ruled from one centralized location. However, after the fall of Axum around 1,700 to 1,000 years ago, medieval Ethiopian history was unique in that the region was ruled from migrating capitals. The entire infrastructure of the capital city moved from place to place as needed to ensure a secure resource base and rule over the people. Merchants, soldiers, aristocrats, church officials, laborers, farmers, and servants all moved with the capital; at times up to 100,000 inhabitants migrated. Because what evidence remains that would tell us about life during this period is spread all over the region, archaeological efforts are yet to be focused on this period in Ethiopia's history.

EVOLVING SOCIAL SYSTEMS

Medieval lineage groups, chiefdoms, and kingdoms were hardly static. Despite the fact that there is much archaeological work to be done to reveal the details of life in medieval Africa, colonial writers from the 16th century observed changes and recorded oral histories that indicate modifications in the social structures of the people they encountered. The increased contact with other human groups, city-states, empires, and traders and the changing natural resource base resulted in these variations, and these same conditions were certainly affecting social systems throughout the medieval period. For example, the social structure of the Kongo (also called Bakongo) people of central Africa, who had been farming near the Congo River throughout the medieval period, mutated from a network of lineages to more hierarchical and complex sociopolitical systems. Previously, within a society of loosely connected lineages, chiefs acted more as representatives of the lineages rather than authoritarian rulers, and decisions were made in an egalitarian manner. As the structure of the society changed, chiefs held substantial power and controlled a considerable amount of land. Changes in the social structure of the Kongo are thought to have been related to changes in livelihoods (for example, the spread of agriculture and consequent clearing of the land and increases in trade—including, in particular, increases in slave trade activities). Later in the 16th century it was observed that the lineage system shifted from matrilineal to patrilineal and back to matrilineal, which indicates that these changes may have been present in the earlier medieval period as well.

Another factor that resulted in changes in the social organization of people during the medieval period was the spread of Islam. Some societies converted more completely and others melded their traditional social systems with those of Muslim traders, creating a unique social system. For many of the Hausa people, Islam was not common until the 14th century, but even after converting some of their ancient beliefs and traditions endured and some of the Hausa never converted, retaining their animist religious traditions into present times.

In northern Africa prior to the adoption of Islam in Berber, or Amazigh, society women held high status, including the role of supreme leader. Even after adopting Islam near the end of the medieval period, the men and women of the Tuareg, or Kel Tamasheq (a Berber group), of northern Africa enjoyed free interaction, and women held substantial social and political power. Women were responsible for passing down the poetry and literature.

LESS CENTRALLY ORGANIZED CIVILIZATION CENTERS

The civilization of Jenne-jeno, which originated as early as 250 B.C.E. and was at its height between 400 and 1100 C.E., is a notable example of a densely populated center that was not based on a hierarchical social structure. The inhabitants in this settlement area were supported by agriculture based on rice, millet, and sorghum grown in the surrounding Niger Delta floodplains. Archaeological evidence of Jenne-jeno reveals that there were specialized workers in iron, jewelry, and pottery as well as farmers and herders. Trade with outsiders was well established. Despite the fact that home sites were clustered based on occupational trade, there is no evidence of a powerful ruler or of differing status based on wealth or occupation. Houses were not substantially different in decor or size. It is thought to have been an egalitarian civilization.

In general, the Berbers of North Africa were far less united than a single term implies. They made their living hunting and raising livestock and in less harsh lands near the coast or in a desert oasis by farming. The various groups that fall under the term *Berber* were engaged in trade at times with the different occupiers of the northern coast of Africa, enslaved to work the occupiers' lands, tax-paying farmers to the occupier states, or leaders of repeated resistance movements. Berber peoples became essential to the trans-Saharan trade, particularly after the adoption of the camel in 300, because they had the skills needed to lead caravans across the expansive desert.

The Berber people usually resisted central governance. In the interior of the desert these groups were mostly left to their own systems of organization. There social relationships were more egalitarian, with families being the main organizational unit. Traditionally, Berber herders were nomadic and united into groups consisting of several families on a seasonal basis. This unification of families was weak and changed from season to season. They are said to be a segmentary society, meaning that their main organizational unit was subdivided into clans and then further subdivided into families. Groups were bound together loosely under representational elders. Family descent was patrilineal, so heritage was based on the father's bloodline.

Many of the decisions that affected Berber communities were made through consensus. At each level of Berber society, power was distributed to create a balance where no one person, family, or clan had more power than another. There was also a weak, overarching system that unified Berber groups into federations and that was activated only when necessary for defense and negotiation with outsiders. With increased contact with invaders who employed more complex systems of social and political organization, some Berber groups began to coalesce under the acting leaders, or *aguellid* (war leaders), who became known as kings. Contact with the Romans just before the medieval period left a legacy of Christianity, and kingdoms scattered throughout parts of the Sahara and northern coast.

The Igbo were a people that settled in southern Nigeria sometime during the ninth century. Their social organization was generally thought of as more egalitarian and less authoritarian than the medieval empires and city-states. The Igbo people were usually organized into villages, and adult males from the village were all eligible to meet and discuss community decisions. Although every adult male had a say, individuals could gain respect, titles, and status through accomplished ability and allegiances or loyalties that an individual might have from kinship, wives (polygamy being a symbol of status), and friends. Some Igbo societies did organize under chiefs, but the chief did not have final word and was often challenged by other lineage and family elders. Furthermore, social order was maintain through the existence of secret societies that enforced social norms.

THE AMERICAS

BY MICHAEL J. O'NEAL

Before the Spanish conquest the range of social organization types in the Americas was wide. On the one hand, some cultures had complex, highly stratified social systems, meaning that people were sharply divided into higher and lower classes, each with its own privileges in the case of the upper classes and its own demands in the case of lower classes. Others had more egalitarian social structures, meaning that while the culture had leaders, most people belonged to the same social class, no group enjoyed any particular privileges, and decisions were made by consensus rather than the dictates of a leader.

Social stratification was almost always a marker of social, economic, and governmental complexity in the Americas before European contact, as indeed it was throughout the world. In preceding centuries as cultures evolved from hunter-gatherer societies to sedentary agricultural societies with permanent towns and cities and attachment to the land they farmed, it was inevitable that people would get sorted into classes, each class enjoying a higher level of prestige than the one below it. (Archaeologists and historians use the word *sedentary* not to refer to "laziness" or "unwillingness to work" but to the notion of settled, fixed communities, in contrast to nomadic communities that moved about in search of food.) People be-

came more specialized in their occupations and functions, so classes of craftsmen, artisans, farmers, landowners, serfs, and peasants emerged.

Religion became more complex and organized with emphasis on state-sanctioned rituals, a calendar of religious events, and temples and shrines where religious activity took place. This led to the emergence of a class of priests and shamans who wielded considerable authority and social influence. Further, the mythology of many precontact cultures evolved over time to provide people with a sense of unity—of belonging to a particular people with a unique history and destiny. This mythology supported the notion that the highest social class, including the king or emperor and the nobles that surrounded him, were the descendants of the culture's earliest founders, who themselves were descendants of gods.

Not all American cultures prior to the Spanish conquest, however, shared these views. Many remained far less complex and sophisticated. There was little specialization of labor, so every member of the group played a role in its most important activities, including hunting, gathering, fishing, and the collection and storage of food. While a class of priests and shamans exerted influence, the religious views they taught were directed at creating a set of societal norms to which everyone in the community adhered. And while these more tribal societies had leaders and headmen, these leaders did not rule by divine right or because they were regarded as descendants from the gods; rather, they tended to emerge by consensus because of their leadership abilities.

A common characteristic of many precontact American cultures was that clan and kin relationships were important. Throughout the Americas people identified themselves through membership in a clan, which is defined as any group of people who claim descent from a common ancestor—though in some cases that ancestor was not necessarily a blood relative. In some cultures, but by no means all, this distant ancestor was regarded as a god. Some of these clan relationships were patrilineal, meaning that a person traced his or her ancestry through the father's line and the father's line of descent was regarded as a source of stability. Others were matrilineal, meaning that the mother's ancestors were the basis of clan membership and a new husband went to live with his wife's family rather than the bride going to live with her husband's family.

Clan relationships provided people with an extended social support network that encompassed more than the immediate family. This support network enabled people to survive during hard times and to perform laborious tasks that could be accomplished only with the help of numerous people, such as clearing fields, building irrigation systems, or bringing in the harvest. Identification of clan relationships also helped early cultures avoid the risk of inbreeding. When populations were smaller than they are in modern life and when people were less mobile, a danger existed that close blood relatives, such as cousins, could marry and have children. Before European contact Americans recognized that this had to be avoided, and acknowledgment of clan relationships helped in this regard. Most importantly, clan relationships were a source of identity and belonging.

THE INUIT

One generalization that can be made about social organization in the Americas is that it tended to be more complex and formal in more equatorial regions, less so farther to the north and to the south. The Inuit of the far north, for example, maintained a relatively simple social structure. Because of the forbidding cold of the Arctic, populations were not very dense, and nothing like the modern city emerged. Rather, people lived in small settlements with bands of perhaps 60 to as many as 300 people, who lived primarily from the resources provided by the sea. The word *muit* was used to refer to the people who inhabited a particular geographical area. The Inuit tended to trace their ancestry bilaterally, meaning that the father's and mother's lines of ancestry were equally important; some Inuit groups, however, placed more emphasis on the father's line.

The basic social organization of the Inuit was the nuclear family: father, mother, children, newly married older children and their spouses and children, close relatives such as grandparents, and sometimes more distant, unmarried relatives. Work was allocated along gender lines. Within each band people recognized a leader based on his age, experience, and wisdom. The leader's principal role was to provide advice based on his lifetime of knowledge about the environment. Further, each band had a shaman, or *angakuk*, who was usually a man but could be a woman. Generally, Inuit shamans were disliked. They exercised their power through fear, but they served an important social function by keeping people in line and ensuring that they adhered to social norms. Usually, the Inuit avoided social conflict as much as possible; the precariousness of life in the frozen north made it imperative that people cooperated. When conflict erupted it was often settled by song duels in which the "combatants" composed and sang songs insulting their adversaries. These song duels, witnessed by the community and often a source of laughter, defused tension and restored social order.

The Inuit maintained flexible ties to other bands. While these bands were often in competition with one another for resources, the Inuit also recognized that sometimes they needed to cooperate with and gain the cooperation of other bands. Marriage was one way in which ties were maintained.

A newly married couple typically lived with the woman's family for a period of time, often until the birth of a first child, and then returned to the man's family. In this way ties were established with another band. Gift giving was also important. Sometimes the "gift" could include permission for a man from another band to have sexual relations with a member of one's own band, although the woman always had the right to refuse. Otherwise, material gifts were a way of maintaining loose social ties with another band.

NATIVE AMERICANS

The term *Native American* has different meanings depending on the context; it can apply to any indigenous group of Americans, from the Inuit of the Arctic to the groups at the southern tip of South America. In modern life, though, the term is often applied specifically to the many tribes that inhabited North America in what are now Canada and the United States.

The North American continent was home to hundreds of groups, each with its own culture and form of social organization, making generalizations difficult. One generality that can be made, however, is that the environment often shaped social organization. For example, the Utes of present-day Utah, New Mexico, and Colorado—in contrast to, say, the Woodlands of eastern North America or the Sioux of the central Plains—lived in mountainous regions. These regions were separated from one another by mountain ranges, valleys, and canyons. Like the Inuit, they were spread out over a wide area, and Ute culture was divided into bands; examples include the Moache band, which lived on the eastern slopes of the Rocky Mountains, or the Uncompahgre, whose home was the valleys surrounding Colorado's Uncompahgre Plateau and Gunnison River. These widely separated bands, each adapting to its geographical niche in its own way, never formed a highly organized tribe. Because the region was sparsely vegetated, each band needed a large area to survive, one that would provide the band with enough food. Since people had to spread out over a large geographical area, the most important unit of social organization was the family rather than the band, although membership in a band remained important in Ute life. Bands came together only during the winter months when they held festivals and marriages were arranged. As the weather warmed and the snows melted, the bands dispersed, following the thawing to higher and higher elevations to plant crops and find food.

The Apache, who lived in what is the present-day American Southwest, adhered to a slightly more sophisticated and complex social system than that of the Utes. A typical Apache community consisted of two to six extended families that were matrilocal; that is, upon marriage the groom lived with the bride's mother's kin rather than his own. The purpose of matrilocality among the Apache and other early societies was to avoid inbreeding, for it helped ensure that men would be widely dispersed. This unit of two to six extended families was referred to as a *gota*. Although a *gota* operated communally in such matters as hunting game, it was led by a headman, or chief. The position of headman was not necessarily hereditary; rather, it was conferred on a man by consensus as a result of his leadership qualities. If no hereditary headman was suitable, the group, in effect, elected someone from another family. Although nominal power resided with men, Apache women held a great deal of influence; it was their matrilines that formed the basis of Apache society.

Beyond the chieftainship, there was no real social "order" in Apache society. There was a kind of nobility that consisted of young men identified by the chief who would assume leadership responsibilities as the chief aged and after he died. It is also clear that there was a poor class of Apaches, for the headman organized charitable relief for them by collecting goods and food from more affluent members of the community. The social organization of the Apache extended beyond the *gota*. In addition to being a member of a *gota*, each Apache was also a member of one of 62 matrilineal clans. These clans overlapped the various Apache settlements. Members of these clans did not intermarry. Again, the social organization was communal, with members of the different clans called on to aid one another in times of need.

A major way in which the Apache maintained social order was through magic and the fear of magic. When conflict erupted, particularly conflict between members of different clans, order was maintained by the fear of magic and sorcery. People who behaved according to the social norms of the tribe were said to have power. This power protected a person from magic and sorcery. Power took many forms, including, for example, "fire power," "mountain lion power," "wind power," and "black-tailed deer power." People could invest their time and energy into learning a source of power, usually through a shaman, who taught pupils in exchange for food, horses, and other commodities. Learning this form of power was no mean feat. Acquiring black-tailed deer power, for example, required the student to learn nearly 60 chants; each of these chants had at least 20 verses, and chanting one such verse could take up to a half hour. Acquisition of this power ensured that one had adhered to the norms of Apache society, and that power could be used to keep others in check and to resolve disputes.

Both the Utes and the Apaches lived in the vast mountain and desert regions of the American Southwest, giving rise to a particular type of social organization. In contrast, the Woodlands of the American Northeast and southeastern Canada lived in a very different type of region. As the name suggests, these many tribes inhabited densely forested regions. Because the forests provided them with abundant resources, these tribes led more sedentary lives in larger, more fixed communities. Accordingly, their social structure became yet more complex. Some of these tribes were patrilineal, others were matrilineal, and still others were bilateral. Most recognized clan groups, and each clan was identified by an animal totem. The clan was the basis of social interaction.

Some Woodlands groups were more sedentary than others, depending more on agriculture than on hunting and gathering, and developed more complex social structures. Many had hereditary leaders, often called sachems, sagamores, or *werowances*. This leader, rather than ruling by consensus and agreement, claimed the right to rule by virtue of divine descent. Some groups had one leader for civic affairs and another for military affairs. Land was owned in common, with group members having the right to use it but not to own it. In these more sedentary societies social stratification was more evident, with upper, more privileged classes and lower classes of the poor and agricultural workers. Some of them, notably the Iroquois, were organized matrilineally, and members of a matriline lived together in a large dwelling called a longhouse. While they had male leaders, the social leader of the group was the matron of the line, whose authority extended to religious, ethical, and social matters.

MESOAMERICA

Among the most prominent Mesoamerican cultures was that of the Maya, who inhabited a swath of land in southern Mexico, Yucatán, and parts of Central America. Historians identify three broad periods of Mayan history. The earliest, called the Formative Period, began in about 1500 B.C.E. and extended to about 250 C.E. The Classic Period, when Maya culture in numerous city-states achieved its florescence, extended from about 250 to 900. Finally, the Postclassic Period began in about 900 and extended to about 1500, with the arrival of Europeans. During this time Maya culture began to decline until it lost some 90 percent of its population. About 4 million Maya survive in the 21st century.

Archaeologists do not agree about the nature of Maya social organization. They note that it is difficult to make inferences about an abstraction such as social organization from the material archaeological record. Evidence such as tombs and excavations of housing sites can provide some indication of social stratification. Some historians believe that Maya society was highly stratified; others disagree. Historians cannot even agree, for example, on whether Maya society was organized patrilineally or matrilineally. Nor do they have the same opinion on whether Maya society was unified or segmented—that is, divided and not uniform across the many city-states that made up the Maya culture.

It is known, however, that Maya culture was sedentary, depending on agriculture for survival. Because much of the region was hot and dry, the Maya had to develop sophisticated farming and water-management techniques. In those areas that were wet and forested, the dense forests posed their own impediments to agriculture. This type of activity needed to be organized on a large scale involving hundreds, if not thousands, of people, suggesting that at least some social stratification was inevitable. The archaeological record shows wide differences in wealth and status, differences exhibited in the size and elaborateness of public buildings and of homes. The highest status individuals were probably members of patrilineages, although again this is uncertain.

At bottom, some archaeologists have concluded that there was no uniform system of social organization among the various Maya city-states. Each one existed relatively independently from other Maya communities, and thus its form of social organization was unique to itself. It is likely that some communities were highly stratified, with wide differences in wealth and status. These communities may have needed a rigid social order to survive. Others probably featured more flexible, less stratified societies.

A fuller record exists for the Aztec, the culture that flourished in central Mexico during the centuries before the arrival of the Spanish in the early 16th century but that had its roots in the 12th century. The Aztec developed a stratified and fairly complex social organization, though one that was somewhat fluid and allowed lower class people to rise through hard work and skill. Their social order was a clan-based system that consisted of 20 clans, called *calpulli*, each of which had its own officials and governmental organization. Within this clan-based social structure, each person was born into a particular social class. At the top, of course, was the king, referred to as the *tlatoani* or *tlacatecuhtli*. The king was always reputed to be a descendant of Acamapichtli, a Toltec prince. In turn, Acamapichtli was regarded as a descendant of Quetzalcoatl, the Toltec's principal god. According to Aztec myth, the prince came to Tenochtitlán, the Aztec capital city, to establish the royal line. He did so by mating with 20 wives, possibly one from each of the 20 clans.

Beneath the king and the royal household were the nobles, referred to as *pipiltin*. Every noble was regarded as a descendant of Acamapichtli, and thus was of royal blood. The chief advantage of being an Aztec noble was that one could own land in his own name on achieving adulthood. The nobles were also taught to write, using the Aztec system of glyphs, and they were given educations in religion and the arts. Nobles held the highest religious, judicial, civil, and

military positions. However, in the Aztec social hierarchy being a noble did not guarantee holding an important job. The highest positions were held by nobles who showed skills in leadership. Any member of the nobility who failed to demonstrate leadership skills could end up with a low-ranking job, including that of a servant in the royal household, or even no job at all. Nearly equal to the class of nobles was a class of warriors who achieved a position akin to knighthood by showing valor in warfare. Warriors were typically promoted from lower classes.

The next social class was that of the working class and commoners, referred to as *macehualtin*. These people were educated in trades or farmed the Aztec's communal lands. The land was owned by the clans, so commoners themselves could not own it in their own name. However, they were entitled to ownership of the produce of the land, which they could trade, sell, or consume for their own needs. These commoners were members of the 20 clans, and it was possible for a commoner to rise to office in his clan and thus have more prestige, in fact if not in name, than a low-ranking or unemployed noble. Alongside agricultural workers were a class of landless commoners who normally worked in trades as craftsmen; the less capable among these typically worked as day laborers.

Beneath the commoners was a class of serfs, or *mayeque*, who worked plots of land in return for payment in the form of some percentage of what they produced. They were attached to the land, in effect part of it, so that if a parcel of land was sold, they went with it to the new owner as part of the bargain. In addition to laboring in the fields, males worked as servants and performed such tasks as hauling water or constructing buildings; women were often employed as cooks. Serfs had one advantage: They were not required to pay taxes. Accordingly, some commoners, who were required to pay taxes, tried to pass as serfs. Many, too, were immigrants from conquered territories. A serf who was industrious was able to rise to the class of commoner.

Finally, at the bottom of the social order were slaves. Aztec slave owners did not have life-and-death power over their slaves. They owned a slave's labor but not the slave's person. Slaves could own property, including their own house, and they could not be sold or traded to a new owner without their consent. Slaves could even own other slaves. A person could escape slavery through hard work and meritorious service to his or her master.

SOUTH AMERICA

In discussions of any aspect of South American culture before the Spanish conquest, historians inevitably focus on Andean civilizations—that is, the civilizations of Bolivia, Ecuador, Peru, and parts of Chile that flourished in the Andes and along the western coast and valleys of the continent. The archaeological record for these civilizations is more extensive and more advanced than that of the interior of the continent. Put simply, while a considerable amount is known about the Andean civilizations, little is known about the rain forest civilizations that occupied much of the rest of the continent.

The Andean civilizations depended on agriculture, so they were sedentary rather than nomadic. Further, their agricultural enterprises flourished despite the harsh terrain that hosted wide differences in temperature and elevation. Over the course of many centuries, the people of the Andes developed complex terraced fields along the mountains, irrigation systems, and a network of roads that eased the movement of people and goods through the region. All of this economic activity required a complex social system.

The basic social institution was probably like the *ayllu* of later times. This was a social unit at the village level that was based on kinship. The *ayllu* provided a kind of vertical integration of the families of the unit. Again, climate and geography dictated this form of social organization. Because of the sharp differences in elevation, people at different altitudes had to specialize in certain kinds of crop. Those at the higher elevations, for example, emphasized such crops as tubers and millet, while those at lower heights emphasized more tropical crops. Reciprocal exchange between the families of the *ayllu* at different elevations ensured that everyone had a variety of foodstuffs. In time, these cultures would pay tribute to the more powerful Inca civilization.

Late in the precontact period the Inca became the most dominant Andean civilization and the one that is most studied by modern historians. But the Inca did not emerge from nowhere. Inca civilization was the final florescence of a number of Andean civilizations that had emerged in the preceding centuries. Not a great deal is known about most of these civilizations. Many produced pottery and had sophisticated agricultural systems, including terraces and irrigation canals; one such canal was 75 miles long. It is known that some of these civilizations became increasingly militaristic and had a social class of warriors. One such Andean culture emerged at Tiwanaku in about 500 near Lake Titicaca. The culture was urbanized, and it is known that its society was highly stratified. At about the same time the Huari emerged in southern Peru, and it, too, was socially stratified. Along the northern coast of Peru the later Chimu culture was greatly stratified, with classes from a divine king down to farmers and peasants who worked the land. In the middle was a class of artisans and craftsmen who produced pottery, textiles, and other goods for mass consumption.

Inca culture began about 1200, although its origins are obscure. The Inca Empire expanded rapidly through military conquest, in time encompassing 380,000 square miles. Historians do not know as much about the Inca Empire as they do about the Aztec Empire, primarily because of a lack of written records. It is known that the Inca Empire was highly regimented. It was a socialist state; the state owned the land, access to water, and surplus agricultural production, which it then redistributed as needed. Harvests were transported to large storehouses, where they were used by public servants, the army, priests, and especially the nobility.

At the head of Inca social structure was the emperor, referred to as Sapa Inca, who controlled every aspect of the empire. Next were the nobility, who were members of the royal family. Below the nobility were the state's high priest and the commander in chief of the military. The next level consisted of the *apus*, the military commanders of each of the empire's four regions. Such people as architects, priests, army commanders, and civic administrators made up the next class. Just below them were musicians, artisans, lower ranking military officers, and accountants. The bottom rung of the social order included herders, farmers, sorcerers, and men who had been conscripted into the army.

People did not pay taxes but instead were required to work for the state on such public works projects as the construction of roads. This obligatory service was known as *mita*. Most of this work was done by members of the social class called *runas* or *mitimaes*, essentially the lower classes. Members of the upper classes, including the nobility, craftsmen, and priests, were exempt from *mita*. Another exempt class was the *yanacuna*, or boys who served as permanent aides to the nobility or to the emperor. Physically attractive girls were taken to convents in the capital city, Cuzco, where they would be trained as concubines for the emperor.

The emperor was regarded as a descendant of the sun. To preserve the purity of the bloodline, most Inca emperors took their sisters as wives, and members of the nobility typically married their cousins. Members of the nobility were identified by the heavy jewelry they wore dangling from their ears. For this reason, the Spanish conquerors referred to them as *orejones*, or "big ears."

ASIA AND THE PACIFIC
BY BRET HINSCH

Although Asia is both enormous and diverse, its history nevertheless reveals some clear patterns in the general expansion of its medieval societies. Most important, China and India, the two major cultural centers on the continent, each developed large, complex, literate, prosperous civilizations that exerted enormous influence over surrounding peoples. Korea, Japan, and Vietnam remade their societies while being constantly exposed to Chinese ideas and institutions, whereas the various peoples of Burma, Thailand, Cambodia, and Indonesia developed within the Indian culture zone.

CHINA

The collapse of the Eastern Han Dynasty in 220 C.E. marked the traumatic end of national unity and the emergence of a distinctive medieval social and economic system. Even before the end of the Han, Chinese society had already begun to take on medieval characteristics. With the central government in decline, extended prominent families stepped into the vacuum to maintain local order. They accumulated large estates worked by dependents who were increasingly tied to the land. Peasants were willing to give up their traditional autonomy in return for protection from bandits and foreign raiders.

China went through several centuries of chaos in the early medieval era, marked by a succession of weak regional governments. North China was conquered by the Tuoba, a nomadic Mongol people, while southern China was governed by a succession of fragile states. Social mobility drastically declined as security became more important than opportunity. Although there were still free peasants, large numbers of people worked as tenants on the estates of the great landholding families. Social status became progressively more hereditary, and genealogy was a primary source of prestige. The members of the landed elite maintained their exclusive social status through intermarriage, and they carefully excluded new blood. In fact it became illegal for people of different backgrounds to marry. Social strata resembled hereditary castes. Union between people of different backgrounds was even considered physically unclean. Because of early medieval Chinese society's low mobility and its association of status with both land and pedigree, some scholars classify it as a feudalistic system. However, unlike European feudalism, there was also an active central government, a clear definition of national borders, a literate bureaucracy, an active commerce, and widespread ownership of private property.

The reunification of China under the Tang Dynasty (618–907) marked a period of national recovery, during which society gradually began to change. This era marked a time of struggle for supremacy between the emperors at the center and the traditional local elites who flaunted their exalted ancestry. Although the previous era of chaos had been a low point politically, it did see improvements in agricultural technology. So as society became more stable, the economy grew and social mobility inexorably increased. The monopoly on power of the traditional elite frayed as commerce and urbanization grew. Nevertheless, regional elites continued to maintain their supremacy in many areas and were virtually autonomous for much of the period.

The Song Dynasty (960–1279) marked a major turning point in the history of Chinese society. Most fundamentally, economic growth increased rapidly, fueling widespread urbanization. A new class of prosperous merchants and craftsmen inhabited the growing cities, vying for prestige with the traditional rural elite. An expanding economy brought about rapid social mobility, with an end to fixed social positions. Life became organized increasingly around professions rather than kinship.

Changes in the nature of government affected society as well. The Song system was far more centralized and better organized than earlier eras. Most important, regular examinations recruited talented scholars into official positions. In theory, anyone could now become a high government official, although in practice only the rich could afford the lengthy education necessary to pass these grueling examinations. The exam system severed the traditional link between genealogy and power, forcing changes among the conservative rural elite. Old families began to marry their daughters to parvenu officials to maintain their influence under this new system.

Ming Dynasty (1368–1644) society saw a continuation of these trends. The founder of the Ming, known as the Hongwu Emperor (r. 1368–98) came from peasant stock, and he helped foster even more egalitarianism in the Chinese state and society. Commerce grew so rapidly that some historians argue that China was on the verge of developing a nascent capitalist economy. This prosperity was reflected in the vibrant urban culture of the era. Moreover, the importation of new crops from the Americas, such as sweet potatoes and corn, allowed marginal land to be cultivated, fueling a population explosion that has continued to the 21st century. Rising population and partitive inheritance (inheritance divided among heirs) meant that the number of families with insufficient land steadily increased, fueling immigration to Taiwan and Southeast Asia.

The examination system continued to serve as the most important determinant of elite status. In response, families routinely bought land and used the profits of landlordism to finance the education of their sons. These offspring would intermarry with other scholar gentry families, helping to ensure a degree of prestige regardless of how their sons fared in the examinations. Ideally, a family member eventually would pass the battery of tests and gain official employment. However, as the number of people taking these exams grew, this means to wealth and status became increasingly competitive and frustrating.

EAST ASIA

The expulsion of Chinese armies from the Korean peninsula in the seventh century led to a struggle between three local states: Silla, Paekche, and Koguryo. Although the social structure in each was somewhat different, in general aristocratic families living in the capital dominated society and government, enjoying hereditary privileges. As in contemporary China, the elite painstakingly traced genealogy because ancestral connections served as the basis of exclusive position and power. Most peasants were free and owned small plots of land. Although some agricultural labor was still communal, ordinarily each family was an independent unit of production. However, aristocratic families controlled enormous tracts of land, often farmed by low caste laborers descended from prisoners of war and criminals. Because of constant warfare, a large percentage of society was eventually enslaved by the aristocracy.

In the ninth century the Korean kings tried to subdue the aristocracy by importing Chinese customs that favored centralization, but they were generally thwarted. Regional powers grew in importance, making it impossible for the government to collect taxes in many areas. The heavy burdens imposed by local authorities, however, led to a series of peasant rebellions in the ninth and 10th centuries.

The 10th-century reforms marking the beginnings of the Koryo era gave rise to a new hereditary elite closely linked to government service, in calculated imitation of China's social system. The bulk of society was made up of free peasants, and the lot of slaves improved until it resembled that of tenant farmers. In the 14th century the new Yi Dynasty (1392–1910) undertook radical land reform. Authorities confiscated the large estates, breaking the traditional power of the hereditary aristocracy. Some land was allocated to the new literati class, marking a radical reorganization of society along the lines of China's system centered on government service.

The medieval era saw surprisingly rapid development in Japan because of the cultural stimulus of China and Korea. Initially the monarchy tried to establish a Chinese-style state with strong central government. However, aristocrats and powerful Buddhist monasteries eventually conspired to turn the emperor into little more than a figurehead. During the Heian era (794–1185), Japanese society became decentralized and local aristocrats became more autonomous. Nevertheless, the state still maintained the facade of Chinese-style central bureaucracy and emperorship, and the court aristocracy remained preeminent. Land tenure was progressively more feudalized, and peasants owed both grain and corvée labor to their land's proprietor.

Kamakura-era (1185–1333) society was organized differently. The court aristocracy and the powerful monasteries lost their hold on society. In response, a mature feudal system emerged, organized around a local military aristocracy that reordered society as a complex series of relationships between lords and vassals. Although this aristocracy maintained a symbolic imperial system, true power rested with a supreme military leader who maintained order among the fractious noble houses. Unlike the refined court aristocrats, the new *bushi* elite were primarily warriors. These men were initially quite rough and uneducated and often relied on Buddhist monks as administrators. Common people remained tied to the villages, where they supported the feudal hierarchy with annual payments of rice and labor to the local lord.

Far to the south on the Asian mainland the people of northern Vietnam originally practiced irrigation farming in small communities. By the 10th century, as Vietnamese society became more complex, these groupings coalesced into villages. Ever since its unification, the Chinese Empire had included northern Vietnam, so the Vietnamese elite were encouraged to assimilate Chinese culture and participate in the imperial bureaucratic system. Moreover, there was a great deal of emigration southward from China. Many social forms were inevitably brought in from Vietnam's giant neighbor to the north. For example, the Vietnamese traditionally lived in large extended families, but when Chinese immigrants arrived in nuclear families, some local people began imitating this new model. The Chinese also introduced an "equal-field system" that assigned each farmer an equal amount of land, which he tilled for his lifetime, after which it reverted to the state for reallocation. Despite the extent of Chinese influence, the Vietnamese managed to maintain a distinct culture and identity. For example, women labored in the rice paddies in violation of basic Chinese ideas of sexual propriety.

In the ninth century the decline of the Tang allowed the Vietnamese to become independent, and a new local ruling class emerged. Free peasants practiced rice paddy agriculture in the lowlands, while the highlands were inhabited by various ethnic groups. Vietnam's coastal position gave it a cosmopolitan flavor. International trade grew in importance, merchants became numerous, and coastal settlements developed into regional market centers. Communal ownership of land remained the norm. The large clans of each area were extremely strong and competed with the state for authority. The king took numerous consorts from the major clans, and these palace women acted as conduits between the central authority and local clans. In the 13th century, rulers of the Trân Dynasty (1225–1400) tried to reduce the authority of the clans by marrying their own cousins, thereby reducing the access of the clans to the center of power. The Trân accumulated massive royal estates and sought officials from among the major landowners to help them administer the state.

INDIA

The Indian attitude toward society has been conditioned by deep religious beliefs. Indians saw the universe as consisting of many interlocking levels inhabited by a variety of beings. To the average Indian, society was an extremely complicated place consisting of human beings, heroes, gods, and demons. On a more mundane level, people maintained the ancient division of society into four social categories called *varna*, which were subdivided into thousands of castes or *jati*. Originally this Hindu social model was limited to a section of north India, but in the medieval era it was disseminated throughout India and overseas.

Although Indian social structure consisted of thousands of carefully distinguished hereditary groups, two elite forces were particularly powerful: Kshatriya warriors and Brahman priests. Brahmans were given positions of wealth and privilege, and at court they were employed as royal counselors. They also received large land grants, both as individual families and sometimes to establish Brahman communities. The state actively patronized temples, further boosting the position of Brahmans. In return, Brahmans provided the ideology and values that upheld Kshatriya rule. These two elites usually cooperated to dominate society, and the cooperation between secular and sacred elites became the focus of Indian social structure.

Unlike China, the various regions of India were usually autonomous. Even under the famous empires it was always difficult to control local elites, and central rule was usually weak. This system has been characterized as a type of feudalism, brought about largely by a precipitous reduction in the circulation of currency, which prevented central rulers from paying salaries to local officials. This style of social organization can be seen clearly in the first great medieval empire, that of King Harsa of Kanauj (r. 606–47). Although Harsa controlled the central part of his realm directly, it was mostly decentralized, and each area was under the control of an autonomous local tributary ruler known as a *samanta*. These local princes were obligated to present tribute to Harsa and do his bidding under certain circumstances, although in most matters they remained autonomous. Successful rule consisted of controlling the fractious *samantas* and maintaining their loyalty.

India is incredibly diverse, and in medieval times each region had its own unique traditions and characteristic social structure. For example, as agriculture was adopted in the area of Rajasthan, the local Rajputs—members of the military caste—were able to use this stronghold to gain influence over a large area of north India. This group was divided into small clans, and their exogamous customs meant that they were loosely held together as a people and polity by marital alliances.

The Hindu model of society steadily spread south and east, eventually dominating the subcontinent. Petty tribal chieftains were gradually converted into local Hindu princes and brought into the feudal *samanta* system. These new *samantas* would push out peoples who refused to assimilate into the Hindu world order and invited Brahmans to settle in their realms instead, attracting them with generous land grants. Brahmanization allowed local kings to imitate the ideology and system of the political center to the north. Eventually some of these petty monarchs conquered neighboring states and established larger kingdoms. At the local level, however, villages remained fairly autonomous and most people's lives were relatively untouched by royal decree. If a ruler taxed villagers too heavily, their leaders might foment rebellion and bring down an overambitious *samanta*.

In southern India the extent of maritime trade meant that prosperous merchants were a particularly powerful force. Some merchants gathered together in autonomous self-governing communities (*nagara*). Others lived in ports under the control of monarchs. Their guilds were extremely powerful and even supported independent armies. Nevertheless, the coastal Indian monarchs also benefited from commercial wealth, which they used to patronize temples and finance their activities.

Temple cities became more numerous and were built ever farther south. Although temples were massively expensive, kings still built and patronized them both out of piety and a desire to attract Brahman support. However, these were far more than just religious centers. A temple city remade the local society along both Brahman and *samanta* lines. The king and people gave generous donations to large temples, which also received regular income from landholdings. In return, the temple bureaucracy would lend money to the villages. The emergence of new pilgrimage centers further influenced economic and cultural life.

Beginning in the eighth century Muslim conquerors began making incursions into India. During the 12th century they were able to establish a large empire in northern India. Because Muslim rulers of the new Islamic states relied on Brahmans and temple cities to maintain their sway, they had to create novel institutions. New customs were brought into the heart of daily life when many Indians converted to Islam and embraced its alien lifestyle and values. This transformation challenged many Indian traditions. Buddhism was hit particularly hard. Because Buddhists are technically atheists, some fanatical Muslims persecuted them with an intense ferocity that eventually led to the extinction of Buddhism in the land of its birth.

Islam was limited primarily to the urban administrative and military elite, while the countryside remained mostly Hindu. Nevertheless, large numbers of low-caste people converted to the new religion to escape their degraded status.

The direct rule of the Muslim sultans rarely extended much beyond the hinterland around the capital at Delhi. Otherwise the sultans depended on the cooperation of local rulers, in a new variation on traditional feudalism. Outside of the cities, Muslim military commanders, as a rule, remained in local strongholds, often centered on a military fief. In the villages, life continued much as before, while the sultans conducted local affairs through village headmen. Although Hinduism was still legal, some rulers used high taxes and specific legislation to encourage conversion to Islam.

SOUTHEAST ASIA

Before the 10th century Southeast Asia was a patchwork of ethnic groups and small states. The unique environment of the region originally gave birth to native societies quite different from those in India and China. For example, population density was relatively low, and some scholars claim that the resulting lack of concern for landed property led to higher autonomy for women. Traditionally, women in the medieval kingdoms of Thailand and Cambodia enjoyed prominent roles in domestic commerce. Kinship was often bilateral, with equal inheritance rights for both sons and daughters.

The spread of Indian culture and institutions throughout Southeast Asia transformed those regions, stimulating the development of high culture and complex administration. There has been considerable debate as to how Southeast Asia came to absorb so much Indian influence. Some scholars emphasize the role of trade. They credit the wealth of Indian traders with giving prestige to their religious ideas and customs, leading distant peoples to emulate them. Another view sees the Indianization of Southeast Asia as a continuation of the gradual spread of north Indian values and institutions southward throughout the subcontinent proper. Eventually Brahmans and Buddhist monks settled abroad, bringing with them skills in writing, law, and government. While Indian influence is no longer considered the prime reason for social development in the region, these ideas were eagerly adopted by growing societies in need of paradigms for more complex social groupings. Southeast Asian rulers were often eager patrons of Indian culture, striving to reconstruct their own societies in the image of the complex models to the west. Between the third and eighth centuries, Buddhist and Hindu sculptures began to appear across Southeast Asia, providing concrete archaeological evidence of this dramatic social transformation.

During the 11th and 12th centuries a complex Khmer state emerged in what is now Cambodia. Most of what is known about Angkor comes from inscriptions and archaeological evidence. This society was a matrilineal monarchy that ruled over a large area using a sophisticated bureaucracy, which employed written records and a rigid law code. Hindu and Buddhist clerics provided a religious ideology that legitimized and ordered this society. Distant regions were controlled through force of arms and ruled over by royal governors. As in India, temples became important centers of politics and administration. Khmer rulers constructed vast temple complexes, designating local families as temple slaves to support the upkeep of these gigantic monuments.

The decline of Angkor and Pagan, another large Indianized state located in northern Burma, allowed the rise of new regional powers. Ethnic Thai peoples, known collectively as the Tai, migrated southward into the region of the former empires. In the 13th century they founded a state known as Lan Na (or Lanna), with a capital at Chiang Mai in what is now northern Thailand. The Tai had converted to Buddhism centuries earlier and used Indianized religious and secular ideas as the basis of a complex society. Lan Na was an ethnically diverse state, held together by common political and religious institutions. Although most people lived in villages, the rulers established sizable cities with temples and fortifications. Skilled craftsmen such as metalworkers migrated there from other states, raising the technological level.

The Sukhothai state flourished in southern Thailand in the 13th and 14th centuries. This society coalesced out of cooperation between Tai tributary princes and officials who had originally served Angkor. As the Khmer Empire declined, a series of dynamic local rulers built on existing institutions to create a new state. Buddhism was fundamental to all aspects of Sukhothai rule. The king and senior monks even shared the same throne, officially melding secular and religious authority. The Sukhothai kings actively encouraged trade, guaranteed the security of inheritance, and sought to defuse social tensions through just adjudication of disputes, often by the king himself. Social structure was relatively simple, with a small elite ruling over the vast body of commoners. Foreign peoples were also absorbed into the Sukhothai kingdom. Their leaders became Sukhothai nobles, while the ordinary people were often integrated as slaves or feudal vassals.

The Indonesian archipelago also saw the rise and fall of several notable states, each giving rise to a complex society. The state of Mataram (570–927) in central Java gave birth to a new type of state, which was to be a model for later polities. Fertile volcanic soil allowed prosperous villages to emerge inland, while merchants and sailors resided in trading centers along the coast. Irrigation networks were overseen by powerful village and lineage leaders who became the focus of local power. Competing local elites vied constantly for supremacy, but as they were evenly matched, it was not easy for one group to establish suzerainty over the others. Rather than vanquishing foes through conquest, competing lineages formed complex alliances, often through interlocking marriage ties. The agricultural and mercantile spheres exchanged goods at periodic markets, meshing the two groups into a symbiotic economy that could support a unified state. The importation of Buddhist and Hindu beliefs allowed local leaders to use these sophisticated systems to attract further loyalty, and holy men legitimized and supported the ruler. Both kings and temples received tribute from allies and engaged in trade with coastal commercial hubs. Nevertheless, unlike the civilizations of continental Asia, Mataram never gave rise to a large professional bureaucracy.

Similar states appeared elsewhere on Java, Sumatra, and in the surrounding region during the medieval era. Like the Mataram prototype, these societies mixed productive agriculture with maritime trade, and native cultures were overlaid by imported Indian customs and beliefs. By the 13th century Islam had begun to spread over the same trade routes that had originally brought Indian religions to the region. Eventually, many of the people in Southeast Asia converted to this new religion, re-creating their own societies yet again according to the ideals of a foreign religion.

EUROPE

by Charles W. Abbott

Medieval western Europe represented a fusion of two heritages: Roman and Germanic. From Rome came elaborate administration, Roman law, and Christianity. From Germanic and other barbarian invaders came social fluidity among warriors, the common law from tradition, and improved folk technologies in farming. The Roman Empire had been centered on the Mediterranean, a "Roman lake." (The Romans called it Mare Nostrum, "our sea"). As Rome declined, the empire broke apart into three main pieces. Many of its old provinces became part of the Islamic world, while others remained part of the Byzantine East. The third part of Rome was western Europe, Latin Christendom. Western Europe's economic center of gravity shifted north into cooler and more heavily forested terrain. Many of these lands had never been ruled by Rome, and most of them had never been Rome's core provinces. In this new medieval Europe old and new models clashed; the tensions were never fully resolved but provided ongoing inspiration.

Certain commonalities emerge about medieval Europe during its 1,000-year history and across diverse societies. Political authority was often fragmented and decentralized; frequently it was embodied in personal ties of allegiance rather than bureaucratic command. Economic life was at times similarly fragmented, in some eras with much productivity being household labor for subsistence. At times the major-

ity of Europe's inhabitants were part of an unfree peasantry. Taxes were often paid in labor services rather than in cash. Most people identified themselves with reference to their family, their local society, and their estate—clergy, nobility, and commoner.

The centuries after 1000 saw growth in trade, urbanization, and social complexity. A striking agricultural expansion also took place up to 1300. Europe became less forested and more populous as farms replaced trees, but it also became more complex as new cities were founded and as old ones grew larger. Merchants had more and better institutions to serve them. More monasteries graced Europe, containing more mills and libraries. Monarchs had more direct and predictable influence in their domain. Unfavorable weather after 1300 was followed by famines and then by the Black Death (1348–51), which wiped out over one-third of Europe's population. These developments were bad for social organization but good for social innovation. Urban dwellers were especially hard hit, and new pathways for social advancement opened up in the fourteenth century.

THE THREE ORDERS: THOSE WHO WORK, THOSE WHO PRAY, AND THOSE WHO FIGHT

In England in 995 the Saxon churchman Aelfric (ca. 955–ca. 1010) described his social world as being divided into three groups: those who work, those who pray, and those who fight. These were the three great divisions of medieval Europe. Persons in each group proclaimed separate values, performed their roles as they saw fit, and struggled to rise or to maintain their level in a separate status hierarchy. As history progressed, each group became more internally differentiated. The working class spawned merchants, towns, and the urban nucleus from which modern Europe emerged—but with the military ferocity of the secular leaders, nurtured in a politically fragmented society of sovereign states.

The church ("those who pray") was its own world. It governed itself by its own institutions, relying on a separate bureaucracy, canon law, separate courts, and the assembly of cardinals. It was responsible for salvation in the next world and enforced discipline through religious symbolism and supernatural sanctions. It had strong faith in its own universality—the church was for all, except for the small number of Jews who remained outside of it. (Muslims were also outside the church, but they did not flourish in Christian Europe, though they created a thriving culture in Muslim Spain.) Among members of the church the highest values were piety, faith, mercy, and charity: a concern for the eternal souls of their fellows.

Secular leaders ("those who fight") were also those who ruled. They were the heirs of the fall of Rome and the disintegration of public order that accompanied it. Many were themselves descendants of invaders who fostered a militarized society. Their goal was to survive, to carve out their domain and rule over it, and to protect against further attacks (from Vikings in the north, Magyars in the east, and Saracens in the south). They trained and prepared for war, they fought wars, and they administered justice to those in their domain. When they were not fighting, they held tournaments (mock fights), or they hunted. Secular rulers held land in grant from larger lords; they did not farm the land themselves but required a servile or free peasantry to farm for them. They provided hospitality in their massive halls, the only nonsacred buildings that could hold hundreds of people at once. They prized physical vitality, and their highest values were martial courage, personal loyalty, and the love of justice.

The common people ("those who work") included the mass of peasant farmers and herders but also the various other folk not involved in the church, the government, or war. This group included the families of substantial merchants and skilled craftsmen as well as humble peddlers, milkmaids, fishermen, and domestic servants. About 90 percent of men and women fell into this group. The common people were commoners; that is, rather than being military nobles with political status or bishops, abbots, and monks with religious office, they were people without rank. Some of them were modestly prosperous or even rich, but most of them were quite poor. These people worked with their hands, and it is harder to specify their highest values. Solidarity and mutual aid among villagers were important to commoners. Pragmatic focus on endless practical work was a way of life. People in this station of society valued patience, pragmatism, prudence, and diligence.

The common people were indispensable: They did the work without which society would immediately grind to a halt. Growing grain, herding sheep, catching fish, forging iron, making barrels, milking cows, churning butter, constructing buildings, and transporting goods, members of this group were less likely than the others to leave written records. Except for merchants who kept accounts and guildsmen who regulated themselves, much of what we know about them was written by others, in court dockets and in the accounts of their creditors.

THE BASICS OF FEUDALISM

Feudalism emerged as way of marshaling military power in a society in which land was abundant and the cash economy had unraveled. The nominal ruler of a large area (the lord or a high-ranking retainer at court) needed an army. Only with an army could he hold his territory against invaders and local competing strongmen. However, the lord lacked money to pay his army. The solution was for him to grant estates of land (fiefs) to his regional subordinates (the vassals of the lord), who received their land in return for pledges of military service. A regional fief holder (the lord's vassal) was free to govern his estate as he saw fit, and he would typically grant fiefs internally to his own vassals. The result was a pyramid structure of patron-client relationships, personal relationships between people unequal in power and status who had reached an agreement.

The superior man granted land to his vassal for the vassal's livelihood and swore to protect him. The vassal in turn swore to aid and assist his lord when called upon to do so—to provide military service (typically 40 days of service per year), with the vassal responsible for his own horse, armor, and weapons. The agreement was formalized in a solemn ritual pledge; it was Christian in content and was witnessed by the highest church officials available. The vassal owed his lord such intangibles as ceremonial deference and military service, and he appeared at the lord's court when summoned. In times of service the vassal would bring his own armed retainers and followers with him when called. (The number of one's followers was a key marker of status and leadership ability.) The lowest rank of followers

Seal of the Picot family, wealthy merchants and aldermen of London, mid-14th century; in all classes of society seals were used in formal transactions. (© Museum of London)

would be ambitious young men—pages and squires—who aspired to hold fiefs of their own in due time.

Neither the lord nor the vassals farmed the land; they were dependent on the labor of free peasant farmers or unfree serfs. These subordinate farmers financed a vassal's military capacity by working on the vassal's agricultural plot (the demesne) as well as on their own. Stereotypically, the vassal lived in a manor house and presided over unfree serf farmers, while the manor was largely self-contained as an economic unit. The lord of the manor was a vassal of the higher lord who had granted him his fief, but simultaneously he was lord to his serfs. Serfs worked on his land without pay on certain days. They also paid for the right to use the lord's facilities: the mill, the pond, the forest, and the ovens. All of those resources were the lord's, and serfs paid to use them (either in kind or in cash). In this way an army was financed, and an entire martial class was supported.

Farmers were typically subject to various forms of servitude and inequality. They were serfs and so were not free, but they were far from being slaves. The lord of the manor did not own them and could not sell them. He could not confiscate their property without cause, and he had no right to command them arbitrarily or to deprive them of their land. Serfs had customary rights, but they were not free. They were deprived of the right to move freely. (They could not travel away from the manor without their lord's permission, and if they ran away, they could be returned by force.) They could not choose their own profession, go to court against others, or freely enter contracts; they were generally prohibited from becoming monks (though they might become affiliated with monasteries as laborers). Serfs owed labor services to their lord. They had to go to him for justice, and he often monopolized key functions in general. The court for resolution of disputes was his court, just as the mill and the pond were his. In this sense, feudalism devolved all government functions to local knights, who exercised jurisdiction in their own domain.

The Uncertainties of Feudalism

Feudalism was at the core of medieval society from the early Middle Ages until many serfs had their labor dues commuted to cash rents in the centuries after 1000. On one level the purpose of feudalism was political: It was a system for building political authority and matching it with military power. More generally, it was a form of social and economic organization. Authority over land made the feudal system work. Those who farmed the land could be taxed (usually in labor or in kind) to support one knight. That knight swore allegiance to a greater lord, who might swear allegiance to an even greater lord. In this way a body of fighting men could be raised to fight a neighboring kingdom or to put up a good front against the Vikings so that they would go and plunder elsewhere.

Feudalism also conjures up economic associations: the image of the self-contained manor, for example. At the dawn of the Middle Ages the manor aspired to self-sufficiency. Much production involved household labor. Villagers grew their own food, spun and wove their own cloth, raised their own farm animals, built their own houses, and made their own tools. The balance of production came from within the manor, from local specialists, such as the butcher, the baker, the cooper (barrel maker), the smith, and the tinker (mender).

In medieval Europe serfdom was real, as were knights in armor. The manor as a largely self-sufficient economic institution was real at certain times. (Its self-sufficiency eroded whenever trade revived, since specialization has demonstrable benefits.) Some modern historians have argued that feudalism was not real but a mirage. The knight and the manor are proven historical facts, but feudalism is an idea, a stylized story, an interpretation of reality—not necessarily a historical fact. It existed in some places and at some times in medieval Europe, but it was not a general pattern. While scholars once asserted that the medieval period was the age of feudalism, many now consider feudalism to have been not a stage in history but a stage in historiography (the writing of history).

Peasant Farmers

As is the case with feudalism, which is simple to describe in theory but harder to analyze in reality, the exact status of serfs can be difficult to work out. It is hard to tell hundreds of years later, from fragmentary sources written by their supervisors and adversaries, to what extent a particular group of farmers was free. It can be especially hard to tell what their exact dues to their lord may have been, what their bargaining power was relative to their lords, or when their servile obligations arose and why.

The term *serfdom* is imprecise, covering a variety of unfree and dependent conditions. Historically, it emerged from a variety of earlier statuses, including the outright slavery of the late Roman Empire. At that time senators and magnates often retired from Rome to their large country estates. Such holdings were worked by gangs of slaves, and the senators surrounded themselves with armed retainers and had little need for public order. Later on in the early Middle Ages descendants of slaves became serfs. In the sixth century the church forbade the enslavement of Christians, but slavery endured for centuries. (Slaves are listed in England's Domesday Book of 1086.) Because the largest estates were perceived as inefficient, proprietors often broke up estates into smallholdings where serf families farmed individual plots, the serf operating somewhat like a sharecropper or a tenant farmer.

Not all serfdom arose from people coming out of chattel slavery; in other places free farmers were unable to defend themselves during the general collapse of public order. It was common for them to commend themselves to a local strongman who would protect them, essentially giving their land to a local protector, who then granted it back again in return for labor services. The lord's exact explanation of how he achieved authority over his serfs was often self-serving and differed markedly from the peasants' viewpoint. Successful lords usually gained a territory full of inhabitants, some of whom may have been slaves and some close to free peasants, and then subjected them to relentless pressure for labor services. Sometimes he might bully them; other times he might grant them assistance, but with strings attached. He presented himself as a benefactor, but it was costly to be one of his beneficiaries.

THE CHURCH AND THE CLERGY: CRUSADES AND PERSECUTION

It is relatively easy to imagine the feudal lord in medieval Europe; it is harder to imagine the role of the church. The lord's power flowed from his military prowess, from his potential to contribute to public order (or to disrupt it), by his monopoly over local justice, and by his tax revenue from those who worked the land. The church also drew some of its own power from the ownership of land, for it was one of the largest owners of land in Europe. It had other sources of strength as well.

One source of church influence was its historical continuity. For much of the Middle Ages the church was the greatest source of literacy, brainpower, and bureaucratic continuity. The church had corporate coherence; individuals aged and died, but the church endured. The church could often achieve its long-term goals because of its staying power. The church also drew its strength from the legitimacy it could grant to secular rulers as well as by the reciprocal exchange of favors between church and secular rulers. The emperor of the Holy Roman Empire was by tradition crowned by the pope; lesser kings were invested by lesser religious officers. The church did not need its own military machine to challenge secular rulers. By granting or withholding legitimacy to an individual ruler, it could alter the balance of power, weakening those rulers who challenged church doctrine and prerogatives. The church did not need to attack them itself; ambitious rulers would be happy to launch an attack with the church's blessing.

The grandest example of this practice was the investiture controversy, in which a reform faction of the church withdrew the right of secular rulers to appoint church officers, such as bishops. The conflict culminated with the Holy Roman emperor and the pope proclaiming each other to have been sacked from office. In the long run the church seems to have won that battle. The Holy Roman Empire was weakened, coming to look less and less like a strong monarchy (such as England, France, and Spain would become). Instead, it became more and more a patchwork of smaller states in the aftermath of the controversy.

While European lands were invaded by Vikings, Saracens, and Magyars in the early Middle Ages, after 1000 Europe built up its strength and began to invade lands on its fringes. (Germanic groups drove into the Slavic and Baltic East, and Christian Spain reconquered the peninsula from the Moors.) A notable example is the Crusades, the first of which was launched in 1095 with the blessing of the pope. He proclaimed that those who embarked on the crusade would cleanse themselves of sin in the process and would be assured of reaching heaven.

In addition to the highly visible Crusades to the Holy Land (the eastern shore of the Mediterranean), Europe began to embark on various campaigns against heresy closer to home. After 950 a "persecuting society" arose in Europe, with the goal of enforcing religious orthodoxy, rooting out heresy, segregating Jews and lepers, and protecting society from various social dangers viewed as contagious. The Albigensian Crusade (1209–29) against the Cathars of southern France was thus another crusade closer to home. The persecutory process provided material benefits for those who engaged in it: It increased their power, wealth, and status, even while it provided a chance to eliminate rivals and enemies. There may have been a cynical element to the Crusades as well. It is better for belligerent warriors to go fight in foreign lands than stay nearby and cause trouble at home.

MONASTERIES AND RELIGIOUS FOUNDATIONS

Among the various associations that flourished in the Middle Ages, monasteries were crucially important. The various religious orders included the Benedictines, the Columbans, the Cluniacs, the Carthusians, and the Cistercians, to name a few. The monastic tradition originated with solitary hermits or anchorites in the Egyptian desert and was well developed by the fourth century. As it grew in numbers, organization became necessary, and some monks isolated themselves together in collectives rather than individually, guided and ruled by an abbot (from *abba*, meaning "father" in Aramaic).

It is difficult to generalize about such a movement, but we know that monasteries grew in number and in the number of members, both men and women. Successful monasteries that grew would create new "daughter" monasteries by propagation. Great secular rulers endowed monasteries with land and their benevolent protection. Freemen, many from wealthy families, joined monasteries by taking a vow of obedience. Monasteries also accumulated lay brothers and hangers-on as well as supplicants seeking charity. (Monasteries took seriously Christ's directive to feed the hungry and clothe the naked.) Some joined out of sincere piety, and others joined because doing so was expected of many well-born individuals.

As in any institution that flourished, tensions abounded. Monks took vows of poverty, but many came from wealthy families, and monasteries accumulated substantial wealth and owned large tracts of land. Some peasants considered monasteries to be poor neighbors—grasping, demanding, and expanding landholdings aggressively at the expense of the poor. Monks espoused the goals of simple piety and humility, yet contemporary documents show that many monastic leaders had top-notch classical educations and wrote compelling Latin prose.

Monasteries were to be away from the hustle and bustle of the world, but some served as guesthouses (essentially hotels) for traveling elites. The monasteries with royal patrons had the king or the queen as a most demanding customer, visiting periodically as a guest and expecting to be lodged and fed. Monasteries also functioned as medieval conference centers, where king and barons could all gather at once.

Merchants and Towns: Country Gentry

Because the lord aspired to a monopoly of government, anyone on his manor found it necessary to submit to his justice to enjoy his protection. The merchant guild provided a way out of this situation. Merchants, by uniting among themselves, could lobby for a stable and predictable commercial environment, including low and predictable tolls, freedom from the seizure of their goods, and the right to form contracts and adjudicate them among themselves. Such was the beginning of commercial privileges, which tended to be localized in particular places, normally walled cities governed by themselves.

It was not necessarily hard to move to a city, but it was hard to make a living in one. In theory, towns were governed by the commune, the sworn association of all members. Large merchants tended to dominate town politics over time, and many towns became ruled over by an exclusive, self-confident, upper-class strata, or urban patriciate. This group was able to succeed in business, but in addition, the children might become notaries, lawyers, accountants, and town council functionaries, and they might accumulate landholdings as well. In some countries, such as England, town-based merchants were separate from the rural-based gentry of independent landowners. In Italy the cities tended to dominate the country more; the country elite were essentially the urban-based elite.

The Family

The family is the fundamental building block of society and the enduring unit when all else has crumbled away. Peasant farm families were closest to the modern ideal of the nuclear family; the peasant hovel could not feasibly house more than a married couple, perhaps a grandparent, and their children (as well as the animals that were brought into the house at night and that helped to warm it in the winter). English primogeniture (the passing of land undivided to the oldest son) left the younger sons without significant inheritance. The ideal solution to this problem was to provide younger sons with genteel occupations, such as the priesthood or the law. It was the upper classes for whom family ties meant the most. It was possible to travel and see distant cousins, to engage collectively in business enterprises or war, or carefully to orchestrate marriages so as to gain and maintain control over a city council or a principality.

THE ISLAMIC WORLD

by Massoud Abdel Alim

The conquering armies of Arabian Muslims brought with them a tribal, pastoral-nomadic form of social organization. The Muslim's primary identity was based in blood relationships to family, clan, tribe, and ethnic group. Identity was further derived from places, with people identifying themselves as being from a particular neighborhood, district, village, town, city, province, or country. The final basis of identity was religion first and sect second.

During the conquest, Arab Muslims retained the most elite status and differentiated themselves from their converts and those they governed. The attitude was that free Arab Muslim males carried divine revelation to be distributed to the world. As the conquest spread and conquered lands and conversions increased, the dual-tiered system became untenable; ultimately all Muslims were declared equal, whatever their ethnicity, even though in practice the bias continued.

The most fundamental distinction in Islamic social organization is that between *dar al-Islam* (House of Islam), which contains Muslims regardless of race, ethnicity, or location, and *dar al-harb* (House of War), which houses all others living in lands not under Muslim sovereignty. Muslim government rule and the sharia, or Islamic law based on the Koran, reign supreme and govern the status and relations among Muslims and with non-Muslims. A state of perpetual war exists between Muslims and non-Muslims, to be interrupted by occasional truces that permit Muslim forces to regain strength.

ELEMENTS OF MUSLIM SOCIETY AS DEFINED BY THE SHARIA

Medieval Islam experienced a gradual transformation in the relationship among government, religion, and society. At Islam's inception in the seventh century all three were essentially one unit in that religion spawned a government, which in turn ordered society. By the 15th century government in most Islamic lands was clearly differentiated from religion. Strictures in the sharia regarding taxation, jihad, and political leadership informed government decisions but were hardly enforced without considering contemporary political issues. The same was not true of religion and society: The sharia continued to be the basis for structuring society and regulating personal status with respect to marriage, divorce, inheritance, succession, and commerce. Thus, understanding the Islamic social order requires understanding the social organization defined in the sharia and enforced by the ulema, or the clerical leadership.

The sharia recognized three distinct status categories: free Muslim males, free Muslim females, and slaves. From this three-tiered structure, there emerged specific laws on how classes should interact with one another. The sharia also regulates dealings with non-Muslims in Muslim society. These included the *ahl el-Kitab*, or "people of the book"—Christians and Jews—and all others (Zoroastrians, Manichaeans, Pagans, Sikhs, Hindus, and so on). These non-Muslims were called *dhimmis*. Finally, as trade with non-Muslims expanded (especially with Italian city-states), groups of merchants, emissaries, and other foreigners set up residence in Islamic lands. These people fell outside the Islamic social order.

Medieval Islamic society was a community of belief in which smaller segments of society retained a religious character. Various schools of jurisprudence and theology appeared and disappeared, but all retained an Islamic composition. To the medieval Muslim, nothing existed outside the *umma*, or Islamic community, save small groups of Christians and Jews, whose wealth, power, and influence were perpetually and legally curtailed by both the state and the sharia.

THE ELITES WITHIN THE *UMMA*

The caliph stood at the head of the *umma* and, as successor to Muhammad (ca. 570–632), was Allah's representative. During the Abbasid regime in Baghdad, the caliph, as both religious and political leader, had absolute power. Through him came all position, privilege, and assigned political power. As head of the military, the caliph enforced his rule, often with the power of the sword. Unlike Christianity, with its division between worldly and spiritual obligations (Jesus' admonition to render unto Caesar the things that are Caesar's and to God the things that are God's), Islam does not differentiate the religious from the political; indeed, political problems were often framed as religious problems. This lack of differentiation resulted in three civil wars over the course of the seventh and eighth centuries, stemming from disagreements over caliph succession, which resulted in the murder of three of the first four caliphs by coreligionists.

By the mid-10th century the pressures of administering a far-flung empire and internal strife over succession undermined Abbasid rule and fragmented caliphal power. Political power became increasingly decentralized and uneven, with real power held by regional governors. The caliph continued to be held in esteem, but thenceforth the legitimacy of military leaders was negotiated through the caliph's local representatives, the ulema, who administered the sharia. This accommodation continued after the fall of the Abbasid Caliphate, following the 12th-century Mongol invasion and destruction of Baghdad. Against this background developed the complex and often symbiotic relationship between the ruling military elites and the ulema, or religious elites, a relationship that created the upper tier of medieval Islamic society.

Medieval Islamic military regimes were usually of foreign origin, with officer ranks of Turkish or central Asian origin. Most spoke Turkish dialects, despite the instruction of soldiers in Arabic. Also, many were relatively recent converts to Islam who embraced their new religion with different levels of fervor. From Baghdad to Fès, victorious commanders understood that in practical terms they had to negotiate with local elites to maintain power. Within cities the ulema held the dominant social position, and it was to this group that the military ultimately looked to justify its rule.

What this alliance meant is that the members of the ulema became politically influential, representing local populations and extending their social and religious roles. Their main responsibilities were to formulate Sunni Islam's identity, train their successors, and transmit religious knowledge. They were administrators of charitable activities, enforcers of Islamic law, and intermediaries for the military regimes. They also provided scribes and midlevel bureaucrats for a regime's administration. These activities were distributed among the three main administrative departments of the Islamic state: The chancery was the source of all political correspondence from which a formal literary style developed. The exchequer or treasury concerned itself with the collection of taxes. The third department was the army, which was responsible for all military matters, including recruitment, armament, war making, supplies, logistics, and military finance. With presence in two departments, the ulema established deep local roots; this localization became its main source of power.

As a class, the ulema was neither a clearly defined nor an easily differentiated group. Many members came from wealthy families and were themselves engaged in commerce. Hence, there developed especially close ties between the urban mercantile class and the class of religious scholars. The ulema consolidated power and status by arranging for sons to inherit professorships, by nurturing dynasties of religious scholars, and by allowing individual scholars to sometimes hold professorships at several institutions simultaneously. Especially in the medieval period, the ulema was a fluid group through which wealth and social mobility could be achieved. In addition to prestigious professorships, the top scholar might win appointment as a qadi (judge) or preacher in a large mosque.

The interests of the military and the ulema intersected most notably in the administration of Islamic law, in which members of the ulema served not only as viziers (heads of the state administrative apparatus) and qadi but also in extended bureaucratic roles—especially in the Mamluk era—which included participating in public ceremonies and state occasions, leading emirs on campaigns, and sitting at the sultan's courts. But it was because the ulema defined Islamic identity and developed Islamic thought that its members were the custodians and enforcers of the sharia, establishing what behaviors lay inside and (more significantly) outside the Islamic mainstream; this gave the group its effective and sustained power. Several times from the 11th to the 14th centuries the ulema stepped in during periods of political chaos: in Nishapur (Iran), when the ulema agreed to recognize the Seljuk leader Toghrïl Beg (ca. 990–1063); when ibn al-Kashshad, a qadi from Aleppo (Syria) ruled the city upon the collapse of Seljuk rule; in the 13th century, when the religious leaders of Damascus negotiated surrender terms with the Mongol Ilkhanid ruler Ghazan (r. 1295–1304); and in the 14th century, when yet other religious leaders organized payment of tribute to Timur (1336–1405) after the Mamluk sultan Faraj fled to Cairo.

Given its reach in the exercise of political power, the ulema, as a group, could serve as a source of pressure on the military. Several elements came together to create and maintain this capacity: the foreign roots of the military, its need to negotiate power with local elites, and most significantly from the very understanding of the nature of authority within Islamic ideology. In return for stressing obedience to the state to maintain social order, the military's duty was to implement the sharia, which required the ulema to act in its capacity as enforcer. Prerogatives of the state—such as taxation—had to, at least nominally, nod to the requirements of the sharia. Rulers, for their part, sought to control the ulema largely through control of its financial support and access to facilities. The ulema needed sources of salaries, stipends, and endowments, as well as funds for buildings, schools, mosques, and specialized housing facilities. This ongoing need bound its members to the military.

The net result of this arrangement was that neither the military nor the ulema exercised unchallenged power, and both required the other in order to function, with the military providing sources of finance for the ulema and the ulema legitimizing military rule, an arrangement that remained a characteristic feature of Muslim social organization up to the modern era.

THE URBAN BOURGEOISIE

Islamic government, culture, religion, and society developed largely in urban settings, with towns growing up around the military garrisons formed to house occupying detachments following the Muslim conquest. Towns became cities and some cities became great centers—notably Baghdad, Damascus, al-Fustat (later expanded to become al-Qahirah, or Cairo), Fès (Morocco), and Córdoba (Spain). Urban centers were characterized by the main market and central mosque, the two primary spaces around which city life revolved and which were located close to each other. Beneath the top tier of the military and clergy class, urban centers had a bourgeoisie composed of a merchant class and lesser military officers, government administrators, and mosque attendants. At the lower levels this bourgeoisie also included craftsmen, small businessmen, and various shopkeepers.

A great distinction existed between state-controlled crafts and free crafts. The state controlled the manufacture of armaments and other war-making objects, shipbuilding and maritime armaments, paper making, and construction of luxury fabrics (for example, gold-threaded brocades) for either royal costumes or gift giving. Mintage of coins was, of course, also under state control. The commissions for the manufacture of these items required contact with the upper civilian administration (scribes, translators, and tax collectors) and carried great prestige—as well as lucrative remuneration. Powerful merchant families evolved, carrying on international maritime trade with Europe, India, and Africa. It was from this upper-middle class that families groomed sons to enter the ulema in order to develop their cultural capital and extend their influence.

The free trades included banking and work in precious metals (gold and silver), textiles, and leather. Their relative prestige was defined by how close they were situated to the mosque and market, which was determined by their need for water resources. Generally, the closer a trade was to the market and central mosque, the greater its prestige. Banking and goldsmithing—neither of which needed water—were located closest to the main mosque. The textile industry—with its weavers, spinners, dyers, and launderers—needed some water and was located farther away. The leather industry employed dyers, tanners, and other workers who required ample water resources, and the industry was thus located farthest away. Trade with nomads and peasants occurred just outside a town or near a city's ramparts and carried the least social status. For practical reasons, food purveyors were scattered throughout the city and fell outside this convention. In addition, the lower echelons of the ulema—muezzins (criers), Koran readers, prayer leaders, and rank-and-file soldiers—also populated this middle class. At the bottom were slave soldiers, who, because of their past unbelief, retained this status despite their conversion.

THE RURAL BOURGEOISIE

The countryside was itself stratified, with large landowners and town and village chiefs (who were also tax collectors) representing the upper tier of the rural population. The system of endowments, or *waqfs*, of land grants in lieu of military salaries gradually took hold; here, the income from a piece of property could be used for philanthropic purposes, such as the founding of a madrassa, or school, or the building of a mosque and provision of support for its staff. The owners of such *waqfs* gradually arranged for the income from these land grants to become hereditary; thus, a landed aristocracy evolved. Although officers with large *waqfs* and other large landowners retained a certain prestige, their impact on Islamic culture was limited. At the lower levels were landowning peasants and various agricultural workers—farmers, field hands, and slaves, whose lives were mean, short, and characterized by backbreaking manual labor.

THE SOCIETY OF FREE MUSLIM FEMALES

Medieval Islamic ideology stressed the need for unity and order within the *umma* and thus did not develop notions of individual liberty, freedom of conscience, and the pursuit of happiness—notions that might lead to social anarchy and moral decay. As guardians of the Koran, which they believed was Allah's ultimate revelation to humankind, the members of the ulema retained for themselves legislative power over Islamic law, especially the laws of personal status. Because they could also be appointed as judges or *qadis*, they had an enforcement role as well.

The ulema exercised these prerogatives by implementing three fundamental precepts. First, both men and women were required to declare the *shahada*, or statement of belief: "There is no god but Allah; Muhammad is the messenger of Allah," which forms the core of Islamic prayer. Second, Islamic ide-

Fritware bowl, painted with an enthroned ruler and his attendants, Kashan, Iran, 1187 (© The Trustees of the British Museum)

ology declared patrilineal kinship as a norm and as the primary determinant of personal status. What was important, above all, was paternal certainty and, therefore, female chastity, which was rigorously enforced. Third, the Koran requires that a man support all members of his household, which, in addition to wives, also typically included children, servants, slaves, and elder relatives.

In addition, the lives of women of procreative age were also characterized by modesty strictures on dress and segregation from men to whom they were not related. Public modesty was ensured by complete coverings that hid all body parts except for eyes, hands, and feet. This norm, though widespread, did not apply to prepubescent girls, who were not considered sexual beings, and was much less strictly applied to postmenopausal women, who were not considered sources of temptation to men. The physical segregation of women extended to the private sphere, with separate quarters set up to house women and their servants. However, only the wealthiest families could afford to seclude women completely, and this custom was enforced more rigorously in cities and towns than in the countryside, where the need for women's physical labor prevented either complete covering or total seclusion.

There is a Koranic basis for the unequal treatment of women in marriage, divorce, inheritance, and child custody. Women were allowed to own property before and after marriage, but marriages could be dissolved easily—by a husband's simple verbal repudiation. Given the complications of settling property rights in the event of serial marriage and divorce, women were permitted to keep their property.

Despite segregation and unequal status, medieval Muslim women had a role model in the literary career of Aishah (614–78), Muhammad's child bride, who became an important source of Hadith (customary sayings) after his death. A controversial figure, Aishah was also famous for her presence at the battle of the Camel (656), where she observed the fight between Muhammad's supporters and those of his son-in-law Ali (r. 656–61)—the genesis of the Sunni-Shia split—from a covered litter atop a camel. Sunni Islam revered Aishah for her scholarly contributions, but she remained a symbol of women who meddled in public affairs.

Slaves

Slavery was common to all major traditions in the ancient world, and pre-Islamic Arabia had a slave population. A body of laws pertaining to slave status, trading in slaves, the manumission (or freeing) of slaves, and who could own slaves evolved. Slavery was permitted by Allah and recognized and regulated by the sharia. Both the Koran and sharia permitted Muslim men sexual access to slave concubines. The offspring of such unions could be recognized and legitimized by Muslim fathers, and the same was possible for the slave mother herself. The slave mother achieved a certain status as *umm walad*, or the "mother of a child." The Muslim world soon developed a large number of children of mixed racial and ethnic characteristics.

A person became a slave by being born to a slave woman; by being taken captive in jihad; by being offered as part of an annual tribute paid by the head of state of a conquered land; or by outright purchase. Slaves could only be non-Muslims, because the Koran presumed the natural freedom of human beings, but jurists determined that their original state of "unbelief" (in Islam) justified their continued slave status even after conversion to Islam. Conquered countries provided slaves, among them, Mesopotamia, Egypt, Iran, Africa, central Asia, and Spain. Skilled slaves came from Byzantium, India, China, and Southeast Asia and unskilled labor from Europe, the Eurasian steppes, and Africa.

Slaves were employed as domestic servants, agricultural workers, tradesmen, business agents, military recruits, and civil servants. Military slave commanders were at the top of the social hierarchy. Next were high-ranking slave civil servants, who sometimes rose to positions of influence. Eunuchs were next in the social strata, acting as guards of harems and custodians of mosques, tombs, and shrines. Slaves working for merchants and craftsmen in cities and towns occupied the middle ranks of the hierarchy. Some became

responsible for their masters' businesses and could act as the business owners' agents. Musicians, singers, and dancers were often slaves and were especially well regarded. At the lower levels of society were female slaves, who acted as domestic servants and concubines. At the very bottom were the agricultural workers or slaves working on large public works projects.

The sharia denied slaves any legal rights; they could not hold office, perform or participate at religious functions, have any authority over others, or present testimony in court. The sharia did not fix a penalty for maltreatment, although tradition frowned upon such practice. Slaves required their master's consent to marry. Their rights included food and shelter and duties that were not excessive.

Dhimmis in Muslim Society

Since Christians and Jews originated in the Abrahamic tradition, they were permitted their lives, certain property rights, and limited exercise of their faith, provided they accepted the sovereignty of Islam and the terms established by Caliph Umar ibn al-Khattab (r. 634–44) in the seventh century. But it was also perceived that Christians and Jews had corrupted the divine truths transmitted by God to Abraham, Noah, Moses, David, Solomon, and Jesus. The Koran held that Jews had corrupted the Torah, killed prophets, and falsely claimed to have crucified Jesus. Christians were to be condemned for having corrupted the Gospel, proclaiming Jesus as God's son and, worse for the rigorously monotheistic Muslims, declaring belief in the Trinity, which Muslims maintain is polytheism.

The 12th-century Syrian jurist al-Shayzari (d. ca. 1193) prescribed distinguishing clothing for *dhimmis*. All *dhimmis* were to wear a distinctive cloth, called a ghiyar. Jews had to display a red or yellow cord on their shoulders. Christians wore special belts and hung crucifixes around their necks. In the public baths *dhimmis* kept a steel, copper, or lead band around their necks.

As with the seclusion of women, enforcement of these guidelines differed according to period, region, class, and ruling regime. Despite elasticity, these laws—particularly the payment of protection money—were meant to demonstrate submission to Muslim authority and to enforce the social superiority of Muslims. Over the centuries the economic, social, and political discrimination reduced the *dhimmi* population. Still, Muslims were admonished to limit their interactions with them. Indeed, the 13th-century writer al-Nawawi interpreted one Koranic verse as a sanction against permitting non-Muslims into one's affairs, since anyone who was not a Muslim was to be considered an outsider and not fully trustworthy. Although greatly diminished, small *dhimmi* populations survived, enjoying greater or lesser degrees of liberty, depending on the prevailing attitudes of the ruling elites.

Non-Muslim Foreigners

Islamic society also had small contingents of foreigners—agents of foreign governments, visitors, and international merchants and businessmen. This reality created an awkward situation, since such individuals were *ahl al-Harb* (people of war). Given the ongoing trade with Africa, India, and southern and western Europe and the concomitant need to establish diplomatic relations with foreign governments, embassies of various sizes had to be more or less permanently established in major cities to house ambassadors and support staffs. Theoretically, the goods carried by international merchants were to be taxed according to the religious confession of the merchants. This ideological stricture was often ignored, and commercial transactions were typically completed based on the nature and quality of the merchandise rather than on the theology of the merchant.

See also ADORNMENT; AGRICULTURE; ALCHEMY AND MAGIC; BUILDING TECHNIQUES AND MATERIALS; CHILDREN; CITIES; CLOTHING AND FOOTWEAR; DEATH AND BURIAL PRACTICES; ECONOMY; EDUCATION; EMPIRES AND DYNASTIES; EMPLOYMENT AND LABOR; FAMILY; FESTIVALS; FOREIGNERS AND BARBARIANS; GENDER STRUCTURES AND ROLES; GOVERNMENT ORGANIZATION; HOUSEHOLD GOODS; HUNTING, FISHING, AND GATHERING; LAWS AND LEGAL CODES; LITERATURE; MIGRATION AND POPULATION MOVEMENTS; MILITARY; NOMADIC AND PASTORAL SOCIETIES; OCCUPATIONS; RELIGION AND COSMOLOGY; RESISTANCE AND DISSENT; ROADS AND BRIDGES; SETTLEMENT PATTERNS; SLAVES AND SLAVERY; SOCIAL COLLAPSE AND ABANDONMENT; TOWNS AND VILLAGES; TRADE AND EXCHANGE; TRANSPORTATION; WAR AND CONQUEST; WRITING.

Asia and the Pacific

～ *Ancient Japanese Constitution (604)* ～

1. Harmony is to be valued, and an avoidance of wanton opposition to be honored. All men are influenced by class-feelings, and there are few who are intelligent. Hence there are some who disobey their lords and fathers, or who maintain feuds with the neighboring villages. But when those above are harmonious and those below are friendly, and there is concord in the discussion of business, right views of things spontaneously gain acceptance. Then what is there which cannot be accomplished!

2. Sincerely reverence the three treasures. The three treasures: the Buddha, the Law, and the Priesthood, are the final refuge . . . and are the supreme objects of faith in all countries. What man in what age can fail to reverence this law? Few men are utterly bad. They may be taught to follow it. But if they do not go to the three treasures, how shall their crookedness be made straight?

3. When you receive the Imperial commands, fail not scrupulously to obey them. The lord is Heaven, the vassal is Earth. Heaven overspreads, and Earth upbears. When this is so, the four seasons follow their due course, and the powers of Nature obtain their efficacy. If the Earth attempted to overspread, Heaven would simply fall in ruin. Therefore is it that when the lord speaks, the vassal listens; when the superior acts, the inferior yields compliance. Consequently when you receive the Imperial commands, fail not to carry them out scrupulously. Let there be a want of care in this matter, and ruin is the natural consequence.

4. The Ministers and functionaries should make decorous behavior their leading principle, for the leading principle of the government of the people consists in decorous behavior. If the superiors do not behave with decorum, the inferiors are disorderly: if inferiors are wanting in proper behavior, there must necessarily be offenses. Therefore it is that when lord and vassal behave with propriety, the distinctions of rank are not confused: when the people behave with propriety, the Government of the Commonwealth proceeds of itself. . . .

6. Chastise that which is evil and encourage that which is good. This was the excellent rule of antiquity. Conceal not, therefore, the good qualities of others, and fail not to correct that which is wrong when you see it. Flatterers and deceivers are a sharp weapon for

(continued)

(continues)

the overthrow of the State, and a pointed sword for the destruction of the people. Sycophants are also fond, when they meet, of speaking at length to their superiors on the errors of their inferiors; to their inferiors, they censure the faults of their superiors. Men of this kind are all wanting in fidelity to their lord, and in benevolence toward the people. From such an origin great civil disturbances arise.

7. Let every man have his own charge, and let not the spheres of duty be confused. When wise men are entrusted with office, the sound of praise arises. If unprincipled men hold office, disasters and tumults are multiplied. In this world, few are born with knowledge: wisdom is the product of earnest meditation. In all things, whether great or small, find the right man, and they will surely be well managed: on all occasions, be they urgent or the reverse, meet but with a wise man, and they will of themselves be amenable. In this way will the State be lasting and the Temples of the Earth . . . will be free from danger. Therefore did the wise sovereigns of antiquity seek the man to fill the office, and not the office for the sake of the man. . . .

10. Let us cease from wrath, and refrain from angry looks. Nor let us be resentful when others differ from us. For all men have hearts, and each heart has its own leanings. Their right is our wrong, and our right is their wrong. We are not unquestionably sages, nor are they unquestionably fools. Both of us are simply ordinary men. How can any one lay down a rule by which to distinguish right from wrong? For we are all, one with another, wise and foolish, like a ring which has no end. Therefore, although others give way to anger, let us on the contrary dread our own faults, and though we alone may be in the right, let us follow the multitude and act like men. . . .

11. Give clear appreciation to merit and demerit, and deal out to each its sure reward or punishment. In these days, reward does not attend upon merit, nor punishment upon crime. You high functionaries who have charge of public affairs, let it be your task to make clear rewards and punishments. . . .

15. To turn away from that which is private, and to set our faces toward that which is public—this is the path of a Minister. Now if a man is influenced by private motives, he will assuredly feel resentments, and if he is influenced by resentful feelings, he will assuredly fail to act harmoniously with others. If he fails to act harmoniously with others, he will assuredly sacrifice the public interests to his private feelings. When resentment arises, it interferes with order, and is subversive of law. . . .

16. Let the people be employed [in forced labor] at seasonable times. This is an ancient and excellent rule. Let them be employed, therefore, in the winter months, when they are at leisure. But from Spring to Autumn, when they are engaged in agriculture or with the mulberry trees, the people should not be so employed. For if they do not attend to agriculture, what will they have to eat? If they do not attend the mulberry trees, what will they do for clothing?

17. Decisions on important matters should not be made by one person alone. . . . They should be discussed with many. But small matters are of less consequence. It is unnecessary to consult a number of people. It is only in the case of the discussion of weighty affairs, when there is a suspicion that they may miscarry, that one should arrange matters in concert with others, so as to arrive at the right conclusion.

From: W. G. Aston, trans., *Nihongi: Chronicles of Japan from the Earliest Times to a.d. 697* (London: Kegan, Paul, Trench, Trübner, 1896).

Europe

∼ *Charter of Homage and Fealty (1110)* ∼

In the name of the Lord, I, Bernard Atton, Viscount of Carcassonne, in the presence of my sons, Roger and Trencavel, and of Peter Roger of Barbazan, and William Hugo, and Raymond Mantellini, and Peter de Vietry, nobles, and of many other honorable men, who have come to the monastery of St. Mary of

Grasse, to the honor of the festival of the august St. Mary: since lord Leo, abbot of the said monastery, has asked me, in the presence of all those above mentioned, to acknowledge to him the fealty and homage for the castles, manors, and places which the patrons, my ancestors, held from him and his predecessors and from the said monastery as a fief, and which I ought to hold as they held, I have made to the lord abbot Leo acknowledgment and homage as I ought to do.

Therefore, let all present and to come know that I the said Bernard Atton, lord and viscount of Carcassonne, acknowledge verily to thee my lord Leo, by the grace of God, abbot of St. Mary of Grasse, and to thy successors that I hold and ought to hold as a fief in Carcassonne the following: that is to say, the castles of Confoles, of Leocque, of Capendes (which is otherwise known as St. Martin of Sussagues); and the manors of Mairac, of Albars and of Musso; also, in the valley of Aquitaine, Rieux, Traverina, Hérault, Archas, Servians, Villatiitoes, Tansiraus, Presler, Cornelles. Moreover, I acknowledge that I hold from thee and from the said monastery as a fief the castle of Termes in Narbonne; and in Minerve the castle of Ventaion, and the manors of Cassanolles, and of Ferral and Aiohars; and in Le Roges, the little village of Longville; for each and all of which I make homage and fealty with hands and with mouth to thee my said lord abbot Leo and to thy successors, and I swear upon these four gospels of God that I will always be a faithful vassal to thee and to thy successors and to St. Mary of Grasse in all things in which a vassal is required to be faithful to his lord, and I will defend thee, my lord, and all thy successors, and the said monastery and the monks present and to come and the castles and manors and all your men and their possessions against all malefactors and invaders, at my request and that of my successors at my own cost; and I will give to thee power over all the castles and manors above described, in peace and in war, whenever they shall be claimed by thee or by thy successors. Moreover I acknowledge that, as a recognition of the above fiefs, I and my successors ought to come to the said monastery, at our own expense, as often as a new abbot shall have been

made, and there do homage and return to him the power over all the fiefs described above. And when the abbot shall mount his horse I and my heirs, viscounts of Carcassonne, and our successors ought to hold the stirrup for the honor of the dominion of St. Mary of Grasse; and to him and all who come with him, to as many as two hundred beasts, we should make the abbot's purveyance in the borough of St. Michael of Carcassonne, the first time he enters Carcassonne, with the best fish and meat and with eggs and cheese, honorably according to his will, and pay the expense of shoeing of the horses, and for straw and fodder as the season shall require.

And if I or my sons or their successors do not observe to thee or to thy successors each and all the things declared above, and should come against these things, we wish that all the aforesaid fiefs should by that very fact be handed over to thee and to the said monastery of St. Mary of Grasse and to thy successors.

I, therefore, the aforesaid lord Leo, by the grace of God abbot of St. Mary of Grasse, receive the homage and fealty for all the fiefs of castles and manors and places which are described above: in the way and with the agreements and understandings written above; and likewise I concede to thee and thy heirs and their successors, the viscounts of Carcassonne, all the castles and manors and places aforesaid, as a fief, along with this present charter, divided through the alphabet. And I promise to thee and thy heirs and successors, viscounts of Carcassonne, under the religion of my order, that I will be good and faithful lord concerning all those things described above.

Moreover, I, the aforesaid viscount, acknowledge that the little villages of Cannetis, Maironis, Villamagna, Aiglino, Villadasas, Villafrancos, Vitladenz, Villaudriz, St. Genese, Conguste and Mata, with the farmhouse of Mathus and the chateaux of Villalauro and Claromont, with the little villages of St. Stephen of Surlac, and of Upper and Lower Agrifolio, ought to belong to the said monastery, and whoever holds anything there holds from the same monastery, as we have seen and have heard read in the privileges and charters of the monastery, and as was there written.

(continued)

(continues)

Made in the year of the Incarnation of the Lord 1110, in the reign of Louis. Seal of Bernard Atton, viscount of Carcassonne, seal of Raymond Mantellini, seal of Peter Roger of Barbazon, seal of Roger, son of the said viscount of Carcassonne, seal of Peter de Vitry, seal of Trencavel, son of the said viscount of Carcassonne, seal of William Hugo, seal of lord abbot Leo, who has accepted this acknowledgment of the homage of the said viscount.

And I, the monk John, have written this charter at the command of the said lord Bernard Atton, viscount of Carcassonne and of his sons, on the day and year given above, in the presence and witness of all those named above.

From: Teulet, *Layetters du tresor des Chartres*, trans. E. P. Cheyney. *University of Pennsylvania Translations and Reprints* (Philadelphia: University of Pennsylvania Press, 1898).

FURTHER READING

Jonathan P. Berkey, *The Formation of Islam: Religion and Society in the Near East, 600–1800* (New York: Cambridge University Press, 2003).

Michael Brett and Elizabeth Fentress, *The Berbers* (Oxford, U.K.: Blackwell Publishing Limited, 1996).

Diane Z. Chase and Arlen F. Chase, "Archeological Perspectives on Classic Maya Social Organization from Caracol, Belize," *Ancient Mesoamerica* 15 (2004): 139–147.

Georges Duby, *The Three Orders: Feudal Society Imagined*, trans. Arthur Goldhammer (Chicago: University of Chicago Press, 1980).

John Winthrop Haeger, ed., *Crisis and Prosperity in Sung China* (Tucson: University of Arizona Press, 1975).

Martin Hall, *The Changing Past: Farmers, Kings, and Traders in Southern Africa, 200–1860* (Chicago: University of Chicago Press, 1990).

P. M. Holt, Ann K. S. Lambton, and Bernard Lewis, eds., *The Cambridge History of Islam*. Vol. 2, *The Further Islamic Lands, Islamic Society and Civilization* (Cambridge, U.K.: Cambridge University Press, 1970).

Clifford H. Lawrence, *Medieval Monasticism: Forms of Religious Life in Western Europe in the Middle Ages*, 3rd ed. (New York: Longman, 2001).

James E. Lindsay, *Daily Life in the Medieval Islamic World* (Westport, Conn.: Greenwood Press, 2005).

John Alden Mason, *The Ancient Civilizations of Peru* (Baltimore, Md.: Penguin, 1957).

Patricia McKissack and Frederick McKissack, *The Royal Kingdoms of Ghana, Mali, and Songhay: Life in Medieval Africa* (New York: Henry Holt and Co., 1994).

Robert Montagne, *The Berbers: Their Social and Political Organisation*, trans. David Seddon. (London: Routledge, 1973).

Susan Reynolds, *Fiefs and Vassals: The Medieval Evidence Reinterpreted* (New York: Oxford University Press, 1994).

Emily W.B. Russell, *People and the Land through Time: Linking Ecology and History*, 2nd ed. (New Haven, Conn.: Yale University Press, 1998).

Arthur F. Wright and Denis Twitchett, *Perspectives on the T'ang* (New Haven, Conn.: Yale University Press, 1973).

► sports and recreation

INTRODUCTION

It seems to be a part of the human condition that people want to have fun. It also seems to be part of the human condition that people want to take that which is fun and turn it into ritual, gambling, or symbolic contests of life and death. Sports and recreation had a variety of origins. Some began as children's play. For instance, kicking a ball around could become various sports in which balls are kicked but not touched by hands. In North America the sport of shinny, ancestor of ice hockey and field hockey, was associated with children's play even after grownups made shinny into an adult contest.

Sports and games sometimes arose out of efforts to teach children important ideas. The game *morabaraba*, which was played by cattle-herding cultures in Africa, may have begun as a way to introduce children to techniques for stealing cattle. Another form of African game involved complex thinking that introduced children to mathematics; this was a sowing game, often played with seeds or stones. The many African sowing games are often grouped under the term *mancala*, and they became so popular among adults that variations of them spread from Africa to Europe and all along the southern coast of Asia to Vietnam. Sowing games could involve mathematics so simple that the person who played first was likely to win but could be so complex that people would play them all their lives trying to master them. The elegance of a game can often be seen in how easy it is to set up: games such as *mancala* and eastern Asia's go required no more than open space where outlines of the board could be drawn in dirt and some pebbles as playing pieces. Signs of how much such games were enjoyed can be found in the discoveries by archaeologists of boards and playing pieces carved in valuable hardwoods with beautiful inlays. Games that taught children lessons or helped adults keep their minds limber were useful as well as fun.

Another source for useful games was warfare. In much of the medieval world war was always a danger. It could come all at once in a rush of large armies or sporadically in skirmishes and raids. In either case, people needed to defend themselves and often had to practice their martial skills frequently. Perhaps to turn such skills into fun, certain martial skills inspired sports. In the Islamic world cavalry skills were at the root of exhibitions of horsemanship in which men showed off their control of their mounts and their ability to ride while using their weapons. In Japan this idea manifested itself in mounted archery competitions in which samurai would fire at targets while riding at a gallop. Indeed, archery contests were a common example of how people showed off their martial skills. In India contestants fired at targets that were high on poles; winners often won the right to marry a princess. Hunting was another way for people to show off their skills. In Europe, China, and India the aristocrats hunted for pleasure, often in game reserves created for their use to the exclusion of lower classes.

The stakes in sports and games varied from just finding pleasure in playing the sport or game to the shaping of kingdoms. In many areas where a sport or game was played by most people, those with superior skills were admired and drew audiences. Those who played polo could attract thousands of spectators. Exceptionally gifted runners could draw avid fans to their races—fans who wagered on the outcomes of contests. Wagering was at one time or another considered a problem in most medieval cultures. In India men sometimes squandered their families' fortunes in card games, dice games, or chess. In China addiction to mahjong could cause people to neglect their duties to their families and their government. Almost anything could be wagered on, from insect fights to wrestling to chess tournaments. In India a king lost his kingdom in a game of chance that took the place of waging actual war. Gambling could be very serious business, with contestants even wagering their freedom and, upon losing, becoming slaves. Such serious consequences took some of the fun out of sports and games, turning them into businesses that were often regulated by the state.

The banning of certain gambling contests or of all gambling seldom was effective for long. Even in the Islamic world, among people who took their faith very seriously and where such things were forbidden by Islamic law, gambling with cards and dice flourished. The lure of winning for by simply rolling dice or by betting on someone else's athletic prowess was a powerful attraction for people. Even so, it is worth remembering that for all the seriousness with which people took their sports and games, at bottom the exhilaration of mastering a skill was a major attraction, even for people without athletic or gaming talent. Most people escaped the difficulties of their lives for a little while by running as fast as they could or by figuring out how to move a seed from one square to another to capture more seeds.

AFRICA

BY MICHAEL J. O'NEAL

Historians' knowledge about sports and recreation in medieval sub-Saharan Africa is limited. No written records exist, so much of what is known is based on two primary sources. One source is the reports of European explorers and colonists, who began traveling through the continent in the 17th century. The other is tradition. In the modern world forms of medieval recreation continue to exist; in some cases such items as games and game pieces are still created by craftsmen and are regarded as symbolic of the culture. Additionally, many games played in medieval Africa are still played today.

With regard to sports, little evidence suggests that sports competitions were in any sense organized. It is likely that boys and young men took part in numerous activities that are similar to modern sporting events, but they did so not in the spirit of athletic competition but as a way of learning the skills they would need to survive as adult members of the community. In general, many of these life-skills activities were an outgrowth of medieval African men's perceptions of masculinity and bravery.

Thus, such activities as running, swimming, wrestling and boxing, hunting and fishing, archery, stick fighting, climbing, feats of strength, and so on would be part of a boy's or young man's daily life. It is highly likely that competition developed between individuals to determine who was the fastest runner or swimmer. Some evidence suggests that organized competitions between villages or teams of individuals within villages took place, but this evidence is limited, and such practices became more commonplace after colonization by Europeans.

One competitive form of recreation was dancing, although historians are divided over the question of whether competitive dancing took place before the arrival of Europeans or began later. It is known that competitive dancing, with acrobatic moves, was a form of competition men took part in to compete for spouses.

Stick fighting was a form of competitive sport, one still practiced in Africa. The sport required a great deal of skill and often bore a resemblance to the martial arts. The game was played, of course, with each competitor carrying a large stick. Sometimes the stick was in the nature of a staff and sometimes it was more flexible and whiplike. Each competitor also carried a shield. The fighters wrapped cloths around themselves to provide protection from blows, and many wore hats to protect their heads. Covering the hat in butter was a sign of wealth and status. The game was part of many cultures' spiritual traditions; it was a common activity after harvest time and was a way of giving thanks to the gods for the harvest.

The game typically began with some sort of provocation, usually symbolic. Thus, for example, a member of a village would hold the hand of the fiancée of a member of another village for a few minutes or possibly cut one of the bead bracelets she wore.

The woman's husband-to-be would "hear" about this provocation and respond by tying a piece of cloth somewhere on the "offending" man's house. The stick fight would then take place the following day, sometimes between two people and sometimes between two villages, with each village's men fighting collectively. Prayers were offered, for the game could sometimes be fatal. As the two "warriors" fought, the women of the village chanted and sang, celebrating their heroes as bulls, leopards, and similar noble animals while scoffing at the village's opponents as cowards and hooligans. The goal of the fight was generally to subdue the opponent, though sometimes the goal was more specific, such as leaving behind visible stripes on the opponent's back.

In some cases stick fighting was a means of resolving actual disputes. A judge watched the contest to ensure that each contestant followed the rules, one of which was that fighters had to keep their tempers in check. The contest was declared over when one of the combatants drew blood; the winner tended to his opponent's injuries, and the dispute was regarded as at an end.

Many forms of medieval African sport and recreation were considered to have a divine or spiritual component. Archery provides a good example. A bow, with its ability to bring down enemies or prey from a distance, was regarded as a reflection of the power of the gods. Similarly, music played a key role in medieval African culture in large part because it reflected the will and intentions of the gods. Medieval Africans, in common with people throughout the world, found order in the physical world through its rhythms, and very often these rhythms were aural. They listed to the babble of a stream, the song of birds, the crack of thunder, the roar of a lion, and the patter of raindrops, and all of these sounds gave meaning to their lives. They became part of a pattern in life, a patterning that was reflected as well in calendars, sundials, the zodiac, totem poles, and similar articles that measured and ordered life.

Thus, for example, a musical instrument as simple as a drum had spiritual dimensions. Among medieval Africans, a drum, often made from a piece of a tree trunk, reflected the voice of the ancestors, locked in the trunk but released when a person played a drum made from it. Because of the spiritual dimensions of music, a community would have a repertoire of songs associated with key life events: birth, the arrival of puberty, harvest time. Singing and dancing were usually communal activities, binding the people together during life's major events. In the course of these celebrations, people often wore colorful clothing. Music was thought to be a way to drive off evil, and even in modern life drums often contain something like a small pea or stone representing the evil that is kept in check by the pounding of the drum. Many modern historians of music regard early African music, with its driving beat and strong emphasis on percussive instruments, as a precursor of American jazz.

Similarly, many board games were thought to represent powers of divination, or the ability to read the will of the gods. In this sense, many such games were a form of gambling, and later, after the beginning of the slave trade, many African men lost their freedom as a result of losing a board game or a similar game of chance. One such game, called *nigbé*, involved flipping four white cowrie shells filled with black wax. Winning and losing were determined by the number of shells that landed with the white or black side facing up. The winner collected the other player's cowrie shells. The game could be considered similar to rolling dice, and its element of pure chance could be compared to the simple game of picking a card from a deck.

One of the most popular board-type games in medieval Africa was *mancala*. Versions of this game were played virtually throughout the continent. The primary purpose of the game was to teach children how to count. One common form of the game consisted of two rows of six cups, although different numbers of rows could be used. The cups were placed in an area that included space for captured pieces. The game pieces may have consisted of seeds or balls made of ivory. The goal was to move the cups about, capturing the opponent's pieces. The best players relied not on luck but on mathematical calculations about the likelihood that various cups will contain the most pieces.

Many versions of *mancala* existed. The game had a variety of names—as many as 250—including *awale, awele, ayo, ourin,* and *wari*. In some cases, boards with pegs were used, and the game took on many of the characteristics of chess. Rules varied regionally, but in general the game was played in the same way and with the same goals.

A popular game among the people of east-central Africa was *abbia*. The game was played with chips carved out of either hard nuts or the bark of the calabash tree. Designs on the chips could include animals, people, or abstract forms.

Players sat in a circle and placed bets. One player tried to predict how the chips would fall when they were tossed into the circle. If the player's prediction was accurate, that player won the other players' bets.

Another game that involved tossing was called *panda*. Again, this was a game with a strong mathematical component. One player tossed an agreed-upon number of beans on the ground. The number could be as few as 20, but often many more were used. Then the challenger scooped up a handful of the beans. The other player was give a few moments to examine the beans that remained on the ground and then could request the first player to return one, two, or three beans to the ground, to result in a number of beans that was a multiple of four.

Many of these and other games were played by adults, but a number of games were designed specifically for children. One was called *quakela*. In this game a group of children sat in a circle. One player was sent away so that he or she could not eavesdrop on the group. Each remaining player in the circle hid a small object in his or her hand. Common objects included a bean or a stone. When the exiled player returned, each player in the circle held out two clenched fists. The returning player had to guess which hand contained the object and what the object was. If the child successfully guessed, he or she joined the circle and the player holding the object went to the center to continue the guessing process.

THE AMERICAS

BY RENEE MCGARRY

During the fifth century there were not great changes in sports in the Americas. Many traditional games continued to be played as they had for centuries. Ancient games, such as the Mesoamerican ball game, spread from civilization to civilization. This ball game, which existed more as a ritual than as a game, was still being practiced when the Spanish invaded the Americas in the 15th century. In fact, most written descriptions of the game date to the Aztec version that was played at the time of Hernán Cortés's arrival on the continent. The Spaniards were greatly struck by the use of rubber balls, a material with which they were unfamiliar, as well as by what they perceived as the bloodthirsty nature of the game. Each game ended with a ritual sacrifice of the losing team to the gods. Most archaeologists believe that this was a fertility ritual, seeking to ensure the survival of the Aztec people.

Much like the ball game, foot races were an ancient tradition that continued into the fifth century. In fact, these races became less ritual and more practical. Eventually, South American civilizations and North American tribes organized themselves into running societies in an effort to further communication and trade. One of the most organized of these running societies, formed in Peru, was known as *chasqui*, meaning "to exchange" among the Inca. Young male runners in this society were able to communicate information over a 2,000-mile-long road system in Peru. They carried not only messages but also fresh fish from coastal areas to isolated, inland areas. The ability to navigate such a difficult road system and the stamina to do so were developed in the battery of foot races required of young Inca boys as initiation rites. The *chasqui* running society was more effective than horses, and the Spanish continued to use it after their arrival on the continent with beasts of burden.

While these ancient and traditional sports continued, new sports were developed. Lacrosse, or the racket game, originated around 1000, most likely in the southeastern United States. Lacrosse is clearly not an American Indian word, and there are many theories as to how the game was named. The most popular of these theories suggests that the French witnessed the Croix playing the racket game and named it after them. Lacrosse was generally considered a game only for men and quickly spread with relative consistency and zeal across North America.

Much like the ancient ball game and foot races, lacrosse was more than simply a sport. It also taught young male participants the skills necessary for warfare. It developed ruggedness, speed, and endurance and was believed to have been a fairly brutal and violent game. Unlike the ball game, there is no evidence of ritual sacrifice in games of lacrosse, but some archaeologists argue that it was not uncommon for players to become critically injured or even die during the game. Many members of the tribe spent months in preparation and training for a match, to develop the necessary stamina. During this period certain foods were taboo, including rabbit, which was believed to endow the player with elements of fearfulness. Most tribes danced and held ceremonies before lacrosse matches.

The matches, typically held between tribes, were generally large, with many spectators. Because of this intertribal communication, rules and play of the game were fairly consistent throughout the continent. The main difference was between southern groups, who played the game with two rackets, and northern groups, who used only one. These rackets were made of smooth sticks from 2 to 4 feet long. At the end of each of these sticks was a curved hoop with a net. Each of the players strove to keep the ball in that net and move it down the field from player to player. As with most ball games, contact with the hands was not allowed.

Lacrosse fields were very large, ranging in size from 500 feet to 1 mile long. Each end had goal posts. A team scored points by hitting the ball through the opposing team's goal. Balls were made of either wood, in the southern parts of the

Stone ball game yoke, Aztec culture, Mexico, ca. 550–1150 (Courtesy, National Museum of the American Indian, Smithsonian Institution [catalog number 028212])

country, or buckskin, in northern parts. Games could last from a half day to a full day. Different groups varied play from season to season, with the most frequent lacrosse season being in late summer and early fall, in order to allow for crop harvest. The game was played naked except during the coldest times of the year. While the majority of tribes did not play the game ritualistically, those in the southeastern United States saw lacrosse as a ceremonial contest between teams and used a medicine man to put the ball into play.

Shinny is often understood as the female equivalent to lacrosse, as women were not allowed to play the more violent and brutal game. While lacrosse still exists in the modern sports vocabulary, shinny has evolved into ice hockey and field hockey. Shinny, like lacrosse, was practically universal among Native American groups in North America. Primarily women and children played the game, although on occasion men did play separately. Indians frequently refer to the mythological origins of shinny, but there is no evidence that it had a ceremonial component outside the Makah tribe in the Pacific Northwest, were it was used to celebrate the capture of a whale. The object of shinny is to drive the ball down the field and into the other team's goal using sticks. Again, there is no use of hands in this game. The sticks were 2 to 4 feet long and had a curved end for hitting the ball. The shinny ball was made from buckskin or wood and was decorated. The decoration varied from group to group.

Shinny was played on a long field similar to that of lacrosse, although during the colder months it could be played on frozen rivers and lakes. Each team had 10 to 50 players. The game started midfield, with the ball buried. A member of each team would attempt to dig out the ball and pass it to her teammates as quickly as possible. Although field hockey

and ice hockey today involve a series of small movements to move the ball, the main strategy of shinny was to hit it over the heads of many players, attempting to move it down the field in as few moves as possible.

Cat's cradle is a diversionary game that originated around the same time as lacrosse on the North American continent. Many tribes believed that it had mythological and supernatural origins. The southwestern Zuni and Navaho both believed that ancient spider people taught the skill to their ancestors. This belief led to myriad prohibitions and restrictions on where and when cat's cradle could be played. The Eskimo believed the game could be used to prevent the disappearance of the sun each winter. They sought to catch the sun in the web and keep it shining.

The object of cat's cradle is to use a series of strings to form a web that is patterned after an identifiable object, such as a house. In order to do so, Indians looped string around their hands, using their fingers to manipulate it. Some projects became so involved that children and adults alike resorted to looping the string around their teeth, toes, and other objects. The type of string depended on available material. The Puebla of northwestern Mexico had access to cotton and used cotton fibers in the game. Others used yucca fibers and animal skin to form these elaborate creations. The goal was not simply to form a complex web of string but to remove it from its handheld loom in just one movement.

Another pastime in North America was stilt walking, which became particularly popular among the Hopi of the southwestern United States and Shoshoni of the Great Plains. Stilts were made of sapling branches and kept each player up to 2 feet from the ground. Stilt walking was particularly important to the Maya civilization in Mexico, as it was used to honor their bird deity, Yaccocahmut. Stilt walking is thought to have been illustrated in the Maya manuscript now referred to as the Codex Troano, with those on stilts wearing the costume of this deity.

Just before the colonial period in the Americas the indigenous peoples played a wide variety of games that kept old traditions alive and added new diversions to their communities. Some of these games served simply as leisure activities, and others served more practical and ritualistic purposes. There was a strong culture of sports on the American continents before the arrival of Europeans, and much of that tradition continued into the colonial period.

ASIA AND THE PACIFIC

BY KENNETH HALL

Throughout Asia and the Pacific medieval societies participated in and enjoyed recreational activities that frequently became public competitions having ritual as well as societal significance. One famous literary example is the account in the Indian epic the Mahabharata of a ritualized dice contest between a king and his opponent engaged in as an alternative to going to war, which ended in the king losing his kingdom on a gamble. Numerous festivals marked by merrymaking and procession included rich and poor participants, who temporarily forgot their social status to parade together in the streets with their neighbors.

Contests between animals and men were widely popular. Among the court-sponsored animal contests were spectacular fights between elephants, tigers, buffalo, and smaller animals. South and Southeast Asian kings collected elephants and rode them in real and mock battles that included hundreds of elephants. Thai and Burmese kings were well known for their excellence in elephant jousts. Elephants were also pitted against other animals, such as buffalo, rams, and tigers. Often these matches had ritual significance, as when the elephant, symbolic of royal order, faced a tiger, representative of danger, disorder, wildness, and the enemies of the state. The match was intended to end with the elephant throwing the tiger (usually handicapped in some way by being tied to a stake or having its claws extracted) high in the air with its tusks. The elite of South Asia participated in equally symbolic tiger hunts. Mounted on elephants, aristocrats would pursue a tiger until it was trapped by their servant beaters, who would encircle the tiger until their lords could come and kill it.

Bulls offered lively competitions and were normally victorious against a tiger. Cattle, buffalo, and horses were raced. In southern India a bullfight matched an unarmed male against a bull in a wrestling match; the male competitor attempted to master rather than kill the bull. The event was considered a test of manhood and a demonstration of male virility; unwed girls watched the contests to select suitable husbands.

Mounted horsemen participated in jousts. As with jousts of the medieval West, the object was to force opponents from their mounts with a blunt spear. Medieval records report that competitors regularly died in such tournaments and also in assorted duels on horseback and on foot using spears, swords, and knives. Polo was a favorite recreational and ritual activity of central Asian nomadic tribesmen that spread to southern Asia and Southeast Asia. Legend has it that the original polo ball was the cloth-wrapped head of a vanquished opponent.

Cockfighting was the favorite competition in Southeast Asia, whether held as an individual event or as part of temple feasts and other sacred rituals. The blood sacrifice of a cock was necessary to ensure fertility and success in war and was an alternative to earlier human sacrifices. Cockfighting was extremely popular with the public. Many villagers raised prized roosters, which fought with sharp metal spurs on their feet in a combat circle. Cocks fought to the death or until one cock withdrew from the fight (thus the expression to "chicken out"). A rooster's victory was symbolic of its owner's personal prowess associated with his sexual potency.

Village competitions were lively affairs in which villagers bet on one or another cock. Betting took on social significance when bets would pit two villagers or village factions against each other. To bet against another was a personal

Ladies playing double-sixes, Song Dynasty, China, 10th to 11th centuries (Freer Gallery of Art, Smithsonian Institution, Purchase, F1939-37)

statement and often involved uttering negative proclamations in the midst of battle against an opponent's cock that could not otherwise be spoken in public. Thus the cockfight could be a public airing of previously unspoken rivalries that would have subsequent consequence, but it could also be a means of conflict resolution. It dramatized both the solidarity among kin groups, factions, and villages and the hostilities associated with their ongoing competitions for status. A cockfight might end in the loser resorting to violence or reduced to slavery owing to indebtedness or to the oral violation by insult of a more powerful opponent. To curtail the potential negative consequences, late medieval courts tried with little success to regulate cockfighting. The law code of 15th-century Melaka acknowledged that cockfighting was the occasion for gambling that might get out of hand but did not declare it illegal. However, if a cockfight resulted in a brawl and a consequent appeal to Melaka's authorities, disputed bets could be seized by the court's officials.

Boat races were popular competitions that also inspired heavy betting with social and ritual significance. (Kings expected their boat to win; a win or loss had symbolic implications.) Thousands would line the banks of the local river to root wildly for and bet on their favorites. Southeast Asian villagers prepared for annual boat races against their neighbors. A rowing team received preferential treatment from other villagers when its members were allowed time from their ordinary labors to train in preparation for the annual races. Royal rowers were professionals who were also employed as rowers of royal barges.

Kite flying was a special amusement throughout Asia. In Thailand and Java kites portraying animals had symbolic value that was associated with the changing of the monsoon seasons and the consequent fertility of the soil. Kite-fighting contests in which rivals would try to bring one another's kites down or cut their strings were the source of personal pride as well as heavy betting. Spinning tops was another pastime for boys, and the source of fighting competitions among men—spinning tops were sent flying to knock an opponent's top out. It was also a ritual activity that was associated with the ripening of crops.

Rounded seeds and nuts were widely used as marbles and balls in a variety of games in which a seed or ball was struck in attempts to knock against others. As an alternative to the throwing of dice, which was popular in India and China, in mainland Southeast Asia players cast six cowrie shells, the lowest form of money, and the number landing right side up was counted.

Mah-jongg, go, and Chinese chess were favorite games in medieval China. The object of mah-jongg was to remove more tiles from the board than an opponent, by collecting two tiles with the same kind of markings. Medieval-era go was played on a square board, 19 squares long on each side and defined by nine star points in a rectangle around a central star. Players strategically placed colored stones at the 361 intersections of line points on the board to gain control over the board sections, until there were no opportunities to place another stone. In the Chinese version of checkers (commonly known today as Chinese checkers), game pieces were placed on the intersection of lines rather than in squares.

The Asian version of backgammon (originally a Middle Eastern game), called *nard* (battle on wood), developed in the northwestern borderlands of India in the early medieval era and passed into Southeast Asia and China, where it was called *tashubu*, and Japan, where it was called *sugoroko*; both the Chinese and Japanese versions were played on a circular board. In the Indian version the board had 12 lines, representing the 12 months of the year; 24 points, representing the hours of the day; and 30 points, representing the days of the month. The dice stood for the seven days of the week and the colors of the checker pieces the night and the day.

Card playing, using a 60-card deck, was widely popular in China and was a favorite pastime among women. Chess was being played both at Asia's courts and by commoners when Europeans arrived in the early 16th century. Chess is initially thought to have developed in India using an eight-by-eight square board, requiring four players and the rolling of dice to control the moves. Known as *chaturanga*, "the four elements of an army," the game represented a competition among elephants, horses, chariots, and foot soldiers. In the Southeast Asian version chariots, which were never used in local warfare, were replaced by boats. Chinese claim their version to be older. In China the chessboard was divided in the middle by a river. Elephants ("ministers") advanced to the near riverbank; soldiers ("pawns") achieved promotion when they reached the far bank. Armies guarded and attacked the general and two mandarin officials, who guarded castles and palaces.

In the Sanskrit version of the Indian Gupta era (320–550) the king and his minister (the queen in the English equivalent) were the most powerful among the competitors. The elephant in Indian chess became the bishop in the English version, and the horse the knight, the chariot the castle, and the foot soldier the pawn. While Asia's elite used elaborately carved and jeweled game pieces, commoners played with game pieces made of local materials—in Thailand the soldier was symbolized by a cowrie shell; island Southeast Asians used bamboo game pieces.

A form of kickball, in which participants formed a circle and kept a ball in play by knee or foot kicks, preferably with the inside sole of the foot, was widely popular. In Southeast

Asia the original balls were hollow, made of woven rattan or other natural fibers. A skilled player could keep a ball in play by repeatedly kicking a ball to himself with elaborate kicks hundreds of times before passing it on to another player. Most often this was a display of personal skill and a group exercise rather than a competition; in Japan it became a ritual and meditative activity intended to promote proper thought among court elite and Shinto priests. Southeast Asians modified the ball into a feathered shuttlecock made by sticking chicken feathers into a small bamboo tube, kept in the air by competitors using wooden bats—which became the basis of modern badminton.

Chinese martial arts (wushu), originated as a means of hand-to-hand combat and mental discipline in war and by the medieval era had evolved into popular physical exercise and meditation, based in the rich wushu philosophical tradition. Wushu emphasized foot and leg kicking and tripping, hand strikes at various areas of the body, and throwing an opponent to the ground and gaining control by use of joint locks, tendon and muscle stretching, striking nerve points, and obstruction of breath or blood flow. Modern kung fu is wushu but adds tumbling and rigorous basic training skills to traditional styles.

There were three traditional wushu methods: internal and external styles, southern and northern styles, and Shaolin, Wudang, or Ermei. The latter were specific styles that developed among the medieval-era militant monks at the Shaolin Buddhist Temple in Henan province and at the Wudang Daoist temples in Hubei Province and the Ermei Daoist temples in Sichuan Province. Southern and northern styles also referenced points of origin, while internal and external distinguished whether the natural strength was from the torso and legs (internal, *qi*) or from the training of specific arm and leg muscles (external). Generally, wushu competitions and performance emphasized empty-hand forms, weapon forms, choreographed routines involving two or more people, group practices, sparring competitions, and power demonstrations (*qigong*).

Empty-hand combat was of the long-fist (*chang quan* and Shaolin styles) and southern-fist (*nan quan, Wudang,* and *Ermei*) types, which were external styles, and "spontaneous" shadowboxing or "ultimate fist" (*taiji quan*), "mind fist" (*xingyi quan*), and "eight-directions fist" (*bagua quan*) types, which were internal styles. There were also imitating styles, such as Praying Mantis, Eagle Claw, Monkey, Tiger, Leopard, Drunken, Duck, Snake, and Rooster. Wushu could include the use of 18 standard weapons (out of 400 medieval-era Chinese potentials): several broadswords, straight sword, spear, staff, Kwan sword, double swords, double straight swords, double hook swords, double-ended spear, nine-section whip, rope dart, chained hammer, three-sectional staff, two-sectional staff, daggers, and double short staff.

Wushu training improved physical ability, health, and willpower and became an art form, a means of self-defense, and a competitive sport. Chinese wushu spread to Korea, where it influenced the development of Korean tae kwan do, which emphasized swift kicking techniques. In Japan it was called karate and stressed open-handed punching and kicking techniques as descended from southern Chinese boxing forms; judo, which emphasized throwing techniques derived from Chinese wrestling; and jujitsu, developed from Chinese *qinna*, the art of locking joints or muscles by knowing the pressure points and the body vulnerabilities of an opponent. Similar martial arts traditions developed widely in southern Asia, Southeast Asia, and Tibet. Medieval-era Thai and Burmese courts developed a style of boxing using both the feet as well as the hands.

EUROPE

BY AMY HACKNEY BLACKWELL

Medieval Europeans engaged in many recreational activities. Some of these activities, such as chess, backgammon, and horseshoes, were purely for fun. Others, such as archery contests and tournaments, served as practice for soldiers who needed to keep their skills sharp for battle. Almost all types could include a gambling component. The gambling that went with recreation caused numerous church officials and rulers to try to ban certain activities, efforts that almost always failed.

Medieval people enjoyed playing various casual games. In horseshoes, they would throw horseshoes at a stake, trying to hook the shoes on the stake. Bowls was similar to the modern Italian game called bocce; players would throw balls in an effort to reach a goal and prevent their opponents from reaching it. Skittles was a form of bowling in which players would roll a ball to knock down pins. Javelin throwing and hammer throwing were common tests of skill. Some people enjoyed participating in or watching footraces, horse races, and wrestling matches. There were also some team sports, such as the Irish game known as hurling, which is somewhat similar to lacrosse. Polo was popular in the Byzantine region throughout the medieval period.

An early form of chess seems to have first arrived in Europe in the 800s. The game was probably invented in India and traveled to Europe through the Islamic world. By 1000 it was common in Europe and was a popular game for the aristocracy. Knights enjoyed playing it because it involved battle strategy, but women also learned how. The modern European form of the game developed in Italy or Spain between 1200 and 1475.

A bone ice skate, Britain, 12th century (© Museum of London)

Dice games were extremely popular among all social classes throughout the medieval period. Some people even went to school to improve their skills at dice games. Simple dice games involved throwing dice in the hopes of achieving particular numbers, sometimes for money. The more complicated dice and board game called backgammon was extremely popular in France between the 11th and 13th centuries, and grew so all-consuming that King Louis IX (r. 1226–70) tried to ban the game in 1254. Despite his efforts, the game spread throughout Europe.

Playing cards seem to have first appeared in Europe in the late 1300s. The medieval deck, adapted from a deck created in China in the ninth century, was quite similar to the modern deck, with 52 cards and four suits. The cards for the queen and the knight, now called the jack, appeared in the 1400s. Card games became wildly popular throughout Europe during the late 1300s.

Golf appears to have been invented in the 1100s in Scotland and to have spread from there to the Netherlands. By the 1400s the game had elaborate rules and had already been outlawed in some places. The golf course at Saint Andrews in Scotland had an established route with 11 holes. Golfers would play these holes in order and then turn around and work their way back. The point of the medieval game was the same as the modern one. Golfers used clubs or bats to knock balls into holes in the ground. There is some evidence that medieval Europeans played other games with sticks and leather balls that had to be hit into targets. One example is the French game called mail, which involved a ball and a mallet and might be a predecessor of croquet and cricket. Tennis also existed in medieval times. Players used rackets to hit a ball back and forth in the air. Whoever missed the ball lost the point.

Animal baiting was a popular spectator sport. People would capture a fierce animal such as a bear or a badger, chain it or trap it in a cage, and let dogs attack it. Onlookers would cheer and place bets on the participants. Both dogs and prey could be injured or killed in these events. Horse and chariot racing were well-liked sports in early medieval Europe, especially in southern and eastern Europe, where old Roman circuses still existed. In Constantinople, the Hippodrome was a central element of the city's social life. Huge crowds of people packed into the building to watch chariot races and bet on their favorite teams. The rivalry between the two main teams, the Blues and the Reds, infected the entire population of the city and occasionally led to riots or even civil wars, such as the major riots of 532. The Palio di Siena, an annual event in which horses race around the central piazza of the town, seems to have developed from annual horse races through the entire city in medieval times.

The nobility of medieval Europe loved to hunt. Nobles kept for themselves the right to hunt on the lands they owned, sometimes punishing severely any peasants who dared kill animals on their land. Both men and women hunted. Most hunting was done on horseback. Hunters used a variety of weapons, including bows and arrows, crossbows, spears, clubs, and even swords. Hunters carried horns that they used to communicate with one another while galloping across the countryside. Dogs ran with the hunters to track quarry and hold it at bay. Medieval hunters often carried birds of prey with them to help hunt. Medieval falconers would take months to train hawks and falcons to ride with humans and return to them with the prey they had flown out to capture. Hunters pursued a variety of animals, including deer, boars, and foxes. Hunting, like many medieval sports, was quite dangerous, and numerous hunters were killed or injured by falling off their horses, being accidentally shot, and by other misadventures.

Medieval people enjoyed watching and participating in archery contests. These contests tested the participants' skill at hitting a target with an arrow shot from a bow. Targets could take various forms. One of the most popular was a narrow strip of wood called a wand. The wand was fairly long and positioned vertically, which made the competition especially challenging when wind was blowing. Some competitions resembled a game of golf with a course of different targets. Competitors would shoot at a target such as a flag, a wooden stake, or any other object that could receive arrows. They would then walk to the target, score their shots, and shoot at the next target from there. Sometimes people participated in team archery competitions that simulated battle conditions.

Tournaments, also called tourneys, were mock battles between groups of knights. These events served the double purpose of entertaining spectators and letting soldiers practice their military skills. In the early medieval period, tournaments consisted mainly of groups of soldiers fighting without much organization. They could be divided into two teams or they could simply all fight on their own. This chaotic early form of tournament was called a melée in French. The melée could be quite dangerous and even deadly because the soldiers used their actual weapons and fought without much in the way of rules or referees.

During the 11th century people began making rules for tournaments that made them somewhat less deadly to participants. A tournament might begin with the two teams on horseback, throwing javelins at one another and chasing one another down. The soldiers wore armor, carried shields, and often wore full-face helmets to protect themselves from the onslaught. After the teams finished throwing javelins, the teams would charge at one another, trying to knock their opponents off their horses with lances, and the soldiers would engage in hand-to-hand combat on horseback and on foot. Knights would capture one another for ransom. The fighting could go on for hours and sometimes covered a large area as the melée became less and less organized.

Medieval nobles held tournaments throughout the year except during Lent. Large tournaments attracted hundreds of knights and followers, who might travel for many miles to participate. Teams were generally formed according to loyalties, with the knights from the local area fighting for the home team and visitors from greater distances forming the opposition. Before and after the tournament the participants engaged in feasting and merrymaking, using the opportunity to socialize with people they rarely saw, to flirt, and to make alliances. The feast following the tournament was an occasion to present awards to the bravest and most successful participants.

Tournaments were immensely popular, but they also caused problems. Knights were frequently killed or injured.

They also tended to become drunk and disorderly and were known to rob people, destroy property, and generally cause mayhem. Because of this, several kings and popes in the 12th and 13th centuries tried to outlaw tournaments or at least to regulate them, restricting them to specific sites and requiring participants to use blunted weapons instead of their ordinary swords and knives.

By the beginning of the 14th century, tournaments had become less popular. They disappeared entirely by the end of the century, replaced by the more gentle jousting. Jousting was a competition in which two knights carrying long lances faced each other on horseback. They rode their horses at each other and each tried to knock the other to the ground with his lance. The knights participating in a joust often used weapons blunted for the purpose, such as lances with rings on their ends instead of sharp points. Jousting was still dangerous, but it was much safer and better organized than a melée. Like tournaments, jousts were major social events that attracted huge crowds and provided an occasion for feasting and socializing. Good jousters could win large amounts of money as prizes. Courtly love played an important part in jousts. Knights would solicit favors, gifts such as scarves, from the ladies they loved, and they would carry these items while jousting to show their loyalty.

THE ISLAMIC WORLD
BY KIRK H. BEETZ

In almost the entire medieval Islamic world there were people who took delight in playing sports and games and in competitions. Those who resisted the popularity of recreational activities seem to have been a minority. The pressure to raise children to bring honor to their families sometimes caused parents to restrict their children's lives to studying. Children who were precocious in memorizing the Koran brought prestige to their families; children who became good scholars earned praise for their parents. Both boys and girls could be raised without toys and without playing games inside or outside. Some medieval Muslim scholars thought this was bad for the children, arguing that play taught children valuable social and survival skills that they would be able to use in life outside schools and scholarly retreats. Those who held this view advocated allowing children to play. In most Muslim households play seems to have been encouraged, and toys and games were common.

Pleasure in competition seems to have been an essential part of the Arabian roots of Islam. Before Muhammad's time and after, when Arab tribes gathered, poetry competitions were held. These were not occasions of dry recitations by introverted poets. Instead, they were exuberant events with much showmanship and audiences riveted by words and action. Audiences of poetry competitions hoped to learn some clever new phrases and compelling new images that they could later quote when home or among friends. Professional girl singers, who were often slaves chosen for their voices and dancing skills, were frequently the presenters of the new poems. Music could coincide with the singing and dancing. When Muslim armies conquered most of the Near East, they brought with them the Arabian love of poetry, and poetry competitions became common in their new lands. In the former Sassanian Empire, in particular, poetry competitions contributed to a renaissance for the Persian language as a literary language, and medieval Persian poems written for public presentation remain to this day popular among many Near Eastern readers.

Common outdoor toys included seesaws and balls for kicking. In much of the Near East even grown women continued to enjoy playing on seesaws, and ball games were popular among grownups of both genders as well as among children. The most popular ball game of them all may have been polo, because it combined two passions of medieval Muslims: horses and competition. Displays of horsemanship were common in the Near East, with riders exhibiting skills in maneuvering their horses and in the techniques used in hunting and in battle. Such displays could be put on as parts of festivals, tribal gatherings, or market days. Where polo began is disputed among historians, with good possibilities being China, Persia, and Afghanistan. By no later than the first century and possibly as early as the 500s B.C.E., polo was

played in Iran, and it is likely that Muslims learned the sport from the Sassanians. Another possible source is central Asia, where Chinese troops played the sport when the Muslims invaded the area. It would have been one of many cultural legacies the Islamic world would have absorbed from the Chinese. The word *polo* may have derived from *pulu*, Tibetan for "ball."

Among the Sassanians, both men and women played polo, and this practice continued among Muslims. Among the Muslims of central Asia and the northern Near East, women were especially prominent in the sport. Among Turks and others from central Asia, both girls and boys learned to ride horses before they could walk, making polo a sport that was natural to their way of life. Muslims wrestled with the issue of whether it was proper for women to participate in any kind of sport. In general, the dress code of Islamic law was applied to both men and women competitors. Men had to be covered from their navels to their knees at all times, and women had to be more thoroughly covered. Even in places where polo was played extensively by women, the women wore robes that enveloped them completely below their necks, including their feet. Only their faces were exposed. Even though this must have been uncomfortable on hot days, women from queens to commoners participated in polo contests. Islamic law forbade women from playing sports with men.

Another popular sport was wrestling. It was common in North Africa and much of the Near East and was the favorite sport of Turks and others from central Asia. It was controver-

Glass gaming pieces, Islamic Egypt or Syria, 13th century (Los Angeles County Museum of Art, The Madina Collection of Islamic Art, gift of Camilla Chandler Frost, Photograph © 2006 Museum Associates/LACMA [M.2002.1.516a-c])

sial among Muslims because it tended to require men to be only semiclad and because it was associated in their thinking with the ancient Greeks, who were a pagan people whose sports carried pagan associations. Male wrestlers wore garments that covered them from their navels to their knees. Garments could include straps over the shoulders. Much is known of the history of wrestling among the Turkish peoples because their wrestling tradition continues to be very popular in Turkey. In medieval times wrestlers were often famous and admired for their athletic feats. Turkish wrestlers wore leather garments called *kisbets*; before they made contact with Greeks, they wrestled freestyle. After interacting with Greeks after the 1000s, they took to covering their bodies with olive oil, as had Greek wrestlers. To show their respect for each other, two wrestlers who were about to compete against each other would spread oil on each other. Among the variations of wrestling contests was one in which wrestlers would try to insert their arms under the straps of their opponents. There were no time limits, and contests could continue all day without a winner. Near Edirne in Turkey a wrestling tournament was established in 1362, perhaps because it was near a sultan's summer residence. The tournament is still held for three days each summer.

Among the games for which Muslims had a passion was chess. It was called *shatranj* in Arabic, probably deriving from Sanscrit's *chaturanga*, a term used for the traditional four divisions of an army in Hindu cultures. In India the game was played by four people seated at a square board on a table. Sometimes the table had the squares of the board inlaid into its surface. Iranians learned the game from Indians, and it was probably through them that the Islamic world acquired the game, carrying it across North Africa. It is likely that Europeans had already learned the game from the Sassanians. There were several versions of *shatranj* in the medieval Islamic world, but its general appearance would be familiar to modern players of chess. The contest was between two players. The board would have resembled those used today, and the pieces would have been arrayed similarly to those used in modern times, although the placement of the king varied from region to region.

The pieces in India were *raja, mantri, gajah, ashva, ratha,* and *padati*, meaning "king," "minister," "elephant," "horse," and "soldier," respectively. These pieces corresponded to the modern king, queen, bishop, knight, castle (or rook), and pawn. The term *rook* derived from Persian *rukh*. In Arabic the pieces became *shah, firz, al-phil, fars, ruhk,* and *baidaq*. The word *firz* referred to a sultan's vizier or chief minister. The conversion of the minister into the queen seems to have been a European innovation. In the game as played in the medieval Islamic world the *firz* (the queen piece) was notably

weak. It could move only one space diagonally. The *fars* (the bishop piece) could move only two spaces at a time diagonally. *Baidaqs* (pawns) could move only one space on their first move; upon reaching the far edge of the board, they could only change into *firzes*. Only in the late 1400s in Italy or Spain did pawns first acquire the ability to go two squares on their first moves and gain the maneuver of capture now called "en passant." The maneuver called "castling" was probably a later development.

In the medieval Islamic world the requirements for winning a game of *shatranj* varied from place to place and from time to time, but the idea of winning by checkmate had already developed in Iran. The word *checkmate* probably derived from the Persian phrase *shah mat*, roughly meaning "the king is at a loss," perhaps indicating that the king could not move. Chess games were used to reenact actual battles, and military officers typically were very skilled in the game. The idea of a real battle being reenacted is hard to picture with the traditional board and pieces, but archaeologists have uncovered numerous variations of the board in the Near East, including one with over 100 squares. Thus, it may have been that boards could vary enough to allow scope for reenacting a large battle. Further, the variations of rules regarding movements and requirements for victory may have developed out of the desire to reenact particular battles. Generals would sometimes set up boards and use chess pieces to show their sultans how a particular battle had progressed. The pieces themselves had been figures of people and animals in India, but during the medieval era Islamic pieces became abstract in order to avoid offending those who believed living things should not be depicted in figures.

A more controversial game was backgammon. This game appeared in the Near East in about 3000 B.C.E. The oldest boards known were discovered by archaeologists in Iran. They predate one found in Mesopotamia by about 200 years. Variations of the game were popular in the ancient Mesopotamian civilizations and in ancient Egypt, and it was likely already well known to Arabs before the era of Muhammad. The number of playing pieces, usually just stones, seems to have varied considerably. Although there probably were variations in the rules of the game, little of these rules survives before medieval Muslims wrote about the game. Just as Muslims published studies of the strategy of chess, they also published studies of the strategy of backgammon. Dice carved out of ivory, wood, seeds, or stone were used with the game. The dice were six-sided, looking much like modern backgammon dice. The controversial aspect of backgammon is that it was often used for gambling. Although gambling was forbidden by Islamic law, many medieval Muslims were avid gamblers, betting on athletic contests, horse or camel races, or animal fighting matches as well as gambling with dice or playing cards. People even bet on who would win a chess match. In the case of backgammon, gamblers would agree beforehand on how much a point was worth, and they would play until a player won the game or until each player agreed to stop playing. There was no doubling die.

See also CHILDREN; CLOTHING AND FOOTWEAR; CRAFTS; DRAMA AND THEATER; FAMILY; FESTIVALS; FORESTS AND FORESTRY; HUNTING, FISHING, AND GATHERING; LITERATURE; MILITARY; MUSIC AND MUSICAL INSTRUMENTS; NUMBERS AND COUNTING; RELIGION AND COSMOLOGY; WEAPONRY AND ARMOR.

∼ Excerpt from the Mahabharata (fifth century B.C.E. to fourth century C.E.) ∼

BOOK 2: SABHA PARVA

Sakuni said,—O thou foremost of victorious persons, I will snatch (for thee) this prosperity of Yudhishthira, the son of Pandu, at the sight of which thou grievest so. Therefore, O king, let Yudhishthira the son of Kunti be summoned. By throwing dice a skilful man, himself uninjured, may vanquish one that hath no skill. Know, O Bharata, that betting is my bow, the dice are my arrows, the marks on them my bow-string, and the dice-board my car.

Duryodhana said,—This Sukuni skilled at dice, is ready, O king, to snatch the prosperity of the son of Pandu by means of dice. It behoveth thee to give him permission. . . . Men of the most ancient times invented the use of dice. There is no destruction in it, nor is there any striking with, weapons. Let the words of Sakuni, therefore, be acceptable to thee, and let thy command be issued for the speedy construction of the assembly house. The door of heaven, leading us to such happiness, will be opened to us by gambling. Indeed, they that betake to gambling (with such aid) deserve such good fortune. The Pandavas then will become thy equals (instead of, as now, superiors); therefore, gamble thou with the Pandavas. . . .

Then king Dhritarashtra, possessed of learning, summoning Vidura the chief of his ministers, said:— Bring prince Yudhishthira here without loss of time. Let him come hither with his brothers, and behold his handsome assembly house of mine, furnished with countless jewels and gems, and costly beds and carpets, and let a friendly match at dice commence here. . . .

Vaisampayana said,—When the play commenced, all those kings with Dhritarashtra at their head took their seats in that assembly. And, O Bharata, Bhishma and Drona and Kripa and the high-souled Vidura with cheerless hearts sat behind. And those kings with leonine necks and endued with great energy took their seats separately and in pairs upon many elevated seats of beautiful make and colour. And, O king, that mansion looked resplendent with those assembled kings like heaven itself with a conclave of the celestials of great good fortune. And they were all conversant with the Vedas and brave and of resplendent countenances. And, O great king, the friendly match at dice then commenced.

Yudhishthira said,—O king, this excellent wealth of pearls of great value, procured from the ocean by churning it (of old), so beautiful and decked with pure gold, this, O king, is my stake. What is thy counter stake, O great king,—the wealth with which thou wishest to play with me?

Duryodhana said,—I have many jewels and much wealth. But I am not vain of them. Win thou this stake.

Vaisampayana continued,—Then Sakuni, well-skilled at dice, took up the dice and (casting them) said unto Yudhishthira, Lo, I have won! . . .

Yudhishthira said,—Thou hast won this stake of me by unfair means. But be not so proud, O Sakuni. Let us play staking thousands upon thousands. I have many beautiful jars each full of a thousand Nishkas in my treasury, inexhaustible gold, and much silver and other minerals. This, O king, is the wealth with which I will stake with thee!

Vaisampayana continued,—Thus addressed, Sakuni said unto the chief of the perpetuators of the Kuru race, the eldest of the sons of Pandu, king Yudhishthira, of glory incapable of sustaining any diminution. Lo, I have won!

Vaisampayana said,—During the course of this gambling, certain to bring about utter ruin (on Yudhishthira), Vidura, that dispeller of all doubts, (addressing Dhritarashtra) said, O great king, O thou of the Bharata race, attend to what I say, although my words may not be agreeable to thee, like medicine to one that is ill and about to breathe his last. When this Duryodhana of sinful mind had, immediately after his birth, cried discordantly like a jackal, it was well known that he had been ordained to bring about the destruction of the Bharata race. Know, O king, that he will be the cause of death of ye all. A jackal is living in thy house, O king, in the form of Duryodhana. Thou knowest it not in consequence of thy folly. Listen now to the words of the Poet (Sukra) which I will quote. They that collect honey (in mountains), having received what they seek, do not notice that they are about to fall. Ascending dangerous heights, abstracted in the pursuit of what they seek, they fall down and meet with destruction. This Duryodhana also, maddened with the play at dice, like the collector of honey, abstracted in what he seeketh, marketh not the consequences. Making enemies of these great warriors, he beholdeth not the fall that is before him. It is known to thee, O thou of great wisdom, that amongst the Bhojas, they abandoned, for the good of the citizens a son that was unworthy of their race. The Andhakas, the Yadavas, and the Bhojas uniting together, abandoned Kansa.

From Kisari Mohan Ganguli, trans., *The Mahabharata of Krishna-Dwaipayana Vyasa,* (Calcutta, India: Bharata Press, 1889–1896).

Europe

⌁ *Statuta Armorum (Statutes of Arms, ca. 1260)* ⌁

Here begin the Statutes of Arms.

At the request of the Earls and Barons and of the Chivalry of England, it is ordained and by our Lord the King commanded, that from henceforth none be so hardy, whether Earl, Baron, or other Knight, who shall go to the Tournament, to have more than three Esquires in Arms to serve him at the Tournament; and that every Esquire do bear a Cap of the Arms of his Lord, whom he shall serve that day, for Ensign.

And no Knight or Esquire serving at the Tournament, shall bear a sword pointed, or Dagger pointed, or Staff or Mace, but only a broad sword for tourneying. And all that bear Banners shall be armed with Mufflers and Cuishes, and Shoulder-Plates, and a Skull-cap, without more.

And if it happen that any Earl or Baron or other knight, do go against this statute, that such knight, by assent of all the Baronage, shall lose Horse and Harness, and abide in prison at the pleasure of our Lord Sir Edward the King's son, and Sir Edmund his brother, and the Earl of Gloucester, and the Earl of Lincoln. And the Esquire who shall be found offending against the statute here devised, in any point, shall lose Horse and Harness, and be imprisoned three years. And if any man shall cast a knight to the ground, except they who are armed for their Lord's service, the knight shall have his horse, and the offender shall be punished as the Esquires aforesaid.

And no son of a great lord, that is to say, of an Earl or Baron, shall have other armor than mufflers and cuishes, and Shoulder-Plates, and a skull-cap, without more; and shall not bear a dagger or sword pointed, nor mace, but only a broad sword. And if any be found who, in either of these points, shall offend against the statute, he shall lose his horse whereon he is mounted that day, and be imprisoned for one year.

And they who shall come to see the tournament, shall not be armed with any manner of armor, and shall bear no sword, or dagger, or staff, or mace, or stone, upon such forfeiture as in the case of Esquires aforesaid. And no groom or footman shall bear sword, or dagger, or staff, or stone; and if they be found offending, they shall be imprisoned for seven years.

And if any great lord or other keep a table, none shall bring there any Esquire but those who are wont to mess in their Lord's presence. And no King at Arms or Minstrels shall bear secret arms, nor any other besides their swords without points. And the Kings at Arms shall have their mantles without more, etc.

From: A. Luders, ed., *The Statutes of the Realm: Printed by Command of His Majesty King George the Third, in Pursuance of an Address of the House of Commons of Great Britain, From Original Records and Authentic Manuscripts,* 11 vols. (London: Record Commission, 1810–1828).

FURTHER READING

John Marshall Carter, *Medieval Games: Sports and Recreations in Feudal Society* (Westport, Conn.: Greenwood Press, 1992).

Stewart Culin, *Games of the North American Indian* (New York: Dover Publications, 1975).

Donn F. Draeger, *The Weapons and Fighting Arts of Indonesia* (Rutland, Vt.: Tuttle, 2001).

James E. Lindsay, "Entertainments," in his *Daily Life in the Medieval Islamic World* (Westport, Conn.: Greenwood Press, 2005).

Horace Mann, "Sports, Games, and Recreation in Medieval Muslim Societies." Available online. URL: http://www.sfusd.k12.ca.us/schwww/sch618/Sports/Sports.html. Downloaded on November 3, 2007.

Eugene B. McCluney, "Lacrosse: The Combat of Spirit," *American Indian Quarterly* 1, no. 1 (1974): 34–42.

Peter Nabokov. *Indian Running: Native American History and Tradition* (Santa Fe, N.M.: Ancient City Press, 1987).

Joseph B. Oxendine, *American Indian Sports Heritage*, 2nd. ed. (Lincoln: University of Nebraska Press, 1995).

David Parlett, *The Oxford History of Board Games* (New York: Oxford University Press, 1999).

G. M. Wickens, "What the West Borrowed from the Middle East," in *Introduction to Islamic Civilization*, ed. R. M. Savory (New York: Cambridge University Press, 1976).

Sally E. D. Wilkins, *Sports and Games of Medieval Cultures* (Westport, Conn.: Greenwood Press, 2002).

► storage and preservation

INTRODUCTION

During the medieval era people needed to store and preserve water, textiles, and food, including grains, root and other vegetables, fruits and meats. Continual access to good drinking water was always important, and storing it was vital in areas prone to droughts or those with little annual rainfall or with only seasonal rainfall. Textiles were vulnerable to decay, so preserving and storing them securely mattered, especially to people who could not afford much clothing or bedding. Depending on the environment, people in the medieval period needed to protect foods and textiles from moisture, which could lead to rotting of stored food and decay of fabrics, and from such pests as insects, worms, mice, rats, and squirrels.

For nomadic peoples storage containers were often limited to what could be carried. Burying items in the ground to be recovered later left the items vulnerable to worms. In places as far apart as Australia and southwestern Africa nomadic peoples relied on animal skins to transport water, and they dried or smoked meats to preserve them. Drying was a common way for people to preserve food, and it was used almost everywhere in the medieval world. The drying process usually involved setting out food such as grains and fruits in the sun. Once the moisture evaporated from the food, the food could be stored, sometimes for years, depending on

the dryness of the climate. Meats posed a problem because they were susceptible to rotting during the drying process. People often draped the meat over a spit above a smoky fire or hung the meat inside a smokehouse, often just a hut, in which a slow fire was kept burning. The smoking enhanced the flavor of the meat. This process was a life-and-death matter for people who depended on seasonal meat, as many fishermen did. They needed to have dried fish to help them survive during periods when seasonal fishes such as salmon were unavailable.

The storing of fish sometimes involved keeping the fish alive in ponds or shallow water. In East Africa fishermen sometimes would use netting or basketry to wall off tide pools in which they kept fish that they caught; the water could get in, but the fish could not get out. In the Americas people sometimes made storage ponds in which they kept live fish. A somewhat similar principle was at work for beef, mutton, pork, and other meats from livestock. Sometimes people followed herds such as reindeer in northern Siberia, but usually they directed the movements of their livestock. Whether following or directing their herds, people were in essence storing their meat on the hoof. Nomadic pastoralists were dependent on seasonal rains and open pastures to maintain their herds; settled peoples often kept their livestock fenced in on a particular plot of land and had to provide the animals with food. This led to the need to store and preserve animal feed such as hay.

To do so, people followed practices they used for storing grain safely. They usually built a granary. This was not always the case; for instance, many western and central Africans built huge jars set on the ground or into the ground for holding harvests. The most common granary was built above ground. For instance, the Japanese placed their granaries on stilts to make them difficult for mice and rats to reach. In some societies, granaries served the entire population of a village or town; in others, each farming family had its own granary. Often in medieval times governments took a strong interest in storing grain in an effort to ensure that there was enough stored to get the population through bad harvests.

The importance of water storage varied according to climate. In North Africa and the Near East large basins were maintained underground; water, sometimes directed by aqueducts or canals to a city, drained into the basins from which the water could be withdrawn. Southern Arabia had an ancient tradition of building dams to hold rainwater, enabling the people of Yemen, in particular, to develop a vigorous agricultural economy. During wars one side or the other might poison wells and other sources of water to prevent the enemy from having fresh sources of water. Ice from glaciers could be used to preserve fresh fruits and vegetables in the course of shipping to markets. In some very dry places water would be left in caves and would vaporize so fast that the water temperature dropped faster than the water could evaporate, turning it into ice.

AFRICA

BY BRADLEY A. SKEEN

The agricultural revolution (ca. 10,000–8000 B.C.E) of the Neolithic marked the transition from hunting and gathering wild sources of food to agriculture based on the use of domesticated plants and animals. The reliance of the new farmers on a small number of food crops meant that large amounts of food in general could be reliably obtained only once a year at the harvest; therefore, it was necessary to store and preserve a year's worth of food. This was accomplished by developing several new technologies or new uses for existing technologies. The most basic of these was the granary. This is an architectural structure not fundamentally different from a house or barn. Its purpose was to store large amounts of grain in an enclosed, roofed-over space to protect it from the elements and from the intrusion of large animals, such as wild cattle, that might otherwise eat the grain as well as smaller vermin, such as rats, and, insofar as possible, insects. Of course, storing grain in a tightly enclosed space also created new risks, such as its destruction by molds or fungus if the granary was not kept dry and properly ventilated. Similar to granaries were storage buildings for fruits or vegetables (a larder) or for animal food, such as a hay barn.

Smaller amounts of grain and other foodstuffs, even cooked food for a short period of time, could be stored in woven baskets or ceramic pots. Surprisingly perhaps, the relatively simple technologies of basket weaving and pottery making seem not to have existed in earlier times to store gathered food but were developed as a result of the large surpluses of the agricultural revolution. The earliest pottery was made by joining together coils of clay, but soon the more sophisticated technique of throwing ceramics on a potter's wheel was developed. Most early homes consisted of one or very few rooms; pots and baskets full of food would simply have been stacked on the floor wherever it was convenient. Cooking would have been done at a detached oven away from the house. Separate rooms of the house with built-in ovens and specialized kitchens were a development of urban culture that did not become very widespread in Africa even as late as medieval times. Liquids such as water and wine (where it was available, such as in Egypt and Ethiopia) or palm wine frequently were stored in leather bags. The use of leather and basketry for storage, however, usually has to be deduced from later practices, since these perishable substances rarely show up in the archaeological record.

Egypt was the wealthiest grain-producing region in the world. Because of the fertilizing effect of the annual inundation of the Nile, crops in Egypt generally returned 20 times as much grain as had been planted, compared with returns of 2:1 to 7:1 for most of the rest of the world. Because of this abundance, the country was filled with granaries, from small structures owned by individual farmers through larger structures belonging to great landowners (including temples), with the largest facilities owned by the state used to regulate the grain supply of the whole country and build up surpluses against times of famine. Granaries also existed throughout Egyptian cities to store grain about to be processed into food products for urban dwellers. By late Roman times large granaries also existed in the capital city of Alexandria and other ports to store grain before transport overseas, since Egyptian grain was especially important to supply the large populations of the Roman capitals of Rome and Constantinople.

In the last century and a half before the Arab conquest, Egypt participated fully in the commercial network of the Roman Empire. This means that the main form of storage used in the country (as well as in the rest of Roman North Africa) was the amphora. These were large ceramic jugs made in standard sizes ranging from about 20 to more than 40 inches in length, with long, thin necks and relatively slender bodies tapering to a point on the bottom. They were fashioned with two handles mounted between the neck and body of the jar and could be fitted with a lid. Amphorae were generally mass-produced in industrial-scale workshops. Because of the pointed bottom, they could not stand up by themselves, but because the amphorae were standardized in size for storage, every house and other building that needed amphorae had racks specially built in to hold them. The racks consisted of a wooden or ceramic framework supporting two loops of unequal size that would hold the amphorae in much the same way a modern-day test-tube rack supports its contents. These racks existed not only in buildings but also on ships, since almost all commodities were shipped inside amphorae.

Amphorae held not only grain and other foodstuffs but also salt, oil, water, wine, honey, and almost every other conceivable product, including items like nails. Vendors in markets would naturally store their foodstuffs in amphorae. Taverns stored stews and other cooked foods in racks of amphorae for sale to day laborers and others who could not follow the usual custom of returning home for lunch. Because the infrastructure for the production of amphorae broke down after the Arab conquests and the collapse of the Western Roman Empire, the amphora was quickly replaced by other forms of storage in the seventh and eighth centuries.

Baskets also were used as a common means of storage in late Roman Egypt, probably mostly in households and by small shopkeepers. Basket weaving was a specialized profession, if a very humble one. It was considered decorous for Christian monks who had dedicated themselves to a life of poverty to make and sell baskets as a way to earn the small amounts of money they needed to buy the food with which they infrequently broke their fasts.

Before the Arab conquest the Nubian peoples of the upper Nile (Sudan) enjoyed the same level of storage technology as Egypt, although they did not use the amphora system (though many amphorae entered Nubian and even Ethiopia through commerce). Very high-quality pottery was produced locally using the wheel and was fired in brick kilns. Basketry was also made out of local palm fibers and grasses. A bronze bowl from Kerna made in the period of the kingdom of Meroë (which ended in about 350 C.E.) shows that ceramic jugs were used in milking cattle. (Interestingly, some of the jugs depicted bear decoration meant to make them resemble woven baskets, suggesting, perhaps that ceramic ware was sometimes used to replace basketry in certain functions—though baskets could most likely never held milk.) Although this piece dates from just before the Middle Ages, there is no reason to think that practice changed substantially before the Arab conquest.

Medieval Ethiopia had large urban centers, especially Axum in the early period, and must have had a very sophisticated technology for agricultural storage, but very little in this way has been clarified so far by archaeological research. However, given that wine was fermented locally in rock-cut vats carved out of stone outcroppings, it is likely that Ethiopians turned their remarkable stoneworking skills to making granaries that have not yet been identified as such. The quality of Egyptian pottery was remarkably good, considering that it was coil made without the potter's wheel.

About 9000 B.C.E. the agricultural revolution became widespread among the peoples of the Sahara, which was then a far wetter environment than it is today. The technology to store agricultural produce moved south with agriculture itself and reached almost all of Africa (except for those few tribes that maintained a hunter-gatherer way of life) by the Middle Ages. The ancient town of Nok in central Nigeria seems to have been a point of transition for many technologies that were developed (or at least existed) in the Neolithic Sahara (although Nok itself was abandoned around 200 C.E.). Nok seems to have been the point of origin for the spread of basketry and ceramics to much of sub-Saharan Africa. The pottery types current in Nok in the Middle Ages were handmade from clay coils without the potter's wheel. The quality of ceramic wares at Nok was nevertheless very high. Pots were made in a variety of shapes and were often decorated with painted patterns or impressed textures.

Pottery of the same type and quality spread throughout western Africa during the Middle Ages. By about 1000 C.E. sophisticated coil pottery making had spread into central and southern Africa, though in many areas inferior wares were produced and always with considerable local variation. Most often pots were clamp-fired; that is, they were hardened in an open bonfire rather than in a kiln. Even the civilization of Great Zimbabwe, notable for its stone-coursed walls, did not use any significantly different pottery-making techniques. However, the people of Great Zimbabwe manufactured large numbers of vessels equivalent in size, shape, and use to clay pots, but carved out of soapstone, a soft mineral native to the area.

Granaries used in Sub-Saharan Africa in the early colonial period (postmedieval) were usually made of perishable materials, either unfired mud bricks or timber products, including thatch. The chances of finding such structures from the medieval period are slight, although there is little reason to think they were not in use.

THE AMERICAS
BY MICHAEL J. O'NEAL

Medieval Americans had to store and preserve three primary resources without the benefit of modern refrigeration and materials such as plastic. One was fresh water for drinking and cooking, and often this water had to be preserved through dry seasons and periods of drought. A second was seeds to be used for the following year's planting of crops. The third was food, in the form of short-term storage in the household and longer-term storage for the community as a whole. Their adversaries in storing these vital resources were temperature, moisture, pests (insects and rodents), and microorganisms that produced rot, spoilage, and molds.

Medieval Americans preserved food in ways similar to their ancient ancestors. A common method was drying. Drying food reduces the moisture content that fosters the grown of microorganisms. Meat, for example, was cut into thin slices and dried on racks in the sun or over a fire, similarly to modern-day jerky. Vegetables, too, could be dried and then, throughout the winter months, be rehydrated by adding them to soups and stew or simply soaking them in water.

Smoking had an effect similar to drying. Meats were placed in sealed huts, where a smoky fire was kept burning, preferably using chips of hardwood, which burn hotter than such woods as pine and can be kept smoldering without open flames. This process also reduced the moisture content of the meat so that it would keep for many months, and substances from the smoke itself discouraged the growth of microorganisms. The smoke also added flavor to the meat.

Those who lived in cold climates were able to take advantage of freezing temperatures to preserve meat. In the Arctic north, hunters harvested sea mammals such as seals and then froze the meat until it was ready to be consumed, when it could be thawed over a fire. In the southern Andes of South America, people used a freeze-drying technique to preserve such foods as potatoes. They sliced the potatoes and laid them out to freeze. Freezing reduced the moisture content; the potatoes could be reconstituted by cooking or soaking in water. In less frigid regions, such as Canada and much of North America, deer, bison, and other game animals were harvested late in the autumn and frozen over the winter months. The same technique could be used to preserve fish. Native Americans also preserved meat in the form of pemmican, a mixture of meat, berries, and fat.

In storing vegetable seeds, humidity could be a major obstacle. Native Americans in the desert regions of the American Southwest and Mesoamerica were able to store maize (corn) seeds for up to three years because the air was dry. In contrast, the climate of the Yucatán Peninsula was much more humid, so seeds could be stored for only a year.

The most common method of storage at the household level used pots and baskets. Throughout the Americas, people—usually but not always women—wove baskets out of materials at hand. In the north, for example, baskets were made of such materials as grasses, ash, and birch bark. Those in the Northwest relied on swamp grasses, cedar bark, and spruce roots, while those in California wove baskets of sumac, yucca, and willow. Open-weave baskets were lighter and could be used for such purposes as gathering firewood. Such baskets were also useful for fish and clams because the openings in the weave allowed excess water to run out. More tightly woven baskets, on the other hand, were more suitable for storing seeds and nuts.

In addition to basketry, Native Americans became accomplished potters, particularly as cultures became more sedentary and adopted agricultural ways of life. These pots, often clay-fired but sometimes not, were used to store seeds, nuts, acorns, beans, rice, and similar dry items. Many of these ceramic pots, especially in the Mayan culture, were highly decorated with paintings and hieroglyphic texts. Pots sealed with some type of resin were used to store water, although the Maya of the Yucatán Peninsula in Mexico stored water in reservoirs in the ground. After digging holes, they plastered the bottoms to prevent water from running out the porous limestone bottoms. These reservoirs could hold enough water to last up to 18 months during periods of little or no rain.

Ceramic vessel in the shape of a jaguar, Maya culture, Mexico, ca. 950–1200 (Courtesy, National Museum of the American Indian, Smithsonian Institution [catalog number 236335])

A considerable amount of food storage and preservation took place at the household level. However, in more complex cultures, communal storage of foodstuffs was more the norm, particularly in the larger cities. For example, among the mound-building cultures of the Mississippi River valley, including the Cahokia culture in the region around modern-day Illinois, large granaries were built on the mounds. Similarly, the more highly developed cultures of Mesoamerica and the Inca of South America constructed communal granaries.

A good example is the Paquimé culture. Paquimé, in northern Mexico, was the center of the Casas Grandes culture for some 300 years. It attained the height of its power around the 13th century, and the city may have reached a population of 10,000. Archaeologists have found granary systems in the northern Sierra Madres and at other sites with such names as Schoolhouse Point Mound, Punkin Center, Canyon Creek, as well as in the San Pedro Valley, parts of Arizona, and the Mimbres region of southwestern New Mexico. Many of these granaries are still well preserved.

With respect to Mesoamerica, archaeologists are divided over the question of whether kivas at Chaco, which flourished from about 650 to 1130, were used as granaries. Usually, kivas, or round, underground buildings, have been regarded as strictly ceremonial and cultural centers. Some archaeologists believe that many of these kivas were used for long-term grain storage, specifically for maize. Put differently, they argue that the kivas, in addition to having a ceremonial and religious function, were put to a variety of uses depending on longer-term needs. During periods of prolonged drought, the most critical of those needs was storage of grain.

A major piece of evidence supporting this view is the ventilation systems built into the kivas. This ventilation could control humidity levels and provide air circulation. They also supplied air to the fireplace hearth. Evidence also shows that substances in the wood that was burned, specifically tannins, functioned to preserve the grain from rodents, mildew, molds, and insects. Because the humidity level has to be below 12 percent for corn not to develop mold, the builders of the kivas may have included latticework floors that allowed circulation of warm, dry air. Interestingly, the people had no tools for measuring humidity, but modern-day evidence, in the form of people who use the same techniques, suggests that they somehow just knew when the humidity level was correct. Additionally, the hearth and ventilation systems introduced carbon monoxide into the air. Carbon monoxide is an effective pesticide that has no effect on the food being stored. Very small quantities of charcoal briquettes provided ten times the amount of carbon monoxide needed to eradicate pests.

Again, the notion that kivas were used for grain storage flies in the face of conventional belief—that they were used strictly for religious and ceremonial purposes. Archaeologists who argue otherwise suggest that the religious-ceremonial purposes became predominant only later, after the culture turned away from the storage of surplus grain to more of a subsistence form of agriculture. As the structures were left empty, they were converted to other uses. The archaeologists who take this view also note that throughout the world religious structures are generally (but not always) not round but that granaries almost always are round—just as kivas are. Further, they point to the existence of other structures that clearly were used for religious and ceremonial purposes, suggesting that the kivas had other uses. Another bit of evidence is that the Paquimé kivas are set in rows, similar to the rows of grain-storage facilities throughout Mesoamerica and in other parts of the world.

One way of preserving fish for human consumption is to keep them alive until they are needed. Archaeological evidence suggests that this may have been a common practice in the Bolivian Amazon region of South America. There, archaeologists have found the remains of earthworks that suggest not only a high degree of building and engineering skill but also the ability to convert a poor environment into one that may have supported a larger population than it has in modern times.

In the flat, seasonally flooded Baures region of Bolivia, scientists have found an immense network of artificial earthworks. These earthworks cover an area of 326 square miles.

All of them are interconnected in a zigzag pattern. These structures functioned as fish weirs, or traps. During periods of seasonal flooding the weirs trapped fish that migrated and spawned in the flooded area. These weirs, along with artificial ponds, amounted to a system of aquaculture. They were easily managed and provided the people with a rich source of food high in protein.

The weirs measured about 3 to 6 feet in width. Their height ran from 7 to 20 inches. Every 30 to 100 feet the weirs changed directions. At the places where the structures formed sharp angles, 3- to 6-foot-long openings in the shape of a funnel directed fish into nearby ponds that measured some 90 feet in diameter, where they could be harvested as needed. The Bolivian fish-storage systems are fundamentally different from other such systems throughout the Americas. Generally, such systems of weirs were temporary. They were built on permanent bodies of water and then rebuilt when necessary, usually each year. The Bolivian system was just the opposite: The system of weirs was permanent, but the water was seasonal. The zigzag pattern, while not unique, was denser and more complicated than that of other fish weirs. The structures were abandoned in roughly 1700.

ASIA AND THE PACIFIC
BY MARK W. ALLEN

Archaeologists frequently note that the development of sedentary societies in the past was closely linked to the development of storage and preservation technology. Indeed, one of the key differences between agriculturalists and hunter-gatherers is that the latter usually do not store large quantities of food. An intensive agricultural system that produces vast surpluses absolutely depends on effective ways to store and preserve food. Asia during medieval times was nearly everywhere dependent on large-scale agricultural production of rice, wheat, millet, and other crops. Domesticated animals provided protein. These products were produced through high investments of labor, such as irrigation, fertilization, multi-cropping, and plowing. Over thousands of years a number of food-preparation techniques and technologies evolved to ensure that bountiful harvests of food or drink did not go to waste. They could be set aside for lean times, to be reinvested in supporting armies or other large groups such as workers or craftspeople or used to trade for other commodities.

In the Pacific islands agriculture was generally less intense. It relied mainly on root crops and arboriculture. Irrigation was rare, and most gardening was done with simple digging sticks. Nevertheless, sometimes large surpluses were produced both for food and as political capital to be expended at the right time. Storage and preservation was indeed central to this cultural area, as foods had to survive transplantation across vast ocean distances via double-hull voyaging canoes such as those of the Polynesians.

Asian agriculturalists, like nearly all early agriculturalists, were heavily reliant on one key storage technology—ceramics. Pottery is often a good archaeological indicator of at least some degree of agriculture. It is crucial for storing grains and other crops because it seals and protects food from pests, moisture, and dryness far better than basketry. Jars are typically used as storage containers, while bowls often are used for food preparation or presentation. Medieval Asian ceramic technologies, particularly those of China, produced some of the finest examples of porcelain ever made (used for storage and other functional purposes but often most important as a status good or for trade). In southern Asia areas such as India produced a wide variety of different kinds of pottery to be used for particular kinds of food or liquid storage. Storage facilities, such as granaries and silos, also were used in areas with production of grain such as wheat and millet. Such crops usually were ground into flour to increase their longevity.

Food and drink were also preserved through natural processes augmented with cultural techniques and technologies. In Asia one of the key ways to preserve food and drink was to use fermentation—the natural decay of sugars and carbohydrates into acids and alcohols in anaerobic (without oxygen) environments. Numerous alcoholic beverages were produced through fermentation in medieval Asia, including rice wine. Soy sauce and other similar liquids were also made through fermentation. Fruits and vegetables were preserved by specialists through this process, producing a wide variety of pickled foods. Korean kimchi, or fermented vegetables, is a good example, but there were literally hundreds more types of such preserved foods. Fermented dairy products, such as yogurt, were common in central Asia and India. Grains were fermented with yeasts to produce various forms of bread in many areas. There were other ways to preserve food as well, such as the Chinese method for preserving eggs by coating their shells with salt and ash (though it turns them into blue jelly). Salt was used to preserve meat, fish, and other foods. In short, there was a diverse set of techniques to preserve food and liquid in medieval Asia.

Another key form of Asian storage was the use of large, stone-lined reservoirs to store the monsoon rains in Southeast Asia for use during the dry season. This was an absolutely critical resource for this area, as can be seen by their vast numbers and sizes in the ruins of medieval towns and cities in present-day Cambodia, Thailand, and Vietnam. Such reservoirs often were regarded as the property of rulers or the priestly classes and were viewed as sacred parts of the landscape, particularly within Hindu cultural areas.

When the first ocean voyagers left the relative safety of island Southeast Asia and New Guinea and headed east to explore and colonize faraway islands, their canoes were loaded with stored water and food (for the voyage and for transplanting crops to new islands). Some such voyages covered more than a few thousand miles and lasted several weeks at least. The major period of long-distance exploration and colonization in the Pacific corresponds fairly well to the medieval period, though it began a few centuries before 500 C.E. Micronesians and Polynesians spread out to find and colonize nearly every habitable island in the Pacific Ocean. They relied heavily on technology and knowledge to accomplish this. Double-hulled canoes could be at sea for more than a month with enough provisions and people to begin a new colony on some new island. This meant, of course, that they needed food for the voyage and crops to plant on new islands—they brought their economy with them.

The foods they carried, however, were quite different from those of mainland Asia. They relied mainly on tropical root crops (sweet potato, taro, yams) and arboriculture (coconut, breadfruit, bananas). Some foods for these voyages would be dried or smoked, such as fish and pork. Such products could be stored for months, perfect for long voyages. As in Asia, fruits and other plants in the Pacific often were fermented to last long periods of time.

Another interesting difference from Asia is that for the most part Pacific islanders eventually quit making ceramics for both storage and cooking vessels. They instead turned to wooden containers for storage and serving food and earth ovens for cooking. In addition, Pacific islanders had a fairly wide variety of storage facilities (such as store houses, pits, and racks). In Melanesia elaborate "yam houses" were constructed to house harvested tubers; they were often named and decorated and were considered very much a prestige symbol when jammed full of yams. The yams were adorned with woven masks and were often nearly anthropomorphic. Such storage facilities usually were mounted on poles or stilts to help keep rodents and other pests out of the food supply.

In many islands breadfruit was stored for months or even years. This is a tree crop rich in starches, so when it is placed in pits in the ground the fruit ferments into a paste. Reportedly, it is edible for more than 30 years. Polynesians often stored breadfruit as a backup in case other foods failed. Usually the islands were kind to people, for they provided nearly limitless tree crops, fish, and good gardening locations. On the other hand, catastrophes such as storms, tsunamis, or volcanic eruptions were a very real threat. Any of these natural disasters could wipe out an entire economic system in a matter of minutes. Stored breadfruit was the key insurance for such scenarios.

Perhaps the most involved storage facilities of the Pacific were elaborate covered pits in the Polynesian islands of New Zealand. The Maori (the indigenous Polynesians of New Zealand) were faced with a major problem, since their rugged islands were far south of the equator. Frosty winters and poor soil conditions nearly prevented the successful establishment of the traditional Pacific tree and root crops. The Maori adapted to this by focusing on hunting and gathering and fishing for several hundred years. Around 1500, however, a new storage technology developed that allowed the spread of sweet potatoes to the extent that they became an important food source. Tubers were stored on racks inside subterranean pits covered by insulated roof structures that gave protection from frost and cold winter rains. Drainage ditches were dug around the pits to channel runoff water away from the stored food, since moisture could quickly destroy them. These spread quickly, and the visitor to New Zealand can still see the archaeological remains of pits scattered across the landscape in former gardening areas. The reliability of the storage pits allowed the sweet potato to become an extremely important status food that symbolized productive lands and people. The Maori also smoked and dried fish, birds, and freshwater eels. Airtight gourds were used to seal in some foods such as salted birds for long-term storage.

Of course, there is one more important storage system in the Pacific islands. This one, however, is natural rather than cultural. The coconut was widely available across the vast ocean, as it readily survives long periods of time in the sea. Once washed up on a beach, new trees sprout. Pacific islanders could usually count on finding coconuts on most islands (except New Zealand, which was too cold). The coconut can store its milk and "meat" for long periods of time. It is truly one of the most important foods of the Pacific.

EUROPE

BY CHARLES W. ABBOTT

Food storage is crucial for human communities. Bread (or some form of porridge) was the staple food over much of Europe, yet field crops were harvested once a year. Fruit harvests were similarly concentrated, and vegetables were in season only periodically. All of these products could be eaten outside limited times of harvest abundance only if they could be preserved and stored. With grains this was a matter of the utmost importance, since for the average person they provided most dietary calories throughout the year.

Animals and animal products presented similar challenges. In theory animals might be maintained alive until needed, storing meat "on the hoof" until it was harvested by slaughter for consumer needs. In practice, this could not be fully carried out: There simply was not enough forage to sustain all animals through the winter. Thus the need to preserve crops was partially paralleled by the need to preserve meat. The only perishable items for which storage was not necessarily a problem were animal products that yielded at constant rates, such as milk and eggs. Even with these items, storage and preservation were still desirable for transportation and marketing. Fluid milk was so bulky, unwieldy, and perishable that it could be marketed only within a narrow radius of its production. Cheese and butter were more valuable by weight, kept longer, and existed in more transportable form.

Medieval Europe was a land without modern refrigeration, preservatives, or pest control. Glass was a luxury product and steel a semiprecious metal; hermetically sealed containers had not been invented (modern canning was finally pioneered during the Napoleonic Wars). The preferred containers for many products were wooden barrels or clay-fired pots and jars. Without the availability of modern methods and materials, a variety of simple techniques were used to preserve and store food. Many of the practices predated medieval times. Technologies were generally folk technologies, practiced when necessary by the average household. Certain techniques were limited to artisans—some were craft skills in the hand of experts; others were specialties arising from the division of labor and the concentration of inputs in a limited number of hands. (Fish preservation, for example, was done by specialists soon after the catch was landed in coastal settlements.)

The most common techniques for preservation were few in number and elementary in concept: drying, curing with salt (sometimes combined with smoking), pickling, and sweetening. The goal of each is to alter the food's vulnerability to spoilage by making it less hospitable to the growth of destructive microorganisms (such as bacteria or molds), which would make food inedible. Drying does this by lowering the moisture content and salting by making moisture unavailable. Smoking was combined with salting, and it facilitates moisture reduction and adds chemical resins and flavors. Pickling makes food too acid for decay; the addition of sugars reduces available moisture and makes it too sweet. A few foods were preserved through the opposite technique: controlled spoilage. This involves facilitating the progression of biological changes known to preserve edibility (such as the fermentation of grape juice or a starchy water mix to produce wine or beer or the fermentation of milk curd to produces cheese).

Drying was by far the most common technique and the one used for most vegetable products low in protein, such as grains, legumes, many fruits, and herbs. Sunshine on a warm, dry day was the preferred drying source when possible for bulk crops; barns were used to ward off moisture and preserve and extend the drying process. Small items in regular use, such as herbs, could be hung from the rafters of houses. The drying of higher-value goods was also pursued in a more determined manner through the use of ovens and kilns. Fruits were cut into thin slices to aid drying.

If drying was the technique for products low in protein, salt curing (sometimes combined with smoking) was the technique for meat. Much of medieval Europe walked a tightrope between three simultaneous shortages: grain for people, forage for animals, and animal traction to draw the plow. The forage constraint appeared quickly at the onset of winter, when animals could no longer be fed on green pastures on the outskirts of the village but were turned out to graze on crop stubble. The response was to slaughter all excess animals so that an adequate core of the best ones could be fed till spring arrived and the forage constraint was eased.

The best and most robust technique was to salt meat to the point that it was inedible for people (for also for bacteria). One common mixture, Ann Hagen found, was salt, bay

Red clay jar with green and blue glaze used to store hazardous or precious ingredients, Beauvais, France, ca. 1500 (© Museum of London)

salt (an inferior salt variety with many impurities), saltpeter, honey, and black pepper. The meat would later have the excess salt soaked out of it before it was cooked and served. Smoking was a supplementary technique using with salt curing; the burning of certain types of wood added flavor and beneficial chemicals. Similar techniques were used to preserve ocean-caught fish in large quantities in the vicinities where it was landed. Fish was cleaned, sliced open, salted, and then dried on special racks in the open air, exposed to wind and sun.

Pickling was primarily used for such products as cabbage; in actuality, the sugars in cabbage ferment and produce vinegar, which is acidic and contributes to preservation. Sweetening fruits to produce items such as jams and jellies was constrained by the low supply of sugar (which was an expensive imported good that was treated more like a spice) and the relatively small amounts of honey (the most common source of sweetener) available to the average household. A common technique was to boil fruits down to concentrate them in their own sugars, later adding honey.

Milk was a versatile product and apparently a larger source of protein than meat for the average person. Milk could be drunk fresh or made into yogurt. The cream was often skimmed off and made into butter. Milk could also be kept until it curdled—the whey was then drunk separately, and the curds were used to make cheese. Cheese making was typically performed at the household level; its production requires simply milk and rennet (derived from cow stomachs) to speed and complete fermentation. It is thought that the consumption of aged cheese was a good marker of affluence: The poorer a family was, the fresher the cheese they ate. This is consistent with our knowledge of the production of high-quality cheeses by monasteries.

Storage buildings such as barns were used to hold large amounts of products such as grain and legumes. Wheat was sometimes stored in barns while still in sheaves; beans and peas were usually threshed first. The cellars of houses (if available), root cellars, and various types of pits in the ground (covered with earth and straw) were used to store products when the primary concern was the achievement of a low, predictable temperature. Turnips were stored in this way. Flour, once milled from grain, could be stored in chests or bins that were relatively secure from vermin. Cats were kept to reduce the rodent population.

An overarching technique was also watchfulness—an attitude of vigilance and periodic inspection to detect spoilage in its early stages or pest infestation. Monasteries and lords maintained institutional stores where a steward was responsible for monitoring supplies to detect incipient spoilage. When it was discovered, the impacts of spoilage often could be minimized by disposing of the bad portions before contamination spread. Peasant households were crowded with household stores. Various products would hang from rafters—not just herbs but sausages and fresh cheeses tied up with string and yet to be consumed. Crocks of pickled products and jars would line the walls or be half-buried in the dirt floor. Livestock were sometimes kept inside at night to warm the building and guard against pilferage.

Barrels were the preferred container for wet goods, and they often stored wine at the beginning of their storage life. When beer was made in large quantities (rather than at home), barrels were used to store it and also to transport it if it was not to be sold on the brewing premises. Crocks with well-constructed lids could serve as something close to an airtight environment when sealed with vegetable oil or clarified butter.

Salt was required in large quantities; it was used to cure meat and in cheese and butter making. It extended the life of butter. The exact role of spices in the medieval diet continues to be debated, but some beliefs that were previously conventional wisdom are now questioned. For example, historiography long stressed Europe's craving for exotic spices brought from the Middle East or farther afield through the spice trade. It was asserted that pepper was in high popular demand in Europe partly in order to mask the taste of spoiled meat. This claim is now questioned, though it is yet to be conclusively debunked.

It is difficult to find much evidence of technical progress in storage and preservation during the period. Agriculture was revolutionized by the horse collar, the horse shoe, the three-field system, and the heavy plow, but progress in storage and preservation was minimal. It may be that food technology improvements in medieval Europe were in production, milling, and transport rather than in techniques of storage and preservation.

A robust finding of economic historians is that the interest rates were shockingly high in the High Middle Ages. We can see this trend directly in financial records but also indirectly in the monthly increments in the price of grain after harvest time had passed. Researchers have noted that civic leaders and households struggled endlessly to build up stores of grain and other supplies as insurance against crop failure and disruptions in trade, because society as a whole lived very close to crop failure and hunger if not famine.

THE ISLAMIC WORLD
BY AMY HACKNEY BLACKWELL

The inhabitants of the medieval Islamic world had to be able to store food for long periods of time. Fresh foods were available for only short times every year, right after harvests; in or-

der to have food for the rest of the year, people had to be able to preserve fresh items. They also needed convenient foods that could easily be carried and eaten on journeys. Most preservation techniques involved drying, which took advantage of the climate of much of the region.

Legumes were the main source of protein for people throughout the Islamic world. Every year farmers would grow chickpeas, lentils, split peas, fava beans, and other pulses. These were almost all preserved by drying. After harvest people would spread their legumes on cloths in the sun, which would quickly dry them rock hard. Dried beans would keep for months or even years as long as they were kept away from moisture. People stored them in cloth sacks, baskets, or earthenware jars.

Dried fruits were essential to the Islamic diet. People took fruits such as apricots, grapes, and plums and laid them on cloths in the sun. The resulting dried fruits would keep for months as long as they stayed dry. Salted dried lemons were an essential flavoring to many Arabic dishes. Herbs were perfect material for drying. People collected wild herbs from the countryside or picked them from their own gardens and hung them up in bunches until they were dry.

Dates were a staple food because they were nutritious, cheap, edible to both humans and camels, easy to eat and transport, and readily preserved. Although people ate fresh dates when they were available during the harvest season, for the rest of the year dried dates were essential. Dried dates were so important in some areas that people used them to pay taxes or make charitable contributions as required by Islamic law. Some dates were harvested by hand and dried on the ground. Other dates were left on the tree until the full crop had ripened and dried somewhat, and then the entire growth of fruits and branches would be cut off at once. Sometimes dates were dried individually, harvested, and placed carefully so that they would not be crushed and their skins would remain intact. Ideally, the skins would remain dry and not become sticky with juice from inside the fruit.

Different species of dates had different properties when dried; some kept their shapes better than others. Flesh texture could be soft and syrupy or stringy. To make pressed dates, growers would fill rectangular sacks or baskets woven from date palm leaves with fresh dates. The sacks or baskets would be stacked inside a date press. About 4 to 5 percent of the dates' mass would come out in the form of liquid date syrup, which was a desirable product in its own right. The rest of the dates would be drier and have a higher sugar concentration than fresh dates, between 70 and 85 percent. This sugar concentration helped preserve the dates, which could stay edible for over a year. This process produced food that both humans and camels could eat.

Luster-painted pottery jar, Syria, late 13th century; this jar is thought to have been used for storage and not decoration. (© The Trustees of the British Museum)

Grains such as wheat and barley were a major source of calories. Grain left in seed form did not always keep well, so people devised ways of preserving it by precooking and drying it. These methods had the advantage of creating foods that functioned much like modern instant cereals. One simple method of preserving grains was to toast them in a dry skillet and then grind them into powder. Often people would add spices to the mill to create spiced flour. This could be mixed with water and olive oil to make lumps that could be eaten on the fly, while working or traveling. It could also be made into a drink.

Bulgur was a cereal made from dried wheat, usually durum wheat. The process of making bulgur simultaneously preserved the wheat and precooked it, making it into a sort of instant cereal. Women generally made bulgur once a year, after the wheat harvest. This was often something of a festive event in medieval towns. The women of a town would go out to a special mill in the countryside with many sacks of wheat and would boil the kernels until they were swollen. They would then spread them in the sun to dry, often using flat rooftops for this purpose. Once the kernels were dry, they would grind them in the mill. They would then use a series of sieves to separate the bulgur by grain size. They would use the larger grains in soups and pilafs and the smaller grains for stuffing vegetables and in salads. Properly prepared bulgur would keep for months and made a very convenient foodstuff that could be stored easily in a dry location and also carried on trips.

Couscous was another type of dried wheat cereal. It was the staple foodstuff in much of North Africa starting around the 11th or 12th century. By the 13th century it was known throughout the Mediterranean region and in the Levant. Couscous usually was made with durum wheat, though it could also be made from millet or barley. Ground durum wheat, or semolina, does not keep well in warm weather, quickly growing moldy or attracting weevils, so people had to come up with a method of preserving it. Like bulgur, couscous was made once a year in a big event after the harvest. The women of the town would first grind their semolina into coarse flour. They would then wet the flour and use their hands to roll it into tiny balls. They would place these balls in the sun to dry. Couscous could keep for several months and ideally would last until the next harvest. To eat it, people would steam it and serve it with a stew of vegetables and meat.

The Bedouin and other desert dwellers of Arabia and North Africa looked for food that was easy to carry and readily preserved and that would stay edible in a wide range of temperatures, from below freezing to well over 100 degrees Fahrenheit. Bedouins often carried with them a type of dried ready-made food called *ba-theeth*. This consisted of chopped dried dates, parched flour, and a type of clarified butter called *samn*, mixed together and pressed into lumps or bars. *Ba-theeth* could be eaten without additional cooking, rather like a modern granola bar.

Goats and sheep were common throughout much of the Islamic world, and people devised several ways of preserving their milk. Yogurt was one of the first methods devised for keeping milk from spoiling. The fermentation process that produced yogurt consumed natural sugars in the milk and increased its acidity, which prevented undesirable bacteria from growing and making people sick. Although the earliest yogurts were probably made accidentally, by the medieval period yogurt was largely a household staple. To make yogurt, the cook would heat fresh milk and mix it with some existing yogurt, which contained the bacteria needed to ferment the milk. The bacteria would make the milk thicken and turn sour.

Milk could be made to last even longer by salting and drying. Many people made dried yogurt lumps that were good travel rations. The cook would drain the yogurt by placing it in a cloth and hanging it to let the excess water drain out. She would then salt it and place dabs of it on a cloth in the sun. These lumps would dry rock hard and keep for a long time. They could be reconstituted in water or eaten dry. People made a similar food called *kishk* or *trahana*, which was made with a mixture of yogurt and grain such as bulgur or wheat flour and salt, formed into lumps and allowed to dry.

People also made milk into cheese. They could use either rennet or the whey from existing cheese to make the milk form into curds. A cook would mix the milk with the rennet or whey and heat it, which would cause the milk to separate into liquid whey and solid curds. She could collect the curds and use a weight to press out excess liquid. To store the cheese, she would place the solid cheese into a jar, pour salted whey over it, and seal it to keep air out. This cheese would keep for several weeks.

Butter would not keep in the hot climate, so people made *samn*. To make *samn*, people would churn fresh milk into butter by agitating it. The Bedouin accomplished this by putting the sour milk into a goatskin bag and blowing into it. The resulting butter would be heated with flour and spices such as cumin and coriander. The solid part of the butter would sink to the bottom of the pot, and the cook would skim off the clarified liquid fat with a spoon so as not to mix it with the solids. The *samn* would be placed in a storage container, such as an earthenware jar or a goatskin bag. *Samn* could be stored for months if the container was airtight. *Samn* production was often a winter activity, done while herds were not on the move.

Olives were a staple food throughout much of the Islamic area. To preserve olives, people would soak them in plain water for several days, weighting them down to keep them submerged. They would then drain the olives, place them in an earthenware or glass jar, pour saltwater over them, add flavorings such as garlic if desired, and seal the jars. After sitting in their brine for a few weeks, the olives would be ready to eat. They would keep for several months. It was not unusual for the surface of the olives and brine to develop a coating of mold, but this was not considered cause for concern as long as the olives below the surface had not rotted.

Olive oil was also extremely important. Most olives, in fact, were turned into olive oil and were not eaten whole. To make olive oil, people crushed olives in a mill and then pressed them in an olive press, which pushed out the oil. The olive oil was stored in earthenware or glass jars and would keep for many months.

See also AGRICULTURE; ARCHITECTURE; BUILDING TECHNIQUES AND MATERIALS; CITIES; CLIMATE AND GEOGRAPHY; CRAFTS; ECONOMY; FESTIVALS; FOOD AND DIET; GENDER STRUCTURES AND ROLES; HOUSEHOLD GOODS; HUNTING, FISHING, AND GATHERING; NATURAL DISASTERS; OCCUPATIONS; SACRED SITES; SEAFARING AND NAVIGATION; TRADE AND EXCHANGE.

FURTHER READING

Nell Du Vall, *Domestic Technology: A Chronology of Developments* (Boston, Mass.: G. K. Hall, 1988).

Richard D. Fisher, "Long-term Corn Storage." In *Paquimé: The Anasazi Rosetta Stone.* Available online. URL: http://www.canyonsworldwide.com/fisher/cornStorage.htm. Downloaded on December 7, 2007.

Frances Gies and Joseph Gies, *Cathedral, Forge, and Waterwheel: Technology in the Middle Ages* (New York: HarperCollins, 1995).

Ann Hagen, *Anglo-Saxon Food and Drink: Production, Processing, Distribution and Consumption* (Hockwold cum Wilton, Norfolk, England: Anglo-Saxon Books, 2006).

Kate Melville, Rusty Rockets, and Richard Taylor, "Pre-Columbian Fish Farm." Available online. URL: http://www.scienceagogo.com/news/20001008173027data_trunc_sys.shtml. Downloaded on December 7, 2007.

D. P. S. Peacock and D. F. Williams, *Amphorae and the Roman Economy: An Introductory Guide* (London: Longman, 1986).

Dorie Reents-Budet and Ronald Bishop, "What Can We Learn from a Maya Vase?" *Archeology* 56, no. 2 (2003). Available online. URL: http://www.archaeology.org/0303/abstracts/mayavase.html. Downloaded on December 7, 2007.

Paula Wolfert, *Mediterranean Grains and Greens* (New York: Harper Collins, 1998).

► textiles and needlework

INTRODUCTION

For the study of the lives of people in medieval times, textiles can be more valuable than gold. Gold work is flashy and often shows the best craftsmanship a society had to offer, and it can also reveal something of the wealth of a society. But textiles speak not only to what was valuable but to what was ordinary as well. Textiles decay, usually more quickly even than wood, so when even a fragment of a medieval rug, blanket, or other textile is discovered, archaeologists and historians react with excitement and treat it carefully, because even the fibers can speak to them about who used the textile, where it came from, and why it was made.

Textiles were made from threads. The threads were made from animal hair or plant fibers. One of the fundamental curiosities of medieval cultures is that people in both the Old World and the New World figured out how to spin cotton into fibers, how to turn those fibers into threads, and how to make those threads into textiles. Also curious is that someone worked out in ancient China how to take caterpillar cocoons and turn them into the most coveted thread of the ancient and medieval worlds. Governments of the Western world eagerly sought to learn the secrets of making silk; when they did, they invested much money and resources into mastering both the production of silk and the manufacturing of silk cloth. Although silk was highly desirable for clothing and cotton could be made into light, comfortable cloth, neither

material was always preferable for all purposes, instead often serving for embroidery of textiles made of tougher stuff.

For instance, rugs could be made for decoration, but for everyday use not even monarchs could afford to replace frequently ones made entirely of silk. For most rugs, animal hairs were the stuff of tough threads able to withstand frequent treading of feet. Wool from sheep or alpacas and hair from goats, horses, or llamas were woven together to create sturdy textiles. Even so, such tough textiles, when used as rugs, were valuable enough to occasion the special custom of always removing one's footwear when entering a home, extending the life of rugs in the home.

In the creation of textiles out of threads there were two fundamental techniques: knotting and weaving. In each case medieval textile makers used warp and weft to form their textiles. The warp consisted of threads that formed the muscle of a fabric; it would provide the strength of a textile and therefore was usually made of dense, tough threads. The weft was made up of threads woven into the warp at a right angle. The weft usually gave a textile its color and designs; some medieval cultures strove to make the warp invisible, easier to do with knotting than weaving. Knotting had variations, but its essence was the tying in a knot of weft thread around individual warp threads. This required the intense use of hands and great patience from the textile maker. Weaving used looms, which came in many shapes and sizes. Another of the curiosities of textiles is that looms were invented in different parts of the world seemingly independently of one another. Nomadic peoples tended to use looms made of light wooden frames that could be easily taken apart and carried. Settled peoples tended to use looms made of heavy wood—sturdy devices intended to endure a great deal of use.

Given the amount of labor that went into textiles, they were likely to reflect the needs of their makers. As the medieval world created cash economies, one need was to earn money. This resulted in textiles made to appeal to potential buyers, and the creation of appealing designs and colors became a matter of intense competition in the marketplaces of the medieval world. The frequent use of Arabic script in the textiles of the Islamic world speaks of a buying public interested in the written word; in East Asia the common depiction of dragons and other exotic creatures tells of buyers' interest in mystical symbolism. Many textiles were made not for sale but for family use. In many medieval cultures, looms were a common part of the everyday lives of ordinary people and were used to make fabric for clothing, curtains, pillows, beds, rugs, caps, gloves, and other everyday artifacts. Through these artifacts, people of our time can make an emotional connection to the people of the past, for they speak of the weavers' loved ones, the weavers' sense of duty, and the weavers' disciplined imagination, which created colors and images to be seen and enjoyed each day.

AFRICA

BY MICHAEL J. O'NEAL

The chief problem historians and archaeologists have in studying textiles and sewing from medieval Africa is that the materials involved in textile production do not survive the passage of long periods of time. This applies both to the fabrics and clothing produced and to the means of producing them. Cloth fabrics produced hundreds of years ago could not survive the climate, nor could the wooden looms used to weave cloth or the wooden spindles used to make thread.

Some evidence of weaving and embroidery survive from the kingdom of Meroë in Sudan. Other bits of fabric have been found in the modern-day Republic of Niger, dating from about the second half of the eighth century. Most of the surviving fabrics, though, were produced late in the medieval period and beyond. The earliest archaeological remains are exceptions, so historians have to rely primarily on artwork that depicts the kinds of cloth and dress people wore. They also look at written records, but even written records are unreliable, for many were compiled by Middle Eastern and European explorers based on personal observations that vary widely. In many cases historians have to extrapolate backward from modern hand-weaving practices that are hundreds of years old.

Another factor complicating the issue of weaving and sewing in sub-Saharan Africa is that many woven goods, along with weaving technologies, were imported into the region along extensive trade routes. Many of these goods and the technologies that produced them came from Islamic countries to the north and from the Middle East. Islam played a major role in the production and trading of fabrics with sub-Saharan Africa because of Islamic rules regarding personal modesty and the need to cover the body.

These goods became prestige goods and hence were worn by members of elite classes. However, among the social elites, lack of personal adornment was regarded as a sign of carelessness, a signal that the person was unable to fulfill his or her obligations to those lower in the social order. Members of lower classes had to make do with locally produced cloths and fabrics. Nevertheless, fabrics and items made from fabric were important trade goods because they were useful and easy to transport. Also traded were materials such as plants that were the source of dyes. Examples include saffron, safflower, and various types of woods.

To understand the nature of medieval weaving in Africa, it is necessary to understand a few basic weaving terms. Weaving is done on a frame that interlaces the threads of a piece of fabric. One set of threads, called the warp, is fixed to the frame. The other set, called the weft, is interwoven over and under the threads of the warp. For the process to work, a gap has to be produced between the alternate strings of the warp. This is done by string loops around every other thread. This set of string loops is called a heddle. When only a single set of alternate warps is attached to a heddle, the loom is called a single-headed loom. When two sets are attached, the loom is said to be double-headed. Many textile historians classify medieval African cultures according to whether they used single- or double-headed looms.

Additionally, the weaver can produce different types of cloth depending on the relationship between the warp and the weft. The simplest type of fabric is the plain weave, consisting of single strands, one warp and one weft, similar to a simple potholder. A basket weave is made with pairs of threads, and various types of patterning and "brocade" can be made by changing the proportions of threads in the warp and weft. In some instances African weavers were able to produce cloth that gave the appearance of virtually no warp, giving the fabric a sense of extreme delicacy.

Other forms of classification are used as well, and generally, one scheme of classification does not exclude others. For example, historians note whether a culture relied on horizontal "ground looms" or upright looms used primarily to produce raffia, a type of cloth made from the raffia palm, primarily in rain forest regions. Some historians believe that both of these

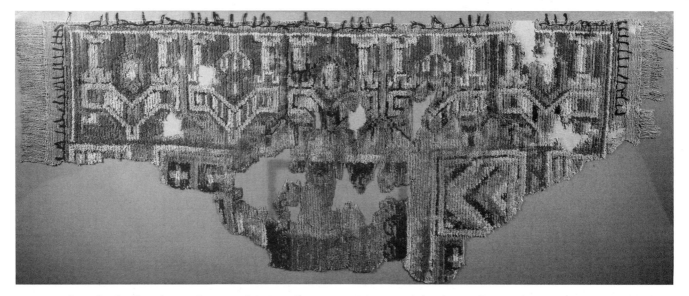

Fragment of a multicolored woolen rug from a tomb at Qasr Ibrim, Egypt, Coptic Period, fourth to sixth centuries (© The Trustees of the British Museum)

variants originated somewhere in the Nigeria/Cameroon area. The chief evidence supporting this view is fragments of cloth from these regions that date to the ninth century.

Another scheme of classification is whether the loom produces narrow strips of cloth or wider ones. Historians have found evidence of both types in Sierra Leone, which may have been where the oldest narrow-strip looms originated. In burial caves in Mali, along the Bandiagara cliffs, archaeologists have found bits of cloth dating to the 11th century, the oldest cloths produced by a narrow-strip loom. An example of the use of written records to shed light on the history of African weaving is the work of al-Bakri, an Arab traveler who recorded his observations. He wrote that he watched a narrow-strip loom being used in the town of Silla, in Mauretania, in 1068.

The labor of weaving and sewing was often divided by gender. For example, it is likely that most of the weaving on double-headed looms was done by men. Additionally, men in East Africa did the work using what is called a pit loom, or a loom positioned over a pit dug into the ground, giving the operator a place to put his legs (rather than having to lean over the loom). In contrast, women were more likely to operate upright looms in such places as Nigeria and Cameroon, though in these regions raffia and ground looms were operated by men.

The jobs of spinning and weaving also were allocated by gender. Typically, in such places as Sierra Leone, women did most of the spinning of thread, typically with handheld spindles. These spindles throughout western Africa consisted of a thick stick with a baked clay whorl at the lower end. The

whorl was a round or trapezoid-shaped section that served as a kind of pulley. The spinner then gathered a cluster of fibers and drew them out, twisting them into yarn as they pulled. Depending on the use to which the yarn and any fabric made from it would be put, the spinner pulled the fibers more or less tight, creating a yarn that was more or less dense. Women, as spinners, were often thought of as the "owner" of the project, and they hired others to turn the thread into woven cloth. That said, in some cases weavers, usually men, purchased thread from women; often their own wives and daughters worked as spinners. The weaver, then, was regarded as the owner of the project.

Weaving was related to the social structure of the culture. In such places as Mali weaving was an occupation that was practiced by a member of a hereditary caste, or social class. In this respect, weaving was analogous to pottery making or blacksmithing. Weaving was thought to bring the weaver into contact with the spiritual world. Very often, weavers were, in effect, slaves of noble families. In other cultures, though, weaving occupied no particular social niche; it was regarded as simply an occupation one followed, although many people became spinners, weavers, dyers, and sewers because they were members of a family that had traditionally practiced the trade. Typically, in a family compound, all boys would be taught the arts of weaving, while all girls would be taught to spin, dye, and sew. All of these activities would take place under the watchful eye of a master, who supervised younger, less experienced workers.

The earliest fabrics sub-Saharan Africans used were made of tree bark. The bark of certain types of trees was carefully removed, and then an inner layer was pounded with a mallet to make it more flexible, softer, and wider. Later, softer materials, such as raffia, were found, and later still, cotton was the fabric of choice. Not all fabrics were made as a result of the spinning and weaving processes. In some cases, fibers were twisted together into heavier threads by hand, and these threads were woven and plaited into fabrics that could be used as cloths and to make clothing. Articles of clothing commonly manufactured included hats and lengths of cloth wrapped around the body. A typical method of manufacture was to produce squares of cloth that were then sewn together into larger pieces. The cloth could have an infinite range of characteristics, depending on the nature and color of the pieces being assembled.

Many fabrics were not extensively dyed, for medieval Africans lacked binding chemicals that made the dye stick. Nevertheless, indigo was used to produced shades of blue, particularly among the Yoruba, who repeatedly dyed fabrics in a compound that contained high concentrations of the active ingredient in indigo (indigotin) and then beat the fabric until it virtually glowed with a coppery color. In the Congo threads were blackened and used for embroidery on raffia cloth, which was beige. Additionally, a wild silk was used to produce a silvery-beige fabric. Among the Mali iron-rich mud was used to print dark designs on natural cotton fabric.

Medieval Africans also used a technique called resist dyeing, meaning that the fabric was dipped in a dye but the parts the dyer did not want tinted were somehow blocked off to prevent the dye from reaching them. One such technique, similar to modern tie-dye, was called *plangi* and consisted of tying the cloth. Another, similar to modern batik, was to paint the fabric with a dye-resistant substance. One example is a starch paste made with cassava flour. Dyeing was typically regarded as a female activity.

THE AMERICAS

BY JULIA MARTA CLAPP

Textiles are particularly difficult to trace throughout the pre-Columbian history of the Americas because the medium is so perishable. This is compounded by the fact that many regions of the Americas have damp climates, which accelerate deterioration. The greatest knowledge about textiles of the Americas comes from regions that are dry, like much of the Andean region of South America.

The importance of textile production to South American artistic traditions cannot be overstated. From the Moche civilization (ca. 100–700) archaeologists have found fabric woven in cotton and wool (from llama and alpaca). These samples are few, but they are a testament to skillful Moche craftsmanship.

The tapestries were woven with a back-strap loom. Although the colorful and geometrically patterned Moche tapestries may appear abstract, their designs represent specific figures, such as warriors or mythological scenes. The Moche buried textiles and other items of value, such as jewelry and pottery, with elite citizens.

The Wari civilization (ca. 600–1000) flourished during the Middle Horizon period. The Wari, like many South Americans before and after them, tended to weave tapestry in lieu of creating monumental sculpture. Tapestry is created by weaving dyed threads through undyed threads, forming a pattern. The designs that weavers skillfully incorporated into their tapestries are colorful and also appear quite abstract, as did the tapestries of the Moche. The images are not meaningless, however; rather, they are representations of deities or supernatural beings (but never humans). These images are simplified to the extent that it is difficult for us to "read" them.

As in the later Inca period, the culture's government strictly regulated the production of textiles; it is likely that designs were standardized and monitored, though weavers did have a significant degree of artistic license as well. Most important, however, was the importance of textiles for establishing and maintaining political control. It was also a way of demonstrating prosperity: the nearly unimaginable quantities of thread required for the finest Andean weaving indicated the wealth of the ruler who commissioned a given textile. The most common figure depicted in Middle Horizon tapestry is the staff god, a part human, part bird supernatural being who has wings and holds a staff. This figure also appeared on monumental architecture of the period, so he was undoubtedly a central figure in religion or myth.

During the Inca period (ca. 1450–1530s) textiles were used in trade and were socially and culturally important. The Inca were notoriously adept at organizing labor, and textiles were produced in great quantities for the benefit of the empire. When the Spanish arrived in South America in 1533, they were astonished to discover warehouses full of surplus textile goods. Because the Inca Empire was spread over widely varying terrain, from the Andean highlands to the coast, weavers used different materials depending on their location. In the highlands they created thread out of the wool of vicuña, llama, and alpaca. On the coast they used cotton.

Inca textiles had varying degrees of roughness and smoothness. Rougher weaves were used as carpet. A second type of weave formed everyday clothing. Finally, a very fine and soft weave called *cumbi* was used for tapestry and the clothes of elites. *Cumbi* cloth was extremely valuable, and the women who wove the finest of it were sequestered and had been trained since childhood in its production. Occasionally, feathers from tropical birds such as the macaw, parrot, and

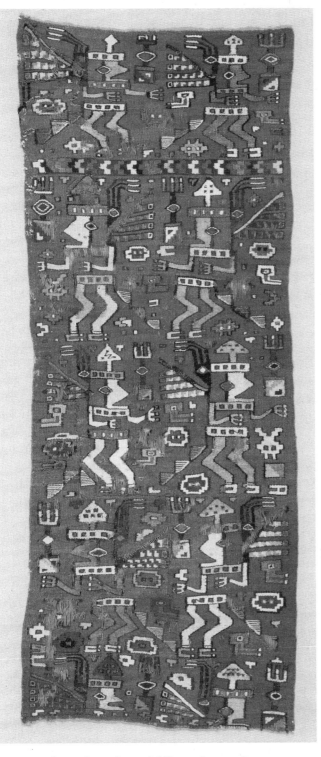

Fragment of a textile panel, camelid fiber and cotton, Peru, ca. 600–850 (Los Angeles County Museum of Art, The Phil Berg Collection, Photograph © 2006 Museum Associates/LACMA [M.71.73.242])

flamingo were attached to *cumbi*. This yielded a fine, vibrant, and soft surface that was a true testament to the skillful weaving and feather working in the Americas at this time. It is

only by virtue of the very dry climate that such delicate pieces have survived over the centuries.

The designs that weavers incorporated into textiles during this later period were also overwhelmingly abstract, often geometric patterns. This reflected a shift from earlier eras, in which ancient South Americans tended to depict various gods and other important figures. In the Inca period designs were extraordinarily complex. In order to create a tapestry or tunic with an intricate pattern, the weaver would have to possess both creative and mathematical facility in order to plan scrupulously in advance. Sometimes a certain pattern would require that the piece be woven sideways or upside down, necessitating even greater proficiency.

In the ancient Andes the arrangement of textiles on the body was performed thoughtfully and held social significance. In other words, Andeans did not drape textiles in the offhand manner in which we might absentmindedly put on a pair of jeans today. Tunics were woven so that certain patterns would be accentuated and sometimes so that the underside of a garment was as finely finished as the front.

It is probable that textiles were a major part of production in Teotihuacán (ca. 1–ca. 650), but they—like other perishable items, such as those made of wood—have not survived. The same is overwhelmingly true of the Maya, though tapestries do appear in Mayan art, giving us at least a glimpse of the skill with which they produced textiles. Weaving was performed by women of varying social statuses, though the materials used would have been commensurate with a woman's position in society. Like many pre-Columbian Americans, they wove on a back-strap loom. Mayan women also made patterns from batik (fabric with designs made through a wax-coating process), tie-dye (fabrics with designs produced through tying part of the material so as not to absorb dye) and embroidery.

Archaeological excavations in the former Aztec Empire (ca. 1300–1500s) in central Mexico have not yielded the fruitful remains that work in the Andes has. Modern-day Mexico City is the site of the former Aztec capital, Tenochtitlan, and its primary temple, the Templo Mayor, which was rediscovered in the 1970s. Excavations from the Templo Mayor have yielded some textiles, and one bundle, in particular, was believed to be part of a priests' wardrobe. Nevertheless, we know from manuscript depictions of the Aztec that elites and warriors were clothed as sumptuously as pre-Columbian South Americans. The Aztec used textiles as currency in economic exchange, as did the Andeans. In the Aztec Empire provinces were required to pay enormous quantities of tribute to the ruling city's leaders in Tenochtitlán; fabric was a major part of this system of taxation and political control. Weaving was the work of Aztec women, particularly commoners.

In the Mississippian era in North America (ca. 750–ca. 1500) native peoples inhabited the eastern portion of the United States. Like other civilizations before them, such as the Adena (ca. 1000 B.C.E.–200 C.E.) and Hopewell (c. 200 B.C.E.–400 C.E.), they were mound builders: They made large hills out of the earth in varying shapes and sizes. These hills had varying functions (often ceremonial); in the case of the Mississippians, many served as burials. From this period archaeologists have found fragments of cloth, such as one from the Craig Mound at a site called Spiro (located in Oklahoma). The fragment, probably from the 13th or 14th century, is a very small piece relative to contemporary examples that have been better preserved in other regions of the Americas. It is too small to be able to interpret, but some scholars believe that it depicts the wings of a bird or someone dressed ceremonially in a bird costume.

We have limited information about Caribbean textile production. We do know that, as in the rest of the Americas, the Taíno (inhabitants of the Caribbean islands between about 1200 and 1500) wove clothing for garments, a task that probably belonged to the women of the society. In addition, a noteworthy and relatively unique aspect of their creative production included woven fibers that were incorporated into art objects. While it is surmised that other pre-Columbian Americans adorned molded or carved figurines with cloth, feathers, human hair, shells, stones, or other materials, often they have been lost or destroyed over the course of time. One *zemi* (a ritualistic object thought to have magical powers) from the Dominican Republic is formed of shell and human bones as well as cotton. The cotton has been fashioned into a material by a means of braiding, and into this bundle is stuffed various materials. The result resembles a doll-like idol.

ASIA AND THE PACIFIC

by Kenneth Hall

Many medieval era Asians and Pacific islanders wore high-quality indigenous textiles made of inner tree and shrub fibers (bast). Bark cloth and other early textiles were made exclusively by women, who cleaned and spun the threads and wove the patterns. Quality local textiles resulted from beating tree bark that had previously been soaked in water until it was soft, with the resulting threads woven into garments. Bark cloth for everyday use was plain or very simply decorated with dyed or painted geometric symbols or stylized depictions of humans or animals. Among tribal groups bark cloth was used in numerous rites of passage: birth, circumcision, tooth filing, tattooing, marriage, and death. Tattooing was a symbolic complement to the minimal coverage afforded by bark cloth. Since bark cloth had to be removed lest it disintegrate in the rain, tattooing was a continuous means of protecting a man (or a woman) from supernatural harm.

Southeast Asian textile weavers initially incorporated magical Indian religious symbols into their bark cloth production and, by the late 15th century, began to duplicate the images of the more durable imported Indian cotton cloth. Silk was generally less popular in island Southeast Asia, although mulberry trees and silk worms were indigenous. By contrast, on mainland Southeast Asia, Burmese and Thai used locally produced silks and cottons. Only in Vietnam, because of its substantial China connection, was silk widely produced, using advanced and meticulous technology similar to that of China, Korea, and Japan.

By the 12th century Southeast Asian and Indian ports were importing Chinese silk for court consumption. In the 15th century India-based merchants were also trading their own silk and cotton cloth for Southeast Asian spices. In this first mass market Indian cotton textiles became the commodity of exchange most demanded by pepper growers and spice collectors. There were technical reasons for the success. The spread of Islam into India in the 14th century introduced carding bows and spinning wheels, which made cotton production more efficient. With this new technology Indian weavers were able to offer greater variety in pattern, color, texture, and size. Southeast Asia did not have to import cotton. Regions with a sufficient dry season, such as eastern Java, central Sumatra, Bali, Lombok, southern Sulawesi, Sumbawa, Luzon, Cebu, and Cambodia, produced and sold raw cotton, which was cultivated alongside wet-rice fields. From the 13th century on some Southeast Asian cotton yarn and cloth was even taken back to China by returning traders from ports in Java, Luzon, and Vietnam.

Making Javanese batik cloth involved the application of wax in designs to prevent dyes from penetrating the protected portions of a cloth. After the wax was removed from the dyed fabric, the pattern created by the wax was apparent. Among the favored designs were floral and symbolic symbols of plants, animals, pavilions, and mountains that replaced previous realistic depictions of humans and animals. Tie-dyeing, where cloth was wrapped, tied, or stitched together before dying so that the bound areas did not absorb dyes, was another local innovation.

Indian *patola* cotton cloth from Gujarat became the market standard by the 15th century. Because of Indian mastery of permanent dyes, these were more brightly colored than local cloth and came in wider widths. Owing to market competition for Indian, Chinese, and local cloth, local populations could dictate their market preferences for colors and designs. Commonly, the base colors were the colors of life itself: brown of the earth, blue of the heavens, and white of the air.

The 13th-century Italian traveler Marco Polo was fascinated with the embroidery designs he observed on Asian carpets, robes, wall hangings, pillows, curtains, and table covers. While evidence of Chinese embroidery dates to the third century B.C.E., the use of embroidery reached its peak in the era of the Tang Dynasty (618–907). Chinese embroidery was influenced by China's silk culture, which made available high-quality threads and fabrics to artisans who adorned garments and other items with flowers, birds, bold flowing lines, and abstract motifs. Among the most exquisite embroideries were those on the Chinese emperors' and bureaucrats' robes, which were lavishly decorated with traditional motifs on a dark silk background, the color and embroidery of which distinguished the individual's rank. China's styles of embroidery set the standard for others. Its embroidery especially inspired Japan's artisans, who also decorated colored silks with long soft stitches of untwisted silk threads, as demonstrated in the embroidery of women's kimonos in the late medieval era.

Yue embroidery, often called Cantonese embroidery because it originated in the southern regions of China, became popular in the era of the Tang Dynasty. This style is known for its complicated variety of visual accents using silk or cotton threads that draw attention to a central subject. It is smooth embroidery on silk or cotton, with little of the three-dimensional texturing found in other styles. Commonly, Yue embroidery featured several objects or animals, such as birds and dragons. Early Yue artisans used twisted pieces of peacock feathers as their thread, to produce accents and to blend separate objects together. Yue artisans also used course thread derived from the tail of a horse to stitch outlines that accentuated the patterns, colors, and objects of the main design.

Xiang embroidery, which had its origin in the earliest embroidery tradition of China's Hunan Province, used loose threads and rich colors on transparent chiffon silk. The silk threads were dyed and then soaked in water containing oil to make the thread soft. Stitching was seemingly random and uneven but produced colors and textures that were effectively mixed. Animals, people, and landscapes were brought alive by the colors and three-dimensional effect created by thick knots and stitching. The most famous examples of Xiang embroidery used tigers as their subject. Xiang embroidery was usually two-sided, with different patterns or images on each side of the transparent chiffon.

Shu (Shuzhou) embroidery, which developed in Sichuan Province, became prominent in the Song Dynasty (960–1279). Shu embroidery is characterized by its very detailed silk thread depictions of a variety of subjects on silk and satin cloth, although panda bears and fish (especially carp) were favorites. Some Shu pieces were two-sided, in this case repeat-

Tapestry: fruit trees and hollyhocks, China, Ming Dynasty, 1368–1644 (Freer Gallery of Art, Smithsonian Institution, Gift of Charles Lang Freer, F1916-542)

ing the same pictured embroidery on both sides. The stitching was done with fine silk threads that were almost impossible to see. Repetitive stitching resulted in very dense embroideries. Shu embroidery was so detailed and intricate that it was often considered artwork and was prominently displayed. It also was used to produce embroidered silk maps, wall hangings, screens that separated rooms, and curtains.

So-called Oriental carpets were produced in medieval-era China, Egypt, India, and Persia (now Iran). The Chinese carpet had its origin among the seminomadic populations of China's northwest Xinjiang steppe region. Drawing on the common practice among central Asian tribal populations, traditional Chinese carpets were made of wool or goat and camel hair. Later Chinese carpet weavers frequently used silk to add distinctive colors as the light source changed. Since silk threads were also cool to the touch, Chinese carpets were often thought to be "magic carpets."

Chinese carpet designs were largely symbolic rather than decorative and used colors that were considered to be both elegant and in good taste, such as black, blue, red, white, beige, and yellow. Red indicated great joy and happiness, yellow symbolized royalty and longevity, white represented mourning and death, blue meant immortality, and black and beige conveyed the sense of solitude. Chinese carpets were initially small wool temple floor mats, prayer rugs, and wall hangings that were feltlike in texture and which held Daoist and Buddhist sacred symbols, such as the swastika and the yin and yang motif.

During the medieval era the manufacture of wool pile carpets spread from its original Silk Road roots, as regional styles developed among carpet-weaving centers in northern China. In common with the earliest ritual use of carpets, medieval-era Chinese carpets displayed designs that had precise meanings and were not meant to be primarily decorative. Among these designs were three script characters that represented long life, luck, and wedded bliss, which were contained in central medallions. Animals and objects each also had symbolic meaning, as in the case of the dragon, the symbol of a powerful deity, the sovereignty of the forces of nature, and the emblem of the emperor. The bat was popular, since the word bat (*fu*) was the same as that of the script symbol for good fortune. Other common depictions included the phoenix, elephants, and horses. The chrysanthemum, a symbol of longevity, and the peony, the symbol of nobility, wealth, and affection, were favored flowers.

Indian carpets, which became popular in the post-1000 era, mimicked the symbolism of their Iranian neighbors. Small floral designs, such as plants, rosettes, and leaves, were repeated over the carpet surface. Border motifs were similar to the featured designs. Maroon was a favored color, as were light and dark green and burnt orange.

EUROPE

by Jean Shepherd Hamm

After gaining significance as early as 1000, the manufacture of textiles during the Middle Ages gave rise to Europe's first major industrial development. Fabric had long been crafted by individuals to make their own clothing and to sell in local markets. In their manors lords and ladies appropriated the best raw materials and weavers for their own fine garments. However, not all textiles used in a region were indigenous products. Even during the Middle Ages trade ships carried textiles from one country to another so that woolen, linen,

silk, and hemp fabrics could be found almost anywhere on the continent.

With the expansion of trade routes to the East and the development of new shipping lanes through European waters, the demand for textiles increased. Nobles not only willingly paid for fine fabrics for garments but also began to decorate their homes with textiles. Woven rugs and tapestries adorned manor houses and castles and helped make them warmer by closing off chilly drafts. The production and trade of textiles in all forms contributed significantly to the economy of medieval Europe by providing a livelihood for individuals at all levels of society. In 1297, during a dispute with Edward II (r. 1307–27), English barons purported that one-half the country's wealth was in its wool. Although this proportion was exaggerated, wool exports represented a major part of England's economy. The Italian Medici family's rise to prominence began with the textile trade. They purchased raw wool and sold it to spinners. Then they purchased thread from the spinners to sell to the weavers and bought fabric from weavers to sell throughout the world. In Germany the Fugger family followed much the same route to wealth with the production of linen from flax.

Certain regions of Europe became known for the quality of their raw products or textiles. For example, English wool generally garnered the highest prices because of its superiority; however, prior to the Hundred Years' War (1337–1453) most of the wool was exported to Flanders for weaving into fabric. The woolen cloth produced in Flanders was then the most desired. Cloth manufacturing did not become a major industry in England until the 14th century. Although the population of Europe decreased dramatically as a result of the Black Death, rising wealth increased demand for textile products and led the industry to seek better production methods.

Spinning, weaving, embroidering, knitting, and other textile-related labors provided women with one of the few occupations considered suitable for them. These textile arts began in homes as women prepared clothing for their own families. When it became profitable to trade in textiles, men entered into the manufacture of textile products at all levels. Male weavers formed guilds in towns and villages, worked with other related guilds, and gained control of the manufacture and distribution of textiles. Nevertheless, women were still employed as spinners, weavers, and seamstresses. Contemporary art depicts women at looms and spinning wheels, and several representations of the Madonna show her knitting or constructing garments. Geoffrey Chaucer's (ca. 1342–1400) 14th-century Wife of Bath, a weaver by trade, boasts that she made fine fabrics that "rivaled those of Ipres and of Gaunt (Ypres and Ghent)."

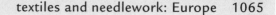

Ribbon, tablet-weave gold metal thread, Great Britain, ca. ninth century (Los Angeles County Museum of Art, Los Angeles County Fund, Photograph © 2006 Museum Associates/LACMA [55.57.1])

In the 13th century groups of women known as the Beguines formed. They lived in communal houses but were not nuns and were not under the authority of bishop or church. Many of the women were from middle- and lower-class families who could not afford the dowry required for becoming a nun. Many Beguines supported themselves by weaving.

Early weavers practiced their craft in small cottages on horizontal looms. Weaving had to be done from the sides of the loom and produced long, narrow pieces of fabric. With the development of the broad loom in the 13th century, yarn could be woven more quickly into fulled or felted "broadcloth." The increased speed of weaving created a demand for yarn to be spun more quickly. Wool, flax, and cotton were combed into yarn with the use of a distaff and a spindle. The raw material was wrapped around the distaff, and a thread was pulled from it and spun with the turn of the distaff and whorl. The carding of yarn, begun in the early 14th century, shortened the time for its production and yielded thread suitable for wefts. The introduction of the spinning wheel in the late 13th century also aided the manufacture of textiles by making it possible to spin greater quantities of thread. About 50 years later a foot treadle was added to the wheel, again speeding the process of spinning. Water-powered fulling mills also reduced the time and labor involved in textile production. By this time weaving had moved from primarily a cottage industry to a manufacturing concern that was controlled by guilds.

Usually, different guilds developed for the different steps in the manufacturing process: spinners, weavers, fullers, dyers, and wool merchants. In the late Middle Ages merchants gained more control over the process in what was known as the "putting out" system. Cloth sellers purchased wool from farmers and hired spinners, weavers, and dyers; then they sold the finished product. This system was the first step in what later became factory production of textiles by a single company.

Basic fabric could be altered by several methods, including adding other materials during the weaving process, dyeing before or after weaving, and adding needlework to the fabric or garment. Early weavers produced an amazing variety of fabric, from sheer silks to heavily felted woolens. They also experimented with combining materials to create diverse effects and patterns. Fustian fabric was created by combining linen and cotton threads. Substances as varied as horsehair and even metals, such as thin strands of silver and gold, were woven into some of Europe's finest textiles. Using yarns that were dyed prior to weaving could produce stripes, plaids, and wonderfully intricate patterns.

After the 13th century, and using artists' drawings for patterns, the most skilled weavers created complex tapestries depicting biblical, mythological, and hunting scenes. They used a technique known as weft-faced weaving, which hid the warp threads and allowed only the weft to show in the patterns. The resulting tapestry was not only decorative but also stronger and heavier. The seven Unicorn Tapestries (15th century), showing scenes of a group of nobles pursuing and capturing a unicorn, hang in the Metropolitan Museum of Art in New York. A similar series called the *Lady and the Unicorn* survives at the Musée de Cluny in Paris.

Fabric dyeing developed into an industry of its own, with its artisans carefully guarding their secrets for producing signature colors. As dyestuffs could be very rare and expensive, the colors added to yarn or fabric could significantly increase its price. Red, the most expensive dye, was derived from several sources, each yielding a different hue. Sumptuary laws, enacted in many areas, prohibited the lower classes from wearing certain garments or colors, particularly scarlets. These laws had little actual effect on what was worn, however, since few nonnoble individuals could afford the expensive fabrics they were denied by law.

Dyes were produced from both plant and animal substances. Purples were produced from mollusks belonging to the whelk family. Dyers also experimented with exposure to sunlight and different combinations of additives to the mollusk mucus to create a wide range of colors. Several small insects from the Coccidae family (shield lice, kermes, cochineals, and others) provided sought-after deep-red dyes and were actually cultivated for the textile industry. Indigo and the common woad plant provided dyers with shades of blue. Weld and saffron yielded tints of orange and yellow. Browns and greens could be obtained from several types of lichens. Various combinations of dyestuffs and more than one dye bath could be used to make a wide spectrum of other shades.

The term *scarlet*, which today describes a shade of red, originated not as a color but as an indication of the best grade of fabric produced. Wool merchants identified the softest and highest-quality raw wool to be sold for weaving into scarlets, longer and wider than other fabrics. Thus, medieval sources mention scarlets in various colors, including white scarlets. Modern usage derives from the fact that the expensive red dyes added more value, making red scarlets the most highly prized fabrics.

Knitting, crocheting, and lace making (tatting) were all popular in the Middle Ages. In addition, embroidery using all types of thread embellished the garments of clergy and nobility, and its extent and intricacy, as well as the base fabric, indicated one's relative wealth.

The best-known example of medieval textile art, the Bayeaux Tapestry, is not a tapestry at all but an embroidery piece. The tapestry is a piece of linen approximately 20 inches high and more than 230 feet long. Woolen embroidery creates more than 70 scenes that tell the story of the Norman Conquest of England in 1066. The narrative covers the time from the visit of King Harold III (r. 1045–66) to Normandy in 1064 to the death of Harold at the Battle of Hastings in October 1066. The last scene shows his troops fleeing. The end of the tapestry is missing, so it is impossible to tell whether there were more scenes in the original. Legends report that the embroidery was completed by Matilda (d. 1083), the wife of William the Conqueror (r. 1066–87), but there is no reliable evidence to support these assertions. Some historians suggest that Odo (ca. 1036–97), William's half brother and bishop at Bayeaux, commissioned the work. Still others believe that the work was embroidered in England. The Bayeaux Tapestry is housed in the former bishop's palace at Bayeaux and serves as a rich source of historical evidence of clothing, battle gear, ships, and other aspects of life in 11th-century Europe.

THE ISLAMIC WORLD
BY KIRK H. BEETZ

Studies of medieval Islamic textiles tend to focus on rugs and carpets, because many people throughout the world have a passion for the beauty of Islamic rugs and carpets. Much is known of Islamic textiles from about 1500 on, because this passion has fueled many studies of Islamic fabrics. Information for rugs and other textiles is thin for the period prior to 1500, because textiles are perishable, not only from environmental causes but because they were intended to be used by people and they wore out from use. In general, the hotter and drier the climate, the better chance for fragments of textiles to survive, although the oldest-known textile was saddle covering from a cold grave in central Asia. Part of its significance, apart from its beauty and the skill that was required to make it, is that it used a knotting technique that was later used in Islamic societies and is still used in Turkey today.

Rugs were very important from the beginning of the Islamic era. Rugs were useful to nomadic Arabs because they could be carried on pack animals, and they were also used for praying. Thus, rugs often had niches in their designs that could be pointed toward Mecca when the rug was laid out in preparation for prayer. Medieval Islamic rug makers used two different techniques to manufacture their products: the knotting technique and the weaving technique. The knotting technique had the advantages of requiring only a little equipment that was easy to carry; moreover, it had the flexibility to be used almost anywhere by one person or several people. A drawback was that it required very painstaking work that was harsh on the maker's hands. A single rug could require several months of working long hours every day. In the first few centuries of the Islamic era the knotting technique was used primarily by nomads and was common among central

Asian and Iranian tribes. It was a production process almost completely controlled by women and often was a source of income for women, who were excluded from most commercial activities.

Important to understanding how medieval Islamic people made their textiles are the concepts of warp and weft. The warp consisted of the lengthwise, usually vertical, threads in textiles, and the weft were the threads that were interlaced crosswise, or horizontally, in the warp. The warp for rugs usually consisted of wool. Woolen thread or yarn was made with hand-twisted spinners that were dangled in the air from a hand; spinning wheels were rarely used. The two most important kinds of wool in the medieval Islamic world were from Persian sheep and merino sheep. Sheep were probably first domesticated in northern Iran, and the first use of wool in textiles most likely occurred in Iran. The yarn made from Persian sheep tended to be coarse; in central Asian Islamic societies, it was often mixed with the hair of goats, making for coarse but tough textiles. Merino sheep were bred in Spain, and during the second half of the medieval era their wool was the finest in the Islamic world and was favored for making fabrics for clothing, draperies, and the best rugs.

The weft was wool, cotton, or silk. Among Turkish societies wool tended to be used for the weft, but in much of the rest of the Islamic world cotton was preferred. Silk was reserved for special textiles, such as those intended to be rugs for caliphs or sultans. It was used primarily to give rugs a glistening appearance that was much desired during medieval times. In knotted rugs the weft was interlaced with the warp in one of two ways: the double loop and the single loop. With the double loop the weft had two loops per knot per thread of the warp, whereas the single loop dipped and rose once around each thread. Single-loop knotting was easier than double-loop knotting. In this process, it was helpful to have the upper ends of the warp thread weighted down or held together by someone. Both kinds of knotted rugs were usually laid out flat, and the maker moved along the rug as she made the weft. The single looping went much faster than double looping, and it resulted in flatter, smoother rugs. Double knotting resulted in a thicker, more durable pile.

A pile was the fabric that projected out at right angles to the warp and weft. Part of the manufacturing process for both kinds of knotted rugs was to lay out the finished product and use shears to even the pile and remove stray bits of thread. Although knotted rugs were usually manufactured inside or outside homes or inside or outside tents, sometimes factories were established in villages or cities, typically to mass-produce carpets; these workshops were often controlled by monarchs, because textiles such as rugs were a valuable

Tiraz textile fragment, silk tapestry weave on plain weave linen, Islamic Egypt, 12th century (Los Angeles County Museum of Art, Mr. and Mrs. Allan C. Balch Fund, Photograph © 2006 Museum Associates/ LACMA [M.55.12.11])

commodity for international trade. Double-knotted rugs predominated in northern areas of the Islamic world, and single-knotted ones prevailed elsewhere.

Woven textiles are likely to be more familiar to modern readers than knotted ones, because they more easily lend themselves to modern industrial manufacturing methods. In the medieval Islamic world looms were used to weave not only rugs and carpets but draperies, clothing, and blankets as well. There were two basic kinds of looms: the horizontal loom and the vertical loom. The horizontal loom is often called the nomadic loom because it was favored by nomads. The horizontal loom was fairly simple and light. As its name implies, it was laid out flat, usually on the ground. Its frame consisted of four pieces of wood that were easy to assemble and to take apart and bundle together. There were two long pieces that went the length of the warp and two somewhat shorter pieces that were set as crossbars through holes in the long pieces and set with pegs. These crosspieces limited the width of the product. Another bar was set through the warp threads, separating odd from even, and another bar was set across the frame with warp threads across it held tight to keep them taut for the weaver. Usually the weaver using a horizontal loom moved along the fabric as she interlaced her weft threads.

In the case of a vertical loom, the weaver almost always remained in place while the fabric was moved toward her. Vertical looms were favored in settled communities and in workhouses in cities. There were many variants of vertical looms. The simplest configuration had two large, heavy wooden posts set vertically in the ground. The main crossbars were also stout and tended to be rounded, with pegs at their ends that passed though holes in the posts. Both were intended to be turned during the manufacturing process. The bar that separated the odd and even warp threads tended to be left freely suspended amid the threads, although it could be fixed to the posts. The bar used to keep the warp threads taut tended to be in front of the weaver, where she could easily control it. The weaver would usually sit before the loom, passing the weft threads amid the warp threads. A common variation did not have the warp threads wound around the top crossbar, moving when the crossbar was turned, but instead had the threads stretched over the top crossbar, with the ends of the warp threads gathered in bundles and tied to weights. One process required an assistant, probably a child, to hold the upper ends of the warp threads.

By and large weavers did their own dyeing, using a variety of organic sources. In India a coveted red was created from crushed insects. Purple often came from crushed mollusk shells. Red dye derived from madder roots and henna, blue from indigo plants, and other colors from fruit skins, tree bark, and nut shells. Before being dyed, silk required a soapy process of cooking in water to strip it of its stickiness.

Two techniques were favored for weaving several colors together. One was the slit weave, and the other was dovetailing. Each was used to achieve different visual effects.

The slit weave has the colored weft thread interlaced only with the warp threads for its pattern, and the weft thread does not link with warp thread outside of its designated area. This method results in a slit or gap between warp threads where different weft colors meet. This technique was used for draperies, sheets, and light clothing. Slit weaves would not hold up well with heavy use. Dovetailing may have been the most common alternative to the slit weave. Where different fields of color met, the colored weft threads would each loop around the same warp thread that marked their boundaries. This worked well for heavy clothing and rugs. In general, slit weaving would have been favored for silken textiles in which sharp images or patterns would be required.

When a fabric was fully woven, its edges would be stitched together or tied in decorative knots. Rugs were often laid out in the sun to set their dyes and to fade colors that were too bright. Other textiles might be stiff when removed from the loom and were handed over to fullers, who would process the fabrics to soften them. Plain white and plain black cloth frequently was favored, and white cloth would sometimes be left out in the sun to bleach it whiter.

Not much is known about medieval Islamic needlework, such as embroidery. In general, needlework on textiles seems to have been favored in India and the western Near East. In the 700s metalsmiths in Syria began producing very finely pointed needles that enabled people to stitch silk and fine cotton threads into detailed patterns in fabrics. Silk tended to be reserved for fine garments or coverings for special objects. In general, the use of silk in men's clothing was frowned upon, perhaps because it seemed feminine. Little needlework from medieval Islamic societies survives, so historians typically have to rely on depictions of textiles in paintings and illustrations. Some lace fabric has survived. Most needlework seems to have been done by women at home for textiles to be used by family members. Needlework in clothing, curtains, and covering cloths for sale may have been done in shops by men rather than women in Iran and the regions of modern-day Pakistan and Afghanistan.

See also ALCHEMY AND MAGIC; ADORNMENT; ARCHITECTURE; ART; CLIMATE AND GEOGRAPHY; CLOTHING AND FOOTWEAR; CRAFTS; DEATH AND BURIAL PRACTICES; ECONOMY; EMPLOYMENT AND LABOR; FAMILY; GENDER STRUCTURES AND ROLES; HOUSEHOLD GOODS; INVENTIONS; OCCUPATIONS; RELIGION AND COSMOLOGY; SOCIAL ORGANIZATION; TRADE AND EXCHANGE.

Europe

∼ Procopius: "The Roman Silk Industry" (ca. 550) ∼

About the same time there came from India certain monks; and when they had satisfied Justinian Augustus that the Romans no longer should buy silk from the Persians, they promised the emperor in an interview that they would provide the materials for making silk so that never should the Romans seek business of this kind from their enemy the Persians, or from any other people whatsoever. They said that they were formerly in Serinda, which they call the region frequented by the people of the Indies, and there they learned perfectly the art of making silk. Moreover, to the emperor who plied them with many questions as to whether he might have the secret, the monks replied that certain worms were manufacturers of silk, nature itself forcing them to keep always at work; the worms could certainly not be brought here alive, but they could be grown easily and without difficulty; the eggs of single hatchings are innumerable; as soon as they are laid men cover them with dung and keep them warm for as long as it is necessary so that they produce insects. When they had announced these tidings, led on by liberal promises of the emperor to prove the fact, they returned to India. When they had brought the eggs to Byzantium, the method having been learned, as I have said, they changed them by metamorphosis into worms which feed on the leaves of mulberry. Thus began the art of making silk from that time on in the Roman Empire.

From: *Procopii Caesariensis historiarum temporis sui tetras altera. De bello Gothico*, trans. Claudius Maltretus, rpt. Roy C. Cave and Herbert H. Coulson, eds., *A Source Book for Medieval Economic History* (Milwaukee: Bruce Publishing Co., 1936).

The Islamic World

∼ Excerpt from The Itinerary of Benjamin of Tudela (late 12th century) ∼

Thence it is two days to Bagdad, the great city and the royal residence of the Caliph Emir al Muminin al Abbasi of the family of Mohammed. He is at the head of the Mohammedan religion, and all the kings of Islam obey him; he occupies a similar position to that held by the Pope over the Christians. . . . Within the domains of the palace of the Caliph there are great buildings of marble and columns of silver and gold, and carvings upon rare stones are fixed in the walls. In the Caliph's palace are great riches and towers filled with gold, silken garments and all precious stones. He does not issue forth from his palace save once in the year, at the feast which the Mohammedans call El-id-bed Ramazan, and they come from distant lands that day to see him. He rides on a mule and is attired in the royal robes of gold and silver and fine linen; on his head is a turban adorned with precious stones of priceless value, and over the turban is a black shawl as a sign of his modesty, implying that all this glory will be covered by darkness on the day of death. He is accompanied by all the nobles of Islam dressed in fine garments and riding on horses, the princes of Arabia, the princes of Togarma and Daylam (Gilan) and the princes of Persia, Media and Ghuzz, and the princes of the land of Tibet, which is three months' journey distant, and westward of which lies the land of Samarkand. He proceeds from his palace to the great mosque of Islam which is by the Basrah Gate. Along the road the walls are adorned with silk and purple, and the inhabitants receive him with all kinds of song and exultation, and they dance before the great king who is styled the Caliph. They salute him with a loud voice and say, "Peace unto thee, our Lord the King and Light of Islam!" He kisses his robe, and stretching forth the hem thereof he salutes them. Then he proceeds to the court of the mosque, mounts a wooden pulpit and expounds to them their Law. . . . He does not leave the palace again for a whole year. He is a benevolent man.

From: Marcus Nathan Adler, *The Itinerary of Benjamin of Tudela: Critical Text, Translation and Commentary* (New York: Phillip Feldheim, Inc., 1907).

FURTHER READING

Jose J. Arrom, Ricardo E. Alegria, and Fatima Berch, *Taíno: Pre-Columbian Art and Culture from the Caribbean* (New York: Monacelli Press, 1997).

Rita Bolland, *Tellem Textiles: Archaeological Finds from Burial Caves in Mali's Bandiagara Cliff* (Amsterdam, Netherlands: Royal Tropical Institute, 1991).

David S. Brose, James Allison Brown, and David W. Penney, *Ancient Art of the American Woodland Indians* (New York: Harry N. Abrams, 1985).

Young Yang Chung, *Silken Threads: A History of Embroidery in China, Korea, Japan, and Vietnam* (New York: Harry N. Abrams, 2005).

Elizabeth Crowfoot, Frances Pritchard, and Kay Staniland, *Textiles and Clothing, c. 1150–c. 1450*, new ed. (Rochester, N.Y.: Boydell Press, 2001).

Frances Gies and Joseph Gies, "The Arabs, Transmitters and Inventors," in their *Cathedral, Forge, and Waterwheel: Technology and Invention in the Middle Ages* (New York: HarperCollins, 1994).

"Islamic Textile History," *TextileAsArt.com*. Available online. URL: http://www.textileasart.com/weaving.htm. Downloaded on November 8, 2007.

"Islamic Textiles," *Islamic Architecture*. Available online. URL: http://www.islamicarchitecture.org/art/islamic-textiles.html. Downloaded on November 15, 2007.

Désirée G. Koslin and Janet Snyder, eds., *Encountering Medieval Textiles and Dress: Objects, Texts, Images* (New York: Palgrave Macmillan, 2002).

Colleen E. Kriger, *Cloth in West African History* (Lanham, Md.: AltaMira Press, 2006).

Venice Lamb, *West African Weaving* (London: Duckworth, 1975).

Robyn Maxwell, *Textiles of Southeast Asia: Tradition, Trade, and Transformation* (Hong Kong: Periplus, 2003).

David Nicolle, "Textiles as Treasure," in his *Historical Atlas of the Islamic World* (New York: Checkmark Books, 2003).

Manouchehr Saadat Noury, "Origins of Carpet Weaving in Iran," IranDokht. Available online. URL: http://www.irandokht.com/editorial/print.php?area=pro&sectionID=8&editorialID=1116. Downloaded on November 8, 2007.

Sheila Paine, *Embroidery from India and Pakistan* (Seattle: University of Washington Press, 2001).

Esther Pasztory, *Pre-Columbian Art* (New York: Cambridge University Press, 1998).

John Picton, "Tradition, Technology, and Lurex: Some Comments on Textile History and Design in West Africa." In *History, Design and Craft in West African Strip-Woven Cloth* (Washington, D.C.: National Museum of African Art, 1992).

John Picton and John Mack, *African Textiles: Looms, Weaving and Design*, 2nd ed. (New York: Harper and Row, 1989).

Charles Rostov and Jia Guanyan, *Chinese Carpets* (New York: Harry N. Abrams, 1983).

Rebecca Stone-Miller, *To Weave for the Sun: Ancient Andean Textiles in the Museum of Fine Arts, Boston* (New York: Thames and Hudson, 1992).

James C. Y. Watt and Anne E. Wardwell, *When Silk Was Gold: Central Asian and Chinese Textiles* (New York: Metropolitan Museum of Art, 1998).

► towns and villages

INTRODUCTION

The reasons people created villages were manifold, affected by their culture, their environment, and the politics of their region. In general, in the medieval world villagers lived lives apart from people in cities; their outlook on society could be very different from that of city dwellers. Villages sometimes arose only reluctantly, when people were pressed to form social units larger than the nuclear family. For instance, in Britain, even when it was ruled by the Roman Empire, most people preferred to live in homesteads: a house, perhaps a barn, and sometimes a surrounding wall, far from their neighbors. During the medieval era the British were compelled to form villages and towns for mutual protection from bandits and warlords as well as for cooperating on public works such as irrigation.

Indeed, some historians and archaeologists think that public works projects may have given rise to the first towns in ancient Mesopotamia, where building and maintaining irrigation canals required people to work together and enabled them to farm more land that allowed more people to live close together, eventually giving rise to full-blown cities. This complex process whereby people came together to form ever-larger settlements can be oversimplified, as if homesteads that were clustered together became villages, which prospered and attracted enough people to become towns, which in their turn became cities. This seemingly linear development rarely happened; indeed, sometimes urban cultures such as that of the Maya transformed themselves into rural cultures. An ecological disaster (and possibly relentless wars) seems to have made Mayan urban life unbearable, and the Maya left their cities to live in villages in forests and fields.

What makes a village, and what makes a town? Sometimes archaeologists try to define villages and towns by their populations. A village would rarely have more that a few thousand residents, whereas a town would have as many as 10,000 residents. Cities have populations larger than 10,000 people. This way of defining settlements is intended to be a simple shorthand for classifying social units that could vary greatly in their structure from one culture to another. Another way of distinguishing villages and towns would be by their political structure. In many parts of the medieval world villages were composed of related families, in the form of clans—that is, people claiming descent from a common ancestor, real or mythological. The laws governing a village would be kinship rules that defined who was to be respected and what duties a person was expected to perform based on his or her gender and relationship to other members in the village. In some African and central Asian cultures this resulted in a language that made refined distinctions in how someone was to address another person based on that person's relation as uncle, aunt, cousin, in-law, and so on. In that sense, a village was a place where everyone knew everyone else and everyone's place in the society of the village.

Thus, a town could be defined in part as a settlement where not everyone knew everyone else, related or otherwise. In a town, social structure would have to account for the possibility that two people upon meeting would not know each other. In a western African village, it was possible for a person to be acknowledged the village leader based on his or her standing in the community. In a process anthropologists call *social banking,* a person would do favors for others and accumulate a social debt that everyone in a village would know about. In a town it would not be possible for everyone to keep track of everyone else's status in that way. Some towns in the medieval world tried. For instance, towns in the Islamic world often were subdivided into districts that were inhabited and governed by particular clans. This often resulted in a social breakdown in which no one had control of a town. Muhammad was invited into Medina to resolve just such a problem.

Therefore, a town in most of the medieval world was a settlement in which a political structure existed that allowed people to know who was in charge of what. In those cases, there would be a civil authority that was either elected or appointed. Replacing incompetent leaders could be difficult, because towns could develop small bureaucracies and politically elite families that would strive to hold on to power. This could result in civil unrest, in which case in cultures as diverse as those of China, India, and the Islamic world outside authorities would impose a political structure on the town. Governors or monarchs were expected to remove bad political leaders and replace them with better political leaders in towns. Sometimes towns organized themselves in ways intended to enable them to avoid such actions by governors or local nobility, perhaps because the townspeople preferred their leaders to the unknown leadership that could be imposed from outside. For instance, in medieval Europe craftspeople in towns sometimes formed communes through which they asked for charters from monarchs that would make the towns independent of local nobility.

AFRICA

by Amy Hackney Blackwell

Medieval Africa was a rural society predominantly. Most people supported themselves through agriculture, herding, or hunting and gathering. They did not trade extensively with one another. Because of this, African towns and villages were small, located near fields or pastures, and inhabited by people who were closely related, such as brothers and their wives and children. In many cases, people lived in settlements that could only barely be described as villages; they were very small and often temporary.

People who engaged in agriculture built the largest and most permanent towns and villages. There were a number of towns and villages in Ethiopia. These towns were home to a thriving Muslim and Christian population. Houses were built of stone, and neighborhoods were divided by paved roads. These towns were often surrounded by stone walls. Within the towns were cemeteries, mosques or churches, and courtyards. In 2006 archaeologists found traces of three Muslim towns that they believe date from the 10th through the 16th centuries. These towns seem to have been sparsely populated and surrounded by stone walls.

The Ibo people of present-day eastern Nigeria lived in villages that housed between 100 and 2,000 people. Each village was part of a larger group of villages that were connected by kinship, culture, and shared government. The villages within a group were typically less than a mile away from one another. The village was surrounded by farmland that was divided into several sections, most of which were allowed to lie fallow to regain their fertility. The village was surrounded by a band of palm trees grown for oil and raffia fibers. These palms also lined the paths between villages.

The houses of a village were built around a central area or two areas if the village was large. People used the open space for group meetings and ceremonies, placing logs around the perimeter of the square to serve as seating during festivities. The men of the village would also build and maintain a mud hut with a thatched roof in the square as a place for male social gatherings. Surrounding the square were several groups of houses. Family groups all lived in the same part of town, often in formally defined compounds. A family compound contained numerous mud-and-thatch houses that shared walls with one another. The houses opened onto narrow alleys, and the compounds themselves opened onto the central town squares. Families adorned the entrances to their compounds with decorated gateways.

The Hausa people of what is now northern Nigeria had numerous towns and villages in addition to a number of larger settlements that could be classified as cities. Towns and villages were made up of compounds, each of which housed a large number of people. A compound was surrounded by a high mud wall. At its entrance was a hut where visitors could announce themselves. Just inside the entrance to the compound was a courtyard where animals were stabled and young men slept. Beyond this was a wall leading to an inner courtyard. Inside it were a number of mud huts with thatched roofs, one hut for each wife of the compound's owner. These huts could be round or rectangular and might have porches and were separated from the compound's entrance by interior walls and courtyards. The women's quarters were arranged in such a way that it was difficult for someone standing outside to see into them. The inner courtyard contained a cooking area where the women prepared food for the family. It might also have a well. Off to the side were a latrine and bathing area.

The outer walls of the town's or village's compounds defined streets. Most towns and villages were surrounded by large walls designed to keep out invaders. Each town had a market area, often on its periphery. Here merchants and customers gathered every week or so. Towns and villages within the same area would coordinate their market days so that they would not overlap. Towns also contained mosques and palaces for chiefs. Villages formed the smallest unit of local administration. Villages themselves were divided into wards, each with its own head who would handle land distribution and other matters.

The Ganda people of present-day Uganda built villages that contained between 30 and 80 houses. These houses were circular beehive-shaped structures about 20 feet in diameter made entirely of thatched cane. Each house had a front and a back room. A family might inhabit several houses and small huts, all encircled by a fence to form a compound. Some of the family's farmland would be enclosed inside its compound. A chief's compound contained many houses and huts that accommodated all the chief's wives, children, and servants. The chief's compound served as the social center of the village, and the village people would congregate there to eat, drink, and talk with one another. Ganda territory was typically hilly or swampy. The villages were built on the sides of hills. The people used the rougher hilltops and swamps as pasture or marginal farmland. Although people tended to live near relatives, it was not uncommon for the Ganda to move from village to village to escape bad chiefs, unfriendly neighbors, or sorcery. The Ganda built their villages in clusters surrounding the homes of their chiefs. This semicentralized building structure made it easier for chiefs to collect tribute from their subjects.

The Swazi of what is now South Africa organized their dwellings into homesteads that housed the dependents of headmen or chiefs, and these homesteads, in turn, were grouped into villages. A Swazi homestead was built around a large enclosure where cattle were kept and grain was stored. The living quarters, which consisted of a number of huts made of reeds, stood at one end of the enclosure. The largest hut was the home of the most important woman, usually the chief's mother. The man's wives lived in the surrounding huts. Each woman had her own space in which to sleep, cook, and store her food. Boys and men lived in separate huts.

Kings and chiefs used this village structure to spread their power across large territories. A king had many wives, and he would try to distribute them in different villages. This allowed him to control a large amount of surrounding farmland and made it possible to separate wives or other relatives who could not get along with one another. People who sustained themselves by herding lived in clusters of dwellings but usually did not build permanent towns as farmers did. The herders of present-day Kenya, such as the Masai, lived in small, temporary villages that they could easily abandon when they moved their herds to new grazing areas. When a group decided to stay in one place to let the cattle graze, the women would build small, round houses out of sticks and cattle manure. They would build a fence around the cluster of houses out of thorny sticks. Women and children were the primary occupants of the village, while the men spent most of their time out with the cattle.

The nomadic pastoralists of modern-day Somalia built temporary settlements within the territory that their clans grazed. They abandoned their hamlets and moved to new locations whenever they needed to find better pastures or water sources. They did not think of settlements as permanent fixtures of the landscape. A Somali settlement consisted of several huts made of wood frames and animal skins. Each wife owned her own hut, which could be dismantled and moved on the back of a camel when necessary. The settlement was encircled by a fence made of thorn bushes that kept out animals and threatening humans. In the center of the settlement were pens for sheep and goats. The inhabitants of a hamlet might include several related families, such as the wives and children of several brothers, but more often they were just three or four nuclear families living together. Boys and men spent most of their time out in the pastures with the herds, leaving the settlements to their womenfolk.

The Jie, a seminomadic people of present-day Uganda, lived in small collections of houses called homesteads. A Jie homestead typically housed several extended families who all belonged to one clan; it might contain 100 to 200 people. The residents lived in round beehive-shaped thatched grass huts. Each hut was the home of one of the wives and her children. Each hut was inside its own fenced yard, where the woman who owned it cooked over an open fire and did her other work. Within the yard the woman would erect another grass hut to shelter her calves and serve as a kitchen during rainstorms. The fenced enclosures were arranged in a horseshoe shape. Cattle and goats spent their nights inside the horseshoe. Although the women owned the houses, the men of the homestead's family were the real owners of the settlement. The Jie would typically build several homesteads near one another, forming a settlement. The inhabitants of the settlement shared local resources, such as ponds. They also shared rituals and came to one another's defense.

The hunter-gatherers of the Kalahari desert did not build permanent settlements. They did, however, build temporary houses close to one another. Women occasionally built huts called *scherms* to provide shade for themselves and their children. Although they usually did not bother with this work, preferring to sleep in the bush, if they were staying in one place for a while and there was no good natural shelter, they would build several *scherms* that the group would live in for a time. The !Kung were particularly likely to build *scherms* for special occasions such as a wedding or a girl's first menstruation.

The small-statured hunter-gatherer peoples of the central African forests likewise did not build real towns or villages. They would build temporary settlements when they stopped at a particular place in a forest. A settlement would include huts inhabited by couples and their young children and huts occupied by bachelors.

THE AMERICAS

BY J. J. GEORGE

The Aztec city of Tenochtitlán in what is now Mexico, with its population of 200,000 in 1521 (when Hernán Cortés arrived), represents the maximum extent of Mesoamerican urbanism. Towns and villages had lower levels of population, complexity, function, form, and urban texture. Towns should be thought of as settlements running to hundreds of acres, with housing structures that number in the hundreds, accompanied by deep middens (or refuse heaps). Towns have heavy structures that have been rebuilt or strengthened over time in one spot. A town's dwellings are arranged in definite patterns and often in relation to ceremonial structures, such as temples, and often with some type of fortification. Towns also have a sense of place, longevity, and continuity that is lacking in villages. They are often distinguished by size and elaborate public architecture, and greater size usually means that new forms of organization develop. (More recently scholars have been simplifying their classification by using such terms as *large settlement*, *center*, or simply *big site*, terms that are effectively neutral.)

A village, broadly speaking, occupies less area than a town. It will occupy an area of several acres where the number of dwellings might run as high as 30 or 40. Structures are suitable for extended periods of time, refuse and midden deposits are in evidence, and some basic form of village planning is common. Early villages often had primitive social hierarchies ruled by chiefs and overlap with chiefdoms in the literature. Towns and villages were ubiquitous throughout the Americas by the period from 500 to 1500.

Anasazi, Hohokam, and Mogollon pit house villages in the North American Southwest before 900 may have shared a common layout—a central clear area, possibly a plaza, with a great kiva, or underground ceremonial structure, to one side, separating northern and southern clusters of residences. By 700 Anasazi towns consisted of lines of linked rooms fronted by pit houses, perhaps foreshadowing the "street" arrangement of later sites, such as Skunk Springs, Yellow Jacket, Snaketown, and even some modern pueblos. Yellow Jacket was assumed to be among the largest towns, and population estimates range from 1,000 to 4,500, partly depending upon the number of outlying villages and hamlets included in the count.

The many separate buildings of Chaco Canyon in present-day New Mexico, jammed into an inhospitable canyon, were long thought to be independent, self-sufficient agrarian pueblos. But research suggests Chaco Canyon was a coherent settlement delineated by roads, walls, mounds, and public architecture. Public architecture, in this sense, could mean plazas, great houses (structures containing up to 700 rooms), kivas, ball courts, platform mounds, canals, and roads. After the fall of Chaco Canyon around 1150, pueblo communities and cliff dwellings became common, such as the familiar Mesa Verde, Zuni, and Kayenta. Generally speaking, pueblo style was defined by massed adobe units surrounding a plaza, and cliff dwellings by stacked-stone enclosures with ritual kivas neatly molded into defensible spaces beneath cliff overhangs. After 1300 pueblos grew very large, with pueblos of 1,000 or more rooms common. The largest settlement of this time, Paquime, had an estimated population of 4,700.

Towns and villages in the Southeast and Midwest emerged within the broader cultural contexts of the Adena and Hopewell traditions of 300 B.C.E to 400 C.E. and the later Mississippian culture of roughly the ninth to 16th centuries. The towns and villages of the Mississippian tradition shared a sedentary lifestyle, a hierarchical social organization of chiefs and warriors, and a unifying ideology involving earth-fertility themes and ancestor veneration. Mississippian towns were defined by a central mound-temple configuration and plazas, resulting in a square plan that symbolized the symbolic four-quarters worldview. Major Mississippian towns include Cahokia, Moundville, Spiro, Lake George, Winterville, Etowah, and Angel. The largest site, Cahokia, had over 100 mounds, multiple plazas, covered more than 2,965 acres, and had a population estimated between 12,000 and 30,000.

Clustered villages and towns were common during the Aztec period (14th–16th centuries), especially in the southern basin. In these settlements, houses were packed rather closely together and the communities had fairly clear boundaries. Towns and some larger villages contained buildings set aside for administrative and religious functions. Large villages, towns, or areas of dispersed settlement often corresponded to a *calpolli*, a social or territorial unit that helped regulate land tenure and tribute payment.

Scholars subdivide Mayan settlements into regional, primary, secondary, tertiary, and quaternary centers based in part on the number of emblem glyphs that show up at a particular site and on the number of plazas. Each Mayan center had its own glyph, like a symbol or seal unique to that center, which when found at another site indicated a relationship between the two. Regional and primary centers were the first to achieve state-level organization and some scholars identify them as cities. The subsequent centers would then overlap with towns and villages. For example, Tikal, Yaxchilan, Copán, and Palenque are primary centers. Secondary centers include Aguateca, Machaquilá, Naranjo, Piedras Negras, and Quiriguá. And tertiary centers include Uaxactún, Bonompak, Jimbal, Ixla, and Miraflores. The largest centers, such as Tikal, extended over 48 square miles, and the smallest may have covered less than a half a square mile.

Mayan centers are dominated by central concentrations of special-purpose architecture including platforms, causeways, temples, ball courts, palaces, occasional fortifications, and plain or sculpted stone monuments. The centers served many functions. There are areas for public gatherings, ceremonies, ball games, and markets; and there are facilities for political and administrative activities. The largest and most elaborate residential structures were often in or near these centers.

Archaeological research in South America favors Andean settlements of larger, more complex entities akin to cities, capital cities, city-states, and empires. Nonetheless towns and villages, like the other areas, were ubiquitous. For instance, the Nazca society, centered on the central coast of Peru from 200 B.C.E. to 700 C.E., is considered by many scholars to be a group of agrarian villages and towns that together controlled a given valley. Other scholars see Nazca as a multi-valley state with its capital at a settlement called Cahuachi, a site with over 40 mounds dispersed over 371 acres whose permanent residential occupation is debated.

Moche was a state-level enterprise on the north coast of Peru that had run its course by 700. The conventional perception of Moche has been of a monolithic state with its capital at a site of the same name, but recent rethinking supports multiple regional political units, not unlike administrative towns with local tributaries, sharing cultural and aesthetic traits broadly identified as Moche.

Like Moche, Tiwanaku culture spread widely and unified a broad area with similar cultural characteristics. It occupied the richest agricultural area of the whole highland region of present-day Peru and Bolivia, adjacent to Lake Titicaca, between the sixth and 11th centuries. Largely a farming population, permanent settlements were established in valleys in small clusters of houses or in villages directly associated with farmland but also connected to the urban center.

The Wari Empire evolved adjacent to and simultaneous with Tiwanaku from the sixth to 11th centuries. It developed to the north in the Ayacucho-Huanta basin of Peru, territory occupied by a group identified as Huarpa. Huarpa life was village-based and at the time occupied the entire basin with a large number of small villages and hamlets scattered over the mountain slopes, which were sculpted with terraces to provide cultivable space and to limit erosion. The most numerous settlements were villages built with tree trunks or clay, coexisting with towns made of rough stone houses, generally round or oval in shape. The largest sites were near irrigated fields.

Finally, Cuzco, the eventual capital of the Inca Empire, was a large town or small city. Much of its pre-imperial history has been wiped out by human action—Inca and Spanish—and natural catastrophe. Settlements in the region prior to the Inca were no more than hamlets and small villages. Many were found on mid-elevation peaks or ridges, implying a concern for defense. By 1434 the Inca imperial campaigns had begun, and a primary concern was the total reorganization of Cuzco, which turned from what was probably a fairly sleepy town into the heart of a massive empire.

ASIA AND THE PACIFIC

BY MARK W. ALLEN

In many human societies the bulk of the population lives not in large urban centers, but in towns and villages. A village can be defined as a distinct community with inhabitants numbering from a few hundred to maybe a thousand and a town as having a few thousand to perhaps 5,000 people. Communities with true urbanism and populations in the tens of thousands are usually regarded as cities. Like cities, towns usually serve functions that villages do not. For example, they might serve as markets and administrative centers, with storage facilities and craft specialists. They might contain religious structures such as temples, shrines, or cemeteries. And they might be fortified, offering protection to which people living nearby might flee.

It is common to find towns surrounded by a number of neighboring villages, which officially or unofficially rely on the town as their social, economic, and political center. Geographers and anthropologists have long noted that the locations and types of settlements provide accurate information about the level of integration of particular human societies. Cities generally indicate the presence of state level governments. States often have considerable hierarchy in types of settlements including hamlets (small, scattered communities with a hundred or fewer inhabitants), villages, towns, regional cities, and true urban centers. Towns without cities might reflect a less integrated system such as a chiefdom or small kingdom. Isolated villages scattered in a wide area probably indicate that communities are largely autonomous and self-reliant. In medieval Asia and the Pacific, a considerable variety in the patterns of towns and villages is evident.

Medieval Asia saw the continuation of states and empires in India and China from ancient times. In other areas, such as Japan, Korea, and Southeast Asia, states arose for the first time starting between 500 and 800 C.E. Thus it should be no surprise that major cities were the capitals or hubs in most of medieval Asia. Towns and villages surrounded these centers and were tied to them through interdependence. They provided agricultural surplus and sometimes labor for the cities. In turn, cities provided administration, special markets and crafts, military protection, and sometimes religious functions or facilities. In many cases it was the cities that got the most out of these relationships.

Towns varied quite a bit depending on their location and culture. In medieval India towns often contained extremely important Hindu temples or other sacred sites despite a relatively small size compared with royal or imperial cities. Such shrines often received pilgrimages from faraway places. In Southeast Asia medieval towns were centers of both Buddhist and Hindu temples, which were often surrounded by walls to delineate sacred areas. Towns there were also fortified and contained large reservoirs of water critical for agriculture. Those located on the coast and along major rivers served as important trading centers. Korean towns from the early and middle medieval period reflect the lack of integration there while three kingdoms battled for supremacy. Nearly all large communities in Korea were located on high hills that provided natural defense, and they were heavily fortified with ditches and walls. Like many Asian towns, they contained the tombs of rulers.

Chinese towns frequently were walled for defense, had large markets, and were key intersections for linking the peasants of their hinterlands into the empire. It is important to note that most Chinese peasants rarely left their own villages and local fields. Towns were usually a day's travel away and were rarely visited by most villagers. Cities were even less visited, as they might be several days of travel away. Village China essentially had its own culture established on ancient traditions based on the *hsu*, or patrilineage. Villages were far indeed, in many senses, from the literate Confucian culture to be found in the cities.

One particularly interesting medieval Asian town is that of the center of the Mongolian Empire in central Asia. Karakorum (also spelled Kharkhorum) was constructed from 1220 to 1260 by order of Genghis Khan (ca. 1162–1227). It was a planned community placed in a strategic point in the center of the empire, well positioned to take advantage of trade and communication routes. The town did not have a large permanent population, but it did contain separate districts for Chinese merchants and Muslim inhabitants. Temples representing a dozen religions were constructed. The key building of the town was the Wan, an imperial palace surrounded by a wall a little over half a mile long. Main streets ran through the town, and the town itself was surrounded by a fortification wall a little under 4 miles long. Much is known about this community from archaeological excavations as well as from the description of the European traveler Willem van Ruysbroeck (ca. 1215–ca. 1295). Thus, even the highly mobile Mongol pastoralists of Asia found it necessary to construct towns to administer their territories, conquests, and trade routes.

In contrast, villages of medieval Asia are fairly similar. These communities lacked fortifications, major temples, market centers, administrative centers, or any of the other special facilities of towns and cities. They served as the residence of peasants, and were largely structured through kinship rather than strict political control. In many ways, these communities maintained basic patterns dating back several thousand years to the beginnings of agriculture. Even in the 21st century Asian villages share much with their medieval counterparts despite the increasing presence of machines, television, and the Internet. In much of Asian history, it would be typical to find that well over 90 percent of the population lived in villages rather than towns or cities. Life in these communities was usually organized along family lineages with elders having important leadership roles.

In the Pacific the cultures of Melanesia, Micronesia, and Polynesia were spread across small islands (with a few exceptions) and supported mostly by growing root crops in small gardens in most cases (again with a few exceptions). Towns were thus very rare in the Pacific during medieval times; people lived in hamlets and villages. Even in the early 21st century such settlements are highly efficient for maximizing the resources of small islands without destroying them, because the population is spread out across both coastal and interior areas. Indeed, many Pacific Island villages specialize in particular resources such as fishing or gardening. Medieval villages here, as in nearly every other part of the world, were organized largely along kinship. To a large degree one's family lineage or lineages determined where one lived. Family elders were usually the key decision makers in villages. Special facilities and functions are limited in such communities.

There were, however, some islands in the Pacific where large communities with populations in the low thousands did develop. These communities often had special functions: they served as administrative centers for chiefdoms; as centers of defense; as locations for food storage, trade, and concentrations of crafts such as canoe-building; and sites of religious temples and monuments.

A good example of extremely large villages or small towns formed for military protection would be the *pa* (hill forts) of the New Zealand Maori. New Zealand's cool and wet climate made the typical Polynesian crops impossible or difficult to grow. Good gardening areas were very limited and highly desirable. Around 1500 the demand for this land brought about intense warfare, which led to the centralization of settlement in some particularly productive areas. Chiefs and their followers constructed *pa* in naturally defensible locations. The construction involved the use of earthwork fortifications and wooden palisades. Inside these strongholds were houses as well as stored food supplies. The largest such communities had perhaps a thousand occupants at times of greatest threat. Similar towns or villages can be found in parts of Micronesia and other Polynesian islands.

In Hawaii agriculture and religion seem to have led to the construction of the largest communities in the most favored locations. Here chiefs had considerable power, to the extent that they were sometimes considered direct descendants of gods. They owned large wedges of islands outright while their followers numbering in the tens of thousands at times owned virtually nothing. Irrigation was used to increase the production of the root crop taro, and this sometimes resulted in the concentration of people in large villages near dependable rivers or streams. Chiefs often established their sizable households in these areas. Another function of these types of communities was religious as Hawaiian chiefs competed with one another to build the biggest temple complexes using stone architecture. Still, even the largest of these communities could be regarded as simply a number of adjoining villages and hamlets rather than a centralized town. For the most part, traditional Pacific life was village life.

EUROPE

by Bradley A. Skeen

In the late Roman Empire, as landowners grew more independent, the large estates called *latifundia* became self-sufficient agriculturally, producing enough for their own needs and a surplus for local markets. Workers, who might have been enslaved during the empire, were now free, albeit they were usually dependent on the landowners. As the protective cordon of the Roman frontier collapsed and pillaging

peoples occupied the Western Roman Empire, landowners fortified their isolated villas for protection. These fortified Roman villas became the nucleus of the medieval manorial system. Workers would have lived in one or another of the villages (a term derived from *villa*, as is the Middle English *villein*, meaning "peasant") that sprang up near the fortified manor. Roman towns, on the other hand, had been purposely founded centers placed at strategic locations, either near the frontier for defensive purposes or along the transportation network, without any special relation to the villas.

This system of rural land use remained substantially intact in territories controlled by the Byzantine Empire and also endured surprisingly well in western Europe. In the fifth century the island of Britain was abandoned by the Romans, and most of the villas, palatial country houses that had been increasingly fortified, were sacked by the Anglo-Saxon invaders. Paradoxically, these ruins have features that have been preserved in their original condition, revealing a very detailed picture of rural life in Britain to archaeologists.

At the same time on the Continent the population was declining, which meant that many villas, along with large stretches of the countryside, were virtually abandoned. This was a pattern that was to be repeated in the Middle Ages. When the population dropped, towns might become smaller, but they were not abandoned. Rural estates were abandoned, however; when that happened the land returned to forest. Populations remained as concentrated as possible, since the way of life of European peasants, always on the margin of starvation, required extensive cooperation to ensure survival. In the fifth century the existence of large unpopulated tracts of land allowed the emperors to invite whole Germanic ethnic groups, such as the Visigoths and Burgundians, into the empire and assign them lands held by the local kings in exchange for a pledge of military service. These lands were divided among the ethnic groups into freehold farms following Germanic custom. This practice is the precursor, if not the direct ancestor, of the medieval feudal system. The policy failed disastrously, since the ethnic group leaders, with only the most tenuous ties to Roman civilization, soon preferred independence to the uncertain protection of the waning empire and let it dissolve into a number of independent kingdoms after 476. After his failed invasion of Spain (778), Charlemagne (r. 800–14) settled his veterans on unoccupied farmland in southern France, obliging them to render military service in the future in exchange for the land. This is often seen as the beginning of feudalism.

In the fifth and sixth centuries the population of western Europe plummeted still further in the face of repeated invasions and contagious diseases. The consequent high mortality rate and panic naturally led to famine, and hunger led to susceptibility to other diseases. By the year 800 the total population of Europe is thought to have been no more than 30 million, when it had once been as much as 100 million during the empire. In the sixth and seventh centuries pious landowners with untenanted villas frequently gave them to monastic orders, which would reclaim the land and attract their own peasants to work the estate. Almost all the monasteries established in western Europe at this time, such as the famous Monte Cassino in Italy (529), were founded in this way. New villages and towns would grow up around the monasteries.

First the Carolingian and then the Holy Roman Empire made concerted efforts to expand to the east, even in bad times. After local ethnic groups living beyond the frontier had been defeated, new provinces (marches or marks) would be established with colonists from the interior. There, new towns and villages would be organized. Another support for new towns at this time was the increased volume of trade on the North and Baltic seas. These so-called emporia (trading posts) grew steadily in prosperity and by the later Middle Ages had mostly become imperial cities (free of the interference of local nobles) and had organized themselves into the Hanseatic League, which monopolized trade in the area. In the east the new towns had often been founded, like Lübeck, on the sites of conquered Slavic villages.

After another series of devastating raids by Vikings, Magyars, and Saracens, the general security of Europe began to improve around the year 1000 and with it the level of population and economic prosperity. By 1347 (the eve of the great pandemic of the Black Death), the total population of Europe is thought to have risen to as high as 100 million again. Social organization was now firmly based on the manor system. This consisted of a fortified position (castle), whose lord was the major landowner, in which the local populace took refuge during invasions, with an adjacent village inhabited by agricultural workers dependent on the lord. Peasants worked their own fields, which had been allotted them by their lord, in exchange for a share of the crop. They also worked on common fields and used common lands for grazing livestock. Old regions of forest were redeveloped through the reoccupation of older sites and the establishment of new manors.

In the 10th century and later landowners continued granting lands to found new monasteries, but these lands typically had long been forested by this time and were technically part of the lord's hunting preserves. There was little untenanted farmland. The great monastery of Cluny in France was founded (909) in this way. In Russia, after the devastation of the Mongol invasion and occupation in the 1230s, monasteries were founded in virgin, uninhabited forest to the northeast of the old population centers of Kiev Rus as places

Calendar page of October, showing a street lined with buildings and the village gate in the distance, Belgium, ca. 1510; men negotiate over the sale of an ox. (The Pierpont Morgan Library)

of refuge. Villages, towns, and eventually new cities, such as Moscow, grew up around them.

As new areas of countryside were redeveloped for agriculture and the population increased, new towns came into existence. These generally began as villages that happened to become market centers for trade between nearby villages, and they supported larger populations of traders and craftsmen besides peasants. Some would host regional trade fairs and so grow larger still. Towns produced additional income for their lords, especially income in the form of cash from taxes on business rather than a share of crops taken in kind. For this reason, the growth of towns was encouraged by the nobility, but at the same time the nobility wished to subject the townsmen to exploitative taxes. The townsmen's response to this problem was to form a commune, or society of mutual protection, that acted as a local government, and to try to obtain a charter granting the town fixed rights (especially in regard to economic activity). These charters were not granted by the local lord but by outside authorities, such as the king or emperor, who granted such rights not only to impose a control on the power of the nobility but also in return for a large cash payment from the commune.

The commune movement began in northern Italy where the urban tradition from Roman times was the strongest and the cities had the most independence, but it spread throughout Europe and down to very small communities. The Swiss government, for instance, evolved out of communal pacts made among quite small villages for the maintenance and protection of the Alpine passes. Communes would also finance the construction of city walls and establish a militia for self-protection. The threat was no longer from outside invaders but from the bandits whom the nobles failed to police or from the nobles themselves, who were often not above simply raiding unprotected towns.

An extreme, but not atypical, example of the relations between lord and town was that between Prince Alexander Nevsky (ca. 1220–63) and Novgorod. Novgorod was a wealthy merchant town that handled the transshipment of Russian furs to the Hanseatic League of cities that controlled trade on the Baltic. From 1236 to 1242 the previously independent town submitted itself to Nevsky (Prince of Vladimir) in return for his protection from Swedish and German invaders, greatly increasing his revenues. But in 1259 the commune of Novgorod grew tired of paying taxes to Nevsky and demanded a charter of freedoms and liberties from its prince. Nevsky responded by massacring hundreds of the leading merchants in the city.

From 1347 to 1350, the pandemic of plague known as the Black Death dramatically cut the population of Europe, very probably in half. The population did not begin to grow again for almost another century. Part of the reason was that the feudal governments enacted severe new laws to keep peasants where they were and earning no more than they had before the disaster—whereas a move to the free labor markets in the cities and larger towns would have brought far better prospects for most agricultural workers. In short, the balance of population between the cities and large towns and the countryside (villages) was manipulated for most of a century. The overall standard of living did increase slowly, however, simply because more resources were available, and another dramatic increase in population began in the early modern period that followed the Middle Ages with a shift toward urban centers.

THE ISLAMIC WORLD

BY KIRK H. BEETZ

At its fullest extent the medieval Islamic world encompassed many different cultural traditions in its towns and villages. Especially in India and the regions of modern-day Pakistan and Afghanistan, towns and villages retained much of their original cultural significance and governance. In northern India during the early era of Islamic conquest there was the clearest division between Islamized towns and villages and those that retained traditional Indian functions. Early Muslim rulers distinguished between immigrant Muslims and their descendants and Indian converts to Islam and their descendants. In general, Muslims of local extraction were discriminated against in hiring for government jobs and in social privileges. Many Indian cities had been burned, resulting in new cities or cities rebuilt along traditional Islamic lines, with marketplaces and mosques as the center of civic life. Towns and villages tended to remain as they had been before the imposition of Islamic government, even though most temples and other monuments had been destroyed. In those villages where Muslims dominated, mosques were built. In general, the farther a village was from a capital city, the more likely it was to be run as it had been before the advent of Islam.

An Indian town or village in Islamic territory tended to be run by a headman, by a council, or by both. The headman was usually a wealthy person descended from a family that had a tradition of civic leadership, although a headman could be replaced, usually at the orders of a sultan. A headman was responsible for settling local disputes, for negotiating with other villages over water rights and control of farmland, and for organizing and leading the defense of the town or village. In northern India as well as the regions of Pakistan and Afghanistan, this was very important because of the continuous threat of raids by bandits. It was common for headmen to die in battle against raiders.

Councils consisted of both old and young people, usually chosen for membership in a council by current council members. Councils cooperated with headmen when both were present in city governance. Some villages were organized around a particular craft or business. For instance, there were villages of blacksmiths, carpenters, or foresters, usually on a route to a city where their products could be shipped. These villages were run by guilds whose leaders functioned in the manner of a council, except that the leaders were usually elected by the residents of the village. In villages and towns of converts to Islam, headmen and councils continued to be the governors, with the same responsibilities as before. Villages and towns of Muslim immigrants seem to have been rare, with cities attracting most Muslim immigrants. In almost all cases villages and towns were expected to supply conscripts for public works projects, such as building and maintaining irrigation canals. During the medieval era Muslims gradually became Indianized, growing more tolerant of Hindu and Buddhist customs and more likely to organize their towns and villages in the traditional Indian manner.

To the west and in central Asia towns and villages were more likely to be organized according to the customs of Arabs. Outside of Islamic cities, people of the Near East tended to organize themselves in two ways: by kinship and by economic cooperation. Kinship was especially important among nomads. Individual families were often too weak for self-defense and too small to be economically powerful, so they associated with kinship groups whose members claimed descent from a common ancestor of four or five generations earlier. The limit of four or five generations was mostly the result of lines of descent being preserved as oral tradition and not as written tradition, with about five generations being the outer limit of oral memory. Actual descent from a common ancestor was not required for people to claim descent from a common ancestor and to claim membership of a kinship group. Numerous important kinship groups included people of different ethnic ancestry. For instance, many groups in North Africa consisted of both Berbers and Arabs. The oral history would be revised to include new members as if they actually shared a common descent, even when people knew they did not. Kinship groups provided protection from aggression by outsiders, leaders who could arbitrate disputes within the group, and spokespeople who could represent the group in dealings with government authorities. In towns and villages kinship groups often had their own quarters. Such was the case in some Arabian cities in Muhammad's own time.

Kinship groups could remain nomadic rather than settled, but economic cooperation created pressure for people to settle in one place where they could work together. Many towns and villages had existed before the era of Islam, others developed in response to agricultural needs, and still others grew out of trade. In each case, the more remote the town or village was from a city, the more likely it was that the Islamic faith would have a weak hold on the inhabitants, or no hold at all. Villages of pagans, Jews, and Christians often acknowledged the preeminence of an Islamic central government but pursued their own interests with only rare interference by outside authorities. In most cases during the medieval era, villages in remote mountain or desert areas were on their own, except for paying taxes and providing troops for the defense of the territory.

Historians sometimes write of an Islamic agricultural revolution. This developed out of the efforts of Islamic governments to bring wastelands under cultivation. In the Near East it meant repairing abandoned irrigation canals from previous eras. There and in North Africa and al-Andalus, governments also built new irrigation canals and made it a priority to maintain the canals. This helped bring new areas under cultivation, attracting settlers who became farmers. Different districts produced different agricultural products, perhaps one producing fruits from orchards, another grain, and another meat from sheep and cattle. Where such districts met, sometimes several at a given point, people set up markets. The markets were held as often as once a week or as rarely as once a year. The markets attracted craftspeople, from women hoping to sell the textiles they made to blacksmiths hoping to repair broken pots and pans.

The agricultural revolution was sustainable enough for it to become worth their while for people to settle in such marketplaces. Farmers would set up housing near each other to aid in their cooperation in marketing their goods as well as to provide for mutual defense against bandits or other attackers. Carpenters, fullers, and others would settle in the new village because they found regular work among the farmers and visitors to the local market, called a *suq*. Such villages would almost always have a mosque, and Jews and Christians, if they were numerous enough, might build their own places of worship. Farming communities usually developed the *musha'* system. Under this system, the cultivable local land was held in trust by the community, and perhaps once a year or sometimes more than once a year the land would be divided among the village's farmers according to how much they could cultivate.

Another way for a village or town to arise was when a particular location was suited as a stopping place along a trade route. In particular, rivers and coastlines became lined with settlements where traders could stop. A caravansary was a place set up on land routes to house and provide protection for traders and their goods, and around the caravansary a community could develop, first focused on providing services to travelers such as repairing broken equipment but sometimes developing into places where people from rural areas could come to trade their goods with travelers. In such cases, a spot could become a full-blown city with all the traditions and trappings of medieval Islamic urban areas.

Towns and large villages were often divided into districts, some of which were living quarters for people associated with one another either by a kinship group or by a craft or profession in common. Most villages had *asabiyya*, a community spirit that inspired villagers to work together for the common good. *Asabiyya* was often enough to ensure that villagers settled disputes peacefully and worked together. Such cooperation often derived from the nomadic Arabian traditions of honor that required people to be respectful to one another and to come to one another's aid in times of need.

The concept of honor often united groups of villages in cooperation. This was especially important for villages in areas remote from a central government's authority, because the villages often had only themselves to rely upon for defense. A central government's troops might be days away from being able to come to the aid of remote villages. In mountain valleys in al-Andalus and central Asia, among oases in a dry desert, and on the irrigated plains of the Near East and North Africa, villages near each other often had geography and needs in common.

Among those villages particular kinship groups may have become dominant, and those kinship groups would ally themselves by creating a fictional mutual relationship with a heroic ancestor; out of that alliance would arise leadership for the groups of villages. Applying ancient Arabian rules of honor more often than Islamic law, leaders would make legal rulings, apply punishments, and organize public works projects, such as building roads or maintaining irrigation ditches. Often a single person, usually a man, became the acknowledged leader of the kinship group. He was accepted as leader because of his wisdom, after the fashion of Mohammad in Medina, or because he was elected by village leaders, or because of his military prowess. His leadership position was fragile; if he proved ineffective in mediating a dispute between rival villages or incompetent in military matters, he could be replaced.

Towns and village frequently did a very good job of organizing themselves and looking after the needs of their people. Still, all were potentially subject to social disasters. Towns and villages that were divided into quarters by kinship could become battlegrounds in feuds among the kinship groups. In such cases an outsider might be called upon to take over the police force or to arbitrate. A leader could fall from respect if he failed to bring the feuding groups under control. Sometimes feuds could be so disruptive to civic life that fields went unplanted, traders stayed away, or taxes went unpaid. In such cases the central government's regional governor was expected to use the military forces at his command to quell the violence, meet out punishments, and organize relief. In areas prone to earthquakes or floods, regional governors often had to organize aid to villages. Failure in such duties could result in the governor's dismissal or even his execution. On the other hand, if he did a good job in defending against raiders or organizing communities to help each other, he could cause concern for the caliph or sultan, who would fear his popularity; death was then a common result for a governor.

See also AGRICULTURE; ARCHITECTURE; BUILDING TECHNIQUES AND MATERIALS; CITIES; CLIMATE AND GEOGRAPHY; CRAFTS; ECONOMY; EMPIRES AND DYNASTIES; EMPLOYMENT AND LABOR; FAMILY; FOOD AND DIET; FOREIGNERS AND BARBARIANS; FORESTS AND FORESTRY; GENDER STRUCTURES AND ROLES; GOVERNMENT ORGANIZATION; HOUSEHOLD GOODS; LAWS AND LEGAL CODES; MIGRATION AND POPULATION MOVEMENTS; MILITARY; NATURAL DISASTERS; NOMADIC AND PASTORAL SOCIETIES; OCCUPATIONS; PANDEMICS AND EPIDEMICS; RELIGION AND COSMOLOGY; SETTLEMENT PATTERNS; SOCIAL COLLAPSE AND ABANDONMENT; SOCIAL ORGANIZATION; TRADE AND EXCHANGE.

Asia and the Pacific

∾ *Willem van Ruysbroeck: Account of the Mongols (1253–55)* ∾

Mangu had at Caracarum [Karakorum] a great palace, situated next to the city walls, enclosed within a high wall like those which enclose monks' priories among us. Here is a great palace, where he has his drinkings twice a year: once about Easter, when he passes there, and once in summer, when he goes back (westward). And the latter is the greater (feast), for then come to his court all the nobles, even though distant two months journey; and then he makes them largess of robes and presents, and shows his great glory. There are there many buildings as long as barns, in which are stored his provisions and his treasures. In the entry of this great palace, it being unseemly to bring in there skins of milk and other drinks, master William the Parisian had made for him a great silver tree, and at its roots are four lions of silver, each with a conduit through it, and all belching forth white milk of mares. And four conduits are led inside the tree to its tops, which are bent downward, and on each of these is also a gilded serpent, whose tail twines round the tree. And from one of these pipes flows wine, from another cara cosmos, or clarified mare's milk, from another bal, a drink made with honey, and from another rice mead, which is called terracina; and for each liquor there is a special silver bowl at the foot of the tree to receive it. Between these four conduits in the top, he made an angel holding a trumpet, and underneath the tree he made a vault in which a man can be hid. And pipes go up through the heart of the tree to the angel. In the first place he made bellows, but they did not give enough wind. Outside the palace is a cellar in which the liquors are stored, and there are servants all ready to pour them out when they hear the angel trumpeting. And there are branches of silver on the tree, and leaves and fruit. When then drink is wanted, the head butler cries to the angel to blow his trumpet. Then he who is concealed in the vault, hearing this blows with all his might in the pipe leading to the angel, and the angel places the trumpet to his mouth, and blows the trumpet right loudly. Then the servants who are in the cellar, hearing this, pour the different liquors into the proper conduits, and the conduits lead them down into the bowls prepared for that, and then the butlers draw it and carry it to the palace to the men and women.

And the palace is like a church, with a middle nave, and two sides beyond two rows of pillars, and with three doors to the south, and beyond the middle door on the inside stands the tree, and the Chan sits in a high place to the north, so that he can be seen by all; and two rows of steps go up to him: by one he who carries his cup goes up, and by the other he comes down. The space which is in the middle between the tree and these steps by which they go up to him is empty; for here stands his cup-bearer, and also envoys bearing presents; and he himself sits up there like a divinity. On (his) right side, that is to the west, are the men, to the left the women. The palace extends from the north (southward). To the south, beside the pillars on the right side, are rows of seats raised like a platform, on which his son and brothers sit. On the left side it is arranged in like fashion, and there

sit his wives and daughters. Only one woman sits up there beside him, though not so high as he. . . .

Of the city of Caracarum you must know that, exclusive of the palace of the Chan, it is not as big as the village of Saint Denis, and the monastery of Saint Denis is ten times larger than the palace. There are two quarters in it; one of the Saracens in which are the markets, and where a great many Tartars gather on account of the court, which is always near this (city), and on account of the great number of ambassadors; the other is the quarter of the Cathayans, all of whom are artisans. Besides these quarters there are great palaces, which are for the secretaries of the court. There are there twelve idol temples of different nations, two mahummeries [mosques] in which is cried the law of Machomet, and one church of Christians in the extreme end of the city. The city is surrounded by a mud wall and has four gates. At the eastern is sold millet and other kinds of grain, which, however, is rarely brought there; at the western one, sheep and goats are sold; at the southern, oxen and carts are sold; at the northern, horses are sold.

From: Willem van Ruysbroeck, *The Journey of William of Rubruck to the Eastern Parts of the World, 1253–55, As Narrated by Himself, with Two Accounts of the Earlier Journey of John of Pian de Carpine,* trans. and ed. William Woodville Rockhill (London: Hakluyt Society, 1900).

Europe

∼ *Charles the Bald: A Renewal of the Privileges of a Monastery (874)* ∼

In the name of the Holy and Indivisible Trinity, Charles, by the grace of God, King. If we have granted the requests devoutly raised to us by our faithful servants, doubtless in so doing we have exercised a royal and ancient custom. Therefore be it known to all our faithful, and to the faithful of Holy Church, present and future, that the venerable abbot Hilduin, our most faithful servant and worthy clerk, abbot of the monastery of Sithiu [Saint Omer], situated in the district of Terouenne, built in honor of St. Peter, Prince of the Apostles, where the bodies of the holy confessors

Omer and Bertin are known to be buried, has brought to our attention that in the time of Abbot Hugh, his predecessor, we gave authority to that monastery, placing it and all things pertaining to it under our protection, care and immunity. We also placed under our protection all its cells, villas, and other possessions within the counties, territories, and jurisdiction of our kingdom. And neither we nor our successors would divide them or turn those properties to any other uses, and the monastery would give purveyance to no man. The abbot now seeks a renewal of our authority and

(continued)

(continues)

the naming of each privilege. We therefore, for the love and reverence we have for those saints, have ordered a renewal of our authority over that place, and, at the same time, confirmation of those privileges by this our charter. And we have ordered these royal letters to be written to warn our successors to permit those things we formerly granted to that monastery to remain secure, to make no division of the cells or property or other possessions of the monastery, or to permit such division to be made, or to permit the turning of those possessions to other uses. We further decree by our letters that no public official or person with judicial authority shall at any time dare to go into the churches, fields, places, or possessions of that monastery, neither those possessed in our time, nor those which holy piety shall add in the future, either for hearing cases according to judicial custom, for taking taxes, for

exercising authority, for preparing lodging, for taking food by purveyance, for the taking of pledges, for distraining free or servile men of that monastery, or for requiring other services. Let no judge presume to exact the things mentioned within the monastery itself. The abbot and his successors shall possess in peace, under our protection, the property of the monastery just as we decreed in the charter to Abbot Hugh. We grant also to that monastery that it shall have for all time a market, to be held on Fridays, and whatever profit there is from that market shall be for the shrine of Saints Omer and Bertin. Once a year the abbot shall give a feast to the brethren. And let the brethren who serve God there as His servants pray perpetually for us, the queen, our children, and the stability of our kingdom.

From Roy C. Cave and Herbert H. Coulson, *A Source Book for Medieval Economic History* (Milwaukee: Bruce Publishing Co., 1936).

FURTHER READING

Peter Biller, *The Measure of Multitude: Population in Medieval Thought* (Oxford, U.K.: Oxford University Press, 2001).

Richard Hodges, *Dark Age Economics: The Origins of Towns and Trade* (New York: St. Martin's Press, 1982).

Albert Hourani, "The Countryside," in his *History of the Arab Peoples* (New York: Warner Books, 1992).

Patrick V. Kirch, *On the Road of the Winds: An Archaeological History of the Pacific Islands before European Contact* (Berkeley: University of California Press, 2000).

Archibald R. Lewis, *The Development of Southern French and Catalan Society, 718–1050* (Austin: University of Texas Press, 1965).

Miriam T. Stark, ed., *Archaeology of Asia* (Oxford, U.K.: Blackwell Publishing, 2006).

► trade and exchange

INTRODUCTION

Medieval trade and exchange affected not just merchants and the governments that taxed and regulated them. Trade within a country or culture and trade with people of other lands affected almost everyone. The open, protected trade routes fostered by the early Islamic world, for example, were essential to the agricultural boom that began in the 700s. Few people in Islamic cities went without a good, varied diet, because trade brought fruits, vegetables, and meats from al-Andalus, North Africa, and the Near East and brought them quickly. Well-regulated, protected market-places encouraged merchants to invest their money in such ventures as harvesting ice from mountains and glaciers for preserving the fruit that was transported on the Tigris and Euphrates and other waterways. The healthy diet that was afforded even poor people made trade of significant benefit to the Islamic world.

Still, trade was about more than bringing food to market. Underlying trade was people's desire to purchase goods not to be found locally; merchants who understood what their markets wanted could prosper. The most spectacular examples of this in the medieval world were probably the trade in silk and the trade in spices. Silk was a product that drove much international trade in Asia before the medieval era. In the early medieval period China sought to militarily dominate the trade routes of central Asia, out of a desire to ensure that the trade routes for its silk remained open. In the Near East and Europe governments tried to learn the secret of making silk; when they did, they began silk-making industries in their own lands. In this were elements of modern trade and exchange, because not all silk was equal in quality.

Silk needed to be processed to eliminate the stickiness that could cause itching of the skin. The quality of silk depended on how well it was processed and therefore how smooth the silk was to the touch. Thus, Egyptian silk tended to be better than Syrian silk, but Indian silk was better than both. Chinese silk was much coveted. Although Chinese silk was often supposed to be the best silk, its quality within China varied greatly, and Japanese silk was much desired in China. This meant that a purchaser in one market might have several grades of silk from which to choose. Some grades were preferred for weaving rugs, others for cloth for clothing, and so on. India's silk often originated in China, and it was how the Indians processed the silk and dyed it with special colors not to be found in foreign markets that made it especially desirable in Cairo or Constantinople. Thus, during the medieval era trade began to flourish not only with basic materials but with value-added materials. For instance, the value of Iranian metal goods when sold in North Africa, Europe, or China was not restricted to the raw value of the metal; the ways in which Iranian craftspeople enriched their goods with durability and decoration added to the price.

Medieval traders were usually adventurers. In many parts of the world most people never ventured more than 20 miles from where they were born. Even a local peddler making his rounds from village to village in a backwater rural area faced hazards that others did not face and had to be able to deal with people with varying customs and needs. In some cultures traders were celebrated figures, their adventures the stuff of tall tales. In the Islamic world this was especially true, because Muhammad had been a merchant and merchants were regarded as carriers of the word of God to the world beyond that of Islam. Even in cultures (for example that of China) in which merchants were officially scorned because they did not seem to produce material goods themselves, their status during medieval times was hard to ignore. Their work not only helped feed the cities of China but also supplied consumers with goods that enhanced their quality of life; thus Chinese governments usually took pains to ensure the safety of traders on land and at sea.

Spices were goods that enhanced life. They helped preserve food and often turned nutritious but tasteless food into attractive meals. This inspired heroic efforts on the part of merchants to find, transport, and distribute spices from the farthest reaches of the world. Much has been made of the quest for gold in the Americas and Africa, but for most people in most places the spices found in those lands meant more. Thus, the spice trade inspired exploration by Chinese, Indian, Islamic, and European merchants, opening new avenues for both trade and communication. Some of the greatest explorers in the world were traders from lands with abundant spices, such as Indonesia and Southeast Asia, seeking to profit from their goods.

AFRICA

by Charles W. Abbott

Trade and exchange are based on differences in the relative scarcity of goods and on differences in the valuation of scarce goods. There may be variations in the relative supply of goods or in the demand for them or both. Sometimes goods are exchanged using barter. More commonly exchanges are facilitated through the use of some form of money, which might be coins or paper notes, but in Africa were cowries (shells), iron bars, brass rods, spear tips, fishhooks, hoe heads, cloth, gold dust, measures of grain, or almost anything that was a durable store of value and easily exchangeable for other goods.

Imagine a situation in which pastoralists keep large animals for grazing but do not grow crops, while farmers grow and harvest crops but do not keep large animals. In such a case, trading between the two groups is likely. Members of each group have goods (particular types of food). They can both become better off (other things being equal) by exchanging part of what they possess for something else they value more highly at the margin.

Much African trade took advantage of these differences in comparative scarcities. Pastoralists had a relative abundance of animal products (meat, blood, milk products, skins, and manure), while settled farmers had a relative abundance of plant products (grains, tubers, fruits, vegetables, and grain products, such as beer). These sorts of exchanges (grain for meat or yogurt) commonly occur in local trade—pastoralists and sedentary farmers might live close to one another and see each other regularly. It was typical for them to frequent nearby areas in the same semiarid zone but specialize in different activities. Trade of this type often occurred across ethnic lines because specialization of production was often influenced by ethnicity.

The element of demand for a good or service is crucial. Some cattle-raising groups in southern Africa shunned the consumption of fish and prided themselves on their prowess in growing crops and herding cows. Such peoples did not import fish from their coastal neighbors, despite the comparative scarcity of fish of the local economy. Fish were scarce among such groups, but the people who wished to purchase fish were scarcer.

Long-distance trade refers to the transport of goods in bulk over extended distances by professional merchants to serve distant markets. Such trade seems to have been a crucial source of power and revenue for African states. Africa lacked many hearth areas where land was especially productive and valuable and where cities arose and flourished permanently, hosting durable states that obtained their revenue from a sedentary population. Instead, many African states seem to have derived much of their revenue from their ability to tax trade flows. Instead of taxing farmer-citizens and punishing them for nonpayment, many states found it easier to direct trade flows through their territory and to charge tolls on merchants and traders who passed through.

In Africa the equatorial zone is largely covered by tropical rain forest, and as travelers move toward higher latitudes (north or south) they pass through biomes (ecological zones) that are conditioned by decreasing levels of rain and humidity. Thus the progression northward from the equator is rain forest, monsoon forest, guinea (wet) savanna, sudan (dry) savanna, the Sahel (the fringe of the desert) and then desert. Many agricultural commodities can be economically produced in only one or two of these ecological zones. Long-distance trade connected production within the appropriate biome to consumers who might be elsewhere.

Consider the kola nut. Kola nuts (genus *Cola*) grow only in certain forest areas of western Africa, in portions of what are now countries such as Côte d'Ivoire, Ghana, and Nigeria. They are edible fleshy fruits about the size of an almond, packed with caffeine and other alkaloid stimulants. Many Muslims prize them because they are mildly intoxicating yet nowhere prohibited in the Koran. Various other peoples enjoy them as well for their pleasurable stimulant effects, and in some societies they are used in rituals and in cherished traditions of hospitality. Long-distance trade transported kola to markets hundreds of miles from its growing area. By the time kola nuts reached the Maghreb (the western part of North Africa) they were a luxury good.

The raising and breeding of large animals was (and still is) heavily conditioned in Africa by the tsetse fly, which is endemic to the forest belt and much of the humid savanna. The tsetse fly transmits a disease (trypanosomiasis) that kills cattle, horses, and camels. Therefore, those animals could be raised only elsewhere, in drier regions of the continent. Cows raised outside the tsetse fly's range might be driven into the forest to be killed and eaten, but none could be raised there. The same was true of horses.

One study of the horse in western African history concluded that many societies there had ancient knowledge of the horse, even in places where it could not be bred. (In contrast, linguistic and other evidence has found that most groups in central and southern Africa did not know the horse before the coming of the Arabs or the Portuguese.) It has been estimated that the life expectancy of a horse in the humid savanna was no more than two years—too short for any horse population to sustain itself successfully and to reproduce. Yet elites in these areas desired horses intensely—they were useful in war and brought great status and prestige to their owners. In western Africa, therefore, elites in the moist savanna

who could afford it continually imported horses from regions farther to the north. The range of camels was more limited still (as they were quite vulnerable to the tsetse fly), and their owners or caretakers learned to take them only so far south of the Sahara for trade and no farther.

If some products entered long-distance trade routes because of environmentally specific production requirements, others were traded because they were minerals that were extracted only in certain areas. Gold was produced in western and southern Africa and traded over long distances. Western Africa had three major gold production areas: a large zone in what is currently southern Ghana, a smaller area in the high headwaters of the Niger River, and a small area just south of the Senegal River. From these production sites it often flowed north across the Sahara, where the demand for it was greater.

Salt production was also concentrated, but less so—in many places along the coast it could be produced by boiling seawater. Much was produced in open-cast mines developed in dry lake beds within the Sahara. Whatever the source of salt, it was different from gold in the sense that most inland communities craved predictable quantities of it and had to import it from elsewhere. Trade thus brought small amounts of salt into even the most otherwise isolated communities in Africa.

Goods especially common in long-distance trade included necessities such as salt, pricey items such as livestock and slaves, luxuries and stimulants such as kola nuts, and a variety of household items, among them, clothing, items of adornment (cloth, beads, feathers, dyes, and shea butter, which was used as a moisturizer and skin conditioner). Some items were raw materials (hides, from which a variety of goods could be manufactured), and some were finished consumer goods (elaborate cloth, often dyed and embroidered). A variety of manufactured goods were traded as well, including weapons (swords and spears) and tools (knives and hoe heads). Food products traded over a long distance tended to be mostly high-value, low-weight products such as dried fish. Bulky manufactured and artisanal products, such as containers (fired clay pots, baskets, gourds, calabashes, and eating ware), were more likely to be produced locally and traded over short distances.

Gold exists in a category of its own because of its status as an international valid unit of exchange. To produce gold was tantamount to producing money. One Malian king, Mansa Musa, became infamous for the amount of gold he spent on his journey through North Africa (ca. 1324) on the way to Mecca for the Muslim pilgrimage. Anecdotes in Islamic historical accounts report that he paid for everything with gold, spending so lavishly that the value of gold in North African markets was reduced for years after his journey.

The ubiquitous importance of slaves as trade items merits discussion. There were three trade routes from Africa to points north by 1500 (the Atlantic trade, the Indian Ocean trade, and the trans-Saharan trade). Slaves seem to have been important exports from Africa on all three trade routes. The European-dominated Atlantic route was linked to what has been called a "plantation complex" for sugar production, based in large part on slave labor. The sites of sugar production moved from the western Mediterranean to Atlantic islands (Madeira, the Canary Islands) after the year 1400 before the system eventually migrated to the Caribbean and Brazil.

In part, slaves were valuable and in high demand because the African labor market depended on slaves rather than waged workers. In addition, slaves had the major advantage of transporting themselves when driven along a trade route; in this way they were more like livestock than like inert merchandise that had to be hauled. Slaves were also least prone to escape when transported far from the area where they had been captured. Additionally, much of sub-Saharan Africa was a relatively thinly populated region. Contemporary research on the political economy of war has highlighted the tendency for thinly populated areas without much wealth to be prone to slave raiding. When an area is poor and has little to offer in trade, merciless outsiders throughout history have found a way to make a profit through plunder and enslavement of the local inhabitants.

Along with ethnic specialization in production, Africans often practiced ethnic specialization in transportation and marketing. Some groups, such the Tuareg and Berbers, specialized in managing and supervising the trans-Saharan camel caravans. Others, such as Hausa and Dyula (Dioula), specialized in brokering the flow of goods between the forest and Sudanic ecozones. Hausa and Dyula merchants settled as foreigners where kola nuts were produced, often marrying local women. They advanced credit to producers, bought kola nuts at harvest time, and arranged their shipment north to the Sudanic zone. Islam was often an aspect of the business culture for these groups—it brought a common religion, adherence to a shared commercial code, access to scribes for the production of contracts where necessary, and the services of religious leaders for the adjudication of disputes.

Farther south along the Atlantic coast, around present-day Guinea, Kru canoe men specialized in transportation of kola nuts, salt, and fish. In what is now southern Ghana, these transporters might have been Fante. In the Niger River valley they were often Ijaw. For the most part Islam had not yet reached these groups by 1500, and they had other cultural mechanisms to aid cooperation. The unit of organization among canoe-based traders was often the house, a group of men large enough to outfit a large war canoe that might hold 100 fighters or 50 men plus heavy cargo.

Researchers have commented on contrasts between Africa's and Europe's long-distance trade systems in the centuries approaching 1500. Europe's trade seems to have been more oriented toward bulk commodities (grain, timber, wine, raw wool, and cheese) than Africa's. Comparisons between the two regions can be made in a variety of ways, focusing on analytical constructs such as the relative prevalence of luxury goods versus staples, the prevalence of raw materials versus finished goods, the sophistication of transport methods, and the sophistication of financial institutions (including credit instruments) to finance shipments, clear payments, and insure against loss. Similar comparisons might be made with Indian Ocean or Chinese trading systems, where Europe's differences might not be so marked.

A basic comparison of European and African trading systems points to Africa's greater focus on slaves, its relative underdevelopment in ocean-borne commerce, and the limitations of trade in the interior. (Many of Europe's rivers provide easy transportation between the sea and the continental interior, while very few of Africa's do the same.) Because of Africa's peculiar characteristics, many places were inaccessible to shipping by canoe or camel, limiting transportation to human portage and raising transportation costs far above Europe's.

THE AMERICAS
BY J. J. GEORGE

A very telling event occurred the day Christopher Columbus (1451–1506), on his fourth voyage to the New World, encountered a Mayan trading party in a dugout canoe off the Islas de la Bahía, in the Caribbean near present-day Honduras. This was the first meeting between Europeans and Mesoamerican peoples, and it revealed the complicated intertwining already under way in Mesoamerican society. The Maya, as Columbus discovered, were carrying goods from all over Mesoamerica, including obsidian knives and swords from a highland source, cacao beans from the tropical lowlands, bronze axes and bells quite possibly from the Tarascan state of West Mexico (then a major enemy of the Aztec Empire), crucibles for smelting copper, and intricate cotton textiles. The goods in this single canoe represented all of Mesoamerica, indicating a single economic and cultural zone with a high degree of interaction. Trade and exchange activities in the Americas were varied and complex and differed in form from standard trade (a two-way exchange undertaken with a profit or needs-based motive) to tribute (a kind of tax levied upon a subject polity) to reciprocity (the mutual exchange of privileges or goods).

Trade practices in North America varied by region and often focused on elite or prestige items. For example, elite groups from different cultures traded prestige items in the Northwest. These prestige items included copper, dentalia and other marine shells, whalebone (baleen), obsidian, nephrite (a kind of jade), graphite, galena (lead ore), and certain bird feathers. Scholars have also proposed the presence of an elite merchant class that peddled regional goods among the other elites. Proximity to rivers facilitated trade into the interior, while sea routes were used for trade among coastal communities. The Southwest was believed to be linked by elaborate long-distance exchange networks. Archaeological research of shell remains at numerous sites suggest sources connecting southern California, the Gulf of California, northern Mexico, the Colorado Plateau, and the Gulf of Mexico to Hohokam and Anasazi settlements in present-day Arizona, New Mexico, and southern Colorado.

In the Southeast and Midwest evidence from Hopewell Period (ca. 200 B.C.E.–ca. 300 C.E.) sites in the Ohio and Illinois river valleys indicate extensive long-distance exchange networks focusing on raw materials ranging as far as west as Wyoming and as far east as the South Atlantic. Wide-ranging interaction continued but fluctuated throughout time. Shell and copper items in southeastern mortuary sites support continued long-distance exchange as late as the 13th to 15th centuries. Evidence at Cahokia (ca. 900–ca. 1100), near contemporary Saint Louis, suggests that items from distant sources were available primarily to elite status peoples, distributed unequally by social position, presumably to put people in positions of indebtedness.

In Mesoamerica the breakup of Teotihuacán in the mid-eighth century led to new patterns of exchange and connections less focused on major centers such as Teotihuacán and Monte Albán and incorporating coastal and peripheral areas. By the early Postclassic Period (ca. 950–ca. 1150), after the fall of many lowland Maya cities, Tula in Central Mexico, and Chichén Itzá in the Yucatán, became major centers of exchange. Their collapse in the 12th century again contributed to a reorganization of trade and exchange patterns in Mesoamerica, wherein rising city-states of small size and limited local power contributed to the expansion of commercial exchange.

Various models of exchange at Tula, Mexico, have been proposed based on studies of obsidian. Tula (ca. 950–ca. 1150), the capital of the Toltec Empire, also had primary influence on Mayan development in the Yucatán Peninsula, specifically at the site of Chichén Itzá. The first model suggests that obsidian, used in tool and weapons production, was exchanged outside Tula by local workshops and was thus a private-sector enterprise. Local craftsmen simply diverted part of their production and either carried it themselves on trading expeditions or sponsored such expeditions, or they traded it to professional merchants, comparable to later *pochteca* (Aztec traveling merchants). A second model suggests that obsidian was obtained by the state through a system of taxation on city workshops or market vendors. Subsequently, merchants would have been a kind of state-sponsored trader, acting like *pochteca,* essentially serving the state's elite class. A third model suggests that obsidian workshops were located outside the city, closer to the source of the raw material and principal trade routes. In this model, production and exchange are both under control of the state. In a fourth model, obsidian is exchanged in a kind of tribute system. In this system, Tula controlled a tribute empire wherein subject cities paid their obligation in obsidian.

Much is known about the Aztec tribute and market system from painted manuscripts detailing the empire's tribute system and eyewitness accounts of Spanish chroniclers who described the markets. The Codex Mendoza, a painted manuscript commissioned in the 1540s by the Spanish viceroy Antonio de Mendoza (ca. 1490–1552), is divided into two parts. The first is a pictorial history showing the conquests of Aztec emperors, and the second part is a record of the tribute paid by each province of the empire. Tribute items included large quantities of food staples, such as maize, beans, cacao, honey, salt, and chilies; textiles and clothing items, such as garments, raw cotton, and cochineal dye; jewelry and luxuries, such as colorful feathers, lip plugs, amber, turquoise masks, and gold

Pottery vessel, Cholula, Mexico, 1200–1521; polychrome vessels were intended for use by the elite and were traded widely. (© The Trustees of the British Museum)

bars; and miscellaneous products like copal incense, paper, and pottery bowls. Tribute is a formalized kind of tax paid to the state, indicating fealty to the empire. Tribute was one major form of exchange; similarly, the Aztec also had a major market system that facilitated multiple levels of trade.

During Aztec times (14th–16th centuries), unlike the situation with the contemporary Inca of Andean South America, markets and trade were largely independent of the state. Spanish chroniclers— including Hernán Cortés (1485–1547), the leader of the expedition that conquered the Aztec in 1521, and Bernal Díaz del Castillo (1492–?1581), one of his soldiers—marveled at the size of the main Aztec market at Tlatelolco, which served both Tlatelolco and Tenochtitlán (the Aztec capital) where tens of thousands of people (Cortés figured up to 60,000) gathered to do the business of trading hundreds of different goods, all in an orderly, organized fashion. The Basin of Mexico had what anthropologists call a complex interlocking market system with four levels of markets. Tlatelolco is the sole example of the top level. The second level comprised markets that were larger than most, such as at Texcoco, the second-largest city, and Xochimilco. The third level comprised markets in city-state centers like Otumba, Coyoacán, and Alcoman. Finally, the lowest-level markets were those of small towns and villages. The levels were distinguished by numbers of people buying and selling, the quantity and variety of goods and services offered, and by frequency—the highest-level markets met daily, the city-state markets met once a week, and the smallest markets met even less frequently.

Maya long-distance trade in the Classic Period (ca. 250–ca. 900) was dominated after 400 by the central Mexican power center of Teotihuacán, which had established colonies and alliances in Maya territory, notably at Kaminaljuyu, at contemporary Guatemala City, and Tikal, in northern Guatemala. The decline of Teotihuacán around 750 led to trade realignments and possibly contributed to the failure of some Maya cities such as Tikal. During the Postclassic Period (ca. 1000–1697) coastal trade routes increased their hold over commerce, extending routes all around the Yucatán Peninsula, again possibly contributing to the collapse of Classic Period lowland Maya settlements. While seaborne trade grew significantly, overland trade nonetheless remained important and allowed unconquered Maya groups as late as the end of the 17th century to maintain their independence.

Principal long-distance trade goods were divided among utilitarian items and items that were primarily exotic. Utilitarian items included agricultural products, bark cloth, cotton, dyes and pigments, chert (for stone tools), obsidian, pottery, salt, textiles, and tobacco. Exotic items included amber, cacao, cinnabar, copal, quetzal feathers, jaguar pelts, stingray spines, and shark teeth. The trade system itself was in the hands of several classes of merchants, the majority of whom were members of a nonelite class of peddlers and itinerant traders who bought and sold goods in markets or in interactions with individual producers and consumers. Other people engaged in trade part-time, such as those people who manufactured and sold their own goods. But a smaller group of wealthy merchants, members of the elite class, possessed the means to organize and maintain long-distance trade, and they controlled most of the goods that passed through the Mayan area.

Many aspects of Andean civilization were organized in response to extreme topographic factors, which affected development from the earliest cultural florescence straight through to the 15th-century and 16th-century Inca. Exchange networks linked people living in complementary ecological zones; since not all products can be produced at all zones and vary depending on such factors as altitude and climate, people in one zone would trade their products with people in another zone, thus linking themselves in a complementary and vertical system of exchange. For example, altiplano peoples, or people who lived on the high plains, traded llamas and wool for lowland products including pepper, cotton, and coca.

Similarly, many exchange paradigms evolved alongside imperial cultural developments. The Wari and Tiwanaku empires developed almost simultaneously through the sixth to 11th centuries, the Chimú in the 12th through 14th centuries, and the Inca in the 15th and 16th centuries. Each empire expanded and developed both regional and long-distance exchange networks. In the case of the Inca the entire Andean region from Quito, Ecuador, to Santiago, Chile, was subsumed into one massive zone. A very hands-on authority, the Inca redistributed many staples by means of an elaborate system of storage facilities built throughout the empire. The Inca institution of *mit'a* labor, which was a kind of tax by forced labor, meant that an exchange of labor occurred wherein laborers were forced to leave home for an extended period of time to work on various state projects or to serve as members of the military. Finally, local lords, responsible for political, military, and ritual leadership, sometimes distributed products that could be procured only from great distances.

ASIA AND THE PACIFIC

BY KENNETH HALL

Local Asian and Pacific island trade in the medieval era ranged widely. Highland hunter-gatherers exchanged such forest products as timber, scented woods, bamboo, and lacquer; seminomadic herders of the pastoral steppe and desert

The Story of the Silk Princess, *wooden panel painting, Dandan-oilik, Khotan oasis, Xinjiang Province, China, sixth century. Khotan was a thriving kingdom on the Silk Road; this panel tells the story of a princess who smuggled silkworms into Khotan, defying the emperor's embargo by hiding mulberry seeds and silk moth eggs in her headdress.* (© The Trustees of the British Museum)

regions supplied meats, hides, and transport services; and lowland cultivators added agricultural produce. Salt from the coast, which was essential to the human diet, was a key commodity in these upland-lowland and hinterland-steppe exchanges. Another type of swap took place between settled hinterland farmers and coastal peoples: To the coastal people the farmers supplied grains, fruits, vegetables, specialty agricultural produce (cotton, hemp, and spices), manufactured goods (textiles, ceramics, and handicrafts), and raw materials (iron, gold, gems, and tin), as well as the forest and steppe products supplied by the highlanders and steppe dwellers. The coastal populations in turn sold externally to international traders. This coastal-sector trade brought products of the sea and specialized goods and imports back to the rural communities, who passed these commodities on to their highland- and steppe-dwelling trade partners.

Regional and long-distance trade was a motor for societal development throughout Asia during the medieval era, especially among those regions that had contact with the major international trade routes that connected China to India and the Middle East. Indigenous populations responded to the opportunities provided by these external contacts. They supplied local agricultural, animal husbandry, craft, and jungle products that made their way from the hinterland to the coast through more sophisticated marketing networks. Such trade influenced a society's productive and consumptive patterns. Regional and long-distance trading connections were also an important source of cross-cultural and religious exchange. Traders and travelers brought ideas and technology. In the early medieval era Buddhist pilgrims passed along the commercial routes between China and India, with Christian and Muslim missionaries following in the second millennium hoping to convert Asia's populations.

Transcontinental caravan trade routes connected eastern and western Eurasia by means of a central Asian passageway that lay just north of the rugged Himalaya mountain range separating India from China, central Asia, and southern Russia. Among the major goods carried along the route in addition to silk were jade, jewels, bronze, ceramics, glassware, carpets, cotton, tea, and spices. From the fourth to the eighth centuries central Asian Sogdians based in Suyab (in modern-day Kyrgyzstan) and Talas (in present-day Kazakhstan) were the most prominent among the multiethnic caravan traders; then, in the 11th century, the central Asian Samanids (with ties to newly Muslim Persia) based in Bukhara and Samarqand (in modern-day Uzbekistan) and Herat (in present-day Afghanistan) were preeminent. From the 11th century until the early 13th century political instability on either end of the route led to a decline in its use until Mongol tribesmen took control of the China–to–Middle East portion of the route in the 13th century. During this period, as in others when the route was not safe, travelers shifted to the alternative Indian Ocean maritime route.

Westbound merchants on the Silk Road often began their journeys in China's northern capitals and traveled along a network of urban commercial centers, between China's Gobi Desert in the north and the mountains of Tibet in the south. This portion of the route ended in northern Afghanistan, where the route split. One portion continued west to eastern Europe, another went south to India, while the main route went southwest through Persia (modern day Iran) to Constantinople.

The China–to–central Asia portion of the route depended on alliances negotiated by the representatives of China's and Persia's rulers with the central Asian Xiongnu and Yuezhi peoples (as they were known by the Chinese). These groups were well paid by Chinese and Persian governments to keep the route open, but strategically placed government military outposts served to remind them who was in charge. However when a Persian or Chinese dynasty fell, resulting in a time of inattention and a failure to pay for the protection, these groups collected passage fees directly from the traders—or they seized their goods.

Trade along the Silk Road reached its high point under the 13th-century Mongols who had conquered all the territory from China to modern Turkey. Marco Polo (1254–1324), traveling to China from Venice and back in the late 13th century, was one of many European merchants who benefited from Mongol stewardship of the Silk Road. However, in addition to bringing wealth to Europe, the Silk Road brought the Black Death, or plague, which spread from central Asian cities to Europe in the late 1340s.

In the 15th century the route's volume permanently declined. This decline was the result of several factors: the fall of the Mongol Yuan Dynasty in China in 1368; the subsequent conversions to Islam among the post–Mongol era hordes that controlled the overland passageway; and the increased preference the subsequent Ming Dynasty had for the ocean route in the early years of its reign.

Indian Ocean–based trade was initially driven by the exchanges of Middle Eastern and southern Asian goods for those of China, but during the medieval era Southeast Asia's spices became prominent. Spices were rare items used in culinary, aromatic, and medicinal applications, with their medicinal value initially overshadowing their culinary use. Because these were all very expensive and imported in small quantities, only aristocrats could afford to buy them. They were literally worth their weight in gold to a successful merchant.

The most prized spices were pepper, ginger, cinnamon, turmeric, cardamom, cloves, nutmeg, and mace. Southeast Asia's eastern archipelago Spice Islands (now called the Moluccas) were the source of the most valuable spices: cloves, nutmeg, and mace grew exclusively there. Cloves are the dried, unopened flower bud of an evergreen tree grown on five small islands in the Moluccas; nutmeg and mace are parts of the fruit of a rare evergreen tree native to the Banda Islands. The jungles of Borneo and Sumatra were the source of benzoin and camphor barks, which were considered vital in preparations of Chinese medicines. Benzoin was also in demand for Chinese and Indian religious ritual, as were aloe and sandalwood from Southeast Asia and frankincense and myrrh from the Arabian Peninsula and east coast of Africa. India's southwest Malabar Coast was considered the source of the best pepper; northern Sumatran pepper was a less expensive alternative in the era after 1000.

These commodities made their way from their point of origin to eastern and western markets through the hands of multiethnic traders by way of the Indian Ocean maritime routes. The Strait of Malacca that separated the Malay Peninsula from Sumatra was a key passageway from Southeast Asia to the western marketplaces of India and the Middle East. The South China Sea was equally important in the transit of spices from Java to Vietnam, China, Japan, and Korea. An alternative route from the Moluccas to China passed north through the Sulu Sea by way of the Philippines.

As the international trade developed in the first millennium, Indonesian seamen and their vessels dominated the shipping lanes; India-based and Middle Eastern–sojourning seamen and merchants were then the most common in the western Indian Ocean. By 800 Middle Eastern seamen and merchants were sailing all the way to China. Mixtures of highly skilled and experienced Chinese and Southeast Asian navigators were dominant after 1100, but they were subject to Chinese government restrictions on China-based seamen and on foreign access to China's ports of trade.

Seafaring traders bought deck and cargo space from a ship owner or captain. The crews involved in international shipping were composed of multiethnic professional seamen; in contrast, ships involved in regional and local trade regularly supplemented their professional crews with slaves purchased at regional slave markets or from pirates. The rhythm of the international sea trade depended on the seasonal monsoons, with winds blowing southwest to northeast from roughly June through August, and then reversing to blow northeast to southwest from December through March. Maritime travelers found themselves regularly lying over in a port until the next monsoon season allowed their return voyage. Because it took two to three years to make the complete east–west passage, traders would specialize in one sector of the route. For example, a merchant might trade only between the Middle East and India, India and Southeast Asia, or Indonesia and China. Ports-of-trade, similar to the caravan centers of the Silk Road, were likely to have peaks and lows in their populations as well as in their trading activities, depending not only on the seasonal travels of the merchants but also on the opening and closing of the major international markets.

Indian Ocean and Silk Road merchants would settle for months or years in a foreign port or caravan center, where they might take on wives and raise families. Itinerant traders would sell their goods to local intermediaries at their destination ports or urban centers. These intermediaries would then hold and resell them to merchants arriving later from other regional markets. For example, local intermediaries in Southeast Asia's ports exchanged Middle Eastern glassware and Indian cotton textiles supplied by South Asia–based seafarers for ceramics, silk, and spices brought by Chinese and Southeast Asian merchants.

A mix of administered and open marketplace competition was the norm in the Asian centers of trade. Local marketplaces were administered by members of the local elite in partnership with resident commercial specialists; a visiting merchant's activities and prices were predetermined by his negotiations with local authorities to ensure that the interests of the local community were protected while the merchant made a reasonable, but not abusive level of profit. Indian, Chinese, and Middle Eastern merchant-traders commonly organized themselves into merchant guilds or operated in partnership with other family members at the local and international level to represent and protect their collective interests better.

Most major commercial centers were under the direct control of central government officials or their delegated authorities, who similarly negotiated the terms of local trade access and collected the government's tax or share in cash or in kind prior to allowing visiting merchants to participate in their marketplace. The major commercial centers and ports-of-trade also competed to provide the most agreeable terms of trade; favored market centers offered the security, products (whether their own or acquired from secondary marketplaces), and provisions demanded by traders.

The 11th and 12th centuries witnessed a surge in the volume of Indian Ocean trade, thanks largely to the regional stability established over the Middle East by Muslim Abbasid caliphs (to 1258), the Seljuk Turks (1037–1219), and the Song Dynasty government's development and relocation to south China (1127–1279). Middle Eastern merchants flooded the Indian Ocean, seeking Asian goods in exchange for their own. This, paired with a stable China market, resulted in southern India and Sri Lanka becoming new international commercial hubs, filling roles as strategic intermediaries in the trade between the Middle East and Southeast Asia. In Southeast Asia, Java became prominent because of its central role in providing international access to the Spice Islands. By this time, regional centers began to function as part of one great, integrated Indian Ocean trade network. The increased volume of trade attracted a multiethnic community of trade specialists that included assorted Middle Easterners, Indians, Southeast Asians, and Chinese.

In the early 15th century, the new Ming-Dynasty emperors, who had come to power in China in 1368, sent the eunuch admiral Zheng He and his fleet of Chinese battleships to assert China's interests across the entire maritime network (1405–33). Zheng He purposefully eliminated pirates that were inhibiting trade, and he provided military assistance and promises of continued Chinese support to local political regimes that could guarantee the regular flow of international products to China's ports—for example, in Chinese support of the new Moluccas polity that was empowered to ensure the security of the vital Strait of Malacca passageway. He also reinstated the Chinese tributary trade system, wherein Indian Ocean countries sent periodic embassies to China's courts to present diplomatic gifts of their prize marketplace commodities in return for honorific material symbols and official proclamations that confirmed their local authority. In part in response to these Ming-Dynasty initiatives, Asia's 15th century had substantial increases in trade volume, participants, and the diversity of traded commodities. This prosperity attracted the attention of Europeans, whose desire to acquire Asia's exotic commodities resulted in Europe's 16th century Age of Discovery.

EUROPE

BY TINA THURSTON

Medieval Europe saw significant changes in economic organization, which archaeologists study through analysis of artifacts, features, sites, and landscapes as interpreted through social theory and, since scant texts on markets and trade do not always reflect actual conditions, the careful use of historic documents. Several geographic axes affected markets, trade, and exchange in medieval Europe. The first is the continuum of urban to rural environments. Archaeological rescue work in European cities provides evidence for market activities in former medieval urban centers. Ecclesiastic establishments are also studied for their role in production and trade, and in recent years archaeologists have revealed less distinction between country and town; many who manufactured, marketed, and traded were also farmers. Rural production sites figured importantly in provisioning urban consumers with food animals, dairy, and cloth, and rural markets were tied into larger exchange networks.

Another important axis relates to the territorial boundaries of the former Roman Empire. While all of Europe felt the impact of imperial collapse, former provinces were differently affected than were non-Roman regions to the north and east, effectively shaping the nature of early medieval trade in each area. A final axis is the scale of study: Archaeologists identify the links in the chain of trade and exchange from workshops to marketplaces to trade routes and whole regions. Well-designed research on economic activity takes more than one scale into account.

Many 20th-century historians used only primary documents and scholarly insight to hypothesize about relationships between feudalism, urbanization, markets, and local and long-distance trade in medieval Europe. Some proposed that Roman organization persisted in the medieval period and was only dismantled when Muslim expansion cut Europe off from the Mediterranean, creating a so-called dark age, a view that became widely accepted.

By the 1970s archaeologists began to investigate the accuracy of these assertions. Generalized, predictable processes linked to political, economic, and environmental conditions were studied and compared globally, cross-culturally, and crosscutting time periods. A mandate to ignore historic records in favor of ahistorical interpretations directly from material culture was widely accepted. Such archaeologists deconstructed European historical perspectives, arguing that primary sources were biased by their authors' ideologies. Archaeological evidence alone showed that the Roman panregional market economy collapsed quickly in the fifth century and continued to decline into the seventh century as large-scale manufacturing, import, and export under the aegis of a single government and legal system disappeared.

More recent archaeologists advocate historically contextualized archaeological study that uses different kinds of data as independent threads of evidence. Analyses in this light indicate that while organized, commercial long-distance trade evaporated, local merchants and craftspeople across Europe were in fact busy with a major reorganization of trade that was a model of ingenuity, displaying the ability of human societies to cope with changing conditions and sometimes catastrophic events.

Within former Roman regions during the fifth century archaeological investigations show that harbors fell into disrepair, and steep declines occurred in amphorae traded long distance between distant parts of the former empire. In Rome craftspeople plied their trades and conducted business from ephemeral structures in formerly elegant public spaces like the Campus Martius, while elsewhere market activities were conducted from crude stalls in abandoned forums. In Buthrotum (modern-day Butrint) the insecurity of the post-Roman world is reflected through brief spurts of fortification construction and a short surge of palace building, perhaps to preserve the status quo. Abandonment followed; palaces were left half constructed, and in derelict or unfinished structures small, vernacular houses were built whose refuse shows plenty of market activity but greatly reduced trade with distant regions. Around the onetime Roman world artifacts once traded from afar reverted to local manufacture. Simultaneously, parts of Europe closer to the Byzantine

Baltic amber beads, a precious commodity testifying to Britain's trade with the Baltic region (1400s) (© Museum of London)

sphere saw increased activity in both international trade and market activity.

Outside former imperial boundaries both elites and ordinary people continued to seek market trade, and thus more regionalized trade routes and markets evolved. The Roman era Rhine-Rhone route remained important, augmented with increased activity between the Baltic and Black seas via connecting river routes. Atlantic Europe and Britain, connected for millennia by sea-lanes, saw increased trade, and new North Sea routes connected western Europe with Scandinavia. Some Roman era trading places continued to operate for a time as local markets, but as sea and land routes shifted to reflect new political systems, many eventually were replaced by newly established ports of entry and trading posts.

Conditions had changed by the ninth century; archaeological evidence combined with newly analyzed Islamic texts shows a revival in long-distance trade due to exchange with the East, and the main product traded out of Europe, which might well have fueled European economic development, were slaves of European origin, bought and sold throughout the Byzantine world, the eastern Mediterranean, and western Asia. Between the seventh and 11th centuries commercial trading sites, or emporia, were established across northwestern Europe. The larger of these locations, often coastal ports, have been subjected to much archaeological study: Ipswich and Hamwic in Britain; Birka, Ribe, Kaupang, Uppåkra, Löddeköpinge, and Hedeby in Scandinavia; Quentovic and Dorestad on the Rhine; Staraya Ladoga in Russia; and Wolin in Poland.

The presence of weights and measures, fortifications, and boundary markers were once cited as evidence that kings or bishops closely controlled and administered trade through their unique ability to regulate, organize, and tax—their motive to support themselves and control access to high-prestige items. More recent investigations indicate that local magnates, farmers, or craftspeople producing surplus—indeed all those with goods and means—were permitted to trade at emporia with the stipulation that they pay taxes and tolls to rulers who provided safe and regulated commercial places. Research in central and eastern Europe indicate that similar markets evolved from crafts-working communities associated with local rulers at their fortified settlements, but these eventually developed into urban marketplaces.

Once, large coastal emporia were considered the sole expression of long-distance trade in post-Roman, extra-imperial Europe, but recently small inland trading sites have been discovered and investigated. In contrast to expectations, these places also show evidence of long-distance trade: coins, metalwork, and other materials not usually associated with short-distance trade in subsistence items that typically were bartered.

Early marketplaces were composed of ephemeral structures, sunken-floored stalls, and booths that are identified only by virtue of their location away from settlements or indications of their transient use. More frequently, they are identified through artifacts of manufacture: Artisans producing wares in the marketplace create unique artifact assemblages. Typical finds include weaving tools or bone and horn fragments from the manufacture of pins and combs; fragmentary crucibles, molds, and silver or bronze wasters from jewelry making; slag, iron bars, and rods, and in rare cases tongs and hammers from ironworking. Industrial-scale activity is reflected in the uniform size of fish caught in large commercial nets, and trade in fish, fowl, and other animals is clear from butchery patterns that professionals used to prepare them for market. Other market finds include coins, scales, weights, and keys to merchants' coffers. Serendipitous finds of warehouses or trading shipwrecks occasionally provide information on transport and storage. Even so-called dark earth—a humanly created soil often associated with marketplaces—can be studied.

In the High Middle Ages historical records are more numerous and detailed but were still kept by the upper classes, and many questions still are best viewed from archaeological perspectives. By the 13th and 14th centuries artifacts show that even within the lower classes, social stratification separated the poorest from the less poor, especially after the Black Death, or plague, when wages rose as the result of labor shortages. Early medieval markets were few, and their luxury materials were primarily reserved for the upper classes. In later times a vast network of small and large markets permitted ordinary people to participate in more frequent buying and selling, and this network further linked town and country as products like meat, milk, and the ingredients for ale were produced in the hinterland, processed there, and transported to urban areas.

Different archaeological questions require varying scales of analysis. To understand how needed or desired goods were made and brought to consumers, excavations at a workshop are appropriate. Studies have shown that while many artisans kept full-time workshops in markets, some sold luxury wares to ordinary people as itinerants, moving portable workshops from village to village.

If the taxation or control of trade by rulers is under study, the larger scale of the emporia or marketplace is useful. Some show long-term occupation of the same plot of land by artisans in the same trade. Evaluated as a group, their unchanging boundaries and continuity, often surrounded by a nondefensive demarcation ditch, suggest that those buying and selling on these plots of land were regulated and taxed.

Comparisons of archaeology and history often reveal contradictions as medieval chroniclers rarely wrote objective descriptions of market interactions and noted only information biased toward their own concerns. Landscape-scale study explains this, tracing the paths of rural products to urban markets. Written records discussing commercially produced wool, meat, and milk indicate large populations of cattle and fewer sheep, while archaeologists record much higher numbers of sheep than cattle bones. Sheep, dying more frequently from disease, were disposed of as whole carcasses. Cows with longer life spans were butchered for food after natural death or after live transport to town markets; their bones, fragmented from butchery and cooking, are less frequently preserved. Only study of a large transect from country to town can reveal this. Thus, even in the middle to late medieval periods, when historical records of exchange, taxation, assessment, and individual holdings are more common, questions about products, the paths they found to market, and their eventual depositional contexts are still best answered through archaeological explorations.

THE ISLAMIC WORLD

BY BRADLEY A. SKEEN

The prophet Muhammad was a merchant active in the area of the Red Sea and the eastern Mediterranean. His new religion of Islam found its first home among the mercantile aristocracy of Medina and Mecca, but others of this class opposed him because they thought founding a new, exclusivist religion might be bad for business. Trade, as a profession, always held a more favored position in the Islamic world than in Europe. Trade was for many Muslims almost a necessity, since carrying small amounts of merchandise to sell along the way was a common means of financing the pilgrimage to Mecca that all Muslims had to make in their lifetime.

The Islamic conquest of an empire that stretched from Spain to the borders of China in inner Asia created an enormous economic unit that also linked together the maritime trade of the Mediterranean and the Indian Ocean (the greatest hubs of economic activity in the medieval world). The lack of political barriers in this vast realm aided the movement not only of trade but also of armies, craftsmen, scholars, and pilgrims. Government, cities, agriculture, and long-range trade all nourished each other and consequently flourished. The large cities of the Islamic world needed food and raw materials, while palaces, mosques, and aristocrats required luxuries for the display of wealth and power. Arab merchants were ready to supply them. Contact with Islamic traders by their counterparts in Italy also introduced new words into European languages, among them, check, broker, tariff, traffic, magazine, caravan, and bazaar.

The ease of trade in the Islamic world also meant that new ideas, techniques, and inventions could travel freely. At the most prosaic level, a rug made in China, for instance, could be traded as far as Algeria within a year, and the technique of its manufacture could be examined and copied by local craftsmen. Inventions such as the spinning wheel traveled from China to Europe via the Islamic trade routes. Thanks to trade, books could move just as swiftly across the Islamic world. The revolution in European intellectual history fostered by the reception of Greek and Arabic philosophical works by Christians in Spain depended for the most part on books that had been written or translated in Persia or Baghdad but which were readily available in Spain because of the flourishing book trade.

Although trade was taxed, Islamic government did not generally interfere with commerce and did much to support it. In 695 the caliph Abd al-Malik introduced a new Islamic coinage to replace the older Byzantine and Sassanian coins that had been circulating in the Islamic world. Because of the Koranic ban on representational art, the new coinage did not bear the traditional image of the ruler and other iconographic

Blue-and-white brush rest with Arabic inscription, Jingdezhen, Jiangxi Province, southern China, as early as 1506; such pieces with Islamic decoration would have been made specifically by and for the large Muslim population living in China and were traded and exported.
(© The Trustees of the British Museum)

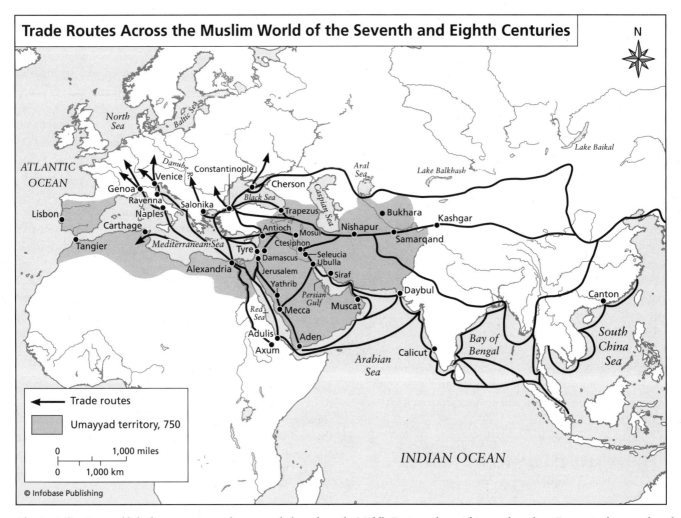

Trade Routes Across the Muslim World of the Seventh and Eighth Centuries

N

Trade routes

Umayyad territory, 750

0   1,000 miles

0   1,000 km

© Infobase Publishing

Islamic civilization established an extensive trading network throughout the Middle East, northern Africa, and southern Europe in the seventh and eighth centuries.

types but was decorated with calligraphic representations of verses from the Koran. The first coinage was the gold dinar (whose name derived ironically from the Roman silver denarius), though the main currency used in trade was, as always, silver: the dirham. These coins rapidly spread throughout the world and have been discovered, for example, as far away from Islamic territory as Sweden. Hundreds of thousands of dirhams were buried in hoards during the Middle Ages, obtained in exchange for furs, amber, and slaves that traded through Kiev Rus (the modern-day Baltic States and Ukraine) to the Islamic world. Archaeologists have also found Islamic coins in China and in Great Zimbabwe in southern Africa.

The Arab conquest did not entail much long-term disruption of the local economies of the conquered peoples (except for the imposition of higher tax rates on non-Muslims) who contributed to the Islamic commercial economy. On the other hand, large commercial enterprises, such as the pearl fishery in the Persian Gulf, were increasingly monopolized by the state, interfering with the development of a capitalist economy. Sharia law prevents Muslims from charging or paying interest (a testimony to the relative primitiveness of the economic system in which Muhammad participated), but this does not seem to have hampered the development of economic activity in the Islamic world compared with that in antiquity or in the contemporary European economy. On the other hand, Islamic courts for the first time favored lawsuits as a realistic means for merchants to find redress.

Arab merchants created new financial institutions and instruments for themselves that had not been available in earlier times. International banks were established for the first time and spread the model of the Sassanian (ancient Persian) banking system. In the Islamic world a bank could accept a deposit in Baghdad and pay out a promissory note or check (derived from the Persian word *sakk*, transmitted to the West as an Arabic loanword) issued against the same deposit at a bank in Córdoba or in China. Arab traders also formed the first simple versions of joint-stock companies. Islamic merchants would trade with capital borrowed from investors, even from Jews and Christians, dividing the profits among the investors. In the earlier Roman Empire, by contrast, aristocrats (who controlled the bulk of the wealth generated from land) were legally proscribed from investing in trade except that conducted by their own freedmen (slaves they had manumitted).

The new Islamic trade practices were quickly copied by their European rivals, first by the Venetians. The crusading order of the Knights Templars operated a system of international banks on the Islamic model, and it was with the goal of erasing debts owed to the Templar bank that the order was destroyed by Philip IV of France beginning in 1307. The important technique of double-entry bookkeeping was also an Islamic invention that was quickly borrowed by Europeans.

In medieval times the primary source of wealth was the agricultural exploitation of land. However, the unification of the trade routes between the Far East and the Mediterranean world in Islamic hands made international trade for the Islamic middlemen far more profitable than it had been in ancient times. This trade conveyed luxury goods, such as silk and porcelain, from east to west, but since there was very little produced in the West that was wanted in China and India, the return was almost entirely in the form of precious metal coinage. The main trade route was from Ceylon (a large island off the southern tip of India) to ports on the Red Sea and Persian Gulf. This trade was facilitated by the annual cycle of monsoon winds, which allowed fleets of merchant ships to sail to Asia from the Horn of Africa across the open ocean to Ceylon and back without the need of sophisticated navigational equipment (although Arab seamen made considerable advances in navigation).

The Indian Ocean trade was monopolized in the 11th through the 13th centuries by the Karimis (an Arabic term for "merchant" but given special meaning in connection with this group), a group of about 50 merchant families organized in a network in Egypt, Yemen (at the mouth of the Red Sea), Ceylon, and India. This group engaged purely in mercantile activity and did not directly profit from, for instance, land owning or tax farming (a practice by which a private contractor will pay a government a sum approximately equal to the expected tax revenues of a province in exchange for the right to collect the actual tax). Their activities were financed as joint-stock ventures with private investors. This same group of merchants ran the largest network of international banks. The Karimis are sometimes viewed as a precursor to modern multinational corporations.

The Indian Ocean trade route was the most important in the Islamic world. In general, shipping was far more efficient and safer than land transport; thus, insofar as possible, local trade was conducted by river barges and on small coast-hugging merchant ships that plied the Persian Gulf, the Red Sea, and the Mediterranean and Indian Ocean along the African coast. Another trade network based on coastal sailing extended eastward from Ceylon and reached as far as Guangzhou in southern China, on the Pearl River estuary near modern-day Hong Kong. This was a city specially built by the Tang government to facilitate Islamic trade. Cross-Mediterranean trade from the Islamic cities of North Africa and the Levant was usually handled by European merchants, especially those from the republics of Venice and Genoa and from Barcelona in Spain.

Caravan routes crisscrossed much of the Islamic world. Regular tracks were followed, but few roads that could have supported wheeled vehicles were built between cities. Caravan traffic was almost exclusively packed on the backs of camels. Individual caravans could be made up of as many as 5,000 camels. The important Silk Road trading routes began at the Chinese western capital of Xi'an, where there was a strong Islamic presence and an impressive mosque, and ran through the inner Asian cities of Samarqand, Bukhara, and Merv and through Persia to Baghdad. Other routes ran through inner Asia to ports on the Black Sea. An extensive trade route also stretched north and south through Russia and supplied goods to the Islamic world. Caravan routes also reached from Baghdad to the Mediterranean and Red Sea across the Arabian Desert. The Western Sahara was also traversed by caravan routes dominated by the Tuareg tribesmen between the Mediterranean coast and the Niger Delta, where great Islamic cities, such as Djenné and Timbuktu, existed. Local commodities such as salt were traded via these routes, but by far the most profitable commodity on them were slaves brought up from western Africa to the Mediterranean.

See also ADORNMENT; AGRICULTURE; CITIES; CLIMATE AND GEOGRAPHY; CLOTHING AND FOOTWEAR; CRAFTS; ECONOMY; EMPIRES AND DYNASTIES; EMPLOYMENT AND LABOR; FOOD AND DIET; GOVERNMENT ORGANIZATION; HUNTING, FISHING, AND GATHERING; INVENTIONS; LAWS AND LEGAL CODES; METALLURGY; MIGRATION AND POPULATION MOVEMENTS; MINING, QUARRYING, AND SALT MAKING; MONEY AND COINAGE; PANDEMICS AND EPIDEMICS; ROADS AND BRIDGES; SEAFARING AND NAVIGATION; SHIPS AND SHIPBUILDING; SLAVES AND SLAVERY; SOCIAL ORGANIZATION; TEXTILES AND NEEDLEWORK; TOWNS AND VILLAGES; TRANSPORTATION; WEIGHTS AND MEASURES.

Asia and the Pacific

Excerpt from the Liang-shu (ca. 629)

In the west of it [India] they carry on much trade by sea to Ta ts'in [Roman Syria] and Ar-hsi [Arsacids, or Parthia], especially in articles of Ta-ts'in, such as all kinds of precious things, coral, amber, chin-pi [gold jadestone], chu-chi [a kind of pearl], lang-kan, Yu-chin [turmeric?] and storax. Storax is made by mixing and boiling the juice of various fragrant trees; it is not a natural product. It is further said that the inhabitants of Ta-ts'in gather the storax plant, squeeze its juice out, and thus make a balsam; they then sell its dregs to the traders of other countries; it thus goes through many hands before reaching Zhongguo [China], and, when arriving here, is not so very fragrant. Yu-chin only comes from the country of Chi-pin [a country near the Persian Gulf].

From Friedrich Hirth, *China and the Roman Orient: Researches into Their Ancient and Mediaeval Relations as Represented in Old Chinese Records* (Shanghai and Hong Kong: Kelly and Walsh, 1885).

Europe

Francesco Balducci Pegolotti: Excerpt from Pratica della Mercatura (ca. 1340)

Goods are sold at Constantinople in various ways.

The indigo called Baccaddeo is (sold in packages) of a certain weight, and the weight you must know should be the cantar. And if the buyer chooses to take it from the seller without weighing it, be it more or less than a cantar, 'tis to the profit or loss of the buyer. But they do almost always weigh it, and then payment is made according to the exact weight, be it more or less than a cantar. And the skin and wrapper are given with it but no tare is deducted; nor is garbling allowed nor do they allow the indigo to be examined except by a little hole, from which a small sample may be extracted. For such is use and wont in those parts.

[The following are sold by the cantar (of 150 Genoese lbs.).]

Wormwood; madder, and the bag goes as madder without any allowance for tare. Alum of every kind, and even if it be Roch-alum, the sack and cord go as alum.

[The following also are sold by the cantar at Constantinople and in Pera.]

Ox hides, buffalo hides, Horse hides: In purchasing these they are shown to the provers up the hill . . . and if the hides smell damp or wet, then a fit allowance is made, and this is the system in Pera and in Constantinople, and they are not put in the sun unless they are exceedingly wet indeed.

Suet in jars; iron of every kind; tin of every kind; lead of every kind. Zibibbo or raisins of every kind, and the mats go as raisins, with no allowance for tare unless they be raisins of Syria. In that case the baskets or hampers are allowed for as tare, and remain with the buyer into the bargain.

Soap of Venice, soap of Ancona, and soap of Apulia in wooden cases. They make tare of the cases, and then these go to the buyer for nothing. But the soap of Cyprus and of Rhodes is in sacks, and the sacks go as soap with no tare allowance.

Broken almonds in bags; the bag goes as almonds; only if there be more than one sack and cord it must be removed, or deducted, so that the buyer shall not have to take more than one sack and cord as almonds, but for any beyond that there shall be tare allowed; and the cord shall go to the buyer gratis.

Honey in kegs or skins; tare is allowed for the keg or skin, but it remains with the buyer gratis.

Cotton wool; and the sack goes as cotton without tare. Cotton yarn; and the sack is allowed as tare, and remains with the buyer for nothing.

Rice; and the bag goes as rice, but if it be tied the cord is allowed as tare and remains with the seller. Turkey galls of every kind; and if they are in bags you weigh bag and all, and do not make tare of the bag. Dried figs of Majorca and Spain in hampers. Orpiment, and the bag goes as orpiment. Safflower, and you make tare of bag and cord, and after that they remain with the buyer gratis.

Henna; and the bag goes as henna, only a tare of four per cent is allowed by custom of trade. Cummin; and the bag goes as cummin, and if tied with rope the rope is allowed as tare but remains with the buyer gratis.

Pistachios; and the bag goes with them with no allowance for tare, unless there be more bags than one, and if there be, then the excess is weighed and allowed as tare, and the buyer has the one bag gratis.

Sulphur; and the bag or barrel in which it is, is allowed as tare, and goes to the buyer gratis. Senna; and the bag is tare and goes to the buyer. Pitch; and the mat is allowed for as tare, and goes to the buyer. Morda sangue; the bag goes with it and no tare allowed. . . .

Saltmeat; cheese; flax of Alexandria and of Romania; Camlet wool; washed wool of Romania; unwashed ditto; washed or unwashed wool of Turkey; chestnuts. . . .

Round pepper; ginger; barked brazil-wood; lac; zedoary; incense; sugar, and powdered sugar of all kinds; aloes of all kinds; quicksilver; cassia fistola; sal ammoniac or lisciadro; cinnabar; cinnamon; galbanum; ladanum of Cyprus; mastic; copper; amber, big, middling, and small, not wrought; stript coral; clean and fine coral, middling and small.

[The following are sold by the pound.]

Raw silk; saffron; clove-stalks and cloves; cubebs; lign-aloes; rhubarb; mace; long pepper; galangal; broken camphor; nutmegs; spike; cardamoms; scam-mony; pounding pearls; manna; borax; gum Arabic; dragon's blood; camel's bay; turbit; silk-gauze; sweet-meats; gold wire; dressed silk; wrought amber in beads. . . .

[By the piece.]

Silk velvets; damasks; maramati; gold cloth of every kind; nachetti and nacchi of every kind; and all cloths of silk and gold except gauzes. . . .

[Then follow details of the different kinds of cloths, with the length of the pieces. And then a detail of special modes of selling certain wares, such as:]

Undressed vairs, and vair bellies and backs; Slavonian squirrels; martins and fitches; goat skins and ram skins; dates, filberts, walnuts; salted sturgeon tails; salt; oil of Venice; oil of the March; oil of Apulia, of Gaeta, etc.; wheat and barley; wine of Greece, of Turpia in Calabria, of Patti in Sicily, of Patti in Apulia, of Cutrone in Calabria, of the March, of Crete, of Romania; country wine.

From: Henry Yule and Henri Cordier,
trans. and eds., *Cathay and the Way
Thither, Being a Collection of Medieval
Notices of China* (London: Hakluyt
Society, 1916).

FURTHER READING

Janet Abu-Lughod, *Before European Hegemony: The World System 1250–1350* (New York: Oxford University Press, 1991).

James H. Barrett, Alison M. Locker, and Callum M. Roberts, "'Dark Age Economics?' Revisited: The English Fish Bone Evidence AD 600–1600," *Antiquity* 78, no. 301 (September 2004): 618–636.

Luce Boulnois, *Silk Road: Monks, Warriors, and Merchants*, trans. Helen Loveday (New York: W. W. Norton, 2006).

Geoffrey Braswell, ed., *Maya and Teotihuacan: Reinterpreting Early Classic Interaction* (Austin: University of Texas Press, 2003).

George E. Brooks, *Landlords and Strangers: Ecology, Society, and Trade in Western Africa, 1000–1630* (Boulder, Colo.: Westview Press, 1993).

K. N. Chaudhuri, *Trade and Civilisation in the Indian Ocean: An Economic History from the Rise of Islam to 1750* (Cambridge, U.K.: Cambridge University Press, 1985).

Olivia Remie Constable, *Medieval Trade in the Mediterranean World* (New York: Columbia University Press, 2001).

Patricia Crone, *Meccan Trade and the Rise of Islam* (Princeton, N.J.: Princeton University Press, 1987).

Andrew Dulby, *Dangerous Tastes: The Story of Spices* (Berkeley: University of California Press, 2002).

Kenneth R. Hall, ed., *Maritime Diasporas in the Indian Ocean and East and Southeast Asia (960–1775)* (Leiden, Netherlands: E. J. Brill, 2006).

Richard Hodges, *Towns and Trade in the Age of Charlemagne* (London: Duckworth and Co., 2000).

John Middleton, *The World of the Swahili: An African Mercantile Civilization* (New Haven, Conn.: Yale University Press, 1992).

Peter Mitchell, *African Connections: Archeological Perspectives on Africa and the Wider World* (Walnut Creek, Calif.: AltaMira Press, 2005).

Anthony Reid, *Southeast Asia in the Age of Commerce*, 2 vols. (New Haven, Conn.: Yale University Press, 1990, 1995).

W. Montgomery Watt, *The Influence of Islam on Medieval Europe* (Edinburgh: Edinburgh University Press, 1972).

Frances Wood, *The Silk Road: Two Thousand Years in the Heart of Asia* (Berkeley: University of California Press, 2004).

► transportation

INTRODUCTION

One of the impressive aspects of medieval transportation is how much was done by people on foot. People carried goods for very long distances. This included not just nomads but also merchants, pilgrims, and farmers. In Australia and Africa nomads took all their belongings with them from place to place. In lands such as China, India, and Europe people often carried on their backs the goods they sold in villages, towns, or cities. Foresters hauled wood for burning, farmers lugged sacks of grain, and fishermen carried their catches to places where they could hope to sell them for coins or for the services of a craftsperson.

In some parts of the world walking was the only reliable form of transportation. In the mountain passes of central Asia, the marshlands of southern India, and the rain forests of Africa and Southeast Asia, transportation by animals or vehicles was impractical. For instance, in western and central Africa, flying insects carried diseases that killed animals such as oxen, horses, camels, and donkeys. Donkeys were the most reliable pack animals in the region, because they seem to have been more resistant to disease, but even they had no use on paths in densely forested areas. People had to carry goods themselves, or the goods did not move.

The use of animals for transportation was often preferable to moving goods on foot, but animals had drawbacks besides not being able to go some places that people could. One was that they were expensive. They had to be fed, groomed, and sheltered. In the grasslands of the Sahel of Africa, for example, a horse had to be housed in a stable, where it was shielded from flying insects, and it needed to be watched and cared for full-time for by several people. For many people pack animals were too expensive to own or were so valuable that it was preferable to have people carry loads rather than to burden the animals with them, as was sometimes the case with donkeys in North Africa.

One of the curiosities of medieval transportation is the use and disuse of the wheel. The Maya knew of the wheel and made toys for children that rolled on wheels, but they did not take the seemingly logical step of applying what they knew about the wheel to transportation. One reason for this may have been their environment, which often included dense, wet forest in which wheels would become entangled. But much of the medieval Mayan world that presently lies under jungle was cleared, open land. The challenge may have been one of emerging technologies: Techniques for building roads were not sufficient for creating reliable avenues for wheeled vehicles.

Perhaps more curious was the region in which the wheel seems to have had its first practical uses as aids to transportation, in the carts and chariots of the Near East. In the medieval Islamic world of the Near East and North Africa wheeled transportation fell into disuse. People walked long distances carrying goods, or they used animal transportation—camels over long distances and donkeys for both long and short distances. Cities of the Near East became ones of narrow streets; a city's space was used as much as possible for personal living in houses. Some historians think that the narrow streets developed because people either walked or rode donkeys rather than riding in carriages.

Even so, in many medieval cultures time was money, and efficient transportation was important to commerce. In China city streets apart from the main avenues were usually narrow and winding. Thus, in Chinese cities peddlers would navigate their way through streets by transporting their goods on wheelbarrows, a Chinese invention. Still, the use of carts to transport goods was essential to many urban areas, because carrying large loads in carts pulled by animals or people was the best way to provide consumer goods to urbanites. Thus, most Chinese cities had wide avenues that led from city gates to marketplaces. In Europe carts seem to have placed a heavy demand on the maintenance of roads, and many governments charged a tax for the use of their roads that varied according to the size of cart and the kind of animal pulling the cart. Some farmers found ways to carry their produce on their backs in order to avoid the taxes, but anyone carrying large loads needed wide avenues for their carts, and many a city made them pay for the roads.

AFRICA

BY CHARLES W. ABBOTT

Sub-Saharan Africa's history is unusual in many ways. It skipped the Bronze Age and went straight from stone to iron. It had few traditions of writing before Islam. Another peculiarity is the absence of the wheel. Africans made little use of the wheel. In many parts of the continent they relied heavily on human portage; that is, goods were carried by individuals on their backs, heads, or shoulders. Where camels were feasible, they were used. Horses were employed as well, but more for military purposes than for long-distance trade.

In the African setting coastal and riverine navigation were relatively unimportant in most places. (Europe and

China, in contrast, had more favorable physical geographies, with some combination of deeply incised coastlines, inviting estuaries, and plentiful rivers providing access deep into continental interiors.) The tsetse fly is endemic to humid Africa (but not to the arid or highland zones) and transmits a deadly disease, trypanosomiasis, to the horse, the cow, and the camel over large swaths of Africa. (The same disease causes sleeping sickness in humans.) In many humid parts of Africa the largest domesticated animal is the goat—a good source of protein and leather but useless for transport or motive power. The most common biome in Africa is the savanna (grassland mixed with trees), a somewhat dry climatic zone and thus unlikely to be well endowed with navigable rivers. Many places in Africa are far from the sort of stream in which one can paddle a canoe easily; much of Africa is high plateau.

The ideal mode of transportation in Africa, where feasible, was the camel. Until recently Western scholars did not fully appreciate the efficiency and flexibility of the camel. After its introduction the camel largely replaced wheeled cartage in the animal's entire range, from Morocco to Afghanistan. Two camels were more efficient than a cart pulled by two oxen. They carried roughly the same amount of cargo. They needed no cart (which was expensive, heavy, and difficult to repair outside an artisan's workshop) and no road. There was no risk of mechanical breakdown. In addition, camels were far more resistant to thirst, and they could graze on materials inadequate for oxen.

The camel was thus most efficient way of transporting goods for the long haul across the Sahara. The relevant areas of Africa served by camel caravan include the range of territory from the southern shores of the Mediterranean Sea to entrepôts (intermediary trade centers) of the Sahel, such as Senegal River trading sites, Timbuktu, Gao, and Kano. South of these Sahelian entrepôts goods were transported along the Niger River (at its northernmost bend near Timbuktu) in boats or taken farther south using donkeys or human porters. Research suggests that the southern limit of tolerance for the camel is approximately 14.5 degrees north latitude in the dry season (when the tsetse fly recedes). The ox's limit is a bit farther south: 12 degrees in the wet season and 10 degrees in the dry season. Much more tolerant yet is the donkey, which might be taken as far south as 5 degrees in the dry season.

The freight costs in camel-based trans-Saharan trade were relatively similar to European-controlled Atlantic maritime trade. (Maritime technology improved in efficiency over time, while camel-based technology seems to have been more static.) Exact freight rates for camels are difficult to compare to the Atlantic maritime trade, since some camel trade was not a long haul across the Sahara but rather to interior Saharan sites (for salt and gold) or for east-west trade past Kanem-

Bornu and Darfur toward the Nile Valley. The trans-Saharan trade was not devastated by Atlantic seaborne competition but seems to have grown in subsequent centuries. The coming of the Atlantic trade after 1450 did not eliminate the trans-Saharan trade; the two trade systems coexisted for hundreds of years, one tribute to the efficiency of the camel.

If the camel was the choice where possible for overland trade, within its range the horse was prized for war. The tsetse fly and trypanosomiasis limited the horse's range as well, though it seemed to maintain its health within the humid savanna for up to two years. (The tropical forests of the south were still a deadly zone, and horses died in the humid savanna too quickly for them to be bred there successfully.) The camel was superior for carrying goods, but the horse was superior for military purposes. The horse (with bit, saddle, and stirrups) and rider (with helmet and chain mail) extended the military power of elites who could get it. With horses, one could launch raids against one's neighbors during the dry season (after the harvest was in and the tsetse fly was less prevalent), catch slaves or extract tribute, and use the revenue to pay for more horses when animals sickened and died.

The use of porters for transportation limited the sorts of goods that could be traded long distances within the forest, except where canoe transport was possible. We know that common products traded over long distances in the forest included salt, kola nuts (a stimulant and a luxury good), gold, cloth, brass, and leather goods. Each of these was valuable enough to bear the relatively high transport costs involved in portage. Slaves were usually driven on foot; like livestock, they transported themselves.

For many scholars, the absence of the wheel is perceived as a puzzle that necessitates an explanation. Often it provokes a debate about the judgment of Africans, bringing into question their intelligence or their attitude toward change. Perhaps Africans spurned the wheel for good economic reasons. A wheeled vehicle requires roads to be effective, while camels (as well as donkeys and human porters) can follow paths with unimproved surfaces. Africans adopted many products and technologies as soon as possible: camels, horses, armor, firearms, and iron smelting. Perhaps they rejected the wheel because it made sense to do so.

In the forest Africans spent a lot of time and energy carrying things. If there are no wheeled carts, no roads for them to travel anyway, and no beasts of burden and if the topography is not suitable for canoes, almost everything that is moved must be carried by people. Modern scholars suggest that human porters usually carried between 50 and 80 pounds. Parts of Africa's zone of human portage were relatively economically isolated from the rest of the world—not by culture or values but by the cost of transportation. The logistics of porterage were relentless in their simplicity. Porters expended considerable time and energy in carrying goods, and it was costly to transport goods by portage; therefore, only valuable items could be traded long distances. Such zones were open to outside cultural influences, ideas, and diseases, but trade was limited to only the most valuable goods or those that transported themselves. Africa's transportation options conditioned its access to the rest of the world. Portions of western Africa and the East African coast had had hundreds of years of contact with Europe or the Islamic world by 1500, while large areas of the humid interior were largely isolated.

THE AMERICAS

BY MICHAEL J. O'NEAL

While the wheel had been developed and used for transportation purposes on carts and carriages in other parts of the world, it did not find its way to the precontact Americas until the Europeans arrived in the 16th century. The horse, which holds a firm place in the popular imagination as a major means of transportation for the Plains Indians, for example, also arrived with the Europeans, and Native Americans did not use horses for transportation until the 17th century. While pack animals were used in some parts of the Americas, most transportation was by foot and various kinds of watercraft.

In the frozen reaches of the far north the Inuit, commonly known as Eskimos, used methods of transportation that are thousands of years old. The Inuit depended heavily on the sea for most of their resources, so transportation focused on ways of getting around in the water. The most recognizable form of Inuit transportation was the kayak, a word that comes from an earlier Inuit word, *qajait*. A small, canoelike boat made of a whalebone frame covered with animal skins, usually hides from whales, seals, or walruses, kayaks were short and tapered toward the front and back. In the center was a kind of cockpit where the rower sat and propelled himself with a single double-bladed paddle. Sometimes the rower was strapped in with hides tightly bound around his waist such that the boat was entirely waterproof and the rower could easily right himself even if the kayak rolled over in the water. Normally Inuit women never used kayaks.

The umiak was a larger, more open boat. It, too, was made of a whalebone frame. The umiak was often covered with animal hides, but sometimes the covering was bark that was stitched together with root fibers. Unlike the kayak, which was entirely rounded somewhat like a submarine, the umiak had a gunwale, or an upper edge, making it more like a sailing ship. The umiak was more suitable for use in the open seas and was often used to hunt whales, walrus, and other larger

sea mammals. The umiak was also the boat of choice when an Inuit woman had to take to the sea.

On land the Inuit often used dogsleds for transportation, particularly for hunting. Again, the sea provided resources for making these sleds. The runners typically were made of whalebone, while the rest of the sled was generally made with hides; in the more southern reaches of Inuit territory, where some wood was available, the rider stood on planks made of wood. The dogs that pulled the sled, typically six to 12, were arranged in a fan formation, with the strongest, most powerful dogs in front. These dogs were typically Alaskan malamutes; other breeds associated with Alaskan sledding, such as the Siberian husky and the Eskimo dog, did not appear until the 19th and 20th centuries. When goods had to be transported, sled dogs pulled a toboggan, or a wooden platform with a curled-up nose that rested on the snow.

When the Inuit had to walk, they often used snowshoes made of a bone or sometimes a wood frame and a web made of leather straps. Snowshoes enabled people to walk on top of the snow rather than sink into it. More northern groups preferred long, narrow snowshoes that worked well on preexisting tracks. These tracks tended to be more permanent because the extreme northerly regions remained frozen for most of the year. Also, the region was so bitterly cold that it often did not snow. Such snowshoes functioned almost like

Ceramic model palanquin, Colima culture, Mexico, ca. 200–600 (Courtesy, National Museum of the American Indian, Smithsonian Institution [catalog number 237830])

skis. In the south, where temperatures were a bit milder and it snowed more often, people preferred more rounded snowshoes that worked better on fresh snow. These kinds of snowshoes also were used by Native American people in regions that are now lower Canada and the United States. The Inuit became very adept at navigating their way through an environment that provided few natural landmarks for travelers to get their bearings.

The Native American Indian societies of North America employed transportation technologies that were essentially similar to those of the Inuit, although like people throughout the Americas, they relied day to day on foot trails and game trails through forests, over the plains, and in the ravines and canyons of mountains. The Indians of the Southwest desert, of course, had little use for water vessels, but Native American societies that lived along rivers or the ocean coasts depended heavily on watercraft for fishing and transportation. A common form of transportation was the canoe, although Native American Indians constructed canoes in their own way and with different materials from those of the Inuit. The best canoes, because they were lighter and more maneuverable, were built by the Algonquian nation of northern New England, who lived in regions that were dense with white birch trees. The bark of these trees comes off in sheets rather than small chunks. These sheets were carefully removed from the trunks of trees in large sections and then sewn together with plant fibers over a wooden framework to form the outer hull of canoes. The Iroquois, on the other hand, used elm bark, and other societies used whatever materials lay at hand, including animal hides. California Indians used light and buoyant balsa wood.

North American Indians (other than the Inuit) had a greater variety of vessels. Many used dugout canoes—that is, canoes made from a single log that was carved out to form a boat. The cultures of the Northwest in modern-day United States were especially skilled at carving dugout canoes. The Haida of the Northwest constructed large (up to 70 feet long) canoes using giant cedar logs hollowed out using both hand tools and fire. In the American Southeast archaeologists have discovered at least 400 dugout canoes. Some date from ancient times, but many date from later and demonstrate that during the medieval period the societies of the Southeast, with its extensive coastline and numerous rivers and lakes, maintained a vigorous boatbuilding tradition. Another type of boat was the bull boat, a rounded vessel made with a wicker frame and buffalo hides. Plains Indians used bull boats to transport goods across rivers; often at the helm of these boats were women.

For moving goods, Native Americans used the travois, an A-shaped litter made with two poles. The poles were har-

INUKSUIT

On the frozen tundra of the far north the landscape provides few, if any directional markers. On such a vast, white, flat, open area a traveler could easily become disoriented and lost. To navigate their way in these regions, the Inuit built *inuksuit*. These stone structures that served as way markers for the precontact Inuit are still used today. The word translates into English roughly as "something that acts or substitutes for a person."

These stone monuments came in various sizes and shapes, but generally they tended to vaguely represent a human figure. Their most prominent feature was their "arms," which pointed the traveler in a particular direction. Sometimes *inuksuit* were erected on the shore of a body of water to mark the place where the fishing was best; these would be set up at a distance from shore equal to the distance into the water where fish could be found. They were also used to mark dangerous places, spots where food was stored, the location of caribou herds, sacred sites, and places where significant events had occurred. Some were built to point toward the North Star, and some were positioned in such a way that a traveler could look through a peephole through which he could just see the next marker on his way.

The *inukshuk* has deep cultural significance to the Inuit. It served as more than a way marker. It became a spiritual symbol of friendship, safety, cooperation, and hope. Building them was a community effort, with close attention being paid to the balance and positioning of each stone. So deep does the significance of the *inukshuk* run that one is depicted on the flag and coat of arms of the Canadian territory of Nunavut, home to most of Canada's Inuit population. It was also chosen as a symbol to appear on the flag of the 2010 Winter Olympics in Vancouver, British Columbia.

nessed to the chest and shoulders of a dog and dragged on the ground behind the dog. They were connected by crossbars and covered with hides that provided a platform for goods as well as for children, the elderly, or people who were injured or too sick to walk.

Before European contact Mesoamericans relied almost entirely on their feet for purposes of transportation. Some islanders in Central America, people along the ocean coasts and throughout the Caribbean, and those on the shores of lakes used dugout canoes. For example, remains of dugout boats have been found on the Yucatán Peninsula and along the shores of Lake Texcoco near Mexico City. Some of these boats survive because they were made of logs from the chico sapote tree, the hardest wood in Central America. Otherwise, almost all transportation occurred by foot. While the Maya constructed some roads that linked larger cities, rough trails were the norm. People who wanted to travel simply set out on foot. Those who needed to transport goods loaded them into backpacks and began walking. Numerous commodities were transported in this way, including maize (corn), beans, animal skins, cotton, and firewood. Porters who carried feathers in backpacks were the most fortunate.

Later the Aztec of central Mexico constructed a more extensive system of roads. Again, they did not employ pack animals, so transportation was on foot. The roads were built to make them comfortable for foot travelers, with resting places, food, and even latrines available every 6 to 10 miles. The roads were maintained by tribute, a form of taxation, and were traveled by officials who continuously monitored their condition. Because these roads were so closely scrutinized, it was possible for women to travel alone safely. Both the Aztec and the Maya constructed causeways that linked population centers with ceremonial sites. These causeways were paved roads that made it easier for people to travel to attend religious ceremonies.

Prior to the Spanish conquest Andean civilizations—that is, the civilizations that lived along the Andes Mountains in western South America—had the most sophisticated system of transportation in the Americas, although again the wheel was not used. The forbidding rocky terrain of this region, with sharp changes in elevation, would have rendered the wheel useless anyway, so once again most transportation was on foot. In contrast to the Mesoamericans, though, the South Americans used pack animals, primarily the llama, for transporting loads.

It fell to the Inca to build the most extensive road system in all of the Americas, though such a system had been begun by the Caral-Supe civilization in ancient Peru from 3000 to 1600 B.C.E. Incan civilization began to form in about the 12th century, and by the time the Spanish arrived in the 16th century the Inca ruled over an empire that may have encompassed as much as 400,000 square miles. By the time the empire ended, the Inca had constructed a road system that included at least 10,000 miles of roads and perhaps more than twice that many. While many of these "roads" were simply paths that wound through the rocky terrain, about half were paved with stones. Fruit trees were planted along them to offer travelers refreshment, and way stations, called *tampos*,

provided resting places every couple of miles or so. Of vital importance to the Inca Empire was communication along this transportation network. Positioned at each of these way stations was a runner who had been trained from childhood to remember and repeat messages. The runners relayed messages from way station to way station, often transporting a message 150 miles a day. This relay system could carry a message from the Inca capital at Cuzco to the farthest border of the empire in about a week.

In general, water transportation would not have occurred very extensively in the highlands of South America. Some examples of reed and balsa wood boats have been found, but lowlanders in the Amazon rain forests relied more heavily on water transportation, again using dugout canoes to navigate the river and its tributaries.

ASIA AND THE PACIFIC

BY KENNETH HALL

Medieval transport in Asia and the Pacific included ocean voyages, river navigation, and human and animal overland travel. Since the Pacific islands did not have domesticated horses, donkeys, or cows at that time, river navigation or transport on foot were their only alternatives. Asians had the options of transport by local watercraft and barges on rivers and canals or human, animal, or cart transport on roadways. Most medieval-era road transport was used for small-volume carrying trade of local handicrafts (for instance, cloth) or exotic jungle products (for example, spices), the movements of government officials and priests, migrations of populations in times of natural or political crisis, and the relocation of military and their supplies in times of war. Employment, family, pilgrimage, communication, and human curiosity also contributed to travel and transportation of goods in this period.

Since there was no state-sponsored delivery system at that time, Asian societies had to use individual and animal transport networks to move goods and information. Transport and means of transport depended on the local road surface and access to inclusive market centers, warehouses to store goods, facilities to house and care for animals, and hostelries. Most roads were unpaved and little more than cart paths, but there were also major transportation arteries sponsored and maintained by powerful kings in India, Southeast Asia, and East Asia. Transport might be seasonal, to avoid the harsh winters of the northern regions of Asia and the severe tropical storms at the height of the monsoon season in Asia's tropical regions. Roads were first and foremost built for their military rather than their economic importance. In times of turmoil roads were purposely left in disrepair to

Earthenware model of a cart with bullock and human figures, China, sixth century (© The Trustees of the British Museum)

protect against the raids of opponents or were reconstructed to support local military ambitions. Travel could be pleasant, with companionship at nightly stopover hostelries and in private homes that took in travelers to earn additional income. Fearing that itinerant travelers and porters who were traveling through a region might cause trouble, local communities forced merchants, artisans, and travelers in general to abide by rigid codes of conduct that were meant to preserve local stability and prevent the outbreak of violence and violation of local laws and customs.

Owing to the inadequate transportation infrastructure; the limited numbers of public roads, cart paths, and bridges; irregular road maintenance; the difficulty of travel in mountainous terrain and wetlands; and the availability of human labor versus the use of the few available large animals not needed for farming, human porters were often the transport of choice. Humans, who might be accompanied by donkeys in nontropical regions, could go where it was impossible or inefficient to use horses or oxcarts, such as on steep mountain trails.

Professional transporters included merchants, artisans, or itinerant traders who carried their merchandise to the most remote areas of the hinterland on their backs and returned with locally produced goods that they would pass along their exchange networks. Transportation of larger amounts of goods depended on a mix of professional and part-time workers. There were professional wage-earning porters, who

were usually based in the major commercial centers or ports of trade. There they were employed in the loading and unloading of ship and boat cargoes and the transport of goods to and from the urban marketplaces. This was especially the case among southern China's ports of trade throughout the medieval era; in southern India from 1000 to 1300, where professional porters worked for itinerant merchant guilds that transacted long-distance trade in southern India and the Bay of Bengal region; and in the 15th-century Melaka international trade emporium.

The slaves and bondsmen of merchants and artisans also served as full-time porters. Part-time porters included farmers, who could make additional income during the slower periods of the agricultural year or who were otherwise obligated to provide portage as required by their service agreements with local elites or temples. Historians estimate that in a day a porter could carry 80 pounds about 15 miles; in contrast, a mule could carry 132 pounds and a bullock 132 to 220 pounds. To enable human porters to move a greater weight of goods, the wheelbarrow was adapted to the needs of the transportation network first in China during the Tang era (589–907) and then elsewhere in Asia.

Carts for the transport of goods were usually two-wheeled rather than four-wheeled, because the four-wheeled carts were more difficult to engineer in a way that allowed the moveable front wheels to turn within an appropriate radius on narrow roads and were hard to navigate in the tight spaces of the marketplace. Four-wheeled vehicles without moveable front wheels were common in ceremonial use, where ritual or political processions moved slowly. Horse-drawn carts were lighter than oxcarts. Bullock and oxen carts were the major means of animal transport on land, since oxen could carry heavy loads. The basic oxcart was similar to those still used in Asia today, with oxen tied to a central yoke pulling the cart behind them using the strength of their front shoulders. Carts and their wheels were usually made of wood but occasionally of metals and stone. Temple and royal carts used in public celebrations or rituals were especially ornate; temple carts paraded an image of a Hindu or Buddhist divinity around a community on festival days. Military carts transported the supplies necessary to provision warriors in the battlefield: foods, weapons, and gunpowder.

Oxen were best in transportation over level land, but horses could better negotiate hilly terrain, whether pulling a cart or in a pack train. Horse transport was favored in the more commercial economies, since horses provided greater flexibility and faster transport of perishables and small-volume luxuries. However, horses required a greater investment. Horses did not breed in the Asian tropics and had to be imported at great expense from the central Asian steppes, the

Middle East, or northwestern India; horses also required special feeds rather than openly grazing, as was the case with oxen.

Cart transport was time consuming and potentially dangerous. Carts were inherently unstable, with wheels getting caught in ruts in the road, and frequently overturned or fell into ditches and waterways, crushing humans and causing them to drown. As Asian commerce became more sophisticated, rulers desiring commodities and tax revenues funded the construction of better roads and bridges, guarded cargo transport from bandits, and sponsored ferries and ferrymen who provided river passage.

China's military adopted the two-wheeled version of the wheelbarrow, nicknamed the "wooden ox," which required two men to propel and steer. At first they were a closely guarded military secret. China's generals believed that these military carts gave China's armies an advantage in moving goods and wounded soldiers by eliminating the need for slow and costly pack animals.

The Venetian traveler Marco Polo (1254–1324) described his travel to China across central Asia over marshy land covered with layers of ice, which was inaccessible to horses or carts and crossed only by dogsleds. Six dogs pulled the sleds from one to another outpost, where a fresh dog team provided transport for the traders and their hides to the next transfer station. Dog transport was unusual; most of the transport across central Asia depended on camel caravans. Asia's Bactrian camels were efficient transporters that could walk on soft sand and stone and could carry from 250 to 650 pounds of cargo, travel about 2 to 3 miles per hour, and cover about 20 to 25 miles per day.

Caravans might consist of several dozen to 1,000 camels and other pack animals (horses and mules), accompanied by as many as 5,000 men. Transport across the caravan route was risky and demanded that the caravan carry food and water reserves to ensure survival against uncertain weather conditions and other negative circumstances. If food ran out, travelers killed their baggage animals for food, but they did so only with extreme reluctance, since the death of an animal reduced their profits. The Berber scholar and chronicler Ibn Battuta (1304–ca. 1377), who traveled the caravan route after Marco Polo, claimed that several hundred horsemen and accompanying archers guarded his caravan, in contrast to Marco Polo's report, which highlighted the Mongol rule that had provided security and uniform accountability of the regional tribesmen, which encouraged Italian merchants to make the trek to China.

The Silk Road consisted of networked trading posts where travelers replenished their supplies and where their camels, horses, and other livestock rested. Caravan travelers and their animals usually stayed and had stables and warehouse facilities in a walled enclosure just outside the inner walls of a fortified market town. There they lodged and unloaded, watered, and repacked their animals; an open space provided to them could accommodate 300 to 400 camels and mules. Local guides specialized in leading caravans from one post to another. Similarly, few merchants traveled the entire route but instead specialized in one route sector and depended on the natural passage of goods along the route or in the transit of goods through the agency of their business partnerships.

Silk Road transport costs were lower on the overland route than on the Indian Ocean maritime route. Historians draw on early 16th-century European historical records to estimate that the cost of Silk Road transport was roughly 3 percent of the sale price of silk and other valuables carried from China to the West. However, there were additional costs, such as protection fees, customs duties, and bribes that made the caravan trade more expensive than the sea route.

Southeast Asian caravans exclusively used oxcarts for transport and mules rather than horses in pack trains. As in neighboring India, bandits and tigers were the greatest threat, along with wild boars, rhinoceros, and poisonous snakes. Owing to the heat, caravans moved in the cool of the morning and rested during the heat of the afternoon before resuming their travel in the late afternoon and early evening. At nightfall they formed into a protective ring of carts. Travelers slept in the carts or under palm-leaf tents at the ring's protected center. Thai records report that caravans of 60 to 100 carts could move 360 miles from the Mekong River on the modern-day Thai-Laos border in the east to the Ayut-

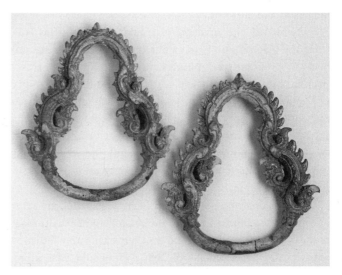

Palanquin rings, gilt copper alloy, Cambodia, 13th century
(Los Angeles County Museum of Art, Indian Art Special Purpose Fund, Photograph © 2006 Museum Associates/LACMA [AC1993.125.1.1-.2])

thya capital on the lower Chaophraya River in the west in five months with a full load and in three months with lesser loads. An individual could make the trip in 15 days in peacetime. Oxen could make the trip without carts in a month but had to carry food for their feed, and this limited the volume of merchandise they could transport. In contrast, travel across the Malay Peninsula, a distance of 60 miles took two to three months in the rainy season.

Sedan chairs were common in China, India, Japan, and Korea throughout the medieval era, and their use spread to other Asian regions by the end of the medieval era. The sedan chair, formed by a seat that was lifted onto the shoulders of the bearers by means of long horizontal poles, was a traditional vehicle of human transport. In East Asia it was usually made of bamboo. The chairs moved the person being carried above the worst of the dust, smell, and noise of a busy streets and unpaved roads. The elite maintained their own private sedan chairs and porters, but private operators also hired them out for public use. These were also traditionally used by rich and poor in Chinese wedding rituals, to carry the bride from her home to the place of the wedding.

Traditional Chinese sedan chairs were of two sorts: the official sedan and the private sedan. The sedan chairs of Chinese government officials carried their emblems of rank on the outside to indicate their occupant's importance. Their decoration was regulated by strict rules that dictated their elaborateness as appropriate to the various levels of the government hierarchy. The Chinese emperor had several sedan chairs, one highly ornate chair for his transport to court, another for his inspection tours around the court compound, a light sedan chair for his participation in hunts or travels outside the court compound, and a spare that was carried for his use while on boat trips to distant places. The chair furnishings would change with the seasons, to provide warmth in the winter and protection from the sun and heat in the summer. Private sedans were less elaborate and were owned by aristocrats and the urban wealthy, including merchant princes. Use of a sedan chair was a public proclamation of social privilege. Sedan chairs, surrounded by accompanying attendants, and carried by two to 16 bearers, were preceded by the beating of gongs or other musical instruments to clear their way and to draw public attention. Commoners meeting the procession were expected to show their reverence, minimally by their quiet and stepping out of the way.

Sedan chairs used in Chinese weddings were covered with brightly colored embroidered silk and gems. Their designs proclaimed good luck. In the medieval era, to ensure that the bride was not to be seen by outsiders, a double sedan had an inner chamber built within the outer chamber. When the chair reached the wedding site (often the house-hold of the groom), the inner chamber was carried inside the house, where the bride finally revealed herself to her husband's relatives.

EUROPE

BY AMY HACKNEY BLACKWELL

Transportation in medieval Europe was slow and difficult. The road system had deteriorated after the Roman Empire ended (in 476), and it was not rebuilt. Methods of transportation were limited. Carts were no longer practical in many areas, especially for long-distance transport, and horses were rare and expensive, so most people made do with their feet to transport themselves and their goods. Oxen were much more common than horses and often were used instead of horses to pull carts or carry goods. Water transportation was in many ways more efficient than ground transportation, though even that was less than ideal.

Different types of transportation were used, depending on the length of the trip and the items being transported. Carts were most commonly used for short distances over land and mainly to transport goods, not people. For long journeys people used ships and barges, rode horses, or walked. The difficulty of transportation did not prevent people from undertaking long journeys. People regularly embarked on journeys that took months if not years. Those who made the pilgrimage from Canterbury, England, to the Holy Land might spend several years along the way; many of them did the entire trip on foot. Armies rode horses and marched vast distances to wage war. Merchants managed to transport their goods hundreds of miles for sale.

Many people habitually walked long distances. Walking for a full day to reach a destination was not considered unreasonable. If people had luggage or goods to sell, they carried it on their backs or in their arms. Parents carried small children, often affixing them to their backs with cloth slings. There are some fictitious accounts of adults carrying other adults on their backs, such as the story of Friar Tuck carrying Robin Hood across a stream, and this may be evidence that this sort of thing did actually happen.

As a practical matter, in much of Europe the condition of roads made any sort of transportation other than foot traffic impossible. Most European roads were narrow dirt tracks wide enough to permit one or two people to walk abreast or to allow people to lead pack animals in single file. There were some wider roads, but even they were usually only rough dirt. They became very muddy after rainstorms and often were obstructed with fallen branches or potholes. Human and animal feet negotiated these hazards better than wheels did.

Medieval travelers regularly encountered other dangers. Roads were owned by the lords whose land they crossed, and these landowners sometimes demanded that travelers pay tolls. If a merchant's cart toppled over or one of his mules' packs ripped open and his goods spilled out, the landowner could claim those goods as his own. Brigands and highwaymen lurked in the forests, ready to prey on unsuspecting or defenseless travelers.

Crossing rivers and streams presented difficulties. In many rural areas people normally crossed rivers at fords. These were shallow places where it was possible to wade across or step from rock to rock. Water levels varied; when they were high, fords might become impassable. Occasionally people would swim across rivers, but swimming was not a universal skill, and most medieval Europeans avoided deep water if possible. In places where there were bridges, people could continue to walk or ride as usual, though they often had to pay a toll before crossing. Ferries were common. These were boats or rafts run by men who would take passengers across a river for a fee.

When people did not walk, they rode animals. Medieval Europeans only rarely rode in other forms of land transportation, such as carts. The horse was the main riding animal, though people also rode on mules. Only the wealthy had riding horses, and even pack horses were expensive and uncommon. Both men and women rode, and women, like men, typically rode astride instead of in the sidesaddle that became popular later.

A horse could walk about 4 miles per hour and trot about twice as fast. Riders and drivers did not ordinarily make their horses move at faster gaits, such as the canter or gallop because a horse cannot maintain those speeds over a long distance. Traveling by horseback presented various inconveniences. Horses needed food and water, and if they stopped for the night, they had to be secured or housed in some way. A horse could ordinarily carry only one person at a time; if a group wanted to travel together, everyone needed a horse or the group had to move at a walking pace. Riding a horse required skill and training and reasonably good physical conditioning. Riders often met with accidents, such as falling off, which could leave them injured or dead.

Horses were bred for different traits, depending on what they were expected to do. Any wealthy person who wanted a horse for general riding and travel would buy a palfrey. Palfreys were bred to have a comfortable gait and to be fairly gentle. Some mules that were specially bred to be ladies' mounts were called palfreys or jennets. Jennets could also be horses, particularly a type of small, quiet horse originally bred in Spain. Rounceys were cheaper, more ordinary horses that could either carry riders or pull carts. Coursers were

Horseshoes, Britain, 12th century; horses were essential for transport and hauling. (© Museum of London)

strong horses with a steady gait and good endurance. They were used by soldiers who needed to travel long distances. Destriers were large war horses that were highly trained, uncommon, and so expensive that only the richest knights and nobles could afford them.

Medieval Europeans used several types of pack animals. Oxen were the most common. They were strong but slow and could be used to pull carts and carry loads, though they could not be ridden. Horses could also carry cargo or pull carts. During the later medieval period some farmers owned pack horses that they used to plow their fields (after the development of the horse collar around the 13th century) and to transport their goods to market. These horses were often bred to be heavy, strong, and slow. Occasionally, horses and oxen were hitched together to carts. Mules were another typical pack animal. Mules are stronger and more patient than horses and do not mind carrying heavy weights. Merchants often carried their goods overland in mule trains, which were lines of many mules all carrying loads on their backs. Donkeys were used to transport small loads and in mountainous areas, where their surefootedness made them superior to horses.

Carts were essential for the transportation of goods, especially in local areas, but they were not much used for human transportation. Carts often were used to transport goods locally, within and between towns. Medieval roads were far too rough and narrow for carts with no suspension, making them uncomfortable as passenger vehicles; few people chose to ride in them. Carts came in various sizes and could have either two or four wheels. One or several horses or other animals could be made to pull them. Women, sick people, and dignitaries such as bishops sometimes rode in litters. A litter was a box or a chair suspended between two long poles. Two or four men would lift the poles and carry the litter from place to place.

Much of medieval transportation was done by water—down rivers, across lakes, and in seas. Carts were useful only for local trips; for long distances, transportation was better done on water. Most long journeys involved a combination of land and water transport. Large rivers such as the Rhine and the Danube functioned as highways. The Mediterranean, the Atlantic Ocean, the North Sea, and the Baltic Sea were all the sites of regular voyage of ships carrying people and cargo.

The people of northern Europe were known to be excellent seamen. The Vikings regularly sailed ships throughout the Baltic Sea, the North Sea, and across the North Atlantic. Viking ships were more technologically advanced than boats in other parts of medieval Europe and included both cargo ships and lighter vessels. Northern Europeans used their boats to colonize the Faroe Islands, Iceland, and Greenland before 1000 C.E. During the early medieval period many boats were rafts made of logs or frame boats covered with animal skins. They could not carry much in the way of passengers or cargo. By the 11th century, however, boats were much bigger and better crafted.

The majority of ships sailing the oceans and seas were commercial vessels dedicated to transporting goods and passengers. Round ships, with round hulls, met this need. They were primarily cargo vessels. They did not venture far into open seas, partly because of the dangers of the seas and winds and partly because of the ever-present threat of pirates. Merchant ships carried with them soldiers to fight off those pirates if they ventured near. They were quite slow because they could not sail without favorable winds. They had several decks inside. The heaviest items would be loaded into the lowest deck to keep the ship from becoming top heavy.

Armies and crusaders sometimes pressed these merchant ships into service to transport them to their destinations. Merchants looked favorably on these events as a way of making money, though sometimes crusaders turned out to be unable to pay for their passage. Ships carrying crusaders to the Holy Land needed to be able to carry up to 600 tons of cargo, including soldiers, horses, weapons, and provisions.

Most heavy cargo was placed on barges and sailed on inland waterways. Vessels designed as barges for inland transport could be simpler and smaller. In the 12th century barges were still sometimes made of logs lashed together. Other barges were built out of planks. They had flat bottoms for smooth transport in shallow water, and they were built so as to maximize cargo space. During the explosion of cathedral building in the 12th and 13th centuries, vast numbers of stone were moved this way.

Carriers would use natural waterways, such as streams and rivers, when they could. Natural waterways presented some of the same hazards as roads on land. Ships and barges had to pay tolls to pass under bridges. If cargo fell off a barge, an unscrupulous lord could lay claim to it. Robbers sometimes attacked barges floating down rivers. When there were no natural waterways in an area, the people would dig canals to allow heavy goods to move more easily. These canals often included locks to regulate the water level. Locks allowed barges to travel uphill by alternately filling and draining ponds until the barge had reached the highest water level. When a cargo ship reached its destination, it had to be docked so that its goods could be unloaded. Some ships were too large to reach the docks; they had to be unloaded piecemeal into smaller boats that could dock. Many docks were equipped with cranes that could lift goods into or out of barges. Once a barge had been unloaded, its contents could be placed onto carts or mules and carried overland to their destination.

THE ISLAMIC WORLD
BY TIA WHEELER

The Middle East has an extensive history of long-distance travel dating back to early civilization, when ancient Egyptians and Babylonians traded with one another. Long-distance travel was strenuous and time consuming; travel between the Mediterranean coast and Samarkand could take more than a year. Environmental factors such as extreme heat in the deserts, frequently snow-blocked passes, and the lack of constant and reliable water sources all made transportation perilous. In ancient times trade mainly took place by horse and cart, but the domestication of camels provided a stronger, more economical option. Unlike most other societies that embraced and advanced their civilizations by using the wheel, large portions of the Middle East and the Islamic world abandoned the wheel for transportation, replacing it with donkeys and walking in urban settings and camels and horses for long-distance travel.

Donkeys were the preferred method for transporting goods within towns and cities because goods could be gathered on top of the animal while a small child sat astride the items and steered the donkey. Larger animals, such as oxen and camels, were less frequently used in urban settings because their bulkier stature limited movement through small passageways. Walking was frequently the method used when traveling short distances to a large city or capital for administrative duties, such as paying annual taxes.

Wagons and carts had commonly been used in the ancient Middle East, but they fell out of favor for the more economical camel in long-distance travels. Furthermore, carts were difficult to pull across sandy dunes, meaning that travelers had to follow designated paths. By the advent of Islam carts and wagons were uncommon. Muslim and European traveler accounts rarely mention travel by wheeled transport, and in the few accounts that exist the writers express surprise at seeing wheeled transportation. This notion is augmented by the lack of wheeled vehicles in medieval Islamic art; there are a few instances of pictorial representation of carts, but the physical structure is implausible, and the representations are most likely figments of the artist's imagination based on vague descriptions from historical texts. Additionally, there was only one primary word in the Arabic language to describe vehicles—*araba*. The one exception where wheeled transportation was used in the greater Islamic world was in central Asia, where nomads used wagons in transporting their households when relocating across the steppes. Carts that were used most often were pulled by horses or oxen, but the Arab traveler and scholar Ibn Battutah (1304–1368 or 1369) does mention a cart pulled by a camel.

For a long-distance journey most travelers would join a caravan because of the many advantages offered by traveling with a group, particularly safety and navigation. Thieves were common along the routes, as were both individuals and rulers exacting a "protection fee." Because of the dangers of traveling through many tribal areas, most caravans included armed guards and local guides. The Islamic world did not have set roads for transportation, and those that had been established during the Roman era had fallen into disrepair. Without the assistance of a guide and sometimes even with a guide, it was easy for travelers to become lost in the desert landscape. An early-20th-century account by the Earl of Ronaldshay notes the difficulties of navigating the ever-changing desert landscape. He became separated from his caravan and found himself miles away from his intended caravanserai; his camels and guides, who were also lost, did not arrive until the following day.

Camels, the ships of the desert, are so called because they are able to travel long distances with minimal requirements.

It was largely an economic factor that initiated the replacement of wheeled vehicles by camels. The animals can carry a 300- to 500-pound load, and the maintenance cost for one camel is considerably less than an animal plus vehicle. In the third century the Roman emperor Diocletian's edict on prices noted that camel transport was 20 percent cheaper than wagons. On average, a camel caravan travels at 3 miles per hour and can accumulate 25 miles per day. Commonly, camels were owned by camel drivers, who leased the animals to the merchants for the duration of the travel. A great advantage of camel transportation was the ability to use them as transport for both people and goods. Riding camels astride was most common, but occasionally elite travelers were borne in litters. Goods were transported in double-sided, woven saddle bags that were placed over the camel's back.

Horses were much less frequently used for transportation, because they required greater maintenance and carried smaller loads than camels. However, horses were advantageous when transportation and travel were under time constraints, since they are much faster than camels or walking. The use of horses was limited to military campaigns, postal and communication services, and elite travelers. Transportation for royals and elite included luxuries, whether riding on more comfortable horseback or riding in a litter. The Abbasid caliph Harun ar-Rashid (r. 786–809) and his wife, Zubaydah, traveled from Baghdad to Mecca for the annual hajj, but as befitting their status they walked along a pathway of laid carpets.

Trade, pilgrimage, and scholarship were the primary reasons for long-distance travel. The spread of Islam increased the need for transportation of pilgrims and scholars. One of

Headstall, the part of the bridle or halter that encompasses a horse's head, Granada, Spain, late 15th or early 16th century (© The Trustees of the British Museum)

the five tenets of Islam is performing the hajj, or pilgrimage to the holy city of Mecca. Other cities around the Islamic world also became pilgrimage centers with shrines of saints, companions of the Prophet, and various imams, or Muslim leaders. Under Islam long-distance travel increased, as the religion encouraged the gathering of knowledge. Centers of Islamic education included Damascus, Baghdad, and Cairo. Muslims wanting to become religious scholars traveled to these cities to learn from masters or to study particular schools of thought or law. Scholars and pilgrims often traveled with trade caravans because it afforded them physical protection and an opportunity to engage in trading of their own to offset the expense of travel. Some wandering scholars, including

Ibn Battutah, Ibn Jubayr, and al-Muqaddasi, kept diaries of their travels and studies, providing accounts of transportation and travel. Unfortunately, many of these sources remain untranslated from Arabic or Persian.

See also ART; BUILDING TECHNIQUES AND MATERIALS; CITIES; CLIMATE AND GEOGRAPHY; EDUCATION; ECONOMY; EMPIRES AND DYNASTIES; FESTIVALS; GENDER STRUCTURES AND ROLES; HUNTING, FISHING, AND GATHERING; INVENTIONS; MIGRATION AND POPULATION MOVEMENTS; MILITARY; RELIGION AND COSMOLOGY; ROADS AND BRIDGES; SACRED SITES; SEAFARING AND NAVIGATION; SHIPS AND SHIPBUILDING; TRADE AND EXCHANGE; WAR AND CONQUEST.

| *Asia and the Pacific* | ∼ *Description of the West by a Chinese Envoy (1220)* ∼ |

In the seventh month (August) of the year 1220, Wu-ku-sun Chung tuan, vice- president of the Board of Rites, was entrusted by the emperor (U-tu-bu of the Kin dynasty) with a mission to the northern court. An T'ing chen, secretary in the Academy, was appointed his assistant. Wu-ku-sun returned in the tenth month (October or November) of 1221, when he addressed me in the following terms:

"I have been sent a distance of ten thousand li west of the border of heaven, and not wishing all the curious things I saw in my travels to remain unrecorded, I therefore request you to write down my narrative.

"In the twelfth month (January) of 1220 I passed the northern Frontier (of the Kin empire), and proceeded in a north-western direction, where the ground rises gradually. Advancing parallel with (the northern frontier of) the Hia empire, after having travelled seven or eight thousand li, I arrived at a mountain. East of it all rivers flow to the east; west of it they run to the west, and the ground gradually descends. Farther on, after travelling four to five thousand li, the climate becomes very hot. I passed through more than a hundred cities; not one of them had a Chinese name. Inquiring about the country, I was told that many tribes were living there, namely, the Mo-li-hi, the Mo-k'o-ti, the Ho-li-ki-sz', the Nai-man, the Hang-li, the Gai-gu, the T'u-ma, and the Ho-lu; all are barbarian tribes.

"Farther on I travelled over several tens of thousands of li, and arrived at the city of I-Ii in the country of the Hui-ho. There is the residence of the king of (or of a king of) the Hui- ho. We were then in the first decade of the fourth mouth (beginning of May).

"The empire of Ta-shi, or the great K'i-tan, was formerly in the middle of the country of the Hui-ho (Mohammedans). Ta-shi Lin-ma belonged to the people of the Liao. T'ai tsu liked him for his intelligence and eloquence, and gave him a princess as wife. But Ta-shi secretly bore the emperor ill-will. At the time the emperor moved his arms to the west, Ta- shi was at first with him, but afterwards he took his family and fled beyond the mountains (probably Altai). Then he assembled the tribes on the frontier and emigrated to the north- west. On their wanderings they rested at places abounding in water and pastures. After several years they arrived at the Yin shan mountain, but could not penetrate owing to the rocks and the snow. They were obliged to leave their carts behind, and to carry their baggage on camels. Thus they arrived in the country of the Hui-ho (Mohammedans), took possession of the land and founded an empire. From day to day Ta-shi's power increased; he reigned some thirty years and more, and after death was canonised as Te tsung. When he died his son succeeded. The latter was canonised as Jen tsung. After his death, his younger sister, by name Kan, took charge of the regency; but as she held illicit

(continued)

(continues)

intercourse and killed her husband, she was executed. Then the second son of Jen tsung came to the throne. Owing to his appointing unworthy officers, the empire fell into decay, and was finally destroyed by the Hui-ho.

At the present day there are few of these people left, and they have adopted the customs and the dress of the Hui-ho."

From: E. Bretschneider, trans., *Mediaeval Researches from Eastern Asiatic Sources* (London: Trübner, 1888).

Europe

∾ *Excerpt from* The Travels of John de Marignolli (1339–53) ∾

We set out from Avignon in the month of December, came to Naples in the beginning of Lent, and stopped there till Easter (which fell at the end of March), waiting for a ship of Genoa, which was coming with the Tartar envoys whom the Kaan had sent from his great city of Cambalec to the Pope, to request the latter to dispatch an embassy to his court, whereby communication might be established, and a treaty of alliance struck between him and the Christians; for he greatly loves and honours our faith. Moreover the chief princes of his whole empire more than thirty thousand in number, who are called Alans, and govern the whole Orient, are Christians either in fact or in name, calling themselves the Pope's slaves, and ready to die for the Franks. . . .

Howbeit on the first of May we arrived by sea at Constantinople, and stopped at Pera till the feast of St. John Baptist. We had no idle time of it, however, for we were engaged in a most weighty controversy with the Patriarch of the Greeks and their whole Council in the palace of St. Sophia. . . .

Thence we sailed across the Black Sea, and in eight days arrived at Caffa, where there are Christians of many sects. From that place we went on to the first Emperor of the Tartars, Usbec, and laid before him the letters which we bore, with certain pieces of cloth, a great war-horse, some strong liquor, and the Pope's presents. And after the winter was over, having been well fed, well clothed, loaded with handsome present, and supplied by the King with horses and travelling expenses, we proceeded to Armalec [the capital] of the Middle Empire. There we built a church, bought a piece of ground, dug wells, sung masses and baptized several; preaching freely and

openly, notwithstanding the fact that only the year before the Bishop and six other Minor Friars had there undergone for Christ's sake a glorious martyrdom, illustrated by brilliant miracles. . . .

Towards the end of the third year after our departure from the Papal Court, quitting Armalec we came to the Cyollos Kagon, to the Sand Hills thrown up by the wind. Before the days of the Tartars nobody believed that the earth was habitable beyond these, nor indeed was it believed that there was any country at all beyond. But the Tartars by God's permission, and with wonderful exertion, did cross them, and found themselves in what the philosophers call the torrid and impassable zone. Pass it however the Tartars did; and so did I, and that twice. . . . After having passed it we came to Cambalec, the chief seat of the Empire of the East. Of its incredible magnitude, population, and military array, we will say nothing. But the Grand Kaam, when he beheld the great horses, and the Pope's presents, with his letter, and King Robert's too, with their golden seals, and when he saw us also, rejoiced greatly, being delighted, yea exceedingly delighted with everything, and treated us with the greatest honour. And when I entered the Kaam's presence it was in full festival vestments, with a very fine cross carried before me, and candles and incense, whilst Credo in Unum Deum was chaunted, in that glorious palace where he dwells. And when the chaunt was ended I bestowed a full benediction, which he received with all humility.

From: Sir Henry Yule, *Cathay and the Way Thither: Being a Collection of Medieval Notices of China* (London: Hakluyt Society, 1913–1916).

FURTHER READING

Ralph A. Austen, "Marginalization, Stagnation, and Growth: The Trans-Saharan Caravan Trade in the Era of European Expansion." In *The Rise of Merchant Empires: Long-Distance Trade in the Early Modern World, 1350–1750*, ed. James D. Tracy (New York: Cambridge University Press, 1990).

Ibn Battuta, *The Travels of Ibn Battuta in the Near East, Asia and Africa, 1325–1354*, trans. and ed. Samuel Lee (Mineola, N.Y.: Dover Publications, 2004).

Richard W. Bulliet, *The Camel and the Wheel* (Cambridge, Mass.: Harvard University Press, 1975).

John Crandall, "The Inca and their Roads." Available online. URL: http://transportationhistory.suite101.com/article.cfm/the_inca_and_their_roads. Downloaded on November 29, 2007.

John Block Friedman, and Kristen Mossler Figg, eds. *Trade, Travel, and Exploration in the Middle Ages* (New York: Garland, 2000).

Robin Law, *The Horse in West African History: The Role of Horses in the Societies of Pre-Colonial West Africa* (Oxford, U.K.: Oxford University Press for the International African Institute, 1980).

Albert C. Leighton, *Transportation and Communication in Early Medieval Europe, A.D. 500–1100* (Newton Abbott, U.K.: David and Charles, 1972).

Eleanor Sims, "Trade and Travel: Markets and Caravanserais," in *Architecture of the Islamic World*, ed. George Michell (London: Thames and Hudson, 1978).

David W. Tschanz, "Journeys of Faith, Roads of Civilization," *Saudi Aramco World* (Jan./Feb. 2004): 2–11. Available online. URL: http://www.saudiaramcoworld.com/issue/200401/journeys.of.faith.roads.of.civilization.htm

Michael Woods and Mary B. Woods, *Ancient Transportation: From Camels to Canals* (Minneapolis, Minn.: Runestone Press, 2000).

► war and conquest

INTRODUCTION

The Middle Ages is often thought of as a period of military amateurism. Much of the fighting in cultures all over the world had a "heroic" quality in the sense of the heroes of the *Iliad*, such as Achilles or Hector, fighting individual duels on the battlefield in a grand contest for honor, as opposed to a clash of disciplined formations of troops. The perception is most true in the case of western Europe, the culture that, however unrepresentative it might be of other areas, does the most to inform our view of the Middle Ages. The knightly ideal of chivalry was an elaborate code for heroic warfare or, viewed differently, of military amateurism.

Knights were indeed professional soldiers, but they trained for single combat. The ritualized fighting of the tournament was as important for their prestige and reputation as actual warfare. Medieval armies and warfare were not marked by brilliant maneuvers on the battlefield or by long campaigns of attrition, which are always the preferred form of campaigning (as being less risky) for professional soldiers. The largest components of feudal armies (serving as infantry), gathered by levy, were hardly trained at all and usually served for very short periods, as little as 40 days. When a force of knights met a disciplined force of mercenaries (for example, the Welsh peasant longbowmen deployed at the battle of Agincourt), the knights did not usually fare well. Still, if a knightly army could deliver a charge of heavy cavalry, it was nearly irresistible.

In the Americas warfare often served a purpose other than mere military victory over the enemy. Among the chiefdoms of North America chiefs fought each other to gain prestige, not typically for the sake of conquest or even plunder. This very ancient style of warfare is the very antithesis of military professionalism. It can find no better expression than in the practice of counting coup. In this custom of the Plains nations, a warrior would approach an enemy warrior and simply touch him, without making any attack. If he could do this and get away unharmed, he could boast that he had utterly overcome and humiliated his foe. Even in Mesoamerica the primary reason for Aztec aggression (as successful as it often was in conquest) was for individual members of the elite military class to capture enemy soldiers as prisoners for human sacrifice and augment their own status within Aztec society. Even in the Americas, however, the Inca seem to have practiced a more methodical form of warfare based on superiority in logistics rather than the bravery of the individual fighters.

In sub-Saharan Africa most warfare was of a very "heroic" character, conducted between individual clans or villages. By the end of the Middle Ages the kingdom of Kongo in central Africa had developed a more sophisticated military system able to field larger forces and utilize them for conquest or profitable raiding. However, just as the Kongo state was organizing, it had the misfortune to become entangled with the Portuguese, first as allies but, inevitably after the Middle Ages, as enemies. Kongo simply could not match the superior military technology and doctrines of the Europeans, who used firearms and more easily held command of the sea.

The most dramatic story of medieval warfare concerns the waves of conquest both east and west by the nomadic tribes of the inner Asian steppe. The pressure was first felt in the West by the Roman Empire when Asiatic tribesmen began forcing Germanic peoples westward out of the Ukraine. Unfortunately, this came at a time when Rome was near collapse from civil wars and other internal dislocations. If the invasions had come earlier, at the empire's height, the Roman Empire's professional army would probably have been able to deal with the problem. As it was, the Romans were forced to increase the size of their forces by admitting German tribesmen and then whole tribes into the army. Eventually, the western part of the empire dissolved more than fell, as the barbarian chiefs to whom the security of its provinces had been entrusted simply declared themselves kings in their own right. Much the same thing happened in the seventh century when the relatively poorly organized Arab tribesmen invaded and overwhelmed the Byzantine and Sassanian empires at precisely the moment the two empires had exhausted each other by decades of costly and inconclusive war.

The greatest triumph of the steppe tribesmen was to come later and in the East, in the person of Genghis Khan. An unlikely military genius, he came from an illiterate society with a tradition of raiding rather than conquest. His military and political education was entirely practical, first in the struggles to secure his heredity position among the Mongols and then to unify the steppe tribes. Owing to the relatively simple level of technology that existed during antiquity and the Middle Ages, even in a sophisticated state like China, Genghis's troops had the advantage of technological parity with their foes that nomadic tribesmen always enjoyed vis-à-vis advanced urban cultures until modern times. In fact, using the stirrup and compound bow, his troopers were more effective fighters than the soldiers of the Chinese and his other enemies. Genghis's conquest of northern China and particularly the states of inner Asia shows a profound grasp of the strategic realities of war in terms of intelligence, planning, logistics, and psychological warfare. Although there was no native tradition of Mongol siege warfare, Genghis immediately recognized its importance and organized a siege train using the best Chinese engineers and equipment. He was also blessed with a circle of subordinate commanders who were themselves brilliant generals. Genghis's quality and fortune as a general can be compared only to such figures as Alexander the Great or Napoléon. His system of warfare allowed his successors to go on conquering for a century, taking southern China, most of the Middle East, Russia, and northern India, but eventually the inherently impoverished

way of life of the steppe and the failure to modernize brought Mongol rule to an end.

AFRICA

BY KIRK H. BEETZ

In 500 North Africa was still primarily under the control of the Byzantine Empire. Outside of that region the most powerful African military was probably that of the kingdom of Axum. To the west of Axum were the Christian kingdoms of Nubia: Nobatia, Makuria, and Alwa. These nations had well-organized armies. Archaeological evidence indicates that there were polities farther west and south, but little is known of their ways of waging war. In general, more information about warfare survives from later in the medieval era than from earlier in the period. In 500 the forests were populated by hunter-gatherers and homesteads of farmers migrating from western Africa. The plains of East Africa and southern Africa were populated mostly by pastoralists, with fishing villages along the coasts. The southwestern reaches of Africa were populated mostly by the San, who were primarily hunter-gatherers. Out of many of these peoples would emerge kingdoms and empires, with well-organized military forces; some pastoral and hunter-gatherer cultures would retain already ancient forms of aggression and defense.

AXUM AND ETHIOPIA

The medieval society of Ethiopia had a strong interest in history, and its government tried to preserve documents about the kingdom's history. Medieval clerics who maintained libraries and copied decaying texts to fresh pages preserved some details of how war was waged during medieval times.

At the start of the medieval era the Horn of Africa was dominated by Axum. This kingdom had originated thousands of years before as a city-state whose main seaport was Adulis, about a six-day journey from the city of Axum. Axum had a powerful military. A navy had proven essential to maintaining seagoing trade, and Axum's navy was unrivaled on the southern seas between India and Africa. Little is known of how the Axumite navy functioned, although its ships were known well enough for poets to refer to them as large and swift. Naval ships transported Axumite soldiers to places on the Arabian Peninsula. The navy fought battles against pirates and seems to have been usually victorious. The eclipse of Axum's military by Muslims occurred in land battles.

Axum's society was the result of a mix of local African and Sabean cultures, and it controlled not only much of northeastern Africa but almost all of southern Arabia, where the Sabeans originated. The Arabian provinces of Axum were governed by a viceroy who commanded a standing army that often supported friendly Arab princes in their wars and even interfered in wars of succession in eastern Arabia. In the era of Muhammad (ca. 570–632) Axum was able to protect Muslim refugees from Mecca.

The king of Axum maintained a standing army that was divided into regiments, each probably led by a member of the nobility. This army moved swiftly on the roads of Axum. This core of professionals would be supplemented in times of war by levies of troops from Axum's provinces and subject states. These were usually poorly equipped people armed with spears, bows, and swords. It was the responsibility of regional nobility and village chiefs to raise these troops when called upon by the king. Even though the king of Axum had protected Muslims from their enemies, the nemesis of Axum proved to be Muslims. Muslims settled on the coasts and within Axum, and beginning in the eighth century they tried repeatedly to overthrow the Axumite government. Although Axum's army had controlled much of northeastern Africa and southern Arabia for hundreds of years, it does not appear to have kept pace with military developments in the Near East. Arabian armies were better armed and wore full chain mail; they were also ably led. Axum had long been able to import supplies from abroad, but the fall of Egypt to Muslim armies cut off supplies from the Byzantine Empire, and Muslim armies cut off supplies from the south. The invaders had better access to supplies, and in conflicts that lasted into the 10th century they were able to outlast the Axumite defenders, seizing control of Axum's ports. The Axumite government had been slowly moving westward for 100 years or so and finally withdrew into the Ethiopian highlands, beginning a new era as the empire of Ethiopia.

In the highlands the Ethiopian army's quick responses to attacks and a system of fortresses defending mountain passes repelled attempts by outsiders to invade the country. Further, the army opened and protected routes to the west, giving Ethiopia access to the Nubian kingdoms of the upper Nile and to trade routes into Africa's interior. In 1270, when Yekuno Amlak (r. 1270–85) founded the Solomonid Dynasty, Ethiopian kings abandoned the practice of having a fixed capital and chose to live in a mobile tent city. The kings were essentially war leaders, and their tent cities allowed them to move themselves, their governments, and their central army to wherever there was fighting. Ethiopia's wars were not always defensive. Often they were intended to expand the kingdom or to turn troublesome neighbors into vassals who paid tribute and contributed soldiers to the Ethiopian army. Much of the professional army consisted of soldiers who had been taken as prisoners of war.

The Ethiopian standing army was divided into regiments. Each regiment was led by someone close to the emperor of Ethiopia, often a son or another relative. Brothers were usually not favored because they were threats to the sovereignty of the monarch. Each regiment had its own colors. Members competed for honors and participated in displays of courage with other regiments. The soldiers were often raised in the military service and taught to regard the emperor as their father. The army continued to suffer in conflicts against Muslim armies because of the inferiority of its weapons and armor until the era of Emperor Amda Tseyon (r. 1314–ca. 1344). His standing army was outfitted in chain mail and helmets and was provided with a variety of weapons. Some units focused on archery. Some had crossbows that fired darts. Others were equipped with long, narrow shields and swords for close fighting. The principal weapon was the long spear; the highly disciplined infantry units could blunt a cavalry charge by forming lines with their spears bristling forward. In Ethiopia's own cavalry the spears could unhorse rivals or be thrust over the shields of infantrymen. The cavalry seems to have been a small part of the army. For example, in 1322 the Muslim governor of Ifat murdered one of the envoys Amda Tseyon had sent to Egypt to protest persecution of Christians in Egypt; Amda Tseyon's forces reportedly had only seven horses when they invaded Ifat in reprisal.

THE NUBIAN KINGDOMS

The kingdoms of medieval Nubia fought wars against each other, against the Egyptians, and against Arab pastoralists, who continually tried to migrate into the lands of Nobatia and Makuria and drive out the local farmers. Christianity came to these kingdoms in the sixth century, and in their early years these peoples traded with the Byzantine Empire. Then Muslim armies seized Egypt and the rest of North Africa; in 651 the Muslim army invaded Nubia but was defeated in 652. Even so, the Nubian kingdoms took to paying the caliph in Baghdad annual tribute in slaves. Makuria paid 365 slaves per year. It is possible that in the late seventh century or the eighth century Makuria conquered Nobatia, although the merger may have been friendly; it is also possible that Nobatia maintained its independence but acknowledged Makuria's supremacy. From about 750 to about 1150 the Nubian kingdoms were stable, and their armies fended off raids and invasions. In 833 they actually invaded Egypt, defeated Egypt's army, and ceased paying tribute. Able to negotiate from a stronger position than before, Makuria persuaded the caliph to forgive tribute that had been unpaid and to reduce future tribute to just once every three years.

One of the duties of the army of each kingdom was to patrol the borders. Bandits and pastoralists trying to seize territory were constant problems, and troops were stationed in fortresses along the borders. Each province seems to have had

A trophy head representing a powerful defeated enemy, Benin Kingdom, Nigeria; 15th to early 16th century (National Museum of African Art, Smithsonian Institution, Photograph by Franko Khoury, Purchased with funds provided by the Smithsonian Collections Acquisition Program, 82-5-2)

a principal lord, who maintained a castle on high ground as well as an army that kept his lands clear of invaders and that would join the national army during a crisis. The army was essential to maintaining the kingdoms' independence and the security of their subjects.

The elite force of the armies was composed of archers on horseback. Able to move swiftly and fire accurately at the same time, they were well respected by their adversaries. Nubian cavalry seems to have resembled European cavalry. The men were equipped with chain mail that was imported from the Byzantine Empire or Egypt, and they wore steel helmets and tunics over their armor with their insignia on them, much as Europeans did. Their weapons included iron swords and long spears. In the sixth and seventh centuries Nubian cavalrymen rode bareback, but by 750 they had saddles, and their stirrups resembled those used in the Islamic world.

The Christians of Upper Egypt regarded the Nubian kingdoms as their protectors, and Makuria in particular sometimes intervened in Egypt when Christian communities were attacked. The period of the Fatimid rule of Egypt seems to have been especially peaceful for the Nubian kingdoms; the Fatimids faced much hostility elsewhere in the world, and they valued the trade and diplomatic relations they developed with the kingdoms to the south. This situation changed in 1171, when the Ayyubids took over Egypt; Makuria seems to have sent troops in support of the Fatimids. They were defeated, and the Ayyubids occupied much of Makuria for several years before withdrawing. The effect on the Nubian kingdoms was dramatic. The Nubians built walls around cities that had had no walls. They invested much time and wealth in building castles after Byzantine models. Their cavalry shifted from light, swift horses to heavier, larger horses.

In 1250 the Mamluk Dynasty took over Egypt and negotiated a military treaty with Makuria in which Makuria promised to help protect Egypt's southern border. Makuria was unable to prevent bandits from raiding across the border into Egypt and in 1272 actually invaded Egypt on behalf of Christians in Upper Egypt. This action resulted in Mamluk invasions of Makuria, and the Mamluks placed a puppet on the Makurian throne before being driven out by a Christian rival. In the 14th century there was a prolonged invasion of the Nubian kingdoms from Egypt. The Nubian armies proved remarkably resilient while battling one of the world's foremost military powers. The Nubians gave up ground grudgingly, fighting a war of attrition that they seemed almost doomed to lose. Makuria fell apart in 1376 because it was no longer able to provide its troops with supplies. In 1287 Alwa was reduced to a group of small, independent principalities, ruled by military nobility. These lords fought long, defensive wars against the Muslim invaders before being overwhelmed in the 15th century.

Thereafter the Nubians either migrated to other lands or continued to fight. Their military organization resembled the traditional organizations of central Africa, with villages led by chiefs who were selected as leaders because of their military skills. Each village had a small, part-time militia that assembled to fight wars or to fend off pastoralists who tried to move into the Nubians' farmlands. The warriors no longer had the armor and shining helmets worn by the knights of the past, but they probably still used horses in battle. Their arms consisted primarily of spears and swords, and they carried light shields with light frames and probably animal skin stretched across the surface. It would have taken skill to use the shields because they would have been effective only against glancing blows and would not have endured direct blows from swords or hammers.

THE EMPIRES OF THE WEST

During the medieval era numerous small kingdoms formed, survived, and then collapsed to be replaced by new kingdoms in western Africa. They often were created by someone who was believed to have magical powers. Their kings were not necessarily regarded as gods themselves, but in general they were regarded as having special connections to God or to the world of spirits. The armies of these kingdoms tended to be run by members of nobility, who usually fought as armored knights on horseback. Horses were difficult to maintain in forested lands, but during the medieval era people learned to house horses in stalls to keep out flies that carried disease; the horses often were cared for and protected by several people. Even so, the rulers of the kingdoms regularly had to import horses from North Africa to replace the horses that died from disease.

Northeast of Lake Chad the kingdom of Kanem was formed in the ninth century. In about 1068 a Muslim overthrew the last king of the Zaghawa Dynasty and founded the Sayfawa Dynasty. Although the monarchs were officially Muslim, the commoners of Kanem resisted Islam, and this resistance led to occasional rebellions. The principal mission of Kanem's army was to protect the trade routes that ran through the kingdom. By 1259 Kanem had an army of 40,000 horsemen, led by 3,000 knights. In times of war infantry consisted of conscripted (drafted) peasants. The infantry was armed with bows and spears. The armored knights wore chain mail made in North Africa or in Kanem itself; the armor covered them from neck to ankles. They were armed with spears, swords, and war hammers. In large battles the knights bore the brunt of the fighting. For patrolling the trade routes, lightly armored cavalry could chase down bandits and harass intruding pastoralists.

The most powerful monarch of Kanem was probably Dunama Dibalami (r. 1210–48). He organized his government around the kingdom's military. Government posts had been filled on the basis of loyalty to the *mai* ("king"), but Dunama Dibalami gave government posts to military nobility and made the posts hereditary. Further, he destroyed the *mune*, a supernatural object that linked Kanem to its non-Islamic past. The results were disorder among the peasants, who were angered at the loss of the *mune*, and frequent rebellions by hereditary governors of provinces. The rebellions created enough turmoil for Arabs successfully to invade Kanem from the north and drive the kingdom's government out of its capital, Njimi. To the south and west of Kanem the refugees founded the kingdom of Bornu. Most of the 15th century was spent in civil strife, but by about 1472 a new capital, Ngazargamu, had been established. It was a fortified city, and much of Bornu seems to have been dotted by fortified settlements. It had a military government consisting of knights, and its focus was on conquest. Ali Gaji (r. 1497–1515) reconquered Njimi.

Farther to the west was the Ghana Empire, which arose around 700 and fell in 1078 to Almoravid invaders. In 1140 the Almoravids were driven out by an army from the kingdom of Kaniaga. A rebellion drove out the Kaniagan troops in 1230, but the new government of Ghana allied itself with Mali and by 1240 had become just another part of the Mali Empire. Ghana's economy depended on trade with North Africa, and much of its military was devoted to protecting that trade. Its soldiers were not well equipped; most of them were peasants hastily conscripted when a war began. Even so, in the 11th century Ghana was reported by Muslim geographers to be able to muster over 200,000 troops, mostly peasant conscripts, led by war chiefs. The number may be an exaggeration, but part of Ghana's military success may have been its army's ability to overwhelm many enemies with the size of its army in an open range. The infantry fought in columns, bristling with spears. Kaniaga's army may have focused on a small core of armored cavalry, with the bulk of the army consisting of archers on horseback and spear-carrying infantry.

The Mali Empire became legendary in the medieval world, famous for its wealth, its system of government, and its military power. Throughout its existence it depended on its military for survival; the military not only protected the many trans-Saharan trade routes through Mali but also had to fight rebellious provinces and invasions by raiders. The growth of Mali into an empire began with an exceptionally gifted military commander, Sundiata Keita (ca. 1217–55), one of the sons of the king of Mandinka. He was a very sickly child who began walking at age seven, with the aid of metal canes that were said to bow under his weight. When Kaniaga conquered many of the tributary kingdoms of the Ghana Empire, the king of Kaniaga had all of Sundiata's family put to the sword except Sundiata and Sundiata's mother. One account of the events says that Sundiata was spared because he was so sickly that he seemed to pose no danger; another says that he and his mother had already been forced into exile by a jealous brother.

Sundiata was a charismatic leader even when he was a teenager, and he attracted followers. He also turned out to have a gift for organizing people. He combined armies from the kingdom of Mema, the city-states of the Mandinkans, and the remnants of Ghana's nobility, and he set the pattern for future armies of the Mali Empire. His cavalry consisted of armored warriors, mostly from the aristocracy, and of infantry armed primarily with spears and bows with poison-tipped arrows. The battle of Kirina (ca. 1235) took place in a region with several rivers, so it is likely that both sides used war canoes. The Kaniagan forces were outmaneuvered; Sundiata was able to put the bulk of his cavalry against Kaniagan infantry. Throughout the years of the Mali Empire at its zenith, its army would maneuver its heavy cavalry into positions that allowed it to charge the massed infantry of its enemies. Not much is known of how Sundiata laid siege to cities held by his enemies, but he seems to have preferred to try to breach the walls of cities rather than to wait out his enemies. It took several months of persistent attacks to breach the walls of Kaniaga's capital city.

After Sundiata's time the Mali Empire continually fought rebels and invaders. Even raiders from the southern forests were persistent, attacking annually and being defeated annually by Mali's highly disciplined heavy cavalry. Mali's cavalry of the 13th and 14th centuries had the most advanced armor in western Africa. Like the knights of Kanem, Mali's cavalry wore chain mail from neck to ankle. They wielded long spears and heavy shields during charges but could fight from horseback or on foot with their swords. They rode large, heavy horses that had padded armor. These horses were themselves weapons, their size and weight bearing down on enemy infantry. During the 13th and 14th centuries Mali may have had 30,000 professional heavy cavalrymen. Mali also had horse archers, but Mali's generals seemed to prefer to use infantry as archers.

Enemies from southern kingdoms often tried to lure the heavy cavalry into dense forest or swamps, where mounted troops could be picked off by archers who hid behind trees. However, Mali rarely sent horsemen into forests, preferring to penetrate the forests with war canoes and infantry or to stay out of them altogether. Mali had a core army of infantry that served as garrisons in cities and fortresses and protected the emperor. Although the emperor and his family were technically Muslims, the emperor continued to practice traditional African magic and to tolerate other traditional customs, including having women in positions of authority. In times of war the mother of the emperor or one of the emperor's wives could be an intimidating military leader, often entrusted with defending important cities and territory. For most military campaigns, Mali relied on its extensive roads to move its troops quickly. Often, even when moving very rapidly, the main body of the army arrived too late to aid a frontier outpost or a city near the empire's borders. This weakness was worsened by a reliance on summoning infantry from peasants, who usually were equipped only with whatever they could grab.

During a period in which Mali suffered a food shortage in its large cities, fended off several attacks from small polities, and lost Timbuktu to Tuareg invaders, a small kingdom with a well-organized military was able to take advantage. The Songhai Empire began as a small kingdom in the northwest of modern-day Nigeria. The kingdom had been a perpetual problem for the Ghana Empire and then the Mali Empire. In 1465 the Songhai conquered Mema. In 1468 they drove the Tuareg out of Timbuktu. The Songhai were joined by troops from rebellious provinces and tributary kingdoms. Their foremost leader was Sonni Ali (r. ca. 1464–92). At his command was an exceptionally well-disciplined army of professional soldiers, veterans of many battles. These full-time soldiers were notable for their hardiness and courage. A Songhai infantryman would stand his ground even if surrounded by the enemy, moving only if ordered by a superior officer to change his position. Cavalry charges that would have scattered other troops often failed against the Songhai infantry. However, the behavior of Songhai's troops after the taking of Timbuktu was very undisciplined, and Malian civilians were slaughtered, the women raped, and their homes looted.

The siege of Jenne-jeno proved to be different. The city of Jenne-jeno was surrounded by swamps in the rainy season and had numerous waterways that enemies had to cross to reach the city itself. In fact, it had successfully resisted all attempts by the Mali Empire to conquer it. Sonni Ali decided against a direct assault on the city, choosing instead to surround it and prevent outside supplies from reaching the city. During the dry season Songhai's army surrounded the city. During the rainy season the army had to withdraw because swamps expanded. Sonni Ali's navy consisted of hundreds of war canoes, and they were used to patrol waterways in an effort to prevent the smuggling of supplies into Jenne-jeno. In open battle Sonni Ali was able to deploy his diverse military units very effectively. His cavalry was fast and could quickly turn enemy flanks. His infantry used spears and swords. For aerial attacks he had not only archers with bows and arrows but also troops who could fire poisoned darts and who were skilled sharpshooters. The terror inflicted by the darts had much to do with defeating the Tuareg because a prick of the skin could mean death.

The leaders of Jenne-jeno were canny, letting their walls and swamps keep the enemy out while not sending their troops out for open battle. After seven years of the siege both sides were ready to give up, but the leaders of Jenne-jeno surrendered first. What then passed was a display of the discipline that would become the hallmark of Songhai's armies. The people of Jenne-jeno were unmolested. The troops of the Songhai remained in formation and under the supervision of their officers. This tactic allowed Sonni Ali to display generosity and magnanimity toward his conquered enemies, something that may have encouraged other potential foes to submit voluntarily to Songhai, saving many lives.

CENTRAL AFRICA

There were kingdoms in the area of the Congo River, but little is known of them. In late medieval times there were kingdoms between western Africa and the southern city-states of East Africa. Little is known about these kingdoms except that their kings could guarantee safe passage to merchants, suggesting some type of military power. The hunter-gatherers of the rain forest were under constant pressure from farmers migrating southward. As the north of Africa became drier and as the dry lands spread southward, people who depended on reliable sources of water for their crops also moved south. How often there was conflict is uncertain. The hunter-gatherers had bows and blowguns. The poisons of the arrows and darts could exact frightful tolls. In some cases, the hunter-gatherers assimilated into the small armies of their northern neighbors; in other cases, the hunter-gatherers retreated. When they chose to fight, they would unite warriors from several different groups, probably related by kinship, but they did not field large armies.

Indeed, for most of the medieval era an army of 3,000 men and women would have been enough to dominate a kingdom. Military leaders were usually people believed to have supernatural powers. Blacksmiths, in particular, became military leaders and even kings. Blacksmiths were traditionally thought to have a supernatural connection to deceased ancestors and to gods, and their work involved secret rituals passed on from father to son. Further, in much of central Africa they were traveling workers. They took their tools with them from village to village on narrow paths through the rain forest. They were subject to robbery while traveling and therefore formed groups of bodyguards. Keeping the paths open for travel even when the blacksmiths were not there required even more guards. These guards became armies, capable of fighting small wars. Blacksmiths with armies could take control of villages. Many chiefs began as blacksmiths with private armies, and some of these chiefs became kings, ruling over many villages.

Wars were seldom long, usually lasting no more than three days. Most conflicts could be settled in a day. Battles were fought according to rules well understood among the different cultures that populated the region. Usually an open area was selected. The object was to force the opposing side to retreat. The warriors would form lines facing each other; they were armed with spears or short swords and carried tall, light shields. Each side would try to outmaneuver the other in order to turn the enemy's flanks. In the process, the warriors would clash, and blood would be shed, but the affair was conducted so as to minimize bloodshed. Once one side had nearly encircled the other, fighting could become fierce, but there was always an opening in the ranks near the forest edge through which the encircled forces could retreat. The battle began in late afternoon so that after an hour of two of fighting, the losing side could retreat under cover of darkness. In general, it was shameful for the victors to loot the enemy's villages, but seizing a moderate amount of livestock, without leaving the enemy destitute, was considered honorable. On rare occasions, when an enemy was especially scorned, the victor would seize the loser's territory, allowing a kingdom to expand a little.

THE EASTERN CITY-STATES

Even though the trading cities of the eastern seaboard of Africa and on northern Madagascar were famous, not much is known about their militaries. Almost all had a navy, usually small and used for protecting sea traffic from pirates. Kilwa may have had a notably large and well-equipped navy that helped it control much of the eastern coast of southern Africa. Kilwa and other cities were surrounded by walls, but the walls do not seem to have been very effective. When Portuguese crews began destroying the cities in the late 15th century, they were able to sail into Kilwa's port like merchants; they then came out during the night, murdering much of the population and carrying many people away for slavery in Europe.

Only Mogadishu managed to fight off the Portuguese, but the details of the feat are unclear. Mogadishu had a fortress on high ground near the city, to which many of the city's people fled; others fled inland. Assaults on the fortress by the Portuguese and Africans allied with the Portuguese failed; the loss of life for the invaders was enough for them to have to retreat from the region. It is unlikely but not impossible that the defenders of Mogadishu had firearms, which could have been imported from the Mediterranean; these defenders more likely had bows, spears, and swords, and wore armor similar to that worn by Ethiopian soldiers.

SOUTHERN AFRICA

To the west of the city-states was Great Zimbabwe, an empire that dominated several kingdoms. The empire had many well-kept roads that seem to have been organized according to an overall plan. Several roads led out of the city of Great Zimbabwe. These roads led to towns. From each town roads connected to villages. The empire relied on the roads for swift movement of its troops, who were likely to have been entirely infantry. Small fortresses along the roads could have housed garrisons whose duty was to keep the roads clear of bandits. Spreading west from Great Zimbabwe were small vassal kingdoms that shared the Zimbabwean culture and that probably required occasional suppression by the army of Great Zimbabwe. Also of concern were the herders of the southern plains. They may have been required to pay tribute for driving their herds of cattle on territory controlled by Great Zimbabwe and other kingdoms. A small but disciplined regular army that used the roads to patrol the borders of the kingdoms could have defeated any but a similarly well-disciplined force from the pastoralists.

The herders were mostly the Khoi. To the west of the grasslands on which the Khoi migrated were drylands occupied primarily by the San. Both peoples had similar weapons: bows and spears. These were used mostly for hunting but could double as military weapons. The Khoi may have had the stronger position in wars between the two groups because they could gather warriors in a group more quickly than could the San. Usually Khoi and San war parties were small, consisting of several men, often related kinsmen. Battles could have consisted more of shouting and posturing than physical combat.

The San, in what is modern-day Angola, sometimes became warriors in the armies of central African kingdoms. Sometimes they fought against the southward expansion of kingdoms. They were valued for their skills with the bow and were tough fighters with spears and short-bladed swords or knives.

THE AMERICAS
BY J. J. GEORGE

Many aspects of war in the Americas during the Middle Ages show great developmental continuity with earlier periods, especially in the areas where hunter-gatherer, nomadic, or chiefly cultures persisted. Areas such as the Arctic, the Great Plains, the Caribbean, southern Central America, and South America outside the Andes generally experienced small-scale but nonetheless intense warfare and raiding. These conflicts were in large part due to smaller scales of political coordination. Between the 10th and 16th centuries, however, the situation changed dramatically, especially in Mexico and the Andes, with the rise of overarching political-economic-military entities, such as the Toltec, Aztec, and Inca empires, all of which were highly organized and able to mobilize war and conquest as deft and persuasive tools. Four major events in this period broadly shaped the ebb and flow of the cultural landscape. War is certainly implicated among them, shaping and being shaped by the intricate and often devastating turning of events.

The first event was the fall of the central Mexican empire centered at Teotihuacán around 750, dissolving numerous practical ties and alliances stretching across Mexico into the Mayan territory of Guatemala and Honduras. The ensuing void gave rise to a number of city-states, struggling against one another for greater power and control. The second event was the collapse of the Classic Period lowland Mayan civilizations in southeast Mexico and neighboring Central America around 925. Scholars have yet to agree on the exact reason for the collapse but agree that any number of factors contributed to their decline; climate change, warfare, and agricultural sustainability are a few of the reasons typically offered. The third major event was the rise of the Aztec Empire in the 14th to 16th centuries. The Aztec, who looked backward to Teotihuacán and the Toltec Empire (10th–12th centuries) for validation, evolved from a warrior tribe to an empire of warriors. Sustaining their tribute empire mandated more or less continuous warfare. The fourth major event was the consolidation of the Inca Empire from 1434 to 1532 along the spine of Andean South America. Centered at the highland city of Cuzco, the Inca eventually conquered all of the territory from roughly Quito, Ecuador, to Santiago, Chile, spanning approximately 3,000 miles and including perhaps 10 million subjects. War and conquest were crucial components in all of these events. Mixed with their social, economic, and political nuances, they amount to highly complex historical processes.

NORTH AMERICAN WARFARE

Warfare was common throughout North America during the period 500–1500, just as it was in many other parts of the world. Some of the best early information regarding indigenous warfare comes from the late 16th century in the form of paintings, sketches, and written accounts by European explorers detailing not only native war practices but general ethnographic information as well. Complementing this information, archaeology has provided data allowing for deeper historical context such that practices witnessed in the 16th century can convincingly be traced further back in time. Native North Americans lacked writing and written texts, unlike their neighbors to the south in the Mayan and Aztec cultures, who developed their own form of pictorial writing. Nevertheless, the picture of North American warfare is becoming clearer as research continues.

Among the Mississippian Period cultures of the Southeast and the greater Midwest, Spanish and French explorers from the 1530s to the end of the 16th century offered pictorial evidence and witness accounts indicating that war and war rituals were both important and common. Chiefly warfare had spread throughout the midcontinent by the end of the first millennium. Intense chiefly rivalries were a main reason for going to war and were a way for a chief to extend influence, not necessarily for the conquest of land but as a way to extend his financial and political base and to defend it against aggressive actions by rival chiefs. According to European sources, preparations prior to military campaigns included war feasts and declarations of war. War chiefs consulted with priests over the likelihood of success; one engraving by Theodor de Bry (1528–98), after an original 1564 painting by

Jacques Le Moyne (ca. 1533–88), shows a chief consulting a shaman about plans for his battle against a neighboring enemy. Behind the chief stand warriors holding clubs, spears, and bows and arrows, evidently awaiting word on whether the battle will ensue.

Another engraving by de Bry is particularly illuminating because it shows a chief named Holata Outina marching to war against an enemy neighbor. What is particularly informative about the image is that it shows Outina at the center of organized troops, who are lined up about 10 deep on each side of him, forming around him a large, open, rectangular space from which he commands and in which he is protected. The troops are dressed minimally in loincloths and carry spears, clubs, and bows and arrows. Many of them are covered in body painting. Another complementary image, also an engraving by de Bry, after an original watercolor by an Englishman named John White (d. ca. 1593), depicts what these advancing troops might have faced once they engaged their target. It shows a small village of huts surrounded by a wooden palisade—a row of sharpened logs planted vertically in the ground forming a defensive barricade around the village. In the middle of the village a number of men appear to engage in some sort of ceremony around a fire, possibly in preparation for war. These images indicate that warfare was often on a smaller scale than was common among other cultures, such as the Aztec and the Inca, in which scores of thousands of troops could be gathered for any particular deployment.

Across North America tribal and chiefly cultures existed in a variety of cultural and settlement patterns, including nomadic, hunter-gatherer, semisedentary, seasonal, and landed agricultural communities, each of which reflects a different relationship to warfare and the kind of warfare that each could wage. Raiding was probably the most common type of aggression and involved small numbers of minimally armed warriors essentially crashing and dashing, perhaps to avenge an insult or a death or perhaps to pillage the food supply or to steal an enemy's women.

Evidence from the Southwest, among the Anasazi, Hohokam, and Mogollon cultures, is consistent with considerable conflict. At the household level archaeologists have found trophy skulls and pottery depicting weapons, body armor, and arrows embedded in human figures. At the community level skull burials, decapitated burials, skeletal evidence of violence, defensive walls on compounds, and site destruction all suggest the proliferation of conflict. In addition, evidence at the spatial scale of the polity and inter-polity, including signal towers, hilltop sites and small sites located for defensive reasons, and uninhabited buffer zones similarly suggest an abiding preoccupation with conflict. The reasons for the conflicts that did occur and the form the conflicts took vary. Furthermore, scholars suggest that conflict in the Southwest was perhaps not endemic but rather happened at some times in some places but not everywhere all of the time.

Mexican Warfare

The decline of the central Mexican empire at Teotihuacán around 750 had far-reaching consequences for all of Mesoamerica. At its height, between 450 and 650, its resident population was at least 125,000, though some estimates reach as high as 200,000. Its political and economic ties stretched to the Mayan territory, where depictions of warriors in Teotihuacán-style garb are known from carved stelae, indicating a clear military influence. Scholars differ on the exact nature of Teotihuacán's military and how much war was promoted within the society, but to maintain extensive trade contacts and to influence Mayan society, at least the impression of power was necessary. Defensive-minded architectural construction within the city itself indicates a preoccupation with or concern over conflict. The exact reason for its decline is still a matter of some conjecture. Nevertheless, it appears that the resulting power vacuum led to the emergence of various regional centers, including Xochicalco, Cacaxtla, and Teotenango, all of which were situated on hilltops and were fortified, again suggesting conditions of conflict. Following the fall of Teotihuacán, the Toltec Empire rose and maintained political-military dominance in central Mexico.

Following the fall of the Toltec and a period of reorganization that involved power struggles between competing city-states, eventually the Aztec rose to power. The word Aztec derives from Aztlan ("place of the herons"), which is the quasi-mythical land from which the ethnic Mexica migrated to the basin of Mexico sometime around 1250. "Aztec" is thus a modern label assigned to the Mexica. The basin of Mexico, or what is today the vast, sprawling metropolis of Mexico City, was then home to numerous independent city-states settled by earlier immigrant groups. By 1325 the Aztec had settled on a swampy island in Lake Texcoco and there began building what would eventually become Tenochtitlán, the capital of the Aztec Empire. After 1325 the Aztec allied themselves with the more powerful states of Azcapotzalco and Texcoco as a tribute-paying entity and aided them in wars. Simultaneously, the Aztec themselves were becoming a powerful entity.

Finally, beginning in 1428 the Aztec made a push for greater power and established a military-economic alliance with Texcoco and Tlacopán, commonly referred to as the Triple Alliance, in which they agreed not to wage war on one another and to cooperate in wars of conquest against other towns or city-sates. The goal of the Triple Alliance was to

Wooden slit drum decorated with scenes from a battle between two cities, Mixtec culture, Mexico, ca. 14th century (© The Trustees of the British Museum)

conquer other city-states in order to force them to pay tribute. A secondary goal of war was to capture enemy soldiers for sacrifice, which was a fundamental element of the Aztec worldview. The Triple Alliance first set about consolidating control throughout the basin of Mexico, conquering city-states to the south at Coyoacán, Xochimilco, and Cuitláhuac. Next they looked to expand outside of the basin of Mexico and turned to Cuauhnáhuac and Huaxtepec, in the modern state of Morelos; they won a major victory over Chalco after Montezuma I (r. 1440–69) assumed the Aztec throne in 1440. This pattern of expansion continued until the arrival of the Spanish in 1521.

However, the Triple Alliance did not advance without setbacks and difficulties. Outright rebellion in subject polities was common, necessitating a strong military response by the Aztec. More devastating, however, was when the Tarascan state to the west of the Aztec Empire, which had remained independent of Aztec hegemony (dominance), delivered one of the Aztec's most crushing defeats. In 1479–80, following a series of ongoing border disputes and incursions, the Aztec leader Axayacatl (r. 1469–81) led an army of 32,000 soldiers into ethnic Tarascan territory. After initial success, taking a major fortress, the Aztec marched deep into Tarascan territory, to within 50 miles of the Tarascan city of Tzintzuntzan, where they were decimated by a combined Tarascan-Mat-latzinca force of 50,000. The Aztec retreated, trailed by the Tarascan, and lost all gained territory west of the town of Taximaroa. Conflict between the two states remained fairly constant up until the Spanish arrival, at which time Aztec desperation was so acute that emissaries were sent to request Tarascan support against the Spanish.

The Aztec did not maintain a standing army, but all young men were trained in military skills at military schools called *calmecac*. Social prestige and advancement were possible for both commoners and nobles through military exploits. Social status depended, in part, on the number of captives taken in battle. With each additional captive, a man gained new privileges. The most successful warriors were called eagle warriors and jaguar warriors, and they enjoyed special privileges, such as being allowed to dine at the royal palace, drink pulque (a fermented alcoholic beverage), and keep concubines. They were the leaders and commanders in battle. The taking of captives for ritual sacrifice reflected Aztec creation myths and religious beliefs, which mandated sacrifices to feed the sun to ensure that the world would keep moving. These so-called "flowery wars" were thus entirely different than any typical modern conception of war. Similarly, the wars were ritualized and followed a strict protocol. The ruler with expansionistic desires sent emissaries with gifts to request the surrender of the targeted town or city-state. Accepting the conditions often meant that the *tlatoani*, or local ruler, would remain in power so long as the mandated tribute was paid. Rejecting the offer meant that war, and possibly destruction, was imminent.

The battles themselves must have been quite spectacular to witness. The war leaders, typically members of the eagle and jaguar societies, adorned themselves in elaborate costumes befitting their rank, often with feather tunics, headdresses, armbands, and other decorative clothing. For example, an image from Fray Bernardino de Sahagún's (ca. 1499–1590) Florentine Codex, one of the most important primary sources for Aztec scholarship, depicts warriors heading into battle dressed in jaguar skin, carrying shields and standards, and bearing the favored Aztec weapon, the *maquahuitl*, a long, flat wooden handle fitted with rows of obsidian blades. Finally, victory on the battlefield came when enough enemy soldiers had been captured or killed to subdue and demoralize the opponent. Sometimes defeat meant the partial destruction of a city. Thereafter tribute quantities were set, and so long as they were met, the victors usually avoided meddling in the internal affairs of the subject polity.

Mayan Warfare

Warfare among the Maya was common, a reality that ran contrary to some early scholarship that held the Maya to be an idealized, peaceful society. Furthermore, it appears that warfare only increased as time passed, such that by the Late Classic and Terminal Classic periods, or roughly between 600 and 925, warfare as an institution was an integral and pervasive element in Mayan society. Much is known about Mayan warfare for two essential reasons: Mayan representations of war on carved stone stelae, murals, painted codices, and painted vessels are prolific, and scholars are now able to decode with great accuracy Mayan glyphic texts, which illuminate names, dates, and events. Inscriptions detailing the capture of a rival king, indicating victory in battle, are found at many Classic Period cities, including Tikal, Palenque, Yaxchilán, Dos Pilas, Quiriguá, Copán, Bonampak, Seibal, and Piedras Negras. Hence, the monuments the Maya used to commemorate warfare were diverse, and now they are intelligible.

Depictions of warfare emphasize garments and weaponry, reveal stages of ritual preparation, such as the presentation of captives, and show that victory was not easily achieved but happened through aggressive hand-to-hand combat, after which captives were stripped of their battle gear and taken back to the city of the victors. The events depicted in Mayan art frequently represent rituals performed at home, such as the display of captives to the public, thereby emphasizing presentation and public validation. Unlike the Aztec and the Inca, the Maya never coalesced into a single empire. Mayan warfare occurred between city-states of varying hegemonic authority, and the public presentation and display of victims worked to reinforce a sense of public pride as well as to validate the authority of the rulers. The public monuments, then, serve to validate localized power and often detail the exploits of individual rulers in the context of the glory of the city.

The city of Yaxchilán, to take one example, seemed particularly focused on detailing the stages of warfare. Yaxchilán is situated in the central area of Mayan territory along the Usumacinta River, astride what is today the border area of Chiapas, Mexico, and Guatemala. Two Yaxchilán rulers in particular figure prominently in the depictions on carved stone lintels on structures they themselves commissioned. They are known as Shield Jaguar, who died in 742, and his son, Bird Jaguar, who succeeded his father to the throne 10 years later. Shield Jaguar constructed a building, referred to as Structure 44, that details his victories in battle and the humiliation of his foes. In another building, referred to as Structure 23, a series of carved lintels depict bloodletting, vision quest, and the capture of an enemy ruler, all of which reinforced the ritual nature of Mayan warfare.

Similarly, Bird Jaguar, following his ascension to the throne and after victory in battle, commissioned his own structures and then chose to depict a series of events that were essentially the same as those his father chose, thereby commemorating both his father's and his family's glory. One particular lintel, referred to as Lintel 41, represents Bird Jaguar donning ritual attire in preparation for battle, presented with arms, wearing cotton armor and a round pectoral with a jaguar inscribed within it, possibly a reference to his father as well as a symbol of power. Representations similar to these were common throughout the Mayan area.

Another interesting aspect of Mayan war, especially during the Classic Period, is that powerful rulers considered the position of the planet Venus to be of crucial importance as a guide to victory. It appears that the planet was invoked for assistance in war by a special skeletal mask worn by royal figures on carved stelae. On one such stela from the Classic Period site of Dos Pilas the text proclaims the Dos Pilas lord victorious against the rival city of Seibal. The text associates the day this event occurred, 3 December 775, with a particular glyph, and this glyph, a shell-star, shows up again and again on days attributed to Venus and is thus read to be a providential day for war, usually when Venus makes its first appearance as the evening star, when Venus passes behind the sun.

Many questions about Mayan warfare remain. Whether the goal of war was to benefit materially or territorially is still debated, but there is evidence that at least some cities had territorial aspirations. Records show that Ruler 3 of Dos Pilas, for example, who ruled from 727 to 41, conquered numerous neighboring sites during his reign, kept their rulers hostage, and controlled a kind of superstate greater in extent than any other Classic Mayan city-state. Though the Maya did not promote material acquisition in their representations of warfare, material gain may still have been an important consequence of or reason for going to battle. Nevertheless, Mayan depictions cast warfare in terms of rituals that upheld the cycle of kingship.

SOUTH AMERICAN WARFARE

The best information on warfare in South America comes from the 16th century and reflects the period of the Spanish conquest, when the Spanish confronted Incan armies and thus witnessed Incan war practice firsthand. Similarly, Spanish chroniclers interviewed and recorded details about Incan life that might have been otherwise forgotten. As useful as the chronicles have proven to be, they must be read with a discerning eye because of their biases. Warfare during the Inca Empire was tied to the empire's extraordinary expansion. Militarism was not the only method by which the Inca expanded, but it certainly was pivotal. Diplomacy, reward, and enculturation were also essential ingredients of their conquest strategy. Nevertheless, to meet their military goals, the Inca created a network of internal garrisons, frontier forts, and a logistical system of roads, support facilities, and depots. Their imperial success is due as much to logistics and organization as it is to training, tactics, or technology.

Before their imperial expansion the Inca, whose civilization was centered at the highland city of Cuzco, were not the most populous, the most powerful, or the wealthiest people of the central Andes. Other groups, such as the Qolla and the Lupaqa of the Lake Titicaca basin, and the vastly larger and more complex coastal Chimú polity, surpassed the Inca in most ways. Early conflict and militarism were probably more in the nature of pillaging and raiding for booty as well as glory, the success of which dissuaded attacks and raised the Incan profile. Policy shifts emphasizing annexation over looting are usually ascribed to the Incan rulers Viracocha Inca (r. ca. 1410–38) and Pachacuti (r. 1438–71), and early imperial successes probably owed much to alliances, conscription (military draft), and selective confrontation backed by overwhelming force. Despite the Incas' reliance on overwhelming force, it is probably also true that the inability of *señorios*, or polities ruled by a native lord, to coordinate resistance facilitated their own annexation. The Incan victory over the Chancas, whose telling usually includes a mythical event in which stones transform into warriors in aid of the Inca, is generally regarded as the springboard for the explosive territorial expansion that followed.

Communities were first offered the opportunity of peaceful annexation. Incan messengers arrived with charitable terms of surrender. If the terms were accepted, subject elites received gifts and could expect to retain their status, and the community would be allowed to keep many of its resources. In return, the new subjects pledged loyalty to the Sapa Inca, or chief Inca, agreed to supply labor service, and paid homage to the sun. In this manner, following combinations of diplomacy or forced coercion, the Inca rapidly expanded. As their systems of support and control matured, including the construction of garrisons or forts, forced resettlement, and the development of provincial centers, the Inca's ability to maintain control and stability greatly improved. Nevertheless, rebellion on differing scales was endemic throughout the empire.

Incan military organization was not complex even by standards of ancient empires. The lack of a standing army, the reliance on conscripted peasants as soldiers, and the difficulties in communication because of great distances and because of the linguistic groups in the empire resulted in a simple military structure. The king was the commander in chief and occasionally a field general. A hierarchy of officers followed below him with the highest officers usually being royal kin. The king's military role shifted as the empire moved through its expansion phase. For example, many Spanish chroniclers

Ceramic vessel in the form of a trophy head, Huastec culture, Mexico, ca. 900–1200 (Courtesy, National Museum of the American Indian, Smithsonian Institution [catalog number 243351])

wrote that Pachacuti delegated authority to his brothers before finally ceding military command to his son, Tupac Yupanqui (r. 1471–93). Beneath them two or four commanders led a campaign or an army, with their units composed of soldiers from particular ethnic groups. Incan oral history and Spanish accounts state that the Inca could raise armies in excess of 100,000 at a time, although these estimates should be viewed with some skepticism as both sides were prone to exaggeration for effect.

Battles themselves relied on preplanning and the use overwhelming force. The Inca scouted the battlefield before engagement and created clay models of the terrain. Once the entire army was in place, they advanced on the point of attack with overwhelming force and numbers. Most battles were described as melees on open terrain or assaults on fortified strongholds. Two favorite tactics were feigned withdrawals coupled with pincer attacks and flanking maneuvers, both of which indicate that the Inca used the element of surprise to their advantage. Typically, a barrage of arrows, sling stones, and javelins preceded hand-to-hand combat by warriors wielding maces, clubs, and spears.

The overall effect of the Incan imperial war machine was a vast reorientation of Andean civilization toward Cuzco, the seat of the royal throne. While many preexisting social and political structures were left alone, the Inca made use of vast resettlements of persons to aid in economic and political goals and to prevent uprisings. When the Spanish arrived in 1532, the empire was in a state of informal disintegration, in which a dynastic war of succession was being waged between Huáscar (d. 1532) and Atahuallpa (ca. 1502–33). Atahuallpa emerged victorious, though he was soon captured by the Spanish and held for ransom. The ransom was paid, but Atahualpa was garroted (strangled) anyway. Finally, Spanish hegemony rapidly ensued, thereby initiating the colonial period of Andean history.

ASIA AND THE PACIFIC
BY MARK W. ALLEN

Warfare and conquest played key roles in Asia and the Pacific during the medieval period. However, the nature of violent conflict varied drastically across this huge expanse of two continents (Asia and Australia) and thousands of islands scattered across the South Seas. In the western deserts of Australia hunter-gatherers continued to fight with simple stone and wooden weapons that appeared tens of thousands of year ago. At the other end of the spectrum the Chinese and others were experimenting with the use of gunpowder and even artillery to bring down city walls during the last centuries of the medieval period. Between these extremes Polynesian chiefs on high volcanic islands in the remote Pacific Ocean led armies of thousands of warriors in attacks on rivals in order to build their own personal power and to conquer the land and labor of other leaders.

The more complex forms of Asian warfare, though of a much larger scale, were not necessarily more deadly than the battles, raids, and skirmishes of traditional societies in Australia or the Pacific islands. Anthropologists have documented that warfare in hunter-gatherer groups or simple farming village societies often resulted in some of the highest casualty rates, particularly among noncombatants. Clearly, though, the warfare of Asian states or empires during the medieval period is far more familiar to us today than that of simpler societies. Medieval Asian warfare involved large standing armies, specialized units, standard-issue weapons, uniforms, distinct hierarchies from lowly foot soldiers to exalted generals, and weapons of mass destruction (relatively speaking) in the form of siege engines and eventually gunpowder and even artillery.

One issue related to warfare is the role of leaders and the elite in deciding when to go to war and with whom, the goals of conflict, and how the victors should treat the vanquished. Other important issues include the role of technological changes in war, for there were many during the medieval period, and how societies employed warfare as a political strategy as they dealt with rival groups in their own society as well as peoples with very different cultures. Warfare was frequently a means to various political ends and could spur on or inhibit other cultural achievements, such as technology, religion, architecture, art, or social organization. Warfare and conquest are central to understanding how Asia and the Pacific progressed from ancient to modern times.

For much of Asia during the medieval period there are written texts, such as bureaucratic records and official imperial histories. Such is especially true of India and China. In contrast, writing did not develop in Southeast Asia, Korea, or Japan until fairly late in the medieval period. It was not present in the Pacific islands at all until European contact. Archaeological evidence is highly abundant for some areas but much less so for others. Such information is often imprecise in terms of pinning down the date of a particular event, but it often gives insight and detail that history cannot match.

WARFARE AND CONQUEST IN ASIAN STATES AND EMPIRES

In Asia during medieval times warfare continued the course developed earlier in the ancient world: Wars were usually waged by states and empires against their neighbors both near and far. They were fought by armies of thousands of soldiers using standardized iron and later steel weapons and armor. These were standing armies organized hierarchically, with powerful generals and other ranks of officers at the top. Specialist units, such as bowmen, cavalry, or engineers, were usual. Naval combat also further developed during this time as ships were sometimes used to transport large forces or to serve as floating fortresses packed with archers and war machines, such as ballistae (large crossbows used for hurling missiles) or catapults. A frequent goal of warfare was the destruction of fortified rival cities or towns to remove competition and to seize resources, such as mineral wealth, trade routes, or productive land. The primary benefactors of this type of war were usually the rulers and other elites who often relied on militaristic themes and symbols as well as plunder and tribute secured through war to support their privileged status.

In India a bewildering number of medieval Hindu states and empires rose and fell through military conquest. The first of these appeared around 500 B.C.E. Hindu armies were particularly effective in the use of war elephants that could crush through nearly any defensive line. The sight of a line of them moving forward was often enough to cause understandable panic in enemy armies. Elephants were often equipped with fighting platforms for archers and other soldiers. Indian armies also used fortifications for defense and war machines, such as catapults and ballistae, to knock down strong points. One of the best-known medieval Hindu empires is that of Vijayanagara (ca. 1350–ca. 1650), which began in central India and spread south to cover the entire southern half of the peninsula. Written texts and archaeological sites reveal that the empire grew rapidly, spurred on by military conquest and by its role as a Hindu counter to Muslim kingdoms to the north. Eventually, several Muslim armies came together to attack the empire in 1566. After a major battle at Talikota, the city of Vijayanagara was sacked and destroyed by Islamic armies despite seven lines of fortification. The ruins of the capital's walls can still be seen today, as the city was never reoccupied as an urban center.

China has one of the oldest traditions of military conquest and professional armies in the world, going back at least 3,000 years. Dozens of states and empires managed to conquer or subdue their neighbors by threat, only to see their own dynasty weaken or fall apart. At the beginning of the medieval period China was trying to recover from fairly dire straits, particularly in the north as waves of tribal warriors from the north and northwest attacked the outer parts of the empire and sometimes even deep into its interior. By the time of the Sui Dynasty (581–619) and the Tang Dynasty (619–907), however, China had managed to reunify its territory and reestablish firm control of the borders, often through rebuilding or improving ancient fortifications, like the Great Wall (really a number of massive fortifications more or less employed as a defensive system rather than a single protective wall). Nevertheless, Chinese armies also were on the offensive, sometimes against rivals within China and sometimes against other cultural areas, such as Korea or Japan.

One military transformation put in place by the early medieval period was to draft peasant farmers into military units (called *fubing*) organized by their local villages to serve at time of need. The later Song Dynasty (960–1279) added further innovations, including the first Chinese standing navy, and experimented with gunpowder as a weapon. By late medieval times, however, Chinese armies were largely outmatched by the speed and ferocity of mounted warriors from the steppes of central Asia, and even the Great Wall and other defenses could not keep them at bay. China itself came to be ruled by outsiders during the Yuan Dynasty (ca. 1271–1368).

Unfortunately, quite a bit less is known about Korea during this period, owing to a lack of indigenous written histories (there are accounts in Chinese documents, but these, of course, are from the Chinese point of view) and less archaeological investigation. While China has a long history of states and empires, complex societies were much more recent developments in the Korean peninsula. Three kingdoms eventually arose there about 300, referred to as Koguryo, Paekche, and Silla. This development seems to have happened during a period when China was self-absorbed with internal conflicts, as before China had essentially not allowed a rival state to exist so near its borders. Archaeology demonstrates that all three Korean kingdoms arose through conquering neighbors and amalgamating their territory and human labor by force. They continued to compete with one another during the first few centuries of the medieval period, as shown by the presence of fortified cities and other fortresses, many of which were destroyed by battles. Eventually, with the assistance of Tang Dynasty China, the Silla Kingdom came out on top and by 688 had successfully united the Korean peninsula through conquest.

To the east of Korea the islands of Japan present a similar history. In fact, the histories of Korea and Japan were closely connected during the early medieval period, and Japanese forces actively participated as allies in some of the Korean kingdom battles. Also, as in the Korean case, China had a heavy hand in at first preventing or discouraging the development of state-level society and in later shaping how the earliest states took shape. Imperial power in Japan was limited compared with that of China, and by the 12th century a series of civil wars had broken out to limit the power of the emperor even more. Clan warlords called shoguns seized power and led their military forces against each other. Different clans rose and fell, largely through military success and failure. The various shoguns could, however, unite their armies to face outside invasion, as they did against the Mongols in the 13th century. Key figures in these wars up until the 18th century were a class of professional warriors known as samurai. They perhaps epitomized the militarized nature of elite medieval Asian society. The way of the samurai was doomed when contact with Europeans began at the end of the medieval period, but widespread adoption of firearms was resisted for centuries as a more ancient form of warfare continued to be fought in Japan while the outside world moved much more quickly toward industrialized warfare—that is, to war of the gun and the canon.

Finally, the wars and conquests of mainland and island Southeast Asia provide other examples of these same processes. This region is a very different environment from central Asia, one of dense tropical forests, lowlands, rivers with large floodplains and deltas, and numerous islands (some of which, such as Sumatra, Borneo, and Java, were very large). States and empires were also slower to develop here than in India or China, and these two Asian powers both had strong influences on developments in this area. Cities with large stone monuments, such as temples, had appeared in Vietnam, Cambodia, and Thailand by 600, and states really began to take off a century or two later. Early medieval warfare is indicated in art showing soldiers and by the presence of city walls, but information about medieval Southeast Asia is still fairly limited because of the scarcity of historic texts and the relatively low level of archaeological research. (This area has been a difficult place in which to conduct research given the environment and modern conflicts, such as the Vietnam War). Fortunately, more information exists about the rise of the Angkor kingdoms in modern Cambodia, which clearly rose by conquest under the first ruler, Jayavarman I, around 800. Over the next few centuries there were continued civil wars, struggles against rival states, and occasional battles with outsiders. War elephants, navies, and fortifications were important in these conflicts, but the use of the horse was not—probably because of the tropical forest environment. No single state ever built a long-lasting empire in this part of Asia during the medieval period.

A NEW MEANS OF WAGING WAR IN ASIA: THE CONQUESTS OF THE STEPPE HORSEMEN

It might come as a bit of surprise that the most devastating armies of all in medieval Asia were formed of nomadic pastoralists from central Asia and not from the ancient walled cities of China or India. This situation came about because of an altogether new type of warfare in Asia from 500 to 1500—one with dramatic effects. Sweeping out of the steppes of central Asia, a succession of relatively nomadic horse-mounted war-

riors struck fear into their more settled neighbors to the west, south, and east. These steppe warriors included the Turks (sixth–eighth centuries), the Uighurs (eighth–ninth centuries), the Khitans (10th–12th centuries), and, finally and most devastatingly, the Mongols (1206–1368).

Of course, cavalry had been used for centuries in the ancient world but never so effectively as with these central Asian horsemen. Mounted warriors took advantage of speed, deadly accurate composite bows that could be fired while maneuvering, and the stirrup. It is unclear when and where the stirrup first appeared and whether it was independently invented more than once; nevertheless, it was employed to great effect by the Mongols and their successors. Stirrups allowed a horseman to stand up in the saddle and deliver powerful blows to the enemy and also allowed a more stable platform for horse archers. With tens or even hundreds of thousands of such skilled horsemen, Genghis Khan (ca. 1162–1227) and his successors created the Mongol Empire, the largest contiguous land empire ever formed (and the second largest ever, after the British Empire), in a very short period of time. The impact of this empire and its successors was such that neighbors as far away as Europe and the Middle East lived in constant fear of invasion for centuries. In some instances, fearful populations neglected to build cities or large monuments since attractive targets would surely invite an onslaught of Mongol horsemen. Despite the Great Wall and other massive fortifications, much of China eventually came to be ruled for a time (the Yuan Dynasty) by the Mongols, starting with Kublai Khan (1215–94), the grandson of Genghis Khan. The Mongols readily adopted other military technologies and approaches, such as naval and siege warfare. They even attempted unsuccessfully (thanks largely to several large storms at sea, which sank hundreds of ships) to conquer the islands of Japan and Java in Indonesia with huge invasion fleets.

NEW TECHNOLOGY OF WARFARE: GUNPOWDER AND ITS EFFECTS

The progression of Asian military technology and capability further accelerated toward the end of the medieval period. Gunpowder was first developed in China around 1000 and was gradually employed in weapons, such as bombs and simple artillery to bring down fortifications. This technology spread to Europe and the Middle East, where further modifications were applied. By the end of the medieval period canons, other types of artillery, and firearms were rapidly spreading through Asia and Europe. This development would lead to a wholesale change in warfare, as city walls were no longer a major deterrent to attack and as warfare moved from a profession that required years of training to use a bow, ride a warhorse, or wield a sword to one that involved standing in formation and pulling a trigger. The transition to firearms and artillery was without question a major factor in the transition from the medieval period to the Renaissance and the Enlightenment.

WAR AND CONQUEST IN THE PACIFIC ISLANDS AND AUSTRALIA

Moving from the Asian continent to island Southeast Asia and the vast area of the Pacific Ocean, warfare and conquest did not involve standing armies, iron weapons, experimentation with gunpowder, or the struggles of fortified cities or empires. Instead, the older weapons of stone and wood continued to be used in conflicts among small-scale farming societies in some areas and chiefdoms in others. It is likely, however, that the effects of warfare on the lives of individuals and on their societies were just as significant as they were on those of Asian societies.

On the largely arid continent of Australia people continued to live by hunting, fishing, and gathering wild plant foods until colonization by the British in the 19th century. In traditional times such simple tools as throwing sticks and stone tools were combined with intimate knowledge of plant and animal resources. No positions of formal leader were recognized, and groups were very small. Nevertheless, Aborigines nearly always carried large wooden shields and clubs for use as weapons in case of attack. Conflict was not common, but the threat of it likely was. Thus, while huge armies battled for control of Asia during the medieval period, in Australia a form of conflict likely tens of thousands of years old continued to be played out.

The Pacific islands are often grouped into three geographic areas: Melanesia, Micronesia, and Polynesia. Melanesia contains many fairly large islands not too far east of island Southeast Asia. Here for thousands of years small-scale societies based on gardening root crops, like taro and the sweet potato, have packed these often rugged tropical islands. Anthropologists frequently cite the continuation (even into the late 20th century) of "Stone Age" warfare in the highlands of the large island of New Guinea—one of the last places on earth to be explored by the outside world. In these valleys anthropologists witnessed firsthand battles between hundreds of combatants lined up against each other with clubs, spears, and bows and arrows. Large planned battles had few casualties, but the highlanders of New Guinea also engaged in surprise raiding, which might kill a number of people caught unarmed outside of their villages. This warfare was not to support the lives of elites as in Asia; instead, it has been interpreted as competition between groups for land or as an outgrowth of religious concerns, such as appeasing the ghosts of dead ancestors. This obviously ancient form of warfare, how-

ever, should not be regarded as a game or as gamelike; it has been noted that up to one out of four men died violently in some areas of New Guinea, a much higher rate of casualties than in Europe during World War I or World War II.

Micronesia is characterized by hundreds of small islands, many of them small coral atolls built up on the rims of extinct volcanoes. Here warfare was employed as a means of expanding chiefdoms by conquest. Specialized warriors fought each other, sometimes wearing full body armor made of woven fibers and armed with wooden swords lined with sharks' teeth. Attacks were frequently made across large distances as one island attacked another. Some islands have archaeological evidence of fortified villages protected by natural defenses, ditches, stone walls, and wooden palisades.

Polynesia encompasses the most remote and wide-scattered of the Pacific islands. These islands were settled by people with a common culture during a flurry of exploration and colonization with large sailing canoes from around 300 to 1000. Anthropologists interested in warfare frequently discuss the Maori of New Zealand—the Polynesians who settled this large set of islands in the far South Pacific. About 100 years after New Zealand's colonization (estimated by archaeologists around 1000–1300) Maori warfare evolved into a classic example of small chiefdom warfare involving the dominance of strong, fortified villages. Despite deadly, specialized hand-to-hand weapons, fortifications were very effective so long as people were vigilant against their enemies. Wars were fought to acquire or to retain suitable gardening land, to avenge insults, and to gain prestige and status. While warfare was not constant, the never-ending threat of warfare came to be a central part of Maori culture, and nearly all males were prepared to fight from an early age. Maori warfare was a form of stalemate as it was essentially impossible for a chief or another leader to build a kingdom through conquest given the strength of enemy fortifications and the lack of siege or missile weapons that could overcome such defenses.

A second important Polynesian example would be warfare in Hawaii, the remote Pacific islands that likely came closest to the level of states. Here powerful chiefs and their specialist war leaders led armies of thousands in attempts to defeat the forces of rival chiefs on the same island or even across islands. Warriors employed shark-teeth swords and daggers, clubs, slings to hurl deadly stones, and other types of specialized weapons. Woven fiber armor was used here and in some other Pacific island cultures. Victorious chiefs would take the lands of their rivals and appropriate the labor of their former subjects. It is speculated by some that given enough time, an ambitious chief would have eventually built a state comprising all of the Hawaiian Islands through such conquest. However, the coming of Europeans starting in

1769 brought wholesale change, disease, and powerful new players from America, England, France, and Russia. Eventually (1810), supported with guns and sailing ships, the chief Kamehameha I (r. 1795–1819) did indeed unite the islands through conquest into an independent kingdom.

CONCLUSION

Warfare and conquest during the medieval period in Asia and the Pacific involved a tremendous amount of geographic and cultural variability. Warriors were armed with Stone Age weapons in some areas and nearly modern weapons in others. Some wars involved empires of millions of people; others involved only a few families. Aims of war varied from revenge, the desire to seize land and other resources, and the selfish aims of powerful rulers to expand their riches, reputation, and renown. Sometimes war and conquest spurred on the quick development of new military technologies, yet in other cases weaponry remained unchanged for thousands of years. This variability is an excellent example of how cultural, historical, economic, political, and geographic factors affect human societies.

Despite this variability, medieval warfare and conquest in Asia and the Pacific also reveal several common patterns and themes. Everywhere, warfare was deadly and was not a game. Casualties could be small in number for a Pacific island society yet could actually encompass a huge proportion of the population. Likewise, leaders, ranging from chiefs in charge of 1,000 or so people to emperors with hundreds of thousands of soldiers in standing armies, used warfare as a tool to build and to consolidate their political power. In most cases, the rise and fall of leaders were tied closely to their military successes and failures. Warfare also encouraged the development of technology, economic production, and logistical organization. It led to major innovations in agriculture, architecture, metallurgy, engineering, and even the arts and literature. Successful war leaders made sure that their exploits were recorded by monuments of stone, by written inscriptions and texts, or by preservation in oral histories and song. Wars and warriors spread ideas, resources, religions, and genes throughout this region of the world, though the Pacific was clearly far more isolated than Asia.

EUROPE

BY TOM STREISSGUTH

The migration of Germanic tribes through western Europe brought about the collapse of Roman government in the fifth century. Without centralized authority or an organized network of defense, European society fragmented into hundreds of small domains. Land and resources were the object of raiding on the part of local counts and the volunteer militias they organized among the peasantry. Conflict among nobles over land and privileges and their constant efforts to remain independent of titular kings and dukes provided the impetus to war. Defensive strongholds were raised on the foundations of Roman walls and towers. In parts of western Britain hill forts dating to the Iron Age were reoccupied in the fifth century. Construction in stone was rare in the early Middle Ages, and many fortifications were little more than tall earth mounds, surmounted by palisades of wood or rubble. A trench or moat dug around the perimeter served as further protection. As siege engines became more effective, fortifications grew stronger.

By the High Middle Ages western Europe had thousands of such strongholds and fortifications. The defense of a realm was accomplished by setting up a network of fortifications and towers that could not turn back an invasion but could slow any invading force. The defensive network of Alfred of Wessex (r. 871–99) in western England countered the Viking invasions of the ninth century. Levying soldiers for service in the field and for defense of the towns, the king set up 33 fortified strongholds, where the locals were detailed to keep watch and defend the city walls. None of these strongholds lay more than 20 miles from the next, which allowed relief forces and supplies to travel from one place to the next without encamping in the open countryside at night. Similar networks of linked fortifications were set up by Fulk of Anjou and Henry the Fowler of Saxony.

THE THREAT FROM OUTSIDE

By the sixth century only the eastern half of the Roman Empire, with its capital at Constantinople, survived as a remnant of imperial Rome. To defend their long borders against raids and invasion, the Byzantine emperors organized mobile cavalry units and a powerful navy, which controlled the eastern Mediterranean. A professional infantry force of archers and spearmen garrisoned the frontier posts, while the horsemen employed spears, lances, and the bow. The stirrup, introduced from China via the Avars of central Asia, allowed the Byzantine cavalry to fight more effectively, with riders using the device to balance and support themselves while charging with heavy lances.

The Byzantine army defeated the Germanic Ostrogoths in Italy through superior training and coordination of their units—a doctrine foreign to the northern tribes, who fought as individuals rather than in mutually supporting and complementary formations. The empire also relied on a long-range supply network and an intelligence service that probed the strengths and weaknesses of the enemy and by appealing for the loyalty of Roman citizens living under foreign rule.

The goal of reconstructing the empire in Italy ultimately failed, however. The long-range campaigns in Italy and Africa overextended the Byzantine frontiers and resources and left the empire vulnerable to attack in the Middle East and Asia Minor.

Foreign raiders swarmed into coastal towns and farming manors in western Europe, looting and burning and wreaking havoc among the civilian population. Seaborne raiders moved swiftly and struck without warning, preventing local militias from organizing effective resistance. In some places these outsiders established permanent settlements, displacing the landowners and peasantry. The Magyars, nomadic horse-mounted warriors from the steppes of Russia, raided throughout central Europe and the Danube River valley before finally settling on the Hungarian plain in the 10th century. The Arabs raided cities along Mediterranean coasts in Greece, southern Italy, Sicily, and the Iberian Peninsula, where an invasion of Moors from North Africa established a Muslim caliphate in the eighth century.

The most feared of these outsiders, the Scandinavian Vikings, attacked the coasts of England, the river valleys of northern France and Germany, and the plains of northern Russia. The Vikings originated in Scandinavia, where they raised livestock and tilled marginal land through short growing seasons. Their meager livelihoods spurred the Vikings to centuries of exploration in the North Atlantic, settlement of lands as distant as the coasts of North America, and terrifying raids on the European continent. Expert navigators, they used swift longboats that could be run directly onto a beach or sailed upstream for surprise attacks on towns, manors, and monasteries. Wielding broadswords and axes, they spread terror throughout Europe for two centuries before reaching a truce with the king of France, who recognized their claim to the duchy of Normandy. In the 10th century the Vikings began converting to Christianity, establishing farming colonies in the North Atlantic, and ceasing their hostilities on the continent of Europe.

The raids of Vikings and Magyars spurred the construction of new fortifications and the creation of a permanent class of professional soldiers, the knights. These mounted warriors fought on behalf of their feudal overlords; they were traditionally obligated to serve their lords for 40 days each year and during any siege or invasion. Their status rose as power coalesced in the courts of hereditary kings and dukes; their services were in high demand as warfare among feudal lords grew more common in the High Middle Ages. Training and equipping a mounted knight was expensive. For this reason, knights were endowed with fiefs (productive property) so that they could afford to maintain horses, weaponry, and armor; hire a retinue; and keep themselves ready for duty whenever

Bone figure of a knight, Britain, mid-14th century (© Museum of London)

called upon. With their role in military operations increasingly important, the knights gained new status and privileges, including the right to pass on their titles and property to their heirs. Their role as soldiers included the protection of domains from raiding and pillage, attacking rival strongholds, and enforcing feudal obligations and laws.

CASTLES AND SIEGE WARFARE

As medieval building technology improved, stone-walled castles replaced the isolated strongholds of earth and wood that had protected villages and manors in the early Middle Ages. Towers holding a small retinue of knights and archers served mainly as lookouts; larger structures were self-contained cities that sheltered goods, food, livestock, and local civilians when the region was under siege. These strongholds kept a lookout on frontiers and defended the countryside from the pillaging of enemy forces.

MEDIEVAL WARFARE IN MODERN FILM

The most common way that modern people receive an impression of warfare in the Middle Ages is by seeing it recreated in films. The Hollywood image of medieval battle is a charge of two bodies of heavily armored knights into each other. Almost invariably, onscreen we see the front wave of knights from the opposing armies reign in their horses and approach their enemies at a walk. The knights are then shown leaning precipitously out of their saddles to fence with each other on horseback. In propagating this caricature of medieval battle, Hollywood has done a grave disservice to the realities of medieval warfare. This stock scene is even used as the climax of both of the major versions of *Henry V* (one by Laurence Olivier in 1944 and the other by Kenneth Branagh in 1989), despite the fact that the main action of the battle at Agincourt consisted of the French knights repeatedly and almost suicidally charging an entrenched position of Welsh archers.

In reality, a typical medieval army consisted mostly of infantry, and the role of the heavy cavalry (knights) was to break the formation of the enemy infantry and scatter and destroy them. But whether made against infantry or other cavalry, the charge of cavalry depended on what is technically known as its weight, the sheer kinetic energy of the mass of horsemen and armored riders hitting into the line of the opponent, breaking through and riding over the enemy at full gallop. Often the enemy would break and run rather than be charged, but even if they stood, the success of the charging knights depended on hitting and riding through the enemy line; it would have been madness to charge and then to reign in the horses at the last moment.

Undoubtedly, this kind of action would be harder to film than the stock Hollywood scene, but it has been done successfully. Paradoxically, the best depiction of medieval battle is in the fantasy films of the *Lord of the Rings* trilogy (by Peter Jackson, 2001–2003). In those films several cavalry charges are successfully shown riding over enemy bodies of both cavalry and infantry. In the scene of the siege of Minas Tirith, those films also show by far the most realistic depiction of medieval siege warfare ever filmed, with the accurate depiction of trebuchets and the terrible damage their missiles could do to fortifications and formations of enemy soldiers as well as their use by both attackers and defenders in a siege.

Castles were defensive structures designed mainly to withstand enemy sieges. They contained a central keep or tower, which rose above the topmost level of the walls and which served as a treasury and central storage area. To withstand a long siege, castle defenders stored grain and salted meat, kept herds of livestock, and dug deep water wells. The walls were penetrated by one or several gates, which themselves served as barracks and important points of defense. Doors were protected by a heavy iron grille known as a portcullis, which could be lowered to resist enemy troops and battering rams.

Medieval architects devised several ingenious methods for the defense of castles. The high walls protected archers and infantry stationed on walkways. Passages over the tunnel leading into the castle were sometimes given murder holes, through which scalding liquids and arrows could be deployed against attacking foot soldiers. Moats protected the castle against battering rams and siege towers and also prevented underground tunneling. The design of these fortifications grew more complex in the later medieval period. In the 13th century the largest forts were designed in a series of rings. An outer ring prevented the use of battering rams and siege towers with a line of sloping walls, which made it difficult to use scaling ladders or artillery. Towers built at the corners afforded a wide view of the countryside and a better field of fire for defending archers and spearmen. Archers sniped at the enemy from atop the walls or from narrow slits known as loopholes.

Castle sieges were carried out over long periods of time, often months, during which the besieging army occupied the surrounding countryside and attempted to starve out the defenders or lure them outside the walls for a decisive battle. Sieges were sometimes negotiated, with the attackers agreeing to withdraw by a certain date if their own reinforcements did not arrive. In this way a besieging army could ensure they did not have to fight through a winter season, in which castle defenders had a great advantage owing to their stores of food and water. During a siege assault, archers sent a rain of deadly arrows into the yards of the castle, while foot soldiers scaled the walls with ladders. Battering rams and catapults were deployed against the walls and gates. Small roofed structures sheltered the rams and their crews from enemy fire. With adequate time and resources, attackers could also raise siege towers, tall wooden structures built on a set of wheels. The siege tower was covered by planks of wood or fire-resistant hides, allowing attackers protection while the tower was brought against a wall. A drawbridge placed at the top of the tower gave attackers a route into the castle.

Before the assault sappers were sent underneath the walls to undermine them. The tunnels were reinforced with heavy timbers; the attackers then burned out the timbers in order to collapse the tunnels and the walls overhead. Siege engines were used to create a breach in the walls, or bring down a castle tower. The trebuchet, the most fearsome artillery weapon of the Middle Ages, consisted of a long arm built on a central pivot and weighted with stone or boulders held aloft at the forward end. Heavy stones were placed inside a sling at the far end, and the weapon was positioned several hundreds yards from the defending walls. When the forward weights were released, the arm swung on its pivot and hurled its stone several hundred yards at high velocity against its target. There was little defense against the trebuchet, as its great range allowed it to be positioned well outside archery range. The trebuchet could bring down a wall in short order or fling carcasses into a town or castle as a way to spread disease.

Besieging armies were at a disadvantage as time wore on, as they had to live off unproductive surrounding land. A supply train followed the besieging force, moving by road or river, but there was no method for long-distance supply of weapons, food, and other items necessary for a long siege. Peasants would abandon sieges during the fall harvest or the spring planting season, when getting a crop into the ground often meant the difference between survival and famine. This forced armies to move and fight during the summer and early fall and avoid any activity during the barren winters, when there were no crops or livestock for food or forage for animals. As the land around a castle was denuded of its crops, the besieging army was subject to famine as well as contagious diseases, which could move rapidly through the ranks of an army living at close quarters. Cholera, dysentery, plague, and other sicknesses often proved much more destructive to besieging armies than fighting.

KNIGHTS AND COMMONERS

The conquest of Spain by the Moors, who fought as massed, lightly armed cavalry, prompted the Franks to develop a professional army of heavy infantry and mobile cavalry. At the battle of Poitiers in 732, the Frankish king Charles Martel defeated the Moors with massed foot soldiers, many of them dismounted from their horses and fighting with heavy shields, spears, and battle axes. This victory stemmed the tide of the Moorish conquest and played a key role in the establishment of the feudal system. Having successfully defended its borders, the Carolingian kings who ruled the Franks seized productive estates from the church and distributed them to their loyal nobles, who were then obligated to provide troops and military service in time of war.

The feudal system gradually spread throughout Europe and to the British Isles. Armies in the early Middle Ages comprised a select levy of men who were recruited for offensive operations outside the local region and who served alongside the personal retinues of local lords. A general levy of the civilian population was called up for defensive fighting, as when a country was invaded, a town was besieged, or raiders were loose. The disciplined legions of ancient Rome were taken as a model by the Carolingian rulers Pepin (r. 751–68) and his son Charlemagne (r. 768–814), who reigned over the Frankish kingdom in the eighth century. All free men within the Carolingian realm were required to take an oath of loyalty and hold themselves ready for military service. In this way the kings gained effective control over the private retinues of local counts and lords, forcing ordinary soldiers to divide their loyalties and the nobles to pay homage to the throne. When campaign season arrived, the armies were raised through a levy of landowners, with those holding large estates required to furnish their own horses and armor. With these levies Charlemagne brought huge armies to the field and subdued the powerful Lombard kingdom of northern Italy as well as the realm of Saxony, in what is now northeastern Germany.

BATTLE FORMATIONS

The mounted knight and his retinue of servants were central to the popular view of warfare in the Middle Ages. In reality, cavalry by itself was never effective in large-scale battles; the chivalrous notion of single combat between armored knights is more a literary device than historical truth. The battle of

The Burghead Bull, Burghead, Morayshire, Scotland, seventh century; one of six carved slabs found together, this is speculated to be part of a Pictish warrrior cult of strength and aggression. (© The Trustees of the British Museum)

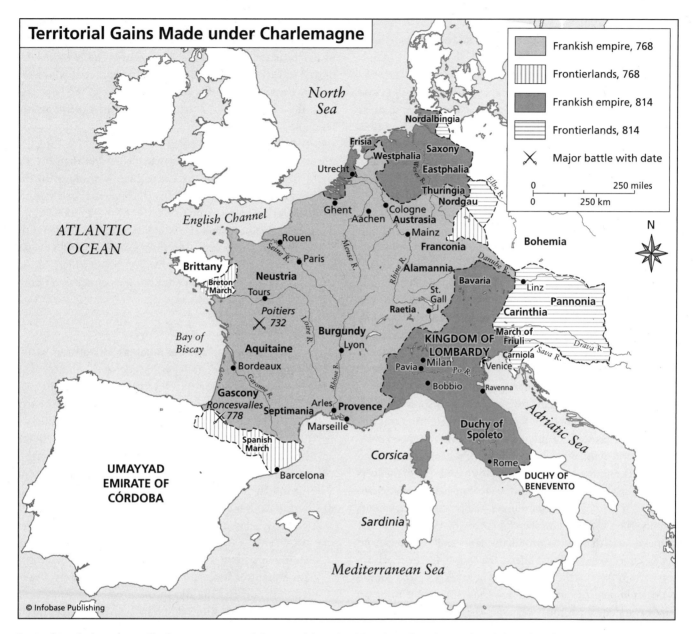

Territorial Gains Made under Charlemagne

Legend:
- Frankish empire, 768
- Frontierlands, 768
- Frankish empire, 814
- Frontierlands, 814
- ✕ Major battle with date

During his rule the emperor Charlemagne conquered the powerful Lombard kingdom of northern Italy and the realm of Saxony, in what is now northeastern Germany; along with other parts of western and central Europe.

Hastings, fought in 1066 between the forces of William the Conqueror (r. 1066–87) of Normandy and King Harold II (r. 1066) of England, was more typical of medieval battle tactics. After a mass of English foot soldiers used their wall of shields to turn back several waves of Norman horsemen, William ordered his archers to send their deadly missiles over the front ranks and into the rear of the English army. Defenseless against the onslaught from the air, the English infantry fell by the hundreds where they stood, after which Harold's army succumbed to a determined cavalry charge.

To bring different forces to bear, medieval generals divided their armies into companies of archers, foot soldiers, and cavalry. The infantry were armed with swords, axes, clubs, or spears, using light armor if their army could afford it, as well as iron helmets and small shields of metal or hides. They fought in a large mass, attempting to hold their formation together as long as possible in order to provide mutual support and create a strong defensive position. Once the group lost its formation, it became much easier for enemy cavalry units to attack and rout them. Archers and crossbowmen were used to fight at long distance, for the attrition of massed enemy units and to send flaming arrows against wooden structures, enemy camps, and siege engines.

Cavalry were placed on the flanks and to the rear, formed up in several ranks to charge against vulnerable points in the enemy line, hoping to panic enemy soldiers and force them to break rank. In a large battle, however, mounted knights usually dismounted for close-quarters combat. Steady discipline was required to control horses in the noise of battle, to avoid disorganized retreats, and to prevent a headlong charge against apparently disorganized or retreating opponents who were in reality laying a trap. A disciplined line of infantry could withstand a charge and easily disperse a cavalry unit with a wall of pikes or halberds (weapons designed specifically to grasp the armor of a horseman and bring him to the ground). This tactic triumphed at the battle of the Lechfeld in 955, when Otto the Great's disciplined foot soldiers defeated the fearsome mounted archers of the Magyars.

THE CRUSADES AND THE MONGOLS

Able knights and military men of medieval Europe enjoyed high prestige. Their deeds were celebrated in songs and poetry that praised bloodshed and mayhem. Fighting was entertainment as well, in the form of jousting (single combat) and the tournament, a form of military rehearsal that pitted teams of knights against each other in combat and maneuvering over a wide stretch of countryside. But as Europe's aristocrats vied for power and resources, the bloody engagements among their retinues cost lives and treasure. Warfare brought considerable damage to productive land and resources, and in an effort to lessen these effects the church forbade warfare on certain days of the week and in holy seasons (the church also attempted to outlaw the crossbow, finding it to be an unfair and unchivalrous weapon). These efforts to redirect martial energies culminated with the call for crusade against the Muslims by Pope Urban II in the late 10th century. The knights of Europe gathered on ships or marched overland to the Middle East in search of glory, land, and riches as well as the blessing of the church.

With the Crusades, European warfare techniques thus arrived in the Middle East, with mixed results. The mounted and armored knight was poorly adapted to the climate of the region and ineffective against the swift and lightly armored cavalry employed by the Arab armies. The siege weapons brought from Europe proved their worth against Muslim strongholds. In Europe the knight gradually went out of style, overpowered by artillery, archers, and the rise of standing armies, which included large masses of foot soldiers that held a great advantage in set battles. A serious blow to the role of the mounted warrior in Europe was the invasion of the Mongols from their homeland in the steppes of northeastern Asia in the 13th century. The Mongols deployed in vast *tumens* of 10,000 mounted archers, who were strictly disciplined, highly skilled in the use of the bow, and carefully coordinated on the battlefield through the use of flags and audible signals.

The Mongols swept through Russia in 1241, defeated an army of Polish knights sent against them, and then turned south through passes in the Carpathian Mountains to the plains of Hungary. The mounted and heavily armored knights of medieval Europe were no match for the more mobile Mongol army, which crushed the Hungarian forces at the battle of Mohacs. At the point of an invasion of western Europe, however, the death of Ogedei, the Mongol khan (ruler), forced the Mongols to withdraw for a traditional council and nomination of the khan's successor.

NAVAL WARFARE

Naval warfare was carried out much as it had been in ancient times, in rowed galleys that carried infantry and archers aboard for close-quarters fighting. Warships maneuvered to ram with a reinforced bow or grapple, board, and fight at close quarters. Ships were built with tall superstructures at the stern and in the bow, which sheltered spearmen and archers. These ships proved effective against the much smaller and lower longboats that had carried the Vikings on their raids. Cannons were added to the decks of the ships at the end of the medieval period. A gun deck immediately below the main deck was built as an artillery platform, with which military ships were able to deliver devastating broadsides.

The Byzantine Empire deployed the most powerful navy of medieval Europe. The Byzantine *dromon* was an oared galley equipped with slings that hurled an incendiary liquid known as Greek fire at opponents. In the 10th century the Byzantine fleet was successful in contesting Arab control of Crete and Sicily by transporting horses across the seas for land operations. Horse transport also played a key role in the conquest of England by the Normans in 1066. During the Hundred Years' War the need of the English to transport their armies by sea and to protect harbors captured in France and the Low Countries provided a spur to England's growing naval power. A key battle took place in 1340 at the Flemish port of Sluys between English and French ships. Archers, crossbowmen, and pikemen hurled their missiles from the decks and towers; with no ground available for retreat, combatants aboard the ships fought desperate hand-to-hand battles with swords, spears, and axes. At Sluys the French lost as many as 20,000 men, both of their commanders, and most of their ships, while the English gained the port of Sluys and a maritime advantage they would exploit for the next century.

THE HUNDRED YEARS' WAR

A destructive scorched-earth campaign that lasted for generations, the Hundred Years' War proved to be a turning point in strategy and tactics of the medieval world. With few set battles, the war progressed in many years as a simple pillaging expedition by the English, who created a new set of effective battle tactics honed in earlier campaigns against the Welsh and Scots. Foot soldiers were drawn up in defensive formations, while cavalry soldiers dismounted and formed up in solid lines of foot soldiers wielding swords and pikes. Longbowmen were dispersed in large blocks, their long range and rapid rate of fire allowing a devastating attack at key points in the enemy line.

The first major battle of the war took place at Crécy, just north of Paris, on August 26, 1346. The English forces numbered 12,000 spearmen, longbowmen, and cavalry, facing a much larger French army. The victory of the English at Crécy helped to end the dominance of mounted knights in medieval Europe. As the war continued, however, the French began to successfully counter the English tactics under the leadership of Bernard du Guesclin, the constable of France under Charles V (r. 1364–80). Du Guesclin avoided open battle with the English and instead employed hit-and-run attacks, ambushes, night raids, and sieges of fortified places by artillery. The new strategy drove the English virtually out of France by 1380, confining them to a few strongholds along the Atlantic coast in the southwest.

Henry V (r. 1413–22) of England returned to France in 1415, capturing the key port of Harfleur, setting up a network of fortified coastal ports, and defeating a large army of French knights and infantry at the battle of Agincourt. The English army employed powerful artillery against French cities and fortifications and returned to their tactic of pillaging the countryside. At Agincourt the English longbowmen used their bows of stout, yet flexible yew wood. Fired in mass at a long distance, their arrows could easily penetrate shields and plate armor, kill a horse, and wreak havoc among massed cavalry and infantry units.

Between battles the English employed the tactics known as the *chevauchée* (meaning "horse charge") in which units of mounted soldiers roamed across the countryside, destroying crops and livestock, burning homes, and killing civilians. The *chevauchée* was an attempt to demoralize the enemy and render the land completely unproductive, thus depriving the French king of tax revenue needed for the upkeep of his military forces. The *chevauchée* was an in-

fantry tactic and had no role for mounted knights, either as attackers or defenders.

NEW MODES OF WARFARE

The French, disorganized and poorly led, found their kingdom threatened with permanent English control when the French king Charles VI (r. 1380–1422) disinherited his own son in favor of Henry's. On the death of both Henry and Charles in 1422, the young English heir Henry VI (r. 1422–53) claimed all of France north of the Loire, except for the royal city of Orléans. A siege of the city in 1428 through 1429, however, was broken by French defenders, inspired by a young and inexperienced peasant girl, Joan of Arc, who claimed a divine mission to restore the French dauphin (heir) to the throne.

After this success the French took the offensive, and Joan witnessed the crowning of the dauphin as Charles VII (r. 1422–61) in the cathedral of Rheims. When Joan was captured and executed as a witch in 1431, the English found they had created a martyr and stirred up a wave of nationalism that swelled the ranks of the French army. Over the next two decades the English were gradually driven out of northern France. A truce in 1444 allowed the French to regroup and reorganize their armies. The effort helped the French king and his advisers centralize their authority and reduce the power of the local dukes and counts.

The French army was reorganized, with each unit given a clearly defined role and a set of uniform battle tactics. The men were paid regularly, and their rations were increased. The French also invested in up-to-date weaponry and integrated their artillery force into the operations of the army. The cannons were put on carriages for better mobility and were improved with trunnions, which were used to balance the guns and allow them more accurate fire. Iron cannon balls were introduced, more reliable and effective than the stones previously used; careful experimentation also improved the effectiveness of gunpowder.

The new tactics and improved condition of the army and artillery allowed the French to quickly go on the offensive. They invaded Normandy and soon had besieged and defeated English strongholds, most of them in a matter of a few days. In set battles their cannon were able to overcome the English longbows. At the battle of Formigny in April 1450 a cannonade by the French provoked a charge in which the English infantry was cut down by the French spearmen and crossbowmen. This was the first major battle in which artillery played a decisive role.

The use of gunpowder, invented in China, transformed military science at the close of the Middle Ages. The first iron bombards were deployed in the 14th century against gates, towers, and wooden structures and in battle primarily to startle and intimidate the enemy horses and foot soldiers. They were used in combination with trebuchets and other siege engines to destroy walls and fortified cities, and the French used them to recapture Harfleur and other key English-occupied cities late in the Hundred Years' War. Cannon also played a key role in the recapture of Spain by Castile in the late 15th century.

As the barrel length of cannon increased, artillery gained range and accuracy, and the use of iron projectiles proved far more destructive than the stone shot used by the traditional siege engines. Artillery emerged as a central weapon in siege warfare in the Italian campaigns of the 1490s. A small hand-held cannon known as the harquebus was introduced at the close of the medieval era, but a poor rate of fire and accuracy made this early rifle still less effective than archers and crossbowmen.

The companies of "freebooters" and mercenaries who roamed France during the Hundred Years' War still depended largely on swift cavalry to make sudden strikes and evade organized pursuit. These companies arrived in Italy late in the 15th century to serve the lords and towns of the Italian peninsula as mercenaries. Freebooters held prisoners for ransom and blackmailed cities not wishing to go to the expense and trouble of levying an army and fighting. Although they were much despised by military strategists and political thinkers such as Niccolò Machiavelli, who saw them as a destructive influence on Italy's political life, mercenaries played an important transitional role between the medieval and the modern age, as the armies of levied soldiers and knights of the Middle Ages developed into the national "standing" armies that came into use during the Thirty Years' War of the early 17th century.

THE ISLAMIC WORLD
BY KIRK H. BEETZ

Much of the medieval Islamic world was defined by war and conquest. The consequences of wars against the Sassanian Empire, the Byzantine Empire, the kingdoms of India, the nomads of Asia, the knights of Spain and France, and the crusaders are written large in history, because they reshaped the culture of the world profoundly. A general trend of Islamic war in medieval times was conservatism, a tendency to cling to outmoded tactics or weapons even when faced with new dangers. Another trend was the tendency of Muslims to turn their military skills against one another. This sometimes led to disaster, because wars among Muslims distracted them from imminent outside dangers that more than once could have swept away their armies.

THE ARABIAN BEGINNINGS

During Muhammad's life (ca. 570–632), Muslim battles were small; they loom large for their consequences. There were three battles of importance for understanding how Muslims waged war in the 600s: the battle of Badr in March 624, the battle of Uhud in March 625, and the battle of the Trench in March 627. In the first of these one can see the full influence of Arabian-style warfare of the era. Leaders in Mecca had conspired to murder Muhammad. Medina had welcomed him as a wise man who could arbitrate disputes among the clans of the city. He used his power base in Medina to retaliate against those who had wronged him.

Badr was a place with many water wells, and it was a customary stop for caravans. Muhammad had most of the wells poisoned so that a Meccan caravan that stopped at Badr had little drinking water. This was a common tactic in the medieval world. In a nasty fight Muhammad's champions triumphed. Then the main battle commenced. The Meccans had 100 horses to Muhammad's two, and these horses seem to have nearly won the battle for the Meccans, but Muhammad's fighters stubbornly held their ground, killing many of the enemy with arrows as well as swords. The result was a victory for Muhammad's troops over superior forces. The victors attributed their triumph to God's intervention. The booty they won was worth over 50,000 dinars.

On the other hand, the battle of Uhud was nearly a catastrophe for the Muslims. In general, Arabs regarded fighting from behind fortifications to be cowardly; they preferred to fight on open ground. At Uhud, Muhammad's forces were again outnumbered, and this time he had no horses, not even for himself. The Meccans had more than 200 horsemen who were cut down. Muhammad was wounded. He and some of the survivors fled to the top of a rocky outcrop where the enemy's horses had trouble getting footing, and there he held out until the Meccans called it a day.

Muhammad adapted. For the battle of the Trench, he had a defensive trench dug around Medina. He had a few thousand poorly equipped troops at his command, whereas the Meccans arrived with thousands of allies from nomadic tribes. Siege warfare was almost unknown to the Arabs in the 600s. In the battle of the Trench the Meccans had the Medinans cut off from fresh supplies. In a patient, long siege the Medinans had to lose, but the Meccans were not interested in spending a long time away from home in uncomfortable conditions while fighting an enemy that would not do the honorable thing and come out to do battle on open ground. They lost interest in the siege and went home.

After Muhammad's death came the Ridda Wars, or the Wars of Apostasy. Some tribes that had pledged their support to Muhammad refused to transfer that support to Muhammad's successors. Further, Muslims themselves disagreed over who should become their new leaders. This led to several battles in which many of Muhammad's original followers were killed. One of their battles was the battle of the Camel in 656. One side was led by Aishah (614–78), the youngest of Muhammad's wives and the most beloved. She rode on the back of a camel as the battle swirled around her. Her side lost, and she retired to her home to write about her husband. It was unusual for Arab women to participate in battles, and Muslim scholars would cite the battle of the Camel as an example of why women should not have positions of leadership. Traditionally, women were motivators in military camps. Before battle they would play their tambourines and taunt men by challenging their courage and manhood, in an effort to excite the men and motivate them to fight valiantly. After a battle the women would sometimes mutilate the enemy dead, taking ears and noses as trophies, as well as caring for and comforting their side's wounded.

When the word *jihad* was used, it usually referred to a phrase from the Koran: *jihad fi sabil Allah*, roughly meaning "striving in the path of God." Each person was responsible for his or her own jihad, a lifetime of striving to live a moral life. Early Islamic soldiers had to pay for their own equipment, meaning most had little except their weapons, and they all dressed differently from one another. This did not lessen their cohesion as fighting units; after all, Alexander the Great had conquered a huge empire with troops who also outfitted themselves individually. One helpful element from Islam was a unifying sense of a higher purpose. This meant that even if they did not fully understand why, and even if they were motivated by the prospect of looting enemy settlements, they were also always serving God, and they were always responsible for working with their fellow Muslims to advance the word of God.

The noun *jihad* has had different meanings for different people. Early in the history of Islam, it acquired a new implication: that Muslims were to advance the word of God throughout the world, because Islam was a universal religion. It never lost the implication that individual people led their own jihads by striving to be good, but it also became greater jihad and lesser jihad. Greater jihad was the preaching of the word to people who did not know of God's word as revealed to Muhammad. Imams and missionaries journeyed to India and eventually along the southern coast of Asia to as far as Indonesia; they were very successful at winning converts. Lesser jihad was the advancing of Islam through military conquest. This last idea fell into disuse in the 800s but was revived in the 1000s, when bandits raiding the Byzantine Empire and pillaging India used it as an excuse for their incursions. When

The siege of a Turanian stronghold by the forces of Kai Khusraw, from a Shahnama (Book of Kings) by Firdawsi, opaque watercolor, ink, and gold on paper; 15th century (Freer Gallery of Art, Smithsonian Institution, Purchase, F1928-11)

the Crusades began in the 1190s, Muslim clerics in the Near East recalled lesser jihad as a way to rally Muslim governments to fight the European invaders.

OPENING A WIDER WORLD

The motivations for the rush of armies out of Arabia in the early medieval era were mixed and somewhat clouded. Although the notion that the expansion was an example of lesser jihad has been common in histories, it may not have seemed that way at all to the early Muslims. During the 40 years before the era of Muhammad's ministry, the Sassanian Empire had overwhelmed two Arabian kingdoms in the north of the Arabian Peninsula and had seized Yemen, apparently in an effort to monopolize both land and water trade routes to and through the Near East. These actions disrupted traditional

Arabian trade routes. Matters became further aggravated when Muslims encountered problems with authorities of the Byzantine Empire while making pilgrimages to Jerusalem.

Initial attacks against the Sassanian Empire involved troops mostly from towns and cities in Arabia. The Muslim army depended on its infantry for most of its success. Camels were used for transporting supplies; camels had the ability to carry heavy loads for hundreds of miles relatively quickly. Horses were rarely ridden between battles; their owners would ride camels or walk rather than risk tiring their horses.

The tactics of Muslim generals were familiar to the Sassanians. Both sides had infantries composed mostly of archers. Among the Sassanians were soldiers devoted to protecting archers with shields that blocked enemy arrows and with swords and spears meant to blunt charges into their ranks. Most of the Muslim infantry was made up of archers who could drop their bows and arrows and fight with swords, knives, and javelins. The Sassanians had professional soldiers who were well trained and experienced. The Muslim soldiers were volunteers, although many had experience as mercenaries. During battle the Muslims maneuvered to get their archers massed on high ground, protecting them with other infantry and using their cavalry to harass Sassanian moves against the archers. Given the Sassanians' impressive professionalism, their well-trained troops, and their experienced officers, they would appear to have been able to quash the army of Islam. Yet the Sassanian generals had recently lost several battles to the Byzantine Empire and may have been less than competent. Further, both the troops and the Sassanian Empire's economy were tired and recovering from a long war against the Byzantine Empire. The Islamic army proved to have a decisive advantage: the extraordinary discipline of its troops. Its soldiers went where they were told to go with relentless determination, and they stood their ground unflinchingly. They wore down the Sassanian troops and eventually broke the morale of the Sassanian soldiers, who either abandoned the fight altogether or fled into eastern Iran, where provinces of the Sassanian Empire held out for several more decades until it was clear the Muslims were not going away. The Muslim conquests put a permanent end to the Sassanian Empire.

The Byzantine army presented different problems for the Muslims. For one thing, under the charismatic leadership of an emperor who was a gifted military strategist, it had defeated the Sassanians and recovered most of the territory that had been lost to the Sassanians a few generations earlier. Byzantine cavalry rode big, heavy steeds that were not intended to be as adroit as were the horses of the Muslims. The Muslim infantry was no match against a charge of the heavily armored Byzantine knights. The old Arabian practice of lining up in parallel lines before battle was easy for the Byzantines to exploit.

The principal reason for eventual Muslim success may have been superior leadership. Muslim generals adapted to the unfamiliar ways of warfare of the Byzantines, while the Byzantine political leaders seem to have believed the Muslim invasion to be only a large raid for booty, much like countless other raids from Arabia. Another factor in the Muslim army's favor was the attitude of the local populations in Palestine and Syria; for centuries empires had come and gone, and some Near Eastern populations changed their religion according to whoever happened to be ruling them. Moreover, Islam did not seem much different from Christianity and Judaism; the ideas and general worldview of Islam was comfortably familiar. Thus many local peoples did not help the Byzantines and sometimes even welcomed the Muslim conquerors.

Umar the Great (Umar ibn al-Khattab, r. 634–44) may have been the most brilliant strategist of his era in the Near East. Under his directions, a Muslim army invaded Egypt, cutting off important supplies of grain to the Byzantine army. This was an accomplishment of far-reaching importance. Because the permanent loss of Egypt's harvests limited the Byzantine army in how far its military operations could range, it helped restrict the Byzantine army to Anatolia and Europe.

THE UMAYYADS AND THE NEW REALITY OF WARFARE

The Umayyad Dynasty lasted only from 661 to 750, but during that time it managed to organize the Islamic world into a cohesive whole. At first, Arabs dominated the officers of the army; traditional kinship groups tried to keep the positions of military power in the hands of pure-blooded Arabs of distinguished ancestry. Muslims were about 5 percent of the population of the Near East and North Africa. To prevent their being assimilated into local populations, Umar the Great had garrison towns built from which Muslims would rule and where Muslim strongholds could be established. The Umayyads created towns solely for soldiers and their families, but they made the soldiers full-time paid professionals, rather than part-time soldiers, and they built an army out of people from ethnic groups other than Arabs. Turks, sub-Saharan Africans, and others were beholden to the caliph, who cared for them, and not to the traditions of Arabian clans.

In the 740s a rebellion in the eastern part of the Islamic world proved to be the undoing of the Umayyads. This rebellion brought with it a style of fighting that was unfamiliar to the Umayyad army. From the region of modern-day Afghanistan and central Asia came cavalry troops that depended on fast attacks that moved too quickly for enemy troops to respond. The invaders rode in open formation, using their horses to break apart ranks of enemy infantry. This sort of tactic would be repeated by the Seljuk Turks and the Mongols in later years. When the Abbasid Dynasty (750–1258) supplanted the Umayyad Dynasty, the reconstitution of the army with non-Arab troops and officers became permanent, and the new officers of the Abbasids chose to emphasize the cavalry over the infantry. Under the Umayyads, warhorses were outfitted with felt armor. During the centuries of the Abbasid Dynasty, arms and armaments improved, although as the Islamic world broke into sultanates, the extent and quality of Islamic armies varied from place to place.

FIGHTING THE CRUSADERS FROM EUROPE

By the late 1000s the various claimants of power in the Islamic world were very antagonistic toward one another, and their interminable wars had weakened them, much as the frequent wars between the Byzantine Empire and the Sassanian Empire had weakened them. Normans invaded Sicily, which had been in Muslim hands for about 200 years, and by 1090 had taken control of the entire island. It was a harbinger of what was to come.

While speaking in Clermont, France, in 1095, Pope Urban II (ca. 1035–99) called upon western European nobility to aid the Byzantine Empire, which was struggling against the Seljuk Turks. When a western European military force, united under German and French leaders, crossed through the Byzantine Empire and into the Islamic world, they appeared to the Muslims as though they were just plunderers who would be gone once they had some booty to take home. The crusaders' speaking of a religious mission probably was familiar to the sultans of the Islamic world. Some Muslim leaders had also justified their raids on the world outside Islam as promoting their own religion. It took months, perhaps even a few years, before the political and military leaders of the Islamic world realized that the crusaders intended to remain in the Near East indefinitely.

The armies that faced the crusaders were ill prepared for the challenge. Each Muslim army received little or no help from other Muslim armies because of their suspicion of one another. Further, the Seljuk Turks were perceived as a far greater threat than were knights from Europe, and some sultanates welcomed the crusaders as allies against the Seljuks. Muslim generals continued to use outdated tactics. They were not prepared for the tactics of the crusaders. The crusaders rode warhorses that were heavier than the warhorses of the Muslims. Their troops were well armored. A knight was a formidable war machine, clad in chain mail from the top of his head to his feet, with plate metal for helmets and shields.

In early battles Muslim cavalry allowed mounted European knights close to them. The Muslims carried light shields and gleaming curved swords made of Indian steel. These blades had cut apart many enemies in India and central Asia, and the swords impressed the enemy, who noted how the blades could cut into chain mail. Even so, tactics that had worked for Islamic armies in the past were failures against the Europeans, who crushed opposing horses under their own, who spitted horsemen on spears, and whose long swords could cut men in half.

The crusaders also brought with them advanced siege techniques. Since the 600s the Islamic world had used mostly catapults and testudos, devices with armored roofs under which soldiers could rush at an enemy's wall. At the battle of Antioch (1098), the Crusaders faced the challenge of a walled city manned with determined defenders. The walls were perhaps 60 feet high and wide enough at their tops for horsemen riding three abreast in each direction to pass one another comfortably. In every direction, defenders could rain *naft* (Greek fire, an incendiary concoction that burst into flames) on their enemies. The crusaders cut off access to the city and built a fortification nearby where they could resist attacks from the city. It seems that the Muslims regarded Antioch as impregnable, but the crusaders built trenches ever closer to the walls, allowing their troops to draw nearer and nearer without being exposed to arrows. The crusaders also built tall wooden towers on which archers and other soldiers perched. Meanwhile, a relief army had been sent to drive the crusaders away from Antioch. By the time it arrived it was one day too late; the crusaders had surmounted the walls, opened the gates, and entered the city.

THE MAMLUK TRADITION

The word *mamluk* translates roughly as "one who is owned." There were other words for different kinds of slave during the medieval era, but *mamluk* was used to designate military slaves and eventually included soldiers who had once been slaves but had been freed. The *mamluks* were begun during the reign of the Abbasid Caliph al-Mamun (r. 813–33) by al-Mutasim (r. 833–42), who used them to help him become caliph. They were bought when they were around the ages of 10 to 12, old enough to have survived childhood diseases but young enough to be molded into fiercely loyal fighting men. They were purchased exclusively in *dar al-harb*, meaning "the abode of war." Islamic nations belonged to *dar al-Islam*, meaning "the abode of submission." These were legal concepts, not military ones, with *dar al-Islam* being where Islamic law prevailed and *dar al-harb* being where Islamic law did not prevail. Islamic law restricted the buying of free people as slaves, so the boys who were to become *mamluks* were purchased in lands outside of the Islamic world from people who were not Muslims. Most came from central Asian nomadic tribes and from sub-Saharan Africa, although Indians and Europeans could be part of the mix. Boys from central Asia were especially valued because they could be counted on to know how to ride horses and how to use bows and spears. This made training them easier, because *mamluks* were expected to be cavalrymen.

SALADIN

Saladin (ca. 1137–93) was in the right place at the right time with the right experience and skills united with a fine mind. He had been a student of theology but became a military officer. He proved adept at political intrigue and by about 1170 he had managed to become master of Egypt. There, he improved the training of the Egyptian army. In 1174 he proclaimed himself sultan of Egypt, starting the Ayyubid Dynasty (1174–1260). At first, his military adventures were against other Muslim states, slowly absorbing Near Eastern states into his new empire. He did not wage war against the crusaders' Kingdom of Jerusalem, instead using the Kingdom of Jerusalem as a buffer between him and the northern Turks, who seem to have been his principal target. He developed tactics that took advantage of the speed of Near Eastern horses. Mamluk troops were adept at using bows while riding horseback, but Saladin used his cavalry in close-quarters fighting.

When Saladin faced armies from the Kingdom of Jerusalem, he often avoided pitched battles. His strategy was to hit quickly and then retreat quickly. Even when this happened, Muslim casualties were often high, because the enemy knights had lifetimes of training in close combat. In the battle of Montgisard in November 1177 about 90 percent of his forces were killed.

For many years thereafter the crusader states and Saladin's empire fought sporadically. He executed almost all prisoners of war. At the battle of Hattin in July 1187, Saladin's troops defeated a sizable army and opened the way to Jerusalem, which he took in October 1187. These events prompted the Third Crusade, among whose leaders was Richard the Lion-Hearted of England (r. 1189–99). Richard I and Saladin reflected different temperaments and different skills. Richard I was a master battlefield tactician. In the battle of Arsuf in September 1191, Richard was able to place the weight of his knights on enemy troops on open ground, and Saladin's forces were soundly defeated. On the other hand, Saladin was master of long-term strategy and often seemed to be thinking months ahead of his opponents. In the case of the Third Crusade, he scorched the earth between the Europeans and Jerusalem. Wells were poisoned, crops ruined, and livestock killed and thrown in the wells or led away. Richard I may have had a golden opportunity; had he immediately marched to Jerusalem, he might have defeated its defenders. Instead he

worried about the lack of clean drinking water, and the moment passed. Eventually he and Saladin made a treaty that left Jerusalem in Muslim control but required that Christians be allowed to make pilgrimages to Jerusalem unmolested. Saladin had much impressed the crusaders, who returned to Europe with stories of Saladin's gallantry in battle.

RETRENCHMENT

When the Mongols invaded the Near East in the 1240s, Islamic governments were still divided and often warring against one another. The major powers were the Seljuk Turks, who controlled much of the north, including Anatolia, having inflicted severe defeats on the Byzantine Empire, and the Mamluk Dynasty (1250–1517) that began with a coup in Egypt. The Mongols were a terrifying force that had slaughtered entire populations of cities. By the time they confronted the Seljuks, they had ended the central Asian civilization that had existed along the Silk Road. The Seljuks recruited Europeans into their army and adopted the tactics of Europeans. The core of the Mongols' army was a cavalry consisting of master horsemen who could shoot arrows accurately at a full gallop. Their swift ponies would sweep into opposing armies on the open plains that the Mongol generals preferred for their battles. Along with their frightening cavalry, the Mongols had siege engines and knew how to bring down a fortification's walls.

In the Seljuks the Mongols met a true test of their might. Seljuk generals knew their territory, and they were experienced in commanding swift cavalry such as that of the Mongols. The Seljuks relied on the discipline of their troops, facing the Mongols with infantry bristling with spears behind shields and trying to bring their heavy cavalry to bear on the Mongols' lightly armored horse archers. It seems that the Mongols were no match for the formations of heavily armored lancers in direct confrontations, but the mobility of Mongol forces allowed them to outflank their enemy, and at Köse Dagh in 1243, outnumbered and outgeneraled, the Seljuks were defeated. The Mongols were able to sweep through the Near East almost all the way to Egypt.

The Great Khan died, and the leader of the Mongol army in the Near East left for the Far East to vote on a successor for the leader of the Mongols. He took with him a large force, perhaps to protect himself. The only military force capable of stopping the Mongols' advance into North Africa was that of the Mamluks. In the Mamluks, the Mongols faced a sophisticated foe whose core troops were great horsemen who were a match for the Mongol horsemen. Mamluk cavalrymen were trained from boyhood to use bows, spears, and swords on horseback; each was trained to be a single-handed army. They were utterly dedicated to their leaders; unlike other forces of often well-trained men, they would not break into flight even when seemingly overwhelmed by opposition cavalry. A Mamluk also could dismount and fight as infantry. As individuals, each was trained in battlefield tactics and could act as an officer when none were to be found; together, they could organize themselves into improvised fighting units even in the midst

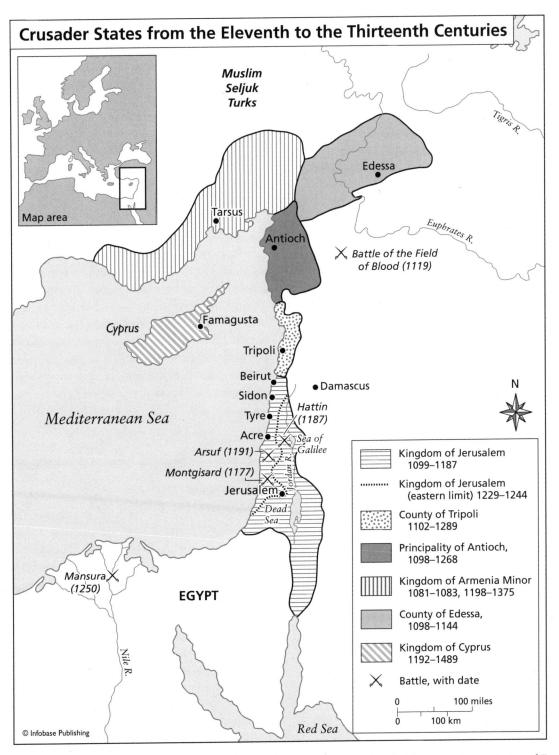

Crusader States from the Eleventh to the Thirteenth Centuries

Muslim Seljuk Turks

Edessa

Map area

Tigris R.

Tarsus

Euphrates R.

Antioch

✕ *Battle of the Field of Blood (1119)*

Cyprus

Famagusta

Tripoli

Mediterranean Sea

Beirut

• Damascus

Sidon

Tyre

Hattin (1187)

Acre

Sea of Galilee

Arsuf (1191) ✕

Jordan R.

Montgisard (1177)

Jerusalem

Dead Sea

N

Mansura ✕
(1250)

EGYPT

Nile R.

Red Sea

Legend	
▦	Kingdom of Jerusalem 1099–1187
┈	Kingdom of Jerusalem (eastern limit) 1229–1244
▦	County of Tripoli 1102–1289
▦	Principality of Antioch, 1098–1268
▦	Kingdom of Armenia Minor 1081–1083, 1198–1375
▦	County of Edessa, 1098–1144
▦	Kingdom of Cyprus 1192–1489
✕	Battle, with date

0 ———— 100 miles
0 ———— 100 km

© Infobase Publishing

Between the 11th and 14th centuries, Christian Europe took up nine military expeditions against the Muslims in Greater Syria and Egypt and established Crusader States that were defended by armies of pilgrim settlers, military-religious knights, and European kings and nobles. Most of the mainland territory was abandoned by Christians by 1291.

of battle. The confrontations between the two sides were bitterly contested, and the Mamluk army was hard-pressed to halt the Mongol advance into Egypt. But the army's persistent resistance mired down the enemy, and the Mamluks eventually defeated the Mongols in 1260 at the battle of Ain Jalut in Palestine. This opened a new era in history not only by ending the Mongol threat to North Africa but also by pushing the Mongols north and out of Syria, leaving the Mamluks to become the foremost power in the Near East.

In al-Andalus, the forces of Islam were not faring as well. A prolonged period of persecuting Christians had sent refugees into the northern Christian kingdoms where their presence had inspired an ideology of *Reconquista*, the term for the campaign of Christians to take back the Iberian Peninsula from the Muslims. The armies of al-Andalus looked very much like those of the Christians. Muslims and Christians had fought on the same side in some wars and had learned the same battle tactics. Both sides had elite horsemen who wore full chain mail armor and wielded lances, swords, axes, and maces, and both sides had infantry that was often drawn from the peasantry and equipped with helmets and spears. For the most part, the governments of al-Andalus failed to cooperate to meet the threat of a determined and usually unified enemy, allowing the Christians to conquer the small states of al-Andalus one by one, until the only major opposition to the Christian forces came from Granada.

Access to Granada was mostly by sea or through mountain passes. The government of Granada built fortifications at the passes to block invaders. Tactics usually focused on small raiding forces that would try to sneak through the mountains and attack enemy outposts and destroy enemy villages and crops. When Christian forces finally broke into open ground in Granada, they faced determined defenders of towns and cities who made the laying of sieges difficult. The Christians tried to lure the Granadan army out into open country, where Christian forces outnumbered the Granadans. When Granadan officers led their cavalry and infantry into direct confrontations with the enemy, they lost, and casualties were usually high. The resolution of the war was as much a matter of enemy patience as military skill, with the city of Granada eventually being cut off from help. The troops of Granada either became part of the army of the new rulers, retired to civilian life, or fled to North Africa or Anatolia.

See also ARCHITECTURE; ART; BORDERS AND FRONTIERS; BUILDING TECHNIQUES AND MATERIALS; CITIES; CLIMATE AND GEOGRAPHY; EMPIRES AND DYNASTIES; EXPLORATION; FOREIGNERS AND BARBARIANS; GOVERNMENT ORGANIZATION; HEALTH AND DISEASE; MILITARY; NOMADIC AND PASTORAL SOCIETIES; OCCUPATIONS; RELIGION AND COSMOLOGY; RESISTANCE AND DISSENT; SEAFARING AND NAVIGATION; SHIPS AND SHIPBUILDING; SOCIAL ORGANIZATION; SPORTS AND RECREATION; STORAGE AND PRESERVATION; TRADE AND EXCHANGE; TRANSPORTATION; WEAPONRY AND ARMOR.

Europe

⮞ Abbo Cernuus: "Wars of Count Odo with the Northmen in the Reign of Charles the Fat" (ca. 890s) ⮜

The Northmen came to Paris with 700 sailing ships, not counting those of smaller size which are commonly called barques. At one stretch the Seine was lined with the vessels for more than two leagues, so that one might ask in astonishment in what cavern the river had been swallowed up, since it was not to be seen. The second day after the fleet of the Northmen arrived under the walls of the city, Siegfried, who was then king only in name but who was in command of the expedition, came to the dwelling of the illustrious bishop. He bowed his head and said: "Gauzelin, have compassion on yourself and on your flock. We beseech you to listen to us, in order that you may escape death. Allow us only the freedom of the city. We will do no harm and we will see to it that whatever belongs either to you or to Odo shall be strictly respected." Count Odo, who later became king, was then the defender of the city. The bishop replied to Siegfried, "Paris has been entrusted to us by the Emperor Charles, who, after God, king and lord of the powerful, rules over almost all the world. He has put it in our care, not at all that the kingdom may be ruined by our misconduct, but that he may keep it and be assured of its peace. If, like us, you had been given the duty of defending these walls, and if you should have done that which you ask us to do, what treatment do you think you would deserve?" Siegfried replied. "I should deserve that my head be cut off and thrown to the dogs. Nevertheless, if you do not listen to my demand, on the morrow our war machines will destroy you with poisoned arrows. You will be the prey of famine and of pestilence and these evils will renew themselves perpetually every year." So saying, he departed and gathered together his comrades.

In the morning the Northmen, boarding their ships, approached the tower and attacked it. They shook it with their engines and stormed it with arrows. The city resounded with clamor, the people were aroused, the bridges trembled. All came together to defend the tower. There Odo, his brother Robert, and the Count Ragenar distinguished themselves for bravery; likewise the courageous Abbot Ebolus, the nephew of the bishop. A keen arrow wounded the prelate, while at his side the young warrior Frederick was struck by a sword. Frederick died, but the old man, thanks to God, survived. There perished many Franks; after receiving wounds they were lavish of life. At last the enemy withdrew, carrying off their dead. The evening came. The tower had been sorely tried, but its foundations were still solid, as were also the narrow bays which surmounted them. The people spent the night repairing it with boards. By the next day, on the old citadel had been erected a new tower of wood, a half higher than the former one. At sunrise the Danes caught their first glimpse of it. Once more the latter engaged with the Christians in violent combat. On every side arrows sped and blood flowed. With the arrows mingled the stones hurled by slings and war-machines; the air was filled with them. The tower which had been built during the night groaned under the strokes of the darts, the city shook with the struggle, the people ran hither and thither, the bells jangled. The warriors rushed together to defend the tottering tower and to repel the fierce assault. Among these warriors two, a count and an abbot, surpassed all the rest in courage. The former was the redoubtable Odo who never experienced defeat and who continually revived the spirits of the worn-out defenders. He ran along the ramparts and hurled back the enemy. On those who were secreting themselves so as to undermine the tower he poured oil, wax, and pitch, which, being mixed and heated, burned the Danes and tore off their scalps. Some of them died; others threw themselves into the river to escape the awful substance.

From: Frederic Austin Ogg, ed., *A Source Book of Mediaeval History: Documents Illustrative of European Life and Institutions from the German Invasions to the Renaissance* (New York: American Book Company, 1907).

The Islamic World

∼ William of Tyre: "The Fall of Edessa," excerpt from History of Deeds Done beyond the Sea (ca. 1150) ∼

In that same year, [1144] during the time which elapsed between the death of King Baldwin's father and Baldwin's elevation to the throne, one Zengi, a vicious man, was the most powerful of the Eastern Turks. His city, formerly called Nineveh, but now known as Mosul, is the metropolis of the region which was earlier called Assur. Zengi, its lord and governor, at this time laid siege to the city of Edessa, more commonly called Rohas, the greatest and most splendid city of the Medes. Zengi did this, relying on the numbers and strength of his men and also on the very dangerous strife which had arisen between Prince Raymond of Antioch and Count Joscelyn of Edessa. The city of Edessa lies beyond the Euphrates, one day's journey from the river. The aforesaid Count of Edessa, contrary to the custom of his predecessors, had ceased to live in the city and made his constant and perpetual abode in a place called Turbessel. He did this both because of the richness of the spot and because of his own laziness. Here, far from the tumult of the enemy and free to pursue his pleasures, the count failed to take proper care of his noble city. The population of Edessa was made up of Chaldeans and Armenians,

(continued)

(continues)

unwarlike men, scarcely familiar with the use of arms and accustomed only to the acts of trade. The city was only rarely visited by Latins and very few of them lived there. The safekeeping of the city was entrusted solely to mercenaries and these were not paid according to the type of service they performed or the length of time for which they were engaged indeed, they often had to wait a year or more for the payment of their stated wages. Both Baldwin and the elder Joscelyn, when they held the county, made their home permanently and customarily in Edessa and took care to have the city supplied with food, arms, and other necessary items from nearby places. They had thus been able both to maintain themselves in safety and also to overawe the neighboring towns with their strength.

There was, as we have said before, bad feeling between Count Joscelyn and the Prince of Antioch a feeling that was not hidden, but rather had become an open hatred. For this reason, each of them took little or no care if the other were attacked or suffered misfortune. Rather they rejoiced at the other's catastrophes and were made glad by the other's mishaps.

The aforesaid great prince, Zengi, took the opportunity offered by this situation. He gathered innumerable cavalry forces throughout all of the East; he even called up the people of the cities neighboring Edessa and brought them with him to lay siege to the day. He blockaded all of the entrances to the city, so that the besieged citizens could not get out and so that those who wished to help them could not get in. The resulting shortage of food aid provisions caused great suffering for the besieged. The city, however, was surrounded by a formidable wall. In the upper town there were high towers and down below there was the lower town where the citizens could take refuge, even if the city itself were taken. All these defenses could be of use against the enemy only if there were men willing to fight for their freedom, men who would resist the foe valiantly. The defenses would be useless, however, if there were none among the besieged who were willing to serve as defenders. . . . Zengi found the town bereft of defenders and was much encouraged. He encircled the town with his forces, assigned the officers of his legions to appropriate stations, and dug in. The catapults and siege engines weakened the fortifications; the continual

shooting of arrows tormented the citizens incessantly; and the besieged were given no respite. It was announced, meanwhile, and the news was also spread by rumor, that the city of Edessa, a city faithful to God, was suffering the agonies of a siege at the hands of the enemy of the faith and the foe of the Christian name. At this news the hearts of the faithful, far and wide, were touched and zealous men began to take up arms to harass the wicked. The Count, when he beard of it, was stricken with anguish. Energetically he assembled his forces. . . . Messengers bearing news of this sinister event came even to the kingdom of Jerusalem, bearing witness to the siege of Edessa and to the misfortunes suffered by its citizens. . . .

The Prince of Antioch, however, rejoiced in Edessa's adversity and paid small attention to his duties for the common welfare. He was little concerned that personal hatred ought not cause public harm and made excuses, while he put off giving the aid which bad been requested.

Zengi, meanwhile, pressed continual assaults on the city. He ran the gamut of attacks and left nothing untried which could harass the citizens and aid him in gaining control of the city. He sent sappers through trenches and underground tunnels to undermine the walls. As they dug passages beneath the walls, they buttressed these with posts, which were afterward set on fire. A great part of the wall was thus broken down. This breach in the wall, more than 100 cubits wide, gave the enemy an entrance into the city. The enemy now had the approach they had desired. Their forces rushed together into the city. They slew with their swords the citizens whom they encountered, sparing neither age, condition, nor sex. . . . The city, therefore, was captured and delivered to the swords of the enemy.

Thus while the Prince of Antioch, overcome by foolish hatred, delayed rendering the help he owed to his brothers and while the count awaited help from abroad, the ancient city of Edessa, devoted to Christianity since the time of the Apostles and delivered from the superstitions of the infidels through the words and preaching of the Apostle Thaddeus, passed into an undeserved servitude.

From William of Tyre, *Historia rerum
in partibus transmarinis gestarum*,
trans. James Brundage, *The Crusades: A
Documentary History*, (Milwaukee, Wis.:
Marquette University Press, 1962).

FURTHER READING

Bernard S. Bachrach, *Armies and Politics in the Early Medieval West* (Brookfield, Vt.: Variorum, 1993).

Thomas J. Barfield, *The Perilous Frontier: Nomadic Empires and China* (Cambridge, Mass.: Blackwell, 1989).

Jim Bradbury, *The Medieval Archer* (New York: Boydell Press, 1996).

Lester Brooks, "The Songhay Ascendancy," in his *Great Civilizations of Ancient Africa* (New York: Four Winds Press, 1971).

Philippe Contamine, *War in the Middle Ages,* trans. Michael Jones (New York: Blackwell, 1984).

Ross Hassig, *Aztec Warfare: Imperial Expansion and Political Control* (Norman: University of Oklahoma Press, 1995).

Ross Hassig, *War and Society in Ancient Mesoamerica* (Berkeley: University of California Press, 1992).

John Keegan, *A History of Warfare* (New York: Alfred A. Knopf, 1993).

Patrick V. Kirch, *On the Road of the Winds: An Archaeological History of the Pacific Islands before European Contact* (Berkeley: University of California Press, 2000).

Steven A. LeBlanc, *Prehistoric Warfare in the American Southwest* (Salt Lake City: University of Utah Press, 1999).

James E. Lindsay, "Warfare and Politics." In his *Daily Life in the Medieval Islamic World* (Westport, Conn.: Greenwood Press, 2005): 57–85.

Harold G. Marcus, "Beginnings, to 1270" and "The Golden Age of the Solomonic Dynasty, to 1500" in his *History of Ethiopia* (Berkeley: University of California Press, 1994).

David Nicolle, *Historical Atlas of the Islamic World* (New York: Checkmark Books, 2003).

Roland Oliver and Anthony Atmore, *Medieval Africa, 1250–1800* (New York: Cambridge University Press, 2001).

Geoffrey Parker, *The Cambridge Illustrated History of Warfare* (New York: Cambridge University Press, 2005).

John Reader, "Part 4: African Civilizations," in his *Biography of the Continent Africa* (New York: Vintage Books, 1997).

Linda Schele and Mary Ellen Miller, *The Blood of Kings: Dynasty and Ritual in Maya Art* (Fort Worth, Tex.: Kimbell Art Museum, 1986).

Barbara Tuchman, *A Distant Mirror: The Calamitous Fourteenth Century* (New York: Ballantine Books, 1987).

► weaponry and armor

INTRODUCTION

At the beginning of the Middle Ages battle was still contested by men at close quarters using edged weapons, hacking at each other with swords, spears, and axes. By the end of the period the battlefield was coming to be dominated by gunpowder artillery and small arms. While we often think of medieval warfare as being an aristocratic pastime, by the end of the Middle Ages popular armies fighting for political and social change had made their appearance, abandoning traditional weapons and tactics in favor of innovations such as the Swiss pike square, the Hussite wagon fortress, and the Korean ironclad gunboats.

In the medieval period cavalry became the dominant arm on the battlefield. While most armies remained predominantly bodies of infantry, the strength of cavalry compared with infantry greatly increased. The stirrup was invented in inner Asia and was borrowed throughout Eurasia. It allowed cavalrymen to remain on a horse for longer periods of time (for days at a time in some cases, as during the long forced marches undertaken by Genghis Kahn) and also to stay in the saddle with much greater security when they were actually clashing with opponents. A cavalryman standing in the stirrups could strike his opponent with much greater force than could an ancient horseman who had to grip the sides of his horse with his thighs and rely on his balance rather than his strength to stay on the horse.

Although most battles were decided with swords or lances, this was conditioned by the inertia of tradition and the relatively low level of professionalism of most medieval armies. The fact is that infantry or cavalry armed with longbows or compound bows could simply stand a hundred yards off from an enemy formation and slaughter them at will. The most decisive victories in medieval warfare—the English successes at Crécy, Poitiers, and Agincourt, and the Mongol conquest of most of Eurasia—were all brought about by archers whose very way of life made them experts in the use of the bow. But the idea of creating long-term service units to train regularly with specialized weapons was foreign to most military institutions in the Middle Ages. In Europe, for instance, the greater bulk of the infantry in any army owed a feudal obligation of 40 days' service a year, so any but the most minimal training was out of the question.

The best swords in the Middle Ages were produced by the craft traditions of Japan and northern India. Indian swords were generally known in Europe as Damascus blades, from the terminus of the caravan routes that brought them westward. The quality of these kinds of swords compared with most medieval weapons is suggested by a legendary story often told about a dinner party held during negotiations between the rival rulers fighting each other in the Third Crusade. Richard the Lionhearted, the king of England, demonstrated his military prowess by splitting the dining table in two with a heavy blow from his broadsword. The Islamic commander Saladin responded by throwing a silk scarf into the air and cutting it into seven pieces with his Damascus sword as it fluttered to the ground.

Armor was certainly useful in medieval battle, but it could rarely protect a soldier from direct attack. Even in the case of the heaviest armor used in late medieval Europe, at Agincourt, arrows often were found to have pierced the armor covering a French knight's thigh, passed entirely through his flesh, pierced another layer of armor on the way out, and then gone through a layer of horse armor and struck deeply enough into the horse to kill it. While the heavy plate armor that evolved in Europe had as much to do with display as practical protection, it was a definite improvement over older chain-mail armor. Mail coats hung all of their weight on the shoulders and so hampered a knight's movements severely. Plate armor, though heavier overall, had its weight suspended equally over the whole body, allowing the wearer much freer movement. Armor was a valuable commodity, and poor knights like William Marshal (1146–1219) helped to make their way through tournament victories: Technically, the defeated knight became the winner's prisoner and had to ransom himself with a suit of armor. At Agincourt one of the chief problems faced by the English king Henry V was keeping his Welsh peasant archers from breaking ranks to go out and strip armor from the growing mound of dead French knights before them.

Armies in the Americas and Polynesia and Australia were hampered by having to use stone and wood to manufacture weapons without metal. Warfare in these areas was able nevertheless to destroy cities and amass great death tolls. But these conditions also encouraged primitive ritual and display elements of warfare such as the Plains Indian practice of "counting coup" (which consisted of a warrior demonstrating his courage by touching an armed aggressive opponent without attacking him) or the sacrifice of prisoners of war in elaborate rituals, as by the Mississippian, Aztec, and Mayan cultures.

AFRICA

BY JUSTIN CORFIELD

The weapons used in medieval Africa varied considerably. In some parts of the continent people used iron, but in others wooden weapons were more common. In many cases the weapons were used primarily for hunting and not for fighting, except in limited areas of the continent. The Bushmen of southern Africa relied heavily on bows and arrows for both hunting and defense. Their bows were up to 5 feet tall—taller than the people using them. They were made from hardwood and bent into a sharp curve, with string made from twisted sinews.

The arrows would 2 to 3 feet in length, usually made from reed, with a heavy point of bone, and with feathers on the tail to steady it in its flight. They were extremely accurate and deadly at less than 20 yards but less so at longer ranges, which made the Bushmen rely on stealth and surprise. The quivers could hold up to 30 arrows. They also carried with them a club known as a *kirri*. It was effectively a cudgel of about 20 inches in length, used for throwing or to kill a wounded animal or as a battle weapon at close quarters.

The Hottentots, also of southern Africa, used bows, similar to those of the Bushmen. By the late medieval period they were using iron as well, and some of their arrows had iron tips, often with barbs. These were attached to arrows that were about 20 inches long, often treated with snake poison to make them deadly in hunting and fighting. The bow generally took second place to the assegai, or hand-held javelin. These were about the height of a man and were sharpened at one end. As with the Bushmen, the Hottentots used the *kirri* and also the *rackum*, which was a longer and pointed version of the club. Made from hardwood, these weapons often were treated with oil to make the wood extremely firm.

Some of the jungle people of central Africa used weapons similar to those of the Hottentots, with the tribes in the Ituri forest region of the modern-day Democratic Republic of Congo making arrows carved from bone, which had up to a dozen barbs. The development of the knife, through use of sharp flints, thigh bone, and hardwood, was an important advance of this period. A knife from the Butua people of modern-day Zimbabwe evidently was made from a human shin bone.

From the early ninth century the empire of Ghana, with its capital at Kumbi Saleh, about 200 miles north of modern-day Bamako, Mali, emerged as one of the great military powers in the region. It gained great wealth from gold and used it to finance wars against its neighbors. During the mid-ninth century the kingdom of Kanem, with its capital at Njimi, northeast of Lake Chad, also emerged as a strong military power, its rulers converting to Islam in the 11th century. Both these states, as well as that of Great Zimbabwe, which also traded gold, relied on large armies, but little information has survived about their weaponry.

The Bantu people during this period clearly used weapons not only for hunting but also for fighting between tribes and within tribes. By the later part of the medieval period they used bronze and iron, and these materials gave them a considerable advantage over their opponents. The Buganda people of modern-day Uganda started using iron as late as 1000, although it seemed to be used in southern Africa before that time, showing a great disparity in the technology of different regions.

During the late medieval period the most advanced African weaponry more closely resembled 11th- and 12th-century European hand weapons, with short daggers; wide, flat-bladed swords; spears; bows and arrows; and clubs. Some surviving daggers from medieval Africa are clearly of Arab design, having a short, curved blade. That these are more common in eastern and northeastern Africa also tends to suggest that the similarities with Arab design were not coincidental. By the late medieval period Arab-style swords became more common in the Horn of Africa (modern-day Somalia), with flat blades that had a stem narrower than the end, making them useful for hacking opponents rather than thrusting at them.

In battle against each other the Bantu tribes tended to make heavy use of spears, many with large, flat blades. When engaging in hand-to-hand fighting, they tended to rely on wooden clubs similar to those that were being used by the Zulus as late as the early 19th century. Often carved from a single piece of hardwood, the clubs had a handle at one end; the other end featured a large round or oval piece of wood for hitting an opponent in battle with considerable force, with the aim of killing rather than stunning. In southern Africa the clubs had a different design: Generally, the handle was made from one piece of polished hardwood and the head from another piece of hardwood or from metal or even bone. High-status warriors, such as rulers and members of ruling families, might carry clubs with bones made from rhino horn, though the more traditional use of rhino horn was for the handles of Yemeni-style daggers popular in parts of the Horn of Africa and in Zanzibar as well as Yemen. The *oba*, or king, in Benin, western Africa, tended to carry a ceremonial hammer with him.

The swords used in western Africa tended to be for thrusting and cutting, like Roman swords, rather than for fencing or parrying, like the European ones of the same period. In fighting, the height of the soldiers and the lengths of the arms as well as the amount of force they could use were just as important as their weaponry. Because of this style of fighting with swords and also to protect soldiers from the use of heavy clubs, many Africans used large, lightweight shields covered with animal hides to deflect the blows of their opponents. The Zulus used civet skin decoration.

From the number of bronze plaques that have survived in Benin, it is possible to elucidate more about their weaponry than for other tribes in the region. Bows shown on these plaques are much smaller than those used elsewhere in Africa, with most hunters specializing in stalking their prey with heavily barbed spears. The daggers were similar in design to spears but with very short shafts. Swords often had large heads, like the cleavers used for cutting branches and undergrowth in western Africa today. Shields were large and mainly rectangular, except for the pointed top. It is also evident that there were certain regional variations in the use of weapons. The Kikuyu preferred the bow and arrow (with iron arrowheads), while the Masai made much greater use of spears.

Camels had been introduced into North Africa in the third century and were used in battle, as were horses. The latter were put to heavy use by the Bornu from central Sudan, who sent cavalry against their opponents each year. Because of the nature of fighting on horseback, the weaponry used by them and also by their opponents was different from that of most of the rest of Africa, where fighting was on foot. The Bornu used Arab-style armor with large numbers of small plates sewn together to form "plate mail." Their primary weapon was the lance, which became longer and stronger over time. Their opponents tended to develop spears and short swords for jabbing at the horses of the Bornu, with large oval shields to protect themselves.

During the 15th century some Europeans, primarily the Portuguese, came into contact with Africans in western Africa, and this often resulted in skirmishes. The part of the armory that the Europeans clearly feared most was the poisoned arrow. These arrows were quite effective, as was made evident when a Portuguese slaving party landed on the western African coast after sailing from the Cape Verde Islands in about 1445 or 1446. Nuno Tristão landed with 21 other men and quickly ran into an ambush from the Africans, who killed 20 of the men with poisoned arrows; only two escaped and made their way to Portugal with the story. Gradually, improvements in European musketry turned battles into unequal contests, with some African tribes trying to buy as many muskets as possible to ensure their own survival or to expand their kingdoms into "secondary empires."

THE AMERICAS
BY J. J. GEORGE

The weaponry and armor of North America during the period 500 to 1500 remained consistent with those of earlier periods, though with a few improvements and additions. The principal weapons used were the spear-thrower (atlatl), sling, spear, and club. Widespread use of the bow and arrow appears to have occurred later, with chipped stone points comparable in size and shape to modern arrows common by about 500. Weapons were normally made of stone, bone, horn, and wood and often were composite, with the point, head, or blade crafted from stone or bone and the handle or shaft from wood.

The atlatl, a device that adds leverage by extending the length of the user's arm and thereby increasing the range, force, and accuracy of the spear, had a particularly wide distribution. Its use was known among the polar Eskimo in the Arctic, the Tlingit of the Northwest Coast, groups in lower California and northwestern New Mexico, Indians at the mouth of the Mississippi and throughout Mesoamerica and in the circum-Caribbean area. Steel weapons did not arrive with the Europeans in the late 15th and early 16th centuries.

Body armor in North America consisted of at least four types. Armor made of slats or plates of bone perforated at the edges and tied together was used among the Eskimo. Similar armor made exclusively of wooden slats was known on the Canadian Plateau and the Northwest Coast. Hide armor was

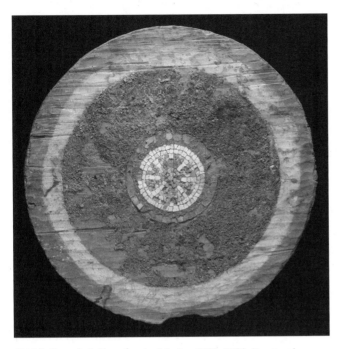

Shield of wood, shell, and resin; Mexico; 1200–1500 (Los Angeles County Museum of Art, Gift of the Art Museum Council in honor of the museum's twenty-fifth anniversary, Photograph © 2006 Museum Associates/ LACMA [M.90.168.27])

more common across much of North America and into Mesoamerica and Central America. Hide armor typically consisted of an untailored hide draped around the body under one arm and tied over the opposite shoulder so that both hands would be free. Shields were also widespread. The most common type, especially in the Plains, was a circular shield made of hide. Other shields were made of rods, slats, or boards fastened together. Helmets also were used and are known from the Arctic, the Northwest Coast, and even in central Mexico, where later Aztec warriors wore helmets as part of elaborate costumes with the insignia of their military orders.

The Mississippian cultures (ca. 750–ca. 1500) of the Midwest and Southeast are known to have been aggressive and warrior-like. According to their mythical worldview, visionary warrior priests journeyed along the Path of Souls to the realm of the dead in search of divine weapons and power. With the use of sacred, spiritual weapons they fought violent battles against powerful mythical creatures, including the Underwater Panther, the Great Serpent, the Old-Woman-Who-Never-Dies, and the Raptor.

Archaeological research and 16th-century European images reflect the preoccupation with war. Axes, knives, clubs, maces, spears, and bows and arrows are known from dig sites and painted imagery. Painted images describe heavily tattooed warriors from the south dressed in loin clothes marching off to battle, some with large medallion-like plates

over their chests and carrying bows and arrows, spears, and wooden clubs with broad, bulbous ends. The Mississippian culture highlighted war imagery in their own practice of representation, favoring repoussé sheet copper, engraved marine shell cups, and engraved marine shell gorgets. One example, an incised shell gorget from the 13th or 14th century, shows two figures engaged in hand-to-hand combat, possibly a ritual war dance, brandishing long flint swords while attempting to decapitate each other with raptor talon–effigy flint knives. Their arms and legs are depicted with protective bands. Although this scene depicts a mythical battle, the actual combat regalia have been recovered from mortuary contexts at Mississippian political centers.

Much farther north, in the Arctic, violence between groups usually involved small bands of men numbering about a dozen and occasionally larger groups in the hundreds, redressing or exacting revenge for an insult or a killing. They often wore protective clothing in the form of special fur or skin vests, and in some regions they wore plate armor manufactured from pieces of bone or ivory linked together with rawhide. Their normal wardrobe of sewn animal furs on its own offered minimal defensive protection. The men were armed with bows and arrows, clubs, spears, and knives and typically meant to catch the entire population of the target settlement involved in a festivity in the *kashim*, or communal structure, at which point the raiding party would send firebrands or smoking debris through the skylight in an attempt to burn or suffocate them to death.

Moving south to central Mexico, Aztec warfare in the 15th and 16th centuries might seem peculiar by comparison. The primary goal of Aztec warfare was to conquer city-states to force them to pay tribute, a kind of tax whereby the conquered territory shipped goods to the Aztec center at Tenochtitlan, now Mexico City. The secondary purpose, however, was to capture warriors for ritual sacrifice. Human sacrifice was a fundamental part of Aztec religion, which to a large extent drove the state. Consequently, to satisfy the sacrificial needs that religion demanded, enemy warriors were captured alive rather than killed.

The primary offensive weapons of the Aztec were thrusting spears and swords. The Aztec sword (*maquahuitl*) consisted of a long, flat wooden handle into which were fitted rows of obsidian blades, which were extremely sharp and highly effective. Like the rest of the Americas, metallurgy in Mexico was limited to softer metals that were ineffective as far as weaponry is concerned. Steel was unknown by the Aztec until Hernán Cortés and his men rode into Tenochtitlan in 1521. Obsidian was an effective replacement. Later Spanish accounts describe instances in which Aztec soldiers cut off the heads of horses with a single blow of the *maquahuitl*.

The bow and arrow also was used, and some groups made use of clubs and slings. Warriors carried shields made of wood and covered with elaborate decoration, often of feathers. They wore body armor made of thick, quilted cotton cloth that was quite effective at stopping arrows and darts.

Quilted cotton body armor was used earlier at Teotihuacán (ca. 1–ca. 700), a major city 40 miles to the northeast of contemporary Mexico City, where it was called *escuipil*. Painted images from Teotihuacán also depict warriors wielding atlatls, rectangular shields, and thrusting spears and bucklers and wearing helmets. Some Spaniards adopted the use of the cotton armor once they realized that there own armor was not only unnecessary, owing to the lack of metal weapons among the native population, but also repressively hot.

For a long time scholars thought that the Maya were a peaceful and idyllic people. Their weaponry, however, suggests otherwise. Spears, atlatls, darts, and the bow and arrow were common in Classic Period (ca. 200–ca. 900) Mayan civilization. Quilted cotton armor, similar to that from Teotihuacán, was also used. Teotihuacán incursions into Mayan territory at this time suggest that weaponry known at Teotihuacán also would have been known among the Maya. Many images of weaponry are known from Mayan artwork. Archaeologists who opened the tomb of the Tikal (ca. 200–ca. 800) ruler Stormy Sky found that he was flanked by two retainers, who were most likely sacrificed at his death. Stela 31, a large sculpted stone relief, shows Stormy Sky similarly flanked by two guardians dressed in Teotihuacán-style military garb and carrying shields, spear throwers, and feathered darts.

Murals at Bonampak, which date to around 800, depict the horror and confusion of hand-to-hand combat. In one scene a thrown spear penetrates the forehead of a warrior. At the center stands a war leader, dressed in a jaguar tunic and holding a thrusting spear. These are but a few examples representing the Maya and their weapons. Wall paintings at the Postclassic (ca. 900–1521) site of Chichén Itzá show Toltec warriors from central Mexico reconnoitering the Yucatán coast, bearing shields and bows and arrows. Similarly, a gold repoussé disk from Chichén Itzá shows a Toltec warrior wearing an elaborate headdress and attacking Mayan warriors with a thrusting spear.

South American war practice was well advanced by the time of the Inca (ca. 1450–1532). Flurries of arrows, sling stones, and javelins preceded hand-to-hand combat by troops who wielded maces, clubs, and spears. Some stones were reportedly large enough to fell a horse or break a sword in half at a distance of almost 100 feet. The sling was a belt of wood or fiber that one twirled above the head before releasing a stone with both force and relatively good accuracy. Piles of hundreds of sling stones can still be found within the walls of various Incan forts. The Incas' preferred weapon was a stone or bronze star mace mounted on a wooden handle about 1 foot long, often fitted with sharp spikes. Another favorite was a hard, double-edged, palm wood club shaped like a sword. The bow and arrow were a late addition to the Incan army's repertoire, as warriors from tribes in the Amazon jungle were drafted into service. They also employed wooden lances, though these were much shorter than those the Spanish used against Incan forces to such devastating effect.

Defensive armor consisted of quilted cloth that was so effective against Andean weapons that many Spaniards adopted its use, as they did in Mesoamerica, replacing their own metal plate in favor of the lighter cloth. Incan warriors also frequently carried shields and protected their chests and backs with plates of metal and their heads with cane helmets. Troops defending fortified locations responded with a similar array of weaponry, to which they added large boulders rolled down onto advancing forces. Military service was compulsory for all males between the ages of 15 and 50. Finally, ample storage facilities, an extensive road network, and a system of fortresses might also be thought of as war implements because they aided the efficiency of the Incan war machine, allowing them to deploy and maintain vast armies at great distances.

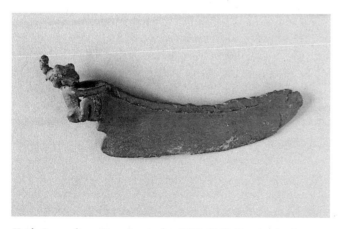

Knife, Inca culture, Peruvian Andes, 1300–1560 (Los Angeles County Museum of Art, The Phil Berg Collection, Photograph © 2006 Museum Associates/LACMA [M.71.73.235])

ASIA AND THE PACIFIC

BY MARK W. ALLEN

There was an astonishing variety of weapons and armor across time and space in Asia and the Pacific during medieval times. At one end of the spectrum, Australian and Melanesian stone and wooden weapons were the same ones used thousands of years earlier, while defensive armor was limited to wooden shields. By contrast, in Asia by 1500 gunpowder was widely used in firearms, artillery, and bombs. Consideration of weapons and armor is instructive, as they shed much light on the goals of war and the ways in which combat was conducted. For example, they can indicate to what extent warriors were professional specialists in the art of warfare or merely members of a group that grabbed their personal weapons to join their kin and neighbors when war threatened. Specialized weapons might take years to master and nearly always indicated formalized positions for warriors. Armor was often a huge expense and usually was restricted to full-time soldiers or the elite members of a society. Weapons and armor are important symbols of the rulers and leaders and demonstrate the protective or threatening nature of military power.

In Australia and the Pacific islands weapons either were of an ancient form, as in the case of Australia and much of the Melanesian islands, or were typical of Neolithic cultures, such as those of Micronesia, parts of Melanesia, and Polynesia. The former type includes simple clubs, stone knives, spears, lances, throwing sticks (like the boomerang of Australia), atlatls, and sometimes the bow and arrow. Defensive armor was limited to the wooden shield, typically used to block spears or arrows rather than for protection during hand-to-hand combat. Warfare involved nearly every male capable of bearing arms; there were no specialist warriors. Thus, each man had his personal weapons of choice, often the same ones he would carry while hunting. These weapons, though simple, must be recognized as lethal. Casualty rates could be very high in this type of warfare, with a very large proportion of deaths coming through conflict.

The situation is considerably more complex in the rest of the Pacific. Here are found a remarkable variety of specialized weapons for warfare rather than the mere use of traditional hunting weapons for combat. Neolithic weapons include polished stone axes hafted onto wooden handles, various forms of clubs efficient for cracking skulls, slings for hurling rocks, wooden swords or clubs with edges made of razor-sharp obsidian or sharks' teeth, and stone projectile points (often with flared or even barbed corners at the base) designed especially for human prey, in that they can do tremendous damage to tissue when they are extracted. Armor was also used, particularly on some islands of Micronesia and Polynesia. It was usually woven out of flax or other vegetation and capable of protecting the wearer from some missiles or blows.

Particularly good examples of specialized Neolithic weapons are those of Fiji, a remote group of hundreds of islands at the very eastern edge of Melanesia. Fiji was ruled by powerful chiefs who used warfare as one of their major forms of social power. They often relied on specially trained warriors, who selected from an amazing variety of wooden hand-to-hand weapons such as clubs, maces, battle-axes, spears, and throwing sticks. Much importance was placed on shock combat rather than the use of missile weapons. Armor was fairly limited. Similarly, the Polynesian New Zealand Maori employed a variety of war clubs with sharp polished edges, called *patu*. These could be made of whalebone, wood, or stone. In the hands of an expert they were deadly. Maori *toa* (warriors) also used the *taiaha*, an unusual wooden spear/sword combination—the tip was used to disarm an opponent, and then the butt end was swung like a sword for an incapacitating or fatal blow. Several other special weapons were used as well. Like the Fijians, armor was eschewed by the Maori, who likewise valued hand-to-hand combat rather than reliance on missiles.

Elsewhere in Polynesia, however, warriors did take to the use of missiles as well as specialized sharks' teeth–lined swords and other lethal close-combat weapons. Hawaii is a good example. Archaeologists often find large caches of sling stones piled near a settlement or in a fortification. These stones were lobbed in mass missile assaults. Prudently, many warriors (particularly specialist fighters and chiefs) wore woven armor and carried light shields to help protect against slings and other weapons.

In a very real way, to understand the history of Asia during medieval times, one must appreciate the significance of a number of offensive innovations in warfare. While we see the most drastic changes in offensive weapons, there were less profound changes in armor and protection as well. By the early to middle medieval period of Asia nearly all parts of Asia were characterized by a very different kind of warfare than that of the Pacific islands. Here, warfare was of a much larger scale, with professional armies comprising up to hundreds of thousands of soldiers armed with standardized iron and steel weapons. Wars were led not by chiefs or kin groups but by emperors or kings together with their generals and other officers. Calvary, war elephants, ships, and early forms of artillery were commonly used.

Hand-to-hand weapons included a wide variety of steel and iron swords, axes, maces, daggers, and longer weapons, such as spears and pole arms for use by infantry against mounted opponents. These weapons have a long history in Asia, particularly in China and India. During the medieval period improvements in metal-forging techniques and technologies did lead to the construction of steel weapons, which were less likely to break and which could keep a sharp edge. Some of the finest swords and armor ever made come from medieval armor, particularly in China and Japan.

To find the greatest advances in weaponry in medieval Asia we have to look elsewhere. One major innovation was the refinement of the stirrup by the early medieval period. Although it is not technically a weapon, it permitted a mounted warrior to be much more dangerous by allowing him to stand

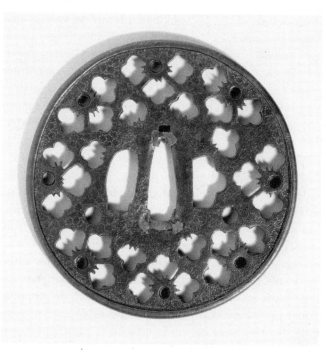

Iron sword guard, Japan, ca. 1400 (Los Angeles County Museum of Art, Gift of Caroline and Jarred Morse, Photograph © 2006 Museum Associates/ LACMA [M.80.219.1])

up and smite down hard on opponents or to have a more stable firing position for bows. This innovation is tied closely to the development of the composite bow, made of different materials bound together to maximize drawing power and thus improve arrow velocity. The small size of this bow, together with the stirrup, made the steppe horsemen of central Asia the most feared of all opponents by late medieval times in Asia. These armies combined great mobility with deadly accurate and rapid missile fire. With these advantages the Mongols (ca. 1206–1368) succeeded in building the largest contiguous land empire in history through military conquest in just a few generations.

The discovery of gunpowder by the Chinese sometime around 1000 meant the slow but sure end of the ancient practices, tactics, and strategies of warfare. This was no revolution in technology. It was a gradual change over three to four centuries as gunpowder came to be used in weapons such as bombs, handheld firearms, and eventually even canons by the end of the medieval period throughout Europe and Asia. This, of course, meant that personal armor and even city walls that had been so vital in warfare for thousands of years were quickly becoming obsolete, as they could not hope to stand up against increasingly deadly weapons. Wholesale changes were made in the size of armies, how they were trained, how they fought, and even the goals of warfare itself. The world would never be the same.

As noted, advances in protective armor during the medieval period of Asia are not nearly as dramatic as those of offensive weapons. Still, before firearms developed, improved metal technology permitted the development of somewhat more effective armor. Nevertheless, these improvements were largely ineffective against the powerful composite bows of the Mongols and their predecessors. Horse warriors of the steppes actually developed a new form of lamellar armor which was made by lacing together patches of lacquered leather, metal, and other materials. It was lighter than metal rings or plates and thus appropriate for horse archers, who shot while moving. It was also more effective protection against arrows than ring armor (chain mail) and better against crushing blows than plate metal armor. One part of Asia where the widespread use of armor did continue into even the 19th century was Japan. *Samurai* and their leaders resisted the introduction of gunpowder weaponry with some success, though it became increasingly important even there.

EUROPE

BY AMY HACKNEY BLACKWELL

Soldiers in medieval Europe used a variety of weapons. A soldier's choice of armor depended on the time during which he lived, the type of fighting he did, and his economic situation. For hand-to-hand combat soldiers typically used swords, axes, clubs, and spears. Crossbows, bows, and javelins served as projectiles for most of the medieval period, though firearms had begun to appear toward the end of the era. Siege weapons such as catapults helped armies break into castles and towns. Many soldiers wore armor to protect them from opponents' weapons. This armor evolved from mail made of metal links to full plate armor as projectile weapons improved.

Medieval soldiers used a variety of weapons for hand-to-hand combat. All knights carried swords with them, and the best soldiers were expected to be skilled at swordplay. A sword consisted of a long blade and a handle called a hilt. Hilts could be made to accommodate one or two hands. Basic hilts were topped with a crosspiece that kept an opponent's sword from sliding down the blade and striking the soldier's hands. Some later swords had more elaborate hand guards. At the end of the hilt was a lump of metal called a pommel, which served as a counterweight to the blade. Sword blades could have one or two cutting edges, and the blades could be curved or straight, depending on how they were meant to be used. Most swords had a sharp point at the end to allow stabbing thrusts. Sword blade lengths varied greatly. The Vikings in the 800s used a sword that was about 3 feet long with a hilt that was usually held in one hand. Blades grew slightly longer during the 11th and 12th centuries. The long sword was common in the 14th through 16th centuries. It had a thinner and lighter blade than earlier swords and a long hilt that allowed the user to swing it with both hands. During the 15th century bastard swords appeared. These swords had a hilt that was short enough to be held in one hand but with a little extra space to accommodate a second hand if necessary, making them more versatile than earlier swords.

Many soldiers carried small blades called daggers in addition to their swords. A dagger had a hilt like a sword and a double-edged blade that was typically between 6 and 12 inches long. Daggers were useful as an extra stabbing weapon during hand-to-hand combat. Soldiers wore both swords and daggers in sheaths hung from their belts. Not all would-be fighters could afford swords, nor could they spend time learning the intricacies of knightly fighting. Still, there were a variety of cheaper weapons available in the medieval period. The most primitive type of weapon was a simple club, a heavy object on a handle designed to batter the enemy. Maces were blunt heavy heads mounted on long handles. They were useful for bludgeoning opponents whose armor could turn aside sword blades. The morning star was a mace with multiple points attached to its head, making it resemble a starburst. The flail was a long handle with a heavy metal ball, sometimes spiked, hanging from it on a chain. The user would swing the ball around and use centrifugal force to magnify the impact of his blows.

Medieval people occasionally fought with long sticks called quarterstaffs. Quarterstaffs were generally not lethal, but they were useful because they were cheap and easy to make and could be used both as clubs and as spears. Battle-axes were cheaper than swords. They were lighter than axes used on wood and had large, sharp blades. Battle-axes could be designed to be held in one or two hands. Some featured points on their ends so that they could be used as stabbing weapons as well. Spears and lances were useful for combat on horseback or on foot when there was a short distance between combatants. Medieval soldiers used throwing spears, or javelins, and spears mounted on longer poles, or pikes, designed to be thrust at the enemy by a stationary soldier. Knights used lances in jousting and in cavalry engagements.

Soldiers used bows and arrows throughout the medieval period. A bow consisted of a piece of wood bent into a curve and held in that position with a length of string that was affixed to each end. Bows shot arrows, which were straight sticks with points at their tips made of metal or another hard substance. Feathers attached to the end of the arrow helped it fly straight. The back end of the arrow had a notch in it. To shoot his bow, an archer would place the notch over the bowstring to hold it in place, pull back the string to increase the tension behind the arrow, and then release the string, sending the arrow flying. For much of the medieval period archers were rather lowly soldiers in armies, ranking far below the knights who fought on horseback. Nevertheless, archers were very useful for quick raids and for attacking an enemy at a distance.

The introduction of the longbow in the 13th century made archery temporarily a powerful military weapon. A longbow could range from 4 to 7 feet long and had a much stronger draw than earlier bows. This gave it a longer range and much greater strength than its predecessors. Armies used groups of longbowmen to shoot large numbers of arrows rapidly, up to 20 arrows a minute. These massed archers did not aim at particular individuals but simply fired their shots rapidly into the opposing army, counting on the number of arrows to do significant damage. The English army made great use of longbows during the Hundred Years' War, and they were a deciding factor in English victories at the battles of Crécy (1346) and Agincourt (1415). The longbow fell into disuse around 1500 as firearms became more common. Longbows were actually more effective weapons than early guns, but they were extremely difficult to use and required years of training and regular practice. Longbow archers were

Viking battle-axes and spears, Britain, ca. 840–1020 (© Museum of London)

expensive specialists, and rulers eventually decided that they were not worth the money.

The crossbow was a common projectile weapon between about 1100 and 1500. It was a small bow with a string mounted horizontally on a stock and an attached mechanism that could draw back the bow and release it when the soldier pulled a trigger. On some crossbows the string was drawn by hand; most bowstrings were too tight for this to be possible, however, so crossbows often had some sort of mechanical device such as a lever or windlass to draw the string back. Starting in the 1300s the trigger was made of metal, such as bronze, iron, or steel. Instead of arrows, crossbows fired short metal bolts. Crossbows had several advantages over ordinary bows. They were easy to use, so a crossbowman did not require lengthy training. They were also small and easy to carry. A crossbow bolt could hit an enemy with a great deal of energy, making them quite effective. Crossbowmen fought both on horseback and on foot.

Firearms arrived in Europe from Asia in the 13th or 14th century. These early guns used gunpowder to fire projectiles. They were not especially efficient or accurate, but when they hit an enemy, they could do more damage than bows or crossbows. The introduction of firearms was the main factor in the escalation of armor into heavy plate during the late medieval period. Medieval armies used some long-range artillery weapons. Catapults were devices that could hurl objects high into the air and some distance, which made them useful for getting weapons into cities or castles under siege. The objects thrown could be nearly anything, including stones, arrows, burning pitch, beehives, dead animals, and the bodies of people who had died of the Black Death. In the early medieval period armies still used the ballista, a type of catapult favored by the Romans. The trebuchet was a large, powerful, and fairly accurate counterweight catapult that was used throughout the medieval period. The culverin was an early type of cannon that appeared in France during the 1400s.

Many medieval soldiers wore armor to protect themselves from the weapons of their enemies. Soldiers who could not afford anything better might wear leather helmets and jackets that offered little protection against sharp blades and projectiles. Roman soldiers had worn solid metal plates as armor, but early medieval smiths lost the technology needed to produce wearable sheets of metal. Instead they made mail, sometimes called chain mail because it appears to be made of metal chains. Mail was a type of armor formed of interlocking metal links. It could be made into a flexible metal shirt that would ward off some blows and stabs. Although mail was fairly heavy because it was made of metal, it was considerably lighter than plate mail and allowed much more freedom of movement.

During the late medieval period smiths began adding bits of solid metal to mail to make it more impervious to blows. Sometimes they affixed numerous metal disks to the chains, similar to a fish's scales. They added larger metal pieces to the arms and legs. During the 1200s soldiers began wearing metal plates attached to leather shirts. By the 1300s armorers could make solid plates to cover the chest, neck, arms, feet, and shins. Knights continued to wear mail under these plates as protection for vulnerable joints, such as the armpits. Finally, starting in the late 14th century, knights encased themselves completely in solid metal armor with full metal helmets. Sometimes horses also wore full plate armor. The reason for this escalation of armor was the invention of better projectile weapons, including improved crossbows and early firearms. Full suits of armor could stop many projectiles, though the soldier wearing plate armor paid a heavy price in money, discomfort, and lost mobility.

Throughout the medieval period knights carried shields. A soldier would hold his shield in his left arm and use it to protect himself from blows while wielding a sword or other weapon in his right arm. A shield was also a convenient place on which to display a coat of arms, a combination of images that identified the soldier.

THE ISLAMIC WORLD
BY KIRK H. BEETZ

In the seventh century the soldiers of the Islamic world had access to weapons and armor brought from India by sea, from Axumite workshops in Yemen, from the Byzantine Empire, and from the Sassanid Empire. Each individual soldier was responsible for purchasing and maintaining his own weapons and armor. Coats of chain mail were the best armor available but were very expensive because of the painstaking work required to make and interlock the small rings of steel. The Islamic army that invaded what is now Afghanistan had more than 50,000 troops and only 350 coats of chain mail. In the era of Muhammad (ca. 570–632) most soldiers had no armor of any kind and were fortunate to have shields. Many had helmets consisting of four bars stretching from an iron rim to meet at a peak at the top, with leather on the interior of the helmet filling the gaps between the bars. Shields tended to be lightweight and small. Some Muslims took it to be a sign of courage and honor not to wear armor into battle. Husayn ibn Ali (626–80) fought without armor in the battle of Karbala in 680, during which he was martyred. Thereafter Muslim leaders who were clearly on the losing side in a war would sometimes enter their final battles without armor in order to be martyred as Husayn ibn Ali had been.

The primary weapon of the infantry was a composite bow, made by interlaying different kinds of wood and ivory to give the bow flexibility and strength where they were most needed. Masses of archers were crucial to success when Muslims left Arabia to invade the Sassanid and Byzantine empires. The principal weapon for hand-to-hand fighting was a short sword, double-edged and pointed for both hacking and thrusting. Many soldiers had only knives. Others carried javelins, iron-tipped spears, or iron maces. Warhorses were rare and well cared for. Their riders were the social elite of the Islamic world; they were men of wealth and high position in their clans or towns. They were the likeliest to have body armor, and they often carried lances as well as swords. The early Islamic army looked like a motley of colors and gear, but even though they had a ragged appearance, they were very disciplined fighters.

During the Umayyad Dynasty (661–750) felt armor for horses and soldiers was introduced. This armor was cloth of wool and fur. It was sufficient to absorb arrows shot from far away and most slashing from swords, but spear thrusts could penetrate it. Battles against the Byzantine Empire had introduced the Muslims to Greek fire, which they called *naft*. Greek fire was a blending of minerals, such as sulfur and petroleum, that could be fired from large squirt guns as if it were water. When ignited, the Greek fire clung to whatever it struck and resisted being put out by water. Had the field generalship of the Byzantines been more competent, this weapon could have turned back the tide of Muslim soldiers. As it was, it contributed to the Byzantine Empire's continuing dominance of the waters of the eastern Mediterranean because it was used to set opposing ships on fire. The military of the Umayyad Dynasty learned to make *naft*, and Muslim armies of the Near East used it through the rest of the medieval era.

The Umayyad Dynasty created a full-time professional army and built garrison towns to house troops and their dependents. Soldiers of all ranks were supplied with helmets, usually of solid iron, with a flap of chain mail that hung from the back of the helmet over the back of the neck. This flap of chain mail would remain a common feature of Islamic helmets. Helmets of the seventh to ninth centuries tended to be open faced, but some had nose guards, which were common features of helmets in enemy armies. Swords became favored for all troops for close-in fighting. Under the Umayyad Dynasty the swords were straight and long, with iron or brass hilts and handles. When not in use, a sword was held in straps so that it was slung over the soldier's back or hung at the soldier's waist.

During the ninth century soldiers fighting in eastern Iran against holdout provinces from the defunct Sassanid Empire introduced a new kind of sword to Muslim troops. These swords were made in India of a special kind of steel, now called damascened steel. The term refers to the city of Damascus in

Armor, forged steel, Turkey, 15th–16th centuries (Los Angeles County Museum of Art, The Madina Collection of Islamic Art, gift of Camilla Chandler Frost, Photograph © 2006 Museum Associates/LACMA [M.2002.1.584a-b])

Syria, where European merchants first saw steel that had been manufactured in India. Archaeologists and modern metallurgists have proposed several possibilities as to why the steel from India was very flexible and very hard. A sword made of damascened steel could bow to either side without breaking or losing strength. In addition, it held an edge so sharp and tough that 13th-century European crusaders said that when wielded by an expert swordsman, the sword could cut though steel helmets and iron chain mail; the sword could cut men in two. The likeliest reasons for the fearsome qualities of damascened swords probably came from two significant factors. One factor that the Indian metallurgists could not control was a trace of vanadium in the steel from where it was mined—about 0.003 percent vanadium. The other factor depended on the exceptionally advanced skills of the people who refined the ore. A process of heating in crucibles, hammering, and annealing repeatedly created layers of vanadium mixed with carbon nanotubes that produced the glistening swirls typical of the side of a damascened sword. This product is called wootz steel.

The swords the Muslims found in eastern Iran were curved and intended for slashing, not thrusting. A top-quality sword from India would have soft, low-carbon iron inside a casing of wootz steel; this construction gave the sword its flexibility while retaining a very sharp edge. The process of dousing in water, hammering, and repeating caused the interior iron to become denser, decreasing its volume and making the sword curve naturally. During medieval times only the swords made in Japan were superior. The scimitar eventually became the blade of choice for most Muslim soldiers during the medieval era. The best scimitars had decorations on their sides and often featured Arabic script that proclaimed the swords' best qualities.

Until about the 1190s, the era of the First Crusade, the Islamic world depended on India and Egypt for its best weapons and armor. Egyptians were especially esteemed for their chain mail, which remained very expensive. Perhaps the disadvantage of Muslim troops who faced better-armored European troops increased demand for chain mail enough for weapons and armor manufacturing industries to arise in Syria and Yemen, where Indian techniques were imitated. Although they were not rated by Islamic soldiers as highly as weapons from India, the weapons from Syria and Yemen were still valued, as were the helmets, shields, and coats of chain mail from these regions.

The use of horses outfitted in chain mail probably began in the 10th century, but only along the border with the Byzantine Empire, where Islamic horsemen faced Byzantine horsemen whose horses were commonly armored. By the 10th century Islamic armies were switching from dependence on infantry to cavalry, and outfitting war horses as well as their riders became an increasing priority because of frequent confrontations with well-armored European knights. When the invasion of the First Crusade began, the armies the crusaders faced were still too lightly armed and armored to fight pitched battles against the Europeans, and a number of battles ended in disasters. To be sure, a general failure of political leadership contributed greatly to the losses of the Muslim armies, but European horsemen were able to absorb more blows and to deliver heavier blows than could their counterparts. Adaptations to the challenges of the European horsemen included lassos, with which to rope and pull down an enemy. Islamic horsemen used lances in ways similar to the Europeans, and they still used swords, maces, spears, and bows.

It took hundreds of years for Islamic armies to retake lands lost to the crusaders. In the process they had to lay siege to walled cities and fortresses. The armies of Islam had never been good at laying siege. Their primary siege weapons were ancient ones: the catapult and the testudo, an armored device with a top under which soldiers could hide while advancing to the wall of an enemy fortification, looking somewhat like turtles. The conquest of Antioch during the First Crusade had demonstrated that just surrounding a city and starving it into submission were not always effective; by overcoming Antioch's formidable defenses with siege engines that enabled European soldiers to enter the city, the crusaders took control of Antioch before a relief army could arrive to aid the city. This siege was a challenge that the armies of medieval Islam did not fully meet; the Christian-held city of Tyre withstood two sieges by Muslim armies during the era of the great commander Saladin (1137 or 1138–93).

Although much of the Islamic world was conservative in its choices of weapons and battlefield tactics, the armies in al-Andalus strove to keep pace with enemies who had access to Europe's latest weaponry. Much of the warring against the Christian kingdoms of the north and among the many Muslim kingdoms of al-Andalus involved traversing mountains. Muslim armies used javelins, slings, bows, and crossbows to defend mountain passes, usually with success. In 1394 Granada used firearms to repel an enemy army. As the Christian kingdoms advanced deeper into al-Andalus, many Muslims and Jews fled, some to North Africa and others to Anatolia, where they may have contributed their knowledge of firearms to the armies of the Turks. Near the end of the medieval era the Ottoman Turks would learn to use canons with effectiveness against opposing fortifications.

See also ART; CLOTHING AND FOOTWEAR; CRAFTS; DEATH AND BURIAL PRACTICES; EMPIRES AND DYNASTIES; HUNTING, FISHING, AND GATHERING; METALLURGY; MILITARY; RELIGION AND COSMOLOGY; WAR AND CONQUEST.

Europe	

∼ Jean Froissart: Excerpt from "On the Hundred Years War" (1337–1453) ∼

THE BATTLE OF CRECY (1346)

The Englishmen, who were in three battles lying on the ground to rest them, as soon as they saw the Frenchmen approach, they rose upon their feet fair and easily without any haste and arranged their battles. The first, which was the prince's battle, the archers there stood in manner of a herse and the men of arms in the bottom of the battle. The earl of Northampton and the earl of Arundel with the second battle were on a wing in good order, ready to comfort the prince's battle, if need were.

(continued)

(continues)

The lords and knights of France came not to the assembly together in good order, for some came before and some came after in such haste and evil order, that one of them did trouble another. When the French king saw the Englishmen, his blood changed, and [he] said to his marshals: "Make the Genoways go on before and begin the battle in the name of God and Saint Denis." There were of the Genoways crossbows about a fifteen thousand, but they were so weary of going afoot that day a six leagues armed with their crossbows, that they said to their constables: "We be not well ordered to fight this day, for we be not in the case to do any great deed of arms: we have more need of rest." These words came to the earl of Alencon, who said: "A man is well at ease to be charged with such a sort of rascals, to be faint and fail now at most need." Also the same season there fell a great rain and a clipse with a terrible thunder, and before the rain there came flying over both battles a great number of crows for fear of the tempest coming. Then anon the air began to wax clear, and the sun to shine fair and bright, the which was right in the Frenchmen's eyes and on the Englishmen's backs. When the Genoways were assembled together and began to approach, they made a great [shout] and cry to abash the Englishmen, but they stood still and stirred not for all that: then the Genoways again the second time made another leap and a fell cry, and stept forward a little, and the Englishmen removed not one foot: thirdly, again they lept and cried, and went forth till they came within shot; then they shot fiercely with their crossbows. Then the English archers stept forth one pace and let fly their arrows so wholly [together] and so thick, that it seemed snow. When the Genoways felt the arrows piercing through heads arms and breasts, many of them cast down their crossbows and did cut their strings and returned discomfited. When the French king saw them fly away, he said: "Slay these rascals, for they shall let and trouble us without reason." Then ye should have seen the men at arms dash in among them and killed a great number of them: and ever still the Englishmen shot whereas they saw thickest press; the sharp arrows ran into the men of arms and into their horses, an many fell, horse and men, among the Genoways, and when they were down, they could not relieve again, the press was so thick that on overthrew another. And also among the Englishmen there were certain rascals that went afoot with great knives, and they went in among the men of arms, and slew and murdered many as they lay on the ground, both earls, barons, knights, and squires, whereof the king of England was after displeased, for he had rather they had been taken prisoners.

From G. C. Macauly, ed., *The Chronicles of Froissart*, trans. Lord Berners (London: Macmillan and Co., 1904).

The Islamic World

∽ Excerpt from De expugatione Terrae Sanctae per Saladinum (*The Capture of Jerusalem by Saladin, 1187*) ∽

The Holy City of Jerusalem was besieged on September 20. It was surrounded on every side by unbelievers, who shot arrows everywhere into the air. They were accompanied by frightening armaments and, with a great clamor of trumpets, they shrieked and wailed, "Hai, hai." The city was aroused by the noise and tumult of the barbarians and, for a time, they all cried out: "True and Holy Cross! Sepulchre of Jesus Christ's resurrection! Save the city of Jerusalem and its dwellers!"

The battle was then joined and both sides began courageously to fight. But since so much unhappiness was produced through sorrow and sadness, we shall not enumerate all the Turkish attacks and assemblies, by which, for two weeks, the Christians were worn down. . . . During this time it seemed that God had charge over the city, for who can say why one man who was hit died, while another wounded man escaped? Arrows fell like raindrops, so that one could not show a finger above the ramparts without being hit. There were so many wounded that all the hospitals and physicians in the city were hard put to it just to extract the missiles from their bodies. I myself was wounded in the face by an arrow which struck the bridge of my nose. The wooden shaft has been taken out, but the metal tip has remained there to this day. The inhabitants of Jerusalem fought courageously enough for a week, while the enemy settled down opposite the tower of David.

Saladin saw that he was making no progress and that as things were going he could do no damage to the city. Accordingly, he and his aides began to circle around the city and to examine the city's weak points, in search of a place where he could set up his engines without fear of the Christians and where he could more easily attack the town. . . .

The tyrant [Saladin] at once ordered the engines to be constructed and balistas to be put up. He likewise ordered olive branches and branches of other trees to be collected and piled between the city and the engines. That evening he ordered the army to take up arms and the engineers to proceed with their iron tools, so that before the Christians could do anything about it, they would all be prepared at the foot of the walls. The cruelest of tyrants also arrayed up to ten thousand armed knights with bows and lances on horseback, so that if the men of the city attempted a foray they would be blocked. He stationed another ten thousand or more men armed to the teeth with bows for shooting arrows, under cover of shields and targets. He kept the rest with himself and his lieutenants around the engines.

When everything was arranged in this fashion, at daybreak they began to break down the corner of the tower and to attack all around the walls. The archers began shooting arrows and those who were at the engines began to fire rocks in earnest.

The men of the city expected nothing of the sort and left the city walls without guard. Tired and worn out, they slept until morning, for unless the Lord watch the city, he labors in vain who guards it. When the sun had risen, those who were sleeping in the towers were startled by the noise of the barbarians. When they saw these things they were terrified and overcome with fear. Like madmen they yelled out through the city: "Hurry, men of Jerusalem! Hasten! Help! The walls have already been breached! The foreigners are entering!" Aroused, they hastened through the city as bravely as they could, but they were power less to repulse the Damascenes from the walls, either with spears, lances, arrows, stones, or with molten lead and bronze.

The Turks unceasingly hurled rocks forcefully against the ramparts. Between the walls and the outer defenses they threw rocks and the socalled Greek fire, which bums wood, stone, and whatever it touches. Everywhere the archers shot arrows without measure and without ceasing, while the others were boldly smashing the walls. . . .

The Chaldeans [Saladin and his army] fought the battle fiercely for a few days and triumphed.

From: *De expugatione Terrae Sanctae per Saladinum*, ed. Joseph Stevenson (London: Longmans, 1875); trans. James Brundage, *The Crusades: A Documentary History* (Milwaukee, Wisc.: Marquette University Press, 1962).

FURTHER READING

James Chambers, *Ancient Weapons: An Illustrated History of Their Impact* (Oxford, U.K.: ABC-CLIO, 2006).

Albert Hourani, "The Making of a World (Seventh–Tenth Century)," in his *History of the Arab Peoples* (New York: Warner Books, 1992).

John Keegan, *A History of Warfare* (New York: Alfred A. Knopf, 1994).

Robert E. Krebs and Carolyn A. Krebs, *Groundbreaking Scientific Experiments, Inventions, and Discoveries of the Ancient World* (Westport, Conn.: Greenwood Publishing Group, 2003).

Steven A. LeBlanc and Katherine E. Register, *Constant Battles: The Myth of the Peaceful, Noble Savage* (New York: St. Martin's Press, 2003).

James E. Lindsay, "Warfare and Politics," in his *Daily Life in the Medieval Islamic World* (Westport, Conn.: Greenwood Press, 2005).

John Powell, *Weapons and Warfare*, vol. 1 (Pasadena, Calif.: Salem Press, 2002).

Eduard Wagner, Zoroslav Drobna, and Jan Durdik, *Medieval Costume, Armour, and Weapons* (Mineola, N.Y.: Dover, 2000).

Weapon: A Visual History of Arms and Armor (New York: DK Publishing, 2006).

Weapons: An International Encyclopedia From 5000 B.C. to 2000 A.D. (New York: St. Martin's Griffin, 2007)

▶ weights and measures

INTRODUCTION

One of the important differences between the medieval world and the modern one may be found in weights and measures. In most cultures of the present, people who buy something that is supposed to be an inch in diameter or weigh 10 pounds know what they are getting and can measure or weigh their purchases to accurately test them. Just imagine considering the purchase of a tool set and not having the matching tools of various sets be of uniform size, instead being the sizes that were determined by each craftsperson who worked on manufacturing the tools. This would make wrenches unusable; how would any home mechanic repair an automobile engine if the tools and the automobile parts did not mesh? But in almost the entire medieval world, standard weights and measures either did not exist or, when a government set standards, the standards were ignored.

An industrial economy with mass production would be almost unattainable without standard weights and measures, and their absence in medieval cultures meant that achieving a modern-style economy was impossible. This did not stop political leaders with foresight from trying to take the step that could have transformed their economies into fully consumer-based economic engines. Certainly, the Chinese tried repeatedly to make the leap, from the short-lived Qin Dynasty (221–206 B.C.E.) all the way through the Ming Dynasty (1368–1644). Instituting universal standards for weights and measures aided China greatly in its industrial development; its craftspeople were able to mass-produce metal and ceramic household goods in factories, thereby not only satisfying the needs of consumers but also creating employment for semiskilled or unskilled workers who did not need to have the experienced eye and skills of a craftsperson in order to help produce goods. Marketplaces were easier to regulate with universal weights and measures in place. But China had difficulty maintaining standardized weights and measures. Wars and rebellions overthrew Chinese governments, and often China was divided in several nations. People who lived outside cities, in places where government regulators had trouble reaching them, tended to prefer their local ways of judging a length or a weight.

During the medieval era several governments recognized the value of standardized weights and measures for their marketplaces. Such weights and measures made taxing people's transactions easier. They increased confidence of both local and foreign traders in the honesty of the marketplace, which in turn inspired more commerce in the marketplace. The empires of Mali and Songhai of western Africa tried to impose standardization but met with determined resistance among the rural peoples of their territories, who clung to their traditional ways of weighing and measuring. The city-states of East Africa were somewhat more successful, although some of their measures remained vague; their prosperity depended on international trade, and at least some broadly recognized that measures were necessary to foster such trade. The Islamic world saw many efforts to standardize weights and measures,

which usually were at least partly unsuccessful because the Islamic world encompassed many diverse local cultures in which people wished to retain their comfortable old ways of weighing and measuring. Even so, the Islamic world did manage to introduce a system of weights that proved valuable from the Near East to sub-Saharan Africa, even though the standards of the system varied somewhat from time to time and place to place.

So how did most medieval people weigh and measure things? The approaches to weighing and measuring had logic to them, despite being vague. People used body parts and the limits of human movement to create loose ways of quantifying their work. The most common measures were spans, cubits, feet, and paces. A span was usually the width of a palm; a cubit was typically the length from the elbow to the tip of the outstretched middle finger; the foot was the length of a person's foot; the pace was the length of a person's stride. Some cultures ignored weighing altogether, instead using volume to measure both liquids and solids. This worked for wine and grains but was unsuitable for solids such as silver. Sometimes a person had to use a trained eye or just lift up goods in order to judge their weight. Such ways of measuring would be maddeningly imprecise for many modern peoples, but for people living in villages and towns, often remote from cities, such ways of measuring could be satisfactory. For instance, if a house were being built with local labor, its size relative to other houses would not be as important as that its own measurements be made by a single craftsperson, perhaps the chief builder, whose feet would be used for measuring all posts, whose hands would be used for measuring all windows, and so on.

AFRICA

BY KIRK H. BEETZ

The peoples of Africa had a multitude of systems of weights and measures. Sometimes weights and measures varied for every village in a region. Most medieval African cultures had weights and measures, but modern scholars usually do not know exactly how these systems compare to modern systems of measurement or even what words were used for specific weights and measures.

It seems that for all African cultures of medieval times, body parts served as the inspirations for measurements. Archaeologists refer to measurements for length and distance as the span, the foot, the cubit, and the pace. A span was the distance across a palm of a hand. This measure was often divided into fingers, often meaning the distance between thumb and forefinger. Such short measurements were used for small manufactured objects, such as wooden images, ivory carvings, and small household goods. In central Africa a post used for building a house was often measured by someone walking next to the post on the ground, heel to toe, giving its length in feet; sometimes the post would be measured in paces, the distance of a person's stride from heel to heel.

Cubits were universally used for measuring textiles, although the definition of a cubit and its actual length varied. In general, a cubit was the distance from a person's elbow to the tip of his or her outstretched finger. In East Africa a cubit was the length from a buyer's elbow to the tip of the middle finger, and buyers often brought long-armed friends with them to market to buy cloth. In Benin the cubit was determined by the length from the seller's elbow to the tip of the middle finger, and consequently the sellers with the longest arms did the most business. Some cultures in western and central Africa used three variations of cubits. A short-armed person's cubit was the length from the elbow to the tip of the outstretched middle finger plus an additional fold back of cloth on the middle finger. An average-armed person would have the standard cubit. A long-armed person would have a cubit ending at one of the knuckles of the middle finger. Even with these modifications of the cubit, sellers who tried to cheat customers on lengths were a persistent problem, even in societies with market inspectors.

A fundamental problem with all these measurements of length is that they were approximations. They worked satisfactorily in many cultures composed of independent villages, each village having people with the basic skills necessary for homebuilding, farming, smithing, and carpentry. In a large trading society with greater specialization of crafts, the absence of universally standard weights and measures could cause difficulties. For example, if a skilled craftsperson in one town made a window frame for a purchaser in another town, the frame might not fit the window opening. This chronic problem was not fully solved in medieval Africa, although some governments periodically tried to impose standardized weights and measures throughout their lands. With much determination, Africans resisted efforts to modify their traditional ways of weighing and measuring; thus, only in the weighing of gold and salt did established standard weights take hold.

Of all the commodities of medieval Africa, gold may have been most in demand wherever there were urban areas. Controlling the trade in gold was part of the business of kingdoms and empires because their economies depended on gold for purchasing goods from traders. The western African empires of Ghana, Mali, and Songhai were the most famous of all gold-trading societies, but Ethiopia and the East African city-states also traded large quantities of gold. In western Africa governments distinguished between two types of gold:

gold dust and solid gold. Gold dust was used for everyday trading in markets, whereas solid gold belonged exclusively to the central government. The government would sometimes render gold nuggets into powder for use in public trading.

Most of these African cultures lacked scales for weighing objects. In general, weight was determined by holding two different objects, one on each outstretched palm, and judging their relative weights. Studies of people of the Congo River area show that they were very good at making such judgments as well as at judging by eye alone the volume of grain. Even so, such fuzzy measurements were inadequate for assuring traders that they were getting their full value in gold for their goods. The Mali and Songhai empires turned to Islamic weights and measures to help them, with the mithqal becoming the most important unit of measurement. The mithqal filtered out of the empires of western Africa through most of central Africa, and it was the primary unit for measuring gold in west Africa and central Africa when the Portuguese began arriving on the west coast of Africa.

Exactly how the mithqal of gold dust was determined by medieval Africans is not known for certain. In the case of Mali and probably Songhai as well, a mithqal probably followed the practice in the Islamic world that 1 mithqal equaled one golden dinar, a coin. The weight of a mithqal of gold dust

Weight for measuring gold dust, Ghana, Côte d'Ivoire, as early as the 15th century (National Museum of African Art, Smithsonian Institution, Photograph by Franko Khoury, Gift of Philip L. Ravenhill in memory of Sylvia H. Williams, 96-42-1.6)

could be determined by comparing it to the weight of a dinar, either a golden coin or an object made to equal a dinar's weight, such as glass coins made in the Islamic world for measuring against real coins. An animal skin could be filled with gold dust, sealed by a market official, and marked with a symbol denoting its value in mithqals. Even in societies that were otherwise nonliterate, such symbols were well understood. During the 15th century and perhaps earlier, people in the Niger River region developed another practice that resulted in the production of frequently charming artifacts: brass or bronze figurines or geometrical images. These are best known from the Asante of the 17th century and later but were apparently in circulation before the Asante culture became prominent. Shaped like people, animals, plants, and household objects, or in symbolic patterns, these generally came in three sizes: A large mithqal was about 0.15 ounces, a small mithqal was about 0.12 ounces, and an ackie was about 0.06 ounces. Every trader carried a set of 10 to 12 of these weights, which could be compared with the weights of customers to determine how much gold was involved in a transaction.

The region of medieval Africa that developed the most refined system of measurements was probably East Africa, whose city-states depended on international trade for their survival and therefore would wish for measurements that everyone could understand. Despite the influence of Islam on the cities, local African measurements seem to have become the basis for the East African measuring system, also sometimes called the Swahili system. The demands of trade called for standardized weights. In much of Africa the terminology for weight varied with the product being weighed. That is, the terms for weight varied depending on whether rice, wheat, or some other grain was being weighed. Examples of how different units of measurement could be used for different products may be found in the practices of the Ganda in modern-day Uganda. For them, salt was measured by lubya, possibly 30 pounds or more; sweet potatoes were measured by lutata, perhaps 30 pounds; and coffee was measured by kiribwa, perhaps 20 pounds. Gandans used gourds to measure liquids.

In East Africa the weights were wakia, about 1 ounce; ratli, 16 wakia; and frasila, 36 ratli. Measuring volume was somewhat more complex; these units of measure included kibaba, about 1 pint; kisaga, 2 kibaba; and pishi, 2 kisaga. In addition were two methods for measuring grain: kibaba cha mfuto, which was a level kibaba, and kibaba cha tele, which was a heaped kibaba. Measuring length had similar complications: Shibiri was 1 span, mkono was 2 shibiri, and pima was 4 mkono. For length of textiles the mkono mkonde was a short cubit, perhaps less the middle finger, and the mkono mkamili was a full cubit. These two lengths were determined by the buyer's arm.

Even though it was an ancient civilization, Ethiopia does not seem to have developed the kind of standardized system used in the East African city-states or attempted by the western African empires of Mali and Songhai. Axum, the kingdom that gave rise to Ethiopia, had developed a standardized system for its coinage by the medieval era. The values of its coins were determined by weight. The most important coin was gold and contained from 0.09 to 0.10 ounces of gold. Silver coins contained from 0.74 to 0.90 ounces of silver. Axum seems to have had market inspectors, suggesting that it had standards for measuring goods, but those standards await more archaeological discoveries. Standardized weights and measures would have been employed mostly in towns and cities, where most of Axum's coins were used. Rural areas would have used local traditional ways of weighing and measuring.

Ethiopia used imprecise measures throughout the medieval era. For short lengths Ethiopians used the span of a palm, four fingers, a finger joint, and the width of a finger. Longer lengths were measured in cubits and fathoms; fathoms were about two arm lengths. For long distances, measurements were expressed in days of travel. For example, the city of Axum was six days' travel from Adulis, the kingdom's main port city. An Ethiopian acre was the area that could be plowed in a day by a farmer using two yoked oxen. Ethiopians did not use weight to measure grain or liquids. Small units of volume were mouthful, handful, and armful, with large units measured as mule loads. Made to hold a particular one of these measurements were baskets, horns, sewn skins, and bowls of gourds, wood, or clay.

THE AMERICAS
Michael J. O'Neal

The existence of a system of weights and measures depends, first, on the development of a mathematical system. Measuring land, weighing commodities, and the like require a system of counting and manipulating numbers, in particular, through multiplication and division. Just as a modern yard is divisible into 3 feet and a foot is divisible into 12 inches (and the reverse: an inch multiplied by 12 equals a foot, and so on), so any meaningful system of measurement depends on small units that make up larger units, which in turn make up yet larger units. Mathematicians typically refer to this process as metrology, the science of measurement and the mathematics of measurement.

Second, the existence of a system of measurement presupposes that the culture that produces it has a reason for having it. Typically, in the Americas before the Europeans arrived, there would have been at least three reasons for measuring and weighing. One was to allocate land and by extension to compute taxes, usually in the form of a percentage of a crop, that a farmer owed to a ruler. But such cultures as the Inuit of the sub-Arctic regions of North America or the numerous Indian nations that inhabited most of North and South America did not allocate land. Land was not regarded as private property; rather, to the extent that it was "owned," it was owned communally, often in the name of a ruler. This would have been particularly true of groups that continued to live primarily by hunting, fishing, and gathering. As might be expected, these groups did not have a system for measuring lengths, nor did they have an understanding of geometry that would have allowed the calculation of the size of a parcel of land, other than in the most general sense.

A second reason for developing a system of measurement would be to underpin the work of engineers and builders. While many bands built such structures as mounds, shelters, and grain-storage facilities, they did not create monumental architecture according to strict and precise specifications. Buildings tended to be improvised, not engineered. Such was not the case, though, with the Maya of Mesoamerica and the Inca of South America, who did design monumental architecture based on a system of measurement that enabled builders and engineers to construct buildings of remarkable symmetry and balance.

A third reason for having a system of weights and measures is to facilitate trade. Trading goods with other people is easier if there is a common system of measurement—if traders can agree on the value of, say, an ounce of gold or a bolt of cloth. But the peoples of North America or the Amazon rain forest, in particular, did not take part in complex trading networks. To the extent that they traded with other people, trade was conducted strictly by barter, where items were traded one at a time, or perhaps in small clusters. No sophisticated system of weights was needed to trade, for example, a particular basket of corn for something of equivalent value.

Since these reasons did not apply to them, many American groups did not have systems of weights and measures that extended beyond counting, or perhaps designating a longer unit of distance, such as the distance that a person could walk in a day. Like their ancient ancestors, they probably used body parts—the hand span, the knuckle, the length of an arm, a stride—to indicate relative lengths, and any items that needed it could be weighed in comparison to stones or other objects. The emphasis was on the particular, not the general.

This lack of a mathematics of measurement did not apply universally, however. The Aztec, for example, had a complex, sophisticated culture that teemed with economic activity. Records of land ownership were kept, with each parcel designated and its area measured. The basic unit of measurement was the quahuitl, a unit about 8 feet in length. Additionally,

Aztec cities featured markets that were often attended by thousands of people. Inspectors mingled with the crowd to ensure that goods were being sold at the proper prices (based not on currency but on units of exchange determined by the value of cloth and cacao beans). These inspectors also ensured that scales and measuring devices were accurate. Any vendor guilty of violating the laws could be fined. Those guilty of serious violations could be beaten to death in the middle of the marketplace. The Maya, too, had complex trade networks that required the ability to weigh commodities.

One of the primary features of Mayan measurement systems is that they seemed to be based on relative measures rather than absolute values. Note that the plural *systems* is accurate, for the surviving evidence shows that there was no single, uniform measurement system throughout the vast Mayan territories. Rather, each city, with its own set of builders, engineers, and land surveyors, applied its own system to its own building and measurement projects. Measurements taken of rooms, wall thicknesses, and the like show that while the system used for a specific building was internally consistent, and usually consistent with other buildings in the community, it differed in small ways from the system used in other locales. This seems strange in modern life where a foot, yard, meter, or any other unit of measurement is always precisely the same. However, in these medieval societies, such uniformity was not necessary. Building materials, for example, were found locally rather than shipped in from elsewhere, hence it sufficed that people in the region agreed on a unit of measurement. In Germany the length of a foot was not decided on until the 19th century, so the Mayan system is not all that unusual.

Despite the local nature of measurements, some generalizations can be made. The Maya appear to have used a system of measurement based on the rod, which was almost 58 inches in length. The rod was divided into either 16 "rules," each divided in turn into 9 "marks" (xóot), or 9 rules divided into 16 marks. The result either way was 144 marks in a rod. This measurement was handy because 144 equals 12 squared. Furthermore, the use of a number such as 16 was useful because 16 can be progressively divided in half, into 8, then 4, then 2, then 1. Similarly, 9 can be conveniently divided into thirds. Note that the square root of 9 is 3, the square root of 16 is 4, and 4 times 3 is 12, the square root of 144. All of these correspondences and mathematical regularities suggest that Mayan builders, as well as land surveyors and others who needed to measure, emphasized the notion of uniform divisibility rather than absolute length.

Like premodern cultures the world over, the Maya of the medieval period used body parts as a basis for measurement. On the Yucatán Peninsula, the oc was a foot, roughly equiva-

THE SPANISH CONQUISTADORES AND UNITS OF MEASUREMENT

Much of what modern historians know about the cultures of Mesoamerica and South America before Europeans arrived is based on chronicles and records produced by the Spanish, usually written in the 1500s after the Spanish had conquered the people in these regions. Many of these documents were written by Spanish priests. Unfortunately, the Spanish destroyed nearly all written materials the Aztec, the Inca, and other peoples had produced. They did this for religious reasons primarily. They wanted to eradicate all elements of indigenous culture that supported the people's religious beliefs so that they could then convert the conquered peoples to Christianity more easily.

Although the various Spanish accounts, chronicles, and histories are written entirely from a Spanish perspective, these works nevertheless provide scholars with insights about the Inca. One of these Spanish writers was Pedro de Cieza de León (1518–60), whose three-part *Chronicle of Peru* has been invaluable to historians. Cieza was able to publish only the first part of his monumental work before he died. Part 3, which details Inca life, was published after his death. Cieza took note of units of weight and measurement that the Inca used, assigning Spanish names to them. Thus, according to Cieza, there was a unit of weight he called the arroba equal to about 25.3 pounds; a larger unit of weight was the quintal, equal to about 101.5 pounds. A fanega was equivalent to about 1.5 bushels, and a carga equaled about 3 to 4 fanegas. For vertical measurements, the Inca used the estado, about 5.5 feet. For longer measurements, the legua, or league, was about 3.5 miles.

Other chroniclers provided similar information. In two works, the *General History of Peru, Origins and Descent of the Inca* (1590–1600) and the similarly titled *General History of Peru* (1605), a priest named Fray Martin de Murúa recorded many details of Inca life. According to his account, the Inca used the thatki, a unit of length equal to about a pace, and there were 6,000 thatki in a tupu. A tupu, though, was a unit of area, not length, so there is an inconsistency that has not been resolved but that is indicative of the difficulties of pinning down these units.

lent to a person's foot, or 16 marks. The chekoc was the footstep, approximately equivalent to a modern yard. A kab was a hand span (9 marks), and the zap or zapal was the distance of outstretched arms. The zapalche, or zap stick, was a common length for a walking cane, which was also used in land measurement.

Archaeological evidence, as well as testimony from 16th-century Spanish conquerors, strongly suggests that the Mesoamericans did not use scales nor did they have a system of weights. Rather, commodities were measured by volume. The Maya used such loose volume measurements as the armload, the fistful, and the load, consisting of a volume of corn, although sets of bowls with progressively descending measurements have been found that suggest, but do not prove conclusively, that they were used in measuring volumes of goods. Some evidence also suggests that the Maya could have used stone weights for measuring commodities.

The later Aztec also measured commodities largely by volume rather than weight. They employed a wooden box called a *quauhchiaquihuitl*, which was divided into 12 parts and used to measure goods such as grain. Additionally, they used sets of jars to measure liquids and cups, roughly equivalent to the modern ounce, to measure gold tribute payments. While surviving buildings allow archaeologists to take measurements and draw inferences about systems of measure-

ment, there is no corresponding way to make inferences about weights. Most of the Mayan written materials, along with those of the Aztec, were destroyed by the Spanish conquerors, so archaeologists continue to debate these matters because the historical record is almost entirely gone.

The Inca, like the Maya, relied more on relative rather than absolute measurements. They, too, used body parts for shorter measurements; the rok'ana, for instance, was about the length of a finger, the k'apa was just under 8 inches, or a hand span; the khococ was about 17 inches, perhaps the length of a forearm; and the rikra was about 5.3 feet, about the height of a person. Longer units, however, were based more on time (for example, the time that it took to walk a certain distance) rather than on a unit of linear measure. For land measurement, the tupu (or topo) was used. Although it remains uncertain what the measurement of a tupu was, it was probably in the range of 300 by 150 feet, or about one-eighth of an acre.

ASIA AND THE PACIFIC
BY KENNETH HALL

The standardization of weights and measures in Asia's medieval age was the result of the appearance of more complexly interdependent societies and economies. Regularization of land measurements that defined property boundaries became necessary when marketplace and governmental activity required greater accuracy regarding income measurement and land-use rights. Governments required taxation, which was more efficiently collected when there was a system of standardized weights and measures. The establishment and regulation of weight and liquid standards and the equitable rates of exchanges of other commodities reflected the increasing volume and greater complexity of marketplace exchanges.

The weights and measures of medieval China were initially set by the Qin Dynasty (221–206 B.C.E.) by standardizing traditional weight and measure units derived from measurements of the human body. The shih unit of weight was equivalent to 132 pounds. The jin, which was roughly equivalent to a pound, was the normal Chinese weight standard, equaling 16 liang; a liang was 24 zhu. The dan unit of mass was associated with measurements of rice. A dan was equal to 10 dou (a peck), and a dou equaled 10 sheng (roughly a liquid quart). In the early records Chinese official's salaries were called dan, since they were paid in units of rice.

Chinese units of length included the cun (roughly 1 inch), the chi (9.8 inches), and the zhang (9.8 feet). Different professions had different standards of length, for example, a carpenter length, a mason length, and a tailor length. Another vital measurement of length was the bolt (pi) of cloth, equal to 4 zhang, which was frequently how peasants were required to pay taxes on their houses (in bolts of silk). The Chinese distance standard, a li, was roughly 1,640 feet. The chi was the basic historical unit of distance, set at 360 paces (bu, or roughly 1,895 feet) by the Qin Dynasty, revised to 1,364 feet by the Han Dynasty, and to 1,060 feet by the Tang Dynasty. The Chinese thought of 10,000 as being "very many."

Land measurements were calculated in mou, which fluctuated according to regional tradition from 0.2 to 0.3 acres. During the medieval era Chinese measurements of liquids and grains were further standardized and achieved greater accuracy through the use of vessels that were defined by their similar weight and pitch. When struck, these vessels produced a uniform pitch according to the weight or volume of their contents.

Japanese and Korean weights and measures were established in the eighth century, based on those then common in Tang China (618–906). The basic unit of length in Japan was the shaku, as demonstrated in a 1-shaku standard ruler displayed in a Nara temple dating to this era. One shaku equaled 0.33 yards, 10 sun, and 100 bu. A cho was 60 ken (1.9 yards) and 360 shaku. A jo was equal to 3.3 yards: 6 shaku equaled 1 ken; 10 shaku equaled 1 jo. The ken was the architectural standard, the measure of the distance between the support poles of a house (about 6 feet). Jo, the equivalent of a tatami mat (used as floor covering), was the vital standard for the measurement of a room.

Japan's volume units were measured in go, equal to 100 shaku (about 0.01 liquid quart and 1.6 dry quarts); 10 go equaled a sho (1.9 liquid quarts and about 7 dry quarts); 10 sho equaled 1 to. A koku (goku) was 10 to, or about 58 liquid gallons or 50 dry gallons. Rice measurements were done in koku, roughly equal to 5 bushels of rice or 160 dry quarts. Koku yields of rice fields were important in determining the income potentials of lands subject to a samurai lord's authority.

Weight was expressed in momme units, equaling 0.1,323 ounce; 160 momme equaled 1 kin (1.3 pounds), which was just larger than a Chinese jin; 1,000 momme equaled 1 kan or 1 kamme (8.25 pounds). Distance was measured in cho, equal to 0.068 miles; 30 cho equaled 2.44 miles. Medieval-era Japanese modified the Chinese standard li to a ri, measuring 36 cho, equal to 2.6 miles. Land was measured in tan (0.2 acre), which equaled 10 se or 300 tsubo. A cho of land equaled 10 tan.

Korean measurements of length included the pun, equal to 0.1 inch; chi, 1 inch; cha, 11.8 inches; and kan, 70.9 inches. The Koreans adopted the Tang li of 1,060 feet as a measurement of distance traveled. Korean weight measures were the pun (0.0075 ounces), ton (0.075 ounces), nyang (0.75 ounces), kun (1.2 pounds), and kwan (8.3 pounds). Volume measurement standards were the hop (0.32 pints), toe (3.2 pints), mal (3.96 gallons), and som (39.6 gallons).

India and Southeast Asia used a variety of regional weight and measurement standards during the medieval era. As in east Asia, concern for measurement standards was related to increased marketplace activity, the need to define local income rights in increasingly hierarchical societies, and the need to determine appropriate rates of taxation payable to new centralizing governments. Indian and Southeast Asian records commonly address standards of gold; liquid and grain measures that quantified local production and marketplace exchanges; and units of land and land use (dry land, wet land, and cultivated and uncultivated lands) as the basis for establishing property rights, validating land transfers, and taxation.

A representative inscription dated 1236 from what is now Myanmar demonstrates the prevailing local use of a silver standard, the klyap, which referred to silver ingots that were weighed and given at each transaction, as the local basis of measurement. This inscription recounted the expenses of the local Buddhist temple, quoted in the marketplace standards: At that time five cows were purchased for 20 klyap, a quantity of toddy juice (coconut liquor) for five klyap, 248 tanale of milk for 25 klyap, 1,350 betel nuts for two klyap, four tan (bushels) of paddy rice for two klyap, and a white cloth for one klyap.

As trade in Southeast Asia became more important, the countries of the region tended to adopt international measures common to their chief trading partners. Burma, Thailand, and Cambodia tended to use Indian standards, while Vietnam and the kingdoms of Indonesia used Chinese standards. In Indonesia, in particular, these were retained even after the spread of Islam.

Polynesia lacked a sophisticated system of weights and measures in the Middle Ages, probably owing to the relatively low volume of trade in the area. Dry and wet measures were taken by using any handy familiar vessel as a temporary standard—a cumbersome but relatively common practice in many isolated areas in the Middle Ages. The basic unit of measure was the fathom (*etaeta* in the Tahitian dialect) or span between the fingers with the arms held outstretched. Large lengths (as in rope making) were reckoned in umi of 10 fathoms. Smaller lengths were just called remnants (*tapê*). Distances were reckoned in the time it took to walk or sail them. Time was calculated according to the rising and falling tides. The passage of time was reckoned in nights rather than days, probably because a lunar calendar was in use.

Steelyard weight, an example of bronze weights that were slid along a balance arm until they counterbalanced the object being weighed, Britain, 13th century (© Museum of London)

EUROPE

BY BRADLEY A. SKEEN

The metric system of measurement now standard throughout the world was devised during the French Revolution and did not exist during the Middle Ages. The so-called English system of measurement still used in the United States in the form of modern U.S. Customary Units was also standardized in modern times to make it suitable for industrial use and so has only a tenuous connection with medieval systems of measurement. What existed during the Middle Ages was an incredible confusion of different standards of weights and measures that might vary among locations within a few miles of one another because of different jurisdictions or just different traditions and might vary again from profession to profession.

Precise measurements are needed to facilitate the trade of goods and in building and manufacturing. The most common measurements are based on the human body—that is, on the body of the person making the measurement. They are very imprecise and not of much use to anyone else because they are not standardized. These include the finger (width), the palm (the length usually from the middle finger tip to the base of the palm), the span or hand (the width of the palm), and the cubit (the length from the tip of the middle finger to the elbow). Although one might logically measure all lengths in the same units or system of units, this was not the case in practice. Different systems of measurement were created for different uses. The hand- and arm-based measures were usually applied to dimensions of objects. Measurement of distances over which one walked were reckoned in feet. The unit was the pace; that is, the distance between the spot where one foot rested on the ground while taking a step and the place that it came down on the ground again after a second step. It was convenient to measure longer distances in units of 1,000 paces (4,850 feet, after the Romans set 1 pace as the equivalent of 4.85 feet), which became known in the Middle Ages as a mile from the Latin word *mille* for "thousand." Instead of miles, leagues were used to measure long distances. In England a league was 7,500 feet, and in France it was 10,000 feet (bearing in mind that the feet in question were not equal in length either).

Thanks to the political unity of the Roman Empire, the Romans had been able to establish some order on basic measurements, fixing standard lengths for each unit involved (although archaeologists have discovered that variation continued in practice), at least in the Western Roman Empire. In the Eastern Roman Empire the Romans had been able to standardize and impose a combination of the old Greek Attic and Olympian systems, which continued to be used into Byzantine times.

Once the Roman Empire collapsed, all practical possibility of standardization disappeared. Individual merchants, stewards, carpenters, and other professionals whose work involved units of measure were cut off from precise knowledge of the old standards and left to devise their own standards and systems. For instance, the city of Paris had its own foot, as did royal officials in England and every city in the Rhineland and Flanders. Merchants from these areas constantly had to convert units when trading with one another. The modern standard foot is 12 inches long, but medieval feet could vary from a little under 10 inches to almost 16 inches. Medieval government officials were aware of the difficulties produced by this confusion of systems and sometimes made attempts to standardize matters. For instance, a new standard foot was based on the actual measurement of Charlemagne's foot (r. 800–14), and later Henry I of England (r. 1100–35) had the distance from the tip of his nose to his thumb measured to fix the yard. At one point the length of the French foot changed with each new monarch. How anyone could have thought such chaotic changing of basic units of measurement would help matters is difficult to see, but it was done because it was traditional. Not only was it traditional, officials for the most part were powerless to enforce any standards even among their own subjects (there was far too little governmental infrastructure to allow a corps of inspectors to be employed), and there was no international body capable of standardizing measures on a European-wide basis.

Despite the lack of standardization, new units of measure were introduced in the Middle Ages. The yard was originally used to measure the volume of large vats by noting the depth of the liquid stored inside and was only later fixed at 3 feet to the yard. The rod (later fixed at 6 feet) was established by Charlemagne's court to measure the dimensions of parcels of land. The fathom, used by sailors and boatmen to measure the depth of waters they navigated, although later also fixed at six feet, was originally the length between the fingertips on the right and left hands when the arms were stretched out. The nautical mile was a length of rope containing 1,000 knots tied at intervals that might be standardized within a given rope but might vary considerably between different sailing traditions (Portuguese or Venetian, for instance). This device was originally used to measure the speed of a ship in the water and only later did it become a measure of distance.

An example from the very end of the Middle Ages of the confusion produced by the lack of standardization had the most profound consequences for the history of the world. Christopher Columbus (1451–1506) had read a Latin translation of a book by the Arab astronomer Alfraganus (d. after 861) in which he very carefully measured the physical distance represented by 1 degree of longitude. The answer Alfraganus obtained was that 1 degree of longitude on the equator covered 56⅔ miles in his system. Reading this gave Columbus the impression that a journey from Portugal to Japan (whose longitudinal positions were approximately known), expressed in modern terms, would be less than 3,100 miles.

It happens that the actual distance from Portugal to the West Indies is about 3,100 miles, but the distance to Japan is nearly 12,420 miles—a distance Columbus's small ships could never have covered without reprovisioning. So, except for the happy accident of discovering the Americas, Columbus's voyage would have been doomed, as most experts at the time thought it was. How did Columbus make this mistake? He failed to make a conversion. He was thinking in terms of the Italian nautical mile, which was much shorter than the Arabic miles Alfraganus used. This mistake led Columbus to miscalculate the distance. If he had understood that he was dealing with different units of distance and had made the conversion accurately, he might well never have sailed. If Alfraganus's calculation is converted into modern units, by the way, he was correct to within 1.2 miles of the actual figure of 68.9 miles.

Volume was originally measured by filling a receptacle with small seeds. A merchant determined whether his vessels were the same size as those of the merchant he was trading with by filling one of his own with seeds (or water) and pouring them into one of his trading partner's vessels. A unit of measure in this system was called the carat: one carob seed. Yet the carat soon shifted from a measure of volume to one of weight, and, as usual, there was no way to standardize it. The measurements of weight and volume were, if anything, more confused than those of length and distance. Besides the lack of standardization, another problem was the use of entirely different systems of measurement by different types of merchants. Cloth and wool, for instance, were both sold by weight, but cloth sellers and wool sellers used entirely different systems of weighing their goods. Yet another problem had been recognized as far back as the time of the Hebrew Bible in which the prophets complain that merchants and landowners routinely used crooked scales to cheat farmers and other customers in order to increase their own profit. The validity of this complaint has been confirmed archaeologically for the Middle Ages as well as antiquity. Scales used in marketplaces (as opposed to those used by a textile maker to measure the ingredients of dye stuffs, for instance) almost always vary from the true weights they were supposed to measure.

THE ISLAMIC WORLD
by Amy Hackney Blackwell

Medieval Muslims were capable of very accurate measurements. Precise measurements and calculations allowed them to build mosques with enormous domes, construct globes depicting the earth, and make numerous astronomical discoveries. Islamic merchants paid close attention to the details of their transactions, measuring out precise amounts of their products when making sales. At the same time, however, for many people, measurements did not need to be especially precise. It did not matter to them how Muslims in another country measured lengths or weights as long as everyone in their locality agreed on standards.

Weights and measures in the medieval world were far from standard. Although people throughout the Islamic region used similar measurements, often with similar names, the actual values of these measurements varied from time to time and place to place. Historians attempting to discern ancient and medieval measurements are often frustrated by the fact that these values were not consistent. Medieval systems of measurement evolved from ancient ones. The Islamic system developed out of existing Persian, Greek, and Roman systems.

The basic length measurement was the foot, which roughly corresponded to the Western foot. This measurement was originally made by placing a person's foot against the object being measured, but this method presented obvious problems of standardization. Once people began using

Weight, mold-pressed glass, eastern Mediterranean, seventh or eighth century (Los Angeles County Museum of Art, The Madina Collection of Islamic Art, gift of Camilla Chandler Frost, Photograph © 2006 Museum Associates/LACMA [M.2002.1.471])

sticks to measure lengths, the foot was standardized at about 12.6 inches. This foot then served as the basis for other measures. An arsh was between 1.5 and 2 Arabic feet. A dirha was about a cubit, or the length of a forearm. An orgye was 6 Arabic feet. A seir, which corresponded to the Latin stadium, was 600 Arabic feet. A farasakh was 18,000 Arabic feet, or about 3 to 4 miles, depending on the size of the foot. On the smaller end of the spectrum, a cabda was one-fourth of an Arabic foot, and an assba was 1/16th of an Arabic foot, or about the length of a finger.

Different places used different names and standards for their measurements. In Baghdad during the ninth and 10th centuries a unit called the habl was about 43 yards long, and 250 habl were equal to about 11,000 yards. One mil was equal to about 2,020 yards. A djarib was equivalent to a square habl, or about 1,900 square yards. Contemporary scholars computed that Bagdhad's total area at the time was about 43,750 djarib.

To provide standards in weights and volumes, towns, merchants, and anyone else who was concerned about weights would own weights of a standard size and weight. Most standard weights were made of glass or bronze, though during the Fatimid era (909–1171) some weights were made of lead. Historians have found some bronze weights in Egypt, many of them shaped like barrels with smooth sides or like octagons with faceted sides. These were similar in shape to contemporary Byzantine weights. Many weights were made with a small punch mark on one side bearing a legend of a weight's value, the name of the current ruler, and a guarantee. These standard weights could vary depending on the commodity being measured; for example, salt might be weighed against one standard, while wheat might be weighed against another. Standard sizes included 1 dirhem, 2 dirhems, 10 dirhems, and 1 ratl.

Many Arabic weights were made of glass, often shaped like coins. Governments maintained standards in weights and measures and in coinage, and often there was considerable overlap between the names and values of weights and coins. Glass coin weights were small, round, and flat with Arabic inscriptions on either side. Modern historians who unearthed medieval coin weights at first thought that they were indeed money but later realized that they were weights. These weights did, in fact, sometimes function as small change between the 10th and 13th centuries, especially when silver was in short supply.

Many Islamic measurements corresponded to earlier Greek and Latin units of measure. For example, the dirhem was a unit of weight in the Middle East. The dirham was also a coin. Historians have suggested that the names *dirhem* and *dirham* came from the ancient Greek coins and units of weight called "drachmas." The dirhem varied in weight by time and place. During economic depressions throughout the medieval period the value of the dirhem was debased, to less than 0.10 ounces. In some areas the dirhem was defined by the weights of seeds. In medieval Egypt a dirhem weighed as much as 60 husked barley seeds.

The awqiyyah, or uqiya, was a unit of weight throughout the Islamic world. It corresponded to the ounce, or uncia in Latin. Its value varied by time and place; it usually weighed about 1 ounce, though it could weigh over 2 pounds. There were 12 uqiyah to a pound. The pound weight was called a ratl in Arabic. It weighed 128 dirhems, or about 14.5 ounces, though this weight varied; historians have reported values for the ratl ranging from less than 1 pound to over 4 pounds. When a ratl weighed 14.5 ounces, an uqiya weighed about 1.2 ounces.

Weight measures were often defined by practical everyday units, such as numbers of seeds or commodities, such as dates. The kirat was 1/16 of a dirhem. It was equivalent to the weight of four barley seeds, approximately 0.007 ounces. This unit was the origin of the carat measurement for gemstones. The miskal or mithqal was the weight of 6,000 mustard seeds, or about 0.15 ounces. It was based on the Byzantine weight called the solidus. The gold coin known as the dinar corresponded with the miskal. A daniq was one-sixth of a dinar; it could also be one-sixth of a dirham. Pearl merchants used a weight called the methkal, which might have been related to the miskal, though historians do not know precisely how much it weighed. Pearl merchants also used units called the yeka and the rthi, which could have come from the Indian unit of weight known as the rati. Muslim pearl merchants imported many of their pearls from India, so it would not be surprising to find Indian units of measure in that trade.

In the Persian Gulf region dates were a common commodity, and the people of the area created several standard measures to quantify dates. These measures took the form of baskets or sacks woven from date palm fronds, and they could hold dried, pressed, or fresh dates. Because the sacks were made to the same size, merchants and customers could count on them holding more or less the right weight of dates. For example, a sack that was about 27.6 inches long and 15.7 inches wide could hold approximately 88 pounds of dates. This unit was known as a jirab. Towns and regions had their own local standards, and these could vary widely.

The main measurement in the Gulf region was the mun, which weighed about 9 pounds. The mun was divided into 24 kiyas, which weighed about 6 ounces each. A family of six needed 20 mun of wheat to survive for six months. That same family needed an additional 12 jirab of dates to make it through the rest of the year.

Measures of volume varied widely. The measure known as the qadah was similar to the liter or quart, though it was not standardized. A mudd also was about 1.8 pints, or perhaps a little more. An ardabb or irdabb was about 20 gallons. Grain and pulse merchants used a type of measuring cup or scoop called a cheeas to measure out precise amounts of wheat, lentils, or other dry items. The cheeas was a wooden scoop that held about 2.7 pints, or half a mun. There were also scoops that would parcel out half or one-quarter of a cheeas.

See also AGRICULTURE; ALCHEMY AND MAGIC; ARCHITECTURE; BUILDING TECHNIQUES AND MATERIALS; CALENDARS AND CLOCKS; ECONOMY; FOREIGNERS AND BARBARIANS; GOVERNMENT ORGANIZATION; HOUSEHOLD GOODS; METALLURGY; MONEY AND COINAGE; NUMBERS AND COUNTING; SCIENCE; SEAFARING AND NAVIGATION; TEXTILES AND NEEDLEWORK; TRADE AND EXCHANGE.

FURTHER READING
François Cardarelli, *Encyclopedia of Scientific Units, Weights and Measures: Their SI Equivalences and Origins* (Berlin: Springer, 2003).
Pedro de Cieza de León, *The Discovery and Conquest of Peru: Chronicles of the New World Encounter*, ed. and trans. Alexandra Parma Cook and Noble David Cook (Durham, N.C.: Duke University Press, 1998).
Francisco Guerra, "Weights and Measures in Pre-Columbian America," *Journal of the History of Medicine and Allied Sciences* 15 (1960): 342–344.
T. Henry, "Ancient Tahiti," *Bernice P. Bishop Museum Bulletin* 48 (1928): 323–335. Available online. URL: http://www.ethnomath.org/resources/henry1928.pdf. Downloaded on December 10, 2007.
Philip Iddison, "Weights, Measures and Money (and Sundry Associated Matters)," Emirates Natural History Group. Available online. URL: http://enhg.4t.com/iddison/weights.htm. Downloaded on October 10, 2007.
Bruno Kisch, *Scales and Weights: A Historical Outline* (New Haven, Conn.: Yale University Press, 1965).
Patricia J. O'Brien and Hanne D. Christiansen, "An Ancient Maya Measurement System," *American Antiquity* 51, no. 1 (1986): 136–151.
F. G. Skinner, *Weights and Measures: Their Ancient Origins and Their Development in Great Britain up to A.D. 1855* (London: HMSO, 1967).
Ian Whitelaw, *A Measure of All Things: The Story of Man and Measurement* (New York: St. Martin's, 2007).
R. A. Young and T. J. Glover, *Measure for Measure* (Littleton, Colo.: Blue Willow, 1996).
Claudia Zaslavsky, "Those Familiar Weights and Measures!" in her *Africa Counts: Number and Pattern in African Cultures*, 3rd ed. (Chicago: Lawrence Hill Books, 1999).

► writing

INTRODUCTION

Writing is a system for recording human speech through symbols drawn on paper (or similar material). In the Middle Ages writing was much nearer its origin in speech than it is now, since texts generally were read aloud even during private study, when reading letters, and in most other circumstances. Writing had been invented independently at least four times in antiquity: in Sumeria, in the Indus Valley (still not deciphered), in China, and in Central America (by the Maya). In other cases entirely new writing systems were devised by people who had some familiarity with an existing writing system. Egyptian hieroglyphs were created this way in reaction to the cuneiform writing of Sumeria. In many other cases, existing scripts were adapted to record new languages that had never before been written down. Many new and modified alphabets came into existence during the Middle Ages. Throughout much of the world the Middle Ages were also a golden age of calligraphy, the transformation of writing into a fine art.

One of the oldest forms of writing and the most widespread in the Middle Ages is the alphabet. Earlier forms of writing had been logographic (each sign representing an individual idea or word), like Egyptian hieroglyphs, or syllabic (each sign representing a discrete syllable), like Sumerian and Akkadian cuneiform. These scripts required hundreds or even thousands of different signs. But the alphabet is phonetic: Each sign represents just one or a few related sounds, so the whole range of human speech can be represented using fewer than 30 letters. The alphabet was invented by speakers of Semitic languages who came from the Levant but were living in Egypt in about 1800 B.C.E (or perhaps even earlier). They had no means of writing their own language, so they borrowed 22 hieroglyphic signs in a simplified form to make the first alphabet. The same signs were constantly transformed over the next thousand years but finally gave rise to the Hebrew alphabet and to the Latin and Greek alphabets. (The name comes from the first two letters in the Greek alphabet: *alpha* and *beta*.) The same system of writing was borrowed by India and became the basis of a whole family of scripts.

In the Middle Ages the Germanic peoples borrowed the Latin alphabet as the basis of their runic system of writing. Later, Christian scholars devised new forms of the alphabet to record the Gothic language and the Cyrillic alphabet to record Slavic languages (a form of which is still in use today). One of the Semitic languages recorded in the alphabet was Aramaic, and the Aramaic alphabet was borrowed and transformed to become the Arabic script. Another branch of the alphabet was used in southern Arabia and Ethiopia from ancient times to record a variety of Semitic and African languages. Persian, one of the most widespread languages in southwestern Asia, never developed its own script but in different periods was written in cuneiform or in Aramaic letters. In the Middle Ages, Persians finally adopted and still use the Arabic alphabet.

Indian forms of the alphabet gave rise to dozens of different writing systems in eastern Asia, from Mongolia to Indonesia. Egyptians eventually devised their own separate alphabetic writing system based on simplified hieroglyphs, known as demotic, and this was combined with the Greek alphabet to produce a script for Coptic, the latest spoken form of the Egyptian language, which is still used as the liturgical language of the Coptic Orthodox Church. The characteristically modern practice of using the Roman alphabet to transcribe indigenous languages began in the late Middle Ages (after 1482) when the Portuguese made contact with the kingdom of Congo in central Africa.

In the Middle Ages most Jews spoke the language of whatever people they happened to live among. While most people were illiterate, an unusual number of Jews learned to read and write Hebrew to a limited degree to fulfill religious requirements. As a consequence, they developed systems of writing their spoken language in Hebrew letters, such as Yiddish (a Germanic dialect) or Ladino (a form of Spanish).

Two logographic systems of writing were important in the Middle Ages—those used to write Chinese and Mayan. Both used thousands of signs to represent individual words but also used other signs to phonetically represent syllables and words. Both were systems widely adopted by neighboring civilizations. In eastern Asia, Korea and Japan also developed their own phonetic systems of writing, though they both used Chinese characters as a prestigious form of writing their own languages. Although earlier groups in Mexico, such as the Toltec, had been influenced by Mayan writing, the Aztec used their own pictographic system, which conveyed information through a series of small sketches but which did not directly record speech.

AFRICA

BY DIANNE WHITE OYLER

Writing in the African society and culture of the medieval world built upon the indigenous and imported writing systems from the Mediterranean basin with the new languages and writing systems arriving from the Middle East and Europe. While northeast Africa and North Africa added to their variety of writing systems through trade and conquest, these new writing systems were also delivered to East Africa and western Africa through trade.

Northeast Africa was the home of Egypt's hieroglyphs, which evolved into the Coptic (Egyptian) script. The Coptic script used Greek letters and a few demotic signs (signs relating to the more ancient hieratic Egyptian writing but simplified) to write the Egyptian language and to translate and transcribe the Bible for a growing Egyptian Christian (Coptic) population in the Byzantine Empire. After the Arab conquest of Egypt in 642 the use of Coptic as a language declined. Medieval Egyptians used the Coptic script and the Greek alphabet as writing systems as they incorporated the new Arabic script. After the Arab conquest, Christian religious texts were written in the Coptic language using Arabic script.

In Axum (present-day Ethiopia) the Ge'ez writing system evolved into the Ethiopic script. This writing system was used for religious and secular reasons; after King Ezana (fourth century) made Christianity Axum's state religion, it also was used to write biblical texts translated from the Coptic language and script. The genealogy of the biblical kings and queens of Axum is recorded in the *Kebra Nagast*, which was written in the Ethiopic script and dates to the 13th century. Other works written in the Ethiopic script include the *Royal Chronicles* and religious sermons by the Orthodox Christian priests.

Axum received its earliest imported writing systems by migration and by trade. The Hebrew alphabet arrived through migration and continues to be used today by the groups identified as the Beta Israel of Ethiopia. The earliest recounting of Jews in Axum is written in the Ethiopic script and relates the creation myth in which the Queen of Sheba from Axum meets King Solomon of Israel (10th century B.C.E.), and their child, Menelik I, and his entourage of Jewish youth bring Hebrew, Judaism, and the Ark of the Covenant to Axum. The Greek alphabet entered Axum through the port of Adulis on the Red Sea and is referred to in the Greek sailor's manual *Periplus of the Erythrean Sea*. In the seventh century the Arabic alphabet was imported to the coastal region by the Beja as this coastal plain was incorporated into the major Muslim empires of the period; Axum reconquered the coastal plain known as Eritrea in ninth century.

North Africa and the Maghreb were home to an indigenous group of people known as the Berbers, who had developed the Tafineq writing system, which may have been influenced by the Punic writing system based on the Phoenician alphabet used in the colony of Carthage. In addition, Greek and Latin writing systems were imported through trade and conquest as a part of both the Roman and Byzantine empires and were used to write religious texts in the Roman Catholic Church.

The Hebrew alphabet arrived in North Africa when many Spanish Jews migrated to the coastal towns of the Byzantine

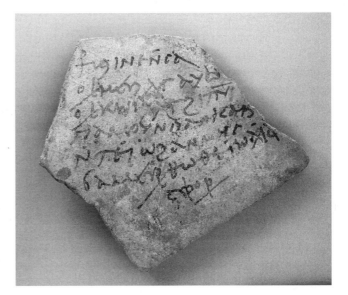

Ostracon with Coptic inscription, Egypt, ca. 250–650 (Los Angeles County Museum of Art, Gift of Jerome F. Snyder, Photograph © 2006 Museum Associates/LACMA [M.80.202.174])

Empire in the seventh century. Writing in Arabic, Ibn Khaldun (1332–1406), a famous Muslim historian from Tunisia, reports that some Jews moved inland to convert the indigenous Berber speakers and that at the end of the seventh century Jews led the resistance to the Muslim conquest; however, after the Jewish Berber defeat many of them converted to Islam. In the 10th century many Jewish traders arrived in present-day Tunisia because the Abbasid Caliphate had become hostile to them, and the largest forced migration of Jews into the region came with the Spanish Inquisition around 1492.

The Arabic alphabet arrived in North Africa in the seventh century as well. Arabic-speaking Muslims conquered the region from Egypt to Morocco, and with this conquest came the use of the Arabic language and writing system for official business. The form of the Arabic alphabet used by the inhabitants of North Africa is the Maghrebi script, a cursive form of Arabic writing that was derived from Iraq and the Hejaz during the eighth and ninth centuries. This alphabet was used by the Moroccan Ibn Battuta (1304–68 or 69), who wrote an epic based on his travels throughout the Muslim world, where Arabic was spoken and where the Arabic alphabet was used. Ibn Battuta wrote his reminiscences of his 14th-century visits to Mali in western Africa and the East African states of Mogadishu (Somalia), Mombasa (Kenya), and Kilwa (Tanzania).

In East Africa the Arabic alphabet arrived by way of the Indian Ocean trade, which was governed by the monsoon winds that blow toward the East African coast from May to October and away from the coast from November to April.

Traders who arrived in East Africa at the beginning of the monsoon season had to remain there until the winds changed, so many lived with their African families in such coastal city-states as Lamu, Pemba, Zanzibar, and Kilwa. Arabic and its script were used for official documents.

This trading system also connected the coastal city-states to the interior using the Swahili trade language, which kept records by using the Arabic script. The word *sawahil* is Arabic for "coast," and incorporating Arabic loan words, the language was understood by the loose association of ethnic groups on the mainland and the coastal islands and as far inland as the Katanga province of present-day Republic of the Congo.

Written in Arabic, the *Lamu Chronicle* shows that the Umayyad Caliphate(661–750) sent traders to the East African coast in the seventh century. The *Kilwa Chronicle* of Zanzibar recounts the story of seven Muslim brothers emigrating from Shiraz, Persia, in the eighth century. This founding myth may attempt to distinguish the Swahili from the Indian Muslims arriving later in the 12th century. These two Arabic chronicles imply that the Arabic script was being taught in Koranic schools on Africa's east coast. The arrival of the Portuguese for trade and eventual conquest brought the Roman alphabet to the region in the early 16th century.

In western Africa the Hebrew and Arabic alphabets arrived early to the interior through the north-to-south trans-Saharan trade from the Maghreb to points south, including Timbuktu (present-day Mali). According to Muslim accounts—the *Tarikh el-Fettash*, written in Arabic—there were several Jewish communities in the Ghana, Mali, and Songhai empires, and in 1402 there was a large Jewish community in Tirdirma. Undoubtedly, these Hebrew speakers were using the Hebrew alphabet for religious and interpersonal communication among themselves and with the regions they had left behind in Egypt, Morocco, Portugal, and Gojjam (present-day Ethiopia). In the 14th century Jews from Portugal and Spain fled these Catholic states and migrated to the trade city of Timbuktu in the Songhai Empire. However, by 1492 Jews were no longer allowed to live freely in the city, and they were forced to convert to Islam or leave.

The Arabic alphabet traveled to Kumbi Saleh, the capital of the ancient kingdom and empire of Ghana, by way of Muslims entering the trans-Saharan trade in the eighth century. While the urban merchants were impressed by the wealth of the traders, the *ghana* (title for the king) was impressed by the writing system. Although there is no evidence of the king's conversion to Islam, he did employ Muslim clerics to use the Arabic writing system to keep governmental records.

Further influence from North African Muslims, the Almoravids, increased the use of the Arabic language and script in the region. The leadership of the Mali and Songhai empires was decidedly Muslim. Mansa (King) Musa (r. ca. 1312–ca. 1332) is renowned for his pilgrimage to Mecca (1324–25) on which he handed out gold to every community through which he traveled. Moreover, he is responsible for bringing Arab Muslim clerics back from al-Ahzar University in Cairo, Egypt, to teach Arabic as a second language (and the alphabet) to black Muslims at the Sankorè University in Timbuktu. The Muslim clerics and scribes of Timbuktu further developed their own form of the Arabic script from the Iraq and Hejaz forms that had been developed in the eighth and ninth centuries. While many books were written or copied in Timbuktu, others were imported through trade, so manuscripts can be found that are written in other forms of Arabic, such as those used in Egypt and Syria.

The Arabic language and alphabet arrived in Hausaland (northern Nigeria and Niger) in the 14th century through merchants and the seminomadic Muslim Fulfulde speakers, who brought Islam with them across western Africa. Arabic writing spread with religion and through trade to the kingdom of Kanem and Bornu (modern-day Chad). In addition to Fulfulde contact, this kingdom traded with the Ottoman Empire on the North African coast. Ibn Furtu of Niger wrote *Mai Idris of Bornu* (late 16th century), about the reign of King Idris Alawma.

In west-central Africa the Portuguese explorer Diogo Cão (b. ca. 1450) introduced the kingdom of Kongo to the Roman alphabet in 1482. Nzinga a Nkuwu, king of the Kongo, established a relationship with King John II of Portugal (r. 1481–95), through which the Kongolese king became enamored with Portuguese culture and civilization. Nzinga a Nkuwu sent four Bakongo men to Portugal to study for the priesthood of the Catholic Church, and Portuguese missionaries baptized the Kongolese king in 1491. The king's son became Afonso I, who spoke Portuguese and wrote the Roman alphabet, while his grandson Henry became even more skilled in the use of the alphabet as a bishop in the Catholic Church.

Writing in African society and culture of the medieval world drew the continent into the widening global economy by developing intricate economic connections with the interior and with sub-Saharan Africa. While the ancient world witnessed writing only in the north and east of the continent, the new forms of writing spread to East Africa, western Africa, west-central Africa, and southern Africa. The Arabic language and writing system bound together large areas of North Africa, western Africa, and East Africa for government documents, business transactions, and correspondence prior to the arrival of the Europeans and the Roman alphabet that came to dominate the world.

THE AMERICAS

BY MIGUEL ARISA

Of all the writing systems that had developed already during the first four centuries of the Common Era, the Incan quipu system in the Andean region and the Mesoamerican systems developed by the Maya and the Zapotec are the most exemplary of a complex form that evolved from ancient times. Amerindian pictographs of the indigenous populations of what are now Canada and the United States did not develop until after the arrival of the Europeans, and especially through the syllabaries that the Sioux and Cherokee tribes introduced in the 19th century.

The knotted cords ordered around a horizontal rope called a quipu became a very sophisticated form of writing for the Inca in South America. Some scholars believe that the black rope, from which the other cords hung, indicated time. The other strings would be uncolored, and at certain gaps knots would be tied, providing meaning to the intervals. The whole system depended on the different colors of the strings and their position within the whole organization. It has been suggested recently that poems or verses could have been stored in the quipu, an assumption based on the fact that Quechuan words are not as abundant as are words in other languages. Such a complex device was probably managed only by dedicated specialists whose expertise was highly regarded.

Shell ornament with series of Mayan hieroglyphs incised on the interior, ca. 600–800 (© The Trustees of the British Museum)

Although writing systems evolved simultaneously throughout the Mesoamerican region during the Preclassic, Classic, and Postclassic periods, it is the Mayan glyphs that have attracted the greatest attention in recent years due to successful decipherment that has taken place since the 1980s. Mayan hieroglyphs are akin to a true writing system in that rather than merely expressing concepts or ideas, they represent actual speech. Great strides have been made in the late 20th and early 21st centuries to decipher Mayan inscriptions. Lacking a Rosetta Stone to help crack the millenary code, modern scholars are coming to grips with this highly complex form of writing.

Even considering that writing did not develop alongside sculptural images at first, some scholars believe that once the dynastic structures were established at the end of the late Preclassic Period and as competition between city-states increased, writing became a principal means to dominate as well as to ascertain legitimacy. In this way, Mayan writing has been discerned to contain a plethora of historical information, including the biographies of the rulers as well as the most important dates of their rise to power and their demise. Rulers were equated to gods, and their rituals included the use of hallucinogens in order to establish contact with the cosmic forces. Fanatical in their attitude toward war and conquest, the inscriptions often represent the capturing of neighboring city-states by power-hungry rulers bent on exercising their dynastic privilege and expanding their territories. Marriages between dynasties were also recorded, regarded as part of continuous cycles.

Emblem glyphs, referring to actual places as well as calendrical dates, and names of historical characters are some of the main features of these representations. In some form Diego de Landa (1524–79), who in 1566 became the first Spaniard to make reference to Mayan writing, had already surmised some of the meanings of the glyphs and described the calendrical usage. These glyphs were carved in stone by scribes, who were often highly educated members of the royal elite. In some cases, kings themselves were also scribes, as is shown in depictions of a number of vases, on which the kings are shown wearing elaborate headdresses made out of pens. It is thought that scribe schools existed where a demanding course of study was required to grasp a thorough knowledge. Judging from their depiction on vases and other monuments, scribes were highly esteemed.

The Classic Period in the Mesoamerican world was characterized by the hegemony (social dominance) of the Teotihuacán urban center, whose writing, pictographic in nature, had evolved from earlier periods into highly geometric forms. The largest city in Mesoamerica, Teotihuacán, was believed never to have had a writing system. However, two different writing systems have been detected in recent discoveries, contemporary to Monte Albán. One resembles Zapotec and Mayan glyphs; the other is more illustrative of the city's own murals. The murals show name glyphs, but it is not certain if they refer to rulers or gods. It also seems that at its height, the city had several quarters in which different languages coexisted, such as Zapotec, Mixtec, Mayan, and Nahuatlan. The metropolis collapsed around 600 to 650, and the meaning of its murals probably influenced future generations, which regarded the site as sacred.

By the late Classic Period the Mayan language was becoming more and more phonetic. It featured squarish blocks that contained more than a pattern representing a sound or a combination of sounds. The Zapotec language, by around the same time, still employed large-format sculpture to display texts that are both pictographic and phonetic. The correspondences between these systems and the ones in the highlands have led scholars to assume that contacts between the Teotihuacáno, the Zapotec, and the Maya were not isolated.

It was from this foundation that the Aztec acquired their system of writing once they had migrated to the Mexican basin in the latter part of the 13th century. The Aztec perfected the system of rebus writing, in which an existing symbol was used to represent a sound and then that symbol represented that sound for other words. This form of abbreviation reduced the need to represent many words. Like the Maya and the Zapotec, the Aztec used this system in their calendrical and divinatory manuscripts, whose manufacture contributed to the elaboration of more complex imagery.

The Maya made a distinction between the scribe (*aj ts'ib*) who used pens to inscribe and the scribe who carved in stone. We know that books existed because many are illustrated on vases; however, few survive. During the Spanish colonization missionaries and government officials forbade the use of the indigenous languages and inscriptions, and many of the historical and divinatory books were burned, as they were deemed diabolical. Once they realized the error of destroying the culture of the people they were trying to dominate, some Spanish friars began the painstaking labor of reconstructing the ancient documents with the aid of natives who had not yet lost the memory of their past, kept alive mostly by oral tradition. In this way the Mayan creation myth Popul Vuh, along with other calendrical and divinatory codices, was commissioned. These works form part of a body of codices produced after the Spanish conquest that are scattered in museums around the world.

A small number of early pre-Columbian manuscripts survived the Spanish conquest. These include Mixtec histories, Mayan religious works, and other books from the highlands, also with religious or divinatory content. Some of these codices were made as screen folds and inscribed on animal skin. Perhaps the most important of the codices are the ones denominated in the Borgia group, which are believed to have been painted just before the conquest and which consist mostly of religious material. Fortunately for scholars, this particular group was spared destruction as it was one of the few that were sent to Europe as a curiosity in the early part of the 16th century.

The best preserved pre-Columbian books are Mixtec codices, beautifully painted in maguey cloth and folded like an accordion. When the books are opened, two pages are visible, each page divided by red or black lines into smaller sections. The complex imagery can be read from top to bottom, although it varies in some codices, in which the order of pictograms can be followed in a zigzag form.

These books resemble European medieval manuscripts in that they seem to have been produced singly and with similar tools. For example, the use of animal skins, the use of organic and mineral pigments, and the fact that the books were of religious nature mark a distinct similarity with their European counterparts. It is hard to ascertain what other kinds of books existed in pre-Columbian times. Some believe that since tribute was a mainstay in the expansion of Aztec as well as Mayan rulers, books designed to keep track of these accounts must have existed, although their existence is hard to prove.

The survival of these codices and their decipherment cast light on a rich and varied culture that originated more than 3,000 years ago. The social structures, language, religion, science, and history were carved or painted in jade, stone, and gold, as well as on monumental pyramids and tombs—evidence of a rich and evolving culture cut short by the advent of the Europeans.

ASIA AND THE PACIFIC

BY KENNETH HALL

During the medieval era the Pacific islands had not yet developed a writing tradition, but in the early first millennium C.E. in mainland and island Asia stone and metal (gold, silver, brass, bronze, iron, tin, and copper) plates were inscribed with official and private records, royal proclamations, land grants, eulogies, and memorials. In the tropical regions of southern Asia and Southeast Asia, most petitions to royal courts and poetic and religious writings were done on strips of palm leaf, using the point of a knife, a sharpened piece of iron, or other pointed object that served as a stylus to carve the script into the palm leaf surface. Books and religious treatises were formed by running a string through strips of palm leaves and connecting it to wooden book covers at the top and bottom. Early mainland Southeast Asians and northern Indians used parchment-like sheets made from animal skins. They also used a less expensive substitute made from tree bark, which was prepared by soaking, pounding, drying, and pressing the bark. The Chinese began to use paper in the second century, and by the sixth century Chinese paper technology had spread to the neighbor countries.

In southern and Southeast Asia inscriptions carved in stone and metal were an important form of local expression and historical record throughout the medieval era. The earliest were the records of the societal elite addressing ancestral and spiritual issues that were foundational to the social and spiritual bonds of a community. In southern India alone there are more than 20,000 inscribed records that remain for the era from 1000 to 1500. Most are temple inscriptions that record gifts to temples, usually of land or money. Many are eulogies for political figures and expressions of local devotion to a specific divine. These surviving inscriptions are a record not only of political and religious piety but also of the local society and its economy. Personal references included places of origin and current residence, occupation, memberships and linkages; above all they were a public record of social superiority or dependency.

The earliest inscriptions portrayed kingship that was heroic rather than institutional; kings were overlords rather than managers. In the 10th and 11th centuries inscriptions became less mythological and more detailed, with a focus on the certification of landholding and income rights. Inscriptions provided public announcements and enduring records of specific political and economic transactions that served as a legal record and allowed government agents to acquire an accurate picture of the standard of local stability and local prosperity, which might justify royal intervention and tax assessments.

According to Chinese tradition, Cai Lun (50?–?118) invented paper in 105 by improving upon previous papermaking techniques, which used only hemp, and developing a process in which a variety of materials could be used, initially tree bark, hemp, and cloth rags but later other barks, grasses, and vegetation. Cai Lun discovered that fibers could be formed into a thin sheet on a screen. He worked with numerous fibers mixed with water in a vat, in which they were washed, soaked, and beaten to a pulp with a wooden mallet. He then submerged a four-sided bamboo-framed cloth screen in the vat and lifted it, catching the fibers on its surface. When dried and pressed with a covering mold, the thin layer of fiber became paper.

Initially, Chinese paper was made from hemp waste from old rugs and fishnets; then, beginning in the second century, the fiber of the mulberry tree was used, which was displaced in favor of rattan from the third to the 12th centuries and bamboo from the eighth century. Bamboo paper, which was soft, smooth, white, absorbent, and durable, was favored by Chinese artists and calligraphers in the Tang Dynasty era (589–907). Specialized paper came from rice and wheat straw, stalks of hibiscus, seaweed, sandalwood bark, and the waste from silkworm cocoons. The vast collection of more than 10,000 rolls of Buddhist manuscripts, which date from 406 to 1035, were written by Buddhist monks at Dunhuang, a pilgrimage center in Chinese Turkestan; here and elsewhere in

Daoist Scripture of Constant Purity and Tranquility, *in standard script, ink on silk, Yuan Dynasty, China, ca. 1292* (Freer Gallery of Art, Smithsonian Institution, Purchase—Regents' Collections Acquisition Program, F1980-8)

CHINESE CHARACTERS AND CALLIGRAPHY

The 26 letters of the Latin alphabet seem like arbitrary representations, each one standing for one or more sounds. They have their origin, however, in ancient Semitic letters and, for the most part, are descended from minute sketches that represented typical words that in northwestern Semitic languages happened to begin with the various letters. The letter *A*, for instance, was originally a picture of a cow: One can still see the triangular face of the animal and the two horns, though the letter has been rotated about 180 degrees from its original form.

The approach to writing in ancient China was completely different, however, and does not express individual sounds. Many Chinese characters are pictographs, that is, small painted sketches of the subject they name (similar to a stick figure for person); others are ideographs, representing abstract ideas, such as a base line and an upright element for the word *up* or three lines for the number 3. Other characters are made by combining signs into larger units. In any case, each character stands for an entire word or idea, and because a good vocabulary consists of at least 4,000 signs (a Song Dynasty dictionary published in 1039 has over 53,000 characters), each one is a remarkably intricate collection of brushstrokes. Moreover, characters were typically painted with a small brush in antiquity and in the Middle Ages. These factors together ensured that calligraphy, the art of painting letters onto paper, would become a fine art in a way that writing never has been among users of the Latin alphabet.

While Western calligraphy aims to produce precise and elegant letterforms that are nevertheless uniform throughout a text, Chinese calligraphy is flowing and demonstrative in a fashion more reminiscent of Western abstract painting, where variation and interpretation of the character forms express emotional and intellectual meanings. Letterforms could be modified to imitate natural beauty. Because the same materials of brush, ink, and paper are used, calligraphy gave rise to ink-and-wash painting, which became the premier graphic art of the East Asian tradition. Frequently, the writing of a poem is made inseparable in form and style from an accompanying painting. Since Chinese characters were adopted for writing Korean and Japanese, calligraphy is equally an important part of those nations' traditions.

the Chinese Buddhist realm, paper replaced other materials for calligraphy. By the third century papermaking technology had been introduced to Vietnam and Tibet, by the fourth century to Korea, and by the sixth century to Japan. In each case paper was ideal for keeping records of the ever-increasing volume and complexity of government, religious, and economic transactions.

Before the invention of paper, however, the earliest Chinese writing was done on wood, bamboo, and silk. The Chinese also erected stone tablets on which the Chinese classics and other public proclamations were inscribed. By the end of the second century these stone texts were transferred to paper by making stone rubbings, an early form of printing. By the early fifth century lampblack ink—a mixture of pine soot and lamp oil blended with the gelatin made from donkey skin and musk (a mixture that became known as "india ink")—was used to blacken the surface of stone-carved hieroglyphics. A sheet of thin white paper was dampened and placed on the stone surface and then rubbed with a small flat stone. Paper pushed down into the carved-out areas remained white, while the raised areas remained black, producing a white-on-black text.

By the mid-fifth century the Chinese were using red and black inks and seals of engraved or carved stone, metal, jade, bamboo, and horn to make their personal marks on paper. Commercial printing evolved from the production of seals; by the seventh century Chinese artisans were carving full-page woodblocks of pictures and texts. Using this technique, in 770 the Japanese empress Koken (r. 749–58) commissioned the printing of *dharani* (prayer charms) on paper made from hemp, using wood, metal, stone, and porcelain stamps. The earliest printed book, the Buddhist Diamond Sutra recovered from Dunhuang, dates to 868. In 953, the first block printing of the Confucian classics was completed after 21 years, and soon all types of printed books were available. These initial books were made up of a series of consecutive printed blocks that produced a scroll text. Block prints were spaced on the long sheets of paper so that they could be folded, and the sheets stitched back to back to produce continuous double-folded pages.

Chinese printing paired with paper production to make scholarship and education potentially available throughout Asia. Standard histories were written in the Tang and Song eras, supplemented by new historical scholarship that addressed how history had and should be written, encyclopedia compilations, gazetteers, and collections of literary works and commentaries on political institutions and economic developments. Printing reinforced the spread of literacy and the development of urban culture.

In about 1041 to 1049 movable type had been introduced to China from Korea, but the complexity and vast number of characters in the Chinese language made it less useful in China than elsewhere. Chinese printers found it more efficient to print books with whole blocks of wood rather than movable type, although they had wood, porcelain, and copper type available. In contrast, in 1390 the reigning Korean emperor established a type foundry to encourage the printing of literature using movable type; the first known Korean printed book dates from 1409. In 1298 the Venetian traveler Marco Polo reported China's use of printed paper money, which was the first printed material seen by Europeans.

The 11th-century Persian scholar al-Biruni (973–1048) provided extensive descriptions of the writing traditions of India. Then, as in rural villages today, students wrote on black wood tablets with pieces of chalk. They also wrote on pieces of the bark of trees—the tuz tree in central and northern India, the inner bark of the bhurja tree in northwestern India—that had been oiled and polished to make them hard and smooth. Southern Indians recorded their manuscripts on palm leaves. Unlike their Middle Eastern neighbors, Indians rarely wrote on animal hides because of their beliefs about ritual pollution. By al-Biruni's time Indians no longer wrote on cloth but instead were just beginning to use paper.

Al-Biruni reports that the earliest Indian paper was attributed to the spread of paper technology from Samarqand in central Asia, where two Chinese papermakers had been taken as war prisoners following a battle near Talas (751). In Samarqand they prepared paper using linen, flax, and hemp rags. Arabian artisans based in Persia improved on the Samarqand paper in the eighth century, producing Khorasani paper using flax and vegetable fibers.

According to one tradition, the production of Khorasani paper spread from Sind to India in the eighth century and took root in the Delhi and Lahore regions. Other traditions assert that the first Indian paper industry developed in Kashmir in the 15th century, following Timur's invasion of the region in 1398. Subsequently, according to the region's *Tarikh-i-Farishta* chronicle, Timur took the local khan's son to Samarqand as his hostage, where Samarqand artisans introduced him to the local papermaking industry. Shahi Khan eventually returned to India, bringing with him numbers of skilled Samarqand papermakers and bookbinders. Soon they were producing high-quality Kashmiri paper, which was the Indian standard. That era's chronicle scribes all wrote on Kashmiri paper. Papermaking spread to other northern Indian production centers. Punjab Sialkot paper was white. Zafarabad in Oudh, which became known as Kaghdi Shahar

("paper city"), produced a glossy polished bamboo paper. Other Indian papers also had glossy surfaces.

Indian papermakers followed the same production techniques as the Chinese, using hammers, screens, teakwood frames, soft date-palm brushes, and polished stones. Indian papermakers were especially proficient in the recycling of waste paper, which they tore into pieces and sorted according to color. The paper scraps were moistened with river water and pounded and repeatedly washed for three days. The pulp was placed in a pit filled with water, soaked until the pulp could be evenly spread into a thin layer on a screen, and then removed to be pressed by a stone cover while it dried. The highest-quality paper was then polished on a wooden board by rubbing it with a shell.

By the third century the Vietnamese were using Chinese paper, later incorporating Chinese woodblock printing. A 13th-century Chinese text reports that China, Korea, and Java made paper. In the 15th century Chinese visitors to Java observed the use of thick paper scrolls made from the fibers of the mulberry tree, known locally as dluwang, that were painted with stories chanted by narrators; but most Javanese writing was still done on palm leaves. In contrast, the western Indonesian archipelago transitioned to the use of dluwang paper in the 15th century, in part because it was difficult to cut the curves and dots of Arabic script into palm leaves. In these regions the Arabic word for "paper" (*kradaat*) was borrowed, as in the Malay *kertas*, as were the Arabic terms for "pen" and "ink." According to the reports of the earliest Portuguese visitors, by the end of the 15th century Melaka was importing quantities of Chinese paper supplied by Ryukyu islanders, and Chinese paper was also being used in Java, Thailand, and Cambodia.

In the 15th century the Thai produced their own paper, which was finer in quality than that of Java. Some Thai paper, similar to that of China and Java, was made from the tree fibers of the *khoi* tree, but Thais also began to produce paper using cotton rags. Long strips of the Thai paper were folded rather than rolled. Court records were written on paper using a clay pen. The Burmese also used a coarse paper but blackened it and wrote on it using a white chalk pencil.

EUROPE

BY JULIE-ANN VICKERS

Handwritten text was one of the primary means of communicating throughout the Middle Ages. The written word was essential for relaying complex information across distances, and, importantly, it was the only method for transmitting information across time to future generations. Yet for most of the medieval period the ability to write was confined to an educated elite, made up primarily of clerics. This situation began to change in the 12th century as literacy levels increased within secular society. Styles of writing also changed a great deal from the early to late Middle Ages. The materials used in the writing process were a fundamental influence on the stylistic forms of letters. But other factors, such as the purpose of the text, local traditions, political influences, and wider cultural trends, also helped form particular styles of writing.

For most of the medieval period, from the fifth century to the 12th century, writing was strongly associated with the church. After the decline of the Roman Empire religious institutions assumed the responsibility for education. The ability to write became a specialized skill associated with the training of some members of the clergy, particularly monks. Many monasteries held rare collections of books and became centers of intellectual and scholarly activity. In the larger monasteries there was usually a dedicated writing room, known as a scriptorium, where the monks studied, wrote, and made copies of manuscripts. Yet even in these highly literate monastic communities not everyone could write. An indication of the degree to which writing skills in the early Middle Ages were restricted to particular groups can be seen in the fact that such an important ruler as Charlemagne (r. 800–14) was unable to sign his name. However, from the 12th century onward, increasing prosperity and wider access to education meant that more and more laypeople acquired the ability to write. Exceptions to this general trend were the Jewish communities, which had maintained high literacy rates throughout the period.

The implements and materials used for writing remained fairly constant during the Middle Ages, although there was some change in the type of material used for writing surfaces. In ancient Rome, papyrus, a material made from the stalk of the papyrus plant, was the most common form of writing surface. But in the fourth century C.E., parchment, which was made from animal skins, gradually replaced the use of papyrus. In both eastern and western Europe parchment soon became the most common type of writing surface. Papyrus did, however, continue to be used for some administrative documents until the 11th century. Paper mills began to spread in Europe only from the 13th century onward. In this early stage of papermaking, paper was generally made from linen rags. But it was not until after the medieval period that the production of paper became widespread; its use in the Middle Ages was generally restricted to writing that was deemed unimportant and insignificant. Wax tablets were also used for day-to-day, casual writing. To make a tablet, a shallow depression was made in a piece of flat wood; the hollow was then filled with wax onto which letters could be scratched and erased. But papyrus, paper, and wax tablets all had a limited use;

Bone writing tablet and leather case of a type typically used as a notebook for jottings, Britain, 14th century (© Museum of London)

throughout the Middle Ages parchment remained the dominant and preferred writing material.

The most commonly used skins for parchment were those of goats, sheep, and calves. Calfskin was particularly valued because of its thinness and suppleness. A writing sheet made from calfskin, or the skin of another young animal, is sometimes referred to as vellum in order to distinguish it from other forms of parchment. Preparing the parchment was a time-consuming process, and large numbers of animals were necessary to supply enough parchment for one codex, or book. Thus, parchment was a highly valued commodity, and every effort was made to ensure that this limited resource was fully used. For instance, medieval scribes developed an elaborate system of abbreviations in order to maximize the amount of text that would fit onto a page. In addition, parchment from books or documents that were no longer in use was sometimes recycled. The surface of the old parchment was scraped down to erase the writing so that the material could be used again for another piece of text; parchment recycled in this way is called a palimpsest.

The pens and inks used for writing on parchment were made from easily accessible natural resources. Quills were the most common form of pen. They were made from the strong flight feathers of a large bird, such as a goose. The feathers were stripped back and then a nib was cut into the pointed end of the feather. These nibs wore down with continuous use and scribes had to periodically sharpen their quill by recutting the nib. Inks were made from a number of different substances, and recipes could vary on a local basis, but the two most common types of ink are known as iron gall ink and carbon ink. To make iron gall ink, oak galls, formed on trees by insect attacks, were mixed with iron vitriol (ferrous sulfate) along with rainwater, wine, or vinegar. Carbon ink was made using either charcoal or soot mixed with gum. Minerals were used to create colored inks.

Besides a pen and writing surface, the medieval scribe needed other materials in order to write. Rulers made of wood, ivory, or stone were employed for laying down the guiding lines on a page. These could be dry-ruled with an implement such as a stylus, which was also used for writing on wax tablets. A tool called a *punctorium*, which made evenly spaced holes along the side of a page, was also used to guide ruled lines. Mistakes in writing were erased using knives or scrapers, and the surface of the page was then smoothed with a pumice stone to prepare it for the corrected text. For holding inks, animal horns were used. Scribes usually did their work at a sloping desk because it is easier to write with a quill on an upright surface. A sloping desk also had the advantage of being better able to catch whatever daylight was available.

The materials used for writing fundamentally influenced the way people wrote in the Middle Ages. Parchment and quills predisposed scribes to form letters with strokes that varied from thick to thin, curved to linear. Elongated flourishes at the end of strokes are another characteristic effect produced by the use of these materials. In contrast, letters formed on wax tablets were made of sharp, straight, and angular lines owing to the consistency of the wax.

The use of the quill and parchment, however, afforded enough flexibility to enable different styles of writing, known as scripts, to develop. Stylistic changes to scripts occurred over time, but within any one period scripts also varied from region to region, and local stylistic traditions tended to develop. In addition, within any one region a variety of different scripts, some more formal than others, were employed at any given time. The choice of one script over another depended largely on the purpose of the written document. For instance, formal scripts were used for important books or legal documents, whereas informal scripts were used for daily correspondence, notes, and draft copies of text. In some cases, scribes employed what is known as a hierarchy of scripts, where different scripts are used for headings or important pieces of text to distinguish them from the surrounding writing.

Scripts can be categorized according to whether they are cursive scripts or book hands. Cursive scripts are those in which letters are joined together, thus requiring less lifting of the pen from the page. These types of script are quicker to execute and therefore were often used in the Middle Ages for less formal types of writing or for administrative documents. However, some cursive scripts were adapted for formal writings as well. Book hands are scripts that contain more formalized characteristics. Separate strokes are used to shape letters in order to produce a consistent, clear, and even style. As the name suggests, these scripts were used in the medieval period for transcribing books. The aesthetic value of formal scripts was important, and some could be highly decorative and difficult to read.

Owing to the number of regional variations, the history of the development of scripts during the Middle Ages is quite complex and constitutes a field of study all its own called medieval palaeography. In western Europe, however, two important general developments took place. In the eighth century, Charlemagne, who ruled over much of western Europe, instigated a number of educational and ecclesiastical reforms, one of which was the standardization of writing. His efforts resulted in a script known as the Caroline minuscule. Renowned for its clarity and harmony of letterforms, this script spread throughout western Europe, and by the 10th century it was the most widely used script of the period. Charlemagne's reforms are an important example of how writing styles were influenced by political directives, as well as by organic change.

While the adoption of Caroline minuscule signaled an era of convergence in script forms, the second major development was one of divergence. In northern Europe during the latter part of the 11th century a new type of script, known as Gothic, began to emerge. More angular, extended, and elaborate than Caroline minuscule, this script signaled a move away from simple letterforms. It also heralded a period of diversification. Gothic script developed in a number of different centers of northern Europe, giving rise to variants that shared some common elements but nevertheless exhibited distinct characteristics. The rise of Gothic variants occurred at the same time that people began to use their local vernacular language, instead of Latin, for some types of writing. Various forms of this script remained in use until the end of the medieval period.

The history of script in the Byzantine Empire is far less complex than that of western Europe because of the cultural and linguistic unity of the region. Yet the developments in scripts there followed a trajectory similar to that of the Latin West. In the early Middle Ages, Byzantine scripts were influenced by the majuscule, or upper-case letterforms used in the classical world. Minuscule scripts, which generally used lower-case letters, developed in the ninth century at the same time that Caroline minuscule was spreading in western Europe. Variations of minuscule scripts dominated Byzantine writing until the end of the Middle Ages and beyond. Unlike the Latin West, the trend to Gothic forms did not happen in the East. The major development in Byzantine scripts during the later Middle Ages was the introduction of more cursive types of minuscule, influenced by the increasing use of paper.

THE ISLAMIC WORLD

BY ROSE ASLAN

The Arabic language is a Semitic language, and its alphabet is written from right to left in cursive form, with rounded characters joined together. Because the language of the Koran is Arabic and the Arabic language was closely tied to Islam, both spoken Arabic and the Arabic alphabet spread with the arrival of Muslims in non-Muslim lands. While a large number of lands adopted the Arabic language and its writing as their own, other regions where people spoke languages such as Persian and Turkish adopted the Arabic alphabet but used it to write their native languages. From Morocco to India the literate used the Arabic alphabet, with Arabic being the language of the Muslim elite; in addition, scribes and calligraphers worked hard to refine the Arabic writing system, creating one of the most beautiful scripts of any language. Because pictorial representation was forbidden in Islam, Muslim calligraphers developed scripts that were literally pieces of art, complete with embellishments and ornate arabesque designs.

Before Islam, very few people were literate. The Arabs were nomads primarily and although they had a rich oral tradition, they did not record most of it, including the poetry that was their most distinguished literary achievement. With the advent of Islam in the early seventh century certain Muslims were assigned to memorize the Koran. It was not until a number of those who had memorized it were killed in battle in 633 that the second caliph, Umar (r. 634–44), persuaded the first caliph, Abu Bakr (r. 632–34), to write down the Koran, which before then had been recorded only on loose leaves of parchment, pieces of bone, and other miscellaneous surfaces. The third caliph, Uthman ibn Affan (r. 644–56), codified the Koran during his reign. At this point, Arabic script was fairly primitive, but very quickly calligraphers endeavored to turn it into a work of art.

While there may have been Arabic scripts earlier, the oldest existing records of the North Arabic script, the forerunner of classical Arabic, go back to the fifth century. Most scholars agree that North Arabic script evolved from Nabataean script, which in turn evolved from Aramaic script. North Arabic script developed in the northeastern region of Arabia among ethnic groups that occupied the areas known as Hira and Anbar. Subsequently, the script spread throughout the western part of Arabia and was introduced by Bishr ibn Abd al-Malik and his father-in-law, Harb ibn Umayyah, into Mecca. The two men were close companions of the prophet Muhammad (ca. 570–632) and learned how to read and write and participated in the early stages of Islam. One scribe named Zayd ibn Thabit was also close to the prophet Muhammad, serving as his secretary; he was responsible for compiling the first written Koran.

The earliest reference to Arabic script refers to it as *Jazm*, and scholars usually agree that it was an evolved version of the Nabataean alphabet. The *Jazm* script became widespread and was the most commonly used script among the Arabs; it eventually became the common script of Islam and the Muslims. Essentially, the Koran laid the ground for Arabic grammar and script. To the devout Muslim, the Koran holds the canon of the Arabic language as revealed by God to the prophet Muhammad through the angel Gabriel and thus is considered to be divine.

Pen box, brass inlaid with copper, silver, and black organic material; Iran, 13th century (Freer Gallery of Art, Smithsonian Institution, Purchase, F1936-7)

In early Islam copies of Uthman's codified Koran were made first in the *Jazm* and its Mecca and Medina variants and later in the Kufic scripts, which were developed in the town of Al-Kufa in present-day Iraq. By this time several other variants of the *Jazm* script had developed in different regions, but ultimately there were three primary script styles: *Tim*, a script with both triangular and rounded letters; *muthallath*, a triangular script; and *mudawwar*, a rounded script. From these, two types of scripts continued to be used, one called *muqawwar*, which was cursive and simplistic, and the other *mabsut*, which was angular and rectangular. These two scripts were dominant on the Arabian Peninsula and were the basis of other styles, such as *maail*, which was a commonly used slanted script; *mashq*, which was an elongated script; and *naskh*, which was elegant and inscriptional. These scripts developed independently at the same time that the Kufic script was rapidly evolving into an extremely refined form.

As Islam became more established in Basra and al-Kufa, both of which are in modern-day Iraq, the cities became cultural and intellectual centers for the Islamic Empire, and calligraphers developed the Mecca and Medina scripts into the Kufic script. With its proportional measurements and angularity, Kufic script gained in popularity, reached its height toward the end of the eighth century, and remained dominant for more than 300 years; it was the only script in which the Koran was written during this time. As Islam spread through the lands of those who did not speak Arabic as their native language, reforms had to be made to simplify the language for them.

Originally the Arabic alphabet did not include any diacritical marks, until Abu al-Aswad al-Duali (d. 688), who was also responsible for establishing a system for Arabic grammar, began using colored dots to help those who were learning Arabic pronounce the words. One problem was that there were a number of consonants that had the same shapes yet had different sounds. It was al-Hajjaj ibn Yusuf al-Thaqafi (661–714), an Umayyad viceroy, who commissioned Nasr ibn Asim (d. 707) and Yahya ibn Yamus (d. 708) to solve this problem. They derived vowel signs and marks from the Syriac alphabet and applied it to Arabic in order to differentiate consonants. Because the colored dots and vowel signs, when used together, were overly complex, al-Khalil ibn Ahmad al-Farahidi (d. 786) exchanged Hajjaj's system of diacritical dots on letters with one using diacritical marks that would complement his letter-pointing system.

The Kufic script was also instrumental in forming the diverse scripts that were to come. It was an oblong script, rectangular and quite plain, although beginning in the early ninth century calligraphers would add embellishments and ornamentations. What made it so unique and momentous was the fact that the height of the letters was almost always much less than their width. Many scholars note that the refinement of the Kufic script developed in accordance with the burgeoning Islamic civilization. The Kufic script was the dominant script in all forms of writing until the late 12th century, when it became mainly ornamental, used in art, while simpler and more functional scripts replaced it for everyday communications.

While several scripts developed up to the ninth century, it was not until the 10th century that Muhammad ibn Muqlah (886–940), an accomplished calligrapher in Baghdad, brought about a momentous change in the Arabic script. Ibn Muqlah developed a perfectly proportioned and elegant script based on his knowledge of geometric and mathematical sciences. Essentially, he was responsible for developing a standard form of the Arabic script based on strict rules. Soon after came Ibn al-Bawwab (d. 1022 or 1031), who further improved Ibn Muqlah's style by giving it more polish and sophistication.

Throughout the medieval period there were six primary Arabic scripts: *thuluth*, *naskhi*, *muhaqqaq*, *rayhani*, *riqa*, and *tawqi*. Outside of the present-day Middle East calligraphers developed their own regional styles of script, such as the Sudani style of sub-Saharan northwestern Africa and the Maghrebi style in present-day Morocco, Libya, Tunisia, and Algeria as well as Islamic Spain.

Because calligraphy was a highly technical occupation and required expertise, students attended special schools to study it for many years. As a refined art, it had special implements that were used to produce the different types of scripts. Scribes worked in the courts as secretaries, recording important documents for the ruling class; in addition, calligraphers were always in demand to produce copies of the Koran and other religious texts. The most important tool for calligraphers was the *qalam*, or pen, which was almost always made from reeds. The reed was cut at an angle and then dipped into ink to write. Differently cut angles on the tip of the pen would produce varying thicknesses of line.

Cutting pens at the most accurate angle to produce the desired effect was a science of its own, and some calligraphers covetously guarded their secret methods of cutting pens and even holding them, only passing their secrets on to close apprentices. The famous calligrapher Yaqut al-Mustasimi (d. 1298) was responsible for inventing a new way of trimming his reed pens, which helped give calligraphic styles even more beauty. Other implements that were essential to the calligraphic trade included a knife for cutting and shaping the pen, brushes, scissors, an ink pot, and a mortar for mixing the ingredients to make ink. These implements would be kept in specially crafted and often

Illuminated opening page from a manuscript of the Hadith, writings concerning the life of the Prophet, ink, watercolor, and gold on paper; Iraq or Iran; 12th to early 13th century (Los Angeles County Museum of Art, The Nasli M. Heeramaneck Collection, gift of Joan Palevsky, Photograph © 2006 Museum Associates/LACMA [M.73.5.556])

so calligraphers might often use a single sheet many times over, writing on both sides and erasing old text. Parchment and paper could be sold as single sheets or, more commonly, as rolls of sheets that were glued together. Parchment made of animal hide was also used, and in the middle of the ninth century paper arrived in the Islamic world from China. Although paper was expensive in relation to other consumer goods, it was widely available and offered a smoother and thus more desirable writing surface than papyrus.

See also ALCHEMY AND MAGIC; ART; CRAFTS; ECONOMY; EDUCATION; EMPIRES AND DYNASTIES; INVENTIONS; LANGUAGE; LITERATURE; MONEY AND COINAGE; OCCUPATIONS; RELIGION AND COSMOLOGY; TRADE AND EXCHANGE; WAR AND CONQUEST.

FURTHER READING

Sheila Blair, *Islamic Calligraphy* (Edinburgh: Edinburgh University Press, 2006).

Michelle P. Brown, *A Guide to Western Historical Scripts from Antiquity to 1600* (London: British Library, 1993).

Vernier W. Clapp, *The Story of Permanent Durable Bookpaper, 1115–1970* (Toronto: University of Toronto Press, 1971).

Christopher de Hamel, *Scribes and Illuminators* (Toronto: University of Toronto Press, 1992).

Department of Medieval Studies at Central European University, Budapest, *Medieval Manuscript Manual*. Available online. URL: http://www.ceu.hu/medstud/manual/MMM/home.html. Accessed on May 15, 2007.

Marc Drogin, *Medieval Calligraphy: Its History and Technique* (Montclair, N.J.: Allanheld and Schram, 1980).

Noboru Karashima, ed., *Indus Valley to Mekong Delta, Explorations in Epigraphy* (Madras, India: New Era Publications, 1985).

Abdelkebir Khatibi, *The Splendour of Islamic Calligraphy* (London: Thames and Hudson, 1976).

Martin Lings, *The Quranic Art of Calligraphy and Illumination* (London: World of Islam Festival Trust, 1976).

Joseph Needham and Tsien Tsuen-Hsuin, *Science and Technology in China.* Vol. 5, *Paper and Printing* (Cambridge, U.K.: Cambridge University Press, 1985).

Y. H. Safadi, *Islamic Calligraphy* (Boulder, Colo.: Shambhala, 1979).

Richard Salomon, *Indian Epigraphy: A Guide to the Study of Inscriptions in Sanskrit, Prakrit, and the Other Indo-Aryan Languages* (New York: Oxford University Press, 1998).

Annemarie Schimmel, *Calligraphy and Islamic Culture* (New York: New York University Press, 1984).

Gary Urton, *Signs of the Inka Khipu: Binary Coding in the Andean Knotted-String Records* (Austin: University of Texas Press, 2003).

elaborately decorated cases that were sometimes made of precious materials, such as ivory or silver.

Ink was usually colored black, using natural plant and mineral ingredients; other colors such as indigo and red were also used, as were expensive silver leaf and gold leaf in illuminated manuscripts. The first materials to which inks were applied were hard surfaces, such as stones and bones. In Egypt papyrus had been common since pharaonic times and continued to be used throughout the Middle East. However, manufacturing papyrus was labor-intensive and very costly,

Glossary

a cappella   Performed or sung without instrumental accompaniment.

abacus   A counting board used to perform simple mathematical calculations by manually sliding counters along wires set in a framework.

ablution   Washing or cleansing of the body as part of a religious rite.

acropolis   A fortified district of a city.

adhan   In Islam, the call to prayer.

adit   Nearly horizontal passage from the surface in a mine.

adobe   A building material made from a mixture of water, clay, and straw, often shaped into bricks and dried in the sun.

adze   A chopping and carving tool made with a thin blade attached at right angles to a handle.

age set   A group of people in the same age range who undergo all life transitions together.

age-grade system   An arrangement in which communities consciously promote internal cohesion within age cohorts; the community delegates some tasks to each age group, and members undergo a rite of passage before succeeding to the next (older) cohort.

agropastoral subsistence   A livelihood based on a combination of farming and herding, often involving the migration of herds between pasturelands.

alchemy   The science of trying to transmute base metals into gold, usually practiced by an elite in medieval laboratories.

alderman   An Anglo-Saxon term meaning "chief" and often used to designate the head of a guild and more generally a member of a town council.

amalgamation   Extraction of precious metals from their ores by treatment with mercury.

amphora   A special type of ceramic pot, manufactured on an industrial scale and used for storage throughout the Roman Empire and later by other cultures.

amulet   A charm, or object meant to ward off evil influences and bad luck.

animism   A belief system that holds that the universe is full of spirits who are mostly indifferent to earth and humanity and that anything can have its own spirit, including rocks, plants, and animals.

anneal   To heat and slowly cool metal to make it less brittle and stronger.

anthropomorphize   To endow an inanimate object, animal, or natural phenomenon with human characteristics.

apostasy   Renunciation of a particular religious faith.

apse   The rounded end of a building, such as a church.

aqueducts   Man-made tunnels that bring water from one place to another.

arabesque   In architecture, a style of ornamentation that involves interlacing plant forms and abstract curvilinear motifs, characterized by a series of counterpoised and leafy stems that split off and return into the main stem.

Arabic numerals   Graphic symbols standing for quantities, developed in India and transmitted to Europe by Arabic scholars in the medieval period.

arboriculture   Cultivation of fruit and other foods from trees.

archaeoastronomy   The study of the ways in which ancient cultures interpreted celestial objects.

archaeofauna   A collection of animal bones from an archaeological site.

archipelago   A geographically linked group of islands.

armillary sphere   A celestial globe or model of the heavenly bodies used as a sighting instrument to determine the relative positions and movements of the stars.

asceticism   Practices to control or discipline the body, such as fasting or refraining from sleep or sexual activity, usually undertaken in connection with religious rites or as a spiritual discipline.

ashlar   An individual piece of dressed stone used in construction.

assay   Analysis of ore for particular components.

astrolabe   An instrument used to mathematically determine the positions of celestial bodies.

astrology   A pseudoscience whose validity was almost universally accepted in the Middle Ages and that proposed that a detailed analysis of the positions of the stars and planets can reveal information about the future or about what actions ought to be taken or not taken.

atlatl   A device for throwing a spear or dart that consists of a rod or board with a projection (as a hook or thong) at the rear end to hold the weapon in place until it is released.

atoll   A coral reef island surrounding a lagoon and set in the open sea.

aurora borealis   A spectacular pattern of lights seen near the North Pole when charged particles from the sun are caught in the earth's magnetic field; also called the northern lights.

autonomous   Independent, not subject to outside control.

bailiff   An official whose job in the medieval age was to supervise the work of farmers, enforce the laws of the manor, and dispense justice on behalf of the lord.

baride   The Islamic mail system.

barrel vault   An architectural feature, usually referring to roofs, that starts with a rounded arch and extrudes it horizontally, creating a barrel effect.

barter   Exchange goods for goods without using money.

base metal   A common metal, like lead or iron, that is less valuable than other metals, such as silver and gold, but that alchemists believed they could transform into the more precious substance.

basilica   A large building built by joining parallel rows of arches, creating a long, relatively narrow space.

bas-relief   A sculptural form in which the projection from the surrounding surface is slight and no part of the modeled form is undercut.

batik   A technique for dying cloth in which portions are left undyed in such a way as to form a pattern or design.

bellows   A device for forcing air through a furnace; essentially a bag or box that releases air under pressure when compressed.

benefaction   A contribution to charity.

berm   An earthen embankment or mound.

bestiary   Collection of stories describing real or imaginary animals and offering moral interpretations of their behavior.

biomass   Estimate of the weight per area of living and dead organisms, which can be limited to specific species.

biome   A particular ecological zone determined by the combination of temperature and precipitation (such as a rain forest, a savanna, or a desert).

Black Death   A medieval epidemic of bubonic and pneumonic plague, an infectious and sometimes fatal bacterial disease transmitted by fleas.

blast furnace   Large furnace in which combustion (and heat) is intensified by a blast of air, especially those used for smelting iron with mineral fuel, resulting in a very efficient extraction.

bloomery furnace   Traditional furnace used for smelting iron in preindustrial times, fueled with charcoal and with relatively low efficiency.

book hand   A term used to describe a number of formal scripts that were used to transcribe books.

bride-price   A fee of money or property given by a prospective groom or his family to the male guardian of a woman as part of the marriage contract, to compensate the family for the loss of the productive powers of their daughter; also called bride-wealth.

brigandage   Highway robbery.

brine   Water saturated with salt.

bubo   A dark swelling under the skin, symptomatic of bubonic plague.

bubonic plague   The most common type of plague that infects humans; transmitted from the bite of infected fleas living on rodents.

bull   An official decree of a pope.

bullion   Bars of gold or silver.

burgage plot   A defined parcel of land usually occupied on a rental basis paid to the town lord or a king.

burgess   Generally an inhabitant of a town but often, in particular, one who enjoys the privileges and duties of a freeman or citizen.

burqa (or burka)   Loose garment made of a single piece of material that covers the entire body, face, and hair.

cabaret shows   In medieval European theater, performances involving singing, dancing, juggling, and magic acts.

cacique   In Latin America, the chief of a clan or tribe.

cadastral survey   A collection of information about individual land parcels, providing information on such variables as location, use, value, and ownership.

calendar round   A period of 52 years.

caliph   Deputy or ruler of the Muslim community, who acts as both religious and political leader; considered to be a successor of Muhammad as a spiritual and secular leader of Islam.

caliphate   A realm established to extend political and religious authority over the entire community of Muslim believers.

camera obscura   A dark enclosure with an opening, possibly fitted with a lens, through which an image can enter, to be projected on the opposite wall of the enclosure.

canon law   The law code of the Catholic Church, based in form on Roman law, that regulates matters such as heresy and discipline of the clergy.

canonical   Belonging to a set of writings, usually religious, that are regarded as authentic and authoritative.

canonization   Process by which a holy person becomes included in the canon, or body, of officially recognized saints.

canopy cover   Measure of the area covered by vegetation.

carat   A measure of the fineness of gold or the unit mass used to measure gemstones.

caravan   A group of travelers and merchants who travel together.

caravansary   A rest station or inn that accommodates caravans along trade routes, usually with a large courtyard and necessary facilities for travelers.

caravel   Small, maneuverable sailing vessel that enables seafaring nations to sail long distances against contrary winds and currents.

carburization   Treatment of iron with charcoal to increase its carbon content, thereby forming steel.

carrack   Small, sturdy boat made of wood and hides.

cartography   The making and studying of maps.

case law   Law based on court interpretations.

cash economy   Economy that primarily uses money for buying and selling goods.

cast iron   Iron and carbon alloy produced as a liquid metal that can be cast into molds but is relatively brittle when hardened.

caste   A subdivision of social class used in medieval India; caste determined a person's occupation and marital choices.

cataphract   A heavy cavalry trooper of the Byzantine Empire.

cavalry   The portion of a military force composed of soldiers mounted on horseback.

celestial navigation   Navigation by the use of the stars in the night sky.

cenote   Natural limestone sinkhole, a source of freshwater in the desert areas of Yucatán Peninsula and considered a sacred place.

censer   A vessel inside which incense is burned.

central place   A settlement that plays a central role in state political authority, economic control, or religious activities (usually the "capital" of a kingdom or empire or one of its provincial "capitals"), often centrally located within the polity.

chain mail   Flexible armor made of small, interlinked metal rings.

chanson de geste   Name given to the French heroic epics of the 12th and 13th centuries, traditionally featuring Charlemagne (742–814) and his barons fighting against the Saracens.

charnel house   A chamber or building in which bodies or bones are deposited.

charter   A document describing the rights, privileges, and duties that define government, usually of a town.

chasing   Indentation or grooving in metal.

chattel   Property; often used in the phrase *chattel slavery*, referring to a slave system in which slaves are regarded as the property of their owners.

chi   In Chinese philosophy, the animating force of the body and of the entire cosmos.

chiefdom   A type of intermediate social and political organization, one that usually numbers in the thousands and is headed by a leader who often has inherited authority from ancestors.

child oblation   The permanent donation of a child to the church by its parents, especially prevalent prior to the 12th century in Europe.

chivalry   The art of acting as a knight; the upholding of the ideals of religion, valor, and charity.

chronometer   A device for measuring time at sea.

churching   The ritual of receiving a mother back into the church after childbirth.

cinnabar   Red mineral consisting of native mercuric sulfide that is used as a cosmetic pigment for coloring cheeks or lips red.

city-state   Independent city and its surrounding territory.

cladding   Metal coating bonded to another metal.

clan   A group of one or more lineages or kin groups related together to a common distant ancestor, sometimes regarded as of divine origin.

clepsydra   A water clock.

clientship   A social relationship between two people in which one acknowledges his or her dependence on and lower social status to that of a wealthy patron in return for the patron's protection.

codex (pl. codices)   Manuscript book, especially scripture, classics, or ancient annals.

codification   Act of organizing rules or laws into a code or prescribed system.

colonnades   Series of columns that support a roof.

colophon   A symbol or symbols printed in a book and representing the publisher or details of publication.

common law   Traditional law system of the Germanic tribes, within which the precedent established by earlier legal decisions is binding on future judgments.

commune   A self-governing city or town, typical of medieval Italy.

compass   An instrument used for navigation that points north–south.

concubine   A woman who serves as a sexual partner to a man but who is not married to him.

conscripts   Soldiers who are forced into involuntary military service by a government or ruling authority.

consecrate   To make sacred or holy.

consumer economy   An economy in which the satisfying of human wants is an important aspect of creating wealth.

coppice   The practice of cutting trees above ground level to create a sprouting stump that yields a significant number of smaller branches.

corbel vault   An arched structure created when stones are offset and project toward the center of the arch to support weight.

corvée   Labor exacted by a local authority for little or no pay; typically a form of taxation.

cosmology   Branch of philosophy dealing with the origin and structure of the universe.

coulter   A vertical blade that breaks up hard earth ahead of a plowshare.

council   A body of church elders including a majority of bishops who meet together to conduct church business.

cowrie shell   The shell of a marine mollusk commonly used as currency in Africa, the Americas, and other parts of the world.

cranial deformation   The practice of using boards, mats, or vices to shape the cranium or skull of an infant before the bone has fused together and hardened.

cresset   A stone or metal basket, typically mounted at the top of a pole, in which fuel is burned.

crucible   A vessel made of a heat-resistant material in which metal or glass is melted into liquid.

cruciform   Having the shape of a cross.

crusade   Military action that serves the ends of the church and is called for by the pope, especially the Crusades by western European knights in the Near East between 1095 and 1291.

cubit   A unit of measure equal to the distance from a man's elbow to the tip of his middle finger.

cuirass   An armored jacket or breastplate that protected a soldier's upper body.

cultigen   A cultivated or domesticated plant or animal.

cuneiform   Script with wedge-shaped characters used in ancient writing systems.

cunning men or women   In medieval Europe, folk healers who cast spells or used herbal remedies to promote healing.

cursive   A script that uses connecting strokes and letters, which means that it can be written rapidly.

customary law   System of law based on common usage and customs of a particular group or community.

dactylonomy   A system of counting and signing numerals using the fingers of the hand.

daimyo   A Japanese feudal lord.

damascening   Ornamentation with wavy lines and shapes or inlaying with various metal compositions (including gold or silver); typically done to iron or steel.

debase   To lower the amount of precious metal in a coin.

debt bondage   Selling oneself into slavery to pay off a debt.

decimal   A system of counting with 10 distinct numerals representing the quantities zero through 9.

demesne   The estate of a feudal lord, which included productive land, forests, pasture, villages, and any income-producing property such as mills and workshops.

denary scale   A system of numeration based on the number 10.

derivation   The formation of a word from another word or from a root in the same or another language.

descant   A musical technique, developed in medieval Europe, in which the upper voice and the lower voice move at approximately the same rate with a steady beat.

dhimma   A covenant or pact originally created by Muhammad following the conquest of Jewish Arab tribes in Khaybar, which formed the model for subsequent treatment of conquered Christians and Jews.

dhimmi   A non-Muslim living in the Muslim world who follows a religion that is tolerated by Islam, mainly Christianity and Judaism.

dhow   A small boat with a triangular sail and a low mast.

diaspora   The dispersal of an ethnic or religious group so that members live as minorities or "strangers" in places seen as the ethnic preserve of other peoples.

didgeridoo   A pipe played by aboriginal Australians.

die   An engraved metal cylinder used to transfer an image to a coin.

diets   Regional assemblies or legislatures.

digvijaya   A series of campaigns conducted by Indian kings to extend their rule in the four major directions, symbolizing conquest of the four corners of the earth.

dike A hill of earth built alongside a river, stream, or other body of water to prevent it from overflowing its banks and flooding the surrounding area.

dimorphic zone A region where both pastoral and sedentary activities and modes of production may overlap.

direct reckoning The direct, sequential numbering of days of the month.

disease climate The general healthiness or unhealthiness of an area, including both indigenous and foreign diseases as well as other factors, such as nutrition and warfare, that affect the body's ability to fight off disease and infection.

divination Any ritual means of consulting the divine about matters that cannot be humanly known, such as foretelling the future.

divine right The belief that God, rather than the people, gives a ruler the right to rule.

diviner A person who divines, or prophesizes, also called a soothsayer or prophet.

doge The chief magistrate of Venice or Genoa.

domestication The biological process by which plant and animal species undergo morphological changes (changes in form), usually coming to depend on human intervention for their survival.

dou gong In Chinese architecture, a bracket that can be placed atop a post to increase its weight-bearing capacity.

dowry The money, lands, or goods that a bride brings to her husband in marriage or the contribution that a woman makes to a convent upon becoming a nun.

drawplate Usually made of iron, a device with holes of different diameters through which hot metal could be drawn to form wires or rods.

dress To carve stone into a desired shape and smoothness.

drought A period in which little or no rain falls, reducing water levels below the level required to sustain crops and natural vegetation.

Druid Ancient Celtic priest or religious leader.

dry farming The practice of raising crops while relying only on natural rainfall as a water source.

drystone walls Walls built of stones fitted together without mortar.

ecliptic Path of the sun across the celestial sphere.

economic recession A decline in economic activity, often during an otherwise prosperous era.

El Niño A cyclical weather phenomenon caused by warming of the waters of the eastern Pacific Ocean, often resulting in drought.

elixir A mixture of ingredients once thought capable of transmuting, or transforming, base metals into gold.

embossing An ornamentation technique that applies a raised pattern of design on the surfaces of metal or wood.

emir A local governor or administrator of an Arab province or state.

emporia Trade and manufacturing settlements connected to long-distance exchange networks, often founded and administered through royal control.

engraving A method of decorating used to create a three-dimensional effect by inlaying gold, silver, or precious stones into a metal surface to create designs.

entrepôts Intermediary trade centers along a trade route.

epicenter The geological center of an earthquake.

epicycle In early astronomy, a planet's circular motion, or orbit, moving around the circumference of another, larger circle with the earth at the center.

epidemiologist Scientist who studies the causes and spread of epidemics.

equant Mathematical concept introduced by Ptolemy to account for the motions of the heavenly bodies.

equator An imaginary line drawn around the middle of the earth, separating the Northern Hemisphere and Southern Hemisphere.

equinox Either of two times each year (in March and September) when the sun crosses the equator and the length of day and night are about equal.

escapement A device in a clock or other timepiece that controls the rate of the clock by advancing the movement of a gear train at regular intervals.

escarpment A cliff or steep slope separating two plateaus or level surfaces, usually formed by erosion or geological faulting.

eschatology A theological discourse concerned with the end of time and the final day of the world, during which human deeds may be examined by God on a day of judgment.

ethnography The scientific study of culture, particularly of the cultural character of various nations and peoples.

etymology The linguistic history of a word.

eunuch A castrated man.

evisceration Removal of the internal organs.

excommunication The order of a bishop cutting off from the sacraments of the church an individual who is deemed not to be in a state of grace.

exedra A domelike structure that forms a recess in a building's facade.

exegesis The interpretation of texts, especially religious formative texts.

exogamous marriage Marrying outside a particular group, usually as prescribed by law or social custom.

falconry The sport of hunting small game with falcons.

fallow   Left unseeded during a growing season to conserve and renew the soil.

fallow forest   The developmental stage and types of forest species that grow up after a forest has been cleared.

fermentation   Controlled chemical change in an organic product (such as food) caused by a microorganism such as a yeast.

feudal law   Body of law that governed the personal relations and mutual obligations between lords and freemen in medieval society.

feudalism   System of governance in which a monarch or other landholder (lord) lets control of a given region to a vassal in return for military service.

fief   A grant of land in return for military service and aid.

filial piety   Respect for one's parents, in-laws, and ancestors, a key virtue in both Confucianism and Hinduism.

finial   Decorative objec placed on the peak or corner of a roof.

flail   A small tool consisting of two stout pieces of wood joined by a rope or chain used to winnow crops or to separate edible grains from inedible stalks and chaff.

flux   Substance used to promote fusion of metals in soldering.

flying buttress   An exterior buttress, or wall reinforcement, that is connected to an interior arch and transfers weight to supports outside the building.

foundry   A place where metal is melted.

four-iwan plan   In medieval Islamic architecture, a plan in which rooms were located around a rectangular or square central courtyard.

fulling mill   A mill, common in medieval Europe, that used waterpower to pound woolen cloth in a process known as fulling.

gable   A triangular section of a roof.

gamelan   An Indonesian orchestra composed primarily of a variety of wood, iron, and bronze drums and gongs.

geocentric theory   The belief that the earth stands motionless at the center of the solar system while the moon, sun, planets, and stars revolve around it.

geoglyph   A symbolic figure sketched in the earth.

geomancy   Study of the landscape and of geographical features, as a way to make predictions about the future.

gesso   A mixture of plaster and glue used as a background for paintings.

ghazal   An Arabic love lyric consisting of five to 12 verses.

ghetto   A walled community within a larger city in which Jews were compelled to live in the latter Middle Ages and after.

gibbet   Upright post with a projecting arm for hanging the bodies of executed criminals as a warning.

gilding   Coating or decorating a metal object with gold or another golden substance.

glaze   Shine and color effects in pottery achieved by applying a mixture of silica, alkaline, or metal oxides to the surfaces of vessels.

glyph   A symbolic figure or a character usually incised or carved in relief.

gorget   An article of armor worn at the throat.

grave goods   Material possessions, which might include food, tools, jewelry, and other people, that are placed with the deceased when they are buried.

griot (female, griotte)   Professional poet, singer, and performer of western Africa.

gristmill   A mill that grinds grain.

groin vault   An architectural feature produced by the horizontal intersection of two barrel vaults at right angles.

guild   An organization of people, based on their occupation, that protects members from competition, standardizes prices and training practices, and provides aid to the families of members in need.

Hadith   The narrative collection of sayings and deeds of Muhammad as passed down by individuals who heard or saw the Prophet's deeds and actions during his lifetime.

hagiography   Biographical account of a saint or revered person written to commemorate and glorify his or her life and for devotional rather than scholarly purposes.

hajj   Pilgrimage to Mecca, considered a sacred duty for Muslims.

halal   In Islam, that which is permitted or fit for use by Islamic law or codes of morality.

hallucinogen   A plant or drug that induces visions or imagined perceptions.

haram   In Islam, that which is forbidden or unfit for use by Islamic law or codes of morality.

harem   In the Middle East, an area inside a home set aside for women and children.

Harmattan   Dry northeast trade wind, found on the Atlantic coast of Africa.

harrowing   The task of covering planted seeds with soil to protect them from wind, rain, and animal predators.

hayward   In medieval Europe, a guardian of the fields and hedges, responsible for preventing damage to the properties from the herds and corralling any stray animals.

hegemony   Authority over others; social domination of one group over another.

hegira   Migration.

heliocentric theory   The belief that the sun lies at the center of the solar system and that the earth revolves around it with the rest of the planets.

henna   Reddish-orange dye that comes from leaves of a plant and is used to dye hair and decorate hands and feet.

herbalist   A physician who seeks to alleviate symptoms through the use of medicine made from plants.

heresy   Beliefs concerning theological matters that are condemned by church authorities as opposing orthodox beliefs.

heterodox   At variance with established or accepted beliefs or practices.

hexadecimal   A system of counting by 16, with symbols representing quantities 1 through 16.

historical linguistics   Study that determines the historical relations between communities by analyzing present-day language.

historiography   Historical writing, or the study of historical writing.

hornbook   An aid used to teach medieval European children to read, consisting of a wooden tablet with a handle at the bottom onto which the alphabet was copied.

humor   In ancient medicine, one of four body fluids that were thought to govern the constitution of the body and a person's basic temperament.

hunter-gatherer   A person who lives by hunting and gathering wild foods instead of cultivating plants or herding domesticated livestock.

hydrological engineers   Experts in the effects of moving water on surfaces.

hypostyle   A building in which the roof rests on rows of columns.

hypotenuse   The side of a right triangle opposite the right angle.

iconography   The pictorial representation of a subject through specific visual symbolic strategies that often become standardized over time.

illumination   Miniature painting that often uses gold, silver, or other bright colors and is placed inside a manuscript alongside text.

imam   Generally denoting a spiritual leader of Islam, such as the person who leads prayers in a mosque.

incantation   A spoken chant that works as a magic spell.

inclusive counting   A system of counting within some calendars in which both the first and the last day are included in the calculation.

incrustation   A method of decorating by applying an additional coat or inlay of enriching material to the surface of an object.

indulgence   In the Roman Catholic Church, the granting of remission by the pope of time spent in purgatory for having committed sins.

infanticide   Killing an infant, usually at birth.

infantry   Soldiers or military units that fight on foot.

infidel   Disparaging term applied by medieval Christians to any group that was not Christian, especially Muslims; derived from the Latin for "faithless."

infix   A formative element inserted in the body of a word.

inlay   Decoration of a metal object achieved by inserting or applying fine layers of different metals on the object's surface.

interdict   An official Roman Catholic censure, banning a person or group from receiving the sacraments and Christian burial.

Ionic numeral system   Sometimes known as the Greek alphabetic system, a number system used in ancient Greece and the Byzantine Empire in which the letters of the Greek alphabet represent numerals.

isostatic rebound   Rise of land masses after the weight of glaciers is removed.

ius commune   Literally, "common law"; in medieval Europe, a common body of civil law that formed out of canon law and Roman law in the 12th century.

Janissaries   Turkish corps of slave soldiers drawn from Christian towns and villages, converted, and given military training.

jihad   An Arabic word denoting a struggle undertaken for the sake of Islam.

jinn   In Islamic belief, spirits or supernatural beings that dwell in various forms on the earth and exercise supernatural powers.

kami   In Shinto, local guardian spirits.

kamikaze   A Japanese word that means "divine wind"; originally a description of the two typhoons that prevented the Mongol rulers of China from invading Japan in the 14th century, it later came to refer to Japanese suicide pilots during World War II.

kana   A script for writing the syllables of Japanese.

khan   Ruler of a Mongol khanate, one of the Asian domains established during the conquests of Genghis Khan and his successors in the 13th century.

kimono   A long, wide-sleeved Japanese robe.

kinship   Ties (either biological or cultural) that determine human groups.

kiva   A North American Indian ceremonial structure that is typically round and partly underground.

labor services   Taxation in the form of unpaid labor rather than through the payment of cash or goods.

laity   Religious worshippers who are not ordained members of the clergy.

lamellar   Composed of small plates laced together.

lateen sail   A triangular sail.

lathe   A device for spinning wood while the wood is carved by a cutting tool.

latitude and longitude   A regular grid of imaginary lines laid over the earth to give precise and consistent references to the locations of geographical features; latitude measures distances north and south of the equator, and longitude measures distances east and west of the prime meridian.

latticework   A decoration technique in which strips of metal or wood are crossed, resulting in a crisscross pattern of design; commonly used in furniture and building ornamentation.

league   Unit of distance equal to about 3 miles.

lexical   Relating to words and word roots.

lexicon   The vocabulary of a language or branch of knowledge.

limbus puerorum   In the Christian religion, the destination of the souls of the unbaptized who have died in infancy.

lineage   Line of descent from a common ancestor.

lingua franca   A common language between speakers whose native languages are different.

linguistics   The study of grammar, syntax, vocabulary, and other aspects of language.

lintel   A horizontal architectural beam spanning and usually carrying the load above an opening (such as a window or door), across vertical posts.

liquation   Method of extracting silver from copper containing silver by treating the metal with lead.

Little Ice Age   A period of cooler temperatures and longer winters that began just after the close of the Middle Ages.

Little Renaissance   In 12th-century western Europe, the reception of a great mass of lost Greek literature in Arabic translation and its effects on learning and civilization.

liturgy   A rite having to do with the Eucharist, the sacrament commemorating Christ's Last Supper.

livery   Distinctive clothing or emblems worn to signal membership in a particular group, such as a guild.

loanword   A word adopted from another language.

lodestone   A piece of intensely magnetic magnetite, a magnetic mineral form of iron, used as an early form of magnetic compass.

loincloth   A piece of cloth wrapped around the hips and groin, typically worn by men in warm climates.

Long Count   A Mesoamerican nonrepeating calendrical system of counting days from a specific origin date.

lost-wax casting   A process in which a wax sculpture is encased in clay, the wax is melted, and the resulting cavity is filled with molten metal and allowed to cool; the clay is then broken, making a metal copy of the original wax sculpture.

lunar calendar   A calendar based on a period of 12 lunar months (approximately 354 days total).

lunation   A lunar month, that is, the period between new moons.

luster paint   A glaze coloring technique in which dissolved gold or other precious metal oxides are applied as a base to the surfaces of pottery or glass vessels, resulting in a metallic shine and color.

macroregion   A large area.

madrassa   A Muslim school, college, or university, typically attached to or associated with a mosque.

mail   Armor made of rings of metal interwoven to make a sort of cloth.

maize   The main staple grain of the Americas, frequently called "corn" in the United States.

majuscule   Any script written using letters of equal height, such as all capital letters.

manna   A divine animating energy.

manor   A system of medieval landholding in which a large agricultural area held by a lord in return for a pledge of military service to a higher authority, such as the king, was worked by peasants bound to the land.

manorial justice   Also called seigneurial justice, part of the economic and administrative system known as manorialism or seigneurialism in medieval Europe, wherein landlords had jurisdictional authority over their estates and held courts in which they dispensed justice.

mansard   A roof with two slopes on each of its four sides.

mantle   A sleeveless cloak.

manumission   The freeing of slaves.

maqamah   A literary genre, popular in the medieval Islamic world, used to tell basically simple and entertaining stories in rhymed prose.

marquetry   A method of inlaying wood with various colors or other materials to achieve elaborate design effects.

mashrabiya   In the Middle East, bay windows enclosed with decorative wood screens that allow cross-ventilation as well as family privacy.

masnavi   A poetic form that originated in Persia and that involves a rhyming couplet; closest to the epic poem in Islamic literature.

materia medica   A variety of natural substances used in medical remedies.

matriarchy   Social organization dominated by women.

matrilineal   Tracing ancestry through a female line of descent.

matrilocal Term used to describe a social custom according to which a groom lives with his bride's mother's kin rather than his own.

mausoleum A large structure that contains one or more tombs.

mead An alcoholic beverage made by fermenting honey boiled with water.

Medieval Warm Period A period of generally high temperatures and longer growing seasons that occurred from the ninth to the 14th centuries in Europe.

melismas Musical devices, common in medieval chants, in which many notes are set to a single syllable of text.

melothesia The belief that the human body is a direct reflection of the universe as a whole, especially of the stars and constellations.

mendicant Begging friar who lives off the alms of others.

mercenaries Soldiers who fight for pay rather than allegiance to a ruler or a national cause.

mestizo A person of mixed European and American Indian ancestry.

middens Heaps of discarded items or refuse; examined in archaelogical contexts to determine materials used by a community.

mihrab A niche in a mosque that indicates the direction of Mecca.

millstone A flat stone with grooves carved in it used as a grinding surface in a mill.

minaret A tower attached to an Islamic mosque and from which a muezzin calls the faithful to prayer.

minbar Pulpit in a mosque.

minuscule A script in which the strokes of letters may include strokes above and below the line (ascenders and descenders) that create letterforms of unequal height, such as lower-case letters.

miracle play A play that focuses on the lives and deeds of Christian saints and heroes.

moldboard A horizontal bar that turns soil after it has been dug by a plowshare.

monastery Secluded house in which monks live and concentrate on living a pious existence.

monolith A large freestanding stone, usually set up for or associated with a religious function.

monolithic Carved of a single block of stone.

monophony Music that has one melodic line with little or no accompaniment; characteristic of medieval chant or plainsong.

monsoon A tropical climate characterized by long, dry winters and rainy summers that arrive predictably; might refer to the climate, the summer rains, or the prolonged winds blowing from the equator and preceding the rains.

monumental With reference to artworks, generally large in scale or created to commemorate an event, such as an important historical occurrence or a death.

morality play An allegorical play with a moralistic message wherein the characters embody abstract qualities, such as Virtue and Vice.

mortar and pestle A hand mill that consists of a bowl (mortar) and a heavy stick with a rounded end (pestle).

mortise A hole in stone, wood, concrete, or some other material that is designed to hold a projecting piece of material called a tenon.

mosaic Image or pattern made by arranging and affixing small pieces of colored tile, stone, glass or other materials to a flat surface.

motet A musical composition in which a fragment of a chant, given a repeated rhythmic pattern, underlies one to three other voices, each with its own text.

movable feast A festival or religious holiday that falls on different days in different years.

nagual The Aztec concept of a human's animal alter ego.

natal family A surrogate kinship group based on an intense bond of loyalty between a mother and her children.

natal horoscopy The idea that a person's future may be known in detail from looking at the position of the planets at the instant of his or her birth.

nave The central aisle of a church or cathedral.

nayaka The military aristocracy of medieval India.

neologism The extended meaning of an existing word.

niello Amalgam of dark metals applied to etched portions of a silver receptacle to create silver patterns against black backgrounds.

night soil Human excrement commonly used as agricultural fertilizer in the Middle Ages; so called because the workmen who dealt with it were allowed to transport it only at night.

niqab Veil that covers the face and leaves a slit for the eyes.

nixtamalization A process in which grain is boiled in limewater, removing the outer husk to make vitamins and proteins more available in finished food products.

nomadic pastoralism A form of pastoralism in which herders are seasonally or constantly mobile to ensure adequate water and pasture for their livestock.

noria A device for lifting water from one level to another using a series of buckets attached to a wheel.

nucleated settlement A compactly settled village or town in which the houses and other buildings are all grouped close to one another, with the main agricultural lands (except kitchen gardens) surrounding the settlement as a sea surrounds an island.

obliquity   Angular deviation from a reference line; the obliquity of the ecliptic (the path of the sun across the celestial sphere) is the angle between the plane of the earth's equator and the plane of its orbit.

occult science   A clearly defined set of practices within a religious or philosophical tradition that usually involves initiation and the teaching of secret information between master and pupil, such as with alchemy.

occultation   Astronomical event wherein a planet passes behind the moon.

ogive   Any pointed shape, figure, or feature; often used to refer to the pointed arches of medieval Gothic architecture.

open-field agriculture   A system of medieval farm management in which households did not fence their individual plots and were subject to the regime of a shared calendar, with plots managed by separate households during the growing season but subject to communal grazing after the harvest.

orthodoxy   Established and accepted practice or belief.

ossuary   A storage container for bones, which might be an urn, a chest, or even the vault of church.

paddle-and-anvil technique   A technique used to form a pottery vessel in which the potter holds a supporting tool, the anvil, on the inside of the vessel while striking the outside with a paddle, usually made of wood.

paduka   Indian sandals with a large knob that was gripped between the toes.

pagan   A Latin word suggesting lack of sophistication; used by Christians to describe Greeks, Romans, and other peoples who practiced traditional religions not related to Judaism, Christianity, or Islam.

pagoda   A tall tower found in eastern Asia, typically built to honor the Buddha.

palimpsest   A piece of parchment used a second time by scraping off the original text before writing on it again.

palisade   A fence of wooden stakes set into the ground and used for enclosure or defense.

pampa   Large, grass-covered plain found in South America to the east of the Andes.

panacea   A substance that can cure all ills and was once thought to restore youth.

pannage   The act of allowing pigs to forage at will in a forest for food; also the law that allows this practice.

papacy   The system of government of the Roman Catholic Church, headed by the pope.

parchment   Animal skin—typically goat, sheep, or calf—that has been cleaned and prepared for use as writing material.

parliament   Popular assemblies in western Europe descended from assemblies of the old Germanic tribes.

partitive inheritance   A system under which each son inherits a share of his father's wealth.

pastoral nomadism   A lifestyle that is migratory in nature and involves the shepherding of animals.

pastoral   Related to the lifestyle of herding animals, such as sheep or goats.

pastoralism   A type of economy emphasizing the raising and tending of livestock such as cattle, camels, goats, and sheep to produce food and utility items, such as skins, for trade and consumption.

pastoralists   People living on an economy of herded domesticated animals, usually associated with extensive grasslands suitable for grazing.

patriarchy   A form of social organization in which men dominate women.

patrilineage   A kinship system based on tracing kin group membership through one's father.

patristic texts   Works pertaining to the writings of the church fathers.

patron-client relations   A system of social relations, common throughout the ancient and medieval Mediterranean world, in which a wealthy and powerful person gave legal and economic protection to a group of dependent clients in exchange for their political support.

pavilion   A large tent like that used by nomadic Arabs.

pectoral   A flat ornament or adornment worn on the chest.

penance   Atonement of sin, generally consisted of a confession to a priest.

pendentive   A triangular segment of a sphere, which tapers to a point at the bottom and flanges outward at the top.

peonage   Forced labor to pay off debts or to be performed in lieu of taxes.

permafrost   Soil whose water is permanently frozen, even in summer.

personality of the law   Legal principle whereby the laws governing individuals were applied according to a person's ethnic origin rather than the territory in which they lived.

petroglyph   A carving or inscription on a rock.

pharmacopoeia   A book that contains descriptions of medications and drugs along with directions for compounding prescriptions.

philosopher's stone   A substance thought to cure all diseases and bestow perpetual life on its user.

phonetics   The system of sounds of speech in a particular language or languages.

physiognomy   The pseudoscience of predicting character from the shape of the head.

pier   A wall support, similar to a column but generally thicker and more massive.

pig iron Iron and carbon alloy produced as a liquid metal in a blast furnace; it can be decarburized to form wrought iron or steel, suitable for smithing into objects.

pilgrimage Journey to a shrine of religious faith, such as Mecca, Santiago, or Jerusalem, for devotional purposes.

pit house An ancient form of dwelling consisting of a pit excavated in the earth and roofed over.

placebo effect The psychological effect that causes patients to feel better after they receive medical treatment, whether or not it is actually effective.

place-value notation Also called positional notation, a numerical system in which the value of a digit is determined by its unit value multiplied by the base raised to the power of its position.

plaque A thin plate or inscribed tablet of metal, porcelain, or other materials used for decoration or commemoration on a piece of furniture, walls, or doors of a building, usually displaying a decoration with a geometric interlace.

play out To exhaust a source of a mineral.

plectrum A pick used to pluck stringed musical instruments.

plowshare The main blade on a plow, designed to dig and loosen soil for later planting.

pneumonic plague The most deadly and contagious type of plague; this type of plague settles in the lungs and is transmitted from person to person.

polder A field recovered from the sea through a system of dikes and drainage canals, enabling farmers in coastal areas of the Netherlands to increase the land under cultivation.

political cycling The cycling of regional political power between competing polities in a region, with the rapid rise and equally rapid collapse of dominant polities due to economic competition, warfare, and other forms of intense interpolity interaction.

polities Organized societies, each with one specific kind of government.

pollard The practice of cutting trees high on the trunk so that young sprouts are out of the reach of grazing animals.

polygyny The practice of marrying more than one woman.

polyphony Music that contains two or more melodic lines.

polytheist Person who worships more than one god.

pontoon bridge A bridge, often military, made by tying boats side by side at a landing stage and covering them with planks.

portcullis An iron grille used to protect the wooden doors of a castle entrance.

portico A porch supported by pillars.

potter's wheel A large stone wheel mounted parallel to the ground so that it could spin freely; its circular motion (long-lasting because of the weight) allowed potters to form clay into pottery.

precession The earlier occurrence of the equinoxes due to a slow variation in the rotation of the earth.

prefecture An administrative division of territory in medieval China.

prefix An element placed at the beginning of a word as an inflection to express a grammatical function or attribute such as tense, mood, person, number, case, and gender.

primogeniture The right of the eldest son to inherit an entire estate without dividing it among younger siblings.

prosody The metrical or rhythmical aspects of verse.

pseudepigraphy The practice of publishing a book under a name other than the actual author's, chosen to attract attention to the work or to suggest continuity with the tradition of the supposed author.

pseudoscience A body of knowledge that is meant to describe or control the physical world but which fails as a science because it relies on unverifiable wisdom rather than on observation and experiment.

psychotropic Type of plant or drug that affects a person's state of mind.

qanat In the Islamic Middle East, an underground irrigation network of wells and canals that brings water to crop fields with minimal loss through evaporation.

qasida An elaborately structured Arabic ode of 20 to 100 verses that opens with a short prelude, usually a love poem, followed by an account of the poet's journey and a tribute to the poet's patron, his tribe, or even himself.

quadrant In early astronomy, an instrument that takes angular and altitude measurements of the stars.

quadrivium The four advanced subjects in medieval education: arithmetic, geometry, astronomy, and music.

quetzal A bird native to Central America whose bright green feathers were used to decorate ceremonial costumes and headdresses.

quinary scale A system of numeration based on the number 5.

quipu A horizontal rope from which hung knotted cords of various colors; used by the Inca in South America for making calculations or indicating time and possibly to record historical and phonetic information.

raffia A textile woven from the soft fronds of a palm tree indigenous to sub-Saharan Africa.

raga A traditional Indian melody.

raja-mandala An ancient Indian geopolitical concept in which rulers attempted to extend their power outward in a circular pattern representing the cosmos.

ramparts   Broad elevations or mounds of earth raised as fortifications.

reeve   In medieval Europe, a supervisor who ensured proper use of the land and payments by the peasantry; the chief authority in a large village or town who served on behalf of the king.

relic   An object said to be part of the physical remains of a holy person or object or the former possession of a holy person, supposedly imbued with spiritual and magical powers and venerated for its spiritual power.

relief carving   Figure that is carved away from a material, such as stone or wood, and is not freestanding but part of the background; low-relief carving is shallow, and high-relief carving is comparatively deep.

reliquary   An object designed to house relics, or holy objects associated with saints and other venerated persons.

repoussé   Metal shaped or ornamented with patterns in relief made by hammering or pressing on the reverse side.

revetment   A facing that holds up an embankment.

rite of passage   A ritual event that marks the change in an individual's social or physical status.

Roman law   Legal system descended from the law of the Roman Empire, within which legal decisions are not based on precedent but on a law code established by the authority of the central government (that is, the king or emperor).

Romance languages   Languages such as Spanish, French, Italian, and Romanian that developed from Latin during the Middle Ages.

roof comb   A highly decorated stone structure placed on top of buildings.

Rosetta Stone   A basalt stone, discovered in 1799, that gives clues to deciphering Egyptian hieroglyphs.

roulette   A small wheel, especially one with sharp teeth, mounted in a handle, for making lines of marks, dots, or perforations.

royal road   The largest type of road in medieval Europe, wide enough to support a great deal of foot traffic and the passing of armies.

rushlight   A type of candle made by coating a rush with tallow or grease.

saga   Heroic poem in Old Norse retelling the deeds of legendary or historical figures or families.

sage   A wise man, philosopher, or scholar whose opinions and pronouncements are generally respected by his culture.

samurai   Professional, aristocratic warriors who formed military regiments in medieval Japan.

sarcophagus   A stone container, often elaborately carved or decorated, used as a coffin.

sarong   A rectangular length of cloth that can be tied in various ways to form a skirt, dress, or cloak.

sawmill   A mill, common during the Middle Ages, that used gears to power saws to cut wood.

scarification   The practice of cutting decorative scars into the skin.

schism   A split within the church occasioned by disagreement over doctrinal matters (as in the great schism between Orthodoxy and Catholicism in 1054) or by confusion over the legitimate head of the church (as in the Western Schism after the period from 1378 to 1417).

scriptorium   A room in a monastery where monks copied out and wrote manuscripts.

secondary burial   A burial in which the remains have been moved from one site to another.

sedentarism   Settled life; shift from an impermanent to a permanent way of living; also called sedentism.

sedentary   Term used by historians to describe cultures that maintain more or less permanent communities, usually because of their dependence on agriculture rather than nomadic hunting and gathering.

segmentary lineage system   A social structure in which different kin descent groups compete for scarce resources, achieving internal cohesion only against a common external threat.

serfdom   The relationship of a person to an elite patron, in which there is an obligation to pay tribute and to perform military, agricultural, craft, or other services but the individual cannot be sold to another patron.

sextant   An instrument used to calculate latitude by measuring the angle between the horizon and the sun.

shahada   The first pillar of wisdom in Islam: that there is no god but God and Muhammad is his messenger.

shaman   A spiritual practitioner who acts as intermediary between the natural and supernatural worlds, using magic or sorcery for purposes of healing, divination, and control over natural events.

sharia   Islamic law derived from the Koran.

shifting cultivation   An agricultural strategy in which farmers cut vegetation to form new fields, burn the vegetation to enrich the field's soil, grow crops in the field for two to three years, and finally leave the field fallow for 10 to 20 years while they move on to make new fields.

shinden-zukuri   Aristocratic style of Japanese architecture featuring a central hall and surrounding symmetrical rooms.

shogun   Any of a line of military leaders who governed Japan during the medieval and early modern periods.

shoin-zukuri   Style of Japanese architecture employed by samurai, featuring gardens and asymmetrical layouts.

sidereal compass   A chart of specific stars that allows a person to determine his or her position relative to them and to known landmarks.

siege   The particular military art of surrounding an enemy fortification such as a castle in order to starve the garrison out and eventually assaulting it if necessary.

sigla   In Islam, scribal abbreviations in the form of symbols that commonly stand for God's holy names.

skraelings   Norse term for Native Americans.

slag   What remains after ore is smelted and the metal is removed.

slash-and-burn agriculture   The cutting and burning of forest or woodlands to create fields for agriculture; also called shifting cultivation.

slip   Thinned potter's clay used to coat ceramics.

sluices   Floodgates.

smelt   To melt ore to separate out the metal from the other parts of the ore.

snuff   A powdered substance that is inhaled, often through the nostrils.

social banking   Building social obligations by giving and receiving help and goods.

social stratification   The division of people into social classes based on birth, wealth, prestige, status, and similar factors.

sod   Surface soil held together by the matted roots of grass.

solar calendar   A calendar based on one full revolution of the earth around the sun.

solstice   Either of the times each year when the sun is at its farthest point from the equator, marking the longest and shortest days of the year (in June and December, respectively).

sphere of influence   An area in which one nation or culture dominates economically, politically, or militarily.

splinter   A thin strip of wood coated in tallow that acted as a type of candle.

spolia   Pieces of architecture from former buildings that are reused to create new monuments.

state   A type of social and political organization involving centralized control, formal territories, large populations, and usually some form of urban settlements.

stateless economy   Economy unregulated by a government.

stela (pl. stelae)   A carved stone marker used to commemorate deaths or historical events.

steppe   A geographic area of flat, semiarid grassland.

stop   In speech, a consonant sound produced by closing off the airflow in the vocal tract.

storm surge   A significant increase in sea levels caused by a storm.

stucco   Plaster made of gypsum or lime used to decorate walls made with statues.

stupa   A hemispherical shrine that holds relics of the Buddha or that lies somewhere the Buddha passed during his life.

stylized   Describing a work in which the artist uses artistic forms to create unnatural effects.

subsistence economy   Economy in which people produce little more than what they need for basic survival from one day to the next.

sudd   In the Middle East, a dam, whether used to divert or store water.

suffix   An element placed at the end of a word as an inflection to express a grammatical function or attribute such as tense, mood, person, number, case, and gender.

sultan   A title assumed by some Muslim rulers after the 11th century that signifies full sovereignty or independence of a higher ruler.

sumptuary laws   Laws that attempt to regulate or prevent extravagant spending and consumption.

sunspots   Dark spots that are cooler than the rest of the sun and appear in a cyclical pattern on the sun's surface.

sura   A chapter of the Koran.

sutras   Teachings of the Buddha.

suttee   The Hindu custom in which a dead man's sonless widow throws herself on her husband's funeral pyre to be cremated with him.

swaddling   The custom of wrapping babies' bodies tightly in cloths or narrow bands with the intention of keeping them warm and preventing their limbs from growing crooked.

syllabaries   Sets of written symbols or characters that represent syllables, or parts of words.

syntax   The organization of words into sentences; the order and structure of sentences.

talionic   Based on the concept of retaliation.

talisman   An object thought to have magical properties, which could be imparted to the person who wore or carried it.

tallow   Rendered animal fat.

talud-tablero   A stepped pyramid design in which each terrace is composed of a vertical panel with recessed inset and a sloping wall (talud) that is topped by a rectangular inset panel (tablero).

tannin   Chemical used for treating animal skin to make leather.

tariff   A payment exacted by a government for the importation or exportation of goods.

tectonic plates   Seven major and numerous minor sections of the outermost part of the earth's interior that slowly float atop a less solid part of the interior of the earth.

tenon   A projection from the side of a piece of stone, wood, or other material that is designed to fit into a hole of similar size and shape called a mortise.

terraced agriculture   Agriculture that uses artificially leveled and stepped hilly or sloped regions, to conserve soil, retain moisture, and make plowing and other aspects of cultivation possible on otherwise marginally productive lands

terra-cotta   Low-fired clay often used for sculpture, ceramics, and architectural elements.

testator   A person who has made a legal will.

theme   An administrative district of the Byzantine Empire.

theocracy   Rule by priests.

three-field system   A method of planting fields in rotation, with two fields devoted to growing crops (spring and fall) and the third allowed to lie fallow to improve its fertility.

tokonoma   A recess in a wall in a Japanese home specially made to display a picture that is often secular.

tonal   Term describing languages in which the speaker raises or lowers the voice when pronouncing words, thus allowing any word to be pronounced a different way and have a unique meaning.

tort   A wrongful act that carries with it relief in the form of damages to the victim.

trabeated pyramid   A building form of successively rising posts and horizontal beams, with the space between posts narrowing with each successively higher level, resembling a side of a pyramid.

transept   In a cruciform church, the area set crosswise to the nave.

transhumance   A form of nomadic pastoralism in which herders keep a home base with a permanent water hole and seasonally leave this base to seek new pastures for their livestock, returning to the base as water and pasture grows scarce.

transmutation   In alchemy, the supposed process of turning one metal into another, as lead into gold.

transubstantiation   Mystical transformation of the bread and wine of the Eucharist into the body and blood of Christ.

trebuchet   A siege engine in the form of a large catapult, which could fling heavy stones or other projectiles several hundred yards against the walls and towers of an enemy castle.

trepanation   The medical procedure of drilling into the skull; one of the oldest forms of surgery, dating far back into prehistory.

tribute   A payment made by a ruler or a country to another ruler or country as a form of submission or as the price of protection.

trickster   A recurrent character in indigenous North American mythology who represents the unpredictability of fate and absurdity of life; also a creator divinity and culture hero or heroine.

triconsonantal   Composed of three consonants.

trigonometry   The mathematical study of triangles.

trivium   The three basic subjects in medieval education: grammar, rhetoric, and logic.

trypanosomiasis   Also known as "sleeping sickness," a disease affecting both animals and humans that is spread by the saliva of the tsetse fly.

tumulus (pl. tumuli)   A mound of earth and stone built over one or more graves.

tundra   Land in the arctic whose soil is permafrost, preventing the growth of large plants and usually unsuitable for human habitation.

tunic   A shirtlike garment that could have short sleeves, long sleeves, or no sleeves; could fall to between the hips and the ankles; and was often belted at the waist.

tuyere   An opening for supplying air to the interior of a furnace.

twining   The technique of twisting plant fibers during the process of weaving.

two-field system   A system of rotating crops between two fields, one of which is allowed to lie fallow in alternating years.

type   An image or other design stamped onto coins.

typhoon   A cyclonic storm identical to a hurricane in force and meteorological characteristics but originating over the Pacific Ocean and traveling westward.

typology   Study, analysis, or classification based on types or categories.

uji   The Japanese term for the aristocratic clans that participated in government administration and other tasks during the early medieval period.

umma   The Muslim community as a whole.

unguent   Cream or lotion applied to the skin to soften or perfume it.

varna   Any of the four major social classifications of medieval India.

vassal   Freeman who rendered services to a sovereign, lord, or other superior in return for land.

vellum   A particular type of parchment made from the skin of a calf or other young animal.

veranda   Covered porch attached to the outside of a building.

vernacular   The everyday language or dialect of a particular region or group.

vigesimal system   A base-20 counting system, using digits of hands and feet to count.

villa   Large rural estate common in the Roman Empire but that survived into the medieval period as the precursor of the manor system.

virgin soil epidemics   Contagious diseases that affect a population group, which has had no previous exposure, with catastrophic results.

visionary experience   Information, often interpreted as religiously significant, that a person receives in a dream, in a trance, or as a result of taking hallucinogenic drugs.

vizier   An executive officer in Muslim societies.

votive   Done to fulfill a vow or as an act of devotion.

wattle and daub   A structure created using a wood latticework covered in a mixture of clay, mud, and straw.

weirs   Dams in waterways designed to divert water or to collect fish.

wet nurse   A woman who breast-feeds another woman's baby for pay.

wootz steel   A form of steel manufactured in medieval India that was famed for its toughness and flexibility.

wrought iron   Form of iron almost entirely free of carbon and having a fibrous structure that is readily forged and welded.

wrought   Produced by beating into shapes with hammer.

xenophobic   Afraid of outsiders or foreign elements.

yin and yang   The two opposing principles in Chinese philosophy—one considered "female" and the other "male"—that also found application in traditional medicine, which sought to keep these principles always in balance within the body to prevent disease; the male principle is hard, bright, and active, while the female principle is soft, dark, and receptive.

yoga   A spiritual and physical discipline developed in India whereby the practitioner, the yogi, seeks to train his or her own consciousness so as to achieve a sort of divine tranquility.

yurt   A tentlike dwelling.

zimbabwe   Term for a stone enclosure among the Shona people of southern Africa.

zodiac   The 12 constellations circling the celestial sphere of fixed stars along the ecliptic, the path of the sun through the sky.

zooarchaeology   The study of animal remains at archaeological sites.

zoomorphic   Taking the form of an animal.

200 – 500	AFRICA	THE AMERICAS

AFRICA

ca. 200: The unexplained end of the Nok civilization in northern Nigeria; this culture was the precursor of many of medieval Africa's achievements in art and technology.

ca. 300: Berber tribesmen from North Africa introduce the domestic camel into the trans-Sahara caravan trade.

ca. 330: The kingdom of Axum (modern-day Ethiopia), an economic power in the early Middle Ages because of its control of Indian Ocean trade, converts to Christianity.

ca. 350: The pseudepigraphic book I Enoch is translated into Ethiopic and becomes a central text of the Ethiopian Orthodox Church.

ca. 400: Iron-smelting technology begins to spread throughout sub-Saharan Africa and is adapted by smiths to local conditions.

ca. 450: The foundation of the kingdom of Ghana in the Niger Delta (Sahel) marks the emergence of a rising economy in the area based on control of the trans-Sahara trade.

THE AMERICAS

ca. 250: The rise of numerous competing Mayan city-states in Mesoamerica.

ca. 450: The Maya develop paper and begin to write their hieroglyphic script (developed about 600 years earlier and used for inscriptions) in manuscripts.

---

500 – 600
(continues)

AFRICA

ca. 500: The Bantu expansion is completed: Bantu-speaking peoples from central Africa spread over much of sub-Saharan Africa, bringing agriculture and metalworking technology with them.

ca. 500: In Egypt, The Emerald Tablet and the *Turba philosophorum*, important alchemical texts influencing Islamic,

THE AMERICAS

ca. 500: Teotihuacán is founded and flourishes as the first urban center and empire in the Valley of Mexico.

ca. 500: Maize cultivation reaches the Eastern Woodlands of North America, completing its pre-Columbian range.

535: The eruption of Krakatau in Indonesia causes temporary climate change that

Chronology by Region

ASIA AND THE PACIFIC	EUROPE	THE ISLAMIC WORLD
499: The Indian astronomer Aryabhata publishes the *Aryabhatiya*, which describes moonlight as reflected sunlight, provides a technique of calculating lunar eclipses, and shows some indirect knowledge of Greek heliocentrism.	**476**: Collapse of the Western Roman Empire in the face of invasions by Germanic tribes that found new kingdoms. **499**: Completion of the Babylonian Talmud, a text destined to become central to the religious life of European Jewry.	**ca. 450**: The Arabic script, later used to write the Koran, is developed from the Nabataean alphabet; it becomes one of the most widespread scripts in the Middle Ages.
535: The volcano Krakatau erupts, affecting world climate; a tsunami may have destroyed the capital city of the Tarumanagara Kingdom on Java. **ca. 540**: The Indian mathematician Brahmagupta develops a means of writing zero and using it in mathematical operations.	**ca. 500**: The promulgation of the Salic law by the Frankish monarchy, one of several bodies of German common law put in writing at about this time. **529**: Saint Benedict founds the monastery of Monte Cassino near Benevento in Italy and shortly thereafter writes the Benedictine rule, the founding document of Western monasticism.	**ca. 570**: The birth of Muhammad, the founder of Islam and author of the Koran.

	AFRICA	**THE AMERICAS**

500 – 600 (continued)

European, and eventually even modern science, are composed.

533–34: Byzantine forces under Count Belisarius conquer and annex the Vandal kingdom in North Africa.

535: The eruption of Krakatau in Indonesia may have affected the annual Indian Ocean monsoon and contributed to the outbreak of plague in the Nile Valley that eventually spread throughout Europe (541–42).

ca. 540: Christian missions sent to Nubia (northern Sudan) by the Byzantine government convert the country, divided into several small states modeling themselves after Byzantium, to Christianity.

results in a severe famine at Teotihuacán and perhaps other areas of the Americas.

562: The Mayan city-state Caracol defeats and supplants the widespread influence of its rival, Tikal.

600 – 700

642: Arab armies occupy Egypt and capture Alexandria after a 14-month siege.

ca. 650: A large-scale slave trade begins to develop between the Indian Ocean coast of Africa and the Islamic world.

665: Arab forces conquer Byzantine North Africa to the west of Egypt (modern-day Libya, Tunisia, Algeria, and Morocco).

ca. 600: Expansion of the Tiwanaku state from the Titicaca plateau in the northern Andes and of the Wari state on the Cuzco plain in South America.

ca. 650: The prototype of the Dresden codex is composed, an astrological handbook concerned with predicting the motion of Venus and lunar eclipses.

ca. 650: Teotihuacán in Mexico is destroyed, its temples and palaces burned, and its population of over 100,000 scattered.

683: The sarcophagus lid of King Pakal of the Mayan city of Palenque, showing the dead king's body flying through the air, is created as one of the great masterpieces of Mayan art.

ASIA AND THE PACIFIC

ca. 550: Collapse of the Gupta Empire in India, under the financial drain of defending the North-West Frontier against Hunic invaders.

ca. 550: Final composition of the Bhagavad Gita, an epic poem connecting ancient Indian literature to medieval Hindu religious practices.

589: After a period of political fragmentation, the Sui Dynasty briefly reunifies China until 618.

593: Buddhism is introduced to Japan by the Prince Regent Shotoku; Japanese society begins to absorb Chinese culture.

605: The introduction of the competitive imperial examination system (based on Confucian philosophy) to select civil servants.

610: Initial completion of the Grand Canal linking northern and southern China.

618: The foundation of the Tang Dynasty in China, which moves the capital to Xi'an in western China and reopens the Silk Road, initiating a period of openness in Chinese culture.

624: The promulgation of the Tang Legal Code, foundation of all medieval Chinese law (revised in 737).

635: Nestorian Christian monks introduce Christianity to China, building a church near the capital of Xi'an.

645: The Chinese monk Xuanzang completes a fifteen-year journey to India and back to secure original Sanskrit copies of Buddhist scriptures and writes a geographical treatise about his journey for the emperor.

ca. 650: In China woodblock printing, in which an entire page of text was printed from a hand-carved wooden master, allowed mass-production of texts; paper is invented in China at about the same time.

ca. 650: Sa`ad ibn Abi Waqqas, one of Muhammad's companions, makes an embassy to the emperor Gaozong, introducing Islam to China.

ca. 660: Yan Liben paints *The Scroll of the Thirteen Emperors*, the earliest surviving masterpiece of Chinese painting.

EUROPE

529–33: Promulgation of the Code of Justinian (*Corpus iuris civilis*), final summary of the body of Roman law.

541–42: A pandemic of bubonic plague kills perhaps 40 percent of the population of the Byzantine Empire and devastates the rest of Europe (called the Plague of Justinian after the ruling emperor).

552: The emperor Justinian sends two Nestorian monks as spies to inner Asia; they succeed in bringing back silkworms and the technique of sericulture.

569: Lombard invasion of Italy: the low point of the depredations caused by the Germanic tribes that destroyed urban culture in western Europe.

626: Combined force of Avars and Sassanians besiege Constantinople.

629: Visigoths drive the Byzantines from southern Spain.

663: Byzantine emperor Constans II (630–68) leads an army against the Lombards, but retreats to Sicily.

673: Visigoth king Wamba (r. 672–81) defeats an Arab fleet near the Straits of Gibraltar.

673–78: Arab armies besiege Constantinople by land and sea.

ca. 675: Byzantine defenders of Constantinople deploy a new weapon, Greek fire—a type of flamethrower.

681: Onogur Huns establish the kingdom of Bulgaria.

687: Victory over dynastic rivals at the Battle of Tertry in northern France extends the power of the Frankish king Pepin II (d. 714).

THE ISLAMIC WORLD

622: The Hijra, or flight, of Muhammad to Medina; this event marks the beginning of the Islamic calendar.

632: The death of Muhammad; the beginning of the rule of the caliphs, with Muhammad's companion Abu Bakr as the first caliph.

636–37: The caliph Omar I wins decisive victories against the Byzantine and Sassanian empires, laying the foundation for Islamic conquest of the entire Middle East.

639: A severe draught and famine in southwestern Arabia require massive shipments of food from the newly conquered Near East and the opening of the old Roman Nile–Red Sea canal.

664: A group of Islamic scholars travel to southern India on the annul monsoon merchant fleet and establish the first mosque in India.

666: Islamic forces raid Sicily, the first Islamic attack against western Europe.

680: Hussein, a descendent of Muhammad's cousin Ali and of Muhammad himself, and a claimant to the caliphate, is killed at Karbala during a revolt, leading to the split of Islam into Sunni and Shii sects.

692: The Dome of the Rock on the Temple Mount in Jerusalem is completed, marking the spot where Muhammad was believed to have ascended to heaven.

695: The caliph Abd al-Malik issues the first specifically Islamic coinage; it does not bear the image of the ruler but is decorated only with calligraphy.

697: Christian Coptic peasants in Egypt revolt against the burden of Islamic taxation; more tax revolts occur in 712 and 725–26.

AFRICA

ca. 750: Part of a Jewish community that had lived in Ethiopia since antiquity may have migrated south (at a very uncertain date) and formed new groups that survive today in South Africa.

THE AMERICAS

ca. 700: The Mayan city of Tikal becomes a dominant manufacturer and trader of obsidian stone tools and weapons.

711: Renewed military triumph in victory over its rival Calakmul and cultural dominance of the Mayan city-state of Tikal.

727: Ruler 3 ascends the throne of the Mayan city of Dos Pilas; before his death in 741 he conquers several Mayan states, making the largest political unit in Mayan history.

ca. 750: The Mayan city of Chetumal in northern Belize, with its maritime station on Ambergris Caye, dominates maritime trade in the Caribbean.

ca. 790: The artistically important Bonampak murals are painted, depicting the Mayan rituals associated with capturing, torturing, and sacrificing enemy warriors.

700 – 800

ca. 800: The last-wax process of metal casting begins to be used to make sculptures at Igbo Ukwu in the Niger Delta (Sahel) and then spreads throughout western Africa.

ca. 800: The coffee bean is domesticated in Ethiopia; according to legend, this occurred after the goatherd Kaldi noticed its stimulating effects on his flock.

ca. 850: The semi-legendary Queen Gudit sacks Axum, turning Ethiopia inward into a period of isolation from the outside world.

ca. 800: The Gate of the Sun (decorated with an early calendar) is erected at Tiwanaku, one of the largest stone monoliths in the world, estimated to weigh 200 tons.

800 – 900

ASIA AND THE PACIFIC

ca. 700: Islamic missionaries, followed shortly by merchants, reach Guangzhou in China, which the Tang opens to international trade.

710: The beginning of the Nara Period in Japan and the transformation of culture based on Chinese models, including the adaptation of Chinese characters (*kanji*).

ca. 750: The Gandhara school of Buddhist religious art flourishes in India, showing heavy influence of Hellenistic (Greek) art.

802: Foundation of the Khmer Empire in Cambodia, a state that endured until 1432.

ca. 850: Gunpowder (probably a recent invention at that time) is first mentioned in a Chinese alchemical text.

EUROPE

782: Charlemagne begins to revive learning in western Europe, bringing the scholar Alcuin to his court and causing surviving texts of ancient books to be copied and distributed.

793: The Vikings make their first great raid on Europe, destroying the monastery on the Northumbrian coast of Britain at Lindisfarne.

800: Pope Leo III crowns Charlemagne as emperor at Rome, restoring the Western Roman Empire in the form of the Holy Roman Empire.

ca. 800: Chess, originally invented in ancient India, is introduced into Europe for the first time and becomes popular among the aristocracy.

835: The "discovery" of relics of Saint James in Spain and the establishment of the pilgrimage center of Santiago de Compostela; the beginning of pilgrimage in medieval Europe.

ca. 800: Modern musical notation is devised as part of the Carolingian Renaissance with its interest in cultural renewal.

842: Charlemagne's empire collapses in civil war; Charles the Bald and Louis the German swear alliance of France and Germany in the first surviving texts in French and German.

ca. 850: Viking trading and conquest in Russia helps to form the Slav state of Kiev Rus, precursor of the modern-day Russian and Ukrainian states.

855: Saints Cyril and Methodius, Orthodox missionaries to the kingdom of Moravia, devise the Cyrillic alphabet, which would become the standard method of writing for Russian and most Slavic languages.

THE ISLAMIC WORLD

ca. 700: As writing copies of the Koran becomes more important, the Arabic alphabet is reformed by adding vowel points and diacritical marks.

711: Islamic forces make their last major conquests, occupying Spain, the Sind (modern-day Pakistan), and the remainder of inner Asia.

750: Abu al-Abbas as-Saffah founds a new dynasty of caliphs; conversion of the conquered populations to Islam is intensified, and Arabic becomes an official administrative language.

755: Al-Muqqana (the Veiled Prophet) inspired a political uprising and long-lasting heretical sect of Islam in Khorasan (Afghanistan), claiming to be the Mahdi (Islamic redeemer).

762: Baghdad is founded by the Abbasid caliphs as a new capital for the Islamic empire; it becomes one of the most important world centers of learning and culture.

ca. 800: The foundation of Kilwa on an island off Tanzania as a result of increasing trade around the Indian Ocean.

803: Birth of Jabir ibn Hayyan (Geber), an important Islamic alchemist, especially influential in western Europe.

810: Establishment of the House of Wisdom at the caliph's court in Baghdad as a library and center for scientific and scholarly research.

833: The astronomer al-Farghani (Alfraganus) precisely measures the distance of 1 degree of longitude and hence of the circumference of the earth.

869: The Zanj revolt of African slaves working on plantations in southern Iraq breaks out and is not suppressed until 883.

880: The Islamic alchemist al-Kindi publishes the first description for the distillation of alcohol from wine.

AFRICA

THE AMERICAS

900 – 1000

ca. 900: Arab traders start to compete with Berber merchants in the trans-Sahara slave trade.

ca. 900: The medieval climate anomaly ushered in a period of warmer than usual temperatures that lasted until ca. 1400; although it was worldwide, it especially fostered the colonization of Greenland.

ca. 900: The Mayan city-states go into decline, and urban centers are abandoned by ca. 1250.

ca. 950: Rise of the Toltec Empire in the Valley of Mexico; its culture spreads to influence the northern Mayan city-states.

1000 – 1100
(continues)

ca. 1000: The Yoruba state forms in western Nigeria; descended from the Nok culture, it flourished until ca. 1700.

ca. 1000: The beginning of the Pavement Period or period of mature artistic and architectural styles in Ife in Nigeria, which declined after 1400.

ca. 1000: The rise of the Chimú Empire in the Moche valley of northern Peru, which established many of the administrative and economic structures of the later Incan Empire.

ca. 1000: The Chimú begin to make quipus: detailed bureaucratic records in which patterns on colored strings indicated numbers and words, a practice taken up by the Inca.

ca. 1000: After a long period of colonization from South America, Arawak peoples organized centralized governments on the islands of the Greater Antilles.

ca. 1000: The Inuit people expand from an isolated homeland in Alaska to colonize the whole of Arctic North America, reaching Greenland by 1300.

ca. 1000: The beginning of a maritime trade along the Pacific coast between Central and South America.

ca. 1000: The invention of lacrosse, a sport developed by Native Americans that is still popular today.

1003: The Viking Leif Ericson founds a short-lived colony in North America on the northern tip of Newfoundland, following up sightings of the American coast by other Vikings in 986.

ASIA AND THE PACIFIC

ca. 900: Chinese merchants begin to use checks, paper money, and simple forms of joint-stock companies.

ca. 900: Chinese shipbuilders introduce watertight compartments into ship design, making sinking much less likely in an accident.

960: The foundation of the Song Dynasty, viewed as the golden age of Chinese culture.

960: The Song make flour milling a government monopoly and widely introduce industrial water-powered mills throughout China.

ca. 1000: The expansion of Polynesian peoples in the South Pacific to Hawaii and New Zealand.

ca. 1000: Burmese, Thai, and Laotian peoples are displaced from Tibet and occupy most of Southeast Asia.

ca. 1000: The composition of *The Tale of Genji* by Murasaki Shikibu, the first Asian novel and an important development on the novelistic form.

1102: China's population reaches 100,000,000, doubling in about a century thanks to newly developed techniques of rice cultivation.

1010: India is invaded by the first of several waves of inner Asia Islamic nomad groups, who eventually take over most of the Ganges valley.

1040: The Chinese artisan Bi Sheng invents the first system of moveable type using a ceramic typeset.

1054: Chinese astronomers notice a spectacular supernova on July 5th that remains visible for 23 days.

EUROPE

ca. 975: Gerbert of d'Aurillac (later Pope Sylvester II), after studying in Spain, introduces Arabic numerals into Europe.

ca. 1000: The troubadour poets begin to work in southern France, introducing Arabic forms of literature to Europe and propagating themes of courtly love and of King Arthur.

ca. 1010: The single manuscript preserving the oral saga *Beowulf* (ca. 700) is written; this is the first important literary work in any vernacular language (Old English).

ca. 1050: The growth of international trade fairs, such as that hosted by the Count of Champaign mark a recovering and later an expanding economy.

1075: Pope Gregory VII begins the Investiture Crisis by claiming the right to appoint bishops; it was settled in the Pope's favor in 1122 after a civil war in the Empire.

1087: The Benedictine monk Constantine the African begins to translate an Arabic version of the work of Greek medical writers into Latin, beginning an important movement in Europe to recover the learning of the ancient world from Arabic sources.

1094: The Byzantine emperor Alexius I requests military aid from the pope against the Seljuk Turks, beginning the period of the Crusades.

THE ISLAMIC WORLD

ca. 900: Ptolemy's *Almagest*, the standard ancient Greek handbook on astronomy, is translated into Arabic; it will be translated into Latin in Spain in 1144.

ca. 900: Shadow puppet theater becomes a prominent art form in the Islamic world, beginning in Egypt but probably based on older Persian traditions.

909: The foundation of the Fatamids, a Shia dynasty that at its height controlled all of North Africa, Syria, and most of Arabia.

920: The caliph al-Muqtadir sends an embassy to the Volga Bulgarians; Ibn Fadlan, the secretary attached to the expedition, leaves a detailed geographic and ethnographic description of the journey.

965: Birth of al-Hassan (Alhazen), an Islamic scientist important in the fields of optics, astronomy, and medicine.

ca. 980: Birth of Ibn Sina (Avicenna), a Persian Neoplatonist philosopher and physician, one of the most influential intellectuals in Islamic history and especially influential in western Europe.

1055: The Seljuk Turks, a tribe originally brought into the Islamic world as mercenaries (1038), quickly seize control of most Islamic territories in Asia, which they rule for two centuries.

	AFRICA	THE AMERICAS
1000 – 1100 (continued)		**ca. 1050**: Beginning of the period of mound building at Cahokia, the largest city of the Mississippian culture; the site was abandoned before 1400. **ca. 1050**: The Anasazi culture in the American Southwest constructs its largest town near the Four Corners at a site now known as Chaco Canyon. **ca. 1070**: The construction of Serpent Mound in modern-day Ohio, a 1,300-foot-long earthwork in the shape of a serpent probably built by a branch of the Mississippian culture.
1100 – 1200	**ca. 1100**: The wooden xylophone, or marimba, is invented in western Africa. **1187**: After the recapture of Jerusalem by Islamic forces, the Ethiopian emperor Gebre Lalibela builds a new capital to serve as a New Jerusalem, constructing a dozen monumental rock-cut churches.	**ca. 1100**: Climate change creates a drier climate in the Great Basin, causing an outmigration of agriculturalists; many become Great Plains nomads, but one group is the ancestor of the Aztec. **ca. 1150**: The Toltec capital of Tula is destroyed by nomadic tribes from northern Mexico, probably including the ancestors of the Aztec.
1200 – 1300 (continues)	**ca. 1200**: The tradition of Ethiopian royal law enshrined in the *Kebra Nagast* and the *Fetha Negast* begins to be composed. **1235**: The Mali Empire dominates the Niger Delta (Sahel) and the trans-Sahara, succeeding Ghana, which had been destroyed by the Almoravid state in North Africa. **ca. 1235**: According to legend (the epic of *Sundiata*), the tradition of bardic western	**ca. 1250**: The replacement of the Anasazi population of the American Southwest by Navajo and Hopi groups.

ASIA AND THE PACIFIC

1162: Birth of Genghis Khan, a military genius who will set in motion the Mongol conquest of most of Eurasia.

ca. 1075: China experiments with land reform and social welfare programs meant to help landless peasants, but they are short-lived owing to opposition from aristocrats.

1086: The first mention in Chinese scientific literature of a compass, a device that seems to have been in use for one or more generations by then.

1192: The beginning of feudalism and the samurai class in Japan as civil disorder escalates and government authority needs more and more soldiers.

ca. 1200: China reaches a new peak of urbanization for any medieval or ancient culture, with five cities of 1,000,000 in population, and 50 cities over 100,000.

ca. 1250: Polynesians colonize Easter Island, the farthest point reached from their homeland in New Guinea.

1209: Genghis Khan attacks China, overwhelming the northern states of Xia and Jin.

EUROPE

ca. 1100: The horizontal loom is introduced from China and is quickly transformed into a mechanized device, allowing weaving to become an industrial process.

ca. 1110: The beginning of miracle, mystery, and morality plays: originally religious dramas, they became increasingly secular and gave rise to modern dramatic traditions, such as that represented by Shakespeare.

1134: Completion of the building of the Abbey of Saint-Denis in Paris, the first building in the Gothic style of architecture.

ca. 1150: Blast furnace developed independently in Europe; together with water-powered mechanical bellows and hammers, this allowed an exponential increase in iron production and laid the foundation for the later Industrial Revolution.

1158: The town of Lübeck is founded on the Baltic coast of Germany; it soon builds a trade network that will became the foundation of the Hanseatic League.

ca. 1175: Europeans used the first counterweight trebuchet during the Crusades; this siege engine was an improvement based on ancient Chinese traction trebuchets.

1209: The foundation of the Franciscan Order, a measure intended to combat popular heresies and which led to important church reforms.

1223: The beginning of the Mongol conquest of Kiev Rus and the period of the so-called Mongol Yoke.

ca. 1250: The magnifying glass and eyeglasses are invented by scholastic

THE ISLAMIC WORLD

1126: Birth of Ibn Rushd (Averröes), an Andalusian Neoplatonist philosopher, physician, and legal scholar especially influential in western Europe.

1165: Birth in modern-day Afghanistan of Abu Bakr, one of the most celebrated calligraphers to produce copies of the Koran.

1206: The Arab scholar and engineer al-Jazari invents the crankshaft to convert continuous circular motion into reciprocating motion, which allowed for a much wider use of milling.

1238: Work begins on the Alhambra Palace in Granada (al-Andalus), one of the finest examples of Islamic architecture in the world.

1200 – 1300
(continued)

1300 – 1400

AFRICA

African poets known as griots begins at the same time as the empire of Mali.

ca. 1250: The penetration of Arabs and later the Portuguese (after 1440) into central and southern Africa spreads strains of smallpox to which the local populations have little immunity, causing epidemics.

ca. 1300: Nomadic cattle herders from the Sudan (including the Tutsi) migrate south to the great lakes region, sometimes conquering local populations of farmers.

1306: Ethiopia sends a diplomatic mission to Europe that visits Rome, Genoa, and Avignon, in an effort to forge an alliance against the Islamic states in North Africa.

ca. 1375: The southern African kingdom of Great Zimbabwe, builder of the largest stone structures in sub-Saharan Africa, reaches its zenith (and goes into sharp decline after 1450).

ca. 1350: Cities on the Indian coast of Africa begin to build stone flood walls to protect themselves from storm surges caused by cyclones (hurricanes).

THE AMERICAS

ca. 1325: The Aztec begin to build their city of Tenochtitlán on an island in Lake Texcoco in the Valley of Mexico.

ca. 1325: The spread of the Kachina religion among the Hopi and Zuni groups of the American Southwest, probably based on Aztec religious ideas.

ca. 1350: The dramatic date of the *Rabinal Achí*, the only intact surviving drama produced by the Mayan culture; it was composed between that time and the Spanish conquest.

1376: The Aztec Empire is established in the Valley of Mexico under its first elected king, Acamapichtli.

ASIA AND THE PACIFIC

1220: Genghis Khan completes the conquest of inner Asia, having subdued Kara-Kitay and the Khwarezmian Empire.

1234: The Korean scientist Choe Yun-ui invents the first set of metal movable type; the first book printed with them is a set of ritual instructions, *Sangjeong yemun*.

ca. 1250: The Mongols systematically rebuild the infrastructure of the Silk Road, building hundreds of caravansaries along the various routes, in order to promote east–west trade, which they taxed.

1271: Kublai Khan, grandson of Genghis Khan, completes the conquest of China and begins the Yuan Dynasty.

1274: Japan repels a Mongol invasion with the help of the *kamikaze*, the "divine wind" (typhoon) that damaged the invasion fleet; another invasion attempt in 1281 was also prevented by storms.

ca. 1280: Chinese drama flourishes during the Yuan Dynasty (also known as the Mongol Dynasty); this is the golden age of Chinese theater.

ca. 1350: The beginning of Japanese Noh drama, a highly stylized literary form influenced by Buddhism and frequently referring to classical Chinese literature.

1368: Native Chinese officials and military officers overthrow Mongol rule and establish the Ming Dynasty.

EUROPE

philosophers investigating the science of optics.

ca. 1250: The foundation of the modern banking system is laid in the Italian city states, especially Venice.

1267: The alchemist and Scholastic philosopher Roger Bacon is the first European to describe the Chinese invention gunpowder.

1274: Thomas Aquinas's publication of the *Summa theologica*, which established the outlines of all later Scholastic philosophy and reconciled Greek philosophical and scientific learning (then being transmitted to Europe through Moorish Spain) with Christian doctrine.

ca. 1275: The ancient Chinese invention of the spinning wheel is introduced into Europe, stimulating the growth of the wool industry and international trade.

ca. 1280: The first mechanical clocks are invented in Europe and installed in churches to keep track of the liturgical hours of the day.

1305: The beginning of the "Babylonian Captivity" of the popes in Avignon, a scandal that eventually led to the election of rival popes and which was not resolved until 1415.

1321: Death of Dante and final publication of his *Divine Comedy*, the first great work of medieval vernacular (Italian) verse.

1324: Gunpowder artillery was first effectively employed at the siege of Metz, rendering all existing fortifications (castles and city walls) obsolete.

1347–50: The great pandemic of bubonic plague known as the Black Death kills as much as half the population of Europe.

1348: Jews, popularly blamed for the Black Death, are massacred in the Rhineland; survivors flee to Poland and lay the foundation for the Ashkenazy communities of Poland and Russia.

ca. 1350: The Merton scholars at Oxford and the French philosopher Nicole Oresme lay the foundation for the graphical representation of mathematical equations.

1356: The Jacquerie (in France) is the first of increasingly serious peasant revolts (rebellion of Wat Tyler in England, 1381; Hussite Wars in Bohemia, 1420–34) occasioned by the grievances of the poor, which looked toward later events such as the Reformation and French Revolution.

THE ISLAMIC WORLD

1250: The Mamluks, slave soldiers who had served the caliphate since the eighth century, rebel and establish an independent government in Egypt.

1258: Mongol invaders destroy the city of Baghdad, massacring the entire population and destroying the royal library (House of Wisdom), thus ending the golden age of Islamic culture.

1270: The Chinese invention of gunpowder is first described by an Arabic alchemist, Hassan al-Rammah.

1282: First mention of the use of the compass in Arabic texts, in the *Treasure Book of Merchants in Travels*.

1299: Osman I begins a series of conquests that would eventually bring the entire Middle East and Balkans under the rule of the Ottoman Turks.

1324: King Mansa Musa of Mali, founder the Sankoré madrassa in Timbuktu, makes a celebrated pilgrimage to Mecca.

1347–50: The great pandemic of bubonic plague kills as much as half the population of the Mediterranean region of the Islamic world.

1365: The Ottoman Empire establishes the Janissary corps as an elite imperial bodyguard, composed of Christian slaves from the Balkans.

1400 – 1600

AFRICA

ca. 1400: In central Africa the rulers of Mpemba Kasi and the Mbata Kingdom enter a federation that creates the kingdom of Kongo.

1441: Representatives of the Ethiopian Orthodox Church attend the Council of Florence held by the Roman Catholic Church.

1444: The Portuguese begin the Atlantic slave trade on the western African coast; the slaves were originally used at sugarcane plantations on São Tomé, an island in the Gulf of Guinea.

1468: The Songhai Empire captures Timbuktu and replaces Mali as the dominant power in the Niger Delta and Sahel regions.

ca. 1470: The city of Benin, founded around 1180, becomes the main imperial power on the western African coast.

1485: After beginning diplomatic relations with the Portuguese, who were trading and exploring in western Africa, Nzinga a Nkuwu, the king of Kongo, converts to Christianity.

1486: Oba Esige, the king of Benin, sends his son to Portugal as an ambassador after several years of trade contacts with the Portuguese.

THE AMERICAS

ca. 1400: Carib colonists from South America displace earlier Arawak populations from the islands of the Lesser Antilles.

ca. 1400: The Aztec make vellum (animal skin) manuscripts written in a pictographic script (practices that may well have begun much earlier).

1431: Nezahuacoyotl is crowned king of Texcoco, the second most important Aztec city, and establishes important legal and artistic traditions.

1438: The foundation of the Inca Empire, which quickly expands to encompass almost all of the Pacific coast of South America and the inland Andes.

1492: Columbus reaches America, ultimately resulting in the complete colonization of North and South America.

1492–1560: Contact with Europeans introduces smallpox and other diseases against which Native Americans have no immunity, causing plagues that wipe out as much as 90 percent of the population.

1502: Creation of the Calendar Stone, a compilation in relief sculpture of Aztec history, mythology, and ideology.

1521: Spanish conquest of the Aztec Empire under Hernán Cortés.

1532: Spanish conquest of the Inca Empire under Francisco Pizarro.

1550: The *Popol Vuh*, a Mayan mythological epic, is written down in the modern Mayan language from now-lost Mayan texts of the Classic Period (before the 10th century).

ASIA AND THE PACIFIC

1402: The foundation of the Sultanate of Malacca on both sides of the straits between Malaysia and Java, a state that would control the increasingly important spice trade.

1405: The emperors of China dispatch treasure fleets of up to 500 immense ships to explore and dominate the Indian Ocean; the voyages are stopped after 1433 because of fears of foreign ideas.

1443: Phonetic alphabet is developed in Korea.

1498: Portuguese explorer Vasco da Gama reaches the port of Calicut, India.

EUROPE

1434: Under King Henry the Navigator of Portugal, explorers begin to sail down the African coast, eventually reaching the Indian Ocean and breaking the Islamic control of trade with India (1497).

1435: Leonbattista Alberti publishes *De pictura*, describing the first geometrically correct system of perspective in painting.

1455: Johannes Gutenberg produces in Mainz the first printed Bible with his invention of the printing press and movable type.

1492: Ferdinand and Isabella complete the Reconquista in Spain by capturing Granada and expel Jews from Spain; Columbus makes contact with the Americas on their commission.

THE ISLAMIC WORLD

1453: The Ottoman Turks capture and destroy the city of Constantinople, bringing the Byzantine Empire to an end and destroying much of the legacy of Greek literature.

1497: The Arab geographer Ahmad bin Majid serves as the Indian Ocean navigator for the Portuguese explorer Vasco da Gama on the first European voyage to round the Cape of Good Hope.

General Bibliography

GENERAL

Jordan, William C. *Dictionary of the Middle Ages, Supplement 1.* New York: Charles Scribner's Sons, 2004.

McKitterick, Rosamond. *Atlas of the Medieval World.* New York: Oxford University Press, 2004.

Strayer, William R. *Dictionary of the Middle Ages.* New York: Charles Scribner's Sons, 1982–1989.

AFRICA

Brooks, George E. *Landlords and Strangers: Ecology, Society, and Trade in Western Africa, 1000–1630.* Boulder, Colo.: Westview Press, 1993.

Connah, Graham. *African Civilizations: An Archaeological Perspective,* 2nd ed. New York: Cambridge University Press, 2001.

Hall, Martin. *Farmers, Kings, and Traders: The People of Southern Africa, 200–1800.* Chicago: University of Chicago Press, 1990.

Davis, Jr., R. Hunt. *Encyclopedia of African History and Culture,* 5 vols. New York: Facts On File, 2005.

Kusimba, Chapurukha. *The Rise and Fall of Swahili States.* Walnut Creek, Calif.: AltaMira, 1999.

Levtzion, Nehemia. *Ancient Ghana and Mali.* New York: Holmes and Meyer, 1980.

McIntosh, Roderick. *Ancient Middle Niger: Urbanism and the Self-Organizing Landscape.* New York: Cambridge University Press, 2005.

Oliver, Roland, and Anthony Atmore. *Medieval Africa, 1250–1800.* New York: Cambridge University Press, 2001.

Oliver, Roland, and Brian Fagan. *Africa in the Iron Age, c. 500 B.C.–A.D. 1400.* New York: Cambridge University Press, 1975.

Tamrat, Taddesse. *Church and State in Ethiopia, 1270–1527.* Oxford, U.K.: Oxford University Press, 1972.

Vansina, Jan. *Kingdoms of the Savanna.* Madison, Wis.: University of Wisconsin Press, 1966.

Vansina, Jan. *Paths in the Rainforests: Toward a History of Political Tradition in Equatorial Africa.* Madison, WI: University of Wisconsin Press, 1990.

Vansina, Jan. *How Societies Are Born: Governance in West Central Africa before 1600.* Charlottesville: University of Virginia Press, 2004.

THE AMERICAS

Ames, Kenneth M., and Herbert D. G. Maschner. *Peoples of the Northwest Coast: Their Archaeology and Prehistory.* London: Thames and Hudson, 2000.

D'Altroy, Terence N. *The Incas.* Malden, Mass.: Blackwell, 2002.

Evans, Susan Toby. *Ancient Mexico and Central America: Archaeology and Culture History.* New York: Thames and Hudson, 2004.

Fagan, Brian M. *Ancient North America: The Archaeology of a Continent,* 4th ed. New York: Thames and Hudson, 2005.

Mann, Charles C. *1491: New Revelations of the Americas before Columbus.* New York: Knopf, 2005.

Moseley, Michael E. *The Incas and Their Ancestors,* 2nd ed. New York: Thames and Hudson, 2001.

Pauketat, Timothy R. *Ancient Cahokia and the Mississippians.* New York: Cambridge University Press, 2004.

Sharer, Robert J., with Loa P. Traxler. *The Ancient Maya,* 6th ed. Stanford, Calif.: Stanford University Press, 2006.

Smith, Michael E. *The Aztecs.* Malden, Mass.: Blackwell, 2003.

Smith, Bruce D. *The Mississippian Emergence,* 2nd ed. Tuscaloosa: University of Alabama Press, 2007.

Wilson, Samuel M, ed. *The Indigenous People of the Caribbean.* Gainsville: University Press of Florida, 1997.

ASIA AND THE PACIFIC

Andaya, Barbara W. *The Flaming Womb: Repositioning Women in Early Modern Southeast Asia.* Honolulu: University of Hawaii Press, 2006.

Andaya, Leonard Y. *The World of Maluku: Eastern Indonesia in the Early Modern Period.* Honolulu: University of Hawaii Press, 1993.

Asher, Catherine B., and Cynthia Talbot. *India before Europe.* New York: Cambridge University Press, 2006.

Embrey, Patricia Buckley. *The Cambridge Illustrated History of China.* Cambridge, U.K.: Cambridge University Press, 1999.

Fischer, Steven Roger. *A History of the Pacific Islands.* New York: Palgrave Macmillan, 2002.

Hall, Kenneth R. *Maritime Trade and State Development in Early Southeast Asia.* Honolulu: University of Hawaii Press, 1985.

Higham, Charles. *The Archaeology of Mainland Southeast Asia: From 10,000 B.C. to the Fall of Angkor.* New York: Cambridge University Press, 1989.

Higham, Charles. *The Civilization of Angkor.* Berkeley: University of California Press, 2004.

Higham, Charles F. W. *Encyclopedia of Ancient Asian Civilizations.* New York: Facts On File, 2004.

Kirch, Patrick Vinton. *On the Road of the Winds: An Archaeological History of the Pacific Islands before European Contact.* Berkeley: University of California Press, 2000.

Reid, Anthony. *Southeast Asia in the Age of Commerce, 1450–1680.* New Haven, Conn.: Yale University Press, 1993.

Thapar, Romila. *Early India: From the Origins to A.D. 1300.* Berkeley: University of California Press, 2003.

EUROPE

Bartlett, Robert. *The Making of Europe: Colonization, and Cultural Change, 950–1350.* Princeton, N.J.: Princeton University Press, 1993.

Bennett, Judith, and C. Warren Hollister. *Medieval Europe: A Short History,* 10th ed. New York: McGraw-Hill, 2006.

Cantor, Norman. *The Civilization of the Middle Ages.* New York: HarperCollins, 1994.

Crabtree, Pam J. *Medieval Archaeology: An Encyclopedia.* New York: Garland, 2001.

Curta, Florin. *East Central Europe and Eastern Europe in the Early Middle Ages.* Ann Arbor: University of Michigan Press, 2005.

Davis, R. H. C. *A History of Medieval Europe: From Constantine to Saint Louis,* 3rd ed. New York: Longman, 2005.

Fitzhugh, William W., and Elisabeth I. Ward, eds. *Vikings: The North Atlantic Saga.* Washington, D.C.: Smithsonian Institution Press, 2000.

Hodges, Richard. *Dark Age Economics: The Origins of Towns and Trade, A.D. 600–1000,* 2nd ed. London: Duckworth, 2004.

Holmes, George, ed. *The Oxford Illustrated History of Medieval Europe.* New York: Oxford University Press, 2001.

Huizinga, Johan. *The Waning of the Middle Ages.* New York: Dover, 1999.

Jordan. William Chester. *Europe in the High Middle Ages.* New York: Viking, 2003.

Keen, Maurice. *The Pelican History of Medieval Europe.* New York: Penguin, 1969.

Le Goff, Jacques. *Medieval Civilization, 400–1500,* trans. Julia Barrow. Oxford: Blackwell, 1988.

McCormick, Michael. *Origins of the European Economy: Communications and Commerce, A.D. 300–900.* New York: Cambridge University Press, 2002.

Pirenne, Henri. *Medieval Cities: Their Origins and the Revival of Trade.* Princeton, N.J.: Princeton University Press, 1969.

Pirenne, Henri. *Mohammed and Charlemagne.* London: Routledge, 2007.

Rosenwein, Barbara. *A Short History of the Middle Ages,* 2nd ed. Orchard Park, N.Y.: Broadview Press, 2004.

Waldman, Carl and Catherine Mason. *Encyclopedia of European Peoples,* 2 vols. New York: Facts On File, 2006.

Wickham, Chris. *Framing the Early Middle Ages: Europe and the Mediterranean, 400–800.* New York: Oxford University Press, 2007.

THE ISLAMIC WORLD

Arnold, Sir Thomas, and Alfred Guillaume, eds. *The Legacy of Islam.* Oxford. U.K.: Clarendon Press, 1931.

Berkeley, Jonathan P. *The Formation of Islam: Religion and Society in the Near East, 600–1800.* New York: Cambridge University Press, 2003.

Bulliet, Richard. *The Case for Islamo-Christian Civilization.* New York: Columbia University Press, 2004.

Campo, Juan E. *Encyclopedia of Islam.* New York: Facts On File Publishing, 2008.

Daniel, Norman. *The Cultural Barrier: Problems in the Exchange of Ideas between Historical Islam and the West.* Edinburgh: Edinburgh University Press, 1975.

Daniel, Norman. *Islam and the West: The Making of an Image.* Edinburgh: Edinburgh University Press, 1960.

Frasseto, Michael and David Blanks, eds. *Western Views of Islam in Medieval and Early Modern Europe: Perception of Other.* New York: St. Martin's Press, 1999.

Ghazanfar, S. M. *Medieval Islamic Economic Thought: Filling the "Great Gap" in European Economics.* London: RutledgeCurzon, 2003.

Ghazanfar, S.M. *Islamic Civilization: History, Contributions, and Influence—A Compendium of Literature.* Lanham, Md.: Scarecrow Press, 2006

Hill, Fred J., and Nicholas Awde. *A History of the Islamic World.* New York: Hippocrene Books, 2003.

Hodgson, Marshall G. S. *The Venture of Islam: Conscience and History in a World Civilization,* 3 vols. Chicago: University of Chicago Press, 1974.

Lapidus, Ira. *A History of Islamic Societies,* 2nd ed. New York: Cambridge University Press, 2002.

Lowney, Chris. *A Vanished World: Muslims, Jews, and Christians in Medieval Spain.* New York: Oxford University Press, 2006.

Menocal, Maria Rosa. *The Ornament of the World: How Muslims, Jews, and Christians Created a Culture of Tolerance in Medieval Spain.* Boston: Little, Brown, 2002.

Morgan, Michael H. *The Enduring Legacy of Muslim Scientists, Thinkers, and Artists.* Washington, D.C.: National Geographic Society, 2007.

Reeves, Minou. *Muhammed in Europe: A Thousand Years of Mythmaking.* New York: New York University Press, 2001.

Schacht, Joseph. *The Legacy of Islam,* 2nd ed. Oxford. U.K.: Clarendon Press, 1975.

Southern, Sir Richard. *Western Views of Islam in the Middle Ages.* Cambridge, Mass.: Harvard University Press, 1962.

Wallace-Murphy, Tim. *What Islam Did for Us: Understanding Islam's Contributions to Western Civilization.* London: Watkins Publishing, 2006.

Watt, W. Montgomery. *The Influence of Islam on Medieval Europe.* Edinburgh: Edinburgh University Press, 1994.

Index